A TEXT BOOK OF

ENGINEERING MATHEMATICS - II

FOR
SEMESTER – II

FIRST YEAR DEGREE COURSE IN ENGINEERING
(COMMON TO ALL BRANCHES)

According to Revised Syllabus of Shivaji University, Kolhapur
With effect from Academic Year 2013-2014

Prof. Dr. NAVNEET D. SANGLE
M. Sc; Ph.D.(Mathematics)
Professor and Head, Department of Basic Sciences
Annasaheb Dange College of Engineering & Technology,
Ashta, (Tal: Walwa; Dist.: Sangli)

N 2401

ENGINEERING MATHEMATICS II (FE SEM. II SU) ISBN 978-93-83971-44-2
First Edition : January 2014

© : Author

The text of this publication, or any part thereof, should not be reproduced or transmitted in any form or stored in any computer storage system or device for distribution including photocopy, recording, taping or information retrieval system or reproduced on any disc, tape, perforated media or other information storage device etc., without the written permission of Authors with whom the rights are reserved. Breach of this condition is liable for legal action.

Every effort has been made to avoid errors or omissions in this publication. In spite of this, errors may have crept in. Any mistake, error or discrepancy so noted and shall be brought to our notice shall be taken care of in the next edition. It is notified that neither the publisher nor the authors or seller shall be responsible for any damage or loss of action to any one, of any kind, in any manner, therefrom.

Published By : **Printed at**
NIRALI PRAKASHAN **Repro Knowledgecast Limited**
Abhyudaya Pragati, 1312, Shivaji Nagar, **India**
Off J.M. Road, PUNE – 411005
Tel - (020) 25512336/37/39, Fax - (020) 25511379
Email : niralipune@pragationline.com

DISTRIBUTION CENTRES
PUNE

Nirali Prakashan
119, Budhwar Peth, Jogeshwari Mandir Lane
Pune 411002, Maharashtra
Tel : (020) 2445 2044, 66022708, Fax : (020) 2445 1538
Email : bookorder@pragationline.com

Nirali Prakashan
S. No. 28/25, Dhyari,
Near Pari Company, Pune 411041
Tel : (022) 24690204 Fax : (020) 24690316
Email : dhyari@pragationline.com
bookorder@pragationline.com

MUMBAI
Nirali Prakashan
385, S.V.P. Road, Rasdhara Co-op. Hsg. Society Ltd.,
Girgaum, Mumbai 400004, Maharashtra
Tel : (022) 2385 6339 / 2386 9976, Fax : (022) 2386 9976
Email : niralimumbai@pragationline.com

DISTRIBUTION BRANCHES

NAGPUR
Pratibha Book Distributors
Above Maratha Mandir, Shop No. 3, First Floor,
Rani Jhanshi Square, Sitabuldi, Nagpur 440012,
Maharashtra, Tel : (0712) 254 7129

BENGALURU
Pragati Book House
House No. 1, Sanjeevappa Lane, Avenue Road Cross,
Opp. Rice Church, Bengaluru – 560002.
Tel : (080) 64513344, 64513355,
Mob : 9880582331, 9845021552
Email:bharatsavla@yahoo.com

JALGAON
Nirali Prakashan
34, V. V. Golani Market, Navi Peth, Jalgaon 425001,
Maharashtra, Tel : (0257) 222 0395
Mob : 94234 91860

KOLHAPUR
Nirali Prakashan
New Mahadvar Road,
Kedar Plaza, 1st Floor Opp. IDBI Bank
Kolhapur 416 012, Maharashtra. Mob : 9850046155

CHENNAI
Pragati Books
9/1, Montieth Road, Behind Taas Mahal, Egmore,
Chennai 600008 Tamil Nadu, Tel : (044) 6518 3535,
Mob : 94440 01782 / 98450 21552 / 98805 82331, Email : bharatsavla@yahoo.com

RETAIL OUTLETS
PUNE

Pragati Book Centre
157, Budhwar Peth, Opp. Ratan Talkies,
Pune 411002, Maharashtra
Tel : (020) 2445 8887 / 6602 2707, Fax : (020) 2445 8887

Pragati Book Centre
Amber Chamber, 28/A, Budhwar Peth,
Appa Balwant Chowk, Pune : 411002, Maharashtra,
Tel : (020) 20240335 / 66281669
Email : pbcpune@pragationline.com

Pragati Book Centre
676/B, Budhwar Peth, Opp. Jogeshwari Mandir,
Pune 411002, Maharashtra
Tel : (020) 6601 7784 / 6602 0855

PBC Book Sellers & Stationers
152, Budhwar Peth, Pune 411002, Maharashtra
Tel : (020) 2445 2254 / 6609 2463

MUMBAI
Pragati Book Corner
Indira Niwas, 111 - A, Bhavani Shankar Road, Dadar (W), Mumbai 400028, Maharashtra
Tel : (022) 2422 3526 / 6662 5254, Email : pbcmumbai@pragationline.com

This Book is dedicated to ...

Adv. Rajendra R. Dange

... Dr. Navneet D. Sangle

PREFACE

This Book is primarily written for the first year students of all technical colleges affiliated to Shivaji University, Kolhapur. Keeping in view the limited time at the disposal of Engineering students preparing for University examinations. The book contains fairly large numbers of solved examples taken from various recently examination papers of different Universities and Autonomous colleges so that the students may not find any difficulty while answering problems in final University Examination. This book is divided in to six units.

Sincere efforts have been made to present the subject matter in a lucid and comprehensive manner so that an average students may follows the subject easily. At the end of each sub topics "Test Your Knowledge" set is given so that the students may try for the problems and assess their confidence of answering the problems after studying the sub topics.

The book covers the new syllabus of **Engineering Mathematics-II**, introduced recently for the second semester (First Year) of Shivaji University, Kolhapur.

I am highly obliged to Executive Director Prof. R. A. Kanai, Principal Dr. A. M. Mulla, Vice-Principal (Adm) Dr. L. Y. Waghmode, Vice-Principal (Acad), Dr. M. M. Awati and Administrative officer D.V. Adsul for their valuable guidance and support.

I would like to thank my family members colleagues and friends for their inspiration and consistent encouragement.

My deepest thanks to Shri Dineshbhai Furia, Shri Jigneshbhai Furia, Shri M. P. Munde, Mrs. Yojana G. Deshpande and entire staff of Nirali Prakashan, for making the publication of this book possible, well in time.

Suggestions, critical evaluations for improvement of this book will be highly appreciated and thankful acknowledged.

Dr. Navneet D. Sangle
navneet.sangale@gmail.com
+919960197519,+918600600711

❖ ❖ ❖

SYLLABUS

SECTION - I

Unit I : Ordinary Differential Equations of First Order and First Degree: (7)
1. Linear differential equations
2. Reducible to Linear differential equations
3. Exact differential equations
4. Reducible to Exact differential equations

Unit II : Applications of Ordinary Differential Equations of First Order and First Degree: (6)
1. Applications to Orthogonal trajectories (Cartesian and Polar equations)
2. Applications to Simple Electrical Circuits
3. Newton's law of cooling
4. Rate of decay and growth

Unit III : Numerical Solution of Ordinary Differential Equations of First Order and First Degree: (8)
1. Taylor's series method
2. Euler's method
3. Modified Euler's method
4. Runge-Kutta fourth order formula
5. Simultaneous first order differential equations by Runge–Kutta method

SECTION - II

Unit IV. Special Functions:
1. Gamma function and its properties
2. Beta function and its properties
3. Differentiation under integral sign
4. Error function and its properties

Unit V. Curve Tracing:
1. Tracing of curves in Cartesian form
   a) Semi cubical parabola, b) Cissiod of Diocles, c) Strophoid, d) Astroid,

e) Witch of Agnesi, f) Common Catenary, g)Folium of Descartes,

2. Tracing of curves in polar form

a)Cardioid, b) Pascal's Limacon, c) Lemniscate of Bernoulli,d) Parabola,

e) Hyperbola, f)Rose curves

3. Rectification of plane curves (Cartesian and Polar form)

Unit VI. Multiple Integration and its applications:

1. Double Integrals and evaluation
2. Change of order of integration
3. Double Integrals in Polar Coordinates
4. Change into Polar
5. Area enclosed by plane curves
6. Mass of a plane lamina
7. Center of Gravity of Plane Lamina
8. Moment of inertia of plane lamina

General Instructions:

1. Batch wise tutorials are to be conducted. The number of students per batch should be as per the university pattern for practical batches.
2. Minimum number of assignments should be 8 covering all topics.

CONTENTS

1. Ordinary Differential Equations of First Order and First Degree............ 1.1 – 1.79

2. Applications of Ordinary Differential Equations of First Order and First Degree .... 2.1 – 2.55

3. Numerical Solution of Ordinary Differential Equations of First Order and First Degree .... 3.1 – 3.64

4. Special Functions .... 4.1 – 4.80

5. Curve Tracing .... 5.1 – 5.81

6. Multiple Integration and Its Applications .... 6.1 – 6.111

✪ Paper Pattern .... P.1 – P.2

✪ List of Formulae .... F.1 – F.2

UNIT - I

ORDINARY DIFFERENTIAL EQUATIONS OF FIRST ORDER AND FIRST DEGREE

INTRODUCTION

Study of differential equations is of prime importance because of its applications in almost all the engineering fields. Analysis of electrical networks, motion of fluid through porous media, heat transfer through spherical or cylindrical shells, decay of radioactive elements, projectile motion are some of the examples. Even medical sciences have not escaped the involvement of differential equations. Concentration of sugar in blood is analyzed by a mathematical model involving differential equation. Studies of blood flow through the arteries, kidneys and the various organs of the body have attracted the attention of scientists working in the fields of Biomedical engineering. Ordinary or Partial differential equations play an important role in different kinds of models representing various phenomena. Differential equations are also used in modeling of day-to-day life situations like concentration of traffic on roads in urban areas, arrival of customers in shopping mauls, landing of planes at the crowded airports and so on.

If an estimation of quantity depends upon only one factor, we come across a situation of one dependent variable and one independent variable and modeling of such phenomena will involve ordinary differential equation. In the case of problems involving more than one dependent variables depending on one independent variable, we come across system of ordinary differential equations. On the contrary if a variable for its variation depends upon two or more independent variables, models of such problems are represented by partial differential equations. Actual modeling takes into account many different factors as the situation demands. In what follows, methods to solve simple ordinary differential equations are discussed. In the next chapter, actual case studies are described.

ENGINEERING APPROACH TO DIFFERENTIAL EQUATION:

For the engineering students the study of a differential equation can be divided in three stages
1. Formation of differential equation from the given physical or engineering problem.
2. To obtain the solution of the differential equation and fixing the values of the arbitrary constants with the help of given conditions.
3. Physical interpretation of the mathematical solution.

For Ex. : Suppose we are dealing with an electrical circuit, containing a resistance R, an inductance L and an e. m. f E all in series.

Let I be the current flowing in the circuit at time t. we need to know the way in which the current varies with time, and how it is affected by the values of the resistance and inductance.

This is the physical engineering problem, in the first stage we transform this into a differential equation. Using Kirchhoff's law for circuit since potential drops across r and L are Ri and $L\dfrac{di}{dt}$, We have $L\dfrac{di}{dt} + Ri = E$. This is the mathematical statement of the electrical circuit.

Next stage is the solve this differential equation by the methods which follow, we obtain the solution of this differential equation as $i = ce^{\frac{-Rt}{L}} + \frac{E}{R}$.

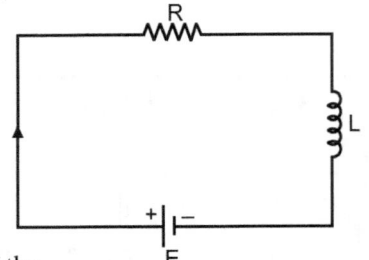

Initial if i = 0 when t = 0
then substituting these in above relation we get c = - E / R

There fore required solution is $i = \frac{E}{R}\left[1 - e^{\frac{-Rt}{L}}\right]$.

In the final stage, we try to interpret this solution in terms of the physical nature of the problem.

we see here that as time t increases, the current i goes on increasing, taking ultimately the maximum value E\R . This relation also help us to note how i is affected by the value of the resistance R and the inductance L in the circuit.

DIFFERENTIAL EQUATIONS

Definition: An equation involving dependent and independent variables and the derivative of dependent variable w. r. t. independent variable is called differential equation (D.E)

Following are some Ex.s of differential equations:

1. $\frac{dy}{dx} - y = 0$ 2. $\frac{dy}{dx} = \cos x$ 3. $\frac{d^2y}{dx^2} = 0$

4. $(2x - y)dx + (y - x)dy = 0$ 5. $\sqrt{1 + \frac{dy}{dx}} = \frac{d^2y}{dx^2}$ 6. $\frac{dy}{dx} = \frac{x + y - 3}{2x - y + 1}$

7. $\frac{dy}{dx} + \frac{2}{x}y = x^2$ 8. $x\frac{\partial z}{\partial x} + y\frac{\partial z}{\partial y} = nz$ 9. $\frac{\partial^2 y}{\partial t^2} = c^2\frac{\partial^2 y}{\partial x^2}$

10. $\frac{\partial^2 u}{\partial x^2} + \frac{\partial^2 u}{\partial y^2} = 0$

Ordinary differential equation: Differential equations involving only one independent variable and one or more dependent variables and their derivatives w. r. t. independent variables are called Ordinary Differential Equations (O.D.E.).

Partial Differential Equations : Differential equations involving two or more independent variables and one or more dependent variables and their partial derivatives w. r. t. independent variables are called Partial Differential Equations (P.D.E.).

Equations (1) to (7) given in above article are ordinary differential equations and equations (8) to (10) are partial differential equations. Differential equations are further classified according to their order and degree.

Order of a Differential Equation: Definition : The order of a differential equation is the order of the highest derivative that appears in the equation.

Degree of a Differential Equation: Definition : The degree of a differential equation is the degree of the highest order differential coefficient or derivative, when the differential coefficients are free from radicals and fractions.

Order and degree of equations (1), (2), (4), (6), (7), (8) of above Article is one.

Order of equations (3), (5), (9), (10) of above Article is two.

Degree of equations (3), (9), (10) of above Article is one.

To find degree of equation (5) i.e. $\sqrt{1+\dfrac{dy}{dx}} = \dfrac{d^2y}{dx^2}$, squaring on both sides, we get

$1+\dfrac{dy}{dx} = \left(\dfrac{d^2y}{dx^2}\right)^2$. Therefore Degree of above equation is two.

Solution of a Differential Equation : Consider the differential equation $\dfrac{dy}{dx} = \cos x$ and the relation $y = \sin x + c$. We observe that the derivative obtained from it satisfies the equation.

Therefore $y = \sin x + c,$ is a solution of the differential equation $\dfrac{dy}{dx} = \cos x.$

Definition: A solution or primitive of a differential equation is any relation between the dependent and independent variables which is free from derivatives and which satisfies the differential equation.

General Solution of a Differential Equation: A relation between the dependent and independent variables, which is free from derivatives, which satisfies a given differential equation and which contains arbitrary constants equal to the order of the differential equation is called the general solution (G.S.) or complete integral.

Hence, the general solution of a differential equation of order n must involve n arbitrary constants.

Particular Solution of a Differential Equation : The solution obtained by assigning particular values to the arbitrary constants in G.S. of a differential equation is called a particular solution or particular integral.

Note: 1. An arbitrary constant may be written in such a form as to make the answer simple. Thus, it may be written as C or $\log C$, $\sin^{-1} C$, $\tan^{-1} C$, e^C etc.

2. Total number of arbitrary constants in the general solution is equal to the order of the equation.

Formation of ordinary Differential Equations: In general, a general solution involving n arbitrary constants will give rise to a differential equation, of order n, free of arbitrary constants. This equation is obtained by eliminating the n constants between the (n + 1) equations consisting of the general solution and the n equations obtained by differentiating the general solution n times w. r. t. the independent variable.

Ex. : Form the differential equation of which general solution is $x = (C_1 + C_2 t)e^t$.

Solution : Here x is dependent variable and t is independent variable.

$x = C_1 e^t + C_2 t e^t$

$\dfrac{dx}{dt} = C_1 e^t + C_2 e^t + C_2 t e^t = x + C_2 e^t$ by above equation

$\dfrac{dx}{dt} - x = C_2 e^t$

$\therefore \dfrac{d^2x}{dt^2} - \dfrac{dx}{dt} = C_2 e^t$ i.e. $\dfrac{d^2x}{dt^2} - \dfrac{dx}{dt} = \dfrac{dx}{dt} - x$

$\therefore \dfrac{d^2x}{dt^2} - 2\dfrac{dx}{dt} + x = 0$ is the required differential equation of order 2, and degree as 1.

Ordinary differential equations of first order and first degree: An ordinary differential equation of first order and first degree is of the form $M + N\dfrac{dy}{dx} = 0$ or $Mdx + Ndy = 0$ where M and N are functions of x and y or constants.

The general solution of such equation will contain only one arbitrary constant.

The method of solving a differential equation of the first order and first degree:

Following are the types of solving differential equation of the first order and first degree
1. Variables separable form (V.S. form).
2. Homogeneous differential equations.
3. Non-Homogeneous differential equations
4. Linear differential equations
5. Equations reducible to the linear form - Bernoulli's form.
6. Exact differential equations.
7. Equations reducible to exact form by using integrating factor.

Types (1) to (3) are known to students, hence we discuss outline of these methods. As per University syllabus we are focusing more on Type (4) to (7).

VARIABLES SEPARABLE FORM (V.S. FORM)

Many first-order differential equations can be reduced to the form $\dfrac{dy}{dx} = \dfrac{f(x)}{g(y)}$ or $\dfrac{dy}{dx} = \dfrac{g(y)}{f(x)}$

by algebraic manipulations. We find it convenient to write $g(y)dy = f(x)dx$ or $\dfrac{dy}{g(y)} = \dfrac{dx}{f(x)}$.

Such an equation is in variables separable form (V.S. form) because the variables x and y are separated so that x appears only on one side of the equation and y appears only on the other side.

The solution is obtained by integrating on both sides giving,

$\int g(y)dy = \int f(x)dx + C$ or $\int \dfrac{dy}{g(y)} = \int \dfrac{dx}{f(x)} + C$.

It is of great importance to introduce the constant of integration immediately when the integration is carried out.

Ex. : Solve $\dfrac{dy}{dx} = \dfrac{x \sin x}{2e^y \sinh y}$.

Solution: Given equation is of the form $\dfrac{dy}{dx} = \dfrac{f(x)}{g(y)}$, hence it can be expressed in the variables separable form as $g(y)dy = f(x)dx$.

$\therefore \dfrac{dy}{dx} = \dfrac{x \sin x}{2e^y \sinh y} \Rightarrow 2e^y \sinh y\, dy = x \sin x\, dx$

General Solution is $2\int e^y \sinh y\, dy = \int x \sin x\, dx + C$

$\int e^y (e^y - e^{-y}) dy = -x \cos x + \sin x + C$

$\dfrac{e^{2y}}{2} - y = -x \cos x + \sin x + C$ i.e. $\dfrac{e^{2y}}{2} - y + x \cos x - \sin x = C$

Homogeneous Differential Equation :

Consider a differential equation in the form $M(x, y)dx + N(x, y)dy = 0$ or $\dfrac{dy}{dx} = \dfrac{M(x, y)}{N(x, y)}$.

The differential equation of the above form is said to be homogeneous if $M(x, y)$ and $N(x, y)$ are homogeneous functions in x and y of the **same degree.**

These equations are reducible to V.S. form by changing the dependent variable from y to u by the substitution $y = ux$ Therefore $\dfrac{dy}{dx} = u + x\dfrac{du}{dx}$.

Ex.: Solve $(y^4 - 2x^3 y)dx + (x^4 - 2xy^3)dy = 0$.

Solution: Given differential equation can be written as

$$\left[\left(\dfrac{y}{x}\right)^4 - 2\left(\dfrac{y}{x}\right)\right] + \left[1 - 2\left(\dfrac{y}{x}\right)^3\right]\dfrac{dy}{dx} = 0.$$

Put $y = ux$ $\therefore \dfrac{dy}{dx} = u + x\dfrac{du}{dx}$

$u^4 - 2u + (1 - 2u^3)\left(u + x\dfrac{du}{dx}\right) = 0$, i.e. $(-u^4 - u) + (1 - 2u^3)x\dfrac{du}{dx} = 0$

$-\dfrac{dx}{x} + \dfrac{(1 - 2u^3)}{u^4 + u}du = 0$ i.e. $\dfrac{dx}{x} = \left(\dfrac{1}{u} - \dfrac{3u^2}{1 + u^3}\right)du$

General Solution is $\int \dfrac{dx}{x} = \int \left(\dfrac{1}{u} - \dfrac{3u^2}{1 + u^3}\right)du$

$\log x = \log u - \log(1 + u^3) + \log C$ i.e. $\dfrac{x(1 + u^3)}{u} = C$

$\therefore x^3 + y^3 = Cxy.$

Non-Homogeneous Differential Equations Reducible to Homogeneous Form

A differential equation of the form

$$\dfrac{dy}{dx} = \dfrac{a_1 x + b_1 y + c_1}{a_2 x + b_2 y + c_2} \quad (I)$$

is called non-homogeneous differential equation.

Case (i) : If $\dfrac{a_1}{a_2} = \dfrac{b_1}{b_2}$ In this case, the expressions $a_1 x + b_1 y$ and $a_2 x + b_2 y$ will always have a common factor of the form $lx + my$. We put $lx + my = u$ then equation (I) reduces to V.S. form in the variables u, x.

Case (ii): If $\dfrac{a_1}{a_2} \neq \dfrac{b_1}{b_2}$ In this case to reduce equation (I) to homogeneous form, we substitute $x = X + h$, $y = Y + k$ where h and k are constants to be determined.

Also $dx = dX$, $dy = dY$ $\therefore \dfrac{dy}{dx} = \dfrac{dY}{dX}$. Equation (I) becomes,

$$\dfrac{dY}{dX} = \dfrac{a_1 X + b_1 Y + (a_1 h + b_1 k + c_1)}{a_2 X + b_2 Y + (a_2 h + b_2 k + c_2)}$$

Choose h and k such that equation will become homogeneous in X and Y i.e. $a_1 h + b_1 k + c_1 = 0$ and $a_2 h + b_2 k + c_2 = 0$

We get $\dfrac{dY}{dX} = \dfrac{a_1 X + b_1 Y}{a_2 X + b_2 Y}$.

which is a homogeneous equation in X and Y. Put $y = ux$ $\therefore \dfrac{dy}{dx} = u + x\dfrac{du}{dx}$.

Finally equation reduces to V.S. form.

Ex. on case-I $\dfrac{a_1}{a_2} = \dfrac{b_1}{b_2}$: Solve $\dfrac{dy}{dx} = \dfrac{x + y + 1}{2x + 2y + 1}$.

Solution: $\dfrac{dy}{dx} = \dfrac{x + y + 1}{2(x + y) + 1}$ Put $x + y = u$ $\therefore 1 + \dfrac{dy}{dx} = \dfrac{du}{dx}$

$\dfrac{du}{dx} - 1 = \dfrac{u + 1}{2u + 1}$ i.e. $\dfrac{du}{dx} = \dfrac{u + 1}{2u + 1} + 1 = \dfrac{3u + 2}{2u + 1}$

$\dfrac{2u + 1}{3u + 2} du = dx \Rightarrow \dfrac{2}{3}\left(\dfrac{3u + 2 - 1/2}{3u + 2}\right) du = dx$

General solution is $\dfrac{2}{3}\int du - \dfrac{1}{3}\int \dfrac{du}{3u + 2} = \int dx + C$

$\dfrac{2}{3} u - \dfrac{1}{9} \log(3u + 2) = x + C$ i.e. $6u - 9x - \log(3u + 2) = C'$

$6(x + y) - 9x - \log(3(x + y) + 2) = C'$ i.e. $6y - 3x - \log(3x + 3y + 2) = C'$.

Ex. on case-II $\dfrac{a_1}{a_2} \neq \dfrac{b_1}{b_2}$: Solve $\dfrac{dy}{dx} + \dfrac{2x + 3y}{y + 2} = 0$.

Solution: Given differential equation can be written as,

$\dfrac{dy}{dx} = \dfrac{-2x - 3y}{y + 2}$ $\therefore \dfrac{a_1}{a_2} \neq \dfrac{b_1}{b_2}$

Put $x = X + h$, $y = Y + k$ Also $dx = dX$, $dy = dY$ $\therefore \dfrac{dy}{dx} = \dfrac{dY}{dX}$.

$\therefore \dfrac{dY}{dX} = \dfrac{-2X - 3Y - 2h - 3k}{Y + k + 2}$

We choose h, k such that $-2h-3k=0$, $k+2=0 \Rightarrow h=3, k=-2$.

$$\therefore \frac{dY}{dX} = \frac{-2X-3Y}{Y} = \frac{-2-3Y/X}{Y/X}$$

Put $Y = uX$, $\frac{dY}{dX} = u + X\frac{du}{dX}$

$$u + X\frac{du}{dX} = \frac{-2-3u}{u} \Rightarrow X\frac{du}{dX} = \frac{-2-3u}{u} - u = \frac{-2-3u-u^2}{u}$$

$$\frac{udu}{u^2+3u+2} = -\frac{dX}{X}.$$

$$\int \frac{udu}{u^2+3u+2} = -\int \frac{dX}{X} + \log C$$

$$\int \frac{2du}{(u+2)} - \int \frac{du}{(u+1)} - \log X = \log C \quad \text{By partial fraction.}$$

$$2\log(u+2) - \log(u+1) + \log X = \log C \quad i.e. \log \frac{(u+2)^2}{(u+1)} X = \log C$$

$$\log \frac{(Y+2X)^2}{(Y+X)} = \log C \quad \therefore X = x-3, \ Y = y+2$$

$$\frac{(y+2+2x-6)^2}{x+y-1} = C \quad i.e. \ (2x+y-4)^2 = C(x+y-1).$$

Note: As per university syllabus we are only concentrating on Linear differential equations of the first order, Equations reducible to the linear form, Exact differential equations, Equations reducible to exact form by using integrating factor.

Linear differential equations: A differential equation is called a linear differential equation, if the dependent variable and its derivative occur in the first degree only.

In other words, no term involves powers of derivatives or powers of dependent variables or product of derivatives and / or dependent variables.

The form of the linear differential equation in y is

$$\frac{dy}{dx} + Py = Q \qquad \text{(A)}$$

where P and Q are the functions of x (or constants) only.

For solving equation (A), we multiply both sides by $e^{\int Pdx}$

$$\therefore \frac{dy}{dx}.e^{\int Pdx} + Py.e^{\int Pdx} = Q.e^{\int Pdx} \qquad \text{(B)}$$

The L.H.S of equation (B) is

$$\frac{dy}{dx}.e^{\int Pdx} + Py.e^{\int Pdx} = \frac{d}{dx}\left[ye^{\int Pdx}\right] \qquad \therefore \frac{d}{dx}\left[e^{\int Pdx}\right] = pe^{\int Pdx}$$

Therefore equation (B) becomes $\dfrac{d}{dx}\left[ye^{\int P\,dx}\right]=Q.e^{\int P\,dx}$

On integration, we get $ye^{\int P\,dx}=\int Q e^{\int P\,dx}\,dx+C$

Note: 1. The term $e^{\int P\,dx}$ is known as integrating factor (I.F) of the differential equation.

2. The solution of linear differential equation can be written as $y(I.F)=\int Q(I.F)\,dx+c$

3. The coefficient of $\dfrac{dy}{dx}$ or $\dfrac{dx}{dy}$ in linear differential equation must be one

4. There are two types of linear differential equations

Type-I $\dfrac{dy}{dx}+Py=Q$, Type-II $\dfrac{dx}{dy}+Px=Q$

Method of Solving Linear differential equation : Type-I $\dfrac{dy}{dx}+Py=Q$

1. First write the given equation in the standard form $\dfrac{dy}{dx}+Py=Q$
2. Find the values of P and Q where P and Q are the functions of x (or constants) only
3. Calculate the value of I.F = $e^{\int P\,dx}$
4. The solution is given by

$y.e^{\int P\,dx}=\int Q.e^{\int P\,dx}\,dx+C$ i.e. $y.(I.F)=\int Q\,(I.F)\,dx+C$

Examples on Linear differential equations: Type-I $\dfrac{dy}{dx}+Py=Q$

Ex. 1: Solve $\dfrac{dy}{dx}=4y+2x-4x^2$

Solution: Given equation can be written in standard form as

$\dfrac{dy}{dx}-4y=2x-4x^2$ Where $P=-4,\ Q=2x-4x^2$

$\therefore I.F=e^{\int P\,dx}=e^{\int -4\,dx}=e^{-4x}$ The solution of given equation is

$y.(I.F)=\int Q\,(I.F)\,dx+C\ \therefore\ ye^{-4x}=\int(2x-4x^2)e^{-4x}\,dx+C$

$ye^{-4x}=\int 2xe^{-4x}dx-\int 4x^2 e^{-4x}dx+C$

Integrating by parts, we get

$ye^{-4x}=2\left[x\left(\dfrac{e^{-4x}}{-4}\right)-\dfrac{e^{-4x}}{16}\right]-4\left[x^2\left(\dfrac{e^{-4x}}{-4}\right)-2x\left(\dfrac{e^{-4x}}{16}\right)+2\left(\dfrac{e^{-4x}}{-64}\right)\right]+C$

$ye^{-4x}=\left[2x\left(\dfrac{e^{-4x}}{-4}\right)-2\left(\dfrac{e^{-4x}}{16}\right)-4x^2\left(\dfrac{e^{-4x}}{-4}\right)+8x\left(\dfrac{e^{-4x}}{16}\right)-8\left(\dfrac{e^{-4x}}{-64}\right)\right]+C$

$ye^{-4x}=\left[x^2 e^{-4x}+x\left(2\dfrac{e^{-4x}}{-4}+8\dfrac{e^{-4x}}{16}\right)-2\left(\dfrac{e^{-4x}}{16}\right)-8\left(\dfrac{e^{-4x}}{-64}\right)\right]+C$

$ye^{-4x}=\left[x^2 e^{-4x}+x\left(\dfrac{-8e^{-4x}+8e^{-4x}}{16}\right)-\left(\dfrac{8e^{-4x}-8e^{-4x}}{64}\right)\right]+C$

$ye^{-4x}=x^2 e^{-4x}+C.$

Ex. 2 : Solve $x \log x \dfrac{dy}{dx} + y = 2 \log x$

Solution: Given equation can be written in standard form as $\dfrac{dy}{dx} + \dfrac{1}{x \log x} y = \dfrac{2}{x}$

where $P = \dfrac{1}{x \log x}$ and $Q = \dfrac{2}{x}$

$\therefore \text{I.F} = e^{\int P dx} = e^{\int \frac{1}{x \log x} dx} = e^{\log t} = t = \log x \qquad \because \log x = t, \dfrac{1}{x} dx = dt$

The solution of given equation is

$y.(\text{I.F}) = \int Q.(\text{I.F}) dx + C$

$y \log x = \int \dfrac{2}{x} \log x \, dx + C$

$= 2 \dfrac{(\log x)^2}{2} + C \qquad \because \int [f(x)]^n f'(x) dx = \dfrac{[f(x)]^{n+1}}{n+1}$

$y \log x = (\log x)^2 + C$

Ex. 3: Solve $xy' + 2y - x \sin x = 0$

Solution: Given equation can be written in standard form as

$\dfrac{dy}{dx} + \dfrac{2}{x} y = \sin x,$ where $P = \dfrac{2}{x}$ and $Q = \sin x$

$\therefore \text{I.F} = e^{\int P dx} = e^{\int \frac{2}{x} dx} = e^{2 \log x} = x^2$

The solution of given equation is $y.(\text{I.F}) = \int Q.(\text{I.F}) dx + C$

$\therefore y x^2 = \int \sin x \, x^2 \, dx + C$

$= x^2 (-\cos x) - 2x(-\sin x) + 2(\cos x) + C$

$y x^2 = -x^2 \cos x + 2x \sin x + 2 \cos x + C$

Ex. 4 : Solve $(y \cos x + 1) dx + \sin x \, dy = 0$

Solution: Given equation can be written in standard form as

$\sin x \dfrac{dy}{dx} = -(y \cos x + 1) \implies \dfrac{dy}{dx} + \dfrac{\cos x}{\sin x} y = \dfrac{-1}{\sin x}$

i.e. $\dfrac{dy}{dx} + (\cot x).y = -\text{cosec} x$

where $P = \cot x$ and $Q = -\text{cosec} x$

$\therefore \text{I.F} = e^{\int \cot x \, dx} = e^{\log \sin x} = \sin x$

The solution of given equation is

$y.(\text{I.F}) = \int Q.(\text{I.F}) dx + C \therefore y \sin x = \int -\text{cosec} x \sin x dx + C$

$y \sin x = -\int dx + C \therefore y \sin x = -x + C$

Ex. 5: Solve $\dfrac{dy}{dx} + y \tan x = x^2 \cos^2 x$

Solution: Given equation is in standard form
where $P = \tan x$ and $Q = x^2 \cos^2 x$

$\therefore \text{I.F} = e^{\int \tan x dx} = e^{\log \sec x} = \sec x$

The solution of given equation is

$y.(\text{I.F}) = \int Q.(\text{I.F}) dx + C$

$\therefore y \sec x = \int x^2 \cos x dx + Cx = \int x^2 \cos^2 x \sec x dx + C$

$y \sec x = \int x^2 \cos x dx + C$

$\qquad = x^2 (\sin x) - 2x(-\cos x) + 2(-\sin x) + C$

$\therefore y \sec x = x^2 \sin x + 2x \cos x - 2 \sin x + C.$

Ex. 6: Solve $\dfrac{dy}{dx} + 2y \tan x = \sin x$ at $y = 0, \; x = \dfrac{\pi}{3}$

Solution: Given equation is in standard form
where $P = 2 \tan x$ and $Q = \sin x$

$\therefore \text{I.F} = e^{\int 2 \tan x dx} = e^{2 \log \sec x} = \sec^2 x$

The solution of given equation is

$y.(\text{I.F}) = \int Q.(\text{I.F}) dx + C \therefore y \sec^2 x = \int \sec^2 x \sin x dx + C$

$y \sec^2 x = \int \sec x \tan x dx + C$

$\therefore y \sec^2 x = \sec x + C \qquad (A)$

At $y = 0, \; x = \dfrac{\pi}{3} \Rightarrow \sec \dfrac{\pi}{3} = 2$, substituting in equation (A), we get

$0 = 2 + C \Rightarrow C = -2 \therefore y \sec^2 x = \sec x - 2$

Ex. 7: Solve $\cos x \dfrac{dy}{dx} + y \sin x = \sec^2 x$ **SUK: May-11**

Solution: Given equation can be written in standard form as

$\dfrac{dy}{dx} + y \tan x = \sec^3 x$

where $P = \tan x$ and $Q = \sec^3 x$

$\therefore \text{I.F} = e^{\int \tan x dx} = e^{\log \sec x} = \sec x$

The solution of given equation is

$y \cdot (I.F) = \int Q \cdot (I.F) dx + C \therefore y \sec x = \int \sec^3 x \sec x \, dx + C$

$y \sec x = \int \sec^4 x \, dx + C$

$y \sec x = \int \sec^2 x \sec^2 x \, dx + C$

$= \int \sec^2 x (1 + \tan^2 x) dx + C$

$= \int (\sec^2 x + \sec^2 x \tan^2 x) dx + C$

$= \tan x + \dfrac{\tan^3 x}{3} + C \therefore 3y \sec x = 3 \tan x + \tan^3 x + C.$

Ex. 8: Solve $\cos^2 x \dfrac{dy}{dx} + y = \tan x$ **SUK: Nov-08**

Solution: Given equation can be written in standard form as

$\dfrac{dy}{dx} + \dfrac{1}{\cos^2 x} y = \dfrac{\tan x}{\cos^2 x}$ i.e. $\dfrac{dy}{dx} + \sec^2 x \cdot y = \tan x \sec^2 x$

where $P = \sec^2 x$ and $Q = \tan x \sec^2 x$

$\therefore I.F = e^{\int \sec^2 x \, dx} = e^{\tan x}$

The solution of given equation is

$y \cdot (I.F) = \int Q \cdot (I.F) dx + C \therefore y e^{\tan x} = \int (\tan x \sec^2 x) e^{\tan x} dx + C$

Put $\tan x = t \therefore \sec^2 x \, dx = dt$

$y e^{\tan x} = \int e^t \, t \, dt + C$

$y e^{\tan x} = t e^t - 1 \cdot e^t + C$

$\therefore y e^{\tan x} = (\tan x) e^{\tan x} - e^{\tan x} + C$

$y e^{\tan x} - (\tan x) e^{\tan x} + e^{\tan x} = C$ i.e. $e^{\tan x}[y - \tan x + 1] = C.$

Ex. 9: Solve $(x^2 e^x - my) dx + mx \, dy = 0$

Solution: Given equation can be written in standard form as

$mx \dfrac{dy}{dx} = -(x^2 e^x - my) \Rightarrow mx \dfrac{dy}{dx} - my = -x^2 e^x$ i.e. $\dfrac{dy}{dx} - \dfrac{1}{x} y = \dfrac{-x e^x}{m}$

where $P = -\dfrac{1}{x}$ and $Q = \dfrac{-x e^x}{m}$

$\therefore I.F = e^{\int P dx} = e^{\int -\frac{1}{x} dx} = e^{-\log x} = \dfrac{1}{x}$

The solution of given equation is

$$y.(I.F) = \int Q.(I.F)\,dx + C \quad \therefore y\frac{1}{x} = \int \frac{-xe^x}{m}\frac{1}{x}dx + C$$

$$y\frac{1}{x} = -\frac{1}{m}\int e^x\,dx + C \quad \therefore y\frac{1}{x} = -\frac{1}{m}e^x + C \text{ i.e. } my + xe^x = xC'.$$

Ex. 10: Solve $(1+x^3)\dfrac{dy}{dx} + 6x^2 y = e^x$

Solution: Given equation can be written in standard form as

$$\frac{dy}{dx} + \frac{6x^2}{1+x^3} y = \frac{e^x}{1+x^3}$$

where $P = \dfrac{6x^2}{1+x^3}$ and $Q = \dfrac{e^x}{1+x^3}$

$$\therefore I.F = e^{\int P\,dx} = e^{\int \frac{6x^2}{1+x^3}dx} = e^{2\log(1+x^3)} = (1+x^3)^2$$

The solution of given equation is

$$y.(I.F) = \int Q.(I.F)\,dx + C \quad \therefore y(1+x^3)^2 = \int \frac{e^x}{1+x^3}(1+x^3)^2\,dx + C$$

$$y(1+x^3)^2 = \int e^x(1+x^3)\,dx + C$$

$$y(1+x^3)^2 = (1+x^3)(e^x) - 3x^2 e^x + 6xe^x - 6e^x + C$$

$$\therefore y(1+x^3)^2 = e^x\left[x^3 - 3x^2 + 6x - 5\right] + C$$

Ex. 11: Solve $x\dfrac{dy}{dx} - y = x^3 \cos x$ given $x = \pi$, and $y = 0$

Solution: Given equation can be written in standard form as

$$x\frac{dy}{dx} - y = x^3 \cos x, \quad \frac{dy}{dx} - \frac{1}{x} y = x^2 \cos x$$

where $P = -\dfrac{1}{x}$ and $Q = x^2 \cos x$

$$\therefore I.F = e^{\int P\,dx} = e^{\int -\frac{1}{x}dx} = e^{-\log x} = \frac{1}{x}$$

The solution of given equation is

$$y.(I.F) = \int Q.(I.F)\,dx + C \quad \therefore y\frac{1}{x} = \int x^2 \cos x \frac{1}{x}\,dx + C$$

$$y\frac{1}{x} = \int x\cos x\,dx + C \Rightarrow y\frac{1}{x} = x(\sin x) - 1.(-\cos x) + C$$

$$y = x^2 \sin x + x\cos x + C \qquad (A)$$

given $x = \pi$, and $y = 0$,

$0 = \pi^2 \sin\pi + \pi\cos\pi + C \Rightarrow C = \pi, \because \cos\pi = -1, \sin\pi = 0,$

Substituting in equation (A), we get $y = x^2 \sin x + x\cos x + \pi$

Ex. 12: Solve $(1-x^2)\dfrac{dy}{dx} + 2xy = x\sqrt{1-x^2}$

Solution: Given equation can be written in standard form as

$\dfrac{dy}{dx} + \dfrac{2x}{1-x^2} y = \dfrac{x\sqrt{1-x^2}}{1-x^2}$ i.e. $\dfrac{dy}{dx} + \dfrac{2x}{1-x^2} y = \dfrac{x}{\sqrt{1-x^2}}$

where $P = \dfrac{2x}{1-x^2}$ and $Q = \dfrac{x}{\sqrt{1-x^2}}$

$\therefore \text{I.F} = e^{\int P dx} = e^{\int \frac{2x}{1-x^2} dx} = e^{-\log(1-x^2)} = \dfrac{1}{1-x^2}$

The solution of given equation is

$y \cdot (\text{I.F}) = \int Q \cdot (\text{I.F}) dx + C \quad \therefore y \dfrac{1}{1-x^2} = \int \dfrac{x}{\sqrt{1-x^2}} \dfrac{1}{1-x^2} dx + C$

$y \dfrac{1}{1-x^2} = \int \dfrac{x}{(1-x^2)^{3/2}} dx + C$

$y \dfrac{1}{1-x^2} = \int x(1-x^2)^{-3/2} dx + C \Rightarrow y \dfrac{1}{1-x^2} = \dfrac{-1}{2} \int -2x(1-x^2)^{-3/2} dx + C$

$y \dfrac{1}{1-x^2} = \dfrac{-1}{2} \dfrac{(1-x^2)^{-1/2}}{\frac{-1}{2}} + C \quad \therefore \dfrac{y}{1-x^2} = \dfrac{1}{\sqrt{1-x^2}} + C.$

Ex. 13: Solve $x^2(x^2-1)\dfrac{dy}{dx} + x(x^2+1)y = x^2 - 1$

Solution: $\dfrac{dy}{dx} + \left(\dfrac{x^2+1}{x(x^2-1)}\right) y = \dfrac{1}{x^2}$ which is linear in y.

$P = \dfrac{x^2+1}{x(x^2-1)}, \quad Q = \dfrac{1}{x^2}, \quad \int P dx = \int \dfrac{x^2+1}{x(x-1)(x+1)} dx$

$\int P dx = \int \left(\dfrac{1}{x-1} + \dfrac{1}{x+1} - \dfrac{1}{x}\right) dx = \log(x-1) + \log(x+1) - \log x = \log\left(\dfrac{x^2-1}{x}\right)$

$\text{I.F.} = e^{\int P dx} = \dfrac{x^2-1}{x}$

Therefore the general solution is given by

$y\left(\dfrac{x^2-1}{x}\right) = \int \dfrac{1}{x^2} \left(\dfrac{(x^2-1)}{x}\right) dx + C = \int \left(\dfrac{1}{x} - \dfrac{1}{x^3}\right) dx + C$

$= \log x + \dfrac{1}{2x^2} + C$

Ex. 14: Solve $\left(\dfrac{e^{-2\sqrt{x}}}{\sqrt{x}} - \dfrac{y}{\sqrt{x}}\right)\dfrac{dx}{dy} = 1$ or $\dfrac{dy}{dx} + \dfrac{y}{\sqrt{x}} = \dfrac{e^{-2\sqrt{x}}}{\sqrt{x}}$ **SUK: Dec-11**

Solution: Given equation can be written in standard form as

$\left(\dfrac{e^{-2\sqrt{x}}}{\sqrt{x}} - \dfrac{y}{\sqrt{x}}\right)\dfrac{dx}{dy} = 1 \Rightarrow \left(\dfrac{e^{-2\sqrt{x}}}{\sqrt{x}} - \dfrac{y}{\sqrt{x}}\right) = \dfrac{dy}{dx}$

$\therefore \dfrac{dy}{dx} + \dfrac{1}{\sqrt{x}} y = \dfrac{e^{-2\sqrt{x}}}{\sqrt{x}}$ Which is linear in y

where $P = \dfrac{1}{\sqrt{x}}$ and $Q = \dfrac{e^{-2\sqrt{x}}}{\sqrt{x}}$

$\therefore \text{I.F} = e^{\int P dx} = e^{\int \frac{1}{\sqrt{x}} dx} = e^{\int x^{-\frac{1}{2}} dx} = e^{2\sqrt{x}}$.

The solution of given equation is

$y.(\text{I.F}) = \int Q.(\text{I.F})\, dx + C$

$\therefore ye^{2\sqrt{x}} = \int \left(\dfrac{e^{-2\sqrt{x}}}{\sqrt{x}}\right) e^{2\sqrt{x}} dx + C \Rightarrow ye^{2\sqrt{x}} = \int \dfrac{1}{\sqrt{x}} dx + C$

$\Rightarrow y.e^{2\sqrt{x}} = \int x^{-\frac{1}{2}} dx + C$ i.e. $y.e^{2\sqrt{x}} = 2\sqrt{x} + C$

Ex. 15: Solve $\sec x \dfrac{dy}{dx} = y + \sin x$

Solution: Given equation can be written in standard form by divide sec x

$\dfrac{dy}{dx} - \dfrac{1}{\sec x} y = \sin x \dfrac{1}{\sec x} \Rightarrow \dfrac{dy}{dx} - \cos x.y = \sin x \cos x$

Where $P = -\cos x$ and $Q = \sin x \cos x$

$\therefore \text{I.F.} = e^{-\int \cos x\, dx} = e^{-\sin x}$

The solution of given equation is

$y.(\text{I.F}) = \int Q.(\text{I.F})\, dx + C \Rightarrow ye^{-\sin x} = \int \sin x \cos x\, e^{-\sin x} dx + C$

$ye^{-\sin x} = \int te^{-t} dt + C$ Put $\sin x = t$, $\therefore \cos x\, dx = dt$

$ye^{-\sin x} = t\left(\dfrac{e^{-t}}{-1}\right) - 1\left(\dfrac{e^{-t}}{1}\right) + C \Rightarrow ye^{-\sin x} = -te^{-t} - e^{-t} + C$

$\therefore ye^{-\sin x} = -\sin x e^{-\sin x} - e^{-\sin x} + C$ i.e. $ye^{-\sin x} = -e^{-\sin x}(\sin x + 1) + C$

Ex. 16: Solve $x(x-1)\dfrac{dy}{dx} - (x-2)y = x^3(2x-1)$

Solution: Given equation can be written in standard form as

$$\frac{dy}{dx} - \frac{(x-2)}{x(x-1)} y = \frac{x^3(2x-1)}{x(x-1)} \quad i.e. \quad \frac{dy}{dx} - \frac{(x-2)}{x(x-1)} y = \frac{x^2(2x-1)}{(x-1)}$$

Where $P = -\frac{(x-2)}{x(x-1)}$ and $Q = \frac{x^2(2x-1)}{(x-1)}$

$$\therefore \text{I.F} = e^{\int Pdx} = e^{-\int \frac{(x-2)}{x(x-1)} dx} = e^{\int \left(\frac{-2}{x} + \frac{1}{x-1}\right) dx} = e^{-2\log x + \log(x-1)} = e^{\log\left(\frac{x-1}{x^2}\right)} = \frac{x-1}{x^2}$$

$$\because \frac{(x-2)}{x(x-1)} = \frac{A}{x} + \frac{B}{x-1} \Rightarrow x - 2 = A(x-1) + Bx \therefore A = 2, B = -1$$

The solution of given equation is

$$y.(\text{I.F}) = \int Q.(\text{I.F}) dx + c \Rightarrow y \frac{x-1}{x^2} = \int \frac{x^2(2x-1)}{x-1} \cdot \frac{x-1}{x^2} dx + C$$

$$y \frac{x-1}{x^2} = \int (2x-1) dx + C \Rightarrow y \frac{x-1}{x^2} = x^2 - x + C.$$

Ex. 17: Solve $x(1-x^2) \frac{dy}{dx} + (2x^2 - 1) y = x^3$

Solution: Given equation can be written in standard form as

$$\frac{dy}{dx} + \frac{2x^2 - 1}{x(1-x^2)} y = \frac{x^3}{x(1-x^2)}$$

Where $P = \frac{2x^2 - 1}{x(1-x^2)}$ and $Q = \frac{x^3}{x(1-x^2)}$

$$\therefore \text{I.F} = e^{\int Pdx} = e^{\int \frac{2x^2-1}{x(1-x^2)} dx} = e^{\int \frac{2x^2-1}{x(1-x)(1+x)} dx} = e^{\int \left(\frac{-1}{x} + \frac{1}{2(1-x)} + \frac{1}{2(1+x)}\right) dx}$$

$$\because \frac{2x^2 - 1}{x(1-x)(1+x)} = \frac{A}{x} + \frac{B}{1-x} + \frac{C}{1+x} \Rightarrow 2x^2 - 1 = A(1-x)(1+x) + Bx(1+x) + Cx(1-x)$$

Put $x = 0 \Rightarrow A = -1$, $x = 1 \Rightarrow B = \frac{1}{2}$, $x = -1 \Rightarrow C = \frac{-1}{2}$

$$\therefore \text{I.F} = e^{-\log x - \frac{1}{2}\log(1-x) - \frac{1}{2}\log(1+x)} = e^{-\log x\sqrt{1-x^2}} = e^{\log\left[x\sqrt{1-x^2}\right]^{-1}} = \frac{1}{x\sqrt{1-x^2}}$$

The solution of given equation is

$$y.(\text{I.F}) = \int Q.(\text{I.F}) dx + C \quad \therefore y \frac{1}{x\sqrt{1-x^2}} = \int \frac{x^2}{1-x^2} \cdot \frac{1}{x\sqrt{1-x^2}} dx + C$$

$$y \frac{1}{x\sqrt{1-x^2}} = \int \frac{x}{(1-x^2)^{3/2}} dx + C \quad \text{Put } 1 - x^2 = t \therefore -2x\,dx = dt$$

$$y \frac{1}{x\sqrt{1-x^2}} = \frac{-1}{2}\int \frac{-2x}{(1-x^2)^{3/2}} dx + C \Rightarrow y\frac{1}{x\sqrt{1-x^2}} = \frac{-1}{2}\int t^{-3/2} dt + C$$

$$y\frac{1}{x\sqrt{1-x^2}} = \frac{-1}{2}\frac{t^{-1/2}}{-1/2} + C \Rightarrow y\frac{1}{x\sqrt{1-x^2}} = t^{-1/2} + C \quad \therefore y\frac{1}{x\sqrt{1-x^2}} = \frac{1}{\sqrt{1-x^2}} + C$$

Ex. 18 : Solve $\cosh x . \dfrac{dy}{dx} = 2\cosh^2 x . \sinh x - y \sinh x$

or $\cosh x . y' + y \sinh x = 2\cosh^2 x . \sinh x$

Solution: Given equation can be written in standard form as

$\dfrac{dy}{dx} + \dfrac{\sinh x}{\cosh x} y = \dfrac{2\cosh^2 x . \sinh x}{\cosh x}$ i.e. $\dfrac{dy}{dx} + \tanh x . y = 2\cosh x . \sinh x$

where $P = \tanh x$ and $Q = 2\cosh x . \sinh x$

$\therefore \text{I.F} = e^{\int P dx} = e^{\int \tanh x . dx} = e^{\log \cosh x} = \cosh x$

The solution of given equation is

$y . (\text{I.F}) = \int Q . (\text{I.F}) dx + C$

$\therefore y \cosh x = \int 2 \cosh x . \sinh x . \cosh x + C$

$= \int 2\cosh^2 x . \sinh x + C$

Thus $y \cosh x = \dfrac{2}{3}\cosh^3 x + C$ $\qquad \because \int [f(x)]^n f'(x) dx = \dfrac{[f(x)]^{n+1}}{n+1}$

Ex. 19: Solve $\dfrac{dy}{dx} + \left(\dfrac{x}{(1-x^2)^{3/2}}\right) y = \dfrac{x(1+\sqrt{1-x^2})}{(1-x^2)^2}$

Solution: Given equation can be written in standard form as

$\dfrac{dy}{dx} + \left(\dfrac{x}{(1-x^2)^{3/2}}\right) y = \dfrac{x(1+\sqrt{1-x^2})}{(1-x^2)^2}$, where $P = \dfrac{x}{(1-x^2)^{3/2}}$ and $Q = \dfrac{x(1+\sqrt{1-x^2})}{(1-x^2)^2}$

$\therefore \text{I.F} = e^{\int P dx} = e^{\int \frac{x}{(1-x^2)^{3/2}} dx} = e^{\frac{-1}{2}\int (1-x^2)^{-3/2}(-2x)dx} \qquad \because \int [f(x)]^n f'(x) dx = \dfrac{[f(x)]^{n+1}}{n+1}$

$\therefore \text{I.F} = e^{\int P dx} = e^{\frac{-1}{2}\left[\frac{(1-x^2)^{-1/2}}{-1/2}\right]} = e^{\frac{1}{\sqrt{1-x^2}}}$

The solution of given equation is

$$y \cdot (I.F) = \int Q \cdot (I.F) dx + C$$

$$y e^{\frac{1}{\sqrt{1-x^2}}} = \int \frac{x(1+\sqrt{1-x^2})}{(1-x^2)^2} \cdot e^{\frac{1}{\sqrt{1-x^2}}} dx + C$$

$$= \int \frac{(1+\sqrt{1-x^2})}{(1-x^2)^{1/2}} \cdot \frac{x}{(1-x^2)^{3/2}} \cdot e^{\frac{1}{\sqrt{1-x^2}}} dx + C$$

Put $\dfrac{1}{\sqrt{1-x^2}} = t \Rightarrow \dfrac{x}{(1-x^2)^{3/2}} dx = dt$

$$y\, e^{\frac{1}{\sqrt{1-x^2}}} = \int e^t (t+1) dt + C$$

$$= (t+1)e^t - e^t + C$$

$$= e^t t + C$$

resubtituting $\dfrac{1}{\sqrt{1-x^2}} = t$

$$y e^{\frac{1}{\sqrt{1-x^2}}} = e^{\frac{1}{\sqrt{1-x^2}}} \frac{1}{\sqrt{1-x^2}} + C \ i.e. \ y = \frac{1}{\sqrt{1-x^2}} + C\, e^{\frac{-1}{\sqrt{1-x^2}}}.$$

Ex. 20: Solve $\sin x \dfrac{dy}{dx} = \cos x - 3y$

Solution: Given equation can be written in standard form as

$$\frac{dy}{dx} + \frac{3}{\sin x} y = \frac{\cos x}{\sin x} \Rightarrow \frac{dy}{dx} + 3(\operatorname{cosec} x)\, y = \cot x$$

where $P = 3(\operatorname{cosec} x)$ and $Q = \cot x$

$$\therefore I.F = e^{\int 3 \operatorname{cosec} x\, dx} = e^{3 \log \tan \frac{x}{2}} = \tan^3 \frac{x}{2}$$

The solution of given equation is

$$y \cdot (I.F) = \int Q \cdot (I.F) dx + C$$

$$y \tan^3 \frac{x}{2} = \int \cot x \, \tan^3 \frac{x}{2} dx + C$$

$$= \int \frac{\cos x}{\sin x} \cdot \frac{\sin^3 x/2}{\cos^3 x/2} dx + C$$

$$= \int \frac{(2\cos^2 x/2 - 1)}{2 \sin x/2 \cos x/2} \cdot \frac{\sin^3 x/2}{\cos^3 x/2} dx + C$$

$$= \frac{1}{2}\int \frac{(2\cos^2 x/2 - 1)}{\cos^4 x/2} \sin^2 x/2\, dx + C$$

$$= \int \left(\tan^2 \frac{x}{2} - \frac{1}{2}\tan^2 \frac{x}{2} \sec^2 \frac{x}{2}\right) dx + C \quad \because 1 + \tan^2 x = \sec^2 x$$

$$y\tan^3 \frac{x}{2} = 2\tan^2 \frac{x}{2} - x - \frac{1}{6}\tan^3 \frac{x}{2} + C.$$

Ex. 21: Solve $\sin 2x \dfrac{dy}{dx} = y + \tan x$

Solution: Given equation can be written in standard form as

$$\frac{dy}{dx} - \frac{1}{\sin 2x} y = \frac{\tan x}{\sin 2x}$$

where $P = \dfrac{1}{\sin 2x}$ and $Q = \dfrac{\tan x}{\sin 2x}$

$$\therefore \text{I.F} = e^{\int \frac{-1}{\sin 2x} dx} = e^{-\int \frac{1}{2\sin x \cos x} dx} = e^{-\frac{1}{2}\int \frac{\sec^2 x}{\tan x} dx} = e^{-\frac{1}{2}\log \tan x} = \frac{1}{\sqrt{\tan x}}$$

The solution of given equation is

$$y.(\text{I.F}) = \int Q.(\text{I.F})\, dx + C$$

$$y\frac{1}{\sqrt{\tan x}} = \int \frac{\tan x}{\sin 2x} \frac{1}{\sqrt{\tan x}} dx + C$$

$$= \int \frac{\sin x}{\cos x . 2\sin x \cos x} \frac{1}{\sqrt{\tan x}} dx + C = \int \frac{1}{2\cos^2 x} \frac{1}{\sqrt{\tan x}} dx + C$$

$$= \int \frac{\sec^2 x}{2} \frac{1}{\sqrt{\tan x}} dx + C$$

$$y\frac{1}{\sqrt{\tan x}} = \sqrt{\tan x} + C \quad \text{i.e } y = \tan x + C\sqrt{\tan x}$$

Ex. 22: Solve $x\cos x \dfrac{dy}{dx} + y(x\sin x + \cos x) = 1$ **SUK: Dec-13**

Solution: Given equation can be written in standard form as

$$\frac{dy}{dx} + \frac{x\sin x + \cos x}{x\cos x} y = \frac{1}{x\cos x} \quad \text{i.e. } \frac{dy}{dx} + \left(\tan x + \frac{1}{x}\right) y = \frac{1}{x\cos x}$$

where $P = \tan x + \dfrac{1}{x}$ and $Q = \dfrac{1}{x\cos x}$

$$\therefore \text{I.F} = e^{\int \left(\tan x + \frac{1}{x}\right) dx} = e^{\log \sec x + \log x} = e^{\log(x\sec x)} = x\sec x$$

The solution of given equation is

$$y.(\text{I.F}) = \int Q.(\text{I.F})\, dx + C \Rightarrow y\, x\sec x = \int \frac{1}{x\cos x} x\sec x\, dx + C$$

$$y\, x\sec x = \int \sec^2 x\, dx + C = \tan x + C$$

TEST YOUR KNOWLEDGE

1. Solve $x(x-1)\dfrac{dy}{dx} - y = x^2(x-1)^2$ Ans: $y\dfrac{x}{x-1} = \dfrac{x^3}{3} + C$

2. Solve $(1+x^3)\dfrac{dy}{dx} + 6x^2 y = e^x$ Ans: $y(1+x^3)^2 = e^x + e^x(x^3 - 3x^2 + 6x - 6) + C$

3. Solve $(2y - x^2)dx + xdy = 0$ Ans: $yx^2 = \dfrac{x^5}{5} + C$

4. Solve $\dfrac{dy}{dx} + \dfrac{1-2x}{x^2}y = 1$ Ans: $y = x^2 + Ce^{1/x}x^2$

5. Solve $\dfrac{dy}{dx} + \dfrac{4x}{x^2+1}y = \dfrac{1}{(x^2+1)^2}$ Ans: $y(x^2+1)^2 = x + C$

6. Solve $(x+y+1)\dfrac{dy}{dx} = 1$ Ans: $y + x + 2 = Ce^y$

7. Solve $\dfrac{dy}{dx} + \dfrac{2x}{x^2+1}y = \dfrac{4x^2}{x^2+1}$ Ans: $3y(x^2+1) = 4x^3 + C$

8. Solve $\dfrac{dy}{dx} + \dfrac{2x}{x^2+1}y = \dfrac{1}{(x^2+1)^2}$ Ans: $y(x^2+1) = \tan^{-1} x - \dfrac{\pi}{4} + C$

9. Solve $\cos x \dfrac{dy}{dx} + y \sin x = \sec^2 x$ Ans: $y \sec x = \tan x + \dfrac{\tan^3 x}{3} + C$

10. Solve $\dfrac{dy}{dx} + 2y \tan x = \sin x$ at $y = 0$, $x = \dfrac{\pi}{3}$ Ans: $y \sec^2 x = \sec x - 2$

11. Solve $\cos^2 x \dfrac{dy}{dx} + y = \tan x$ Ans: $y = \tan x - 1 + Ce^{-\tan x}$

12. Solve $\dfrac{dy}{dx} = x^3 - 2xy$ at $y = 2$ when $x = 1$ Ans: $2y = x^2 - 1 + 4Ce^{-x^2}$

13. Solve $(x+1)\dfrac{dy}{dx} - y = e^{3x}(x+1)^2$ Ans: $\dfrac{y}{x+1} = \dfrac{e^{3x}}{3} + C$

14. Solve $(1-x^2)\dfrac{dy}{dx} + 2xy = x\sqrt{1-x^2}$ Ans: $y = \sqrt{1-x^2} + C(1+x^2)$

15. Solve $\dfrac{dy}{dx} + y \tan x = x^2 \cos^2 x$ Ans: $y \sec x = x^2 \sin x + 2x \cos x - 2 \sin x + C$

16. Solve $\sin y \dfrac{dy}{dx} = \cos y(1 - x \cos y)$ Ans: $\sec y = x + 1 + Ce^x$

17. Solve $(x^2+1)\dfrac{dy}{dx} + 2xy = 4x^2$ Ans: $y(x^2+1) - \dfrac{4}{3}x^3 = C$

18. Solve $\dfrac{dy}{dx}+\dfrac{3x^2}{(1+x^3)}y=\dfrac{\sin^2 x}{(1+x^3)}$ Ans: $y(x^3+1)=\dfrac{x}{2}-\dfrac{1}{4}\sin 2x+C$

19. Solve $\dfrac{dy}{dx}+\dfrac{y}{x}=x^2$ at $y=1$ when $x=1$.   Ans: $4xy=x^4+3$

20. Solve $\dfrac{dy}{dx}+(1+2x)y=e^{-x^2}$ Ans: $ye^{x^2}+2=e^{x^2}+C$

21. Solve $\dfrac{dy}{dx}+y\tan x=\sec x$ Ans: $y=c\cos x+\sin x+C$

Remark: Sometimes the differential equation becomes linear if x taken as the dependent variable and y as independent variable. The differential equation has the following form

$$\dfrac{dx}{dy}+Px=Q$$

where P and Q are the functions of y (or constants) only.

Method of Solving Linear differential equations: Type-II

1. First write the given equation in the standard linear form $\dfrac{dx}{dy}+Px=Q$

2. Find the values of P and Q where P and Q are the functions of y (or constants)

3. Calculate the value of I.F = $e^{\int P\,dy}$

4. There fore the general solution is given by

$$x\cdot e^{\int P\,dy}=\int Q\cdot e^{\int P\,dy}\,dy+C \quad \text{i.e.} \quad x(\text{I.F})=\int Q(\text{I.F})\,dy+C$$

Examples on Linear differential equations Type: II $\dfrac{dx}{dy}+Px=Q$

Ex. 1: Solve $(x+2y^3)dy=y\,dx$ or $(x+2y^3)\dfrac{dy}{dx}=y$.

Solution: Given equation can be written in standard form as

$\dfrac{dx}{dy}-\dfrac{1}{y}x=2y^2$ Which is linear in x

where $P=-\dfrac{1}{y}$ and $Q=2y^2$

$\therefore \text{I.F}=e^{\int -\frac{1}{y}dy}=e^{-\log y}=\dfrac{1}{y}$

The solution of given equation is

$x\cdot(\text{I.F})=\int Q\cdot(\text{I.F})\,dy+C \quad \therefore x\dfrac{1}{y}=\int 2y^2\dfrac{1}{y}dy+C$

$x\dfrac{1}{y}=\int 2y\,dy+C \Rightarrow x\dfrac{1}{y}=y^2+C \quad i.e. \quad x=y^3+yC.$

Ex. 2: Solve $2(x-5y^3)\dfrac{dy}{dx}+y=0$

Solution: Given equation can be written in standard form as

$\dfrac{dx}{dy}+\dfrac{2}{y}x=10y^2$ Which is linear in x

$\therefore \text{I.F} = e^{\int \frac{2}{y}dy} = e^{2\log y} = y^2$

The solution of given equation is where $P=\dfrac{2}{y}$ and $Q=10y^2$

$x.(\text{I.F}) = \int Q.(\text{I.F})dy + C \quad \therefore xy^2 = \int 10y^2.y^2 dy + C$

$xy^2 = 10\int y^4 dy + C \Rightarrow xy^2 = 2y^5 + C.$

Ex. 3: Solve $ydx-(x+2y^2)dy=0$

Solution: Given equation can be written in standard form as

$\dfrac{dx}{dy}-\dfrac{1}{y}x=2y$ Which is linear in x

where $P=\dfrac{-1}{y}$ and $Q=2y$

$\therefore \text{I.F} = e^{\int \frac{-1}{y}dy} = e^{-\log y} = \dfrac{1}{y}$

The solution of given equation is

$x.(\text{I.F}) = \int Q.(\text{I.F})dy + C \quad \therefore x\dfrac{1}{y} = \int 2y.\dfrac{1}{y}dy + C$

$x\dfrac{1}{y} = 2\int dy + C \Rightarrow x\dfrac{1}{y} = 2y + C, \text{ i.e. } x = 2y^2 + yC.$

Ex. 4: Solve $ye^y = (y^3+2xe^y)\dfrac{dy}{dx}$

Solution: Given equation can be written in standard form as

$\dfrac{dx}{dy}-\dfrac{2}{y}x = y^2 e^{-y}$ Which is linear in x

where $P=\dfrac{-2}{y}$ and $Q=y^2 e^{-y}$

$\therefore \text{I.F} = e^{\int \frac{-2}{y}dy} = e^{-2\log y} = \dfrac{1}{y^2}$

The solution of given equation is

$$x.(\text{I.F}) = \int Q.(\text{I.F})\,dy + C \quad \therefore x\frac{1}{y^2} = \int y^2 e^{-y} \cdot \frac{1}{y^2}\,dy + C$$

$$x\frac{1}{y^2} = \int e^{-y}\,dy + C \Rightarrow x\frac{1}{y^2} = -e^{-y} + C, \text{ i.e. } x + y^2 e^{-y} = y^2 C.$$

Ex. 5: Solve $(1+y^2)dx = (\tan^{-1} y - x)dy$

Solution: Given equation contains y^2 term, so it cannot be linear in y. Hence we try to solve it by Type –II. We write the given equation as

$$(1+y^2)\frac{dx}{dy} + x = \tan^{-1} y \text{ i.e. } \frac{dx}{dy} + \left(\frac{1}{1+y^2}\right)x = \frac{\tan^{-1} y}{1+y^2} \quad \text{Which is linear in x}$$

where $P = \dfrac{1}{1+y^2}$ and $Q = \dfrac{\tan^{-1} y}{1+y^2}$

$$\therefore \text{I.F} = e^{\int \frac{1}{1+y^2}dy} = e^{\tan^{-1} y}$$

The solution of given equation is

$$x.(\text{I.F}) = \int Q.(\text{I.F})\,dy + C \quad \therefore x e^{\tan^{-1} y} = \int \frac{\tan^{-1} y}{1+y^2} e^{\tan^{-1} y}\,dy + C$$

Put $\tan^{-1} y = t \quad \therefore \dfrac{1}{1+y^2}dy = dt$

$$\therefore x e^t = \int e^t\, t\, dt + C = t e^t - e^t + C$$

$$\therefore x e^{\tan^{-1} y} = \tan^{-1} y\, e^{\tan^{-1} y} - e^{\tan^{-1} y} + C \quad \text{i.e. } x = \tan^{-1} y - 1 + C e^{-\tan^{-1} y}$$

Ex. 6: Solve $e^{-y} \sec^2 y\, dy = dx + x\,dy$ or $dx + x\,dy = e^{-y} \sec^2 y\,dy$

Solution: Given equation can be written in standard form as

$$(e^{-y} \sec^2 y - x)dy = dx \quad \text{i.e. } \frac{dx}{dy} + x = e^{-y} \sec^2 y$$

where $P = 1$ and $Q = e^{-y} \sec^2 y$

$$\therefore \text{I.F.} = e^{\int 1\,dy} = e^y$$

The solution of given equation is

$$x.(\text{I.F}) = \int Q.(\text{I.F})\,dy + C \quad \therefore x e^y = \int e^{-y} \sec^2 y \cdot e^y\,dy + C$$

$$x e^y = \int \sec^2 y\,dy + C \quad \text{i.e. } x e^y = \tan y + C$$

Ex. 7: Solve $(y+1)dx + \left[x - (y+2)e^y\right]dy = 0$

Solution: Given equation can be written in standard form as

$(y+1)\dfrac{dx}{dy} + x - (y+2)e^y = 0$ i.e. $\dfrac{dx}{dy} + \dfrac{1}{y+1}x = \dfrac{(y+2)e^y}{y+1}$ Which is linear in x

where $P = \dfrac{1}{y+1}$ and $Q = \dfrac{(y+2)e^y}{y+1}$

$\therefore \text{I.F} = e^{\int \frac{1}{y+1}dy} = e^{\log(y+1)} = (y+1)$

The solution of given equation is

$x.(\text{I.F}) = \int Q.(\text{I.F})dy + C$ $\therefore x(y+1) = \int \dfrac{(y+2)e^y}{y+1}(y+1)dy + C$

$x(y+1) = \int (y+2)e^y dy + C$

$\Rightarrow x(y+1) = (y+2)e^y - 1.e^y + C$ i.e. $x(y+1) = (y+1)e^y + C$.

Ex. 8: Solve $(1 + x + xy^2)dy + (y + y^3)dx = 0$

Solution: Given equation can be written in standard form as

$y(1+y^2)\dfrac{dx}{dy} = -(1+x+xy^2) \Rightarrow y(1+y^2)\dfrac{dx}{dy} + x(1+y^2) = -1$

i.e $\dfrac{dx}{dy} + \dfrac{1}{y}x = \dfrac{-1}{y(1+y^2)}$ Which is linear in x

where $P = \dfrac{1}{y}$ and $Q = \dfrac{-1}{y(1+y^2)}$

$\therefore \text{I.F} = e^{\int \frac{1}{y}dy} = e^{\log y} = y$

The solution of given equation is

$x.(\text{I.F}) = \int Q.(\text{I.F})dy + C$ $\therefore x y = \int \dfrac{-1}{y(1+y^2)}dy + C$

$x y = -\int \dfrac{1}{1+y^2}dy + C$ $\Rightarrow x y = -\tan^{-1} y + C$ i.e. $x y + \tan^{-1} y = C$.

Ex. 9: Solve $(1+y^2) + (x - e^{-\tan^{-1} y})\dfrac{dy}{dx} = 0$ or $(1+y^2)dx = (e^{-\tan^{-1} y} - x)dy$

Solution: Given equation contains y^2 term, so it cannot be linear in y. Hence we try to solve it by Type –II. We write the given equation as

$(1+y^2)\dfrac{dx}{dy} + x = e^{-\tan^{-1} y}$ i.e. $\dfrac{dx}{dy} + \left(\dfrac{1}{1+y^2}\right)x = \dfrac{e^{-\tan^{-1} y}}{1+y^2}$ Which is linear in x

where $P = \dfrac{1}{1+y^2}$ and $Q = \dfrac{e^{-\tan^{-1} y}}{1+y^2}$

$\therefore \text{I.F} = e^{\int \frac{1}{1+y^2}dy} = e^{\tan^{-1} y}$

(1.23)

The solution of given equation is

$$x.(I.F) = \int Q.(I.F) dy + C \quad \therefore xe^{\tan^{-1} y} = \int \frac{e^{-\tan^{-1} y}}{1+y^2} e^{\tan^{-1} y} dy + C$$

$$xe^{\tan^{-1} y} = \int \frac{1}{1+y^2} dy + C \Rightarrow xe^{\tan^{-1} y} = \tan^{-1} y + C$$

Ex. 10: Solve $y^2 + \left(x - \dfrac{1}{y}\right) \dfrac{dy}{dx} = 0$

Solution: Given equation contains y^2 term, so it cannot be linear in y. Hence we try to solve it by Type –II. Therefore equation can be written in standard form as

$$y^2 = -\left(x - \frac{1}{y}\right) \frac{dy}{dx} \Rightarrow y^2 \frac{dx}{dy} = -\left(x - \frac{1}{y}\right) \quad i.e. \quad y^2 \frac{dx}{dy} + x = \frac{1}{y}$$

Dividing equation by y^2 $\therefore \dfrac{dx}{dy} + \dfrac{1}{y^2} x = \dfrac{1}{y^3}$

where $P = \dfrac{1}{y^2}$ and $Q = \dfrac{1}{y^3}$

$$\therefore I.F = e^{\int P dy} = e^{\int \frac{1}{y^2} dy} = e^{\frac{-1}{y}}$$

The solution of given equation is

$$x.(I.F) = \int Q.(I.F) dy + C \quad \therefore x\, e^{-\frac{1}{y}} = \int e^{-\frac{1}{y}} \cdot \frac{1}{y^3} dy + C$$

$$xe^{-\frac{1}{y}} = \int \frac{1}{y} e^{-\frac{1}{y}} \left(\frac{1}{y^2} dy\right) + C \quad \text{Put } t = -\frac{1}{y} \therefore dt = \frac{1}{y^2} dy$$

$$= \int (-t) e^t dt + C$$

$$= -(te^t - e^t) + C \Rightarrow xe^{-\frac{1}{y}} = -e^t(t-1) + C$$

$$xe^{-\frac{1}{y}} = -e^{-\frac{1}{y}}\left(-\frac{1}{y} - 1\right) + C \quad \therefore xe^{-\frac{1}{y}} = e^{-\frac{1}{y}}\left(1 + \frac{1}{y}\right) + C \quad i.e. \quad x = 1 + \frac{1}{y} + Ce^{\frac{1}{y}}.$$

Ex. 11: Solve $(1+\sin y) \dfrac{dx}{dy} = \left[2y \cos y - x(\sec y + \tan y)\right]$

Solution: Given equation can be written in standard form as

$$\frac{dx}{dy} = \left[\frac{2y \cos y}{(1+\sin y)} - x \frac{(\sec y + \tan y)}{(1+\sin y)}\right], \quad \frac{dx}{dy} = \left[\frac{2y \cos y}{(1+\sin y)} - x \frac{\left(\frac{1}{\cos y} + \frac{\sin y}{\cos y}\right)}{(1+\sin y)}\right]$$

$$\frac{dx}{dy} = \left[\frac{2y \cos y}{(1+\sin y)} - x \frac{1}{\cos y}\right] \quad i.e. \quad \frac{dx}{dy} + x \sec y = \frac{2y \cos y}{1+\sin y} \quad \text{Which is linear in x}$$

(1.24)

where $P = \sec y$ and $Q = \dfrac{2y \cos y}{1 + \sin y}$

$\therefore \text{I.F} = e^{\int \sec y\, dy} = e^{\log(\sec y + \tan y)} = \sec y + \tan y$

The solution of given equation is

$x \cdot (\text{I.F}) = \int Q \cdot (\text{I.F})\, dy + C \quad \therefore x(\sec y + \tan y) = \int \dfrac{2y \cos y}{1 + \sin y}(\sec y + \tan y)\, dy + C$

$x(\sec y + \tan y) = 2\int \dfrac{y \cos y}{1 + \sin y}\left(\dfrac{1}{\cos y} + \dfrac{\sin y}{\cos y}\right) dy + C$

$= 2\int \dfrac{y \cos y}{1 + \sin y}\left(\dfrac{1 + \sin y}{\cos y}\right) dy + C$

$x(\sec y + \tan y) = 2\int y\, dy + C \quad \text{i.e.} \quad x(\sec y + \tan y) = y^2 + C.$

Ex. 12: Solve $(\sin 2y)\, dx = (\tan y - x)\, dy$

Solution: Given equation can be written in standard form as

$\dfrac{dx}{dy} = \dfrac{\tan y}{\sin 2y} - \dfrac{x}{\sin 2y} \Rightarrow \dfrac{dx}{dy} + \dfrac{1}{\sin 2y} x = \dfrac{\tan y}{\sin 2y},$

$\dfrac{dx}{dy} + x(\operatorname{cosec} 2y) = \dfrac{\sin y}{\cos y}\dfrac{1}{2 \sin y \cos y} \quad \text{i.e.} \quad \dfrac{dx}{dy} + x \operatorname{cosec} 2y = \dfrac{1}{2}\sec^2 y \quad \text{Which is linear in x}$

where $P = \operatorname{cosec} 2y$ and $Q = \dfrac{1}{2}\sec^2 y$

$\therefore \text{I.F} = e^{\int \operatorname{cosec} 2y\, dy} = e^{\frac{1}{2}\log(\operatorname{cosec} 2y - \cot 2y)} = (\operatorname{cosec} 2y - \cot 2y)^{\frac{1}{2}}$

The solution of given equation is

$x \cdot (\text{I.F}) = \int Q \cdot (\text{I.F})\, dy + C \quad \therefore x(\operatorname{cosec} 2y - \cot 2y)^{\frac{1}{2}} = \int \dfrac{1}{2}\sec^2 y\, (\operatorname{cosec} 2y - \cot 2y)^{\frac{1}{2}} dy + C$

As $(\operatorname{cosec} 2y - \cot 2y)^{\frac{1}{2}} = \left(\dfrac{1}{\sin 2y} - \dfrac{\cos 2y}{\sin 2y}\right)^{\frac{1}{2}} = \left(\dfrac{1 - \cos 2y}{\sin 2y}\right)^{\frac{1}{2}} = \left(\dfrac{2\sin^2 y}{2\sin y \cos y}\right)^{\frac{1}{2}} = \tan^{\frac{1}{2}} y$

$x \tan^{\frac{1}{2}} y = \dfrac{1}{2}\int \sec^2 y\, \tan^{\frac{1}{2}} y\, dy + C \quad \text{Put } \tan y = t \therefore \sec^2 y\, dy = dt$

$x\sqrt{\tan y} = \dfrac{1}{2}\int t^{\frac{1}{2}}\, dt + C$

$x\sqrt{\tan y} = \dfrac{1}{3} t^{\frac{3}{2}} + C \quad \text{substituting } \tan y = t \quad \therefore 3x\sqrt{\tan y} = (\tan y)^{\frac{3}{2}} + C'$

TEST YOUR KNOWLEDGE:

1. Solve $(1+y^2)dx = (e^{\tan^{-1}y} - x)dy$ Ans: $2xe^{\tan^{-1}y} = (\tan^{-1}y)^2 + C'$, Hint: put $e^{\tan^{-1}y} = t$

2. Solve $(y-x)\dfrac{dy}{dx} = a^2$ Ans: $x = y - a^2 + Ce^{-y/a^2}$

3. Solve $(x + 2y^3)\dfrac{dy}{dx} = y$ Ans: $x = y^3 + yC$

4. Solve $\dfrac{dy}{dx} = \dfrac{y}{2y\log y + y - x}$ Ans: $x = y\log y + \dfrac{C}{y}$

5. Solve $dx + xdy = e^{-y}\sec^2 y\, dy$ Ans: $xe^y = x^3 + x + C$

6. Solve $(e^{-y}\sec^2 y - x)dy = dx$ Ans: $xe^y = \tan y + C$

7. Solve $ye^y(y^3 + 2xe^y)\dfrac{dy}{dx}$ Ans: $\dfrac{x}{y^2} + e^{-y} = C$

Equation Reducible to Linear Form (Bernoulli's Equation)

An equation of the type $\dfrac{dy}{dx} + Py = Qy^n$, $n \neq 1$.

Where P and Q are functions of x (or constants), is called Bernoulli's equation and can be made linear by dividing by y^n and putting $\dfrac{1}{y^{n-1}} = v$

Method of solving Bernoulli's equation

Consider the equation $\dfrac{dy}{dx} + Py = Qy^n$, $n \neq 1$.

dividing by y^n, we get $\dfrac{1}{y^n}\dfrac{dy}{dx} + \dfrac{1}{y^{n-1}}P = Q$ (A)

Putting $\dfrac{1}{y^{n-1}} = v$, $\therefore (1-n)\dfrac{1}{y^n}\dfrac{dy}{dx} = \dfrac{dv}{dx}$, $n \neq 1$

Substituting in equation (A), we get

$\dfrac{1}{(1-n)}\dfrac{dv}{dx} + Pv = Q$,   i.e. $\dfrac{dv}{dx} + (1-n)Pv = (1-n)Q$. $n \neq 1$

Which is linear in v. Now solve it earlier method, and re-substitute $\dfrac{1}{y^{n-1}} = v$

Examples On Bernoulli's Equation

Ex. 1: Solve $x^2 y - x^3 \dfrac{dy}{dx} = y^4 \cos x$

Solution: The given equation can be written as

$x^3 \dfrac{dy}{dx} + y^4 \cos x = x^2 y$ i.e. $\dfrac{dy}{dx} - \dfrac{1}{x} y = -y^4 \dfrac{\cos x}{x^3}$

Diving by y^4, we get $\dfrac{1}{y^4} \dfrac{dy}{dx} - \dfrac{1}{x} \dfrac{1}{y^3} = -\dfrac{\cos x}{x^3}$, i.e. $y^{-4} \dfrac{dy}{dx} - \dfrac{1}{x} y^{-3} = -\dfrac{\cos x}{x^3}$

Putting $y^{-3} = v$, $\therefore -3y^{-4} \dfrac{dy}{dx} = \dfrac{dv}{dx}$ i.e. $y^{-4} \dfrac{dy}{dx} = -\dfrac{1}{3} \dfrac{dv}{dx}$

$\dfrac{-1}{3} \dfrac{dv}{dx} - \dfrac{1}{x} v = -\dfrac{\cos x}{x^3}$ $\therefore \dfrac{dv}{dx} + \dfrac{3}{x} v = \dfrac{3 \cos x}{x^3}$ which is linear differential equation in v

where $P = \dfrac{3}{x}$ and $Q = \dfrac{3 \cos x}{x^3}$ $\therefore \text{I.F} = e^{\int P dx} = e^{\int \frac{3}{x} dx} = e^{3 \log x} = x^3$

The solution of given equation is

$v.(\text{I.F}) = \int Q.(\text{I.F}) \, dx + C$ $\therefore v.x^3 = \int \dfrac{3 \cos x}{x^3} x^3 \, dx + C$

$v.x^3 = 3 \int \cos x \, dx + C$ i.e. $v.x^3 = 3 \sin x + C$

Thus $\dfrac{x^3}{y^3} = 3 \sin x + C$. $\because y^{-3} = v$

Ex. 2: Solve $2xyy' = y^2 - 2x^3$, with $y(1) = 2$.

Solution: The given equation can be written as

$2xy \dfrac{dy}{dx} = y^2 - 2x^3 \Rightarrow \dfrac{dy}{dx} - \dfrac{y^2}{2xy} = \dfrac{-2x^3}{2xy}$, i.e. $\dfrac{dy}{dx} - \dfrac{1}{2x} y = -y^{-1} x^2$

Multiplying by y, we get $y \dfrac{dy}{dx} - \dfrac{1}{2x} y^2 = -x^2$

Putting $y^2 = v$, $\therefore 2y \dfrac{dy}{dx} = \dfrac{dv}{dx}$ i.e. $y \dfrac{dy}{dx} = \dfrac{1}{2} \dfrac{dv}{dx}$

$\dfrac{1}{2} \dfrac{dv}{dx} - \dfrac{1}{2x} v = -x^2$

$\therefore \dfrac{dv}{dx} - \dfrac{1}{x} v = -2x^2$ which is linear differential equation in v

where $P = -\dfrac{1}{x}$ and $Q = -2x^2$

$\therefore \text{I.F} = e^{\int P dx} = e^{\int -\frac{1}{x} dx} = e^{-\log x} = \dfrac{1}{x}$

The solution of given equation is

$v.(\text{I.F}) = \int Q.(\text{I.F}) \, dx + C$ $\therefore v. \dfrac{1}{x} = \int -2x^2 \dfrac{1}{x} \, dx + C$

$v \cdot \dfrac{1}{x} = -2 \int x \, dx + C$ i.e. $v \cdot \dfrac{1}{x} = -2 \dfrac{x^2}{2} + C$

Thus $\dfrac{y^2}{x} = -x^2 + C$. $\because y^{-2} = v$. i.e. $y^2 = -x^3 + xC$ \quad (A)

As $y(1) = 2 \Rightarrow x = 1, \; y = 2$

Therefore substituting in equation (A), we get

$2^2 = -1^3 + 1 \cdot C \Rightarrow C = 5$ $\therefore y^2 = -x^3 + 5x$.

Ex. 3 : Solve $x\dfrac{dy}{dx} + y = y^2 \log x$.

Solution: The given equation can be written as

$\dfrac{dy}{dx} + \dfrac{1}{x} y = y^2 \dfrac{\log x}{x}$.

dividing by y^2, we get $\dfrac{1}{y^2} \dfrac{dy}{dx} + \dfrac{1}{x} \dfrac{1}{y} = \dfrac{\log x}{x}$, i.e. $y^{-2} \dfrac{dy}{dx} + \dfrac{1}{x} y^{-1} = \dfrac{\log x}{x}$

Putting $y^{-1} = v$, $\therefore -1 y^{-2} \dfrac{dy}{dx} = \dfrac{dv}{dx}$ i.e. $y^{-2} \dfrac{dy}{dx} = -\dfrac{dv}{dx}$

$-\dfrac{dv}{dx} + \dfrac{1}{x} v = \dfrac{\log x}{x}$

$\therefore \dfrac{dv}{dx} - \dfrac{1}{x} v = \dfrac{-\log x}{x}$ which is linear differential equation in v

where $P = -\dfrac{1}{x}$ and $Q = \dfrac{-\log x}{x}$

$\therefore \text{I.F} = e^{\int P dx} = e^{\int -\frac{1}{x} dx} = e^{-\log x} = \dfrac{1}{x}$

The solution of given equation is

$v \cdot (\text{I.F}) = \int Q \cdot (\text{I.F}) \, dx + C$ $\therefore v \cdot \dfrac{1}{x} = -\int \dfrac{\log x}{x} \dfrac{1}{x} dx + C$

$v \cdot \dfrac{1}{x} = -\int t e^{-t} dt + C$ Put $\log x = t \Rightarrow x = e^t$, $\therefore \dfrac{1}{x} dx = dt$

$v \cdot \dfrac{1}{x} = -(t+1) e^{-t} + C$ $\therefore \dfrac{1}{xy} = -(\log x + 1) e^{-\log x} + C$. $\because y^{-1} = v$

Thus $\dfrac{1}{xy} = -(\log x + 1) \dfrac{1}{x} + C$, i.e. $(\log x + 1) y = xyC$.

Ex. 4: Solve $\dfrac{dy}{dx} + \dfrac{y}{x} \log y = \dfrac{y}{x^2} (\log y)^2$. \hfill **SUK: May-10**

Solution: The given equation can be written as

$\dfrac{1}{y}\dfrac{dy}{dx}+\dfrac{1}{x}\log y=\dfrac{1}{x^2}(\log y)^2$ Dividing by y

Putting $\log y=v$, $\therefore \dfrac{1}{y}\dfrac{dy}{dx}=\dfrac{dv}{dx}$

$\dfrac{dv}{dx}+\dfrac{1}{x}v=\dfrac{v^2}{x^2}$ Which is Bernoulli's equation

Dividing by v^2

$\dfrac{1}{v^2}\dfrac{dv}{dx}+\dfrac{1}{x}\dfrac{1}{v}=\dfrac{1}{x^2}$

Put $\dfrac{1}{v}=u$, $\therefore \dfrac{-1}{v^2}\dfrac{dv}{dx}=\dfrac{du}{dx}$

$\therefore \dfrac{-du}{dx}+\dfrac{1}{x}u=\dfrac{1}{x^2}$

$\Rightarrow \dfrac{du}{dx}-\dfrac{1}{x}u=\dfrac{-1}{x^2}$ which is linear differential equation in u

where $P=\dfrac{-1}{x}$ and $Q=\dfrac{-1}{x^2}$

$\therefore \text{I.F}=e^{\int Pdx}=e^{\int \frac{-1}{x}dx}=e^{-\log x}=\dfrac{1}{x}$

The solution of given equation is

$u.(\text{I.F})=\int Q.(\text{I.F})\,dx+C$ $\therefore u.\dfrac{1}{x}=-\int \dfrac{1}{x^2}\dfrac{1}{x}dx+C$

$u.\dfrac{1}{x}=-\int \dfrac{1}{x^3}dx+C=\dfrac{1}{2x^2}+C$

$\therefore \dfrac{1}{x\log y}=\dfrac{1}{2x^2}+C.$

Ex. 5: Solve $\dfrac{dy}{dx}-x^2 y=y^2 e^{\frac{x^3}{3}}$

Solution: Dividing by y^2, $\dfrac{1}{y^2}\dfrac{dy}{dx}-x^2\dfrac{1}{y}=e^{\frac{x^3}{3}}$, i.e. $y^{-2}\dfrac{dy}{dx}-x^2 y^{-1}=e^{\frac{x^3}{3}}$

Putting $y^{-1}=v$, $\therefore -1.y^{-2}\dfrac{dy}{dx}=\dfrac{dv}{dx}$ i.e. $y^{-2}\dfrac{dy}{dx}=-\dfrac{dv}{dx}$

$\therefore -\dfrac{dv}{dx}-x^2 v=e^{\frac{x^3}{3}}$ i.e. $\dfrac{dv}{dx}+x^2 v=-e^{\frac{x^3}{3}}$ which is linear differential equation in v

where $P=x^2$ and $Q=-e^{\frac{-x^3}{3}}$ $\therefore \text{I.F}=e^{\int Pdx}=e^{\int x^2 dx}=e^{\frac{x^3}{3}}$

(1.29)

The solution of given equation is

$$v.(I.F) = \int Q.(I.F)\,dx + C \quad \therefore v.e^{\frac{x^3}{3}} = \int -e^{-\frac{x^3}{3}}.e^{\frac{x^3}{3}}\,dx + C$$

$$\therefore v.e^{\frac{x^3}{3}} = \int -1\,dx + C \Rightarrow v.e^{\frac{x^3}{3}} = x + C \quad \therefore \frac{e^{\frac{x^3}{3}}}{y} = x + C, \quad e^{\frac{x^3}{3}} = yx + yC, \quad \because \frac{1}{y} = v.$$

Ex. 6: Solve $xy - \dfrac{dy}{dx} = y^3 e^{-x^2}$

Solution: The given equation can be written as $\dfrac{dy}{dx} - xy = -y^3 e^{-x^2}$

Dividing by y^3, $\dfrac{1}{y^3}\dfrac{dy}{dx} - x\dfrac{1}{y^2} = -e^{-x^2}$, $y^{-3}\dfrac{dy}{dx} - xy^{-2} = -e^{-x^2}$

Putting $y^{-2} = v$, $\therefore -2.y^{-3}\dfrac{dy}{dx} = \dfrac{dv}{dx}$ i.e. $y^{-3}\dfrac{dy}{dx} = -\dfrac{1}{2}\dfrac{dv}{dx}$

$\therefore -\dfrac{1}{2}\dfrac{dv}{dx} - xv = -e^{-x^2}$ i.e. $\dfrac{dv}{dx} + 2xv = 2e^{-x^2}$ which is linear differential equation in v

where $P = 2x$ and $Q = 2e^{-x^2}$

$\therefore I.F = e^{\int P\,dx} = e^{\int 2x\,dx} = e^{x^2}$

The solution of given equation is

$$v.(I.F) = \int Q.(I.F)\,dx + C \quad \therefore v.e^{x^2} = \int 2e^{-x^2}.e^{x^2}\,dx + C$$

$$v.e^{x^2} = 2\int dx + C, \quad v.e^{x^2} = 2x + C$$

$$\dfrac{e^{x^2}}{y^2} = 2x + C. \text{ i.e. } e^{x^2} = 2xy^2 + y^2 C.$$

Ex. 7: Solve $x\dfrac{dy}{dx} + 2y = y^2 x^3$

Solution: The given equation can be written as $\dfrac{dy}{dx} + 2\dfrac{1}{x}y = y^2 x^2$

Dividing by y^2, $\dfrac{1}{y^2}\dfrac{dy}{dx} + 2\dfrac{1}{xy} = x^2$, i.e. $y^{-2}\dfrac{dy}{dx} + 2\dfrac{1}{x}y^{-1} = x^2$

Putting $y^{-1} = v$, $\therefore -y^{-2}\dfrac{dy}{dx} = \dfrac{dv}{dx}$ i.e. $y^{-2}\dfrac{dy}{dx} = -\dfrac{dv}{dx}$

$-\dfrac{dv}{dx} + 2\dfrac{1}{x}v = x^2 \Rightarrow \dfrac{dv}{dx} - 2\dfrac{1}{x}v = -x^2$ which is linear equation

where $P = \dfrac{-2}{x}$, $Q = -x^2$

$\therefore I.F = e^{\int P\,dx} = e^{\int \frac{-2}{x}dx} = e^{-2\log x} = \dfrac{1}{x^2}$

The solution of given equation is

$v.(I.F) = \int Q.(I.F) \, dx + C \quad \therefore v.\dfrac{1}{x^2} = \int -x^2 . \dfrac{1}{x^2} dx + C$

$v.\dfrac{1}{x^2} = -\int dx + C, \quad v.\dfrac{1}{x^2} = -x + C \quad \therefore \dfrac{1}{x^2 y} = -x + C$

Ex. 8: Solve $3y^2 \dfrac{dy}{dx} + 2y^3 x = 4xe^{-x^2}$.

Solution: The given equation is

$3y^2 \dfrac{dy}{dx} + 2y^3 x = 4xe^{-x^2}$

Putting $y^3 = v$, $\therefore 3y^2 \dfrac{dy}{dx} = \dfrac{dv}{dx}$

$\dfrac{dv}{dx} + 2xv = 4xe^{-x^2}$ which is linear equation

where $P = 2x$, $Q = 4xe^{-x^2}$

$\therefore I.F = e^{\int P dx} = e^{\int 2x dx} = e^{x^2}$

The solution of given equation is

$v.(I.F) = \int Q.(I.F) \, dx + C \quad \therefore v.e^{x^2} = \int 4xe^{-x^2}.e^{x^2} dx + C$

$v.e^{x^2} = \int 4x \, dx + C, \quad v.e^{x^2} = 2x^2 + C$

$\therefore y^3 e^{x^2} = 2x^2 + C$

Ex. 9: Solve $\dfrac{dy}{dx} = 2y(1-2xy)$.

Solution: The given equation can be written as

$\dfrac{dy}{dx} - 2y = -4xy^2$

Dividing by y^2, $\dfrac{1}{y^2}\dfrac{dy}{dx} - 2\dfrac{1}{y} = -4x, \quad y^{-2}\dfrac{dy}{dx} - 2y^{-1} = -4x$

Putting $y^{-1} = v$, $\therefore -y^{-2}\dfrac{dy}{dx} = \dfrac{dv}{dx}$, i.e. $y^{-2}\dfrac{dy}{dx} = -\dfrac{dv}{dx}$

$-\dfrac{dv}{dx} - 2v = -4x, \Rightarrow \dfrac{dv}{dx} + 2v = 4x$ which is linear equation

where $P = 2$, $Q = 4x$

$\therefore I.F = e^{\int P dx} = e^{\int 2 dx} = e^{2x}$

The solution of given equation is

$v.(I.F) = \int Q.(I.F)\,dx + C \quad \therefore v.e^{2x} = \int 4x.e^{2x}\,dx + C$

$v.e^{2x} = 4\left[x\left(\dfrac{e^{2x}}{2}\right) - \dfrac{e^{2x}}{4}\right] + C, \quad \dfrac{e^{2x}}{y} = 2xe^{2x} - e^{2x} + C, \quad \therefore e^{2x} = 2xye^{2x} - e^{2x}y + yC.$

Ex. 10: Solve $x\dfrac{dy}{dx} + 3y = x^4 e^{1/x^2} y^3$. **SUK: May-09**

Solution: The given equation can be written as

$\dfrac{dy}{dx} + \dfrac{3}{x} y = x^3 e^{1/x^2} y^3$

Dividing by y^3, $\dfrac{1}{y^3}\dfrac{dy}{dx} + \dfrac{3}{x}\dfrac{1}{y^2} = x^3 e^{1/x^2}$, i.e. $y^{-3}\dfrac{dy}{dx} + \dfrac{3}{x} y^{-2} = x^3 e^{1/x^2}$

Putting $y^{-2} = v$, $\therefore -2y^{-3}\dfrac{dy}{dx} = \dfrac{dv}{dx}$, i.e. $y^{-3}\dfrac{dy}{dx} = -\dfrac{1}{2}\dfrac{dv}{dx}$

$-\dfrac{1}{2}\dfrac{dv}{dx} + \dfrac{3}{x} v = x^3 e^{1/x^2}, \quad \Rightarrow \dfrac{dv}{dx} - \dfrac{6}{x} v = -2x^3 e^{1/x^2}$ which is linear equation

where $P = -\dfrac{6}{x}, \quad Q = -2x^3 e^{1/x^2}$

$\therefore \text{I.F} = e^{\int P\,dx} = e^{\int -\frac{6}{x}\,dx} = e^{-6\log x} = \dfrac{1}{x^6}$

The solution of given equation is

$v.(I.F) = \int Q.(I.F)\,dx + C \quad \therefore v.\dfrac{1}{x^6} = \int -2x^3 e^{1/x^2}.\dfrac{1}{x^6}\,dx + C$

$v.\dfrac{1}{x^6} = \int e^{1/x^2}.\dfrac{-2}{x^3}\,dx + C, \quad \text{put } \dfrac{1}{x^2} = t, \ x^{-2} = t \ \therefore -2x^{-3}\,dx = dt, \text{ i.e. } -2\dfrac{1}{x^3}\,dx = dt$

$v.\dfrac{1}{x^6} = \int e^t\,dt + C \Rightarrow v.\dfrac{1}{x^6} = e^t + C, \quad \dfrac{1}{x^6 y^2} = e^{1/x^2} + C.$

Ex. 11: Solve $\dfrac{dy}{dx} = x^3 y^3 - xy$.

Solution: The given equation can be written as $\dfrac{dy}{dx} + xy = x^3 y^3$

Dividing by y^3, $\dfrac{1}{y^3}\dfrac{dy}{dx} + x\dfrac{1}{y^2} = x^3, \quad y^{-3}\dfrac{dy}{dx} + xy^{-2} = x^3$

Putting $y^{-2} = v$, $\therefore -2y^{-3}\dfrac{dy}{dx} = \dfrac{dv}{dx}$, i.e. $y^{-3}\dfrac{dy}{dx} = -\dfrac{1}{2}\dfrac{dv}{dx}$

$-\dfrac{1}{2}\dfrac{dv}{dx} + xv = x^3, \quad \Rightarrow \dfrac{dv}{dx} - 2xv = -2x^3$ which is linear equation

where $P = -2x, \quad Q = -2x^3$

$\therefore \text{I.F} = e^{\int P\,dx} = e^{\int -2x\,dx} = e^{-x^2}$

The solution of given equation is $v.(I.F) = \int Q.(I.F)\, dx + C$

$\therefore v.e^{-x^2} = \int -2x^3.e^{-x^2}\, dx + C$

$v.e^{-x^2} = -\int e^{-t}.t\, dt + C$, put $x^2 = t$, $2x\,dx = dt$

$v.e^{-x^2} = -\left[t.\left(\dfrac{e^{-t}}{-1}\right) - 1e^{-t}.\right] + C$, $v.e^{-x^2} = e^{-t}t + e^{-t} + C$

$\Rightarrow \dfrac{e^{-x^2}}{y^2} = e^{-x^2}x^2 + e^{-x^2} + C \quad \therefore \dfrac{1}{y^2} = x^2 + 1 + Ce^{x^2}$.

Ex. 12: Solve $x\dfrac{dy}{dx} + y = x^3 y^6$.

Solution: The given equation can be written as

$\dfrac{dy}{dx} + \dfrac{1}{x}y = x^2 y^6$

Dividing by y^6, $\dfrac{1}{y^6}\dfrac{dy}{dx} + \dfrac{1}{x}\dfrac{1}{y^5} = x^2$, $y^{-6}\dfrac{dy}{dx} + \dfrac{1}{x}y^{-5} = x^2$

Putting $y^{-5} = v$, $\therefore -5y^{-6}\dfrac{dy}{dx} = \dfrac{dv}{dx}$, i.e. $y^{-6}\dfrac{dy}{dx} = -\dfrac{1}{5}\dfrac{dv}{dx}$

$-\dfrac{1}{5}\dfrac{dv}{dx} + \dfrac{1}{x}v = x^2$, $\Rightarrow \dfrac{dv}{dx} - \dfrac{5}{x}v = -5x^2$ which is linear equation

where $P = -\dfrac{5}{x}$, $Q = -5x^2$

$\therefore I.F = e^{\int P\,dx} = e^{\int -\frac{5}{x}dx} = e^{-5\log x} = \dfrac{1}{x^5}$

The solution of given equation is

$v.(I.F) = \int Q.(I.F)\, dx + C \quad \therefore v.\dfrac{1}{x^5} = \int -5x^2.\dfrac{1}{x^5}\, dx + C$

$v.\dfrac{1}{x^5} = -5\int \dfrac{1}{x^3}\, dx + C$, $v.\dfrac{1}{x^5} = -5\int x^{-3}\, dx + C$

$v.\dfrac{1}{x^5} = -5\dfrac{x^{-2}}{-2} + C \Rightarrow \dfrac{1}{x^5 y^5} = \dfrac{5}{2x^2} + C$.

Ex. 13: Solve $y - \cos x \dfrac{dy}{dx} = y^2(1 - \sin x)\cos x$.

Solution: The given equation can be written as

$\cos x \dfrac{dy}{dx} - y = -y^2(1 - \sin x)\cos x$, $\dfrac{dy}{dx} - \dfrac{1}{\cos x}y = -y^2(1 - \sin x)$

Dividing by y^2, $\dfrac{1}{y^2}\dfrac{dy}{dx}-\dfrac{1}{\cos x}\dfrac{1}{y}=-1+\sin x$, $y^{-2}\dfrac{dy}{dx}-\dfrac{1}{\cos x}y^{-1}=-1+\sin x$

Putting $y^{-1}=v$, $\therefore -y^{-2}\dfrac{dy}{dx}=\dfrac{dv}{dx}$, i.e. $y^{-2}\dfrac{dy}{dx}=-\dfrac{dv}{dx}$

$-\dfrac{dv}{dx}-\dfrac{1}{\cos x}v=-1+\sin x$, $\Rightarrow \dfrac{dv}{dx}+\sec x\cdot v=1-\sin x$ which is linear equation

where $P=\sec x$, $Q=1-\sin x$

$\therefore$ I.F $=e^{\int P\,dx}=e^{\int \sec x\,dx}=e^{\log(\sec x+\tan x)}=\sec x+\tan x$

The solution of given equation is

$v\cdot(\text{I.F})=\int Q\cdot(\text{I.F})\,dx+C$ $\therefore v\cdot\sec x+\tan x=\int(1-\sin x)(\sec x+\tan x)\,dx+C$

$v\cdot\sec x+\tan x=\int(1-\sin x)\left(\dfrac{1}{\cos x}+\dfrac{\sin x}{\cos x}\right)dx+C$

$v\cdot\sec x+\tan x=\int(1-\sin x)\left(\dfrac{1+\sin x}{\cos x}\right)dx+C$, $v\cdot\sec x+\tan x=\int\dfrac{1^2-\sin^2 x}{\cos x}dx+C$

$v\cdot\sec x+\tan x=\int\dfrac{\cos^2 x}{\cos x}dx+C$, $v\cdot\sec x+\tan x=\int\cos x\,dx+C$

$v\cdot\sec x+\tan x=\sin x+C$, $\therefore \dfrac{\sec x+\tan x}{y}=\sin x+C$, i.e. $\sec x+\tan x=y\sin x+yC$

Ex. 14: Solve $x\dfrac{dy}{dx}+y=y^3 x^n$.

Solution: The given equation can be written as

$\dfrac{dy}{dx}+\dfrac{1}{x}y=y^3 x^n$

Dividing by y^3, $\dfrac{1}{y^3}\dfrac{dy}{dx}+\dfrac{1}{x}\dfrac{1}{y^2}=x^n$, i.e. $y^{-3}\dfrac{dy}{dx}+\dfrac{1}{x}y^{-2}=x^n$

Putting $y^{-2}=v$, $\therefore -2y^{-3}\dfrac{dy}{dx}=\dfrac{dv}{dx}$, i.e. $y^{-3}\dfrac{dy}{dx}=-\dfrac{1}{2}\dfrac{dv}{dx}$

$-\dfrac{1}{2}\dfrac{dv}{dx}+\dfrac{1}{x}v=x^n$, $\Rightarrow \dfrac{dv}{dx}-\dfrac{2}{x}v=-2x^n$ which is linear equation

where $P=-\dfrac{2}{x}$, $Q=-2x^n$ $\therefore$ I.F $=e^{\int P\,dx}=e^{\int -\frac{2}{x}dx}=e^{-2\log x}=\dfrac{1}{x^2}$

The solution of given equation is

$v\cdot(\text{I.F})=\int Q\cdot(\text{I.F})\,dx+C$ $\therefore v\cdot\dfrac{1}{x^2}=\int -2x^n\cdot\dfrac{1}{x^2}dx+C$

$v\cdot\dfrac{1}{x^2}=-2\int x^{n-2}dx+C$, $v\cdot\dfrac{1}{x^2}=-\dfrac{2x^{n-1}}{n-1}+C$ $\therefore \dfrac{1}{x^2 y^2}+\dfrac{2x^{n-1}}{n-1}=C$.

Ex. 15: Solve $\dfrac{dy}{dx} + y\cos x = y^n \sin 2x$.

Solution: dividing by y^n, $\dfrac{1}{y^n}\dfrac{dy}{dx} + \dfrac{1}{y^{n-1}}\cos x = \sin 2x$, $y^{-n}\dfrac{dy}{dx} + y^{-n+1}\cos x = \sin 2x$

Putting $y^{-n+1} = v$, $\therefore (-n+1)y^{-n}\dfrac{dy}{dx} = \dfrac{dv}{dx}$ i.e. $y^{-n}\dfrac{dy}{dx} = \dfrac{1}{(-n+1)}\dfrac{dv}{dx}$

$\dfrac{1}{(-n+1)}\dfrac{dv}{dx} + \cos x \, v = \sin 2x$, i.e. $\dfrac{dv}{dx} + (-n+1)\cos x \, v = (-n+1)\sin 2x$ which is linear equation

where $P = (-n+1)\cos x$, $Q = (-n+1)\sin 2x$

$\therefore \text{I.F} = e^{\int P dx} = e^{\int (-n+1)\cos x \, dx} = e^{(-n+1)\sin x}$

The solution of given equation is $v.(\text{I.F}) = \int Q.(\text{I.F})\, dx + C$

$\therefore v.e^{(-n+1)\sin x} = \int (-n+1)\sin 2x \cdot e^{(-n+1)\sin x}\, dx + C$

$v.e^{(-n+1)\sin x} = \int (-n+1)2\sin x \cos x \cdot e^{(-n+1)\sin x}\, dx + C$

Put $(-n+1)\sin x = t$, $\therefore (-n+1)\cos x \, dx = dt$

$\therefore v.e^{(-n+1)\sin x} = \int \dfrac{2t}{(-n+1)}e^t dt + C$, $v.e^{(-n+1)\sin x} = \dfrac{2}{(-n+1)}\int t.e^t dt + C$

$v.e^{(-n+1)\sin x} = \dfrac{2}{(-n+1)}\left[e^t.t - e^t\right] + C$,

$v.e^{(-n+1)\sin x} = \dfrac{2}{(-n+1)}\left[e^{(-n+1)\sin x}.(-n+1)\sin x - e^{(-n+1)\sin x}\right] + C$

$\dfrac{e^{(-n+1)\sin x}}{y^{n-1}} = \dfrac{2}{(-n+1)}\left[e^{(-n+1)\sin x}.(-n+1)\sin x - e^{(-n+1)\sin x}\right] + C$

Ex. 16: Solve $\dfrac{dy}{dx} - xy = y^2 e^{-(x^2/2)} \log x$

Solution: Dividing by y^2, $\dfrac{1}{y^2}\dfrac{dy}{dx} - x\dfrac{1}{y} = e^{-(x^2/2)}\log x$, i.e. $y^{-2}\dfrac{dy}{dx} - xy^{-1} = e^{-(x^2/2)}\log x$

Putting $y^{-1} = v$, $\therefore -y^{-2}\dfrac{dy}{dx} = \dfrac{dv}{dx}$ i.e. $y^{-2}\dfrac{dy}{dx} = -\dfrac{dv}{dx}$

$\therefore -\dfrac{dv}{dx} - xv = e^{-(x^2/2)}\log x$ i.e. $\dfrac{dv}{dx} + xv = -e^{-(x^2/2)}\log x$ which is linear differential equation in v

where $P = x$ and $Q = -e^{-(x^2/2)}\log x$

$\therefore \text{I.F} = e^{\int P dx} = e^{\int x dx} = e^{x^2/2}$

(1.35)

The solution of given equation is

$$v.(I.F) = \int Q.(I.F)\,dx + C \therefore v.e^{x^2/2} = -\int \left(e^{-(x^2/2)} \log x\right).e^{x^2/2}dx + C$$

$$v.e^{x^2/2} = -\int \log x\,dx + C, \quad v.e^{x^2/2} = -\int 1.\log x\,dx + C$$

$$v.e^{x^2/2} = -\left[\log x.(x) - \int \frac{1}{x} x\,dx\right] + C, \quad v.e^{x^2/2} = -(x\log x - x) + C$$

$$\frac{e^{x^2/2}}{y} + x\log x - x = C$$

Ex. 17: Solve $\dfrac{dy}{dx} + y\tan x = y^3 \sec x$

Solution: Dividing by y^3, $\dfrac{1}{y^3}\dfrac{dy}{dx} + \dfrac{1}{y^2}\tan x = \sec x$, i.e. $y^{-3}\dfrac{dy}{dx} + y^{-2}\tan x = \sec x$

Putting $y^{-2} = v$, $\therefore -2.y^{-3}\dfrac{dy}{dx} = \dfrac{dv}{dx}$ i.e. $y^{-3}\dfrac{dy}{dx} = -\dfrac{1}{2}\dfrac{dv}{dx}$

$\therefore \dfrac{-1}{2}\dfrac{dv}{dx} + \tan x.v = \sec x$ i.e. $\dfrac{dv}{dx} - 2\tan x.v = -2\sec x$ which is linear differential equation in v

where $P = -2\tan x$ and $Q = -2\sec x$

$$\therefore I.F = e^{\int P dx} = e^{\int -2\tan x\,dx} = e^{-2\log \sec x} = e^{\log \sec^{-2} x} = \sec^{-2} x = \frac{1}{\sec^2 x}$$

The solution of given equation is

$$v.(I.F) = \int Q.(I.F)\,dx + C \therefore v.\frac{1}{\sec^2 x} = \int -2\sec x.\frac{1}{\sec^2 x}dx + C$$

$$v.\frac{1}{\sec^2 x} = -2\int \frac{1}{\sec x}dx + C, \quad v.\frac{1}{\sec^2 x} = -2\int \cos x\,dx + C$$

$$v.\frac{1}{\sec^2 x} = -2\sin x + C, \therefore \frac{1}{y^2 \sec^2 x} = -2\sin x + C, \because \frac{1}{y^2} = v$$

$$\frac{1}{y^2}\cos^2 x + 2\sin x = C, \text{ i.e } \cos^2 x + 2y^2 \sin x = y^2 C.$$

Ex. 18: Solve $y(2xy + e^x)dx - e^x dy = 0$

Solution: The given equation can be written as

$$-e^x \frac{dy}{dx} + e^x y = 2xy^2 \text{ i.e. } \frac{dy}{dx} - y = -\frac{2xy^2}{e^x}$$

Dividing by y^2 $\dfrac{1}{y^2}\dfrac{dy}{dx} - \dfrac{1}{y} = -\dfrac{2x}{e^x}$, i.e. $y^{-2}\dfrac{dy}{dx} - y^{-1} = -\dfrac{2x}{e^x}$

(1.36)

Putting $y^{-1} = v$, $\therefore -y^{-2}\dfrac{dy}{dx} = \dfrac{dv}{dx}$ i.e. $y^{-2}\dfrac{dy}{dx} = -\dfrac{dv}{dx}$

$\therefore -\dfrac{dv}{dx} - v = -2xe^{-x}$ i.e. $\dfrac{dv}{dx} + v = 2xe^{-x}$ which is linear differential equation in v

where $P = 1$ and $Q = 2xe^{-x}$

$\therefore \text{I.F} = e^{\int Pdx} = e^{\int 1 dx} = e^{x}$

The solution of given equation is

$v.(\text{I.F}) = \int Q.(\text{I.F})\,dx + C \;\therefore v.e^{x} = \int 2xe^{-x}.e^{x}\,dx + C$

$v.e^{x} = \int 2x\,dx + C \Rightarrow v.e^{x} = x^{2} + C$

$\therefore \dfrac{e^{x}}{y} = x^{2} + C$, i.e. $e^{x} = x^{2}y + yC$. $\;\;\because \dfrac{1}{y} = v$.

Ex. 19: Solve $3x(1-x^{2})y^{2}\dfrac{dy}{dx} + (2x^{2}-1)y^{3} = ax^{3}$

Solution: The given equation can be written as

$\dfrac{dy}{dx} + \dfrac{(2x^{2}-1)}{3x(1-x^{2})y^{2}}y^{3} = \dfrac{ax^{3}}{3x(1-x^{2})y^{2}}$

$\dfrac{dy}{dx} + \dfrac{(2x^{2}-1)}{3x(1-x^{2})}y = \dfrac{ax^{2}}{3(1-x^{2})y^{2}}$

$y^{2}\dfrac{dy}{dx} + \dfrac{(2x^{2}-1)}{3x(1-x^{2})}y^{3} = \dfrac{ax^{2}}{3(1-x^{2})}$

Putting $y^{3} = v$, $\therefore 3y^{2}\dfrac{dy}{dx} = \dfrac{dv}{dx}$ i.e. $y^{2}\dfrac{dy}{dx} = \dfrac{1}{3}\dfrac{dv}{dx}$

$\dfrac{1}{3}\dfrac{dv}{dx} + \dfrac{(2x^{2}-1)}{3x(1-x^{2})}v = \dfrac{ax^{2}}{3(1-x^{2})}$ i.e. $\dfrac{dv}{dx} + \dfrac{(2x^{2}-1)}{x(1-x^{2})}v = \dfrac{ax^{2}}{(1-x^{2})}$

which is linear differential equation in v

where $P = \dfrac{2x^{2}-1}{x(1-x^{2})}$ and $Q = \dfrac{ax^{2}}{(1-x^{2})}$

$\therefore \text{I.F} = e^{\int Pdx} = e^{\int \frac{2x^{2}-1}{x(1-x^{2})}dx} = e^{\int \frac{2x^{2}-1}{x(1-x)(1+x)}dx} = e^{\int \left[\frac{-1}{x} + \frac{1/2}{(1-x)} - \frac{1/2}{(1+x)}\right]dx} = e^{\left[-\log x + \frac{1}{2}\log(1-x) - \frac{1}{2}\log(1+x)\right]}$

$$= e^{\frac{-1}{2}\left[\log x^2(1-x)(1+x)\right]} = \left[x^2(1-x^2)\right]^{\frac{-1}{2}} = \frac{1}{\sqrt{x^2(1-x^2)}} = \frac{1}{x\sqrt{(1-x^2)}}$$

$$\therefore \frac{2x^2-1}{x(1-x)(1+x)} = \frac{A}{x} + \frac{B}{(1-x)} + \frac{C}{(1+x)} \Rightarrow 2x^2 - 1 = A(1-x)(1+x) + Bx(1+x) + Cx(1-x)$$

Put $x = 0 \Rightarrow A = -1$, $x = 1 \Rightarrow B = \frac{1}{2}$, $x = -1 \Rightarrow C = \frac{-1}{2}$

The solution of given equation is

$$v.(I.F) = \int Q.(I.F)\, dx + C \quad \therefore v.\frac{1}{x\sqrt{(1-x^2)}} = \int \frac{ax^2}{(1-x^2)} \cdot \frac{1}{x\sqrt{(1-x^2)}}\, dx + C$$

$$v.\frac{1}{x\sqrt{(1-x^2)}} = \int \frac{ax}{(1-x^2)^{\frac{3}{2}}}\, dx + C = \frac{a}{-2}\int -2x(1-x^2)^{\frac{-3}{2}}\, dx + C$$

$$= \frac{a}{-2}\frac{(1-x^2)^{\frac{-1}{2}}}{-1/2} + C$$

$$\therefore \frac{y^3}{x\sqrt{1-x^2}} = \frac{a}{\sqrt{1-x^2}} + C$$

Ex. 20: Solve $2\sin x \dfrac{dy}{dx} - y\cos x = xy^3 e^x$.

Solution: The given equation can be written as

$\dfrac{dy}{dx} - \dfrac{\cos x}{2\sin x} y = \dfrac{xy^3 e^x}{2\sin x}$, i.e. $\dfrac{dy}{dx} - \dfrac{1}{2}\cot x \cdot y = \dfrac{1}{2} xy^3 e^x \operatorname{cosec} x$

Multiplying by y^3, we get

$\dfrac{1}{y^3}\dfrac{dy}{dx} - \dfrac{1}{2y^2}\cot x = \dfrac{1}{2} xe^x \operatorname{cosec} x$, i.e. $y^{-3}\dfrac{dy}{dx} - \dfrac{1}{2} y^{-2} \cot x = \dfrac{1}{2} xe^x \operatorname{cosec} x$

Putting $y^{-2} = v$, $\therefore -2y^{-3}\dfrac{dy}{dx} = \dfrac{dv}{dx}$ i.e. $y^{-3}\dfrac{dy}{dx} = \dfrac{-1}{2}\dfrac{dv}{dx}$

$\dfrac{-1}{2}\dfrac{dv}{dx} - \dfrac{1}{2} v\cot x = \dfrac{1}{2} xe^x \operatorname{cosec} x$

$\therefore \dfrac{dv}{dx} + \cot x \cdot v = -xe^x \operatorname{cosec} x$ which is linear differential equation in v

where $P = \cot x$ and $Q = -xe^x \operatorname{cosec} x$

$\therefore I.F = e^{\int P\, dx} = e^{\int \cot x\, dx} = e^{\log \sin x} = \sin x$

The solution of given equation is

$v.(\text{I.F}) = \int Q.(\text{I.F})\, dx + C \quad \therefore v.\sin x = \int -xe^x \text{cosec}\, x.\sin x\, dx + C$

$v.\sin x = -\int xe^x\, dx + C$

$v.\sin x = -(x-1)e^x + C \quad \therefore y^{-2}\sin x = -(x-1)e^x + C. \quad \because y^{-2} = v$

TEST YOUR KNOWLEDGE:

Solve the following differential equation

1. $\dfrac{dy}{dx} - \dfrac{y}{x} = \dfrac{y^2}{x^2}$ Ans: $x = -y\log x + yC$

2. $\dfrac{dy}{dx} + \dfrac{y}{x} = x^2 y^6$ Ans: $x^{-5}y^{-5} = \dfrac{5}{2x^2} + C$

3. $x\dfrac{dy}{dx} + y = xy^3$ Ans: $(2 + Cx)xy^2 = 1$

4. $x - y^2 + 2xy\dfrac{dy}{dx} = 0$ Ans: $cx = e^{y^2/x}$.

5. $x\dfrac{dy}{dx} - y\tan x = y^4 \sec x$ Ans: $y^{-3}\sec^3 x + 3\tan x + \tan^3 x = C$

6. $x\dfrac{dy}{dx} + y = y^2 \log x$ Ans: $\dfrac{1}{y} = \log e^x + xC$

7. $xy^2 \dfrac{dy}{dx} - y^3 = x^2$ Ans: $y^3 = x^2 + x + xC$.

8. $x\dfrac{dy}{dx} + 3y = y^3 x^4 e^{x^{1/2}}$ Ans: $x^6 y^2 \left(e^{x^{1/2}} + C\right) = 1$

9. $x\dfrac{dy}{dx} + xy = y^2 e^{x^2/2} \log x$ Ans: $y^{-1} e^{-x^2/2} = -x\log x + x + C$

10. $\dfrac{dy}{dx} + \dfrac{y}{x}\log y = (\log y)^2$ Ans: $\dfrac{cx}{x\log y} = \dfrac{1}{2x^2} + C$.

11. $\dfrac{dy}{dx} = y\tan x - \dfrac{y^2}{\cos x}$ Ans: $\dfrac{1}{y} = \sin x + \cos x.C$

EQUATION REDUCIBLE TO LINEAR FORM (GENERALIZED BERNOULLI'S EQUATION)

An equation of the type

$$f'(y)\dfrac{dy}{dx} + P.f(y) = Q.$$

Where P and Q are functions of x can be reduced to linear differential equation by substituting $f(y) = v$ and the equation becomes

$\dfrac{dv}{dx} + P.v = Q.$ Which is Linear differential equation in v

Its solution is $v.(\text{I.F}) = \int Q.(\text{I.F})\, dx + C$

Similarly the equation $f'(x)\dfrac{dx}{dy} + P.f(x) = Q.$

Where P and Q are functions of y can be reduced to linear differential equation by substituting $f(x) = v$ and the equation becomes

$\dfrac{dv}{dy} + P.v = Q.$ Which is Linear differential equation in v

Its solution is $v.(I.F) = \int Q.(I.F)\, dy + C$

Examples on Equation Reducible to Linear Form: Generalized Bernoulli's Equation

Ex. 1: Solve $x\dfrac{dy}{dx} + y\log y = xye^x$.

Solution: Dividing given equation by xy, we get $\dfrac{1}{y}\dfrac{dy}{dx} + \dfrac{1}{x}\log y = e^x$

Put $\log y = v$, $\therefore \dfrac{1}{y}\dfrac{dy}{dx} = \dfrac{dv}{dx}$

There fore the equation becomes $\dfrac{dv}{dx} + \dfrac{1}{x}v = e^x$, which is Linear in v

Here $P = \dfrac{1}{x}$, $Q = e^x$

$\therefore I.F = e^{\int P dx} = e^{\int \frac{1}{x} dx} = e^{\log x} = x$

Hence the solution is $v.(I.F) = \int Q.(I.F)\, dx + C$

$v.x = \int e^x.x\, dx + C$, $\quad v.x = e^x.x - e^x + C$

$\therefore x\log y = e^x(x-1) + C$

Ex. 2: Solve $\sin y \dfrac{dy}{dx} = (1 - x\cos y)\cos y$.

Solution: The given equation can be written as

$\sin y \dfrac{dy}{dx} = \cos y - x\cos^2 y$

Dividing equation by $\cos^2 y$, we get $\dfrac{\sin y}{\cos^2 y}\dfrac{dy}{dx} = \dfrac{\cos y}{\cos^2 y} - x$

i.e. $\sec y \tan y \dfrac{dy}{dx} - \sec y = -x$

Put $\sec y = v \Rightarrow \sec y \tan y \dfrac{dy}{dx} = \dfrac{dv}{dx}$

There fore the equation becomes $\dfrac{dv}{dx} - v = -x$, which is Linear in v

Here $P = -1$, $Q = -x$

$\therefore I.F. = e^{\int -1\, dx} = e^{-x}$

Hence the solution is $v.(I.F) = \int Q.(I.F)\, dx + C$

$$v.e^{-x} = \int -x.e^{-x}\,dx + C \Rightarrow v.e^{-x} = -\left[-x.e^{-x} - e^{-x}\right] + C$$

$$\therefore \sec y.e^{-x} = x.e^{-x} + e^{-x} + C \text{ i.e. } \sec y = x + 1 + Ce^{x}.$$

Ex. 3: Solve $\tan y \dfrac{dy}{dx} + \tan x = \cos y \cos^3 x$.

Solution: Dividing equation by $\cos y$, we get

$$\dfrac{\tan y}{\cos y}\dfrac{dy}{dx} + \dfrac{\tan x}{\cos y} = \cos^3 x \Rightarrow \sec y \tan y \dfrac{dy}{dx} + \sec y \tan x = \cos^3 x$$

Put $\sec y = v \Rightarrow \sec y \tan y \dfrac{dy}{dx} = \dfrac{dv}{dx}$

There fore the equation becomes $\dfrac{dv}{dx} + \tan x.v = \cos^3 x$, which is Linear in v

Here $P = \tan x,\ Q = x^3$

$$\therefore \text{I.F.} = e^{\int P\,dx} = e^{\int \tan x\,dx} = e^{\log \sec x} = \sec x$$

Hence the solution is $v.(\text{I.F}) = \int Q.(\text{I.F})\,dx + C$

$$v.\sec x = \int \cos^3 x \sec x\,dx + C \Rightarrow v.\sec x = \int \cos^2 x\,dx + C$$

$$v.\sec x = \dfrac{1}{2}\int (1 + \cos 2x)\,dx + C \therefore v.\sec x = \dfrac{1}{2}\left[x + \dfrac{\sin 2x}{2}\right] + C$$

$$\sec y \sec x = \dfrac{x}{2} + \dfrac{\sin 2x}{4} + C.$$

Ex. 4: Solve $y\dfrac{dx}{dy} = x - yx^2 \cos y$

Solution: The given equation can be written as

$$\dfrac{1}{x^2}\dfrac{dx}{dy} = \dfrac{1}{xy} - \cos y, \text{ i.e. } \dfrac{1}{x^2}\dfrac{dx}{dy} - \dfrac{1}{xy} = -\cos y$$

Put $\dfrac{-1}{x} = v,\ \therefore \dfrac{1}{x^2}\dfrac{dx}{dy} = \dfrac{dv}{dy}$

There fore the equation becomes $\dfrac{dv}{dy} + \dfrac{v}{y} = -\cos y$, which is Linear in v

Here $P = \dfrac{1}{y},\ Q = -\cos y \therefore \text{I.F} = e^{\int P\,dy} = e^{\int \frac{1}{y}dy} = e^{\log y} = y$

Hence the solution is $v.(\text{I.F}) = \int Q.(\text{I.F})\,dx + C$

$$v.y = \int -\cos y.y\,dy + C, \qquad v.y = y(-\sin y) - \cos y + C$$

$$\dfrac{-y}{x} + y\sin y + \cos y = C, \Rightarrow xy\sin y + x\cos y - y = xC.$$

(1.41)

Ex. 5: Solve $\sec y \dfrac{dy}{dx} + 2x \sin y = 2x \cos y$

Solution: The given equation can be written as

$\dfrac{\sec y}{\cos y} \dfrac{dy}{dx} + 2x \dfrac{\sin y}{\cos y} = 2x, \quad \sec^2 y \dfrac{dy}{dx} + 2x \tan y = 2x$

Put $\tan y = v, \therefore \sec^2 y \dfrac{dy}{dx} = \dfrac{dv}{dx}$

There fore the equation becomes $\dfrac{dv}{dx} + 2x.v = 2x$, which is Linear in v

Here $P = 2x, \quad Q = 2x$

$\therefore I.F = e^{\int P dy} = e^{\int 2x dy} = e^{x^2}$

Hence the solution is $v.(I.F) = \int Q.(I.F)\, dx + C$

$v.e^{x^2} = \int 2x.e^{x^2}\, dx + C, \quad v.e^{x^2} = \int e^t\, dt + C \quad$ Put $x^2 = t, \therefore 2x dx = dt$

$v.e^{x^2} = e^t + C \Rightarrow e^{x^2} \tan y = e^{x^2} + C.$

Ex. 6: Solve $\sec^2 y \dfrac{dy}{dx} + 2 \tan x \tan y = \sin x$

Solution: Put $\tan y = v, \therefore \sec^2 y \dfrac{dy}{dx} = \dfrac{dv}{dx}$

There fore the equation becomes $\dfrac{dv}{dx} + 2 \tan x.v = \sin x$, which is Linear in v

Here $P = 2 \tan x, \quad Q = \sin x$

$\therefore I.F = e^{\int P dy} = e^{\int 2 \tan x dy} = e^{2 \log \sec x} = \sec^2 x$

Hence the solution is $v.(I.F) = \int Q.(I.F)\, dx + C$

$v.\sec^2 x = \int \sin x \sec^2 x\, dx + C, \quad v.\sec^2 x = \int \tan x \sec x\, dx + C$

$v.\sec^2 x = \sec x + C \quad \therefore \tan y.\sec^2 x = \sec x + C.$

Ex. 7: Solve $x \dfrac{dy}{dx} - 1 = xe^{-y}$.

Solution: Dividing by xe^{-y}

$\dfrac{1}{e^{-y}} \dfrac{dy}{dx} - \dfrac{1}{xe^{-y}} = 1, \quad$ i.e. $\quad e^y \dfrac{dy}{dx} - \dfrac{1}{x} e^y = 1$

Put $e^y = v, \therefore e^y \dfrac{dy}{dx} = \dfrac{dv}{dx}$

There fore the equation becomes $\dfrac{dv}{dx} - \dfrac{1}{x}.v = 1$, which is Linear in v

Here $P = -\dfrac{1}{x}$, $Q = 1$

$\therefore \text{I.F} = e^{\int P dx} = e^{\int -\frac{1}{x} dx} = e^{-\log x} = \dfrac{1}{x}$

Hence the solution is $v.(\text{I.F}) = \int Q.(\text{I.F}) \, dx + C$

$v.\dfrac{1}{x} = \int \dfrac{1}{x} dx + C$, $v.\dfrac{1}{x} = \log x + C$, $\therefore \dfrac{e^y}{x} = \log x + C \Rightarrow e^y = x\log x + xC$.

Ex. 8: Solve $y\sin x \dfrac{dx}{dy} - \cos x = 2y^3 \cos^2 x$.

Solution: The given equation can be written as $\sin x \dfrac{dx}{dy} - \dfrac{1}{y}\cos x = 2y^2 \cos^2 x$

Dividing by $\cos^2 x$

$\dfrac{\sin x}{\cos^2 x}\dfrac{dx}{dy} - \dfrac{1}{y}\dfrac{\cos x}{\cos^2 x} = 2y^2$, i.e. $\sec x \tan x \dfrac{dx}{dy} - \dfrac{1}{y}\sec x = 2y^2$

Put $\sec x = v$, $\therefore \sec x \tan x \dfrac{dx}{dy} = \dfrac{dv}{dy}$

Therefore the equation becomes $\dfrac{dv}{dy} - \dfrac{1}{y}.v = 2y^2$, which is Linear in v

Here $P = \dfrac{-1}{y}$, $Q = 2y^2$

$\therefore \text{I.F} = e^{\int P dx} = e^{\int \frac{-1}{y} dy} = e^{-\log y} = \dfrac{1}{y}$

Hence the solution is $v.(\text{I.F}) = \int Q.(\text{I.F}) \, dx + C$

$v.\dfrac{1}{y} = \int 2y^2.\dfrac{1}{y} dy + C$, $v.\dfrac{1}{y} = 2\int y\,dy + C$, $v.\dfrac{1}{y} = y^2 + C$,

$\therefore \dfrac{\sec x}{y} = y^2 + C \Rightarrow \sec x = y^3 + yC$.

Ex. 9: Solve $x\cos y \dfrac{dy}{dx} - \sin y = x\sin^2 y$.

Solution: Dividing by $x\sin^2 y$

$\dfrac{x\cos y}{x\sin^2 y}\dfrac{dy}{dx} - \dfrac{\sin y}{x\sin^2 y} = 1$, i.e. $\cot y \operatorname{cosec} y \dfrac{dy}{dx} - \dfrac{\operatorname{cosec} y}{x} = 1$

Put $-\operatorname{cosec} y = v$, $\therefore \operatorname{cosec} y \cot y \dfrac{dy}{dx} = \dfrac{dv}{dx}$

(1.43)

There fore the equation becomes $\dfrac{dv}{dx}+\dfrac{1}{x}.v=1,$ which is Linear in v

Here $P=\dfrac{1}{x},\quad Q=1$

$\therefore \text{I.F} = e^{\int Pdx} = e^{\int \frac{1}{x}dx} = e^{\log x} = x$

Hence the solution is $v.(\text{I.F}) = \int Q.(\text{I.F})\, dx + C$

$v.x = \int 1.x\, dx + C,\quad v.x = \dfrac{x^2}{2}+C,\ \Rightarrow \operatorname{cosec} y.x = \dfrac{x^2}{2}+C.$

Ex. 10: Solve $e^x(x+1)dx + (y^2 e^{2y} - xe^x)dy = 0$

Solution: The given equation can be written as $e^x(x+1)\dfrac{dx}{dy} - xe^x = -y^2 e^{2y}$

Put $xe^x = v,\ \therefore (xe^x + e^x)\dfrac{dx}{dy} = \dfrac{dv}{dy}$

There fore the equation becomes $\dfrac{dv}{dy} - v = -y^2 e^{2y},$ which is Linear in v

Here $P = -1,\quad Q = -y^2 e^{2y}$

$\therefore \text{I.F} = e^{\int Pdy} = e^{\int -1 dy} = e^{-y}$

Hence the solution is $v.(\text{I.F}) = \int Q.(\text{I.F})\, dx + C$

$v.e^{-y} = \int -y^2 e^{2y}.e^{-y} dx + C,\qquad v.e^{-y} = -\int y^2 e^y dx + C$

$v.e^{-y} = -\left[y^2(e^y) - 2y(e^y) + 2(e^y)\right] + C$

$v.e^{-y} = -e^y\left[y^2 - 2y + 2\right] + C,\ \therefore xe^x.e^{-y} = -e^y\left[y^2 - 2y + 2\right] + C$

i.e. $xe^{x-y} = e^y\left[2y - y^2 - 2\right] + C.$

Ex. 11: Solve $\dfrac{dy}{dx} + \dfrac{1}{x}\tan y = \dfrac{1}{x^2}\tan y \sin y.$

Solution: Dividing by $\tan y \sin y$

$\dfrac{1}{\tan y \sin y}\dfrac{dy}{dx} + \dfrac{1}{x}\dfrac{\tan y}{\tan y \sin y} = \dfrac{1}{x^2},$ i.e. $\operatorname{cosec} y \cot y\dfrac{dy}{dx} + \dfrac{1}{x}\operatorname{cosec} y = \dfrac{1}{x^2}$

Put $\operatorname{cosec} y = v,\ \therefore \cot y \operatorname{cosec} y \dfrac{dy}{dx} = \dfrac{dv}{dx}$

There fore the equation becomes $\dfrac{dv}{dx} + \dfrac{1}{x}.v = \dfrac{1}{x^2},$ which is Linear in v

(1.44)

Here $P = \dfrac{1}{x}$, $Q = \dfrac{1}{x^2}$

$\therefore \text{I.F} = e^{\int P dx} = e^{\int \frac{1}{x} dx} = e^{\log x} = x$

Hence the solution is $v.(\text{I.F}) = \int Q.(\text{I.F})\, dx + C$

$v.x = \int \dfrac{1}{x^2}.x\, dx + C$, $\quad v.x = \int \dfrac{1}{x}\, dx + C$, $\quad v.x = \log x + C$ i.e. $\operatorname{cosec} y.x = \log x + C$

Ex. 12: Solve $x - y^2 + 2xy\dfrac{dy}{dx} = 0$.

Solution: The given equation can be written as $2xy\dfrac{dy}{dx} - y^2 = -x$ i.e. $2y\dfrac{dy}{dx} - \dfrac{1}{x}y^2 = -1$

Put $y^2 = v$, $\therefore 2y\dfrac{dy}{dx} = \dfrac{dv}{dx}$

Therefore the equation becomes $\dfrac{dv}{dx} - \dfrac{1}{x}v = -1$, which is Linear in v

Here $P = \dfrac{-1}{x}$, $Q = -1$

$\therefore \text{I.F} = e^{\int P dx} = e^{\int \frac{-1}{x} dx} = e^{-\log x} = \dfrac{1}{x}$

Hence the solution is $v.(\text{I.F}) = \int Q.(\text{I.F})\, dx + C$

$v.\dfrac{1}{x} = \int -1.\dfrac{1}{x}\, dx + C$, $\quad v.\dfrac{1}{x} = -\log x + C$

$\therefore y^2 \dfrac{1}{x} = -\log x + C$, $\Rightarrow y^2 + x\log x = xC$.

Ex. 13 : Solve $\dfrac{dy}{dx} + x\sin 2y = x^3 \cos^2 y$.

Solution: Dividing equation by $\cos^2 y$, we get

$\dfrac{1}{\cos^2 y}\dfrac{dy}{dx} + x\dfrac{\sin 2y}{\cos^2 y} = x^3 \Rightarrow \dfrac{1}{\cos^2 y}\dfrac{dy}{dx} + x\dfrac{2\sin y \cos y}{\cos^2 y} = x^3$

i.e. $\sec^2 y \dfrac{dy}{dx} + 2\tan y.x = x^3$

Put $\tan y = v \Rightarrow \sec^2 y \dfrac{dy}{dx} = \dfrac{dv}{dx}$

Therefore the equation becomes $\dfrac{dv}{dx} + 2xv = x^3$, which is Linear in v

Here $P = 2x$, $Q = x^3$

$\therefore \text{I.F.} = e^{\int 2x\, dx} = e^{x^2}$

(1.45)

Hence the solution is $v.(\text{I.F}) = \int Q.(\text{I.F})\,dx + C$

$v.e^{x^2} = \int x^3.e^{x^2}\,dx + C \Rightarrow v.e^{x^2} = \int t.e^t\,\dfrac{dt}{2} + C$ Put $x^2 = t$, $2x\,dx = dt$

$v.e^{x^2} = \dfrac{1}{2}\left[t.e^t - e^t\right] + C$, $v.e^{x^2} = \dfrac{1}{2}e^t\left[t.-1\right] + C$

$\tan y.e^{x^2} = \dfrac{1}{2}e^{x^2}\left[x^2 - 1\right] + C$ i.e. $\tan y = \dfrac{1}{2}\left[x^2 - 1\right] + e^{-x^2} C.$

Ex. 14: Solve $e^x(x+1)dx + (ye^y - xe^x)dy = 0$.

Solution: The given equation can be written as

$e^x(x+1)\dfrac{dx}{dy} - xe^x = -ye^y$

Put $xe^x = v$, $\therefore e^x(x+1)\dfrac{dx}{dy} = \dfrac{dv}{dy}$

There fore the equation becomes $\dfrac{dv}{dy} - v = -ye^y$, which is Linear in v

Here $P = -1$, $Q = -ye^y$

$\therefore \text{I.F} = e^{\int P\,dy} = e^{\int -1\,dy} = e^{-y}$

Hence the solution is $v.(\text{I.F}) = \int Q.(\text{I.F})\,dx + C$

$v.e^{-y} = \int -ye^y.e^{-y}\,dx + C$, $v.e^{-y} = -\int y\,dx + C$

$\therefore v.e^{-y} = -\dfrac{y^2}{2} + C$ i.e. $xe^x e^{-y} = -\dfrac{y^2}{2} + C \Rightarrow 2xe^{x-y} + y^2 = C'.$

Ex. 15: Solve $\dfrac{dx}{dy} = e^{x-y}(e^x - e^y)$

Solution: The given equation can be written as

$\dfrac{dx}{dy} = \dfrac{e^x}{e^y}(e^x - e^y)$ i.e. $e^y \dfrac{dx}{dy} + e^x e^y = e^{2x}$

Put $e^y = v$, $\therefore e^y\dfrac{dy}{dx} = \dfrac{dv}{dx}$

There fore the equation becomes $\dfrac{dv}{dy} + e^x v = e^{2x}$, which is Linear in v

Here $P = e^x$, $Q = e^{2x}$

$\therefore \text{I.F} = e^{\int P\,dy} = e^{\int e^x\,dy} = e^{e^x}$

Hence the solution is $v.(\text{I.F}) = \int Q.(\text{I.F})\,dx + C$

$v.e^{e^x} = \int e^{2x}.e^{e^x} dx + C$, $\quad v.e^{e^x} = \int e^x.e^{e^x}.e^x dx + C$, put $e^x = t$ $e^x dx = dt$

$v.e^{e^x} = \int t.e^t dt + C$, $\quad v.e^{e^x} = (t.e^t - e^t) + C$

$\therefore e^y.e^{e^x} = e^{e^x}(e^x - 1) + C \Rightarrow e^y = e^x - 1 + e^{-e^x}C$.

Ex. 16: Solve $\dfrac{dy}{dx} - \dfrac{\tan y}{1+x} = (1+x)e^x \sec y$.

Solution: Dividing by $\sec y$

$\dfrac{1}{\sec y}\dfrac{dy}{dx} - \dfrac{\tan y}{(1+x)\sec y} = e^x(1+x)$, i.e. $\cos y \dfrac{dy}{dx} - \dfrac{\sin y}{(1+x)} = e^x(1+x)$

Put $\sin y = v$, $\therefore \cos y \dfrac{dy}{dx} = \dfrac{dv}{dx}$

Therefore the equation becomes $\dfrac{dv}{dx} - \dfrac{1}{(1+x)}.v = e^x(1+x)$, which is Linear in v

Here $P = -\dfrac{1}{1+x}$, $\quad Q = e^x(1+x)$

$\therefore \text{I.F} = e^{\int P dx} = e^{\int -\frac{1}{1+x}dx} = e^{-\log(1+x)} = \dfrac{1}{1+x}$

Hence the solution is $v.(\text{I.F}) = \int Q.(\text{I.F})\, dx + C$

$v.\dfrac{1}{1+x} = \int e^x(1+x).\dfrac{1}{1+x}dx + C$, $\quad v.\dfrac{1}{1+x} = \int e^x dx + C$,

$v.\dfrac{1}{1+x} = e^x + C$, i.e. $\sin y = (1+x)e^x + (1+x)C$

Ex. 17: Solve $y\dfrac{dx}{dy} = x + yx^2 \log y$

Solution: The given equation can be written as

$\dfrac{1}{x^2}\dfrac{dx}{dy} = \dfrac{1}{xy} + \log y$ $\therefore \dfrac{1}{x^2}\dfrac{dx}{dy} - \dfrac{1}{xy} = \log y$

Put $\dfrac{-1}{x} = v$, $\therefore \dfrac{1}{x^2}\dfrac{dx}{dy} = \dfrac{dv}{dy}$

Therefore the equation becomes $\dfrac{dv}{dy} + \dfrac{v}{y} = \log y$, which is Linear in v

Here $P = \dfrac{1}{y}$, $\quad Q = \log y$

$\therefore \text{I.F} = e^{\int P dy} = e^{\int \frac{1}{y}dy} = e^{\log y} = y$

Hence the solution is $v.(I.F) = \int Q.(I.F)\,dx + C$

$v.y = \int \log y . y\,dy + C$, $\quad v.y = (\log y)\left(\dfrac{y^2}{2}\right) - \int \dfrac{1}{y}\left(\dfrac{y^2}{2}\right) dy + C$

$v.y = \dfrac{y^2}{2}\log y - \dfrac{1}{2}\int y\,dy + C$

$\dfrac{-y}{x} = \dfrac{y^2}{2}\log y - \dfrac{y^2}{4} + C$

Ex. 18: Solve $\tan y \dfrac{dy}{dx} + \tan x(1 - \cos y) = 0$.

Solution: The given equation can be written as

$\tan y \dfrac{dy}{dx} + \tan x - \tan x \cos y = 0$, $\therefore \tan y \dfrac{dy}{dx} + \tan x = \tan x \cos y$

Dividing by $\cos y$

$\dfrac{\tan y}{\cos y}\dfrac{dy}{dx} + \dfrac{\tan x}{\cos y} = \tan x,\ \Rightarrow\ \sec y \tan y \dfrac{dy}{dx} + \sec y \tan x = \tan x$

Put $\sec y = v$, $\therefore \sec y \tan y \dfrac{dy}{dx} = \dfrac{dv}{dx}$

There fore the equation becomes $\dfrac{dv}{dx} + \tan x . v = \tan x$, which is Linear in v

Here $P = \tan x$, $\quad Q = \tan x$

$\therefore I.F = e^{\int P\,dx} = e^{\int \tan x\,dx} = e^{\log \sec x} = \sec x$

Hence the solution is $v.(I.F) = \int Q.(I.F)\,dx + C$

$v.\sec x = \int \tan x . \sec x\,dx + C$, $\quad v.\sec x = \sec x + C$

$\sec y . \sec x = \sec x + C$.

Ex. 19: Solve $\cos x \dfrac{dy}{dx} + y \sin x = (y \sec x)^{1/2}$

Solution: Divide equation by $\sqrt{y}\,\cos x$

$\dfrac{1}{\sqrt{y}}\dfrac{dy}{dx} + \sqrt{y}\,\tan x = \sec^{3/2} x \qquad (I)$

Put $\sqrt{y} = v\ \Rightarrow\ \dfrac{1}{2\sqrt{y}}\dfrac{dy}{dx} = \dfrac{dv}{dx}$

Then equation (I) becomes

$\dfrac{dv}{dx} + \dfrac{1}{2}\tan x\,v = \dfrac{1}{2}\sec^{3/2} x$

which is in linear form, so

$$I.F. = e^{\frac{1}{2}\int \tan x\, dx} = e^{\frac{1}{2}\log(\sec x)} = \sec^{\frac{1}{2}} x$$

So the solution of the equation (I) is

$$v \sec^{\frac{1}{2}} x = \frac{1}{2} \int \sec^{\frac{3}{2}} x \sec^{\frac{1}{2}} x\, dx + C = \frac{1}{2}\tan x + C$$

By putting the value of v, the general solution of the given equation is

$$\sqrt{y}\sqrt{\sec x} = c + \frac{1}{2}\tan x \quad \text{or} \quad 4y \sec x = (2c + \tan x)^2$$

TEST YOUR KNOWLEDGE

1. $\dfrac{dy}{dx} + x\sin 2y = x^3 \cos^2 y$ Ans: $4x \tan y = x^4 + C'$

2. $\dfrac{dx}{dy} = e^{y-x}(e^y - e^x)$ Ans: $e^{e^y}(e^x - e^y + 1) = C$

3. $2x\,dx - y^2(y^3 + x^2)dy = 0$ Ans: $e^{-y^3/3}(x^2 + y^3 + 3) = C$

4. $xy(1 + xy^2)\dfrac{dy}{dx} = 1$ Ans: $e^{y^2/2}(2x - 1 - xy^2) = xC$

5. $\dfrac{dy}{dx} + \dfrac{y}{x}\log y = y(\log y)^2$ Ans: $\dfrac{1}{x\log y} + \log x = C$

6. $\dfrac{dy}{dx} + (2x\tan^{-1} y - x^3)(1 + y^2) = 0$ Ans: $e^{x^2}(2\tan^{-1} y - x^2 + 1) = C'$

7. $\cos y - x \sin y \dfrac{dy}{dx} = \sec^2 x.$ Ans: $x\cos y = c + \tan x$

EXACT DIFFERENTIAL EQUATION

Definition: A differential equation which is obtained from its primitive by differentiation only and without any operation of elimination or reduction is called an exact differential equation. Or A differential equation of the form $M(x,y)dx + N(x,y)dy = 0$ is said to be exact if there exits a function $u(x,y)$ such that $M(x,y)dx + N(x,y)dy = du$. Where $du = \dfrac{\partial u}{\partial x}dx + \dfrac{\partial u}{\partial y}dy$

e.g $u = x^2 + y^2 = c$, then $du = \dfrac{\partial u}{\partial x}dx + \dfrac{\partial u}{\partial y}dy = 2x\,dx + 2y\,dy$. equation $du = 0$, we get the equation $x\,dx + y\,dy = 0$ which is exact.

Condition for exactness: Theorem: A necessary and sufficient condition that $M(x,y)dx + N(x,y)dy = 0$ be exact is $\dfrac{\partial M}{\partial y} = \dfrac{\partial N}{\partial x}$.

When the condition of exactness is satisfied, the general solution can be obtained by the following formulae.

1. $\int\limits_{y \text{ Constant}} M \, dx + \int [\text{Term of } N \text{ free from } x] \, dy = C.$

Some times, we may use the following formulae for general solution

2. $\int\limits_{x \text{ Constant}} N \, dy + \int [\text{Term of } M \text{ free from } y] \, dx = C.$

Method of solving Ex.s by exact differential equation:

1. Consider the equation $M(x, y) \, dx + N(x, y) \, dy = 0$

2. From M and N values, find $\dfrac{\partial M}{\partial y}$ and $\dfrac{\partial N}{\partial x}$

3. If $\dfrac{\partial N}{\partial x} = \dfrac{\partial M}{\partial y}$, then given equation is exact. (If not then apply Non Exact method rules)

4. Solution is obtained by the formulae $\int\limits_{y \text{ Constant}} M \, dx + \int [\text{Term of } N \text{ free from } x] \, dy = C$

Remark: If the equation $M(x, y) \, dx + N(x, y) \, dy = 0$ is exact, then its general solution is also obtained by the formulae:

$\int\limits_{x \text{ Constant}} N \, dy + \int [\text{Term of } M \text{ free from } y] \, dx = C.$

Examples on Exact differential equation

Ex. 1: Solve $\dfrac{dy}{dx} = \dfrac{x - 2y + 5}{2x + y - 1}$

Solution: $(x - 2y + 5) \, dx - (2x + y - 1) \, dy = 0$

here $M = x - 2y + 5$ and $N = -(2x + y - 1)$, $\dfrac{\partial M}{\partial y} = -2$, and $\dfrac{\partial N}{\partial x} = -2$. Hence $\dfrac{\partial M}{\partial y} = \dfrac{\partial N}{\partial x}$

Thus the given equation is exact, hence Solution is

$\int\limits_{y \text{ Constant}} M \, dx + \int [\text{Term of } N \text{ free from } x] \, dy = C$

$\therefore \int\limits_{y \text{ Constant}} (x - 2y + 5) \, dx + \int (-y + 1) \, dy = C \Rightarrow \dfrac{x^2}{2} - 2yx + 5x - \dfrac{y^2}{2} + y = C$

$\therefore x^2 - 4yx + 10x - y^2 + 2y = C'$

Ex. 2: Solve $\dfrac{dy}{dx} = \dfrac{y + 1}{(y + 2)e^y - x}$

Solution: $(y + 1) \, dx - \left[(y + 2)e^y - x \right] dy = 0$

Here $M = y + 1$ and $N = x - (y + 2)e^y$, $\dfrac{\partial M}{\partial y} = 1$, and $\dfrac{\partial N}{\partial x} = 1$. Hence $\dfrac{\partial M}{\partial y} = \dfrac{\partial N}{\partial x}$

Thus the given equation is exact, hence Solution is

$$\int\limits_{y\ \text{Constant}} M\ dx + \int [\text{Term of } N \text{ free from } x] dy = C$$

$$\therefore \int\limits_{y\ \text{Constant}} (y+1)dx + \int -(y+2)e^y\ dy = C \Rightarrow xy + x - \left[(y+2)e^y - e^y(1)\right] = C$$

$$\Rightarrow xy + x - e^y(y+1) = C \Rightarrow (y+1)(x-e^y).$$

Ex. 3: Solve $\left(y^2 e^{xy^2} + 4x^3\right)dx + \left(2xye^{xy^2} - 3y^2\right)dy = 0$

Solution: Here $M = y^2 e^{xy^2} + 4x^3$ and $N = 2xye^{xy^2} - 3y^2$

$\dfrac{\partial M}{\partial y} = 2ye^{xy^2} + y^2 e^{xy^2}(2xy)$, and $\dfrac{\partial N}{\partial x} = 2ye^{xy^2} + 2xye^{xy^2}(y^2)$. Hence $\dfrac{\partial M}{\partial y} = \dfrac{\partial N}{\partial x}$

Thus the given equation is exact, hence Solution is

$$\int\limits_{y\ \text{Constant}} M\ dx + \int [\text{Term of } N \text{ free from } x] dy = C$$

$$\therefore \int\limits_{y\ \text{Constant}} \left(y^2 e^{xy^2} + 4x^3\right)dx + \int -3y^2\ dy = C \Rightarrow y^2 \dfrac{e^{xy^2}}{y^2} + 4\dfrac{x^4}{4} - 3\dfrac{y^3}{3} = C \Rightarrow e^{xy^2} + x^4 - y^3 = C$$

Ex. 4: Solve
$\left(12x^2 y + 2xy^2 + 4x^3 - 4y^3 + 2ye^{2x} - e^y\right)dx + \left(2x^2 y + 4x^3 - 12xy^2 + 3y^2 - xe^y + e^{2x}\right)dy = 0$

Solution: Here $M = 12x^2 y + 2xy^2 + 4x^3 - 4y^3 + 2ye^{2x} - e^y$

and $N = 2x^2 y + 4x^3 - 12xy^2 + 3y^2 - xe^y + e^{2x}$

$\dfrac{\partial M}{\partial y} = 12x^2 + 4xy - 12y^2 + 2e^{2x} - e^y$ and $\dfrac{\partial N}{\partial x} = 12x^2 + 4xy - 12y^2 + 2e^{2x} - e^y$

Hence $\dfrac{\partial M}{\partial y} = \dfrac{\partial N}{\partial x}$ Thus the given equation is exact, hence Solution is

$$\int\limits_{y\ \text{Constant}} M\ dx + \int [\text{Term of } N \text{ free from } x] dy = C$$

$$\int\limits_{y\ \text{Constant}} \left(12x^2 y + 2xy^2 + 4x^3 - 4y^3 + 2ye^{2x} - e^y\right)dx + \int 3y^2\ dy = C$$

$$\therefore \dfrac{12x^3 y}{3} + \dfrac{2x^2}{2}y^2 + \dfrac{4x^4}{4} - 4xy^3 + \dfrac{2ye^{2x}}{2} - xe^y + \dfrac{3y^3}{3} = C$$

$$\Rightarrow 4x^3 y + x^2 y^2 + x^4 - 4xy^3 + ye^{2x} - xe^y + y^3 = C$$

Ex. 5: Solve $(2x+3y+5)dx + (3x+2y-5)dy = 0$ **SUK: May-09**

Solution: Here $M = 2x + 3y + 5$ and $N = 3x + 2y - 5$

$\dfrac{\partial M}{\partial y} = 3$, and $\dfrac{\partial N}{\partial x} = 3$, $\therefore \dfrac{\partial M}{\partial y} = \dfrac{\partial N}{\partial x}$

(1.51)

Thus the given equation is exact, hence Solution is

$$\int_{y\,\text{Constant}} M\,dx + \int [\text{Term of } N \text{ free from } x]\,dy = C$$

$$\int_{y\,\text{Constant}} (2x+3y+5)\,dx + \int 2y-5\,dy = C$$

$$2\frac{x^2}{2} + 3xy + 5x + 2\frac{y^2}{2} - 5y = C$$

$$\Rightarrow x^2 + y^2 + 5x - 5y + 3xy = C$$

Ex. 6: Solve $(x^2 - 4xy - 2y^2)\,dx + (y^2 - 4xy - 2x^2)\,dy = 0$.

Solution: Compare given equation with $M\,dx + N\,dy = 0$ then
$$M = x^2 - 4xy - 2y^2 \quad \text{and} \quad N = y^2 - 4xy - 2x^2$$
$$\frac{\partial M}{\partial y} = -4x - 4y \quad \text{and} \quad \frac{\partial N}{\partial x} = -4y - 4x \quad \Rightarrow \frac{\partial M}{\partial y} = -4x - 4y = \frac{\partial N}{\partial x}.$$

Hence the given equation is an exact. On integrating the equation the solution of the equation is

$$\int (x^2 - 4xy - 2y^2)\,dx + \int (y^2)\,dy = C$$

$$\frac{x^3}{3} - 2x^2y - 2xy^2 + \frac{y^3}{3} = C \quad \text{or}$$

$$x^3 - 6x^2y - 6xy^2 + y^3 = 6C = C'$$

Ex. 7: Solve $(\tan y + x)\,dx + (x\sec^2 y - 3y)\,dy = 0$

Solution: Here $M = \tan y + x$ and $N = x\sec^2 y - 3y$

$$\frac{\partial M}{\partial y} = \sec^2 y \quad \text{and} \quad \frac{\partial N}{\partial x} = \sec^2 y \quad \therefore \frac{\partial M}{\partial y} = \frac{\partial N}{\partial x}$$

Therefore given equation is exact, hence Solution is

$$\int_{y\,\text{Constant}} M\,dx + \int [\text{Term of } N \text{ free from } x]\,dy = C$$

$$\therefore \int_{y\,\text{Constant}} (\tan y + x)\,dx + \int -3y\,dy = C \Rightarrow x\tan y + \frac{x^2}{2} - 3\frac{y^2}{2} = C.$$

Ex. 8: Solve $(\sin x \cos y + e^{2x})\,dx + (\cos x \sin y + \tan y)\,dy = 0$

Solution: Here $M = \sin x \cos y + e^{2x}$ and $N = \cos x \sin y + \tan y$

$$\frac{\partial M}{\partial y} = -\sin x \sin y \quad \text{and} \quad \frac{\partial N}{\partial x} = -\sin x \sin y, \Rightarrow \frac{\partial M}{\partial y} = \frac{\partial N}{\partial x}$$

Therefore given equation is exact, hence Solution is

$$\int_{y\,\text{Constant}} M\,dx + \int [\text{Term of } N \text{ free from } x]\,dy = C$$

$$\therefore \int_{y\,\text{Constant}} \sin x \cos y + e^{2x}\,dx + \int \tan y\,dy = C \Rightarrow -\cos x \cos y + \frac{e^{2x}}{2} + \log \sec y = C$$

Ex. 9: Solve $\dfrac{dy}{dx} = \dfrac{y}{2y \log y + y - x}$

Solution: $(y)dx - (2y \log y + y - x)dy = 0$

$M = y$ and $N = -(2y \log y + y - x)$, $\dfrac{\partial M}{\partial y} = 1$, and $\dfrac{\partial N}{\partial x} = -(-1) = 1$. Hence $\dfrac{\partial M}{\partial y} = \dfrac{\partial N}{\partial x}$

Thus the given equation is exact, hence Solution is

$$\int_{y\ \text{Constant}} M\ dx + \int [\text{Term of } N \text{ free from } x]dy = C$$

$$\therefore \int_{y\ \text{Constant}} (y)dx + \int -(2y \log y + y)dy = C$$

$$xy - 2\left[\log y \left(\dfrac{y^2}{2}\right) - \dfrac{y^2}{4}\right] + \dfrac{y^2}{2} + C \Rightarrow xy - y^2 \log y - \dfrac{y^2}{2} + \dfrac{y^2}{2} + C$$

$$\Rightarrow xy - y^2 \log y = C$$

Ex. 10: Solve $\left(y^2 e^{xy^2} + 4x^3\right)dx + \left(2xye^{xy^2} - 3y^2\right)dy = 0$

Solution: Here $M = y^2 e^{xy^2} + 4x^3$ and $N = 2xye^{xy^2} - 3y^2$

$\dfrac{\partial M}{\partial y} = 2ye^{xy^2} + y^2(2xy)e^{xy^2}$, and $\dfrac{\partial N}{\partial x} = 2ye^{xy^2} + 2xy\cdot y^2 e^{xy^2}$. Hence $\dfrac{\partial M}{\partial y} = \dfrac{\partial N}{\partial x}$

Thus the given equation is exact, hence Solution is

$$\int_{y\ \text{Constant}} M\ dx + \int [\text{Term of } N \text{ free from } x]dy = C$$

$$\int_{y\ \text{Constant}} \left(y^2 e^{xy^2} + 4x^3\right)dx + \int \left(-3y^2\right)dy = C$$

$$\therefore \dfrac{y^2 e^{xy^2}}{y^2} + 4\dfrac{x^4}{4} - 3\dfrac{y^3}{3} = C \Rightarrow e^{xy^2} + x^4 - y^3 = C$$

Ex. 11: Solve $\left[y\left(1 + \dfrac{1}{x}\right) + \cos y\right]dx + [x + \log x - x \sin y]dy = 0$

Solution: $\left[y\left(1 + \dfrac{1}{x}\right) + \cos y\right]dx + [x + \log x - x \sin y]dy = 0$

Here $M = y\left(1 + \dfrac{1}{x}\right) + \cos y$ and $N = x + \log x - x \sin y$

$\dfrac{\partial M}{\partial y} = 1 + \dfrac{1}{x} - \sin y$, and $\dfrac{\partial N}{\partial x} = 1 + \dfrac{1}{x} - \sin y$. Hence $\dfrac{\partial M}{\partial y} = \dfrac{\partial N}{\partial x}$

Thus the given equation is exact, hence Solution is

$$\int_{y\text{ Constant}} M\,dx + \int [\text{Term of } N \text{ free from } x]\,dy = C$$

$$\therefore \int_{y\text{ Constant}} y\left(1+\frac{1}{x}\right) + \cos y\,dx + \int 0\,dy = c \Rightarrow y(x + \log x) + x\cos y = c$$

Ex. 12: Solve $[\cos x \tan y + \cos(x+y)]dx + [\sin x \sec^2 y + \cos(x+y)]dy = 0$

Solution: $[\cos x \tan y + \cos(x+y)]dx + [\sin x \sec^2 y + \cos(x+y)]dy = 0$

Here $M = \cos x \tan y + \cos(x+y)$ and $N = \sin x \sec^2 y + \cos(x+y)$

$\frac{\partial M}{\partial y} = \cos x \sec^2 y - \sin(x+y)$, and $\frac{\partial N}{\partial x} = \cos x \sec^2 y - \sin(x+y)$. Hence $\frac{\partial M}{\partial y} = \frac{\partial N}{\partial x}$

Thus the given equation is exact, hence Solution is

$$\int_{y\text{ Constant}} M\,dx + \int [\text{Term of } N \text{ free from } x]\,dy = C$$

$$\therefore \int_{y\text{ Constant}} \cos x \tan y + \cos(x+y)\,dx + \int 0\,dy = C \Rightarrow \sin x \tan y + \sin(x+y) = C$$

Ex. 13: Solve $\left(1+e^{\frac{x}{y}}\right)dx + e^{\frac{x}{y}}\left(1-\frac{x}{y}\right)dy = 0$, Given $y(0) = 4$

Solution: $\left(1+e^{\frac{x}{y}}\right)dx + e^{\frac{x}{y}}\left(1-\frac{x}{y}\right)dy = 0$. Given $y(0) = 4$

Here $M = 1 + e^{\frac{x}{y}}$ and $N = e^{\frac{x}{y}}\left(1-\frac{x}{y}\right)$

$\frac{\partial M}{\partial y} = e^{\frac{x}{y}}\left(\frac{-x}{y^2}\right)$, and $\frac{\partial N}{\partial x} = e^{\frac{x}{y}}\cdot\frac{1}{y}\left(1-\frac{x}{y}\right) + e^{\frac{x}{y}}\left(-\frac{1}{y}\right) = e^{\frac{x}{y}}\left(\frac{-x}{y^2}\right)$. $\therefore \frac{\partial M}{\partial y} = \frac{\partial N}{\partial x}$

Thus the given equation is exact, hence Solution is

$$\int_{y\text{ Constant}} M\,dx + \int [\text{Term of } N \text{ free from } x]\,dy = C$$

$$\int_{y\text{ Constant}} 1 + e^{\frac{x}{y}}\,dx + \int 0\,dy = C \therefore x + \frac{e^{\frac{x}{y}}}{1/y} = c \Rightarrow x + ye^{\frac{x}{y}} = C$$

Put $x = 0$ and $y = 4 \Rightarrow C = 4$ $\therefore$ Particular solution is $x + ye^{\frac{x}{y}} = 4$.

Ex. 14: Solve $(1 + \log xy)dx + \left(1 + \frac{x}{y}\right)dy = 0$

Solution: Here $M = 1 + \log xy$ and $N = 1 + \dfrac{x}{y}$, $\dfrac{\partial M}{\partial y} = \dfrac{1}{xy} \cdot x = \dfrac{1}{y}$, and $\dfrac{\partial N}{\partial x} = \dfrac{1}{y}$. Hence $\dfrac{\partial M}{\partial y} = \dfrac{\partial N}{\partial x}$

Thus the given equation is exact, hence Solution is

$$\int_{y\,\text{Constant}} M\,dx + \int [\text{Term of } N \text{ free from } x]\,dy = C$$

$$\therefore \int_{y\,\text{Constant}} (1 + \log xy)\,dx + \int 1\,dy = C \therefore \int 1\,dx + \int \log xy\,dx + \int 1\,dy = C$$

$$\Rightarrow x + \dfrac{1}{y}\left[(xy)\log xy - xy\right] + y = C \Rightarrow x + x\log xy - x + y = C \Rightarrow x\log xy + y = C$$

Ex. 15: Solve $(ye^{xy} - \tan x)\,dx + (xe^{xy} - \sec y)\,dy = 0$

Solution: $(ye^{xy} - \tan x)\,dx + (xe^{xy} - \sec y)\,dy = 0$

Here $M = ye^{xy} - \tan x$ and $N = xe^{xy} - \sec y$

$\dfrac{\partial M}{\partial y} = e^{xy} + xye^{xy}$, and $\dfrac{\partial N}{\partial x} = e^{xy} + xye^{xy}$. Hence $\dfrac{\partial M}{\partial y} = \dfrac{\partial N}{\partial x}$

Thus the given equation is exact, hence Solution is

$$\int_{y\,\text{Constant}} M\,dx + \int [\text{Term of } N \text{ free from } x]\,dy = C$$

$$\int_{y\,\text{Constant}} (ye^{xy} - \tan x)\,dx + \int -\sec y\,dy = C$$

$$\therefore y\dfrac{e^{xy}}{y} - \log \sec x - \log(\sec y + \tan y) = C \Rightarrow e^{xy} - \log \sec x - \log(\sec y + \tan y) = C$$

Ex. 16: Solve $\left(x\sqrt{1 - x^2 y^2} - y\right) dy + \left(x + y\sqrt{1 - x^2 y^2}\right) dx = 0$

Solution: Here $M = x + y\sqrt{1 - x^2 y^2}$ and $N = x\sqrt{1 - x^2 y^2} - y$

$\dfrac{\partial M}{\partial y} = \sqrt{1 - x^2 y^2} - \dfrac{x^2 y^2}{\sqrt{1 - x^2 y^2}}$, and $\dfrac{\partial N}{\partial x} = \sqrt{1 - x^2 y^2} - \dfrac{x^2 y^2}{\sqrt{1 - x^2 y^2}}$. Hence $\dfrac{\partial M}{\partial y} = \dfrac{\partial N}{\partial x}$

Thus the given equation is exact, hence Solution is

$$\int_{y\,\text{Constant}} M\,dx + \int [N \text{ free from } x]\,dy = C \therefore \int_{y\,\text{Constant}} \left(x + y\sqrt{1 - x^2 y^2}\right) dx + \int -y\,dy = C$$

Lets put $xy = u \Rightarrow y\,dx = du$

$$\therefore \int x\,dx + \int y\sqrt{1 - u^2}\,dx - \int y\,dy = C$$

$$\dfrac{x^2}{2} + \dfrac{u}{2}\sqrt{1 - u^2} + \dfrac{1}{2}\sin^{-1} u - \dfrac{y^2}{2} = C \qquad \because \int \sqrt{a^2 - x^2}\,dx = \dfrac{x}{2}\sqrt{a^2 - x^2} + \dfrac{a^2}{2}\sin^{-1}\dfrac{x}{a} + C$$

$$\dfrac{x^2}{2} + \dfrac{xy}{2}\sqrt{1 - x^2 y^2} + \dfrac{1}{2}\sin^{-1} xy - \dfrac{y^2}{2} = C \Rightarrow x^2 + xy\sqrt{1 - x^2 y^2} + \sin^{-1} xy - y^2 = C'$$

Ex. 17: Solve $\dfrac{dy}{dx} = -\dfrac{4x^3y^2 + y\cos xy}{2x^4y + x\cos xy}$

Solution: $(4x^3y^2 + y\cos xy)dx + (2x^4y + x\cos xy)dy = 0$

Here $M = 4x^3y^2 + y\cos xy$ and $N = 2x^4y + x\cos xy$

$\dfrac{\partial M}{\partial y} = 8x^3y + \cos xy - xy\sin xy$, and $\dfrac{\partial N}{\partial x} = 8x^3y + \cos xy - xy\sin xy$. Hence $\dfrac{\partial M}{\partial y} = \dfrac{\partial N}{\partial x}$

Thus the given equation is exact, hence Solution is

$$\int_{y\,\text{Constant}} M\,dx + \int [\text{Term of } N \text{ free from } x]\,dy = C$$

$$\therefore \int_{y\,\text{Constant}} (4x^3y^2 + y\cos xy)\,dx + \int 0\,dy = C$$

$4y^2 \dfrac{x^4}{4} + y\dfrac{\sin xy}{y} = C \Rightarrow x^4y^2 + \sin xy = C$

Ex. 18: Solve $\left(\dfrac{2x}{y^3}\right)dx + \left(\dfrac{y^2 - 3x^2}{y^4}\right)dy = 0$

Solution: Here $M = \dfrac{2x}{y^3}$ and $N = \dfrac{y^2 - 3x^2}{y^4}$

$\dfrac{\partial M}{\partial y} = \dfrac{-6x}{y^4}$, and $\dfrac{\partial N}{\partial x} = \dfrac{-6x}{y^4}$. Hence $\dfrac{\partial M}{\partial y} = \dfrac{\partial N}{\partial x}$

Thus the given equation is exact, hence Solution is

$$\int_{y\,\text{Constant}} M\,dx + \int [\text{Term of } N \text{ free from } x]\,dy = C$$

$$\therefore \int_{y\,\text{Constant}} \left(\dfrac{2x}{y^3}\right)dx + \int \dfrac{1}{y^2}\,dy = C$$

$\dfrac{2x^2}{2y^3} - \dfrac{1}{y} = C \Rightarrow \dfrac{x^2}{y^3} - \dfrac{1}{y} = C$

Ex. 19: Solve $(\sec x \tan x \tan y - e^x)\,dx + (\sec x \sec^2 y)\,dy = 0$ **SUK: May-12**

Solution: Compare given equation with $M\,dx + N\,dy = 0$ then

$M = \sec x \tan x \tan y - e^x$ and $N = \sec x \sec^2 y$

$\dfrac{\partial M}{\partial y} = \sec x \tan x \sec^2 y$ and $\dfrac{\partial N}{\partial x} = \sec x \tan x \sec^2 y$

$\dfrac{\partial M}{\partial y} = \sec x \tan x \sec^2 y = \dfrac{\partial N}{\partial x}$

Hence the given equation is an exact. On integrating the equation the solution of the equation is

$$\int (\sec x \tan x \tan y - e^x) \, dx + \int (0) \, dy = C$$

$$\sec x \tan y - e^x = C$$

TEST YOUR KNOWLEDGE
Solve the following ordinary differential equation

1. $x\,dx + y\,dy = \dfrac{a(x\,dy - y\,dx)}{x^2 + y^2}$ Ans: $x^2 + y^2 + 2a \tan^{-1}\dfrac{x}{y} = C$

2. $(2x - y + 1)dx + (2y - x - 1)dy = 0$ Ans: $x^2 + y^2 - xy + x - y = C$

3. $(3x^2 - y)dx - x\,dy = 0$ Ans: $x^3 - xy = C$

4. $\dfrac{dy}{dx} + \dfrac{y\cos x + \sin y + y}{\sin x + x\cos y + x} = 0$ Ans: $y\sin x + x\sin y + xy = C$

5. $(y + x\sin x)dx + (x - 2e^y)dy = 0$ Ans: $xy - x\cos x + \sin x - 2e^y = C$

Equation Reducible to exact form [using Integrating Factor(I.F)]

A differential equation of the type $M(x, y)dx + N(x, y)dy = 0$ which is not exact $\left(i.e. \dfrac{\partial M}{\partial y} \neq \dfrac{\partial N}{\partial x}\right)$ can some times become exact by the help of some other function of x and y.

Integrating Factor : A non-exact differential equation can be made exact by multiplying it by a suitable function of x and y, such a function is called as integrating factor (I.F).

Ex.: $y\,dx - x\,dy = 0$, $\dfrac{\partial M}{\partial y} = 1$ and $\dfrac{\partial N}{\partial x} = -1 \Rightarrow \dfrac{\partial M}{\partial y} \neq \dfrac{\partial N}{\partial x}$ is not exact

But if we multiply it by $\dfrac{1}{xy}$, or $\dfrac{1}{x^2}$ or $\dfrac{1}{y^2}$ it becomes exact thus I.F are $\dfrac{1}{xy}$, or $\dfrac{1}{x^2}$ or $\dfrac{1}{y^2}$

The following rules are useful in finding integrating factors for differential equations.

Rule I: If the equation $M(x, y)dx + N(x, y)dy = 0$ is homogeneous and $xM + yN \neq 0$, then $\dfrac{1}{xM + yN}$ is an I.F.

Rule II : If the equation is of the form
$yf_1(x, y)dx + xf_2(x, y)dy = 0$ or $f_1(x, y)y\,dx + f_2(x, y)x\,dy = 0$ and $xM - yN \neq 0$,

then $\dfrac{1}{xM - yN}$ is an I.F.

Rule III: Let $M(x,y)dx + N(x,y)dy = 0$ be the given differential equation.

If $\dfrac{\partial M}{\partial y} - \dfrac{\partial N}{\partial x} \bigg/ N$ is a function of x only, say $f(x)$ then $I.F = e^{\int f(x)dx}$

Rule IV: Let $M(x,y)dx + N(x,y)dy = 0$ be the given differential equation.

If $\dfrac{\partial N}{\partial x} - \dfrac{\partial M}{\partial y} \bigg/ M$ is a function of y only, say $f(y)$ then $I.F = e^{\int f(y)dy}$

Rule V: Some times integrating Factor can be found just by inspection

Rule VI: For a differential equation of the form

$$x^a y^b (Mydx + Nxdy) + x^c y^d (Pydx + Qxdy) = 0$$

where a, b, M, N, c, d, P, Q are constants. Integrating Factor is taken as $x^h y^k$, where h, k are constants and can be determined by using the condition that the equation becomes exact after it is multiplied by $x^h y^k$.

Note : 1. An equation can have many I. F.

2. If $\Psi M(x,y)dx + \Psi N(x,y)dy = 0$ is exact, then Ψ is said to be I.F of the equation $M(x,y)dx + N(x,y)dy = 0$

Remark: A differential equation $M(x,y)dx + N(x,y)dy = 0$ is said to be homogeneous if M and N are homogeneous function in x and y of same degree. i.e degree of every term is the same.

Ex.: $x^2 + y^2$, $xy^3 + x^4$, $x^2 y + y^3$

Examples based on Rules I:

Rule I: If the equation $M(x,y)dx + N(x,y)dy = 0$ is homogeneous and $xM + yN \neq 0$,

then $\dfrac{1}{xM + yN}$ is an I.F

Ex. 1: Solve $x^2 y dx - (x^3 + y^3)dy = 0$ **SUK: May-08**

Solution: The given equation is homogeneous of degree 3.

$M = x^2 y$ and $N = -(x^3 + y^3) \Rightarrow xM + yN = x^3 y - x^3 y - y^4 = -y^4 \neq 0$

$\therefore I.F = \dfrac{1}{xM + yN} = -\dfrac{1}{y^4}$

Multiplying the given equation by I.F, we get

$$\left(\dfrac{x^2 y}{-y^4}\right)dx - \left(\dfrac{x^3}{-y^4} + \dfrac{y^3}{-y^4}\right)dy = 0 \quad \therefore \left(-\dfrac{x^2}{y^3}\right)dx + \left(\dfrac{x^3}{y^4} + \dfrac{1}{y}\right) = 0$$

Which is exact, solution is

$$\int_{y\ Constant} M dx + \int [Term\ Free\ from\ x\ in\ N] dy = C$$

$$\therefore \int \left(-\frac{x^2}{y^3}\right) dx + \int \frac{1}{y} dy = C \Rightarrow -\frac{x^3}{3y^3} + \log y = C$$

Ex. 2: Solve $(3xy^2 - y^3) dx + (xy^2 - 2x^2 y) dy = 0$

Solution: The given equation is homogeneous of degree 3.
$M = 3xy^2 - y^3$ and $N = xy^2 - 2x^2 y$
$xM + yN = 3x^2 y^2 - xy^3 + xy^3 - 2x^2 y^2 = x^2 y^2 \neq 0$

$$\therefore I.F = \frac{1}{xM + yN} = \frac{1}{x^2 y^2}$$

Multiplying the given equation by I.F, we get

$$\frac{1}{x^2 y^2}(3xy^2 - y^3) dx + \frac{1}{x^2 y^2}(xy^2 - 2x^2 y) dy = 0 \therefore \left(\frac{3}{x} - \frac{y}{x^2}\right) dx + \left(\frac{1}{x} - \frac{2}{y}\right) dy = 0$$

Which is exact, solution is

$$\int_{y\ Constant} M\ dx + \int [Term\ in\ N\ which\ do\ not\ involve\ x] dy = c$$

$$\therefore \int_{y\ Cons\tan t} \left(\frac{3}{x} - \frac{y}{x^2}\right) dx + \int -\frac{2}{y} dy = c$$

$$\therefore 3\log x + \frac{y}{x} - 2\log y = c$$

Ex. 3: Solve $(x^2 y - 2xy^2) dx - (x^3 - 3x^2 y) dy = 0$ **SUK: May-10, Nov-12**

Solution: The given equation is homogeneous of degree 3.
$M = x^2 y - 2xy^2$ and $N = -(x^3 - 3x^2 y) \Rightarrow xM + yN = x^3 y - 2x^2 y^2 - x^3 y + 3x^2 y^2 = x^2 y^2 \neq 0$

$$\therefore I.F = \frac{1}{xM + yN} = \frac{1}{x^2 y^2}$$

Multiplying the given equation by I.F, we get

$$\frac{1}{x^2 y^2}(x^2 y - 2xy^2) dx - \frac{1}{x^2 y^2}(x^3 - 3x^2 y) dy = 0 \therefore \left(\frac{1}{y} - \frac{2}{x}\right) dx + \left(-\frac{x}{y^2} + \frac{3}{y}\right) dy = 0$$

Which is exact, solution is

$$\therefore \int \left(\frac{1}{y} - \frac{2}{x}\right) dx + \int \frac{3}{y} dy = C \therefore \frac{x}{y} - 2\log x + 3\log y = C$$

$$\Rightarrow \frac{x}{y} + \log \frac{y^3}{x^2} = \log C' \Rightarrow \log \frac{y^3}{c'x^2} = -\frac{x}{y} \Rightarrow y^3 = C'x^2 e^{-\frac{x}{y}}$$

Ex. 4: Solve $(x^3 + y^3)dx - xy^2 dy = 0$ OR Solve $\dfrac{dy}{dx} = \dfrac{x^3 + y^3}{xy^2}$ **SUK: May-12**

Solution: Since this is an homogeneous equation of degree 3, so the integration factor is
$$Mx + Ny = x(x^3 + y^3) + y(-xy^2) = x^4 + xy^3 - xy^3 = x^4$$

I.F. $= \dfrac{1}{Mx+Ny} = \dfrac{1}{x^4}$

Multiplying the given equation by I.F.,

$$\dfrac{(x^3+y^3)dx}{x^4} - \dfrac{xy^2 dy}{x^4} = 0 \Rightarrow \left(\dfrac{1}{x} + \dfrac{y^3}{x^4}\right)dx - \dfrac{y^2}{x^3}dy = 0$$

This is an exact differential equation, on integrating it, the solution of the given differential equation is $\log x - \dfrac{y^3}{3\,x^3} = C \qquad \therefore 3x^3 \log x - y^3 = x^3 C$.

Ex. 5: Solve $(x^2 - 3xy + 2y^2)dx + (3x^2 - 2xy)dy = 0$

Solution: The given equation is homogeneous of degree 2.
$M = x^2 - 3xy + 2y^2$ and $N = 3x^2 - 2xy \Rightarrow xM + yN = x^3 - 3x^2 y + 2xy^2 + 3x^2 y - 2xy^2 = x^3 \neq 0$

$\therefore$ I.F $= \dfrac{1}{xM + yN} = \dfrac{1}{x^3}$

Multiplying the given equation by I.F, we get

$$\dfrac{1}{x^3}(x^2 - 3xy + 2y^2)dx + \dfrac{1}{x^3}(3x^2 - 2xy)dy = 0 \therefore \left(\dfrac{1}{x} - \dfrac{3y}{x^2} + \dfrac{2y^2}{x^3}\right)dx + \left(\dfrac{3}{x} - \dfrac{2y}{x^2}\right)dy = 0$$

Which is exact, solution is

$$\int_{y\,\text{Constant}} M dx + \int [\text{Term Free from x in } N] dy = C$$

$$\therefore \int \left(\dfrac{1}{x} - \dfrac{3y}{x^2} + \dfrac{2y^2}{x^3}\right)dx + \int 0\,dy = C \therefore \log x + 3\dfrac{y}{x} - \dfrac{y^2}{x^2} = C$$

Ex. 6: Solve $y(x+y)dx - x(y-x)dy = 0$

Solution: The given equation is homogeneous of degree 2.
$M = xy + y^2$ and $N = -xy + x^2$
$xM + yN = x^2 y + xy^2 - xy^2 + x^2 y = 2x^2 y \neq 0$

$\therefore$ I.F $= \dfrac{1}{xM+yN} = \dfrac{1}{2x^2 y}$

Multiplying the given equation by I.F, we get

$$\dfrac{1}{2x^2 y}(xy+y^2)dx + \dfrac{1}{2x^2 y}(-xy+x^2)dy = 0 \therefore \left(\dfrac{1}{2x} + \dfrac{y}{2x^2}\right)dx - \left(\dfrac{1}{2x} - \dfrac{1}{2y}\right)dy = 0$$

Which is exact, solution is

$$\int_{y\ Constant} M dx + \int [\text{Term Free from x in N}] dy = C$$

$$\therefore \int \left(\frac{1}{2x} + \frac{y}{2x^2}\right) dx + \int \frac{1}{2y} dy = C \therefore \frac{1}{2}\log x - \frac{y}{2x} + \frac{1}{2}\log y = C \Rightarrow \log \sqrt{xy} - \frac{y}{2x} = C$$

TEST YOUR KNOWLEDGE

Solve the following ordinary differential equations

1. $(3xy - 2ay^2) dx + (x^2 - 2axy) dy = 0$ Ans: $x^2 y(x - ay) = c$

2. $(y^4 - 2x^3 y) dx + (x^4 - 2xy^3) dy = 0$

3. $(x^3 + y^3) dx - xy^2 dy = 0$ Ans: $cx = e^{y^3/3x^3}$

4. $y^2 dx + x(x - y) dy = 0$ Ans: $cy = e^{y/x}$

5. $(x^2 - xy + y^2) dx - xy dy = 0$ Ans: $\log(x - y) + \frac{y}{x} = c$

6. $(x^4 + y^4) dx - xy^3 dy = 0$ Ans: $4x^4 \log x - y^4 = x^4 c$

7. $x(x - y) dy + y^2 dx = 0$ Ans: $cy = e^{y/x}$

8. $x(x - y) \frac{dy}{dx} = y(x + y)$ Ans: $xy^2 = c$

Examples based on Rule II: If the equation is of the form

$yf_1(x, y)dx + xf_2(x, y)dy = 0$ or $f_1(x, y)y dx + f_2(x, y)x dy = 0$ and $xM - yN \neq 0$,

then $\dfrac{1}{xM - yN}$ is an I.F

Ex. 1: Solve $y(xy + 2x^2 y^2) dx + x(xy - x^2 y^2) dy = 0$ **SUK: Dec-11**

Solution: Given equation is of the form $yf_1(x, y)dx + xf_2(x, y)dy = 0$

Here,

$M = y(xy + 2x^2 y^2)$ and $N = x(xy - x^2 y^2)$

$xM - Ny = x^2 y^2 + 2x^3 y^3 - x^2 y^2 + x^3 y^3 = 3x^3 y^3 \neq 0 \therefore \text{I.F} = \dfrac{1}{3x^3 y^3}$

Multiplying given equation by I.F

$\therefore \dfrac{1}{3x^3 y^3}[y(xy + 2x^2 y^2)]dx + \dfrac{1}{3x^3 y^3}[x(xy - x^2 y^2)]dy = 0 \Rightarrow \dfrac{1}{3}\left(\dfrac{1}{x^2 y} + \dfrac{2}{x}\right)dx + \dfrac{1}{3}\left(\dfrac{1}{xy^2} - \dfrac{1}{y}\right)dy = 0$

Which is exact, hence Solution is

$$\int_{y\text{ Constant}} M\,dx + \int [\text{Term Free from x in N}]\,dy = C$$

$$\therefore \int \frac{1}{3}\left(\frac{1}{x^2 y} + \frac{2}{x}\right) dx + \int -\frac{1}{3}\frac{1}{y}\,dy = C \Rightarrow -\frac{1}{3}\frac{1}{xy} + \frac{2}{3}\log x - \frac{1}{3}\log y = C \therefore -\frac{1}{xy} + 2\log x - \log y = C'$$

Ex. 2: Solve $(xy\sin xy + \cos xy)y\,dx + (xy\sin xy - \cos xy)x\,dy = 0$ **SUK: May-12**

Solution: Given equation is of the form $f_1(x,y)y\,dx + f_2(x,y)x\,dy = 0$

$$M = (xy\sin xy + \cos xy)y \text{ and } N = (xy\sin xy - \cos xy)x$$

Here, $xM - Ny = x^2 y^2 \sin xy + xy\cos xy - x^2 y^2 \sin xy + xy\cos xy = 2xy\cos xy \neq 0$

$$\therefore \text{I.F} = \frac{1}{2xy\cos xy}$$

Multiplying given equation by I.F

$$\therefore \frac{1}{2xy\cos xy}\left[(xy\sin xy + \cos xy)y\right]dx + \frac{1}{2xy\cos xy}\left[(xy\sin xy - \cos xy)x\right]dy = 0$$

$$\Rightarrow \frac{1}{2}\left(y\tan xy + \frac{1}{x}\right)dx + \frac{1}{2}\left(x\tan xy - \frac{1}{y}\right)dy = 0 \Rightarrow \left(y\tan xy + \frac{1}{x}\right)dx + \left(x\tan xy - \frac{1}{y}\right)dy = 0$$

Which is exact, hence Solution is

$$\int_{y\text{ Constant}} M\,dx + \int [\text{Term Free from x in N}]\,dy = C$$

$$\therefore \int \left(y\tan xy + \frac{1}{x}\right)dx + \int -\frac{1}{y}\,dy = c$$

$$\Rightarrow y\frac{\log\sec xy}{y} + \log x - \log y = \log C \Rightarrow \log\sec xy + \log\frac{x}{y} = \log C \Rightarrow \frac{x}{y}\sec xy = C$$

Ex. 3: Solve $(x^2 y^2 + 2)y\,dx + (2 - 2x^2 y^2)x\,dy = 0$

Solution: Given equation is of the form $f_1(x,y)y\,dx + f_2(x,y)x\,dy = 0$

Here, $M = (x^2 y^2 + 2)y$ and $N = (2 - 2x^2 y^2)x$

$$xM - Ny = x^3 y^3 + 2xy - 2xy + 2x^3 y^3 = 3x^3 y^3 \neq 0$$

and

$$\therefore \text{I.F} = \frac{1}{3x^3 y^3}$$

Multiplying given equation by I.F

$$\therefore \frac{1}{3x^3 y^3}(x^2 y^2 + 2)y\,dx + \frac{1}{3x^3 y^3}(2 - 2x^2 y^2)x\,dy = 0 \Rightarrow \left(\frac{1}{3x} + \frac{2}{3x^3 y^2}\right) + \left(\frac{2}{3x^2 y^3} - \frac{2}{3y}\right) = 0$$

Which is exact, hence Solution is

$$\therefore \int\left(\frac{1}{3x} + \frac{2}{3x^3 y^2}\right)dx + \int -\frac{2}{3y}\,dy = C$$

$$\therefore \frac{1}{3}\log x - \frac{2}{6x^2 y^2} - \frac{2}{3}\log y = C \Rightarrow \log x - \frac{1}{x^2 y^2} - 2\log y = C'$$

Ex. 4: Solve $y(1+xy)dx + x(1+xy+x^2y^2)dy = 0$

Solution: Given equation is of the form $yf_1(x, y)dx + xf_2(x, y)dy = 0$

Here, $M = y(1+xy)$ and $N = x(1+xy+x^2y^2)$

$xM - Ny = xy + x^2y^2 - xy - x^2y^2 - x^3y^3 = -x^3y^3 \neq 0$

$\therefore \text{I.F} = \dfrac{-1}{x^3y^3}$

Multiplying given equation by I.F

$\therefore \dfrac{-1}{x^3y^3}[y(1+xy)]dx + \dfrac{-1}{x^3y^3}[x(1+xy+x^2y^2)]dy = 0$

$\Rightarrow \left(-\dfrac{1}{x^3y^2} - \dfrac{1}{x^2y}\right)dx + \left(-\dfrac{1}{x^2y^3} - \dfrac{1}{xy^2} - \dfrac{1}{y}\right)dy = 0$

Which is exact, hence Solution is

$\underset{y\ \text{Constant}}{\int} M dx + \int [\text{Term Free from x in N}] dy$

$\therefore \int\left(-\dfrac{1}{x^3y^2} - \dfrac{1}{x^2y}\right)dx + \int -\dfrac{1}{y}dy = C \therefore \dfrac{1}{2x^2y^2} + \dfrac{1}{xy} - \log y = C$

Ex. 5: Solve $y(xy - 2x^2y^2)dx + x(xy - x^2y^2)dy = 0$

Solution: Given equation is of the form $yf_1(x, y)dx + xf_2(x, y)dy = 0$

Here,

$M = y(xy - 2x^2y^2)$ and $N = x(xy - x^2y^2)$

$xM - Ny = x^2y^2 - 2x^3y^3 - x^2y^2 + x^3y^3 \neq 0 \therefore \text{I.F} = \dfrac{-1}{x^3y^3}$

Multiplying given equation by I.F

$\therefore \dfrac{-1}{x^3y^3}[y(xy-2x^2y^2)]dx + \dfrac{-1}{x^3y^3}[x(xy-x^2y^2)]dy = 0 \Rightarrow \left(\dfrac{-1}{x^2y} + \dfrac{2}{x}\right)dx + \left(\dfrac{-1}{xy^2} + \dfrac{1}{y}\right)dy = 0$

Which is exact, hence Solution is

$\underset{y\ \text{Constant}}{\int} M dx + \int [\text{Term Free from x in N}] dy = C$

$\therefore \int\left(\dfrac{-1}{x^2y} + \dfrac{2}{x}\right)dx + \int \dfrac{1}{y}dy = C \Rightarrow \dfrac{1}{xy} + 2\log x + \log y = C$

Ex. 6: Solve $y(2xy+1)dx + x(1+2xy-x^3y^3)dy = 0$

Solution: Given equation is of the form $yf_1(x, y)dx + xf_2(x, y)dy = 0$

Here, $M = y(2xy+1)$ and $N = x(1+2xy-x^3y^3)$

$xM - Ny = 2x^2y^2 + xy - xy - 2x^2y^2 + x^4y^4 \neq 0 \therefore \text{I.F} = \dfrac{1}{x^4y^4}$

(1.63)

Multiplying given equation by I.F

$$\therefore \frac{1}{x^4 y^4}\left[y(2xy+1)\right]dx + \frac{1}{x^4 y^4}\left[x(1+2xy-x^3 y^3)\right]dy = 0$$

$$\Rightarrow \left(\frac{2}{x^3 y^2} + \frac{1}{x^4 y^3}\right)dx + \left(\frac{1}{x^3 y^4} + \frac{2}{x^2 y^3} - \frac{1}{y}\right)dy = 0$$

Which is exact, hence Solution is

$$\int \frac{2}{x^3 y^2} + \frac{1}{x^4 y^3} dx + \int -\frac{1}{y} dy = C$$

$$\frac{-1}{x^2 y^2} - \frac{1}{x^3 y^3} - \log y = C$$

Ex. 7: Solve $(x^2 y^2 + xy + 1) y\, dx + (x^2 y^2 - xy + 1) x\, dy = 0$.

Solution: This is of the form $f_1(x, y) y\, dx + f_2(x, y) x\, dy = 0$, so the integration factor is

$$I.F. = \frac{1}{Mx - Ny} = \frac{1}{xy(2xy)} = \frac{1}{2x^2 y^2}$$

Multiplying the given equation by I.F.,

$$\frac{(x^2 y^2 + xy + 1) y\, dx}{2x^2 y^2} + \frac{(x^2 y^2 - xy + 1) x\, dy}{2x^2 y^2} = 0$$

$$\Rightarrow \left(y + \frac{1}{x} + \frac{1}{x^2 y}\right)dx + \left(x - \frac{1}{y} + \frac{1}{xy^2}\right)dy = 0$$

This is an exact differential equation, on integrating it, the solution of the given differential equation is $xy + \log x - \frac{1}{xy} - \log y = C \Rightarrow xy + \log\left(\frac{x}{y}\right) - \frac{1}{xy} = C$

TEST YOUR KNOWLEDGE

Solve the following ordinary differential equations

1. $y(1+xy)dx + x(1-xy)dy = 0$ Ans: $xy - \log\frac{x}{y} = C$ SUK:Aug-13

2. $(1+2xy)ydx + (1-xy)xdy = 0$ Ans: $\log\frac{x^2}{y} = \frac{1}{xy} + C$

3. $y(1+xy+x^2 y^2 + x^3 y^3)dx + x(1-xy-x^2 y^2 + x^3 y^3)dy = 0$ Ans: $xy - \frac{1}{xy} - \log y^2 = C$

4. $y(xy + 2x^2 y^2)dx + x(xy + x^2 y^2)dy = 0$ Ans: $\log x^2 y = \frac{1}{xy} + C$

5. $y(1+xy)dx + x(1-xy)dy = 0$ Ans: $xy - \log\frac{x}{y} = C$

6. $y(xy-3)dx + x(3xy+7)dy = 0$ Ans: $y^7 (xy+5)^8 = x^3 C$

7. $(x^2 y^2 + 5xy + 2)ydx + (x^2 y^2 + 4xy + 2)xdy = 0$ Ans: $x^5 y^4 = Ce^{\frac{2}{xy}-xy}$

8. $(xy + 2x^2 y^2)ydx + (xy - x^2 y^2)xdy = 0$ Ans: $x^2 = ye^{\frac{1}{xy}}C$

9. $(xy-3)ydx+(3xy-3)xdy=0$ Ans: $\log(xy^3)+\dfrac{3}{xy}=C$

10. $y(1+2xy)dx+x(1-xy)dy=0$ Ans: $\log(x^2/y)-\dfrac{1}{xy}=C$

11. $y(\sin xy+xy\cos xy)dx+x(xy\cos xy-\sin xy)dy=0$ Ans: $x\sin xy=yC$

12. $y(1+xy+x^2y^2)dx+x(1-xy+x^2y^2)dy=0$ Ans: $xy-\dfrac{1}{xy}+\log x/y=C$

13. $y(2xy+1)dx+x(1+2xy-x^3y^3)dy=0$ Ans: $\dfrac{1}{x^2y^2}+\dfrac{1}{3x^3y^3}+\log y=C$

Examples based on Rule III: Let $M(x,y)dx+N(x,y)dy=0$ be the given differential equation.

If $\dfrac{\partial M}{\partial y}-\dfrac{\partial N}{\partial x}\bigg/N$ is a function of x only, say $f(x)$ then I.F $=e^{\int f(x)dx}$

Ex. 1: Solve $(x^4e^x-2mxy^2)dx+2mx^2ydy=0$

Solution: Here $M=x^4e^x-2mxy^2$ and $N=2mx^2y$

$\dfrac{\partial M}{\partial y}=-4mxy,\quad \dfrac{\partial N}{\partial x}=4mxy,\quad \therefore \dfrac{\partial M}{\partial y}\neq\dfrac{\partial N}{\partial x}$

So given equation is not exact, but

$\dfrac{\partial M}{\partial y}-\dfrac{\partial N}{\partial x}\bigg/N=-4mxy-4mxy\bigg/2mx^2y=\dfrac{-8mxy}{2mx^2y}=\dfrac{-4}{x}=f(x)$ Say

$\therefore$ I.F $=e^{\int\frac{-4}{x}dx}=e^{-4\log x}=\dfrac{1}{x^4}$

Multiplying given equation by I.F

$\dfrac{1}{x^4}(x^4e^x-2mxy^2)dx+\dfrac{1}{x^4}(2mx^2y)dy=0 \Rightarrow \left(e^x-\dfrac{2my^2}{x^3}\right)dx+\dfrac{2my}{x^2}dy=0$

Which is exact, hence Solution is

$\displaystyle\int_{y\text{Constant}} Mdx+\int[\text{Term Free from x in N}]dy=C$

$\therefore \displaystyle\int\left(e^x-\dfrac{2my^2}{x^3}\right)dx+\int 0\,dy=C \Rightarrow e^x+\dfrac{2my^2}{2x^2}=C \Rightarrow x^2e^x+my^2=x^2C$

Ex. 2: Solve $(x^2+y^2+x)dx+xydy=0$ SUK: May-09, Nov-09

Solution: Here $M=x^2+y^2+x$ and $N=xy$, $\dfrac{\partial M}{\partial y}=2y,\quad \dfrac{\partial N}{\partial x}=y,\quad \therefore \dfrac{\partial M}{\partial y}\neq\dfrac{\partial N}{\partial x}$

So given equation is not exact, but

$\dfrac{\partial M}{\partial y} - \dfrac{\partial N}{\partial x} \Big/ N = 2y - y\Big/xy = y/xy = \dfrac{1}{x} = f(x)$ Say

$\therefore \text{I.F} = e^{\int \frac{1}{x}dx} = e^{\log x} = x$

Multiplying given equation by I.F

$x(x^2 + y^2 + x)dx + x(xy)dy = 0 \Rightarrow (x^3 + xy^2 + x^2)dx + x^2 ydy = 0$

Which is exact, hence Solution is

$\displaystyle\int_{y\ \text{Constant}} Mdx + \int [\text{Term Free from x in N}]dy = C$

$\therefore \int (x^3 + xy^2 + x^2)dx + \int 0\,dy = C \Rightarrow \dfrac{x^4}{4} + \dfrac{x^2 y^2}{2} + \dfrac{x^3}{3} = C \Rightarrow 3x^4 + 6x^2 y^2 + 4x^3 = C'$

Ex. 3: Solve $(x^2 + y^2 + 1)dx - 2xy\,dy = 0$ **SUK: Dec-13**

Solution : Here $M = x^2 + y^2 + 1$ and $N = -2xy$

$\dfrac{\partial M}{\partial y} = 2y,\quad \dfrac{\partial N}{\partial x} = -2y,\qquad \therefore \dfrac{\partial M}{\partial y} \ne \dfrac{\partial N}{\partial x}$

So given equation is not exact, but

$\dfrac{\partial M}{\partial y} - \dfrac{\partial N}{\partial x} \Big/ N = 2y + 2y\Big/ -2xy = \dfrac{-2}{x} = f(x)\quad \therefore \text{I.F} = e^{\int \frac{-2}{x}dx} = e^{-2\log x} = \dfrac{1}{x^2}$

Multiplying given equation by I.F

$\dfrac{1}{x^2}(x^2 + y^2 + 1)dx - \dfrac{1}{x^2}2xy\,dy = 0 \Rightarrow \left(1 + \dfrac{y^2}{x^2} + \dfrac{1}{x^2}\right)dx + \left(-\dfrac{2y}{x}\right)dy = 0$

Which is exact, hence Solution is

$\displaystyle\int_{y\ \text{Constant}} Mdx + \int [\text{Term Free from x in N}]dy = C$

$\therefore \int \left(1 + \dfrac{y^2}{x^2} + \dfrac{1}{x^2}\right)dx + \int 0\,dy = C \Rightarrow x - \dfrac{y^2}{x} - \dfrac{1}{x} = C \Rightarrow x^2 - y^2 - 1 = Cx$

Ex. 4: Solve $(y - 2x^3)dx - x(1 - xy)dy = 0$

Solution: Here $M = y - 2x^3$ and $N = -x(1 - xy)$

$\dfrac{\partial M}{\partial y} = 1,\quad \dfrac{\partial N}{\partial x} = -1 + 2xy,\qquad \therefore \dfrac{\partial M}{\partial y} \ne \dfrac{\partial N}{\partial x}$

So given equation is not exact, but

$\dfrac{\partial M}{\partial y} - \dfrac{\partial N}{\partial x} \Big/ N = 1 + 1 - 2xy \Big/ -x(1-xy) = \dfrac{2 - 2xy}{-x + x^2 y} = \dfrac{2(1-xy)}{-x(1-xy)} = \dfrac{-2}{x} = f(x)$

$\therefore \text{I.F} = e^{\int \frac{-2}{x}dx} = e^{-2\log x} = \dfrac{1}{x^2}$

Multiplying given equation by I.F

$$\frac{1}{x^2}(y-2x^3)dx+\frac{1}{x^2}[-x(1-xy)]dy=0 \Rightarrow \left(\frac{y}{x^2}-2x\right)dx+\left(-\frac{1}{x}+y\right)dy=0$$

Which is exact, hence Solution is

$$\therefore \int\left(\frac{y}{x^2}-2x\right)dx+\int y\,dy=C \Rightarrow -\frac{y}{x}-2\frac{x^2}{2}+\frac{y^2}{2}=C \Rightarrow -\frac{y}{x}-x^2+\frac{y^2}{2}=C$$

Ex. 5 : Solve $\left(xy^2-e^{1/x^3}\right)dx-x^2y\,dy=0$

Solution: Here $M=xy^2-e^{1/x^3}$ and $N=-x^2y$,

$\dfrac{\partial M}{\partial y}=2xy, \quad \dfrac{\partial N}{\partial x}=-2xy, \qquad \therefore \dfrac{\partial M}{\partial y}\neq \dfrac{\partial N}{\partial x}$

So given equation is not exact, but

$\dfrac{\partial M}{\partial y}-\dfrac{\partial N}{\partial x}\bigg/N=2xy+2xy\bigg/-x^2y=\dfrac{4xy}{-x^2y}=\dfrac{-4}{x}=f(x)$ Say

$\therefore \text{I.F}=e^{\int \frac{-4}{x}dx}=e^{-4\log x}=\dfrac{1}{x^4}$

Multiplying given equation by I.F

$$\frac{1}{x^4}\left(xy^2-e^{1/x^3}\right)dx+\frac{1}{x^4}\left(-x^2y\right)dy=0$$

$$\Rightarrow \left(\frac{y^2}{x^3}-\frac{e^{1/x^3}}{x^4}\right)dx-\frac{y}{x^2}dy=0$$

Which is exact, hence Solution is

$$\int_{y\text{Constant}} M\,dx+\int[\text{Term Free from }x\text{ in }N]dy=C$$

$\therefore \int\left(\dfrac{y^2}{x^3}-\dfrac{e^{1/x^3}}{x^4}\right)dx+\int 0\,dy=C \Rightarrow -\dfrac{y^2}{2x^2}+\dfrac{e^{1/x^3}}{3}=C \quad \therefore \int e^{f(x)}f'(x)dx=e^{f(x)}$

Ex. 6: Solve $\left(y+\dfrac{y^3}{3}+\dfrac{x^2}{2}\right)dx+\left(\dfrac{x+xy^2}{4}\right)dy=0$

Solution: Here $M=y+\dfrac{y^3}{3}+\dfrac{x^2}{2}$ and $N=\dfrac{x+xy^2}{4}$

$\dfrac{\partial M}{\partial y}=1+y^2, \quad \dfrac{\partial N}{\partial x}=\dfrac{1+y^2}{4}, \qquad \therefore \dfrac{\partial M}{\partial y}\neq \dfrac{\partial N}{\partial x}$

So given equation is not exact, but

$\dfrac{\partial M}{\partial y}-\dfrac{\partial N}{\partial x}\bigg/N=1+y^2-\dfrac{1+y^2}{4}\bigg/\dfrac{x+xy^2}{4}=\dfrac{4+4y^2-1-y^2}{4}\bigg/\dfrac{x(1+y^2)}{4}$

$=\dfrac{3(1+y^2)}{4}\bigg/\dfrac{x(1+y^2)}{4}=\dfrac{3}{x}=f(x)$ Say $\therefore \text{I.F}=e^{\int \frac{3}{x}dx}=e^{3\log x}=x^3$

Multiplying given equation by I.F

$$x^3\left(y+\frac{y^3}{3}+\frac{x^2}{2}\right)dx+x^3\left(\frac{x+xy^2}{4}\right)dy=0 \therefore \left(x^3y+\frac{x^3y^3}{3}+\frac{x^5}{2}\right)dx+\left(\frac{x^4+x^4y^2}{4}\right)dy=0$$

Which is exact, hence Solution is

$$\therefore \int\left(x^3y+\frac{x^3y^3}{3}+\frac{x^5}{2}\right)dx+\int 0\,dy=C \Rightarrow \frac{x^4y}{4}+\frac{x^4y^3}{12}+\frac{x^6}{12}=C \Rightarrow 3x^4y+x^4y^3+x^6=C'$$

TEST YOUR KNOWLEDGE

Solve the following ordinary differential equations

1. $(x^2+y^2+2x)dx+2y\,dy=0$ \qquad Ans: $e^x(x^2+y^2)=C$

2. $(x^2+y^2)dx-2xy\,dy=0$ \qquad Ans: $x^2-y^2=xC$

3. $y(2xy+e^x)dx-e^x dy=0$ \qquad Ans: $x^2+e^{\frac{x}{y}}=C$

4. $(2x\log x-xy)dx+2y\,dy=0$ \qquad Ans: $2y\log x-\frac{y^2}{2}=C$

5. $(x^3e^x-my^2)dx+mxy\,dy=0$ \qquad Ans: $x^2e^x+my^2=x^2C$

6. $(x^2+y^2+2x)dx+2y\,dy=0$ \qquad Ans: $e^x(x^2+y^2)=C$

7. $(y-2x^2)dx-x(1-xy)dy=0$ \qquad Ans: $xy^2-2y-4x^2=xC$

8. $(xy^3+y)dx+2(x^2y^2+x+y^4)dy=0$ \qquad Ans: $3x^2y^4+2y^3+2y^6=C'$

Examples based on Rule IV:

Let $M(x,y)dx+N(x,y)dy=0$ be the given differential equation.

If $\dfrac{\partial N}{\partial x}-\dfrac{\partial M}{\partial y}\Big/M$ is a function of y only, say $f(y)$ then $I.F=e^{\int f(y)dy}$

Ex. 1: Solve $(x+2y^3)\dfrac{dy}{dx}=y$

Solution: Here $(x+2y^3)\dfrac{dy}{dx}=y \Rightarrow y\,dx-(x+2y^3)dy=0$

$M=y$ and $N=-(x+2y^3) \therefore \dfrac{\partial M}{\partial y}=1,\ \dfrac{\partial N}{\partial x}=-1,\ \therefore \dfrac{\partial M}{\partial y}\neq\dfrac{\partial N}{\partial x}$

So given equation is not exact, but

$\dfrac{\partial N}{\partial x}-\dfrac{\partial M}{\partial y}\Big/M=-1-1/y=\dfrac{-2}{y}=f(y)$ Say $\therefore I.F=e^{\int\frac{-2}{y}dx}=e^{-2\log y}=\dfrac{1}{y^2}$

Multiplying given equation by I.F

$$\frac{1}{y^2}(y)dx + \frac{1}{y^2}\left[-\left(x+2y^3\right)\right]dy = 0 \Rightarrow \frac{1}{y}dx - \left(\frac{x}{y^2}+2ydy\right) = 0$$

Which is exact, hence Solution is

$$\int_{y\,\text{Constant}} Mdx + \int[\text{Term Free from x in N}]dy = C$$

$$\therefore \int\left(\frac{1}{y}\right)dx + \int -2y\,dy = c \Rightarrow \frac{x}{y} - 2\frac{y^2}{2} = C \qquad \Rightarrow x - y^3 = yC$$

Ex. 2: Solve $y(xy + e^x)dx - e^x dy = 0$

Solution: Here $M = y(xy + e^x)$ and $N = -e^x$

$$\frac{\partial M}{\partial y} = 2xy + e^x, \quad \frac{\partial N}{\partial x} = -e^x, \quad \therefore \frac{\partial M}{\partial y} \neq \frac{\partial N}{\partial x}$$

So given equation is not exact, but

$$\frac{\partial N}{\partial x} - \frac{\partial M}{\partial y}\bigg/M = -e^x - 2xy - e^x \bigg/ y(xy + e^x) = \frac{-2e^x - 2xy}{y(xy+e^x)} = \frac{-2(e^x + xy)}{y(xy+e^x)} = \frac{-2}{y} = f(y) \text{ Say}$$

$$\therefore \text{I.F} = e^{\int \frac{-2}{y}dx} = e^{-2\log y} = \frac{1}{y^2}$$

Multiplying given equation by I.F

$$\frac{1}{y^2}\left[y(xy+e^x)\right]dx + \frac{1}{y^2}\left[-e^x\right]dy = 0 \Rightarrow \left(x + \frac{e^x}{y}\right)dx + \left(\frac{-e^x}{y^2}\right)dy = 0$$

Which is exact, hence Solution is

$$\int_{y\,\text{Constant}} Mdx + \int[\text{Term Free from x in N}]dy = C$$

$$\therefore \int\left(x + \frac{e^x}{y}\right)dx + \int 0\,dy = c \Rightarrow \frac{x^2}{2} + \frac{e^x}{y} = C$$

Ex. 3: Solve $y(2x^2y + e^x)dx - (e^x + y^3)dy = 0$

Solution: Here $M = y(2x^2y + e^x)$ and $N = -(e^x + y^3)$

$$\frac{\partial M}{\partial y} = 4x^2y + e^x, \quad \frac{\partial N}{\partial x} = -e^x, \quad \therefore \frac{\partial M}{\partial y} \neq \frac{\partial N}{\partial x}$$

So given equation is not exact, but

$$\frac{\partial N}{\partial x} - \frac{\partial M}{\partial y}\bigg/M = -e^x - 4x^2y - e^x \bigg/ y(2x^2y + e^x) = \frac{-2e^x - 4x^2y}{y(2x^2y + e^x)}$$

$$= \frac{-2(e^x + 2x^2y)}{y(2x^2y + e^x)} = \frac{-2}{y} = f(y) \text{ Say}$$

(1.69)

$$\therefore \text{I.F} = e^{\int \frac{-2}{y}dx} = e^{-2\log y} = \frac{1}{y^2}$$

Multiplying given equation by I.F

$$\frac{1}{y^2}\left[y(2x^2y+e^x)\right]dx + \frac{1}{y^2}\left[-(e^x+y^3)\right]dy = 0 \Rightarrow \left(2x^2 + \frac{e^x}{y}\right)dx - \left(\frac{e^x}{y^2}+y\right)dy = 0$$

Which is exact, hence Solution is

$$\int_{y\text{Constant}} Mdx + \int [\text{Term Free from x in N}]dy = C$$

$$\therefore \int\left(2x^2 + \frac{e^x}{y}\right)dx + \int -y\,dy = C \Rightarrow \frac{2x^3}{3} + \frac{e^x}{y} - \frac{y^2}{2} = C$$

Ex. 4: Solve $(y^4 + 2y)dx + (xy^3 + 2y^4 - 4x)dy = 0$

Solution: Here $M = y^4 + 2y$ and $N = xy^3 + 2y^4 - 4x$

$$\frac{\partial M}{\partial y} = 4y^3 + 2, \quad \frac{\partial N}{\partial x} = y^3 - 4, \quad \therefore \frac{\partial M}{\partial y} \neq \frac{\partial N}{\partial x}$$

So given equation is not exact, but

$$\frac{\partial N}{\partial x} - \frac{\partial M}{\partial y} \Big/ M = y^3 - 4 - 4y^3 - 2 \Big/ y^4 + 2y = \frac{-6-3y^3}{y^4+2y} = \frac{-3(2+y^3)}{y(y^3+2)} = \frac{-3}{y} = f(y) \text{ Say}$$

$$\therefore \text{I.F} = e^{\int \frac{-3}{y}dx} = e^{-3\log y} = \frac{1}{y^3}$$

Multiplying given equation by I.F

$$\frac{1}{y^3}\left[y^4 + 2y\right]dx + \frac{1}{y^3}\left[xy^3 + 2y^4 - 4x\right]dy = 0 \Rightarrow \left(y + 2\frac{1}{y^2}\right)dx + \left(x + 2y - \frac{4x}{y^3}\right)dy = 0$$

Which is exact, hence Solution is

$$\int_{y\text{ Constant}} Mdx + \int [\text{Term Free from x in N}]dy = C$$

$$\therefore \int\left(y + 2\frac{1}{y^2}\right)dx + \int 2y\,dy = C \Rightarrow xy + 2\frac{x}{y^2} + 2\frac{y^2}{2} = C \Rightarrow xy + 2\frac{x}{y^2} + y^2 = C$$

Ex. 5: Solve $(3x^2y^4 + 2xy)dx + (2x^3y^3 - x^2)dy = 0$

Solution: Here $M = 3x^2y^4 + 2xy$ and $N = 2x^3y^3 - x^2$

$$\frac{\partial M}{\partial y} = 12x^2y^3 + 2x, \quad \frac{\partial N}{\partial x} = 6x^2y^3 - 2x, \quad \therefore \frac{\partial M}{\partial y} \neq \frac{\partial N}{\partial x}$$

So given equation is not exact, but

$$\frac{\partial N}{\partial x}-\frac{\partial M}{\partial y}\bigg/M = 6x^2y^3 - 2x - 12x^2y^3 - 2x\Big/3x^2y^4 + 2xy = \frac{-6x^2y^3 - 4x}{3x^2y^4 + 2xy}$$

$$= \frac{-2(3x^2y^3 + 2x)}{y(3x^2y^3 + 2x)} = \frac{-2}{y} = f(y) \text{ Say}$$

$$\therefore \text{I.F} = e^{\int \frac{-2}{y}dx} = e^{-2\log y} = \frac{1}{y^2}$$

Multiplying given equation by I.F

$$\frac{1}{y^2}\Big[3x^2y^4 + 2xy\Big]dx + \frac{1}{y^2}\Big[2x^3y^3 - x^2\Big]dy = 0 \Rightarrow \left(3x^2y^2 + \frac{2x}{y}\right)dx + \left(2x^3y - \frac{x^2}{y^2}\right)dy = 0$$

Which is exact, hence Solution is

$$\int_{y \text{ Constant}} Mdx + \int [\text{Term Free from x in N}]dy = C$$

$$\therefore \int \left(3x^2y^2 + \frac{2x}{y}\right)dx + \int 0\,dy = C$$

$$\Rightarrow 3y^2\frac{x^3}{3} + 2\frac{x^2}{2y} = C \Rightarrow x^3y^2 + \frac{x^2}{y} = C \Rightarrow x^3y^3 + x^2 = Cy$$

Ex. 6: Solve $y\log y\,dx + (x - \log y)dy = 0$

Solution: Here $M = y\log y$ and $N = x - \log y$

$$\frac{\partial M}{\partial y} = y\frac{1}{y} + \log y \cdot 1 = 1 + \log y, \quad \frac{\partial N}{\partial x} = 1, \quad \therefore \frac{\partial M}{\partial y} \neq \frac{\partial N}{\partial x}$$

So given equation is not exact, but

$$\frac{\partial N}{\partial x}-\frac{\partial M}{\partial y}\bigg/M = 1 - 1 - \log y/y\log y = \frac{-\log y}{y\log y} = \frac{-1}{y} = f(y) \text{ Say}$$

$$\therefore \text{I.F} = e^{\int \frac{-1}{y}dx} = e^{-\log y} = \frac{1}{y}$$

Multiplying given equation by I.F

$$\frac{1}{y}[y\log y]dx + \frac{1}{y}[x - \log y]dy = 0 \Rightarrow (\log y)dx + \left(\frac{x}{y} - \frac{\log y}{y}\right)dy = 0$$

Which is exact, hence Solution is

$$\int_{y\text{Constant}} Mdx + \int [\text{Term Free from x in N}]dy = C$$

$$\therefore \int (\log y)dx + \int -\frac{\log y}{y}dy = C \Rightarrow x\log y - \frac{(\log y)^2}{2} = C \quad \because \int [f(x)]^n f'(x)dx = \frac{[f(x)]^{n+1}}{n+1}$$

TEST YOUR KNOWLEDGE

Solve the following ordinary differential equations

1. $y(x^2 y + e^x) dx + e^x dy = 0$ Ans: $\dfrac{x^3}{3} + e^{\frac{x}{y}} = C$

2. $(2xy^2 - y) dx + x dy = 0$ Ans: $x^2 y - x = yC$

3. $(xy^3 + y) dx + 2(x^2 y^2 + x + y^4) dy = 0$ Ans: $3x^2 y^4 + 6xy^2 + 2y^6 = C$

4. $(y^4 + 2y) dx + (xy^3 + 2y^4 - 4x) dy = 0$ Ans: $xy^3 + 2x + y^4 = y^2 C$

5. $(x^2 y + e^x) dx - e^x dy = 0$ Ans: $x^3 y + 3e^x = yC$

6. $(2x \log x - xy) dy + 2y dx = 0$ Ans: $4y \log y - y^2 = C'$

7. $xe^x(dx - dy) + e^x dx + ye^y dy = 0$ Ans: $\dfrac{xe^x}{e^y} + \dfrac{y^x}{2} = C$

8. $y(x^2 y + e^x) dx + e^x dy = 0$ Ans: $\dfrac{x^3}{3} + e^{x/y} = C$

Rule V: Some times integrating Factor can be found just by inspection

Integrating Factors Found by Inspection

Integrating factors may sometimes be seen at a glance for some differential equations. For this purpose the following integrable combinations will be found useful in guessing the integrating factors.

1. $xdy + ydx = d(xy)$

2. $\dfrac{xdy + ydx}{xy} = d[\log(xy)]$

3. $\dfrac{xdy - ydx}{x^2} = d\left(\dfrac{y}{x}\right)$

4. $\dfrac{xdy - ydx}{xy} = d\left[\log\left(\dfrac{y}{x}\right)\right]$

5. $\dfrac{xdy - ydx}{x^2 + y^2} = d\left(\tan^{-1} \dfrac{y}{x}\right)$

6. $\dfrac{xdy - ydx}{x^2 - y^2} = d\left[\dfrac{1}{2}\log\left(\dfrac{x+y}{x-y}\right)\right]$ 1

7. $\dfrac{ydx - xdy}{y^2} = d\left(\dfrac{x}{y}\right)$

8. $\dfrac{ydx - xdy}{x^2 + y^2} = d\left(\tan^{-1} \dfrac{x}{y}\right)$

9. $\dfrac{ydx - xdy}{xy} = d\left(\log \dfrac{x}{y}\right)$

10. $\dfrac{xdx + ydy}{x^2 + y^2} = \dfrac{1}{2} d[\log(x^2 + y^2)]$

11. $\dfrac{xdx+ydy}{\sqrt{x^2+y^2}}=d\left(\sqrt{x^2+y^2}\right)$ 12. $xdx+ydy=\dfrac{1}{2}d\left(x^2+y^2\right)$

13. $dx+dy=d(x+y)$ 14. $\dfrac{dx+dy}{x+y}=\dfrac{1}{2}\log(x+y)$

15. $\dfrac{xdy+ydx}{x^2y^2}=d\left(\dfrac{-1}{xy}\right)$ 16. $\dfrac{y.2xdx-x^2dy}{y^2}=d\left(\dfrac{x^2}{y}\right)$

17. $\dfrac{x.2ydy-y^2dx}{x^2}=d\left(\dfrac{y^2}{x}\right)$ 18. $\dfrac{2x^2ydy-2y^2xdx}{x^4}=d\left(\dfrac{y^2}{x^2}\right)$

19. $\dfrac{2xy^2dx-2yx^2dy}{y^4}=d\left(\dfrac{x^2}{y^2}\right)$ 20. $\dfrac{ye^xdx-e^xdy}{y^2}=d\left(\dfrac{e^x}{y}\right)$

21. $(x+y)^n(dx+dy)=d\left[\dfrac{(x+y)^{n+1}}{n+1}\right]$ if $n\ne -1$

Examples on I.F. found by Inspection :

Ex. 1: Solve $(x+y)^2\left(x\dfrac{dy}{dx}+y\right)=xy\left(1+\dfrac{dy}{dx}\right)$.

Solution: Given $(x+y)^2\left(\dfrac{xdy+ydx}{dx}\right)=xy\left(\dfrac{dx+dy}{dx}\right)$

General solution is $\displaystyle\int\left(\dfrac{xdy+ydx}{xy}\right)=\int\left(\dfrac{dx+dy}{(x+y)^2}\right)$

$$\log xy = \dfrac{-1}{x+y}+C.$$

Ex. 2 : Solve $ydx-xdy+3x^2y^2e^{x^3}dx=0$.

Solution : Divide by y^2

$\dfrac{ydx-xdy}{y^2}+e^{x^3}3x^2dx=0 \Rightarrow d\left(\dfrac{x}{y}\right)+d\left(e^{x^3}\right)=0$

$\dfrac{x}{y}+e^{x^3}=C.$

Ex. 3 : Solve $xdy-ydx=(4x^2+y^2)dy$

Solution : $\dfrac{xdy-ydx}{4x^2+y^2}=dy$ i.e. $\dfrac{xdy-ydx/x^2}{4+y^2/x^2}=dy$

General solution is $\int \dfrac{d(y/x)}{4+(y/x)^2} = \int dy + C$

$\therefore \dfrac{1}{2}\tan^{-1}\left(\dfrac{y}{2x}\right) = y + C.$

Ex. 4: Solve $e^{x+y}\left(x\dfrac{dy}{dx}+y\right) = e^{xy}\left(1+\dfrac{dy}{dx}\right).$

Solution: $e^{x+y}(xdy + ydx) = e^{xy}(dx + dy) \Rightarrow \dfrac{xdy + ydx}{e^{xy}} = \dfrac{dx + dy}{e^{x+y}}.$

General solution is $\int e^{-xy} d(xy) = \int e^{-(x+y)} d(x+y)$

$e^{-xy} = e^{-(x+y)} + C.$

TEST YOUR KNOWLEDGE

Solve the following differential equations

1. $xdy - ydx = (x^2 + y^2)(dx + dy)$ Ans: $\tan^{-1}\dfrac{y}{x} = x + y + C$

2. $y(2xy + e^x)dx = e^x dy$ Ans: $x^2 + \dfrac{e^x}{y} = C$

3. $(x^4 e^x - 2mxy^2)dx + 2mx^2 ydy = 0$ Ans: $e^x + \dfrac{my^2}{x^2} = C$

4. $(y + x^3 y^2)dx + xdy = 0$ Ans: $\dfrac{-1}{xy} + \dfrac{x^2}{2} = C$

5. $x\dfrac{dy}{dx} = x^2 y^2 - y$ Ans: $\dfrac{-1}{xy} - x = C$

6. $(xy^2 - e^{1/x^3})dx - x^2 ydy = 0$ Ans: $\dfrac{y^2}{x^2} - \dfrac{2}{3}e^{1/x^3} = C$

7. $(y + y^2 \cos x)dx - (x - y^3)dy = 0$ Ans: $\dfrac{x}{y} + \sin x + \dfrac{y^2}{2} = C$

Rule VI: For a differential equation of the form

$x^a y^b (Mydx + Nxdy) + x^c y^d (Pydx + Qxdy) = 0$

where a, b, M, N, c, d, P, Q are constants. Integrating Factor is taken as

$x^h y^k$, where h, k are constants and can be determined by using the condition that the equation becomes exact after it is multiplied by $x^h y^k$.

Note: 1. An equation can have many I.F.

2. If $\Psi M(x, y)dx + \Psi N(x, y)dy = 0$ is exact, then Ψ is said to be I.F of the equation $M(x, y)dx + N(x, y)dy = 0$

Remark : A differential equation $M(x, y)dx + N(x, y)dy = 0$ is said to be homogeneous if M and N are homogeneous function in x and y of same degree. i.e degree of every term is the same.

Ex. 1: Solve $(x^2y + y^4)dx + (2x^3 + 4xy^3)dy = 0$

Solution : Here $M = (x^2y + y^4), N = (2x^3 + 4xy^3)$ and $\dfrac{\partial M}{\partial y} \neq \dfrac{\partial N}{\partial x}$

Given equation is not exact. The above equation can be put in the form
$(x^2 ydx + 2x^3 dy) + (y^4 dx + 4xy^3 dy) = 0$ i.e. $x^2(ydx + 2xdy) + y^3(ydx + 4xdy) = 0$
which is of the form $x^a y^b (Mydx + Nxdy) + x^c y^d (Pydx + Qxdy) = 0$
$a = 2, b = 0, M = 1, N = 2, c = 0, d = 3, P = 1, Q = 4$.

Hence, the integrating factor must be $x^h y^k$.

Multiplying the original equation by the I.F $= x^h y^k$.

$x^h y^k (x^2 y + y^4) dx + x^h y^k (2x^3 + 4xy^3) dy = 0$

$(x^{h+2} y^{k+1} + x^h y^{k+4}) dx + (2x^{h+3} y^k + 4x^{h+1} y^{k+3}) dy = 0$

$\dfrac{\partial M}{\partial y} = (k+1) x^{h+2} y^k + (k+4) x^h y^{k+3};$

$\dfrac{\partial N}{\partial x} = 2(h+3) x^{h+2} y^k + 4(h+1) x^h y^{k+3}$

But $\dfrac{\partial M}{\partial y} = \dfrac{\partial N}{\partial x}$ for exactness, which requires,

$k + 1 = 2(h+3)$ and $k + 4 = 4(h+1) \Rightarrow h = \dfrac{5}{2}, k = 10$.

$\therefore$ I.F $= x^h y^k = x^{5/2} y^{10}$.

Multiplying by the I.F. to the original differential equation, we get
$(x^2 y + y^4) x^{5/2} y^{10} dx + (2x^3 + 4xy^3) x^{5/2} y^{10} dy = 0$

$\therefore (x^{9/2} y^{11} + x^{5/2} y^{14}) dx + (2x^{11/2} y^{10} + 4x^{7/2} y^{13}) dy = 0$

Hence above equation is exact. Its general solution is

$y^{11} \int x^{9/2} dx + y^{14} \int x^{5/2} dx = C$

$\therefore \dfrac{2 y^{11} x^{11/2}}{11} + \dfrac{2 y^{14} x^{7/2}}{7} = C.$

$\Rightarrow 7 x^{11/2} y^{11} + 11 x^{7/2} y^{14} = C'.$

Ex. 2: Solve $(y^3 - 2x^2y)dx + (2xy^2 - x^3)dy = 0$

Solution: Here

$M = y^3 - 2x^2y$, $N = 2xy^2 - x^3$ and $\dfrac{\partial M}{\partial y} \neq \dfrac{\partial N}{\partial x}$

Given equtaion can be written as

$y^3 dx + 2xy^2 dy - (2x^2 ydx + x^3 dy) = 0$

$y^2(ydx + 2xdy) + x^2(-2ydx - xdy) = 0$

Here $a = 0, b = 2, M = 1, N = 2, c = 2, d = 0, P = -2, Q = 1$.

$\therefore$ I.F $= x^h y^k$

$\therefore x^h y^k (y^3 - 2x^2y)dx + x^h y^k (2xy^2 - x^3)dy = 0$

$\therefore (x^h y^{k+3} - 2x^{h+2} y^{k+1})dx + (2x^{h+1} y^{k+2} - x^{h+3} y^k)dy = 0$

$\dfrac{\partial M}{\partial y} = (k+3)x^h y^{k+2} - 2(k+1)x^{h+2} y^k$; $\dfrac{\partial N}{\partial x} = 2(h+1)x^h y^{k+2} - (h+3)x^{h+2} y^k$

But $\dfrac{\partial M}{\partial y} = \dfrac{\partial N}{\partial x}$ for exactness, which requires,

$k + 3 = 2(h+1);\ -2(k+1) = -(h+3) \Rightarrow h = 1, k = 1$.

$\therefore$ I.F $= x^h y^k = xy$.

Multiplying the given equation by xy, we get,

$(xy^4 - 2x^3 y^2)dx + (2x^2 y^3 - x^4 y)dy = 0$, which is exact.

Hence solution is $y^4 \int x\,dx - 2y^2 \int x^3 dx = C$

$y^4 x^2 - y^2 x^4 = C'$.

TEST YOUR KNOWLEDGE

1. $y(3y + 10x^2)dx - 2x(y + 3x^2)dy = 0$ Ans: $x^3 y^{-2} + 2x^5 y^{-3} = C$ I.F $= x^2 y^{-4}$

2. $(y^2 + 2yx^2)dx + (2x^3 - xy)dy = 0$ Ans: $6\sqrt{xy} - x^{-3/2} y^{3/2} = C$ I.F $= x^{-5/2} y^{-1/2}$

3. $(2x^2 y^2 + y)dx - (x^3 y - 3x)dy = 0$ Ans: $4x^{10/7} y^{-5/7} - 5x^{-4/7} y^{-12/7} = C$ I.F $= x^{-11/7} y^{-19/7}$

4. $(2x^2 y - 3y^4)dx + (3x^3 + 2xy^3)dy = 0$ Ans: $5x^{-36/13} y^{24/13} - 12x^{-10/13} y^{-15/13} = C$ I.F $= x^{-49/13} y^{-23/13}$

5. $(2y + 6xy^2)dx + (3x + 8x^2 y)dy = 0$ Ans: $x^2 y^3 + 2x^3 y^4 = C$ I.F $= xy^2$

6. $(3x + 2y^2)ydx + 2x(2x + 3y^2)dy = 0$ Ans: $x^3 y^4 + x^2 y^6 = C$ I.F $= xy^3$

7. $(3xy + 8y^5)dx + (2x^2 + 24xy^4)dy = 0$ Ans: $x^3 y^2 + 4x^2 y^6 = C$ I.F $= xy$

8. $(y^3 - 2x^2 y)dx - (2xy^2 + x^3)dy = 0$ Ans: $x^{-6/5} y^{12/5} + 3x^{4/5} y^{2/5} = C$ I.F $= x^{-11/5} y^{-3/5}$

9. $(x^7 y^2 + 3y)dx + (3x^8 y - x)dy = 0$ Ans: $2xy^3 - x^{-6} y^2 = C$ I.F $= x^{-7} y$.

YEAR WISE UNIVERSITY QUESTION PAPERS -13 SEMESTERS

Dec-2013(10/12/2013)

Solve 1. $(\tan y - 2xy - y)dx + (x\sec^2 y - x^2 - x)dy = 0$	5
2. $(x^2 + y^2 + 1)dx - 2xy\,dy = 0$	6
3. $(x\cos x)\dfrac{dy}{dx} + y(x\sin x + \cos x) = 1$	5
4. $\dfrac{dy}{dx} + 2x\tan^{-1} y(1+y^2) = x^3(1+y^2)$	5

August-2013(16/08/2013) Re-exam

Solve the following differential equations.

1. $e^y\left(\dfrac{dy}{dx} + 1\right) = e^x$	6
2. $(a^2 - 2xy - y^2)dx - (x+y)^2 dy = 0$	5
3. $(1+xy)y\,dx + (1-xy)x\,dy = 0$	6
4. Solve $2\dfrac{dy}{dx}\cos x + 4y\sin x = \sin 2x$ given $y=0$ when $x = \pi/3$	5

May-2013(18/05/2013)

1. Solve $(x^2 - 4xy - 2y^2)dx + (y^2 - 4xy - 2x^2)dy = 0$	5
2. Solve $(2xy^2 + e^x y)dx - e^x dy = 0$	6
3. Solve $\dfrac{dy}{dx} + y\cot x = 5e^{\cos x}$	5
4. Solve $\sqrt{1-y^2}\,dx = (\sin y - x)dy$	5

May-2012 (29/05/2012)

1. Solve $(\sec x \tan x \tan y - e^x)dx + (\sec x \sec^2 y)dy = 0$	6
2. Solve $\dfrac{dy}{dx} = \dfrac{x^3 + y^3}{xy^2}$	5
3. Solve $(xy\sin xy + \cos xy)y\,dx + (xy\sin xy - \cos xy)x\,dy = 0$	6

Nov-2012(20/11/2012)

1. Solve $(ye^{xy} - 2y^3)dx + (xe^{xy} - 6xy^2 - 2y)dy = 0$	4
2. Solve $\dfrac{dy}{dx} + x\sin 2y = x^2 \cos^2 y$	4
3. Solve $\sin 2y\,dx = (\tan y - x)dy$	4

	4. Solve $(x^2y - 2xy^2)dx + (x^3 - 3x^2y)dy = 0$	4
	Dec-2011(16/12/2011)	
	1. Solve $\left[\dfrac{e^{-2\sqrt{x}}}{\sqrt{x}} - \dfrac{y}{\sqrt{x}}\right]\dfrac{dx}{dy} = 1$	6
	2. Solve $(5x^4 + 3x^2y^2 - 2xy^3)dx + (2x^3y - 3x^2y^2 - 5y^4)dy = 0$	5
	3. Solve $\cos x \dfrac{dy}{dx} + y \sin x = \sec x$	6
	4. Solve $y(xy + 2x^2y^2)dx + x(xy - x^2y^2)dy = 0$	5
	May-2011(25/05/2011)	
	1. Solve $(xy^3 + y)dx + 2(x^2y^2 + x + y^4)dy = 0$	5
	2. Solve $\cos x \dfrac{dy}{dx} + y \sin x = \sec^2 x$	6
	3. Solve $\dfrac{dy}{dx} = 2y(1 - 2xy)$	6
	4. Solve $(1 + 2xy\cos^2 x - 2xy)dx + (\sin^2 x - x^2)dy = 0$.	5
	Nov-2010 (18/11/2010)	
	1. Solve $(1 + x^2)dy = (e^{\tan^{-1}x} - y)dx$	6
	2. Solve $ydx - (y - x)dy = 0$	5
	3. Solve $2xydx - (x^2 + 4)dy = 0$	6
	4. Solve $e^y \dfrac{dy}{dx} = xe^y + 10x$	5
	May-2010 (19/05/2010)	
	1. Solve $(x^2y - 2xy^2)dx - (x^3 - 3x^2y)dy = 0$	6
	2. Solve $(1 + x^2)\dfrac{dy}{dx} + y = e^{\tan^{-1}x}$	5
	3. Solve $\dfrac{dy}{dx} + \dfrac{y \log y}{x} = \dfrac{y(\log y)^2}{x^2}$	6
	4. Solve $\dfrac{dy}{dx} = \dfrac{1 + y^2 + 3x^2y}{1 - 2xy - x^3}$.	5
	May-2009 (19/05/2009)	
	1. Solve $(x^2 + y^2 + x)dx + xydy = 0$	5

2. Solve $(2x+3y+5)dx+(3x+2y-5)dy=0$	5
3. Solve $\dfrac{dx}{dy}=x+y+1$	6
4. Solve $x\dfrac{dy}{dx}+3y=x^4 e^{1/x} y^3$	5
Nov-2009 (16/11/2009)	
1. Solve $\dfrac{dy}{dx}-\dfrac{\tan y}{1+x}=(1+x)e^x \sec y$	6
2. Solve $(x^2+y^2+x)dx+xydy=0$	6
3. Solve $e^{-y}\sec^2 y\, dy = dx+xdy$	5
4. Solve $\left(3x^2 y+\dfrac{y}{x}\right)dx+(x^3+\log x)dy=0$	6
May-2008 (17/05/2008)	
1. Solve $x^2 y dx-(x^3+y^3)dy=0$	6
2. Solve $\dfrac{dy}{dx}=2y+3e^x$	5
3. Solve $y(1+xy)dx+x(1+xy+x^2 y^2)dy=0$	5
4. Solve $ydx+(x+2y^3)dy=0$	5
Nov-2008 (10/11/2008)	
1. Solve $(x+y-1)dx-(x+1)dy=0$	6
2. Solve $y(1+xy)dx+(1-xy)xdy=0$	5
3. Solve $\cos^2 x\dfrac{dy}{dx}+y=\tan x$	6
4. Solve $(x^3 y^3+xy)dy=dx$	5

UNIT - II

APPLICATIONS OF ORDINARY DIFFERENTIAL EQUATIONS OF FIRST ORDER AND FIRST DEGREE

INTRODUCTION

Differential equations are of great importance in engineering, because many physical laws and relations appear mathematically in the form of differential equations.

In the first chapter we discussed methods to solve ordinary differential equations of the first order and first degree. In this chapter, we shall show how these methods enable us to study many interesting problems, such as orthogonal trajectories, Rate of growth and decay, Newton's Law of cooling and some problems related to simple electrical circuits.

It will be quite interesting to see, how methods of chapter one are able to solve the above mentioned problems of practical importance. Taking into account the importance of differential equations in mathematical modeling, we briefly discuss the technique of modeling.

The Technique of mathematical modeling

Mathematical modeling essentially consists of translating real world problems into mathematical problems, solving the mathematical problems and interpreting these solutions in the language of the real world. i.e.

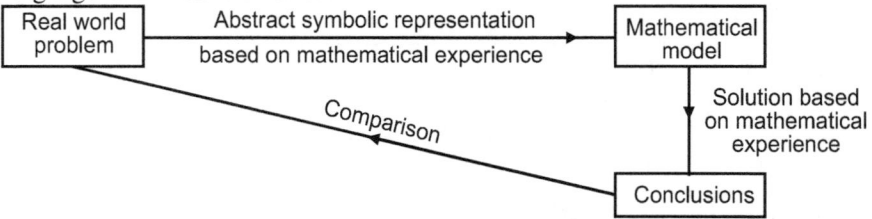

Differential equations arise in many engineering and other applications as mathematical models of various physical and other systems.

For Ex., if we drop a stone then its acceleration $y'' = \dfrac{d^2 y}{dt^2}$ is equal to the acceleration of gravity g (a constant). Hence the model of this problem of "free fall" is $y'' = g$ (neglecting air resistance). We have velocity $y' = \dfrac{dy}{dt} = gt + v_0$, where v_0 is the initial velocity with which the motion is started (e.g. $v_0 = 0$).

We get the distance travelled $y = \dfrac{g}{2} t^2 + v_0 t + y_0$,

where y_0 is the distance from 0 at the beginning (e.g. $y_0 = 0$).

We shall consider physical problems which lead to a differential equation
of first order and first degree.

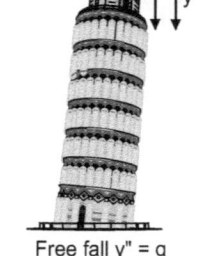

Free fall y" = g

Trajectory : A curve which cuts every member of a given family of curve according to some definite law is called a trajectory.

Orthogonal Trajectory : A curve which cuts every member of a given family of curves at right angles is called an orthogonal trajectory of the family.

Orthogonal Trajectories : Two families of the curves are said to be orthogonal, if every member of one family cuts each member of other family at right angles.

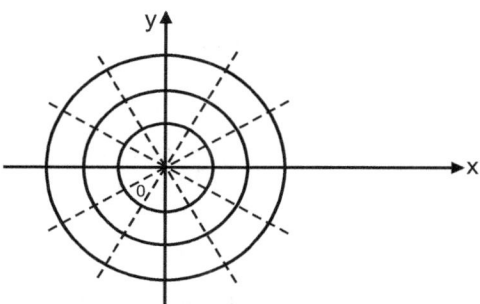

I. Method of finding the equation of Orthogonal Trajectory: For Cartesian Curves

Step-1: Let $f(x, y, c) = 0$ be the equation of the family of given curves.

Step-2: Differentiate $f(x, y, c) = 0$ w. r. t. x to eliminate constant c and forming differential equation $\psi\left(x, y, \dfrac{dy}{dx}\right) = 0$

Step-3: Replacing $\dfrac{dy}{dx}$ by $\dfrac{-dx}{dy}$ and forming differential equations for family of orthogonal trajectories as $\psi\left(x, y, \dfrac{-dx}{dy}\right) = 0$

Step-4 : Solving this differential equation, we get the family of orthogonal trajectories in terms of x,y and an arbitrary constant.

Remarks : 1.The equation $f(x, y, c) = 0$ representing a family of curves for different values of c, where c is an arbitrary constant and is also called as parameter.

2. If a curve cuts every member of the given family at a constant angle, then it is called oblique trajectory.

To find oblique trajectory(not orthogonal trajectories), we proceed as follows:

We replace $\dfrac{dy}{dx}$ in the differential equation by the expression $\left[\dfrac{\dfrac{dy}{dx} + \tan \alpha}{1 - \tan \alpha \dfrac{dy}{dx}}\right]$ to obtain the differential equation of the required oblique trajectory. Here α is the angle made by a curve c of the oblique trajectory with a given family of curves.

Ex. 1: Find orthogonal trajectories of the family of straight lines $y = mx$

Solution: Given $y = mx$ \hfill (1)

Differentiating w.r.t. x , we get

$$\dfrac{dy}{dx} = m \quad (2)$$

Eliminating constant m from equation (1) and (2), we get

$$\frac{dy}{dx} = \frac{y}{x} \qquad (3)$$

Since equation (2) does not involve arbitrary constant, which is the differential equation for the family (1). Replacing $\frac{dy}{dx}$ by $\frac{-dx}{dy}$ in (3), we get

$$-\frac{dx}{dy} = \frac{y}{x} \quad \Rightarrow xdx + ydy = 0 \qquad (4)$$

Which is differential equation for the family of orthogonal trajectories.
Integrating equation (4), we get $x^2 + y^2 = k$.
Which is the required family of orthogonal trajectories.

Ex. 2: Find orthogonal trajectories of the family of parabolas $y = ax^2$.

Solution: Given $y = ax^2$ \hfill (1)

Differentiating w.r.t. x, we get

$$\frac{dy}{dx} = 2ax \qquad (2)$$

Eliminating constant a from equation (1) and (2), we get

$$\frac{dy}{dx} = 2\frac{y}{x} \qquad (3)$$

which is the differential equation for the family (1).

Replacing $\frac{dy}{dx}$ by $\frac{-dx}{dy}$ in (3), we get

$$-\frac{dx}{dy} = 2\frac{y}{x} \quad \Rightarrow xdx + 2ydy = 0 \qquad (4)$$

Which is differential equation for the family of orthogonal trajectories.
Integrating equation (4), we get

$$\frac{x^2}{2} + y^2 = c.$$

Which is the required family of orthogonal trajectories.

Ex. 3: Find orthogonal trajectories of the family of hyperbolas $xy = c^2$

Solution: Given $xy = c^2$ \hfill (1)

Differentiating w. r. t. x, we get

$$x\frac{dy}{dx} + y(1) = 0 \Rightarrow \frac{dy}{dx} = -\frac{y}{x} \qquad (2)$$

Since equation (2) does not involve arbitrary constant, which is the differential equation for the family (1).

Replacing $\frac{dy}{dx}$ by $\frac{-dx}{dy}$ in equation (2), we get

$$-\frac{dx}{dy} = -\frac{y}{x} \Rightarrow xdx - ydy = 0 \quad (3)$$

Which is differential equation for the family of orthogonal trajectories.

Integrating equation (3), we get $\frac{x^2}{2} - \frac{y^2}{2} = k \Rightarrow x^2 - y^2 = k'$, where $k' = 2k$..

Which is the required family of orthogonal trajectories.

Ex. 4 : Find orthogonal trajectories of the family of parabolas $y^2 = 4ax$

Solution: Given $y^2 = 4ax$ \hfill (1)

Differentiating w.r.t. x, we get

$$2y\frac{dy}{dx} = 4a \Rightarrow \frac{dy}{dx} = \frac{2a}{y} \quad (2)$$

Eliminating constant a from (1) and (2), we get

$$\frac{dy}{dx} = \frac{2}{y}\frac{y^2}{4x} = \frac{y}{2x} \quad (3)$$

which is the differential equation for the family (1).

Replacing $\frac{dy}{dx}$ by $\frac{-dx}{dy}$ in equation (3), we get

$$-\frac{dx}{dy} = \frac{y}{2x} \Rightarrow 2xdx + ydy = 0 \quad (4)$$

Which is differential equation for the family of orthogonal trajectories.
Integrating equation (4), we get

$$x^2 + \frac{y^2}{2} = c, \quad i.e. \ 2x^2 + y^2 = 2c..$$

Which is the requires family of orthogonal trajectories.

Ex. 5 : Find orthogonal trajectories of the family of ellipses   **SUK: May-09, 12, 13**

$$\frac{x^2}{a^2} + \frac{y^2}{b^2 + \lambda} = 1, \ \lambda \text{ is a parameter.}$$

Solution: Given $\dfrac{x^2}{a^2} + \dfrac{y^2}{b^2 + \lambda} = 1$ \hfill (1)

Differentiating w. r. t. x, we get

$$\frac{2x}{a^2} + \frac{2y}{b^2 + \lambda}\frac{dy}{dx} = 0$$

$$\Rightarrow \frac{x}{a^2} + \frac{y}{b^2 + \lambda}\frac{dy}{dx} = 0 \quad (2)$$

Eliminating λ from equation (1) and (2),
we equate the values of $b^2 + \lambda$, from equation (1)

$$\frac{y^2}{b^2+\lambda} = 1 - \frac{x^2}{a^2} = \frac{a^2-x^2}{a^2}$$

$$\Rightarrow b^2+\lambda = \frac{a^2 y^2}{a^2-x^2} \quad \quad (3)$$

From equation (2), $\quad b^2+\lambda = -\frac{a^2 y}{x}\frac{dy}{dx} \quad (4)$

From equation (3) and (4)

$$\frac{a^2 y^2}{a^2-x^2} = -\frac{a^2 y}{x}\frac{dy}{dx}$$

$$\Rightarrow \frac{xy}{a^2-x^2} + \frac{dy}{dx} = 0 \quad \quad (5)$$

which is the differential equation for the family (1).

Replacing $\frac{dy}{dx}$ by $\frac{-dx}{dy}$ in equation (5), we get

$$\frac{xy}{a^2-x^2} - \frac{dx}{dy} = 0$$

$$\Rightarrow ydy - \frac{a^2-x^2}{x}dx = 0 \quad \quad (6)$$

Which is differential equation for the family of orthogonal trajectories.

Integrating equation (6), As equation (6) is in variable separable form, we get

$$\frac{y^2}{2} - a^2 \log x + \frac{x^2}{2} = c \Rightarrow x^2+y^2 = 2a^2 \log x + c', \quad c' = 2c..$$

Which is the requires family of orthogonal trajectories.

Ex. 6: Find orthogonal trajectories of $ay^2 = x^3$

Solution: Given $ay^2 = x^3 \quad \quad (1)$

Differentiating w.r.t. x, we get

$$2ay\frac{dy}{dx} = 3x^2 \quad \quad (2)$$

Eliminating constant a from equation (1) and (2), we get

$$\frac{3x^2}{2y\frac{dy}{dx}} y^2 = x^3 \Rightarrow \frac{3}{2x} = \frac{1}{y}\frac{dy}{dx} \quad \quad (3)$$

which is the differential equation for the family (1).

Replacing $\frac{dy}{dx}$ by $\frac{-dx}{dy}$ in equation (3), we get

$$\frac{3}{2x} = -\frac{1}{y}\frac{dx}{dy} \Rightarrow 2xdx + 3ydy = 0 \quad (4)$$

Which is differential equation for the family of orthogonal trajectories.

Integrating equation (4), we get $x^2 + 3\frac{y^2}{2} = c \Rightarrow 2x^2 + 3y^2 = c'$.

Which is the requires family of orthogonal trajectories.

Ex. 7: Find orthogonal trajectories of $2x^2 + y^2 = ax$

Solution: Given $2x^2 + y^2 = ax$ \quad (1)

Differentiating w.r.t. x, we get

$$4x + 2y\frac{dy}{dx} = a \quad (2)$$

Eliminating constant a from equation (1) and (2), we get

$$2x^2 + y^2 = \left(4x + 2y\frac{dy}{dx}\right)x$$

$$\Rightarrow -2x^2 + y^2 - 2xy\frac{dy}{dx} = 0 \quad (3)$$

which is the differential equation for the family (1).

Replacing $\frac{dy}{dx}$ by $\frac{-dx}{dy}$ in equation (3), we get

$$-2x^2 + y^2 + 2xy\frac{dx}{dy} = 0$$

$$2x^2 - y^2 - 2xy\frac{dx}{dy} = 0$$

$$\Rightarrow (2x^2 - y^2)dy - 2xydx = 0 \quad (4)$$

Which is differential equation for the family of orthogonal trajectories.

Now, here $M = -2xy$ & $N = 2x^2 - y^2$

$\frac{\partial M}{\partial y} = -2x$ & $\frac{\partial N}{\partial x} = 4x \Rightarrow \frac{\partial M}{\partial y} \neq \frac{\partial N}{\partial x}$ non exact equation.

But $\dfrac{\frac{\partial N}{\partial x} - \frac{\partial M}{\partial y}}{M} = \dfrac{4x + 2x}{-2xy} = \dfrac{-3}{y} = f(y)$ Say

$\therefore$ I.F $= e^{\int \frac{-3}{y}dy} = e^{-3\log y} = y^{-3}$.

Multiplying equation (4) by y^{-3}

$$y^{-3}(2x^2 - y^2)dy - y^{-3}(2xy)dx = 0 \Rightarrow \left(\frac{2x^2}{y^3} - \frac{1}{y}\right)dy - \frac{2x}{y^2}dx = 0$$

Hence solution is

$$\int -\frac{2x}{y^2}dx + \int -\frac{1}{y}dy = \log c$$

$$\Rightarrow \frac{x^2}{y^2} + \log y + \log c = 0, \quad x^2 + y^2 \log y + y^2 \log c = 0.$$

Which is the requires family of orthogonal trajectories.

Note: Above equation is also solvable by homogeneous method

Ex. 8: Find orthogonal trajectories of $x^2 + 4y^2 = a^2$ **SUK: Nov-10, Dec-13**

Solution: Given $x^2 + 4y^2 = a^2$ (1)

Differentiating w.r.t. x, we get

$$2x + 8y\frac{dy}{dx} = 0 \quad (2)$$

Since equation (2) does not involve arbitrary constant, which is the differential equation for the family (1).

Replacing $\frac{dy}{dx}$ by $\frac{-dx}{dy}$ in equation (2), we get

$$2x - 8y\frac{dx}{dy} = 0 \quad \Rightarrow x = 4y\frac{dx}{dy}$$

$$\therefore \frac{x}{dx} = 4\frac{y}{dy} \quad i.e \frac{dx}{x} = \frac{dy}{4y} \quad (3)$$

Which is differential equation for the family of orthogonal trajectories.

Integrating equation (3), we get

$$\log x = \frac{1}{4}\log y + \log c \quad \Rightarrow y = x^4 c.$$

Which is the requires family of orthogonal trajectories.

Ex. 9 : Find orthogonal trajectories of $x^2 + y^2 = a^2$

Solution: Given $x^2 + y^2 = a^2$ (1)

Differentiating w.r.t. x, we get

$$2x + 2y\frac{dy}{dx} = 0 \quad (2)$$

Since equation (2) does not involve arbitrary constant, which is the differential equation for the family (1). Replacing $\frac{dy}{dx}$ by $\frac{-dx}{dy}$ in equation (2), we get

$$2x - 2y\frac{dx}{dy} = 0 \quad \Rightarrow x = y\frac{dx}{dy}$$

$$\therefore \frac{x}{dx} = \frac{y}{dy} \Rightarrow \frac{dx}{x} = \frac{dy}{y} \quad (3)$$

Which is differential equation for the family of orthogonal trajectories.
Integrating(3), we get
$\log x - \log y = \log c \Rightarrow x/y = c$.
Which is the requires family of orthogonal trajectories.

Remark: To show self orthogonal family, we show that the differential equation of given family of curves and the differential equation of orthogonal trajectories obtained by replacing $\dfrac{dy}{dx} = \dfrac{-dx}{dy}$ both are equal.

Ex. 10 : Prove that system of confocal and coaxial parabolas $y^2 = 4a(x+a)$ is self orthogonal. **SUK: Dec-11**

Solution: Given $y^2 = 4a(x+a)$ (1)

Differentiating w.r.t. x, we get

$2y\dfrac{dy}{dx} = 4a \Rightarrow y\dfrac{dy}{dx} = 2a$ (2)

Eliminating a from equation (1) and (2), we get

$y^2 = 2y\dfrac{dy}{dx}\left(x + \dfrac{1}{2}y\dfrac{dy}{dx}\right)$

$\Rightarrow y^2\left(\dfrac{dy}{dx}\right)^2 + 2xy\dfrac{dy}{dx} - y^2 = 0$ (3)

which is the differential equation for the family (1).

Replacing $\dfrac{dy}{dx}$ by $\dfrac{-dx}{dy}$ in equation (3), we get

$y^2\left(\dfrac{-dx}{dy}\right)^2 - 2xy\dfrac{dx}{dy} - y^2 = 0 \Rightarrow y^2\left(\dfrac{dx}{dy}\right)^2 - 2xy\dfrac{dx}{dy} - y^2 = 0$

$y^2 - 2xy\dfrac{dy}{dx} - y^2\left(\dfrac{dy}{dx}\right)^2 = 0 \Rightarrow -y^2 + 2xy\dfrac{dy}{dx} + y^2\left(\dfrac{dy}{dx}\right)^2 = 0$

$\therefore y^2\left(\dfrac{dy}{dx}\right)^2 + 2xy\dfrac{dy}{dx} - y^2 = 0$ (4)

Which is differential equation of the orthogonal trajectories. Since equation (4) is as same to equation (3) the system of confocal and coaxial parabolas is self orthogonal i.e. each member of (1) cuts every other members orthogonal family.

Ex. 11: Find orthogonal trajectories of $x^2 - c + 4y = 0$

Solution: Given $x^2 - c + 4y = 0$ (1)

Differentiating w.r.t. x, we get

$2x + 4\dfrac{dy}{dx} = 0$ (2)

Since equation (2) does not involve arbitrary constant, which is the differential equation for the family (1).

Replacing $\dfrac{dy}{dx}$ by $\dfrac{-dx}{dy}$ in equation (2), we get

$$2x - 4\dfrac{dx}{dy} = 0 \Rightarrow x = \dfrac{2dx}{dy} \Rightarrow dy = \dfrac{2}{x}dx \qquad (3)$$

Which is differential equation for the family of orthogonal trajectories. Integrating equation (3), we get $y = 2\log x + c$. Which is the requires family of orthogonal trajectories.

Ex. 12 : Find orthogonal trajectories of $x^3 - 3xy^2 = a$

Solution: Given $x^3 - 3xy^2 = a \qquad (1)$

Differentiating w.r.t. x, we get

$$3x^2 - 3\left(y^2 + 2xy\dfrac{dy}{dx}\right) = 0$$

$$\Rightarrow x^2 - y^2 - 2xy\dfrac{dy}{dx} = 0 \qquad (2)$$

Since equation (2) does not involve arbitrary constant, which is the differential equation for the family (1).

Replacing $\dfrac{dy}{dx}$ by $\dfrac{-dx}{dy}$ in equation (2), we get

$$x^2 - y^2 + 2xy\dfrac{dx}{dy} = 0 \Rightarrow 2x\dfrac{dx}{dy} + \dfrac{x^2}{y} = y \qquad (3)$$

Which is generalized Bernoulli's equation of the form $f'(y)\dfrac{dy}{dx} + Pf(y) = Q$.

Put $x^2 = v$ $\therefore 2x\dfrac{dx}{dy} = \dfrac{dv}{dy}$

Substituting in equation (3) $\therefore \dfrac{dv}{dy} + \dfrac{v}{y} = y \qquad (4)$

Which is linear differential equation here $P' = \dfrac{1}{y}$ & $Q' = y$

$I.F = e^{\int \frac{1}{y}dy} = e^{\log y} = y.$

Hence the solution is $v.I.F = \int I.F.Q'dy + c$

$v.y = \int y.ydy + c \Rightarrow vy = \dfrac{y^3}{3} + c$

$\Rightarrow x^2 y = \dfrac{y^3}{3} + c,$ i.e. $y^3 - 3x^2 y = 3c.$

Which is the requires family of orthogonal trajectories.

Ex. 13 : Find orthogonal trajectories of co axial circles $x^2 + y^2 + 2gx + c = 0$ where g is parameter.

Solution: Given $x^2 + y^2 + 2gx + c = 0$ \hfill (1)

Differentiating w.r.t. x, we get

$$2x + 2y\frac{dy}{dx} + 2g = 0 \qquad (2)$$

which is the differential equation for the family (1).

Replacing $\frac{dy}{dx}$ by $\frac{-dx}{dy}$ in equation (2), we get

$$2x - 2y\frac{dx}{dy} + 2g = 0 \qquad (3)$$

We write $2g = -\left(2x - 2y\frac{dx}{dy}\right)$

Substituting in equation (1) $\quad x^2 + y^2 - \left(2x - 2y\frac{dx}{dy}\right)x + c = 0$

$$x^2 + y^2 - 2x^2 + 2xy\frac{dx}{dy} + c = 0$$

$$-x^2 + y^2 + 2xy\frac{dx}{dy} + c = 0$$

$$2xy\frac{dx}{dy} - x^2 = -(y^2 + c)$$

$$\Rightarrow 2x\frac{dx}{dy} - \frac{x^2}{y} = -\left(\frac{y^2 + c}{y}\right) \qquad (4)$$

Which is generalized Bernoulli's equation of the form $f'(y)\frac{dy}{dx} + Pf(y) = Q$

Put $x^2 = v \quad \therefore 2x\frac{dx}{dy} = \frac{dv}{dy}$

Substituting in equation (4) $\frac{dv}{dy} - \frac{v}{y} = -\left(y + \frac{c}{y}\right) \qquad (5)$

Which is linear differential equation here $P' = -\frac{1}{y}$ & $Q' = -\left(y + \frac{c}{y}\right)$

$$I.F = e^{-\int \frac{1}{y}dy} = e^{-\log y \, dy} = \frac{1}{y}.$$

Hence the solution is $v.I.F = \int I.F.Q'dy + k$

$$v.\frac{1}{y} = -\int \frac{1}{y}\left(y + \frac{c}{y}\right)dy + k \Rightarrow v.\frac{1}{y} = -\int \left(1 + \frac{c}{y^2}\right)dy + k$$

$$v\frac{1}{y} = -y + \frac{c}{y} + k \Rightarrow v + y^2 - c = ky \quad \therefore x^2 + y^2 = c + ky$$

Which is the requires family of orthogonal trajectories.

Ex. 14 : Find orthogonal trajectories of $x^p + cy^p = 1$, where p is a given constant and c is the parameter.

Solution: Given $x^p + cy^p = 1$ \hfill (1)

Differentiating w.r.t. x, we get

$$px^{p-1} + cpy^{p-1}\frac{dy}{dx} = 0 \Rightarrow x^{p-1} + cy^{p-1}\frac{dy}{dx} = 0 \quad (2)$$

which is the differential equation for the family (1).

Replacing $\frac{dy}{dx}$ by $\frac{-dx}{dy}$ in equation (2), we get

$$x^{p-1} - cy^{p-1}\frac{dx}{dy} = 0 \quad (3)$$

From equation (1), $c = \frac{1-x^p}{y^p}$

Substituting in equation (3) $x^{p-1} - \left(\frac{1-x^p}{y^p}\right)y^{p-1}\frac{dx}{dy} = 0 \therefore x^{p-1} - \frac{1-x^p}{y}\frac{dx}{dy} = 0$

$$\left(\frac{1-x^p}{y}\right)\frac{dx}{dy} = x^{p-1} \therefore \left(\frac{1-x^p}{x^{p-1}}\right)dx = ydy$$

$$\therefore \left(x^{1-p} - x\right)dx = ydy \quad (4)$$

Integrating equation (4), we get

$$\int (x^{1-p} - x)dx = \int ydy \therefore \frac{x^{2-p}}{2-p} - \frac{x^2}{2} = \frac{y^2}{2} + c \therefore \frac{2x^{2-p}}{2-p} - x^2 - y^2 = c_1.$$

Which is the requires family of orthogonal trajectories.

Ex. 15 : Find orthogonal trajectories of $y = ax^n$, where a is parameter.

Solution: Given $y = ax^n$ \hfill (1)

Differentiating w.r.t. x, we get

$$\frac{dy}{dx} = nax^{n-1} \therefore -\frac{dx}{dy} = nax^{n-1} \quad (2)$$

Eliminating constant a from equation (1) and (2), we get $\frac{y}{x^n} = a$

$$-\frac{dx}{dy} = n\left(\frac{y}{x^n}\right)x^{n-1} \Rightarrow -\frac{dx}{dy} = \frac{ny}{x} \therefore xdx + nydy = 0$$

Integrating $\int xdx + n\int ydy = c$ $\therefore \frac{x^2}{2} + n\frac{y^2}{2} = c$ $\therefore x^2 + ny^2 = c_1$ Which is the requires family of orthogonal trajectories.

TEST YOUR KNOWLEDGE

(I) Find orthogonal trajectories of the family of co axial circles $x^2 + y^2 - 2gx = 0$ where g is parameter. Ans: $x^2 + y^2 = yc$

(II) Find the orthogonal trajectories of following the family
1. $x^3 - 3xy^2 = a$ Ans: $y^3 - 3yx^2 = c$ 2. $x^2 + y^2 = a^2$ Ans: $y = xc$
3. $x^2 - c + 4y = 0$ Ans: $y + 2\log x = c$ 4. $x^2 + 4y^2 = a^2$ Ans: $y = x^4 c$
5. $2x^2 + y^2 = xc$ Ans: $x^2 + y^2 \log cy = 0$ 6. $x^2 + (x-a)^2 = a^2$ Ans: $y^2 + (x-c)^2 = c^2$
7. $x^2 = 4a(y+a)$ Ans: $x^2 = 4c(y+c)$ 8. $2x^2 - y^2 = x^4 c$ Ans: $y = k - \frac{1}{4}\log|x|$
9. $xy = a^2$ Ans: $x^2 - y^2 = c$ 10. $y = x + ae^x$ Ans: $e^{-y}(x-y-2) = c$

II. METHOD OF FINDING THE EQUATION OF ORTHOGONAL TRAJECTORY: FOR POLAR CURVES

Step-1: Let $f(r, \theta, c) = 0$ be the given family.

Step-2: Differentiating $f(r, \theta, c) = 0$ w.r.t. θ, eliminate c and forming differential equation for the given family as $\psi\left(r, \theta, \frac{dr}{d\theta}\right) = 0.$ (1)

Step-3: Replacing $\frac{dr}{d\theta}$ by $-r^2 \frac{d\theta}{dr}$, we get differential equation for the family of orthogonal trajectories as $\psi\left(r, \theta, -r^2 \frac{d\theta}{dr}\right) = 0.$ (2)

Step-4: Solving differential equation (2), we get the solution in term of r, θ and arbitrary constant. This equation is the orthogonal trajectories.

Remark: The equation $f(r, \theta, c) = 0$ representing a family of curves for different values of c, where c is an arbitrary constant and is also called as parameter.

Ex. 1: Find orthogonal trajectories of $r = a(1 - \cos\theta)$ **SUK: May-10**

Solution: Given $r = a(1 - \cos\theta)$ (1)

Differentiating (1) w.r.t. θ, we get

$$\frac{dr}{d\theta} = a\sin\theta \quad (2)$$

Eliminating constant a from equation (1) and (2), we get

$$\frac{1}{r}\frac{dr}{d\theta} = \frac{\sin\theta}{1-\cos\theta} = \cot\frac{\theta}{2} \qquad (3)$$

which is the differential equation for the family (1).

Replacing $\frac{dr}{d\theta}$ by $-r^2\frac{d\theta}{dr}$ in equation (3), we get

$$\frac{1}{r}\left(-r^2\frac{d\theta}{dr}\right) = \cot\frac{\theta}{2} \Rightarrow \frac{dr}{r} + \tan\frac{\theta}{2}d\theta = 0 \qquad (4)$$

Which is differential equation for the family of orthogonal trajectories.
Equation (4) is in variable separable form, Integrating equation (4), we get

$$\int\frac{dr}{r} + \int\tan\frac{\theta}{2}d\theta = \log c$$

$$\log r - 2\log\cos\frac{\theta}{2} = \log c$$

$$\Rightarrow \log r = \log\left(c\cos^2\frac{\theta}{2}\right) \therefore r = c(1+\cos\theta)$$

Which is the requires family of orthogonal trajectories.

Ex. 2: Find orthogonal trajectories of $r^2 = a^2\cos 2\theta$

Solution: Given $r^2 = a^2\cos 2\theta \Rightarrow r = a\sqrt{\cos 2\theta}$ \qquad (1)

Differentiating equation (1) w. r. t. θ, we get

$$\frac{dr}{d\theta} = a\frac{1}{2\sqrt{\cos 2\theta}}(-2\sin 2\theta)$$

$$\Rightarrow \frac{dr}{d\theta} = -a\frac{\sin 2\theta}{\sqrt{\cos 2\theta}} \qquad (2)$$

Eliminating constant a from equation (1) and (2), we get

$$\frac{dr}{d\theta} = -\frac{\sin 2\theta}{\sqrt{\cos 2\theta}} \cdot \frac{r}{\sqrt{\cos 2\theta}}$$

$$\Rightarrow \frac{dr}{d\theta} = -r\tan 2\theta \qquad (3)$$

which is the differential equation for the family (1).

Replacing $\frac{dr}{d\theta}$ by $-r^2\frac{d\theta}{dr}$ in equation (3), we get

$$-r^2\frac{d\theta}{dr} = -r\tan 2\theta$$

$$\Rightarrow r\frac{d\theta}{dr} = \tan 2\theta \Rightarrow \frac{dr}{r} = \frac{d\theta}{\tan 2\theta} \qquad (4)$$

Which is differential equation for the family of orthogonal trajectories.

Equation (4) is in variable separable form, Integrating equation (4), we get

$$\int \frac{dr}{r} - \int \frac{d\theta}{\tan 2\theta} = \log c$$

$$\log r - \frac{1}{2}\log \sin 2\theta = \log c$$

$$\Rightarrow \log r^2 - \log \sin 2\theta = \log c^2$$

$$\therefore \frac{r^2}{\sin 2\theta} = c^2 \Rightarrow r^2 = c^2 \sin 2\theta$$

Which is the requires family of orthogonal trajectories.

Ex. 3 : Find orthogonal trajectories of $\frac{2a}{r} = (1+\cos\theta)$ **SUK: Nov 08, May-11**

Solution: Given $r = \frac{2a}{1+\cos\theta} = \frac{2a}{2\cos^2\frac{\theta}{2}} = \frac{a}{\cos^2\frac{\theta}{2}}$ $\therefore r\cos^2\frac{\theta}{2} = a$ (1)

Differentiating equation (1) w. r. t. θ, we get

$$\frac{dr}{d\theta}\cos^2\frac{\theta}{2} + r \cdot 2\cos\frac{\theta}{2}\left(-\frac{1}{2}\sin\frac{\theta}{2}\right) = 0$$

$$\frac{dr}{d\theta}\cos^2\frac{\theta}{2} - r\sin\frac{\theta}{2}\cos\frac{\theta}{2} = 0 \quad (2)$$

Since equation (2) does not involve arbitrary constant, which is the differential equation for the family (1).

Replacing $\frac{dr}{d\theta}$ by $-r^2\frac{d\theta}{dr}$ in equation (2), we get

$$\left(-r^2\frac{d\theta}{dr}\right)\cos^2\frac{\theta}{2} - r\sin\frac{\theta}{2}\cos\frac{\theta}{2} = 0$$

$$r\cos\frac{\theta}{2}\frac{d\theta}{dr} + \sin\frac{\theta}{2} = 0. \qquad \text{Cancelling throughout by} - r\cos\frac{\theta}{2}$$

$$\therefore \frac{dr}{r} + \cot\frac{\theta}{2}d\theta = 0 \qquad (3)$$

Which is differential equation for the family of orthogonal trajectories.
Equation (3) is in variable separable form, Integrating equation (3), we get

$$\int\frac{dr}{r} + \int \cot\frac{\theta}{2}d\theta = \log c$$

$$\log r + 2\log \sin\frac{\theta}{2} = \log c$$

$$\Rightarrow r\sin^2\frac{\theta}{2} = c \therefore r = \frac{c}{\sin^2\frac{\theta}{2}} = \frac{2c}{2\sin^2\frac{\theta}{2}} = \frac{2c}{1-\cos\theta}$$

Which is the requires family of orthogonal trajectories.

Ex. 4 : Find the orthogonal trajectories of the circles defined by $r = a\cos\theta$ which all pass through the origin and have their centres on the initial line, a being the variable diameter.

Solution: Given $r = a\cos\theta$ \hfill (1)

Differentiating equation (1) w. r. t. θ, we get

$$\frac{dr}{d\theta} = -a\sin\theta \qquad (2)$$

Eliminating constant a from equation (1) and (2), we get

$$\frac{dr}{d\theta} = -r\tan\theta \qquad (3)$$

which is the differential equation for the family (1).

Replacing $\frac{dr}{d\theta}$ by $-r^2\frac{d\theta}{dr}$ in equation (3), we get

$$\left(-r^2\frac{d\theta}{dr}\right) = -r\tan\theta \Rightarrow r\frac{d\theta}{dr} = \tan\theta$$

$$\therefore \frac{dr}{r} = \frac{d\theta}{\tan\theta} \Rightarrow \frac{dr}{r} = \cot\theta\, d\theta \qquad (4)$$

Which is differential equation for the family of orthogonal trajectories.

Equation (4) is in variable separable form, Integrating equation (4), we get

$$\int\frac{dr}{r} - \int\cot\theta\, d\theta = \log c \qquad \therefore \log r - \log\sin\theta = \log c$$

$$\Rightarrow \log\frac{r}{\sin\theta} = \log c \therefore r = c\sin\theta$$

Which is the requires family of orthogonal trajectories.

Ex. 5 : Find orthogonal trajectories of the family of curve $r = \dfrac{2a}{1+\sin\theta}$

Solution : Given $r(1+\sin\theta) = 2a$ \hfill (1)

Differentiating equation (1) w. r. t. θ, we get

$$r(\cos\theta) + (1+\sin\theta)\frac{dr}{d\theta} = 0$$

$$(1+\sin\theta)\frac{dr}{d\theta} = -r(\cos\theta) \qquad (2)$$

Since equation (2) does not involve arbitrary constant, which is the differential equation for the family (1). Replacing $\frac{dr}{d\theta}$ by $-r^2\frac{d\theta}{dr}$ in equation (2), we get

$$(1+\sin\theta)\left(-r^2\frac{d\theta}{dr}\right) = -r\cos\theta$$

$$\Rightarrow r(1+\sin\theta)\frac{d\theta}{dr} = \cos\theta$$

$$\frac{(1+\sin\theta)}{\cos\theta}d\theta = \frac{1}{r}dr$$

$$\frac{\left(\sin\frac{\theta}{2}+\cos\frac{\theta}{2}\right)^2}{\cos^2\frac{\theta}{2}-\sin^2\frac{\theta}{2}}d\theta=\frac{1}{r}dr$$

$$\frac{\sin\frac{\theta}{2}+\cos\frac{\theta}{2}}{\cos\frac{\theta}{2}-\sin\frac{\theta}{2}}d\theta=\frac{1}{r}dr \Rightarrow \frac{\cos\frac{\theta}{2}+\sin\frac{\theta}{2}}{\cos\frac{\theta}{2}-\sin\frac{\theta}{2}}d\theta=\frac{1}{r}dr$$

$$\frac{1+\tan\frac{\theta}{2}}{1-\tan\frac{\theta}{2}}d\theta=\frac{1}{r}dr \Rightarrow \tan\left(\frac{\pi}{4}+\frac{\theta}{2}\right)d\theta=\frac{1}{r}dr \quad (3)$$

Which is differential equation for the family of orthogonal trajectories.

Equation (3) is in variable separable form, Integrating equation (3), we get

$$\int \tan\left(\frac{\pi}{4}+\frac{\theta}{2}\right)d\theta = \int \frac{1}{r}dr$$

$$2\log\sec\left(\frac{\pi}{4}+\frac{\theta}{2}\right) = \log r + \log c$$

$$\sec^2\left(\frac{\pi}{4}+\frac{\theta}{2}\right) = rc \Rightarrow \frac{1}{\cos^2\left(\frac{\pi}{4}+\frac{\theta}{2}\right)} = rc$$

$$\frac{c}{1+\cos 2\left(\frac{\pi}{4}+\frac{\theta}{2}\right)} = r$$

$$\Rightarrow r = \frac{c}{1+\cos\left(\frac{\pi}{2}+\theta\right)} \Rightarrow r = \frac{c}{1-\sin\theta}$$

Which is the requires family of orthogonal trajectories.

Ex. 6: Find orthogonal trajectories of $r^n = a^n \sin n\theta$ **SUK: May-09**

Solution: Given $r^n = a^n \sin n\theta$ (1)

Differentiating (1) w. r. t. θ, we get

$$nr^{n-1}\frac{dr}{d\theta} = na^n \cos n\theta \quad (2)$$

Eliminating constant a^n from equation (1) and (2) by dividing equation (2) by (1), we get

$$\frac{nr^{n-1}\frac{dr}{d\theta}}{r^n} = \frac{a^n n \cos n\theta}{a^n \sin n\theta}$$

$$\Rightarrow \frac{1}{r}\frac{dr}{d\theta} = \frac{\cos n\theta}{\sin n\theta} = \cot n\theta \quad (3)$$

which is the differential equation for the family (1). Replacing $\dfrac{dr}{d\theta}$ by $-r^2 \dfrac{d\theta}{dr}$ in equation (3), we get $\dfrac{1}{r}\left(-r^2 \dfrac{d\theta}{dr}\right) = \cot n\theta \Rightarrow \tan n\theta d\theta + \dfrac{dr}{r} = 0$ (4)

Which is differential equation for the family of orthogonal trajectories.
Equation (4) is in variable separable form, Integrating equation (4), we get

$$\int \tan n\theta d\theta + \int \dfrac{dr}{r} = \log c$$

$$\dfrac{1}{n} \log \sec n\theta + \log r = \log c$$

$$\Rightarrow (\sec n\theta)^{\frac{1}{n}} r = c$$

$$\therefore \sec n\theta \ r^n = c^n \Rightarrow r^n = c^n \cos n\theta$$

Which is the requires family of orthogonal trajectories.
Note: Find orthogonal trajectories of $r^n = a \sin n\theta$ **SUK: Aug-13**
Use the same technique as that of above Ex.

Ex. 7: Find orthogonal trajectories of $r^n = a^n \cos n\theta$.
Solution: Given $r^n = a^n \cos n\theta$ (1)
Differentiating (1) w. r. t. θ, we get

$$nr^{n-1} \dfrac{dr}{d\theta} = -na^n \sin n\theta \Rightarrow r^{n-1} \dfrac{dr}{d\theta} = -a^n \sin n\theta \quad (2)$$

Eliminating constant a^n from equation (1) and (2) by dividing equation (2) by (1), we get

$$\dfrac{r^{n-1} \dfrac{dr}{d\theta}}{r^n} = \dfrac{-a^n \sin n\theta}{a^n \cos n\theta} \Rightarrow \dfrac{1}{r} \dfrac{dr}{d\theta} = -\tan n\theta \quad (3)$$

which is the differential equation for the family (1).
Replacing $\dfrac{dr}{d\theta}$ by $-r^2 \dfrac{d\theta}{dr}$ in equation (3), we get

$$\dfrac{1}{r}\left(-r^2 \dfrac{d\theta}{dr}\right) = -\tan n\theta \Rightarrow -\cot n\theta d\theta + \dfrac{dr}{r} = 0 \quad (4)$$

Which is differential equation for the family of orthogonal trajectories.
Equation (4) is in variable separable form, Integrating equation (4), we get

$$-\int \cot n\theta d\theta + \int \dfrac{dr}{r} = \log c$$

$$-\dfrac{1}{n} \log \sin n\theta + \log r = \log c$$

$$\Rightarrow (\sin n\theta)^{\frac{-1}{n}} r = c \quad \therefore \sec n\theta \ r^{-n} = c^{-n} \Rightarrow r^n = c^n \sin n\theta$$

Which is the requires family of orthogonal trajectories.

Ex. 8 : Find orthogonal trajectories of $r^n = \dfrac{a^n}{\sin n\theta}$

Solution: Given $r^n = \dfrac{a^n}{\sin n\theta} \Rightarrow r^n \sin n\theta = a^n$ \hfill (1)

Differentiating equation (1) w. r. t. θ, we get

$$r^n(n\cos n\theta) + \sin n\theta \, nr^{n-1}\dfrac{dr}{d\theta} = 0 \Rightarrow r^n \cos n\theta + \sin n\theta \, r^{n-1}\dfrac{dr}{d\theta} = 0$$

$$\sin n\theta \, r^{n-1}\dfrac{dr}{d\theta} = -r^n \cos n\theta \hfill (2)$$

Since equation (2) does not involve arbitrary constant, which is the differential equation for the family (1).

Replacing $\dfrac{dr}{d\theta}$ by $-r^2 \dfrac{d\theta}{dr}$ in equation (2), we get

$$-r^{n+1}\sin n\theta \dfrac{d\theta}{dr} = -r^n \cos n\theta \;\Rightarrow\; r\sin n\theta \dfrac{d\theta}{dr} = \cos n\theta$$

$$\Rightarrow \dfrac{\sin n\theta}{\cos n\theta} d\theta = \dfrac{1}{r} dr \quad \therefore \tan n\theta \, d\theta = \dfrac{1}{r} dr \hfill (3)$$

Which is differential equation for the family of orthogonal trajectories.

Equation (3) is in variable separable form, Integrating equation (3), we get

$$\int \tan n\theta \, d\theta - \int \dfrac{dr}{r} = \log c \;\therefore\; \dfrac{1}{n}\log \sec n\theta - \log r - = \log c$$

$$\Rightarrow \dfrac{(\sec n\theta)^{\frac{1}{n}}}{r} = c \;\therefore\; \sec n\theta = r^n c^n \Rightarrow r^n = \dfrac{c^n}{\cos n\theta}$$

Which is the requires family of orthogonal trajectories.

Ex. 9 : Find orthogonal trajectories of $r = a\sin^n \theta$

Solution: Given $r = a\sin^n \theta$ \hfill (1)

Differentiating equation (1) w. r. t. θ, we get

$$\dfrac{dr}{d\theta} = an\sin^{n-1}\theta \cos\theta \hfill (2)$$

Eliminating constant a from equation (1) and (2), we get

$$\dfrac{dr}{d\theta} = \dfrac{r}{\sin^n \theta} n\sin^{n-1}\theta \cos\theta \Rightarrow \dfrac{dr}{d\theta} = \dfrac{nr\cos\theta}{\sin\theta} \hfill (3)$$

which is the differential equation for the family (1).

Replacing $\dfrac{dr}{d\theta}$ by $-r^2 \dfrac{d\theta}{dr}$ in equation (3), we get

$$-r^2 \frac{d\theta}{dr} = \frac{nr\cos\theta}{\sin\theta} \Rightarrow -r\frac{d\theta}{dr} = n\frac{\cos\theta}{\sin\theta}$$

$$\frac{\sin\theta}{\cos\theta}d\theta = -n\frac{dr}{r} \Rightarrow \tan\theta d\theta = -n\frac{dr}{r} \qquad (4)$$

Which is differential equation for the family of orthogonal trajectories.
Equation (4) is in variable separable form, Integrating equation (4), we get

$$\int \tan\theta d\theta + n\int \frac{dr}{r} = \log c$$

$$\log\sec\theta + n\log r = \log c$$

$$\therefore \sec\theta \; r^n = c \Rightarrow r^n = c\cos\theta$$

Which is the requires family of orthogonal trajectories.

Ex. 10 : Find orthogonal trajectories of $r = a\theta$

Solution: Given $r = a\theta$ \qquad (1)

Differentiating equation (1) w. r. t. θ, we get

$$\frac{dr}{d\theta} = a \qquad (2)$$

Eliminating constant a from equation (1) and (2), we get

$$\frac{dr}{d\theta} = \frac{r}{\theta} \qquad (3)$$

which is the differential equation for the family (1).

Replacing $\frac{dr}{d\theta}$ by $-r^2\frac{d\theta}{dr}$ in equation (3), we get

$$-r^2\frac{d\theta}{dr} = \frac{r}{\theta} \Rightarrow -r\frac{d\theta}{dr} = \frac{1}{\theta}$$

$$\Rightarrow -\frac{1}{r}dr = \theta d\theta \qquad (4)$$

Which is differential equation for the family of orthogonal trajectories.
Equation (4) is in variable separable form, Integrating equation (4), we get

$$\int \theta d\theta + \int \frac{dr}{r} = \log c \Rightarrow \frac{\theta^2}{2} + \log r = \log c$$

$$\therefore r = e^{-\frac{\theta^2}{2}} c$$

Which is the requires family of orthogonal trajectories.

Ex. 11: Find orthogonal trajectories of $r\theta = a$

Solution: Given $r\theta = a$ \qquad (1)

Differentiating equation (1) w. r. t. θ, we get

$$r + \theta\frac{dr}{d\theta} = 0 \qquad (2)$$

which is the differential equation for the family (1).

Replacing $\dfrac{dr}{d\theta}$ by $-r^2 \dfrac{d\theta}{dr}$ in equation (2), we get

$$r - \theta\left(r^2 \dfrac{d\theta}{dr}\right) = 0 \Rightarrow r = \theta r^2 \dfrac{d\theta}{dr}$$

$$\Rightarrow \theta r \dfrac{d\theta}{dr} = 1 \quad \therefore \theta d\theta = \dfrac{dr}{r} \qquad (4)$$

Which is differential equation for the family of orthogonal trajectories.

Equation (3) is in variable separable form, Integrating equation (3), we get

$$\int \theta d\theta - \int \dfrac{dr}{r} = \log c$$

$$\dfrac{\theta^2}{2} - \log r = \log c \Rightarrow \dfrac{\theta^2}{2} = \log c + \log r$$

$$e^{\frac{\theta^2}{2}} = rc \Rightarrow r = e^{\frac{\theta^2}{2}} c_1 \quad \because \dfrac{1}{c} = c_1 \text{ which is the required family of orthogonal trajectories.}$$

Ex. 12: Find orthogonal trajectories of $r^2 = \dfrac{a}{\cos\theta}$ **SUK: Nov-12**

Solution: Given $r^2 = \dfrac{a}{\cos\theta} \Rightarrow r^2 \cos\theta = a$ (1)

Differentiating (1) w. r. t. θ, we get

$$r^2(-\sin\theta) + 2r \dfrac{dr}{d\theta} \cos\theta = 0 \qquad (2)$$

which is the differential equation for the family (1).

Replacing $\dfrac{dr}{d\theta}$ by $-r^2 \dfrac{d\theta}{dr}$ in equation (2), we get

$$-r^2 \sin\theta - 2r^3 \dfrac{d\theta}{dr} \cos\theta = 0 \Rightarrow 2r \dfrac{d\theta}{dr} = -\dfrac{\sin\theta}{\cos\theta}$$

$$\Rightarrow \dfrac{dr}{r} = -2 \dfrac{\cos\theta}{\sin\theta} d\theta \therefore \dfrac{dr}{r} = -2\cot\theta d\theta \qquad (3)$$

Which is differential equation for the family of orthogonal trajectories.

Equation (3) is in variable separable form, Integrating equation (3), we get

$$\int \dfrac{dr}{r} = -2\int \cot\theta d\theta + \log c \Rightarrow \log r = -2\log(\sin\theta) + \log c \Rightarrow \log r + \log(\sin^2\theta) = \log c$$

$$\log(r\sin^2\theta) = \log c \Rightarrow r\sin^2\theta = c \quad \therefore r \dfrac{(1-\cos 2\theta)}{2} = c$$

$$\therefore r(1 - \cos 2\theta) = 2c.$$

Which is the requires family of orthogonal trajectories.

Ex. 13 : Find orthogonal trajectories of $r = a\sin^2\theta$

Solution : Given $r = a\sin^2\theta$ \hfill (1)

Differentiating equation (1) w. r. t. θ, we get

$$\frac{dr}{d\theta} = 2a\sin\theta\cos\theta$$

$$\frac{dr}{d\theta} = 2\frac{r}{\sin^2\theta}\sin\theta\cos\theta = 2r\frac{\cos\theta}{\sin\theta} \quad (2)$$

which is the differential equation for the family (1).

Replacing $\frac{dr}{d\theta}$ by $-r^2\frac{d\theta}{dr}$ in equation (2), we get

$$-r^2\frac{d\theta}{dr} = 2r\frac{\cos\theta}{\sin\theta} \Rightarrow -r\frac{d\theta}{dr} = 2\frac{\cos\theta}{\sin\theta}$$

$$\therefore \frac{2}{r}dr = -\frac{\sin\theta}{\cos\theta}d\theta = -\tan\theta\, d\theta \quad (3)$$

Which is differential equation for the family of orthogonal trajectories.

Equation (3) is in variable separable form, Integrating equation (3), we get

$$2\int\frac{dr}{r} = -\int\tan\theta\, d\theta + \log c$$

$$2\log r = -\log(\sec\theta) + \log c \Rightarrow \log r^2 + \log(\sec\theta) = \log c$$

$$\log(r^2\sec\theta) = \log c \Rightarrow r^2\sec\theta = c$$

$$\therefore r^2 = c\cos\theta.$$

Which is the requires family of orthogonal trajectories.

Ex. 14: Find orthogonal trajectories of $r^2 = a^2\sin 2\theta$

Solution: Given $r^2 = a^2\sin 2\theta$ \hfill (1)

Differentiating equation (1) w. r. t. θ, we get

$$2r\frac{dr}{d\theta} = 2a^2\cos 2\theta \quad (2)$$

Eliminating constant a^2 from equation (1) and (2), we get

$$r\frac{dr}{d\theta} = \frac{r^2}{\sin 2\theta}\cos 2\theta = r^2\frac{\cos 2\theta}{\sin 2\theta} \quad (3)$$

which is the differential equation for the family (1).

Replacing $\frac{dr}{d\theta}$ by $-r^2\frac{d\theta}{dr}$ in equation (3), we get

$$-r^3 \frac{d\theta}{dr} = r^2 \frac{\cos 2\theta}{\sin 2\theta}$$

$$-r \frac{d\theta}{dr} = \frac{\cos 2\theta}{\sin 2\theta}$$

$$\Rightarrow -\frac{\sin 2\theta}{\cos 2\theta} d\theta = \frac{dr}{r}$$

$$-\tan 2\theta \, d\theta = \frac{dr}{r} \quad \quad (4)$$

Which is differential equation for the family of orthogonal trajectories.
Equation (4) is in variable separable form, Integrating equation (4), we get

$$\int \frac{dr}{r} = -\int \tan 2\theta \, d\theta + \log c \Rightarrow \log r = -\frac{1}{2} \log \sec 2\theta + \log c$$

$$2 \log r = -\log(\sec 2\theta) + \log c_1 \quad \therefore \log r^2 + \log(\sec 2\theta) = \log c_1$$

$$\Rightarrow \log(r^2 \sec 2\theta) = \log c_1 \quad \therefore r^2 \sec 2\theta = c_1 \Rightarrow r^2 = c_1 \cos 2\theta$$

Which is the requires family of orthogonal trajectories.

Ex. 15: Find orthogonal trajectories of $r = a(1 + \cos \theta)$

Solution: Given $r = a(1 + \cos \theta)$ \quad (1)

Differentiating equation (1) w. r. t. θ, we get

$$\frac{dr}{d\theta} = -a \sin \theta \quad \quad (2)$$

Eliminating constant a from equation (1) and (2), we get

$$\frac{dr}{d\theta} = -\frac{r}{1 + \cos \theta} \sin \theta \quad \quad (3)$$

which is the differential equation for the family (1).

Replacing $\frac{dr}{d\theta}$ by $-r^2 \frac{d\theta}{dr}$ in equation (3), we get

$$-r^2 \frac{d\theta}{dr} = -\frac{r}{1 + \cos \theta} \sin \theta$$

$$r \frac{d\theta}{dr} = \frac{\sin \theta}{1 + \cos \theta}$$

$$\frac{r}{dr} = \frac{\sin \theta}{1 + \cos \theta} d\theta$$

$$\frac{dr}{r} = \frac{1 + \cos \theta}{\sin \theta} d\theta = \frac{2 \cos^2 \frac{\theta}{2}}{2 \sin \frac{\theta}{2} \cos \frac{\theta}{2}} d\theta$$

$$\frac{dr}{r} = \frac{\cos \frac{\theta}{2}}{\sin \frac{\theta}{2}} d\theta = \cot \frac{\theta}{2} d\theta \quad \quad (4)$$

Which is differential equation for the family of orthogonal trajectories.

Equation (4) is in variable separable form, Integrating equation (4), we get

$$\int \frac{dr}{r} = \int \cot\frac{\theta}{2} d\theta + \log c \quad \therefore \log r = 2\log\sin\frac{\theta}{2} + \log c$$

$$\Rightarrow \log r - \log\sin^2\frac{\theta}{2} + \log c \quad \therefore r = c\sin^2\frac{\theta}{2}.$$

Which is the requires family of orthogonal trajectories.

Ex. 16: Find orthogonal trajectories of $r = a(1+\sin\theta)$ **SUK: May-13**

Solution: Given $r = a(1+\sin\theta)$ (1)

Differentiating equation (1) w. r. t. θ, we get

$$\frac{dr}{d\theta} = a\cos\theta \quad (2)$$

Eliminating constant a from equation (1) and (2), we get

$$\frac{dr}{d\theta} = \frac{r}{1+\sin\theta}\cos\theta \quad (3)$$

which is the differential equation for the family (1).

Replacing $\frac{dr}{d\theta}$ by $-r^2\frac{d\theta}{dr}$ in equation (3), we get

$$-r^2\frac{d\theta}{dr} = \frac{r}{1+\sin\theta}\cos\theta$$

$$-\frac{dr}{r} = \frac{(1+\sin\theta)}{\cos\theta}d\theta$$

$$-\frac{dr}{r} = (\sec\theta + \tan\theta)d\theta \quad (4)$$

Which is differential equation for the family of orthogonal trajectories.

Equation (4) is in variable separable form, Integrating equation (4), we get

$$\int \frac{dr}{r} = -\int \sec\theta d\theta - \int \frac{\sin\theta}{\cos\theta}d\theta + \log c$$

$$\log r = -\log(\sec\theta + \tan\theta) + \log\cos\theta + \log c$$

$$\Rightarrow \log r = \log\frac{\cos\theta}{(\sec\theta + \tan\theta)}c$$

$$\therefore r = c\frac{\cos^2\theta}{(1+\sin\theta)}.$$

Which is the requires family of orthogonal trajectories.

TEST YOUR KNOWLEDGE

Find orthogonal trajectories of following

1. $r = a(1+\sin\theta)$
2. $r = a(1-\sin\theta)$
3. $r = \dfrac{2a}{(1-\cos\theta)}$
4. $r = \dfrac{2a}{1-\sin\theta}$
5. $r = \dfrac{2a}{1+\cos\theta}$
6. $r^2 = \dfrac{a}{\cos\theta}$
7. $r^n = \dfrac{a^n}{\cos n\theta}$
8. $2ar^n \sin n\theta = a^n$
9. $r^n = a^n \cos n\theta$
10. $r = a\cos^n\theta$
11. $r^2 = a^2 \cos 2\theta$
12. $r^2 = a \sin 2\theta$
13. $r^2 = a^2 \sin 2\theta$
14. $r = a \sin^2\theta$
15. $r = a(\sec\theta + \tan\theta)$

SIMPLE ELECTRICAL CIRCUITS

Same important notations

Element	Symbol	Unit
Time	t	Seconds
Quantity of electricity	$q \left(q = \int i\, dt\right)$	Coulombs
Current, rate of flow of electricity	$i \left(i = \dfrac{dq}{dt}\right)$	Ampere (A)
Electromotive force (EMF) or voltage	E	Volts
Resistance	R	Ohms or Ω
Inductance	L	Henry (H)
Capacitance	C	Farad (F) or μF
Electromotive force or voltage (constant), E	Battery, E = constant	volt
Variable voltage generator	Generator, E = Variable voltage	volt

The differential equation of an electrical circuit can be formed by using the following two **Kirchhoff's Laws:**

1. Current Law: At any junction or node of circuit, the current incomes is always equal to outgoing current. Or The algebraic sum of the current flowing into or form any terminal of the circuit is zero.

2. Voltage Law: In a closed loop the algebraic sum of the potential drops or voltage drops is equal to the total electromotive force applied. Or The algebraic sum of the voltage drops around any closed circuits is equal to the resultant emf in the circuits.

Active element : An energy source is voltage source or a current is said to be active element. Ex.- Generator, Battery,UPS.

Passive element : A passive element transform or store energy but not an energy source. Ex. - Resistance Inductance, Capacitance.

Remark : Same important Relations-
If i is the current flowing through a loop, then

a. $i = \dfrac{dq}{dt}$ or $q = \int i\, dt$ 　　　　b. Voltage drop across C is q/C or $\dfrac{1}{C}\int i\, dt$.

c. Voltage drop across R is Ri. 　　　　d. Voltage drop across L is $L\dfrac{di}{dt}$.

We shall consider the following cases:

I. R-L Series Circuit (Circuit involving resistance R and Inductance L along with a voltage source E all in series):

Consider a circuit containing resistance R and Inductance L in series with a voltage source(battery) E. Let i be the current in the circuit at any time t. Then according to Kirchhoff's voltage law:

Sum of the voltage (potential) drops across R and L=Total e. m. f(E) across R and L

$$\therefore L\dfrac{di}{dt} + Ri = E \Rightarrow \dfrac{di}{dt} + \dfrac{R}{L} i = \dfrac{E}{L}.$$

This is the required differential equation of the circuit. Moreover this is linear differential equation.

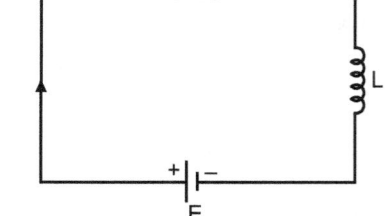

II. R-C Series Circuits (Circuit involving resistance R and capacitor C along with a voltage source E all in series):

Let i be the current flowing in the circuit containing resistance R and capacitor C in series with voltage source (E) at any time t then according to Kirchhoff's voltage law:

$$\therefore Ri + \dfrac{q}{C} = E \Rightarrow Ri + \dfrac{1}{C}\int i\, dt = E.$$

This is the required differential equation of the circuit. Moreover this is linear differential equation.

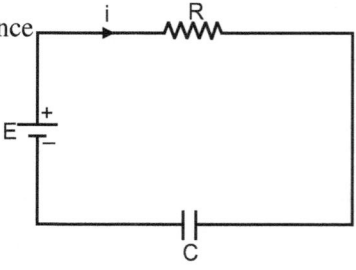

III. L-C Series Circuits (Circuit involving inductance L and capacitor C both in series, after removing source applied e. m. F):

Let i be the current flowing in the circuit containing inductance L and capacitor C with out applied e. m. f, then according to Kirchhoff's voltage law:

$$\therefore L\frac{di}{dt} + \frac{q}{C} = 0 \Rightarrow \frac{di}{dt} = -\frac{q}{LC}.$$

This is the required differential equation of the circuit. Moreover this is linear differential equation.

Remark : Same Important Results:

1. $\int e^{at} \sin bt \, dt = \dfrac{e^{at}}{a^2+b^2}(a \sin bt - b \cos bt)$

   OR $\int e^{at} \sin bt \, dt = \dfrac{e^{at}}{a^2+b^2}(a \sin bt - b \cos bt)$

   $= \dfrac{e^{at}}{\sqrt{a^2+b^2}}\left(\dfrac{a}{\sqrt{a^2+b^2}} \sin bt - \dfrac{b}{\sqrt{a^2+b^2}} \cos bt\right)$

   $= \dfrac{e^{at}}{\sqrt{a^2+b^2}} \sin(bt - \psi)$ by putting $\dfrac{a}{\sqrt{a^2+b^2}} = \cos\psi$ and $\dfrac{b}{\sqrt{a^2+b^2}} = \sin\psi$

2. $\int e^{at} \cos bt \, dt = \dfrac{e^{at}}{a^2+b^2}(a \cos bt + \sin bbt)$

   OR $\int e^{at} \cos bt \, dt = \dfrac{e^{at}}{\sqrt{a^2+b^2}}(\cos bt - \psi)$

Examples on Simple Electrical Circuits :

Ex. 1: The charge Q on the plate of condenser of capacity C charged through a resistance R by a steady voltage V satisfies the differential equation

$R\dfrac{dQ}{dt} + \dfrac{Q}{C} = V$, If $Q = 0$ at $t = 0$, Show that $Q = CV\left(1 - e^{\frac{-t}{RC}}\right)$.

Find the current flowing into the plate. **SUK: Nov-08, Dec-13**

Solution: Given $R\dfrac{dQ}{dt} + \dfrac{Q}{C} = V$, $\Rightarrow \dfrac{dQ}{dt} + \dfrac{Q}{RC} = \dfrac{V}{R}$ which is Linear equation

$I.F = e^{\int \frac{1}{RC} dt} = e^{\frac{t}{RC}}$

Solution is $Q e^{\frac{t}{RC}} = \int \dfrac{V}{R} e^{\frac{t}{RC}} dt + K$

$Q e^{\frac{t}{RC}} = \dfrac{V}{R} \dfrac{e^{\frac{t}{RC}}}{1/RC} + K$

$\Rightarrow Q = CV + K e^{\frac{-t}{RC}}$

At $t = 0$, $Q = 0$ $\therefore 0 = CV + K \Rightarrow K = -CV$

$Q = CV - CVe^{\frac{-t}{RC}}$ i.e. $Q = CV\left(1 - e^{\frac{-t}{RC}}\right)$

Current $= i = \dfrac{dQ}{dt} = CV \dfrac{e^{\frac{-t}{RC}}}{1/RC} = \dfrac{V}{R} e^{\frac{-t}{RC}}$.

Ex. 2: A voltage Ee^{-at} is applied at $t = 0$ to a circuit containing inductance L and resistance R. Show that current at any time t is given by $i = \dfrac{E}{R - aL}\left[e^{-at} - e^{-\frac{R}{L}t}\right]$.

OR A voltage Ee^{-at} is applied at $t = 0$ to a circuit containing inductance L and resistance R, satisfies the differential equation $L\dfrac{di}{dt} + Ri = E e^{-at}$. Show that current at any time t is given by

$i = \dfrac{E}{R - aL}\left[e^{-at} - e^{-\frac{R}{L}t}\right]$.   **SUK: May-08, Nov-10,12**

Solution: Let i be the current at any time t.

By Kirchhoff's law, $L\dfrac{di}{dt} + Ri = E e^{-at}$

$\dfrac{di}{dt} + \dfrac{R}{L}i = \dfrac{E}{L}e^{-at}$ Which is Linear equation

$I.F = e^{\int \frac{R}{L} dt} = e^{\frac{Rt}{L}}$

Solution is i.e $e^{\frac{Rt}{L}} = \int \dfrac{E}{L} e^{-at} e^{\frac{Rt}{L}} + K$

i.e $e^{\frac{Rt}{L}} = \dfrac{E e^{\left(\frac{R}{L} - a\right)t}}{L(R/L - a)} + K$ i.e. i.e $e^{\frac{Rt}{L}} = \dfrac{E e^{\left(\frac{R}{L} - a\right)t}}{(R - La)} + K$

At $t = 0$, $i = 0$

$0 = \dfrac{E e^0}{(R - La)} + K \Rightarrow K = \dfrac{-E}{(R - La)}$

i.e $e^{\frac{Rt}{L}} = \dfrac{E e^{\left(\frac{R}{L} - a\right)t}}{(R - La)} - \dfrac{E}{(R - La)}$ i.e. i.e $e^{\frac{Rt}{L}} = \dfrac{E}{(R - La)}\left(e^{\left(\frac{R}{L} - a\right)t} - 1\right)$

$i = \dfrac{E}{(R - La)}\left(e^{-at} - e^{\frac{-Rt}{L}}\right)$ by dividing $e^{\frac{Rt}{L}}$.

(2.27)

Ex. 3 : The differential equation of the circuit containing inductance L, resistance R and voltage $E = \sin pt$ is given by $L\dfrac{di}{dt} + Ri = E\sin pt$, If $i = 0$ at $t = 0$. Show that

$$i = \dfrac{E}{\sqrt{R^2 + P^2L^2}}\left[\sin(pt - \phi) + e^{\frac{-Rt}{L}}\sin\phi\right], \text{ where } \phi = \tan^{-1}\left(\dfrac{LP}{R}\right).$$

SUK: May-11

Solution: We have $L\dfrac{di}{dt} + Ri = E\sin pt$,

$\dfrac{di}{dt} + \dfrac{R}{L}i = \dfrac{E}{L}\sin pt$ which is Linear equation

$I.F = e^{\int \frac{R}{L}dt} = e^{\frac{Rt}{L}}$

Solution is $i.e^{\frac{Rt}{L}} = \int \dfrac{E}{L}\sin pt \, e^{\frac{Rt}{L}}dt + K$

i.e $e^{\frac{Rt}{L}} = \dfrac{E}{L}\dfrac{e^{\frac{Rt}{L}}}{\sqrt{P^2 - R^2/L^2}}\sin(pt - \phi) + K$ where $\phi = \tan^{-1}\left(\dfrac{LP}{R}\right)$

At $i = 0, \; t = 0$

$0 = \dfrac{E}{\sqrt{R^2 + P^2L^2}}\sin(-\phi) + K, \qquad \therefore K = \dfrac{E}{\sqrt{R^2 + P^2L^2}}\sin(\phi)$

$i = \dfrac{E}{\sqrt{R^2 + P^2L^2}}\left[\sin(pt - \phi) + e^{\frac{-Rt}{L}}\sin\phi\right] \quad \because \phi = \tan^{-1}\left(\dfrac{LP}{R}\right).$

Ex. 4: Prove that the differential equation of a circuit containing a resistance R and a condenser of capacity C in series with e. m. f. E is $E = Ri + \int \dfrac{i}{C}dt$.

Find the current i at any time t, when $E = E_0 \sin \omega t$.

SUK: May-12, Nov-09

Solution: Let i be the current at any time t. By Kirchhoff's law,

$E_0 \sin \omega t = Ri + \int \dfrac{i}{C}dt \quad i.e. \; i + \int \dfrac{i}{RC}dt = \dfrac{E_0}{R}\sin \omega t$

Differentiating w. r. t. t $\quad \dfrac{di}{dt} + \dfrac{i}{RC} = \dfrac{E_0 \omega}{R}\cos \omega t$ which is Linear equation

$I.F = e^{\int \frac{1}{RC}dt} = e^{\frac{t}{RC}}$

$\therefore$ Solution is $i.e^{\frac{t}{RC}} = \int e^{\frac{t}{RC}}\dfrac{E_0\omega}{R}\cos\omega t \, dt + K$

$i.e^{\frac{t}{RC}} = \dfrac{E_0\omega}{R}\dfrac{e^{\frac{t}{RC}}}{\sqrt{1/R^2C^2 + \omega^2}}\cos(\omega t - \phi) + K$ where $\phi = \tan^{-1}\left(\dfrac{\omega}{RC}\right)$

At $t = 0, \; i = 0$

$0 = \dfrac{E_0\omega}{R}\dfrac{e^0}{\sqrt{1/R^2C^2 + \omega^2}}\cos(0 - \phi) + K \;\Rightarrow\; K = \dfrac{-E_0\omega C}{\sqrt{1 + R^2C^2\omega^2}}\cos\phi$

$i.e^{\frac{t}{RC}} = \dfrac{E_0\omega C}{\sqrt{1 + R^2C^2\omega^2}}e^{\frac{t}{RC}}\left[\cos(\omega t - \phi) - \cos\phi \, e^{\frac{-t}{RC}}\right]$

$i = \dfrac{E_0\omega C}{\sqrt{1 + R^2C^2\omega^2}}\left[\cos(\omega t - \phi) - \cos\phi \, e^{\frac{-t}{RC}}\right].$

Ex. 5 : In a circuit of resistance R, self inductance L, the current i is given by
$L\frac{di}{dt} + Ri = E\cos pt$ where E, p are constant. Find the current i at time t.

Solution: Given equation is $L\frac{di}{dt} + Ri = E\cos pt$

$\frac{di}{dt} + \frac{R}{L}i = \frac{E}{L}\cos pt$ which is linear equation

$\therefore I.F = e^{\int \frac{R}{L}dt} = e^{\frac{Rt}{L}}$

Solution is $ie^{\frac{Rt}{L}} = \int \left(\frac{E}{L}\cos pt\right)e^{\frac{Rt}{L}}dt + K$

$ie^{\frac{Rt}{L}} = \frac{E}{L}\frac{1}{\sqrt{p^2 + \frac{R^2}{L^2}}}\left[\frac{R}{L}e^{\frac{Rt}{L}}\cos pt + pe^{\frac{Rt}{L}}\sin pt\right] + K$

$ie^{\frac{Rt}{L}} = \frac{E}{L}\frac{1}{\sqrt{L^2p^2 + R^2}}e^{\frac{Rt}{L}}\left[\frac{R\cos pt + pL\sin pt}{L}\right] + K$

$ie^{\frac{Rt}{L}} = \frac{E}{\sqrt{L^2p^2 + R^2}}e^{\frac{Rt}{L}}[R\cos pt + pL\sin pt] + Ke^{\frac{-Rt}{L}}$

Ex. 6 : A current is flowing in a circuit of resistance $R = 20$ ohms, self inductance $L = 0.05$ henries. If the current of 30 amps flows at the beginning, Find its value after 0.01 sec. there being no external e.m.f.

Solution: Given Resistance = $R = 20$ Ohms, self inductance = $L = 0.05$ Henries, $i = 30$ Amps at time $t = 0$, We have $L\frac{di}{dt} + Ri = 0 \therefore L\frac{di}{dt} = -Ri \quad \therefore \frac{1}{i}di = -\frac{R}{L}dt$

On integration $\int \frac{1}{i}di = -\frac{R}{L}\int dt \Rightarrow \log i = -\frac{Rt}{L} + K$ \hspace{1cm} (1)

At $t = 0$, $i = 30$, $\log 30 = 0 + K \Rightarrow K = \log 30$

Therefore equation (1) becomes

$\log i = -\frac{Rt}{L} + \log 30 \quad \therefore \log i - \log 30 = -\frac{Rt}{L}$

$\therefore \log\left(\frac{i}{30}\right) = -\frac{Rt}{L} \quad \frac{i}{30} = e^{-\frac{Rt}{L}} \quad \therefore i = 30e^{-\frac{Rt}{L}}$

Put $R = 20$ ohms, $L = 0.05$ henry $\therefore i = 30e^{-\frac{20t}{0.05}} \quad \therefore i = 30e^{400t}$.

Ex. 7: Find current i in the circuit having resistance R and condenser of capacity C in series with e. m. f. E sin ωt.

Solution: By Kirchhoff's law.

Sum of potential drops = total e. m. f applied

i.e. $Ri + \dfrac{q}{C} = E \sin \omega t$

$i + \dfrac{q}{RC} = \dfrac{E}{R} \sin \omega t$

$\dfrac{dq}{dt} + \dfrac{q}{RC} = \dfrac{E}{R} \sin \omega t$ which is Linear

$\therefore I.F = e^{\int \frac{1}{RC} dt} = e^{\frac{t}{RC}}$

Hence solution is

$q e^{\frac{t}{RC}} = \int e^{\frac{t}{RC}} \dfrac{E}{R} \sin \omega t \, dt + K$

$= \dfrac{E}{R} \dfrac{e^{\frac{t}{RC}}}{\sqrt{\dfrac{1}{R^2 C^2} + \omega^2}} \sin(\omega t - \phi) + K$

$= EC \dfrac{e^{\frac{t}{RC}}}{\sqrt{1 + \omega^2 R^2 C^2}} \sin(\omega t - \phi) + K$

$q = \dfrac{EC}{\sqrt{1 + \omega^2 R^2 C^2}} \sin(\omega t - \phi) + K e^{\frac{-t}{RC}}$

Now $i = \dfrac{dq}{dt} = \dfrac{EC\omega}{\sqrt{1 + \omega^2 R^2 C^2}} \cos(\omega t - \phi) - \dfrac{1}{RC} K e^{\frac{-t}{RC}}$.

Ex. 8 : The circuit consists of resistance R ohm and a condenser of C farads connected to a constant e. m f. E volts .If q/C is the voltage of the condenser at time t after closing the circuit. Show that the voltage at time t is $E\left(1 - e^{\frac{-t}{RC}}\right)$.

Solution : The differential equation for R-C circuit is

$Ri + \dfrac{q}{C} = E \quad i.e.\ i + \dfrac{q}{RC} = \dfrac{E}{R}$

or $\dfrac{dq}{dt} + \dfrac{q}{RC} = \dfrac{E}{R}$ which is linear equation

$\therefore I.F = \int e^{\frac{1}{RC}} = e^{\frac{t}{RC}}$

Solution is $qe^{\frac{t}{RC}} = \int \frac{E}{R} e^{\frac{t}{RC}} dt + K$

$$qe^{\frac{t}{RC}} = \frac{E}{R} \frac{e^{\frac{t}{RC}}}{\frac{1}{RC}} + K$$

$$\frac{q}{C} e^{\frac{t}{RC}} = E e^{\frac{t}{RC}} + K$$

At $t = 0, q = 0 \Rightarrow 0 = E + K$ $\therefore K = -E$

$$\therefore \frac{q}{C} = E\left(1 - e^{\frac{-t}{RC}}\right).$$

Ex. 9 : The circuit containing inductance L, resistance R and voltage E the current i is given by $L\frac{di}{dt} + Ri = E$ if L = 640 Henry, R = 250 Ohm and E = 500 Volts and i = 0 when t = 0. Find the time that elapses before the current reaches 90% of the maximum value.

Solution : Given $L\frac{di}{dt} + Ri = E$

$\frac{di}{dt} + \frac{R}{L}i = \frac{E}{L}$ Which is linear equation $\therefore I.F. = e^{\int \frac{R}{L} dt} = e^{\frac{Rt}{L}}$

Solution is $ie^{\frac{Rt}{L}} = \int \frac{E}{L} e^{\frac{Rt}{L}} dt + K$

$ie^{\frac{Rt}{L}} = \frac{E}{L} \frac{e^{\frac{Rt}{L}}}{R/L} + K$ i.e. $i = \frac{E}{R} + Ke^{-\frac{Rt}{L}}$

At $t = 0, i = 0$, $0 = \frac{E}{R} + Ke^0 \Rightarrow K = \frac{-E}{R}$

$i = \frac{E}{R} - \frac{E}{R} e^{\frac{-Rt}{L}} = \frac{E}{R}\left(1 - e^{\frac{-Rt}{L}}\right)$

$i_{max} = \frac{E}{R} = \frac{500}{250} = 2$

90% of $i_{max} = \frac{90}{100}(2) = 1.8$

Let at $t = T, i = 90\%$ of $i_{max} = 1.8$

$1.8 = 2\left(1 - e^{\frac{-RT}{L}}\right) \Rightarrow e^{\frac{-RT}{L}} = 1 - \frac{9}{10} = \frac{1}{10}$

$\frac{-RT}{L} = \log\frac{1}{10} \Rightarrow \frac{RT}{L} = \log 10$

$T = \frac{L}{R} \log 10 = \frac{640}{250} \log 10 = 5.89 \sec.$

Ex. 10 : If Q_0 be the initial charge on condenser of a condenser of capacity C having inductance L in series find the charge q and current i at any time t.

Solution : Let i be the current at any time t

By Kirchhoff's law, $L\dfrac{di}{dt} + \dfrac{1}{C}\int i\,dt = 0$

But $i = \dfrac{dq}{dt} \quad \therefore \dfrac{di}{dt} = \dfrac{di}{dq}\dfrac{dq}{dt} = i\dfrac{di}{dq}$

$Li\dfrac{di}{dq} + \dfrac{1}{C}q = 0$, integrating

$\dfrac{i^2}{2} + \dfrac{1}{LC}\dfrac{q^2}{2} = \dfrac{K}{2}$ i.e. $i^2 + \dfrac{q^2}{LC} = K$

At $t = 0$, $q = Q_0$, $i = 0$.

$\dfrac{Q_0^2}{LC} = K \quad \therefore i^2 = \dfrac{Q_0^2 - q^2}{LC}$

$i = \dfrac{dq}{dt} = \pm\dfrac{\sqrt{Q_0^2 - q^2}}{\sqrt{LC}}$

Consider the negative sign, because as time t increases q decreases

$\dfrac{-dq}{\sqrt{Q_0^2 - q^2}} = \dfrac{dt}{\sqrt{LC}}$, integrating

$\cos^{-1}\dfrac{q}{Q_0} = \dfrac{t}{\sqrt{LC}} + K'$

Again at $t = 0$, $q = Q_0 \quad \Rightarrow K' = 0$

$q = Q_0 \cos\left(\dfrac{t}{\sqrt{LC}}\right)$ and $i = -\dfrac{Q_0}{LC}\sin\left(\dfrac{t}{\sqrt{LC}}\right)$.

Ex. 11: A constant e. m. f. is applied a circuit containing a constant resistance R Ohms and constant inductance L henries in series. if initial current is zero. Show that the current builds up to half its theoretical maximum in $\dfrac{L\log 2}{R}$ seconds.

Solution: Let i be the current in the circuit at any time t

Then by Kirchhoff's law we have

$L\dfrac{di}{dt} + Ri = E$ i.e. $\dfrac{di}{dt} + \dfrac{R}{L}i = \dfrac{E}{L}$ which is Linear equation

$I.F = e^{\int \frac{R}{L}dt} = e^{\frac{Rt}{L}}$

Solution is $ie^{\frac{Rt}{L}} = \int \frac{E}{L} e^{\frac{Rt}{L}} dt + K$

$ie^{\frac{Rt}{L}} = \frac{E}{L} \frac{e^{\frac{Rt}{L}}}{R/L} + K, \Rightarrow i = \frac{E}{R} + Ke^{\frac{-Rt}{L}}$

At $t = 0, i = 0 \quad \therefore 0 = \frac{E}{R} + Ke^0 \Rightarrow K = \frac{-E}{R}$

$i = \frac{E}{R} - \frac{E}{R} e^{\frac{-Rt}{L}} = \frac{E}{R}\left(1 - e^{\frac{-Rt}{L}}\right)$

This equation indicate the expression of i at any time t, as t increases $e^{\frac{-Rt}{L}}$ decreases.

i increases and its maximum value is $\frac{E}{R}$

Let the current in the circuit is half of its theoretical maximum $\frac{E}{R}$ after a time T seconds, then

$\frac{1}{2}\frac{E}{R} = \frac{E}{R}\left(1 - e^{\frac{-RT}{L}}\right) \quad i.e.\ 1 - e^{\frac{-RT}{L}} = \frac{1}{2}$

$\frac{-RT}{L} = \log \frac{1}{2} = -\log 2 \Rightarrow T = \frac{L \log 2}{R}$.

Ex. 12 : An electric circuit contains an inductance of 6 H, resistance of 15 Ohm in series with an e. m. f. of $240 \cos(30t)$ Volts. find the current at $t = 0.01$, $t = 0$, $i = 0$

Solution: We have $L = 6H$, $R = 15$ Ohm, $E = 240\cos(30t)$ Volts

Let i be the current at any time t, By Kirchhoff's law

$L\frac{di}{dt} + Ri = E \quad i.e.\ \frac{di}{dt} + \frac{R}{L}i = \frac{E}{L} \Rightarrow \frac{di}{dt} + \frac{15}{6}i = \frac{240\cos(30t)}{6}$

$i.e.\ \frac{di}{dt} + \frac{5}{2}i = 40\cos(30t)$ which is Linear equation $I.F = e^{\int \frac{5}{2}dt} = e^{\frac{5t}{2}}$

Solution is $ie^{\frac{5t}{2}} = \int 40\cos(30t)e^{\frac{5t}{2}} dt + K$

$ie^{\frac{5t}{2}} = 40\left\{\frac{1}{(5/2)^2 + (30)^2}\left[\frac{5}{2}e^{\frac{5t}{2}}\cos(30t) + 30e^{\frac{5t}{2}}\sin(30t)\right]\right\} + K$

$i = \left\{\frac{40}{(25/4)+900}\left[\frac{5}{2}\cos(30t)+30\sin(30t)\right]\right\} + Ke^{\frac{-5t}{2}}$

At $t = 0, i = 0$

$0 = \left\{\frac{40}{(25/4)+900}\left[\frac{5}{2}\cos 0 + 30\sin 0\right]\right\} + Ke^0 \quad i.e.\ 0 = \left\{\frac{40}{(25/4)+900}\frac{5}{2}\right\} + K$

$\Rightarrow K = -0.110$

$$\therefore i = \left\{ \frac{40}{(25/4)+900} \left[\frac{5}{2}\cos(30t) + 30\sin(30t) \right] \right\} - 0.110 e^{\frac{-5t}{2}}$$

Putting $t = 0.01$ $\therefore i = 0.36894$ Ampere.

Ex. 13: When the switch is closed in a circuit containing the battery E, the resistance R and an inductance L, the current i is builds up at rate given by $L\frac{di}{dt} + Ri = E$.

Find i as a function of t. How long it will be, before the current has reached one half its maximum values. If $E = 6V$, $R = 100$ Ohm and $L = 0.1$ Henry.

Solution: Given $L\frac{di}{dt} + Ri = E$.

$\frac{di}{dt} + \frac{R}{L}i = \frac{E}{L}$ Which is linear equation

$I.F = e^{\int \frac{R}{L} dt} = e^{\frac{Rt}{L}}$

Solution is $i e^{\frac{Rt}{L}} = \int \frac{E}{L} e^{\frac{Rt}{L}} dt + K$

$i e^{\frac{Rt}{L}} = \frac{E}{L} \frac{e^{\frac{Rt}{L}}}{R/L} + K \Rightarrow i = \frac{E}{R} + K e^{\frac{-Rt}{L}}$ \hspace{1em} (A)

At $t = 0$, $i = 0$

$0 = \frac{E}{R} + K e^0 \Rightarrow K = \frac{-E}{R}$

Therefore equation (A) becomes

$i = \frac{E}{R} - \frac{E}{R} e^{\frac{-Rt}{L}} = \frac{E}{R}\left(1 - e^{\frac{-Rt}{L}}\right)$

$i_{max} = \frac{E}{R} = \frac{6}{100} = 0.06$

$\frac{1}{2} \text{ of } i_{max} = \frac{1}{2}(0.06) = 0.03$

$t = T$, $i = \frac{1}{2} i_{max} = 0.03$

$0.03 = 0.06 \left(1 - e^{\frac{-RT}{L}}\right) \Rightarrow e^{\frac{-RT}{L}} = 1 - \frac{1}{2}$

$\therefore \frac{-RT}{L} = \log \frac{1}{2}$ i.e. $\frac{RT}{L} = \log 2$

$\therefore T = \frac{L}{R} \log 2 = \frac{0.1}{100} \log 2 = 6.931 \times 10^{-4}$ sec.

Ex. 14: The equation of an L-R circuit is given by $L\dfrac{di}{dt} + Ri = 10\sin t$

If $i = 0$ at $t = 0$. Express i as a function of t.

Solution: Given $L\dfrac{di}{dt} + Ri = 10\sin t$

i.e. $\dfrac{di}{dt} + \dfrac{R}{L}i = \dfrac{10\sin t}{L}$ which is linear equation

$I.F = e^{\int \frac{R}{L} dt} = e^{\frac{Rt}{L}}$.

Solution is $ie^{\frac{Rt}{L}} = \int \dfrac{10}{L}\sin t \left(e^{\frac{Rt}{L}}\right) dt + K$

$ie^{\frac{Rt}{L}} = \dfrac{10}{L} \dfrac{e^{\frac{Rt}{L}}}{\sqrt{1 + \dfrac{R^2}{L^2}}} \sin(t - \phi) + K$

$i = 10 \dfrac{1}{\sqrt{L^2 + R^2}} \sin(t - \phi) + Ke^{\frac{-Rt}{L}}$

At $t = 0, i = 0$

$0 = \dfrac{10}{\sqrt{L^2 + R^2}} \sin(0 - \phi) + Ke^0$

$0 = \dfrac{-10}{\sqrt{L^2 + R^2}} \sin\phi + K \Rightarrow K = \dfrac{10}{\sqrt{L^2 + R^2}} \sin\phi$

i.e $e^{\frac{Rt}{L}} = \dfrac{10}{\sqrt{L^2 + R^2}} \sin(t - \phi) + \dfrac{10}{\sqrt{L^2 + R^2}} \sin\phi$

i.e $e^{\frac{Rt}{L}} = \dfrac{10}{\sqrt{L^2 + R^2}} \left[\sin(t - \phi) + \sin\phi\, e^{\frac{-Rt}{L}}\right]$.

Ex. 15 : A 200 ohms resistor is connected in series with a capacitor of 0.001 farads and e.m.f $400e^{-3t}$. If $q = 0$ at $t = 0$, find the maximum charge on the capacitor.

Solution : Given $R = 200\, ohms,\ c = 0.001\ farads,\ E = 400e^{-3t}$

$Ri + \dfrac{q}{c} = 400e^{-3t}\quad \therefore R\dfrac{dq}{dt} + \dfrac{q}{c} = 400e^{-3t}$

$\dfrac{dq}{dt} + \dfrac{q}{Rc} = \dfrac{400e^{-3t}}{R}$

Put $R = 200\, ohms, c = 0.001\ farad$

$$\therefore \frac{dq}{dt} + \frac{q}{(200)(0.001)} = \frac{400e^{-3t}}{200} \text{ which is a linear equation}$$

Here $P = 5$, $Q = 2e^{-3t}$ $\therefore I.F = e^{\int 5dt} = e^{5t}$

Hence the solution is

$q.I.F = \int I.F.Q dt + c$ i.e. $q.e^{5t} = \int e^{5t}.(2e^{-3t}) dt + K$

$q.e^{5t} = 2\int e^{2t} dt + K \Rightarrow q.e^{5t} = e^{2t} + K$ (1)

At $t = 0$, $q = 0$ $\therefore 0 = 1 + K \Rightarrow K = -1$

Therefore equation (1) becomes $q.e^{5t} = e^{2t} - 1 \Rightarrow q = e^{-3t} - e^{-5t}$.

Ex.16 : In a circuits containing resistance R an inductance L and voltage E, the current i is given by $L\frac{di}{dt} + Ri = E$. find the current i at any time t if $t = 0$, $i = 0$ and L, R, E are constants.

Solution: Given $L\frac{di}{dt} + Ri = E$ $\therefore \frac{di}{dt} + \frac{R}{L}i = \frac{E}{L}$ which is linear eqation

$I.F. = e^{\int R/L\, dt} = e^{Rt/L}$

Solution is $i.e^{Rt/L} = \int \frac{E}{L} e^{Rt/L} dt + K$

$i.e^{Rt/L} = \frac{E}{L} \frac{e^{Rt/L}}{R/L} + K \Rightarrow i = \frac{E}{R} + Ke^{-Rt/L}$

At $t = 0$, $i = 0$ $\therefore 0 = \frac{E}{R} + Ke^0 \Rightarrow K = -\frac{E}{R}$

$\therefore i = \frac{E}{R} - \frac{E}{R} e^{-Rt/L} = \frac{E}{R}\left(1 - e^{-Rt/L}\right)$.

Ex. 17 : A circuit contains a resistance R and a condenser of capacity C farads and is connected to a constant e. m. f. E. Find q given that $q = 0$ when $t = 0$.

Solution: We have $R\frac{dq}{dt} + \frac{q}{c} = E$ $\therefore R\frac{dq}{dt} = E - \frac{q}{c}$ $\therefore R\frac{dq}{dt} = \frac{Ec - q}{c}$

$R\frac{dq}{dt} = -\left(\frac{q - Ec}{c}\right)$ $\therefore \frac{Rc}{q - Ec} dq = -dt$

On integration $Rc \int \frac{1}{q - Ec} dq = -\int dt$ $\therefore Rc \log(q - Ec) = -t + K$ (1)

At $t = 0$, $q = 0$ $Rc \log(-Ec) = 0 + K \Rightarrow K = Rc \log(-Ec)$

Therefore equation (1) becomes

$Rc \log(q - Ec) = -t + Rc \log(-Ec)$

$Rc \log(q - Ec) - Rc \log(-Ec) = -t$

$$\log(q-Ec) - \log(-Ec) = \frac{-t}{Rc}$$

$$\log\left(\frac{q-Ec}{-Ec}\right) = \frac{-t}{Rc} \quad \therefore \left(\frac{q-Ec}{-Ec}\right) = e^{\frac{-t}{Rc}}$$

$$\Rightarrow q = -Ece^{\frac{-t}{Rc}} + Ec \quad \therefore q = Ec\left(1 - e^{\frac{-t}{Rc}}\right).$$

TEST YOUR KNOWLEDGE

1. The current in a circuit containing an inductance L resistance R and voltage $E\sin\omega t$ is given by $L\dfrac{di}{dt} + Ri = E\sin\omega t$. If $i = 0$ at $t = 0$ then show that

$$i = \frac{E}{\sqrt{R^2 + \omega^2 L^2}} \sin(\omega t - \phi) + \sin\phi \, e^{-Rt/L}, \quad \phi = \tan^{-1}\frac{L\omega}{R}.$$

2. A voltage $E\,e^{at}$ is applied at $t = 0$ to a circuit containing inductance L and resistance R. Show that the current at any time t is containing inductance L and resistance R. Show that the current at any time t is $i = \dfrac{E}{R - aL}\left(e^{at} - e^{-Rt/L}\right)$.

3. An electric circuit contains an inductance L and resistance of 12 ohm in series with an e.m.f. $120 \sin(20t)$ volts. Find the current at $t = 0.01$, if it is 0 when $t = 0$.

4. A resistance of 100 ohms an inductance of 0.5 Henry are connected in series with the battery of 20 volts. Find the current in a circuits a function of t. Ans: $i = \dfrac{1}{5}\left(1 - e^{-200t}\right)$.

5. In a circuit containing inductance L, resistance R, and voltage E, the current is given by

$$L\frac{di}{dt} + Ri = E \quad L\frac{di}{dt} + Ri = E$$

Given: L= 640 Henry, R = 250 ohm, E = 500 volts and at $t = 0$, $i = 0$. Find the time that elapses, before reaches 90% of maximum value. Ans: $t = \dfrac{64}{25}\log_e 10$.

6. Find the current I in the circuit having resistance R and condenser having capacity C in series with emf $E\sin\omega t$

$$i = \frac{EC\omega}{\sqrt{1 + R^2\omega^2 C^2}} \cos(\omega t - \phi).$$

7. A 200 ohm resister is connected in series with a capacitor of 0.001 F and emf $40\,e^{-3t}$. If q = 0 at $t = 0$, find maximum charge on capacitor. Ans: $\dfrac{100}{7}\left[\left(\dfrac{1}{15}\right)^{\frac{2}{14}} - \left(\dfrac{1}{15}\right)^{\frac{15}{14}}\right]$.

8. An electric circuit containing a resistance of 12 ohms in series with an e. m. f 120 sin(20t)volts. Find the current at i at t=0.01 if it is zero at t = 0.   Ans: 0.0226 henries.

9. A capacitor of capacitance C is charged through a resistance R by a battery which supplies a constant voltage E, the instantaneous charge Q on capacitor satisfies the differential equation $R\dfrac{dQ}{dt}+\dfrac{Q}{C}=E.$ Find Q as a function of time t, if the capacitor is initially uncharged i.e. if $Q_0=0$. How long will it take before the charge on the capacitor is one half its final value.

$\left\{Let\ at\ t=T\left(Q\ becomes\ \dfrac{Q_{max}}{2}\right)=0.693RC\right\}$ Ans: $Q=EC\left(1-e^{\frac{-t}{RC}}\right)$, where $Q_{max}=EC$.

10. An inductance of 2 henries and resistance of 20 ohms are connected in series with an e.m.f. E volts, if the current is zero when t = 0, find the current at the end of 0.01 sec if
  1. E = 100 volts   2. E = 100 sin150t volts   Ans: 1) 0.475 amp.   2) 0.299 amp.

11. A 20 ohms resistor is connected in series with a capacitor of 0.01 farad and e.m.f. E volts given by $40e^{-3t}+20e^{-6t}$. If q=0 at t=0, show that maximum charge on the capacitor is 0.25 coulomb.

NEWTON'S LAW OF COOLING:

Statement : The rate of change of temperature (T) with respect to time t, $\dfrac{dT}{dt}$, of a body is proportional to the difference between the temperature of the body (T) and that of the surrounding medium (T_0). This principle is known as Newton's law of cooling and is expressed through the following first order and first degree differential equation.

If T_0 is the temperature of the surrounding and T that of body at any time t then by Newton's law of cooling $\dfrac{dT}{dt}\ \alpha\ (T-T_0)$ $\therefore \dfrac{dT}{dt}=-k\ (T-T_0),\ k>0$ (I)

Where k is constant and sign is negative because as time t increases T decreases.

Separating the variables $\dfrac{dT}{(T-T_0)}=-k\ dt$

Integrating, we get $\log(T-T_0)=-kt+\log C \Rightarrow (T-T_0)=Ce^{-kt}$.   (II)

If T_i is the initial temperature of the body when $t=0$, we get $(T_i-T_0)=C$

Substituting the value of C in equation (II), we get

$(T-T_0)=(T_i-T_0)e^{-kt}$ i.e. $T(t)=T_0+(T_i-T_0)e^{-kt}$ (III)

Method of solving Ex.s on Newton's law of cooling

Step-I : Identify T_0, the temperature of the surrounding medium. Then the general solution is given by equation (III)

Step-II : Use two given conditions and find the constant of integration C and the proportionality constant k.

Step-III : Substitute the values of C and k in equation (III). We can determine (i) the value of T for a given time t or (ii) the value of t for a given temperature T from equation (III).

Remark : 1. If the body is cooling at the rate kT and heated at the rate αt then net rate of change is given by $\dfrac{dT}{dt} = -kT + \alpha t$.

2. $\dfrac{dT}{dt} = k(T - T_0)$, for heating process.

EXAMPLES ON NEWTON'S LAW OF COOLING:

Ex. 1 : A body of temperature $100^\circ C$ is placed in a room whose temperature is $25^\circ C$ and cool to $50^\circ C$ in 5 minutes. What will be its temperature after interval of time 5 minutes.

Solution: Let T be the temperature of a body at any time t. given $T_0 = 25^\circ C$

Therefore by Newton's Law of cooling, we have

$$\dfrac{dT}{dt} = -k(T - T_0), \qquad \dfrac{dT}{dt} = -k(T - 25) \qquad \because T_0 = 25^\circ C$$

$$\dfrac{dT}{T - 25} = -k\, dt \qquad\qquad (A)$$

At $t = 0, T = 100^\circ C$ and at $t = 5, T = 50^\circ C$

$\because$ body cools down from $100^\circ C$ to $50^\circ C$ in 5 minutes

Integrating above equation (A), we get

$$\int_{100}^{50} \dfrac{dT}{T - 25} = \int_0^5 -k\, dt$$

$$\left[\log(T - 25)\right]_{100}^{50} = -k[t]_0^5$$

$$[\log 25 - \log 75] = -5k, \quad \therefore k = \dfrac{1}{5}\log 3.$$

Again at $t = 10$, minutes body cools from $100^\circ C$ to $T^\circ C$ (Say)

Hence by equation (A), we get,

$$\int_{100}^{T} \dfrac{dT}{T-25} = \int_0^{10} -k\, dt \Rightarrow \left[\log(T-25)\right]_{100}^{T} = -k[t]_0^{10}$$

$$[\log(T-25) - \log 75] = -10k \Rightarrow [\log(T-25) - \log 75] = -10.\dfrac{1}{5}\log 3.$$

$$[\log(T-25) - \log 75] = -2\log 3 \quad \therefore \log\left(\dfrac{T-25}{75}\right) = \log 3^{-2}$$

$$\dfrac{T-25}{75} = \dfrac{1}{9}, \Rightarrow T - 25 = \dfrac{75}{9}, \quad \therefore T = 33.3333^\circ C.$$

Ex. 2 : A body originally at $80°C$ cools down to $60°C$ in 20 minutes, the temperature of the air being $40°C$. What will be the temperature of the body after 40 minutes from the original?.

Solution: Let T be the temperature of a body at any time t.

Therefore by Newton's Law of cooling

$$\frac{dT}{dt} = -k(T - T_0), \quad \frac{dT}{dt} = -k(T - 40) \quad \because T_0 = 40°C$$

$$\frac{dT}{(T-40)} = -k\,dt$$

$$\log(T - 40) = -kt + C \qquad (I)$$

At $t = 0$, $T = 80°C$

$\log(80 - 40) = 0 + C \Rightarrow C = \log 40$

From equation (I),

$$\log(T - 40) = -kt + \log 40 \Rightarrow \log\left(\frac{T-40}{40}\right) = -kt \qquad (II)$$

Also at $t = 20$, $T = 60°C$

From equation (II), we get

$$\log\left(\frac{60-40}{40}\right) = -20k \Rightarrow \log\left(\frac{20}{40}\right) = -20k \quad \therefore k = \frac{1}{20}\log 2.$$

Again from equation (II), we get

$$\log\left(\frac{T-40}{40}\right) = -\frac{t}{20}\log 2$$

at $t = 40$, $\log\left(\frac{T-40}{40}\right) = -\frac{40}{20}\log 2$ i.e. $\log\left(\frac{T-40}{40}\right) = -2\log 2$

$$\log\left(\frac{T-40}{40}\right) = (\log 2)^{-2} = \log\frac{1}{4}.$$

Taking antilog on both sides, we get

$\frac{T-40}{40} = \frac{1}{4}$ $\therefore T = 50°C$, is the required temperature.

Ex. 3: A metal ball is heated to a temperature of 100^0C and at time $t = 0$. It is placed in water which is maintained at 40^0C. If the temperature of the ball reduces to 60^0C in four minutes. Find the time at which the temperature of the ball is 50^0C.

Solution: Let T be the temperature of a body at any time t.

Therefore by Newton's Law of cooling, we have

$$\frac{dT}{dt} = -k(T - T_0), \qquad \frac{dT}{dt} = -k(T - 40) \qquad \because T_0 = 40^0C$$

$$\frac{dT}{(T-40)} = -k\, dt \qquad (A)$$

Integrating above equation (A), we get

$$\int \frac{dT}{(T-40)} = \int -k\, dt$$

$$\log(T - 40) = -kt + \log C, \Rightarrow -kt = \log \frac{(T-40)}{C} \qquad (B)$$

Given at $t = 0, T = 100^0C$ $\therefore -k.0 = \log \frac{(100-40)}{C}, \Rightarrow 0 = \log \frac{60}{C},$

$\therefore \log C = \log 60 \Rightarrow C = 60.$

Substituting $C = 60$ in equation (B), we get

$$-kt = \log \frac{(T-40)}{60}. \qquad (C)$$

again at $t = 4, T = 60^0C$ $\therefore -k.4 = \log \frac{(60-40)}{60}$

$$-k.4 = \log \frac{1}{3}, \Rightarrow k = \frac{1}{4}\log 3.$$

Hence equation (C), becomes, $-\frac{t}{4}\log 3 = \log \frac{(T-40)}{60}$

at $T = 50$, $-\frac{t}{4}\log 3 = \log \frac{(50-40)}{60} \Rightarrow t = \frac{4\log 6}{\log 3} = 6.5$ minutes.

Ex. 4 : The temperature of the air is 30^0C and the substance cools from 100^0C to 70^0C in 15 minutes, find when the temperature will be 40^0C.

Solution: Let T be the temperature of the substance at any time t and the unit of time be a minute.

Therefore by Newton's Law of cooling, we have

$\dfrac{dT}{dt} = -k(T-T_0)$, $\dfrac{dT}{dt} = -k(T-30)$ $\because T_0 = 30°C$

$\dfrac{dT}{(T-30)} = -k\, dt$ (A)

Integrating above equation (A), we get

$\int \dfrac{dT}{(T-30)} = \int -k\, dt$

$\log(T-30) = -kt + C$ (B)

Given at $t=0$, $T=100°C$ $\therefore \log(100-30) = -k\cdot 0 + C$, $\Rightarrow C = \log 70$,

Substituting $C = \log 70$ in equation (B), we get

$\log(T-30) = -kt + \log 70 \Rightarrow kt = \log 70 - \log(T-30)$ (C)

again at $t=15$, $T=70°C$ $\therefore 15k = \log 70 - \log(40)$ (D)

dividing (C) by (D), we get

$\dfrac{kt}{15k} = \dfrac{\log 70 - \log(T-30)}{\log 70 - \log(40)} \Rightarrow \dfrac{t}{15} = \dfrac{\log 70 - \log(T-30)}{\log 70 - \log 40}$

Now when $T = 40°C$

$\therefore \dfrac{t}{15} = \dfrac{\log 70 - \log 10}{\log 70 - \log 40} = \dfrac{\log 70/10}{\log 70/40} = \dfrac{\log_e 7}{\log_e 7/4} = \dfrac{\log_{10} 7}{\log_{10} 7/4} = 3.48$

$\therefore \dfrac{t}{15} = 3.48 \Rightarrow t = 15 \times 3.48 = 52.20$.

Hence the temperature will be 40°C after 52.20 minutes.

Ex. 5 : The temperature of a body initially at 80°C reduces to 60°C in 12 min. If the temperature of the surrounding air is 30°C. Find the temperature of a body after 24 minutes.

Solution: Let T be the temperature of a body at any time t. given $T_0 = 30°C$
Therefore by Newton's Law of cooling

$\dfrac{dT}{dt} = -k(T-T_0)$, $\dfrac{dT}{dt} = -k(T-T_0)$

$\dfrac{dT}{T-T_0} = -k\, dt$

$\log(T-T_0) = -kt + \log C \Rightarrow (T-T_0) = Ce^{-kt}$ (A)

$T = T_0 + Ce^{-kt} = 30 + Ce^{-kt}$ $\because T_0 = 30°C$

At $t=0$, $T = T_i = 80°C$

$T_i - T_0 = 80 - 30 = Ce^0 \Rightarrow C = 50$ $\therefore T = 30 + 50 e^{-kt}$

When $t = 12$, $T = 60$

$\therefore 60 = 30 + 50 e^{-12k} \Rightarrow k = \dfrac{1}{12} \log \dfrac{5}{3}$

When $t = 24$, $T = 30 + 50 e^{\frac{-1}{12}\log\frac{5}{3}\cdot 24} = 30 + 50 \left(\dfrac{3}{5}\right)^2 = 48$.

(2.42)

Ex. 6 : A body is heated to $105°C$ and placed in air at $15°C$. After one hours its temperature is $60°C$. How much additional time is required for it to cool to $37\frac{1}{2}°C$.

Solution: Let T be the temperature of a body at any time t. given $T_0 = 15°C$
Therefore by Newton's Law of cooling, we have
$$\frac{dT}{dt} = -k(T - T_0), \quad \frac{dT}{dt} = -k(T - T_0)$$
$$\frac{dT}{T - T_0} = -k\, dt$$
$$\log(T - T_0) = -kt + \log C \Rightarrow (T - T_0) = Ce^{-kt} \quad (A)$$
$$T = T_0 + Ce^{-kt} = 15 + Ce^{-kt} \quad \because T_0 = 15°C$$
At $t = 0$, $T = T_i = 105°C$
$$T_i - T_0 = 105 - 15 = Ce^0 \Rightarrow C = 90 \quad \therefore T = 15 + 90e^{-kt}$$
When $t = 1$, $T = 60$ $\therefore 60 = 15 + 90e^{-1k} \Rightarrow e^{-k} = \frac{1}{2}$

When $t = 37\frac{1}{2}$, $37\frac{1}{2} = 15 + 90e^{-kt} = 15 + 90\left(\frac{1}{2}\right)^t \Rightarrow \frac{22\frac{1}{2}}{90} = \left(\frac{1}{2}\right)^t \quad \therefore t = 2.$

Additional time required $= 2\text{ hours} - 1\text{ hours} = 1\text{ hours}.$

Ex. 7 : A body at temperature $100°C$ is placed in a room where temperature is $20°C$, and cool to $60°C$ in 5 minutes. Find its temperature after a further interval of 3 minutes.

Solution: Let T be the temperature of a body at any time t. given T_0 = Room temp = $20°C$.
Therefore by Newton's Law of cooling, we have
$$\frac{dT}{dt} = -k(T - T_0), \quad \frac{dT}{dt} = -k(T - 20)$$
$$\frac{dT}{T - 20} = -k\, dt \quad (I)$$
At $t = 0$, $T = 100°C$ and let at $t = t$; $T = T°C$
Integrating between the above limits
$$\int_{100}^{T} \frac{dT}{T - 20} = -k \int_0^t dt$$
$$\left[\log(T-20)\right]_{100}^{T} = -kt \Rightarrow \left[\log(T-20) - \log 80\right] = -kt \quad \therefore \log\left(\frac{T-20}{80}\right) = -kt \quad (II)$$

Now at $t = 5$ minutes, $T = 60°C$
$$\therefore \log\left(\frac{60-20}{80}\right) = -5k \quad \therefore k = \frac{1}{5}\log 2.$$
And, after further 3 minutes, $t = 5 + 3 = 8$ Minutes,
Substituting in equation (II), we get
$$\therefore \log\left(\frac{T-20}{80}\right) = -8\frac{1}{5}\log 2 \quad \because k = \frac{1}{5}\log 2$$
$$\therefore \log\left(\frac{T-20}{80}\right) = \log\left(\frac{1}{2}\right)^{\frac{8}{5}}$$
$$\frac{T-20}{80} = \left(\frac{1}{2}\right)^{\frac{8}{5}} \quad \therefore T = 20 + 80\left(\frac{1}{2}\right)^{\frac{8}{5}} \approx 46.4°C.$$

Ex. 8 : If a thermometer is taken outdoors where the temperature is 0^0C, from a room in which the temperature is 21^0C, then the reading drops to 10^0C in 1 minutes. How long it will take to record the temperature 5^0C.

Solution: Let T be the temperature of at any time t. given $T_0 = 0^0C$.

Therefore by Newton's Law of cooling, we have

$$\frac{dT}{dt} = -k(T - T_0), \qquad \frac{dT}{dt} = -k(T - 0)$$

$$\frac{dT}{T} = -k\, dt \qquad (I)$$

At $t = 0$, $T = 21^0C$ and let at $t = t$; $T = T^0C$

Integrating between the above limits

$$\int_{21}^{T} \frac{dT}{T} = -k \int_0^t dt$$

$$[\log T]_{21}^T = -kt \Rightarrow [\log T - \log 21] = -kt \therefore \log\left(\frac{T}{21}\right) = -kt \quad (II)$$

Now at $t = 1$ minutes, $T = 10^0C$

$$\therefore \log\left(\frac{10}{21}\right) = -k$$

from (II) $t = \dfrac{1}{-k}\log\left(\dfrac{T}{21}\right) = \dfrac{\log\left(\dfrac{T}{21}\right)}{\log\left(\dfrac{10}{21}\right)} = \dfrac{\log\left(\dfrac{5}{21}\right)}{\log\left(\dfrac{10}{21}\right)} = 1$ minute, 56 seconds $\because T = 5^0C$

Hence time is 1 minute, 56 seconds.

Ex. 9 : Water at temperature 100^0C, cools in 10 minutes, to 80^0C, in a room temperature 25^0C. Find

(i) Temperature of water after 20 minutes.

(ii) Time when the temperature is 40^0C.

Solution : Let T be the temperature of water at any time t. given $T_0 = 25^0C$.

Therefore by Newton's Law of cooling, we have

$$\frac{dT}{dt} = -k(T-T_0), \qquad \frac{dT}{dt} = -k(T-25) \qquad \frac{dT}{T-25} = -k\,dt \qquad (I)$$

At $t=0$, $T=100^\circ C$ and let at $t=t$; $T=T^\circ C$

Integrating between the above limits $\displaystyle\int_{100}^{T}\frac{dT}{T-25} = -k\int_0^t dt$

$$\left[\log(T-25)\right]_{100}^{T} = -kt \Rightarrow \left[\log(T-25)-\log 75\right] = -kt \therefore \log\left(\frac{T-25}{75}\right) = -kt \quad (II)$$

Now at $t=10$ minutes, $T=80^\circ C$

$$\therefore \log\left(\frac{80-25}{75}\right) = -10k \therefore k = \frac{1}{10}\log\left(\frac{75}{55}\right) \text{ i.e. } 10k = \log\left(\frac{75}{55}\right) \therefore e^{10k} = \frac{75}{55} = \frac{15}{11}$$

(i) Let T be the temperature of water after 20 minutes. From (II)

$$\log\left(\frac{T-25}{75}\right) = -20k \therefore \frac{T-25}{75} = e^{-20k} = \left(e^{10k}\right)^{-2} = \left(\frac{15}{11}\right)^{-2}$$

$$\therefore T = 25 + 75\left(\frac{15}{11}\right)^{-2} = 65.33^\circ C.$$

(ii) Let $T = 40^\circ C$. From (II)

$$\log\left(\frac{40-25}{75}\right) = -kt \therefore \log\left(\frac{15}{75}\right) = -kt \Rightarrow -\log 5 = -kt$$

$$\therefore t = \frac{1}{k}\log 5 = \frac{1}{7.85\times 10^{-3}}\log 5 = 52.85 \text{ minutes}.$$

Ex. 10: The temperature of the air is $40^\circ C$ and the substance cools from $80^\circ C$ to $60^\circ C$ in 20 minutes, What will be the temperature of the substance after 40 minutes.

Solution: Let T be the temperature of the substance at any time t and the unit of time be minute. Therefore by Newton's Law of cooling, we have

$$\frac{dT}{dt} = -k(T-T_0), \qquad \frac{dT}{dt} = -k(T-40) \qquad \because T_0 = 40^\circ C$$

$$\frac{dT}{(T-40)} = -k\,dt \qquad (A)$$

Integrating above equation (A), we get

$$\int\frac{dT}{(T-40)} = \int -k\,dt$$

$$\log(T-40) = -kt + C \qquad (B)$$

Given at $t=0$, $T=80^\circ C$ $\therefore \log(80-40) = -k.0 + C, \Rightarrow C = \log 40,$

Substituting $C = \log 70$ in equation (B), we get

$$\log(T-40) = -kt + \log 40 \Rightarrow kt = \log 40 - \log(T-40) \qquad (C)$$

again at $t=20$, $T=60^\circ C$ $\therefore 20k = \log 40 - \log 20 \qquad (D)$

$$\therefore k = \frac{1}{20}\log 2$$

$$\therefore t\frac{1}{20}\log 2 = \log 40 - \log(T-40)$$

Now when $T=40$

$$40\frac{1}{20}\log 2 = \log\frac{40}{T-40} \quad \therefore \log 4 = \log\frac{40}{T-40}$$

$$\therefore 4 = \frac{40}{T-40} \Rightarrow T = 50^\circ C.$$

Ex. 11: Temperature of water initially is $100^\circ C$ and that of surrounding is $20^\circ C$ if water cools down to $60^\circ C$ in first 20 minutes. During what time will it cool to $30^\circ C$.

Solution: Let T be the temperature of a water at any time t.
By Newton's law of cooling, we have

$$\frac{dT}{dt} = -k(T - T_0)$$

$$= -k(T - 20) \quad \because T_0 = 20^\circ C$$

$$\frac{dT}{(T - 20)} = -k\, dt$$

At $t = 0$, $T = 100^\circ C$ and at $t = 20$, $T = 60^\circ C$

$$\therefore \int_{100}^{60} \frac{dT}{(T - 20)} = -k \int_0^{20} dt$$

$$\left[\log(T - 20)\right]_{100}^{60} = -k[t]_0^{20}$$

$$\left[\log(60 - 20) - \log(100 - 20)\right] = -k[20 - 0]$$

$$\log \frac{40}{80} = -20k \quad \therefore k = \frac{1}{20}\log 2 = 0.03466$$

Again at $t = 0$, $T = 100$ and at $t = T$, $T = 30$

$$\int_{100}^{30} \frac{dT}{(T - 20)} = -k \int_0^T dt$$

$$\left[\log(T - 20)\right]_{100}^{30} = -k[t]_0^T$$

$$\left[\log(30 - 20) - \log(100 - 20)\right] = -k[T - 0]$$

$$\log \frac{10}{80} = -kT \Rightarrow \log 8 = kT \quad \therefore T = \frac{1}{0.03466}\log 8 = 59.99 \approx 1 \text{ hours.}$$

Ex. 12: If the temperature of air is $30^\circ K$ and the substance cools from $37^\circ K$ to $34^\circ K$ in 15 minutes. Find when the temperature will be $31^\circ K$.

Solution: Let T be the temperature of substance at any time t. By Newton's law of cooling, we have

$$\frac{dT}{dt} = -k(T - T_0)$$

$$= -k(T - 30) \quad \because T_0 = 30^\circ C$$

$$\frac{dT}{(T - 30)} = -k\, dt$$

As substance cools from $37^\circ K$ to $34^\circ K$ in 15 minutes
integrating between the limits 0 to 15, we get

$$\therefore \int_{37}^{34} \frac{dT}{(T - 30)} = -k \int_0^{15} dt$$

$$\left[\log(T - 30)\right]_{37}^{34} = -k[t]_0^{15}$$

$$\left[\log(34 - 30) - \log(37 - 30)\right] = -k[15 - 0]$$

$$\log \frac{4}{7} = -15k \quad \therefore k = \frac{1}{15}\log \frac{7}{4}$$

Again when temparature is $31^\circ K$

$$\int_{370}^{310} \frac{dT}{(T-300)} = -k\int_0^t dt$$

$$\left[\log(T-300)\right]_{370}^{310} = -k[t]_0^t$$

$$\left[\log(310-300) - \log(370-300)\right] = -k[t-0]$$

$$\log\frac{10}{70} = -kt \Rightarrow \log 7 = \frac{1}{15}\log\frac{7}{4}t \quad \therefore t = \frac{15\log 7}{\log 7/4} = 52 \text{ minutes}.$$

Ex. 13: It the dead body is located in a room that is kept at a constant temperature $68^0 F$. For some time after death, the body will radiate heat into the cooler room causing the body temperature decreases. Assuming that the victim's temperature was normal $98.6^0 F$ at the time of death. Find the murder time if the doctor arrived at 9.40PM and immediately measured the dead body temperature as $94.4^0 F$ and made another measurement at 11.00P.M the body temperature as $89.2^0 F$.

Solution: Let T be the temperature of body at any time t. By Newton's law of cooling,

$$\frac{dT}{dt} = -k(T-T_0) = -k(T-68) \quad \because T_0 = 68^0 F$$

$$\frac{dT}{(T-68)} = -kdt$$

At $t = 0$, $T = 94.4$ and at $t = 80$, $T = 89.2$

$$\therefore \int_{94.4}^{89.2} \frac{dT}{(T-68)} = -k\int_0^{80} dt$$

$$\left[\log(T-68)\right]_{94.4}^{89.2} = -k[t]_0^{80}$$

$$\left[\log(89.2-68) - \log(94.4-30)\right] = -k[80-0]$$

$$\log\frac{21.2}{26.4} = 80k \quad \therefore k = \frac{1}{80}\log 1.242 = 0.0027$$

Again, at the time of death $T = 98.6^0 F$

$$\int_{94.4}^{98.6} \frac{dT}{(T-68)} = -k\int_0^t dt$$

$$\left[\log(T-68)\right]_{94.4}^{98.6} = -k[t]_0^t$$

$$\left[\log(98.6-68) - \log(94.4-68)\right] = -k[t-0]$$

$$\log\frac{30.6}{26.4} = kt \quad \therefore t = \frac{1}{k}\log 1.1591 = 0.0027 \log 1.1591 = 54.6799 \approx 55 \text{ minutes}.$$

Hence the death occurred 54 minutes before first measurement 9.40PM. which is chosen as time zero. This puts the murder at about 8.46 PM.

Ex. 14 : A body of mass m falling from rest is subjected to the force gravity and an air resistance proportional to the square of velocity kv^2.

If it falls through a distance x and possesses a velocity v at that instant. Prove that
$$\frac{2kx}{m} = \log\left(\frac{a^2}{\sqrt{a^2 - v^2}}\right) \text{ where } mg = kv^2.$$

Solution : The force acting on the body is (i) the resistance due to air i.e. kv^2 (vertically upward). By Newton's law of motion, the equation is

$$mv\frac{dv}{dx} = mg - kv^2$$

$$= k\alpha^2 - kv^2 = k(\alpha^2 - v^2)$$

$$\int \frac{vdv}{\alpha^2 - v^2} = \frac{k}{m}\int dx + C$$

$$\frac{-1}{2}\log(\alpha^2 - v^2) = \frac{kx}{m} + C$$

At $x = 0$, when $v = 0$, $\frac{-1}{2}\log \alpha^2 = C$

$$\frac{1}{2}\left[\log \alpha^2 - \log(\alpha^2 - v^2)\right] = \frac{kx}{m}$$

$$\log \frac{\alpha^2}{\alpha^2 - v^2} = \frac{2kx}{m}$$

TEST YOUR KNOWLEDGE

1. The air temperature is 20^0C. A body cools from 140^0C to 80^0C in 20 min. How much time will it take to reach a temperature of 35^0C.   Ans: 60min.

2. If the temperature of the air is 20^0C and the temperature of a body drops from 100^0C to 75^0C in 10 min. what will be its temperature after 30^0C? When will the temperature be 30^0C?   Ans: 46^0C, 55.5 min

3. If water at temperature 100^0C, cools to 80^0C, in 10minutes, in a room maintained at temperature of 30^0C. Find when the temperature of water will become 40^0C.   Ans: 57.9 minutes.

4. The temperature of a body drops from 100^0C to 60^0C in one minutes when the temperature of the surrounding is 20^0C, What will be the temperature of a body at the end of the second minutes.   Ans: 40^0C.

5. If water at temperature 100^0C, cools to 88^0C, in 10 minutes, in a room maintained at temperature of 25^0C. Find the temperature of water after 20 minutes. Ans: 77.9^0C. minutes.

6. If the temperature of the air is 30^0C and the substance cools from 100^0C to 70^0C in 15 min. Find when the temperature will be 40^0C. Ans: 52.5 min.

Rate of Growth and Decay

If the rate of change of a quantity y at any time t is directly proportional to y, then $\frac{dy}{dt} \propto y$.

If k is the constant of proportionality, then the required differential equation is $\frac{dy}{dt} = ky$.

For Growth, $k > 0$ and the differential equation is $\frac{dy}{dt} = ky$, $k > 0$.

For Decay, the differential equation is $\frac{dy}{dt} = -ky$, $k > 0$.

OR This law states that disintegration at any instant is proportional to the amount of material present. If y is the amount of material at any time t, then $\frac{dy}{dt} = ky$.

Examples on Rate of Growth and Decay

Ex. 1: In a certain culture of bacteria, the rate of increase is proportional to the number present. If it is found that, the number doubles in 4 hours. How many be expected at the end of 12 hours.

Solution: Let y be the number of bacteria present at time t hours.

$$\therefore \frac{dy}{dt} = ky \Rightarrow \frac{dy}{y} = kdt$$

Integrating both sides,

$$\int \frac{dy}{y} = k \int dt + C \quad \therefore \log y = kt + C$$

Let y_0 be the bacteria present at time $t = 0$, then

$\log y_0 = C$

$\therefore \log y = kt + \log y_0 \Rightarrow \log y - \log y_0 = kt$

$\therefore \log \left(\frac{y}{y_0} \right) = kt$

$\therefore \frac{y}{y_0} = e^{kt}$

$\therefore y = y_0 e^{kt}$

Now, at time $t = 4$ hours, the number doubles,

Therefore at $t = 4$ hours, $y = 2y_0$

$\therefore 2y_0 = y_0 e^{4k}$

$e^{4k} = 2$

When $t = 12$ hours,

$\therefore y = y_0 e^{12k} = y_0 \left(e^{4k}\right)^3 = y_0 (2)^3 = 8 y_0$

$\therefore y = 8 y_0$ i.e. at the end of 12 hours, bacteria present are 8 times the original numbers.

Ex. 2: In a culture of yeast, at each instant, the time rate of change of active ferment is proportional to the amount present. If the active ferment doubles in two hours, how much can expected at the end of 8 hours at the same rate of growth. Find also, how much time will elapse, before the active ferment grows to eight times its initial value.

Solution: Let y be the quantity of active ferment present at time t.

$\therefore \dfrac{dy}{dt} = ky \Rightarrow \dfrac{dy}{y} = k\, dt$

Integrating both sides,

$\displaystyle\int \dfrac{dy}{y} = k\int dt + C \qquad \therefore \log y = kt + C$

Let $y = y_0$ be the active ferment present at time $t = 0$, then

$\log y_0 = C$

$\therefore \log y = kt + \log y_0 \Rightarrow \log y - \log y_0 = kt$

$\therefore \log\left(\dfrac{y}{y_0}\right) = kt \qquad\qquad (I)$

The active ferment doubles in 2 hours,

$\therefore y = 2 y_0$ at $t = 2$

$\therefore \log\left(\dfrac{2 y_0}{y_0}\right) = 2k \Rightarrow k = \dfrac{1}{2}\log 2$

From equation (I), we get

$\log\left(\dfrac{y}{y_0}\right) = \dfrac{t}{2}\log 2$

$\Rightarrow y = y_0 e^{\frac{t}{2}\log 2}$

(i) When $t = 8$,

$y = y_0 e^{\frac{8}{2}\log 2} = y_0 e^{4\log 2} = y_0 e^{\log 2^4} = y_0 \cdot 2^4$

$y = 16 y_0$

Thus, active ferment grows 16 times of its initial values at the end of 8 hours.

(ii) When $y = 8 y_0$,

$8 y_0 = y_0 e^{\frac{t}{2}\log 2} \Rightarrow 8 = e^{\frac{t}{2}\log 2}$

$$\log 8 = \frac{t}{2}\log 2$$

$$\log 2^3 = \frac{t}{2}\log 2 \Rightarrow 3\log 2 = \frac{t}{2}\log 2 \quad \therefore t = 6 \text{ hours.}$$

Thus, active ferment grows 8 times of its initial values at the end of 6 hours.

Ex. 3: Find the half-life of uranium, which disintegrates at a rate proportional to the amount present at any instant. Given that m_1 and m_2 grams of uranium are present at time t_1 and t_2 respectively.

Solution: Let m grams of uranium be present at any time t.
The equation of disintegration of uranium is

$$\therefore \frac{dm}{dt} = -km \Rightarrow \frac{dm}{m} = -kdt$$

Integrating both sides,

$$\int \frac{dm}{m} = -k\int dt + C$$

$$\log m = -kt + C$$

Let $m = m_0$ be the uranium present at time $t = 0$, then

$$\log m_0 = C$$

$$\therefore \log m = -kt + \log m_0 \Rightarrow \log m - \log m_0 = -kt$$

$$\Rightarrow \log m_0 - \log m = kt \qquad (I)$$

At $t = t_1$, $m = m_1$ and at $t = t_2$, $m = m_2$

$$\log m_0 - \log m_1 = kt_1 \qquad (II)$$

$$\log m_0 - \log m_2 = kt_2 \qquad (III)$$

Subtracting equation (II) from (III), we get

$$\log m_1 - \log m_2 = k(t_2 - t_1) \qquad \therefore k = \frac{\log\left(\frac{m_1}{m_2}\right)}{(t_2 - t_1)}.$$

Let T be the half-life of uranium i.e. at $t = T$, $m = \frac{1}{2}m_0$.

From equation (I), we get

$$kT = \log m_0 - \log \frac{m_0}{2} = \log 2$$

$$\therefore T = \frac{\log 2}{k} = \frac{(t_2 - t_1)\log 2}{\log\left(\frac{m_1}{m_2}\right)}. \qquad \because k = \frac{\log\left(\frac{m_1}{m_2}\right)}{(t_2 - t_1)}$$

Ex. 4 : The rate at which the ice melts is proportional to the amount of ice at the instant. Find the amount of ice left after 2 hours if half the quantity melts in 30 minutes.

Solution: Let m be the amount of ice present at any time t.

$$\therefore \frac{dm}{dt} = km \Rightarrow \frac{dm}{m} = k\,dt$$

Integrating both sides,

$$\int \frac{dm}{m} = k\int dt + C$$

$$\log m = kt + C$$

Let $m = m_0$ at time $t = 0$, then

$$\log m_0 = C$$

$$\therefore \log m = kt + \log m_0 \qquad (I)$$

At $t = \frac{1}{2}$ hours, $m = \frac{m_0}{2}$

$$\log \frac{m_0}{2} = \frac{k}{2} + \log m_0$$

$$\log \frac{m_0}{2} - \log m_0 = \frac{k}{2} \Rightarrow \log \frac{m_0}{2m_0} = \frac{k}{2}$$

$$\log \frac{1}{2} = \frac{k}{2} \Rightarrow k = 2\log \frac{1}{2}$$

From equation (I), we get

$$\log m = \left(2\log \frac{1}{2}\right) t + \log m_0$$

On putting $t = 2$ hours, we get

$$\log m = 4\log \frac{1}{2} + \log m_0$$

$$\Rightarrow \log \frac{m}{m_0} = \log \left(\frac{1}{2}\right)^4$$

$$\therefore \frac{m}{m_0} = \frac{1}{16} \Rightarrow m = \frac{m_0}{16}.$$

After 2 hours, the amount of ice left equal to 1/16 of the amount of ice at the beginning.

TEST YOUR KNOWLEDGE

1. Find the time required for the sum of money to double itself at 5% per annum compounded continuously. **Ans:** 13.9 Years

2. If the population of a country doubles in 50 years, in how many years will it triple under the assumption that the rate of increase is proportional to the number of inhabitants? **Ans:** 79 Years.

F.E. (Sem. II) M II (SU) — Applications of Ordinary Differential Equations of First Order...

3. If the population of a country doubles in 50 years, in how many years will it triple under the assumption that the rate of increase is proportional to the number of inhabitants?
Ans: 79 Years.

4. Radium decomposes at the rate proportional to the amount present. If 5% of the original amount disappears in 50 years, how much will remain after 100 years? **Ans.** 90.25%

5. If 30% of a radioactive substance disappeared in 10 days, how long will it take for 90% of it to disappear? **Ans.** 64.5 days

6. Radium decomposes at the rate proportional to the quantity of radium present. Suppose that it is found that in 25 years approximately 1.1% of certain quantity of radium has decomposed. Determine approximately how long will it take for one half of the original amount of radium to decompose. **Ans.** $1564.66 \approx 1565$ years.

7. Radium decomposes at the rate proportional to the amount present. If a fraction M of the original amount disappears in 1 year, how much will remain at the end of 21 years?
Ans. $(1 - 1/M)^{21}$ times the original amount.

Year Wise University Question Papers -13 Semesters

Dec-2013 (10/12/2013)

1. Find the orthoganal trajectory of the curve $x^2 + 4y^2 = a^2$.	6
2. The charge q on the plate of condenser C chared through a resistance R by a steady voltage V satishfied the differential equation $R\dfrac{dq}{dt} + \dfrac{q}{c} = V$ at $t = 0$ and $q = 0$ initially. Show that charge q at any time t is given by $q = CV[1 - e^{-t/RC}]$.	6

August-2013 (16/08/2013) Re-exam

1. Find the orthoganal trajectory of the family of the curve $r^n = a \sin n\theta$.	6
2. When a switch is closed in a circuit containing a battery of voltage E, Resistance R and an inductance L, the current is built up at a rate $L\dfrac{di}{dt} + Ri = E$, Find i as a function of t.	5

May-2013 (18/05/2013)

1. Find the orthgonal trajectory of the family of curves $\dfrac{x^2}{a^2} + \dfrac{y^2}{b^2 + x} = 1$, where x is a parameter.	6
2. Find the orthoganal trajectory to the curve $r = a(1 + \sin\theta)$	5

May-2012 (29/05/2012)

1. Find the orthogonal trajectories of the family of confocal conics $\dfrac{x^2}{a^2} + \dfrac{y^2}{b^2 + \lambda}$, where λ is parameter.	8
2. The equation of electromotive force in terms of current i for an electric circuit having resistance R and a condenser of capacity C, in series $E = Ri + \int \dfrac{i}{c} dt$. Find the current i at any time t. When $E = E_0 \sin \omega t$.	9

(2.53)

Nov-2012 (20/11/2012)

1. Find the equation of orthogonal trajectories of the family of circle $x^2 - 2hx + y^2 = 4$ [5]

2. Find the orthogonal trajectories of $r^2 = \dfrac{a}{\cos \theta}$, where a is parameter. [5]

3. A voltage Ee^{-at} is applied at $t = 0$ to a circuit containing inductance L, Resistance R satisfies the differntial equation $L\dfrac{di}{dt} + Ri = Ee^{-at}$.

   Show that the current at any time t is given by $i\dfrac{E}{R-at}\left[e^{-at} - e^{\frac{-Rt}{2L}} \right]$. [6]

Dec-2011 (16/12/2011)

1. Show that a system of confocal and coaxial parabolas $y^2 = 4a(x+a)$ itself orthogonal. [6]

2. A 12 V battery is connected to a simple series circuit in which the inductance is $\dfrac{1}{2}H$ and the resistance is 10 Ω, satisfies differential equation $\dfrac{di}{dt} + 20i = 24$. Determine the current i if $i(0) = 0$. [5]

May-2011 (25/05/2011)

1. Find the orthogonal trajectories to the family of curve $\dfrac{2a}{r} = 1 + \cos\theta$; where a is parameter. [5]

2. The current i in an electric circuit containing resistance R and self inductance L satisfies the differential equation $L\dfrac{di}{dt} + Ri = E\sin \omega t$, where R, E, ω are constant. If $i = 0$ when $t = 0$, find the current at time t. [6]

Nov-2010 (18/11/2010)

1. A voltage Ee^{-at} is applied at $t = 0$ to a circuit containing inductance L and resistance R. Find the current at time t if initially at $t = 0, i = 0$. [6]

2. Find the orthogonal trajectories of the curve $x^2 + 4y^2 = a^2$. [5]

May-2010 (19/05/2010)

1. A constant electromotive force E volts is applied to a circuit containing a constsnt resistance R ohms in series and a constsnt inductance L henries. If the initial current is zero, show that the current builds up to half its theoretical maximum in Llog2/R seconds. [5]

2. Find the orthogonal trajectories of the curve $r = a(1-\cos\theta)$.	6
May-2009 (19/05/2009)	
1. When a switch is closed, the current built up in an electric circuit is given by $E = Ri + L\dfrac{di}{dt}$. If $L = 640, R = 250, E = 500$ and $i = 0$ when $t = 0$. Show that the current will approach 2 amp when $t \to \infty$.	6
2. Find the orthgonal trajectory of the family of curves $\dfrac{x^2}{a^2} + \dfrac{y^2}{b^2 + x} = 1$, where x is a parameter.	6
Nov-2009 (16/11/2009)	
1. The equation of electromotive force in terms of current i for an electrical circuit having resistance R and a condenser of capacity c, in series is $E = Ri + \int\dfrac{i}{c}dt$. Find the current i at any time t, when $E = E_0 \sin\omega t$.	6
2. Find the orthogonal trajectories of the curve $r^n = a^n \sin n\theta$.	5
May-2008 (17/05/2008)	
1. A voltage Ee^{-at} is applied at $t = 0$ to a circuit containing inductance L, Resistance R Show that at any time t the current $i\dfrac{E}{R-at}\left[e^{-at} - e^{\frac{-Rt}{2L}}\right]$.	6
2. Find the orthogonal trajectories of the curve $y^2 - x^2 + 4xy - 2cx = 0$.	6
Nov-2008 (10/11/2008)	
1. Find the orthogonal trajectories of $\dfrac{2a}{r} = 1 + \cos\theta$. Where a is a parameter.	
2. The charge q on the plate of a condenser C charged through a resistance R by a steady voltage V satisfies the differential equation $R\dfrac{dq}{dt} + \dfrac{q}{c} = V$. If $q = 0$ at $t = 0$, show that $q = CV\left(1 - e^{-t/RC}\right)$.	5

UNIT - III

NUMERICAL SOLUTION OF ORDINARY DIFFERENTIAL EQUATIONS OF FIRST ORDER AND FIRST DEGREE

INTRODUCTION

Many ordinary differential equations can be solved by analytical methods discussed earlier in first chapter. But in science and Engineering, there arise many problems which can be reduced to the problems of solving differential equation satisfying certain conditions, but all the differential equations cannot be solved analytically. There are many techniques which always exist for finding the solution of such equations. Some times it so happens that problems cannot be solved at all or leads to a difficult situation, in such cases numerical technique is always useful

For Ex. suppose a liquid is poured in to a tank having uniform Cross-sectional area A (Square units) at the rate of Q (cu units/sec). Suppose further that the liquid flows out of the tank through a value of cross sectional area B (Square units) with velocity v. If x_1, x_2 are the height of the liquid at time t_1 and t_2, the effective rise of the quantity of liquid in the tank in this time is equal to the difference between the quantity of liquid that is poured into it and the quantity of the liquid that flows out through the valve. Hence we get

$(x_1 - x_2)A = Q(t_1 - t_2) - Bv(t_1 - t_2)$

i.e. $A \dfrac{(x_1 - x_2)}{(t_1 - t_2)} = Q - Bv$

Taking the limit as $t_1 \to t_2$, We get

$A \dfrac{dx}{dt} = Q - Bv$

By Bernoulli's principle (velocity) $v = \sqrt{2gx}$

g = gravitational Acceleration and

x = height of liquid left in the tank

$A \dfrac{dx}{dt} = Q - \sqrt{2g} \cdot \sqrt{x}$

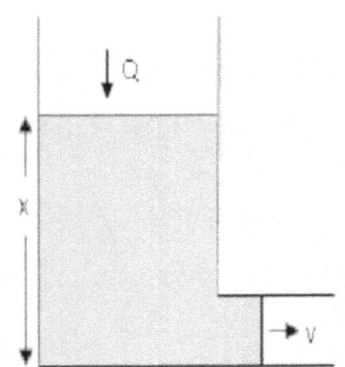

If A is constant, but Q is an unknown function of time then the above equation becomes

$\dfrac{dx}{dt} = f(t) - c_2 \cdot \sqrt{x}$

This equation cannot be solved by analytical method

So we need numerical method for solving such examples.

In this chapter, we shall discuss some of the methods for obtaining numerical solution of first order and first degree ordinary differential equations $\frac{dy}{dx} = f(x, y)$ subject to the condition

$y(x_0) = y_0$ (i.e. $x = x_0, y = y_0$ or $y = y_0$ at $x = x_0$)

The general solution of this equation can be obtained in following two types:

1. The dependent variable y is expressed as a power series in terms of the independent variable x. This method is known as semi-analytic method. Taylor's method belongs to this type.

2. The solution is obtained by using the set of tabulated values of x and y. This method is known as step-by-step method or marching methods, because the values of the dependent variable are calculated by short-steps for equal interval values of the independent variable. Euler's method, Modified Euler's method, Runge-Kutta method belongs to this type.

Note : 1. Differential equation which is solved by analytical methods can be solved by numerically also.

2. In this chapter, we have used the **Calculator** by fixing four digits

(Process for fixing four digits in Calculator: Press mode button three times, then press 1 and then 4 to fix four digits)

TAYLOR'S METHOD

Consider the differential equation, $\frac{dy}{dx} = f(x, y)$ which is to be solved, subjected to the condition $y(x_0) = y_0$ or $y = y_0$ at $x = x_0$ i.e. x_0 and y_0 are initial values of variables x and y respectively.

If $y = f(x)$ is the solution of given equation, then the Taylor's series expansion about $x = x_0$ gives $y = f(x) = f(x_0) + (x - x_0) f'(x_0) + \frac{(x - x_0)^2}{2!} f''(x_0) + \frac{(x - x_0)^3}{3!} f'''(x_0) + \ldots$

Also we can write it as $y = f(x) = y_0 + (x - x_0) y_0' + \frac{(x - x_0)^2}{2!} y_0'' + \frac{(x - x_0)^3}{3!} y_0''' + \ldots$

Find the values $y_0', y_0'', y_0''' \ldots$ by successive differentiation and y_0 is known from initial condition.

Remarks :
1. No Special starting point is required
2. A large interval can be used by increasing the number of terms
3. Method is complicated for calculating high order derivative

EX.S ON TAYLOR'S METHODS

Ex. 1: Using Taylor's series method, obtain a solution of the differential equation $\frac{dy}{dx} = x^2 + y^2$ with $y = 0$ when $x = 0$ at $x = 0.4$

Solution: Given $\frac{dy}{dx} = y' = x^2 + y^2$, $x_0 = 0$, $y_0 = 0$, $x = 0.4$

We know by Taylor's method $y = y_0 + xy'_0 + \dfrac{x^2}{2}y''_0 + \dfrac{x^3}{3!}y'''_0 + ...$ (A)

$y' = x^2 + y^2 \Rightarrow y'_0 = x_0^2 + y_0^2 = 0 + 0 = 0$

$y'' = 2x + 2yy' \Rightarrow y''_0 = 2x_0 + 2y_0 y'_0 = 2.0 + 2.0.0 = 0$

$y''' = 2 + 2y'^2 + 2yy'' \Rightarrow y'''_0 = 2 + 2y'^2_0 + 2y_0 y''_0 = 2 + 2.0 + 2.0 = 2$

$y^{iv} = 0 + 2.2y'y'' + 2yy''' + 2y'y'' = 2[3y'y'' + yy''']$

$\Rightarrow y^{iv}_0 = 2[3y'_0 y''_0 + y'''_0] = 0$

$y^v = 2[(3y'y''' + y''^2) + yy^{iv} + y'y'''] = 8y'y''' + 6y''^2 + 2yy^{iv}$

$\Rightarrow y^v_0 = 8y'_0 y'''_0 + 6y''^2_0 + 2y_0 y^{iv}_0 = 0$

$y^{vi} = 8[y'y^{iv} + y''y''' + 12y''y''' + 2yy^v + 2y'y^{iv}]$

$y^{vi}_0 = 8[y'_0 y^{iv}_0 + y''_0 y'''_0 + 12y''_0 y'''_0 + 2y_0 y^v_0 + 2y'_0 y^{iv}_0] = 16$

$y^{vii} = 8[y'y^v + y''y^{iv} + y''y^{iv} + y'''^2 + 12y''y^{iv} + 12y'''^2 + 2yy^{vi} + 2y'y^v + 2y'y^v + 2y''y^{iv}]$

$y^{vii}_0 = 8[y'_0 y^v_0 + y''_0 y^{iv}_0 + y''_0 y^{iv}_0 + y'''^2_0 + 12y''_0 y^{iv}_0 + 12y'''^2_0 + 2y_0 y^{vi}_0 + 2y'_0 y^v_0 + 2y'_0 y^v_0 + 2y''_0 y^{iv}_0] = 416$

Substituting in equation (A), we get

$y = 0 + x.0 + \dfrac{x^2}{2}.0 + \dfrac{x^3}{3!}.2 + \dfrac{x^4}{4!}.0 + \dfrac{x^5}{5!}.0 + \dfrac{x^6}{6!}.0 + \dfrac{x^7}{7!}.416... = \dfrac{x^3}{3} + \dfrac{x^7}{7!}.416 + ...$

At $x = 0.4$ $y = \dfrac{(0.4)^3}{3} + \dfrac{(0.4)^7}{7!}416 + ... = 0.0215$

Ex. 2 : Using Taylor's series method, obtain a solution of the differential equation $\dfrac{dy}{dx} = 2y + 3e^x$ with $y = 0$ when $x = 0$ at $x = 0.2$

Solution: Given $\dfrac{dy}{dx} = y' = 2y + 3e^x$, $x_0 = 0$, $y_0 = 0$, $x = 0.2$

We know by Taylor's method $y = y_0 + xy'_0 + \dfrac{x^2}{2}y''_0 + \dfrac{x^3}{3!}y'''_0 + ...$ (A)

$y' = 2y + 3e^x \Rightarrow y'_0 = 2y_0 + 3e^{x_0} = 2.0 + 3e^0 = 3$

$y'' = 2y' + 3e^x \Rightarrow y''_0 = 2y'_0 + 3e^{x_0} = 2.3 + 3e^0 = 9$

$y''' = 2y'' + 3e^x \Rightarrow y'''_0 = 2y''_0 + 3e^{x_0} = 2.9 + 3e^0 = 21$

$y^{iv} = 2y''' + 3e^x \Rightarrow y^{iv}_0 = 2y'''_0 + 3e^{x_0} = 2.21 + 3e^0 = 45$

Substituting in equation (A), we get

$y = 0 + x.3 + \dfrac{x^2}{2}.9 + \dfrac{x^3}{3!}.21 + \dfrac{x^4}{4!}.45 + ... = 3x + \dfrac{9x^2}{2} + \dfrac{7x^3}{2} + \dfrac{15x^4}{8} + ...$

At $x = 0.2$ $y = 3(0.2) + \dfrac{9(0.2)^2}{2} + \dfrac{7(0.2)^3}{2} + \dfrac{15(0.2)^4}{8} + \ldots = 0.8110$.

Ex. 3 : Using Taylor's series method, obtain a solution of the differential equation $\dfrac{dy}{dx} = 2y + 3e^x$ with $y = 1$ when $x = 0$ at $x = 0.1$ and $x = 0.2$

Solution: Step-I Given $\dfrac{dy}{dx} = y' = 2y + 3e^x$, $x_0 = 0$, $y_0 = 1$, $x = 0.1$

We know by Taylor's method $y = y_0 + xy'_0 + \dfrac{x^2}{2} y''_0 + \dfrac{x^3}{3!} y'''_0 + \ldots$ (A)

$y' = 2y + 3e^x \Rightarrow y'_0 = 2y_0 + 3e^{x_0} = 2 \cdot 1 + 3e^0 = 5$

$y'' = 2y' + 3e^x \Rightarrow y''_0 = 2y'_0 + 3e^{x_0} = 2 \cdot 5 + 3e^0 = 13$

$y''' = 2y'' + 3e^x \Rightarrow y'''_0 = 2y''_0 + 3e^{x_0} = 2 \cdot 13 + 3e^0 = 29$

$y^{iv} = 2y''' + 3e^x \Rightarrow y^{iv}{}_0 = 2y'''_0 + 3e^{x_0} = 2 \cdot 29 + 3e^0 = 61$

Substituting in equation (A), we get

$y = 1 + x(5) + \dfrac{x^2}{2}(13) + \dfrac{x^3}{3!}(29) + \dfrac{x^4}{4!}(61) + \ldots = 1 + 5x + \dfrac{13x^2}{2} + \dfrac{29x^3}{3!} + \dfrac{61x^4}{4!} + \ldots$

At $x = 0.1$, $y = 1 + 5(0.1) + \dfrac{13(0.1)^2}{2} + \dfrac{29(0.1)^3}{3!} + \dfrac{61(0.1)^4}{4!} + \ldots = 1.5701$.

Step-II Again $\dfrac{dy}{dx} = y' = 2y + 3e^x$, $x_0 = 0.1$, $y_0 = 1.5701$, $x = 0.2$

$y' = 2y + 3e^x \Rightarrow y'_0 = 2y_0 + 3e^{x_0} = 2(1.5701) + 3e^{0.1} = 6.4557$

$y'' = 2y' + 3e^x \Rightarrow y''_0 = 2y'_0 + 3e^{x_0} = 2(6.4757) + 3e^{0.1} = 16.2269$

$y''' = 2y'' + 3e^x \Rightarrow y'''_0 = 2y''_0 + 3e^{x_0} = 2(16.226)9 + 3e^{0.1} = 35.7693$

$y^{iv} = 2y''' + 3e^x \Rightarrow y^{iv}{}_0 = 2y'''_0 + 3e^{x_0} = 2(35.7693) + 3e^{0.1} = 74.8543$

$\therefore y = y_0 + xy'_0 + \dfrac{x^2}{2} y''_0 + \dfrac{x^3}{3!} y'''_0 + \ldots$ becomes

$= 1.5701 + x(6.4557) + \dfrac{x^2}{2}(16.2269) + \dfrac{x^3}{3!}(35.7693) + \dfrac{x^4}{4!}(74.8543) + \ldots$

$= 1.5701 + 6.4557x + \dfrac{16.2269 x^2}{2} + \dfrac{35.7693 x^3}{3!} + \dfrac{74.8543 x^4}{4!} + \ldots$

At $x = 0.2$, $y = 1.5701 + 6.4557(0.2) + \dfrac{16.2269(0.2)^2}{2} + \dfrac{35.7693(0.2)^3}{3!} + \dfrac{74.8541(0.2)^4}{4!} + \ldots$

$= 3.2385$.

Ex. 4: Solve $\dfrac{dy}{dx} = x + y^2$, $y = 0$ when $x = 0$ and find y when $x = 0.5$ by Taylor's method.

Solution: Given $\dfrac{dy}{dx} = y' = x + y^2$, $x_0 = 0$, $y_0 = 0$, $x = 0.2$ **SUK: Nov-08,12**

We know by Taylor's method $y = y_0 + xy_0' + \dfrac{x^2}{2} y_0'' + \dfrac{x^3}{3!} y_0''' + ...$ (A)

$y' = x + y^2 \Rightarrow y_0' = 0$

$y'' = 1 + 2yy' \Rightarrow y_0'' = 1$

$y''' = 2\left[yy'' + y'^2\right] \Rightarrow y_0''' = 0$

Similarly $y_0^{iv} = 0$, $y_0^v = 6$

Substituting in equation (A), we get

$y = 0 + x.0 + \dfrac{x^2}{2}.1 + \dfrac{x^3}{3!}.0 + \dfrac{x^4}{4!}.0 + \dfrac{x^5}{5!}.6 + ... = \dfrac{x^2}{2} + \dfrac{6x^5}{5!} + ...$

At $x = 0.5$, $y = \dfrac{(0.5)^2}{2} + \dfrac{6(0.5)^5}{5!} + ... = 0.1266$.

Ex. 5: Solve $\dfrac{dy}{dx} = y - xy$, $y_0 = 1$ when $x_0 = 0$ and find y when $x = 0.1$ by Taylor's method.

Solution: Given $\dfrac{dy}{dx} = y' = y - xy$, $x_0 = 0$, $y_0 = 1$, $x = 0.1$

We know by Taylor's method $y = y_0 + xy_0' + \dfrac{x^2}{2} y_0'' + \dfrac{x^3}{3!} y_0''' + ...$ (A)

$y' = y - xy \Rightarrow y_0' = 1$

$y'' = y' - xy' - y \Rightarrow y_0'' = 0$

$y''' = y'' - xy'' - y' - y' \Rightarrow y_0''' = -2$

$y^{iv} = y''' - xy''' - y'' - y'' \Rightarrow y_0'''' = -2$

Substituting in equation (A), we get

$y = 1 + x.1 + \dfrac{x^2}{2}.0 + \dfrac{x^3}{3!}(-2) + \dfrac{x^4}{4!}(-2) + ... = 1 + x - \dfrac{x^3}{3} - \dfrac{x^4}{12} + ...$

At $x = 0.1$, $y = 1 + (0.1) - \dfrac{(0.1)^3}{3} - \dfrac{(0.1)^4}{12} + ... = 1.0997$.

Ex. 6 : Solve $\dfrac{dy}{dx} = x^2 y - 1$, $y_0 = 1$ when $x_0 = 0$ and find y when $x = 0.03$ by Taylor's method up to four decimal places. **SUK: Dec-13**

Solution: Given $\frac{dy}{dx} = y' = x^2 y - 1$, $x_0 = 0$, $y_0 = 1$, $x = 0.03$

We know by Taylor's method $y = y_0 + xy'_0 + \frac{x^2}{2} y''_0 + \frac{x^3}{3!} y'''_0 + \ldots$ \hfill (A)

$y' = x^2 y - 1 \Rightarrow y'_0 = -1$

$y'' = 2xy + x^2 y' \Rightarrow y''_0 = 0$

$y''' = 2y + 2xy' + 2xy' + x^2 y'' \Rightarrow y'''_0 = 2$

$y^{iv} = 2y' + 2xy'' + 2y' + 2xy'' + 2y' + 2xy'' + x^2 y''' \Rightarrow y^{iv}_0 = -6$

Substituting in equation (A), we get

$y = 1 + x(-1) + \frac{x^2}{2} \cdot 0 + \frac{x^3}{3!} \cdot 2 + \frac{x^4}{4!}(-6) + \ldots = 1 - x + \frac{x^3}{3} - \frac{x^4}{4} + \ldots$

At $x = 0.03$, $y = 1 - (0.03) + \frac{(0.03)^3}{3} - \frac{(0.03)^4}{4} + \ldots = 0.9700$.

Ex. 7: Solve $\frac{dy}{dx} = x - y^2$, $y = 1$ when $x = 0$ and find $y(0.1)$ by Taylor's series method.

Solution: Given $\frac{dy}{dx} = y' = x - y^2$, $x_0 = 0$, $y_0 = 1$, $x = 0.1$ \hfill **SUK: May-11**

We know by Taylor's method $y = y_0 + xy'_0 + \frac{x^2}{2} y''_0 + \frac{x^3}{3!} y'''_0 + \ldots$ \hfill (A)

$y' = x - y^2 \Rightarrow y'_0 = -1$

$y'' = 1 - 2yy' \Rightarrow y''_0 = 3$

$y''' = -2[yy'' + y'^2] \Rightarrow y'''_0 = -8$

$y^{iv} = -2[yy''' + y'y'' + 2y'y''] \Rightarrow y^{iv}_0 = 34$

Substituting in equation (A), we get

$y = 1 + x \cdot (-1) + \frac{x^2}{2} \cdot 3 + \frac{x^3}{3!} \cdot (-8) + \frac{x^4}{4!} \cdot 34 + \ldots = 1 - x + \frac{3x^2}{2} - \frac{4x^3}{3} + \frac{17x^4}{12} + \ldots$

At $x = 0.1$, $y = 1 - (0.1) + \frac{3(0.1)^2}{2} - \frac{4(0.1)^3}{3} + \frac{17(0.1)^4}{12} + \ldots = 0.9138$.

Ex. 8: Solve $\frac{dy}{dx} = -xy$, $y_0 = 1$ when $x_0 = 0$ and find y when $x = 0.2$.

Solution: Given $\frac{dy}{dx} = y' = -xy$, $x_0 = 0$, $y_0 = 1$, $x = 0.2$

We know by Taylor's method $y = y_0 + xy'_0 + \frac{x^2}{2} y''_0 + \frac{x^3}{3!} y'''_0 + \ldots$ \hfill (A)

$$y' = -xy \Rightarrow y_0' = 0$$

$$y'' = -xy' - y \Rightarrow y_0'' = -1$$

$$y''' = -xy'' - y' - y' = -xy'' - 2y' \Rightarrow y_0''' = 0$$

$$y^{iv} = -xy''' - y'' - 2y'' = -xy''' - 3y'' \Rightarrow y_0^{iv} = 3$$

$$y^{v} = -xy^{iv} - y''' - 3y''' = -xy^{iv} - 4y''' \Rightarrow y_0^{v} = 0$$

$$y^{vi} = -xy^{v} - y^{iv} - 4y^{iv} = -xy^{v} - 5y^{iv} \Rightarrow y_0^{vi} = -12$$

Substituting in equation (A), we get

$$y = 1 + x.0 + \frac{x^2}{2}.(-1) + \frac{x^3}{3!}.0 + \frac{x^4}{4!}.3 + \frac{x^5}{5!}.0 + \frac{x^6}{6!}.(-12) + \ldots = 1 - \frac{x^2}{2} + \frac{3x^4}{4!} - \frac{12x^6}{6!} \ldots$$

At $x = 0.2$, $y = 1 - \frac{(0.2)^2}{2} + \frac{3(0.2)^4}{4!} - \frac{15(0.2)^6}{6!} \ldots = 0.9802$.

Ex. 9 : Solve $\frac{dy}{dx} = x^2 + y^2$ with $y = 0$ when $x = 1$ at $x = 1.3$

Solution : Given $\frac{dy}{dx} = y' = x^2 + y^2$, $x_0 = 1$, $y_0 = 0$, $x = 1.3$

$$y' = x^2 + y^2 \Rightarrow y_0' = x_0^2 + y_0^2 = 1 + 0 = 1$$

$$y'' = 2x + 2y\,y' \Rightarrow y_0'' = 2x_0 + 2y_0 y_0' = 2(1) + 2(0)(1) = 2$$

$$y''' = 2 + 2y'^2 + 2yy'' \Rightarrow y_0''' = 2 + 2y_0' y_0' + 2y_0 y_0'' = 2 + 2(1) + 2(0) = 4$$

$$y^{iv} = 0 + 2.2y'y'' + 2yy''' + 2y'y'' \Rightarrow y^{iv} = 0 + 2.2y_0' y_0'' + 2y_0 y_0''' + 2y_0' y_0''$$

$$= 0 + 2(2)(1)(2) + 2(0)(4) + 2(1)(2) = 12$$

Hence by Taylor's series $y = y_0 + xy_0' + \frac{x^2}{2} y_0'' + \frac{x^3}{3!} y_0''' + \ldots$

$$y = 0 + x.(1) + \frac{x^2}{2}.(2) + \frac{x^3}{3!}.(4) + \frac{x^4}{4!}.(12) + \ldots = x + x^2 + \frac{2x^3}{3} + \frac{x^4}{2} + \ldots$$

At $x = 1.3$, $y = (1.3) + (1.3)^2 + \frac{2(1.3)^3}{3} + \frac{(1.3)^4}{2} + \ldots = 5.8827$.

Ex. 10 : Solve $\frac{dy}{dx} = 0.1(x^3 + y^2)$ with $y = 1$ when $x = 0$

Solution: Given $\frac{dy}{dx} = y' = 0.1(x^3 + y^2)$, $x_0 = 0$, $y_0 = 1$

$$y' = 0.1(x^3 + y^2) \Rightarrow y_0' = 0.1(x_0^3 + y_0^2) = 0.1(0 + 1) = 0.1$$

$$y'' = 0.1(3x^2 + 2y\,y') \Rightarrow y_0'' = 0.1(3x_0^2 + 2y_0 y_0') = 0.1((3)(0) + (2).(1).(0.1)) = 0.02$$

$$y''' = 0.1(6x + 2y'^2 + 2yy'') \Rightarrow y_0''' = 0.1\left(6x_0 + 2y_0'^2 + 2y_0 y_0''\right)$$

$$= 0.1(6(0) + 2(0.1)^2 + 2(1)(0.02)) = 0.006$$

$$y^{iv} = 0.1(6 + 2.2y'y'' + 2yy''' + 2y'y'') = 0.1(6 + 2yy''' + 6y'y'')$$

$$\Rightarrow y_0^{iv} = 0.1(6 + 2y_0 y_0''' + 6y_0' y_0'')$$

$$= 0.1(6 + (2).(1).(0.006) + 6(0.1)(0.02)) = 0.6024$$

Hence by Taylor's series $y = y_0 + xy_0' + \dfrac{x^2}{2} y_0'' + \dfrac{x^3}{3!} y_0''' + \ldots$

$$y = 1 + x.(0.1) + \frac{x^2}{2}.(0.02) + \frac{x^3}{3!}.(0.006) + \frac{x^4}{4!}.(0.6024) + \ldots$$

$$= 1 + (0.1)x + (0.01)x^2 + (0.001)x^3 + (0.0251)x^4 + \ldots$$

Ex. 11: Find the solution of $\dfrac{dy}{dx} = y \sin x + \cos x$ at $x = 0.4$ correct up to four places of decimals by Taylors method, $y(0) = 0$ also find the series for y atleast up to the term of x^5.

SUK: Nov-09, May-12

Solution: Given $\dfrac{dy}{dx} = y' = y \sin x + \cos x$, $x_0 = 0$, $y_0 = 0$

$y' = y \sin x + \cos x \Rightarrow y_0' = y_0 \sin x_0 + \cos x_0 = 0 + 1 = 1$

$y'' = y \cos x + y' \sin x - \sin x \Rightarrow y_0'' = y_0 \cos x_0 + y_0' \sin x_0 - \sin x_0 \Rightarrow y_0'' = 0$

$y''' = -y \sin x + 2y' \cos x + y'' \sin x - \cos x$

$\Rightarrow y_0''' = -y_0 \sin x_0 + 2y_0' \cos x_0 + y_0'' \sin x_0 - \cos x_0$

$\Rightarrow y_0''' = 0 + 2 + 0 - 1 = 1$

$y^{iv} = -y \cos x - 3y' \sin x + 3y'' \cos x + y''' \sin x + \sin x$

$\Rightarrow y_0^{iv} = -y_0 \cos x_0 - 3y_0' \sin x_0 + 3y_0'' \cos x_0 + y_0''' \sin x_0 + \sin x_0 = 0$

$y^v = y \sin x - y' \cos x - 3y' \cos x - 3y'' \sin x + 3y''(-\sin x)$

$\qquad + 3y''' \cos x + y''' \cos x + y^{iv} \sin x + \cos x$

$= y \sin x - 4y' \cos x - 6y'' \sin x + 4y''' \cos x + y^{iv} \sin x + \cos x$

$\Rightarrow y_0^v = 0 - 4 - 0 + 4 + 0 + 1 = 1$

Hence by Taylor's series $y = y_0 + xy_0' + \dfrac{x^2}{2} y_0'' + \dfrac{x^3}{3!} y_0''' + \ldots$

$$y = 0 + x.(1) + \frac{x^2}{2}.(0) + \frac{x^3}{3!}.(1) + \frac{x^4}{4!}.(0) + \frac{x^5}{5!}.(1) + \ldots = x + \frac{x^3}{3!} + \frac{x^5}{5!} + \ldots$$

Ex. 12: Solve $\dfrac{dy}{dx} = 1 + y^2$, $y_0 = 1$ when $x_0 = 0$ and find y when $x = 0.2$ and $x = 0.4$ by Taylor's series method.

Solution: Step-I Given $\dfrac{dy}{dx} = y' = 1 + y^2$, $x_0 = 0$, $y_0 = 1$, $x = 0.2$

$$y' = 1 + y^2 \Rightarrow y'_0 = 1 + (1)^2 = 2$$

$$y'' = 2yy' \Rightarrow y''_0 = 2(1)(2) = 4$$

$$y''' = 2[yy'' + y'^2] \Rightarrow y'''_0 = 2[(1)(4) + (2)^2] = 16$$

$$y^{iv} = 2[yy''' + y'y'' + 2y'y''] = 2[yy''' + 3y'y''] \Rightarrow y^{iv}_0 = 2[(1)(16) + 3(2)(4)] = 80$$

Hence by Taylor's series $y = y_0 + xy'_0 + \dfrac{x^2}{2} y''_0 + \dfrac{x^3}{3!} y'''_0 + ...$

$$= 1 + x(2) + \dfrac{x^2}{2}(4) + \dfrac{x^3}{3!}(16) + \dfrac{x^4}{4!}(80) + ... = 1 + 2x + 2x^2 + \dfrac{8x^3}{3} + \dfrac{10x^4}{3} + ...$$

At $x = 0.2$, $y = 1 + 2(0.2) + 2(0.2)^2 + \dfrac{8(0.2)^3}{3} + \dfrac{10(0.2)^4}{3} + ... = 1.5067$

Step-II Again $\dfrac{dy}{dx} = y' = 1 + y^2$, $x_0 = 0.2$, $y_0 = 1.5067$, $x = 0.4$

$$y' = 1 + y^2 \Rightarrow y'_0 = 1 + (1.5067)^2 = 3.2701$$

$$y'' = 2yy' \Rightarrow y''_0 = 9.8543$$

$$y''' = 2[yy'' + y'^2] \Rightarrow y'''_0 = 51.0821$$

$$y^{iv} = 2[yy''' + y'y'' + 2y'y''] = 2[yy''' + 3y'y''] \Rightarrow y^{iv}_0 = 347.2781$$

Again by Taylor's series $y = y_0 + xy'_0 + \dfrac{x^2}{2} y''_0 + \dfrac{x^3}{3!} y'''_0 + ...$

$$y = 1.5067 + x(3.2701) + \dfrac{x^2}{2}(9.8543) + \dfrac{x^3}{3!}(51.0821) + \dfrac{x^4}{4!}(347.2781) + ...$$

$$= 1.5067 + 3.2701x + \dfrac{9.8543 x^2}{2} + \dfrac{51.0821 x^3}{3!} + \dfrac{347.2781 x^4}{4!} + ...$$

At $x = 0.4$

$$y = 1.5067 + 3.2700(0.4) + \dfrac{9.8537(0.4)^2}{2} + \dfrac{51.0784(0.4)^3}{3!} + \dfrac{347.2458(0.4)^4}{4!} + ... = 6.4804$$

Ex. 13: Solve $\dfrac{dy}{dx} = 1 + xy$, $y_0 = 2$ when $x_0 = 0$ and find y when $x = 0.4$.

Solution: Given $\dfrac{dy}{dx} = y' = 1 + xy$, $x_0 = 0$, $y_0 = 2$, $x = 0.4$

$$y' = 1 + xy \Rightarrow y'_0 = 1 + 0 = 1$$

$$y'' = xy' + y \Rightarrow y''_0 = 0 + 2 = 2$$

$$y''' = xy'' + y' + y' = xy'' + 2y' \Rightarrow y'''_0 = 0 + 2(1) = 2$$

$$y^{iv} = xy''' + y'' + 2y'' = xy''' + 3y'' \Rightarrow y_0^{iv} = 0 + 3(2) = 6$$

Hence by Taylor's series $y = y_0 + xy'_0 + \dfrac{x^2}{2} y''_0 + \dfrac{x^3}{3!} y'''_0 + \ldots$

$$y = 2 + x(1) + \dfrac{x^2}{2}(2) + \dfrac{x^3}{3!}(2) + \dfrac{x^4}{4!}(6) + \ldots = 2 + x + x^2 + \dfrac{x^3}{3} + \dfrac{x^4}{4} + \ldots$$

At $x = 0.4$, $y = 2 + (0.4) + (0.4)^2 + \dfrac{(0.4)^3}{3} + \dfrac{(0.4)^4}{4} + \ldots = 2.5877$

Ex. 14 : Solve by using Taylor's series $\dfrac{dy}{dx} = \dfrac{1}{x^2 + y^2}$ with $y(4) = 4$ at $x = 4.1$ and $x = 4.2$

Solution: Step-I Given $\dfrac{dy}{dx} = y' = \dfrac{1}{x^2 + y^2}$, $x_0 = 4$, $y_0 = 4$, $x = 4.1$

$$y' = \dfrac{1}{x^2 + y^2} \Rightarrow y'_0 = \dfrac{1}{x_0^2 + y_0^2} = \dfrac{1}{(4)^2 + (4)^2} = \dfrac{1}{32}$$

$$y'' = \dfrac{-1}{(x^2 + y^2)^2} (2x + 2yy') = -y'^2(2x + 2yy') = -2xy'^2 - 2yy'^3$$

$$\Rightarrow y''_0 = -2x_0 y'^2_0 - 2y_0 y'^3_0 = -2(4)\left(\dfrac{1}{32}\right)^2 - 2(4)\left(\dfrac{1}{32}\right)^3 = \dfrac{-33}{4096} = -0.0081$$

Hence by Taylor's series $y = y_0 + xy'_0 + \dfrac{x^2}{2} y''_0 + \dfrac{x^3}{3!} y'''_0 + \ldots$

$$y = 4 + x\left(\dfrac{1}{32}\right) + \dfrac{x^2}{2}\left(\dfrac{-33}{4096}\right) + \ldots = 4 + \dfrac{x}{32} - \dfrac{33x^2}{8192} + \ldots$$

At $x = 4.1$, $y = 4 + \dfrac{(4.1)}{32} - \dfrac{33(4.1)^2}{8192} + \ldots = 4.0604$

Step-II Again $\dfrac{dy}{dx} = y' = \dfrac{1}{x^2 + y^2}$, $x_0 = 4.1$, $y_0 = 4.0604$, $x = 4.2$

$$y' = \frac{1}{x^2+y^2} \Rightarrow y'_0 = \frac{1}{x_0^2+y_0^2} = \frac{1}{(4.1)^2+(4.0604)^2} = 0.03$$

$$y'' = \frac{-1}{(x^2+y^2)^2}(2x+2yy') = -y'^2(2x+2yy') = -2xy'^2 - 2yy'^3$$

$$\Rightarrow y''_0 = -2x_0 y'^2_0 - 2y_0 y'^3_0 = -2(4.1)(0.03)^2 - 2(4.0604)(0.03)^3 = -0.0076$$

Hence by Taylor's series $y = y_0 + xy'_0 + \frac{x^2}{2}y''_0 + \frac{x^3}{3!}y'''_0 + ...$

$$y = 4.0604 + x(0.03) + \frac{x^2}{2}(-0.0076) + ... = 4.0604 + 0.03x - 0.0076\frac{x^2}{2} + ...$$

At $x = 4.2$, $y = 4.0604 + 0.03(4.2) - 0.0076\frac{(4.2)^2}{2} + ... = 4.1194$

Ex. 15 : Using Taylor's series method, obtain a solution of the differential equation $\frac{dy}{dx} = y - xy$, with $x_0 = 0, y_0 = 1$ when $x = 0.1$

Solution: Given $\frac{dy}{dx} = y' = y - xy$, $x_0 = 0$, $y_0 = 1$, $x = 0.1$

$\frac{dy}{dx} = y' = y - xy \Rightarrow y'_0 = y_0 - x_0 y_0 = 1 - 0 = 1$

$y'' = y' - xy' - y \Rightarrow y''_0 = y'_0 - x_0 y'_0 - y_0 = 1 - 0 - 1 = 0$

$y''' = (1-x)y'' - y' - y' \Rightarrow y'''_0 = (1-x_0)y''_0 - y'_0 - y'_0 = (1-0)(0) - 1 - 1 = -2$

$y^{iv} = (1-x)y''' - y'' - 2y'' \Rightarrow y^{iv}_0 = (1-x_0)y'''_0 - y''_0 - 2y''_0 = (1-0)(-2) - 0 - 2(0) = -2$

Similarly $y^{iv}_0 = 0$, $y^v_0 = 6$

Hence by Taylor's series $y = y_0 + xy'_0 + \frac{x^2}{2}y''_0 + \frac{x^3}{3!}y'''_0 + \frac{x^4}{4}y^{iv}_0 + ...$

$$y = 1 + x + 0 + \frac{x^3}{3!}(-2) + \frac{x^4}{4!}(-2) + ... = 1 + x - \frac{x^3}{3} - \frac{x^4}{12}$$

$x = 0.1$, $(y)_{0.1} = 1 + (0.1) - \frac{(0.1)^3}{3} - \frac{(0.1)^4}{12} + ...$

$\Rightarrow y = 1.0997.$

TEST YOUR KNOWLEDGE

1. Using Taylor's series method solve $\frac{dy}{dx} = y - xy$ with $x_0 = 0, y_0 = 2$

Ans: $y = 2 + 2x - \dfrac{2}{3}x^3 - \dfrac{1}{6}x^4 + \ldots$

2. Using Taylor's series method solve $\dfrac{dy}{dx} = 2x - y$ with $x_0 = 0$, $y_0 = 0$ also find y at x = 0.2

   Ans: $y = x^2 - \dfrac{x^3}{3} + \dfrac{1}{12}x^4 + \ldots$ At x = 0.2, y = 0.0347

3. Using Taylor's series method solve $\dfrac{dy}{dx} = 3x + y^2$ with $x_0 = 0$, $y_0 = 1$ also find y at x = 0.1
   Ans: y = 1.1272

4. Using Taylor's series solve $\dfrac{dy}{dx} = xy - 1$ with $x_0 = 1$, $y_0 = 2$ at x = 1.02. **Ans:** y = 2.0206

5. Using Taylor's series method solve $\dfrac{dy}{dx} = 4 + y^2$ with $x_0 = 0$, $y_0 = 0$ at x = 0.2 & 0.3
   Ans: y = 0.8454, 1.3683

6. Solve using Taylor's series method the differential equation $\dfrac{dy}{dx} = x + y$ with $x_0 = 1$, $y_0 = 0$ at x = 1.2 & 1.3.   **Ans:** y = 0.1103, 0.2428.

7. Using Taylor's method solve $\dfrac{dy}{dx} = -xy^2$ with $x_0 = 0$, $y_0 = 2$.

   Ans: $y = 2(1 - x^2 + x^4 - x^6 \ldots)$.

8. Solve by Taylor's series $\dfrac{dy}{dx} = 2x - y$ with $x_0 = 0$, $y_0 = 0$. Find y at x = 0.2, 0.4.

   Ans: y = 0.0347, 0.1408.

9. Solve by Taylor's series $\dfrac{dy}{dx} = x - y^2$ for
   $x_0 = 0.2$ to 0.6 with h = 0.2, initially x = 0, y = 1. **Ans:** y = 0.8812, 0.8081, 0.7120.

EULER'S METHOD

Consider the differential equation $\dfrac{dy}{dx} = f(x, y)$, with initial conditions $y(x_0) = y_0$ at $x = x_n$. Suppose we want to obtain the value of y at $x = x_1 = x_0 + h$, $x = x_2 = x_1 + h$, $x = x_3 = x_2 + h, \ldots, x = x_{n+1} = x_n + h$. Writing above equation as $dy = f(x, y)dx$

Integrating both the sides, with limits of y as y_0 to y_1 which correspond to limits of x as x_0 to x_1, we get

$$\int_{y_0}^{y_1} dy = \int_{x_0}^{x_1} f(x, y) dx$$

We assume that for the interval (x_0, y_0), $f(x, y)$ remains stationary as $f(x_0, y_0)$.

$$y_1 - y_0 = f(x_0, y_0)[x]_{x_0}^{x_1}$$
$$= (x_1 - x_0) f(x_0, y_0)$$
$$= h f(x_0, y_0)$$
$$\therefore \quad y_1 = y(x_1) = y_0 + h f(x_0, y_0)$$

Thus value of y at $x = x_1 = x_0 + h$ is calculated from the above formula.

Proceeding in similar fashion, we shall get,

$$y_2 = y(x_2) = y_1 + h f(x_1, y_1)$$
$$y_3 = y(x_3) = y_2 + h f(x_2, y_2)...$$

In general $y_n = y(x_n) = y_{n-1} + h f(x_{n-1}, y_{n-1})$.

Remarks: 1. Take values of n as large as possible to get best approximation of y.

2. Width of the interval is $h = \dfrac{x_n - x_0}{n}$

3. Intermediate points are obtained by the formula $x_r = x_0 + rh$

4. In Euler's method, the value of x_n must be known.

EXAMPLES ON EULAR METHODS

Ex. 1: Using Euler's methods, find the approximate value of y when $x = 0.5$.

Given that $\dfrac{dy}{dx} = x^2 + y^2$, at $y(0) = 0$, $h = 0.1$

Solution: $\dfrac{dy}{dx} = f(x, y) = x^2 + y^2$,

$x_0 = 0 \quad x_1 = 0.1 \quad x_2 = 0.2 \quad x_3 = 0.3 \quad x_4 = 0.4 \quad x_5 = 0.5$

At $x = x_1 = 0.1$

$$y_1 = y(x_1) = y_0 + h f(x_0, y_0) = 0 + 0.1(0 + 0) = 0$$

At $x = x_2 = 0.2$

$$y_2 = y(x_2) = y_1 + h f(x_1, y_1) = y_1 + h\left[(x_1)^2 + (y_1)^2\right] = 0 + 0.1\left[(0.1)^2 + 0\right] = 0.001$$

At $x = x_3 = 0.3$

$$y_3 = y(x_3) = y_2 + h f(x_2, y_2) = y_2 + h\left[(x_2)^2 + (y_2)^2\right] = 0.001 + 0.1\left[(0.2)^2 + (0.001)^2\right]$$
$$= 0.001 + 0.1[0.04 + 0.00001] = 0.005$$

At $x = x_4 = 0.4$

$y_4 = y(x_4) = y_3 + h f(x_3, y_3) = y_3 + h\left[(x_3)^2 + (y_3)^2\right] = 0.005 + 0.1\left[(0.3)^2 + (0.005)^2\right]$

$= 0.001 + 0.1[0.09 + 0.000025] = 0.0140$

At $x = x_5 = 0.5$

$y_5 = y(x_5) = y_4 + h f(x_4, y_4) = y_4 + h\left[(x_4)^2 + (y_4)^2\right] = 0.0140 + 0.1\left[(0.4)^2 + (0.014)^2\right]$

$= 0.0140 + 0.1[0.16 + 0.000196] = 0.03$

Ex. 2 : Using Euler's methods, find the approximate value of y when $x = 0.1$.

Given that $\dfrac{dy}{dx} = x + y + xy$, $y(0) = 1$ taking $h = 0.025$ **SUK: May-12**

Solution: $\dfrac{dy}{dx} = f(x, y) = x + y + xy$, $x_0 = 0$, $y_0 = 1$

$x_0 = 0$ $x_1 = 0.025$ $x_2 = 0.050$ $x_3 = 0.075$ $x = 0.1$

At $x = x_1 = 0.025$

$y_1 = y(x_1) = y_0 + h f(x_0, y_0) = 1 + 0.025(0 + 1 + 0) = 1.0250$

At $x = x_2 = 0.050$

$y_2 = y(x_2) = y_1 + h f(x_1, y_1) = 1.025 + 0.025[0.025 + 1.025 + (0.025)(1.025)] = 1.0518$

At $x = x_3 = 0.075$

$y_3 = y(x_3) = y_2 + h f(x_2, y_2) = 1.0518 + 0.025[0.05 + 1.0518 + (0.05)(1.0518)] = 1.0806$

At $x = x_4 = 0.1$

$y_4 = y(x_4) = y_3 + h f(x_3, y_3) = 1.0806 + 0.025[0.075 + 1.0806 + (0.075)(1.0806)] = 1.1115$.

Ex. 3: Solve by Euler's methods, given that $\dfrac{dy}{dx} = y^2 - \dfrac{y}{x}$ at $y(1) = 1$, $h = 0.1$ when $x = 1.3$.

Or Solve numerically the differential equation $\dfrac{dy}{dx} = y^2 - \dfrac{y}{x}$, $y(1) = 1$ for the interval 1 (0.1) 1.5 by Euler method   **SUK: Aug-13**

Solution: $\dfrac{dy}{dx} = f(x, y) = y^2 - \dfrac{y}{x}$, $x_0 = 1$, $y_0 = 1$

$x_0 = 1$ $x_1 = 1.1$ $x_2 = 1.2$ $x_3 = 1.3$

At $x = x_1 = 1.1$

$$y_1 = y(x_1) = y_0 + h f(x_0, y_0) = y_0 + h\left[y_0^2 - \frac{y_0}{x_0}\right] = 1 + 0.1\left[(1)^2 - \frac{1}{1}\right] = 1$$

At $x = x_2 = 1.2$

$$y_2 = y(x_2) = y_1 + h f(x_1, y_1) = y_1 + h\left[(y_1)^2 - \frac{y_1}{x_1}\right] = 1 + 0.1\left[(1)^2 - \frac{1}{1.1}\right] = 1.0091$$

At $x = x_3 = 1.3$

$$y_3 = y(x_3) = y_2 + h f(x_2, y_2) = y_2 + h\left[(y_2)^2 - \frac{y_2}{x_2}\right] = 1.0091 + 0.1\left[(1.0091)^2 - \frac{1.0091}{1.2}\right] = 1.0268$$

Ex. 4 : Solve $\frac{dy}{dx} = x + y^2$, when $x = 0.05$ at $y(0) = 1$, $h = 0.01$

Solution : $\frac{dy}{dx} = f(x, y) = x + y^2$, $x_0 = 0$, $y_0 = 1$

$x_0 = 0 \quad x_1 = 0.01 \quad x_2 = 0.02 \quad x_3 = 0.03 \quad x_4 = 0.04 \quad x_5 = 0.05$

At $x = x_1 = 0.01$

$$y_1 = y(x_1) = y_0 + h f(x_0, y_0) = y_0 + h\left[x_0 + y_0^2\right] = 1 + 0.01\left[0 + 1^2\right] = 1.01$$

At $x = x_2 = 0.02$

$$y_2 = y(x_2) = y_1 + h f(x_1, y_1) = y_1 + h\left[(x_1) + (y_1)^2\right]$$

$$= 1.01 + 0.01\left[(0.01) + (1.01)^2\right] = 1.0203$$

At $x = x_3 = 0.03$

$$y_3 = y(x_3) = y_2 + h f(x_2, y_2) = y_2 + h\left[(x_2) + (y_2)^2\right]$$

$$= 1.0203 + 0.01\left[(0.02) + (1.0203)^2\right] = 1.0309$$

At $x = x_4 = 0.04$

$$y_4 = y(x_4) = y_3 + h f(x_3, y_3) = y_3 + h\left[(x_3) + (y_3)^2\right]$$

$$= 1.0309 + 0.01\left[(0.03) + (1.0309)^2\right] = 1.0418$$

At $x = x_5 = 0.05$

$$y_5 = y(x_5) = y_4 + h f(x_4, y_4) = y_4 + h\left[(x_4) + (y_4)^2\right]$$

$$= 1.0418 + 0.01\left[(0.04) + (1.0418)^2\right] = 1.0531$$

Ex. 5 : Solve by Euler's methods, $\dfrac{dy}{dx} = 2+\sqrt{xy}$, $y(1)=1$, $h=0.2$ at $x=2$.

Solution: $\dfrac{dy}{dx} = f(x,y) = 2+\sqrt{xy}$, $x_0 = 1$, $y_0 = 1$ **SUK: Nov-08**

$x_0 = 1 \quad x_1 = 1.2 \quad x_2 = 1.4 \quad x_3 = 1.6 \quad x_4 = 1.8 \quad x_5 = 2$

At $x = x_1 = 1.2$

$y_1 = y(x_1) = y_0 + h f(x_0, y_0) = y_0 + h\left[2+\sqrt{x_0 y_0}\right]$

$\qquad = 1+0.2\left[2+\sqrt{1 \cdot 1}\right] = 1.6$

At $x = x_2 = 1.4$

$y_2 = y(x_2) = y_1 + h f(x_1, y_1) = y_1 + h\left[2+\sqrt{x_1 y_1}\right]$

$\qquad = 1.6+0.2\left[2+\sqrt{(1.2)(1.6)}\right] = 2.2771$

At $x = x_3 = 1.6$

$y_3 = y(x_3) = y_2 + h f(x_2, y_2) = y_2 + h\left[2+\sqrt{(x_2)(y_2)}\right]$

$\qquad = 2.2771+0.2\left[2+\sqrt{(1.4)(2.2771)}\right] = 3.0342$

At $x = x_4 = 1.8$

$y_4 = y(x_4) = y_3 + h f(x_3, y_3) = y_3 + h\left[2+\sqrt{(x_3)(y_3)}\right]$

$\qquad = 3.0342+0.2\left[2+\sqrt{(1.6)(3.0342)}\right] = 3.8749$

At $x = x_5 = 2$

$y_5 = y(x_5) = y_4 + h f(x_4, y_4) = y_4 + h\left[2+\sqrt{(x_4)(y_4)}\right]$

$\qquad = 3.8749+0.2\left[2+\sqrt{(1.8)(3.8749)}\right] = 4.8031$

Ex. 6: Solve $\dfrac{dy}{dx} = x+y$, when $x=1$, at $y(0)=1$, $h=0.2$

Solution: $\dfrac{dy}{dx} = f(x,y) = x+y$, $x_0 = 0$, $y_0 = 1$

$x_0 = 0 \quad x_1 = 0.2 \quad x_2 = 0.4 \quad x_3 = 0.6 \quad x_4 = 0.8 \quad x_5 = 1$

At $x = x_1 = 0.2$
$$y_1 = y(x_1) = y_0 + h f(x_0, y_0) = y_0 + h[x_0 + y_0]$$
$$= 1 + 0.2[0 + 1] = 1.2$$

At $x = x_2 = 0.4$
$$y_2 = y(x_2) = y_1 + h f(x_1, y_1) = y_1 + h[(x_1) + (y_1)]$$
$$= 1.2 + 0.2[(0.2) + (1.2)] = 1.48$$

At $x = x_3 = 0.6$
$$y_3 = y(x_3) = y_2 + h f(x_2, y_2) = y_2 + h[(x_2) + (y_2)]$$
$$= 1.48 + 0.2[(0.4) + (1.48)] = 1.856$$

At $x = x_4 = 0.8$
$$y_4 = y(x_4) = y_3 + h f(x_3, y_3) = y_3 + h[(x_3) + (y_3)]$$
$$= 1.856 + 0.2[(0.6) + (1.856)] = 2.3472$$

At $x = x_5 = 1$
$$y_5 = y(x_5) = y_4 + h f(x_4, y_4) = y_4 + h[(x_4) + (y_4)]$$
$$= 2.3472 + 0.2[(0.8) + (2.3472)] = 2.9766.$$

Ex. 7 : Solve $\dfrac{dy}{dx} = 1 - y^2$, at $y(0) = 0$, $h = 0.2$ when $x = 1$

Solution: $\dfrac{dy}{dx} = f(x, y) = 1 - y^2$, $x_0 = 0$, $y_0 = 0$

$x_0 = 0 \quad x_1 = 0.2 \quad x_2 = 0.4 \quad x_3 = 0.6 \quad x_4 = 0.8 \quad x_5 = 1$

At $x = x_1 = 0.2$
$$y_1 = y(x_1) = y_0 + h f(x_0, y_0) = y_0 + h[1 - y_0^2]$$
$$= 0 + 0.2[1 - 0^2] = 0.2$$

At $x = x_2 = 0.4$
$$y_2 = y(x_2) = y_1 + h f(x_1, y_1) = y_1 + h[1 - (y_1)^2]$$
$$= 0.2 + 0.2[1 - (0.2)^2] = 0.392$$

At $x = x_3 = 0.6$

$y_3 = y(x_3) = y_2 + h f(x_2, y_2) = y_2 + h\left[1-(y_2)^2\right]$

$= 0.392 + 0.2\left[1-(0.392)^2\right] = 0.5613$

At $x = x_4 = 0.8$

$y_4 = y(x_4) = y_3 + h f(x_3, y_3) = y_3 + h\left[1-(y_3)^2\right]$

$= 0.5613 + 0.2\left[1-(0.5613)^2\right] = 0.6983$

At $x = x_5 = 1$

$y_5 = y(x_5) = y_4 + h f(x_4, y_4) = y_4 + h\left[1-(y_4)^2\right]$

$= 0.6983 + 0.2\left[1-(0.6983)^2\right] = 0.8008.$

Ex. 8: Solve $\dfrac{dy}{dx} = 1 - 2xy$, at $y(0) = 0$, $h = 0.2$ when $x = 0.6$

Solution: $\dfrac{dy}{dx} = f(x, y) = 1 - 2xy$, $\quad x_0 = 0, \quad y_0 = 0$

$x_0 = 0 \quad x_1 = 0.2 \quad x_2 = 0.4 \quad\quad x_3 = 0.6$

At $x = x_1 = 0.2$

$y_1 = y(x_1) = y_0 + h f(x_0, y_0) = y_0 + h\left[1 - 2x_0 y_0\right]$

$= 0 + 0.2[1 - 0] = 0.2$

At $x = x_2 = 0.4$

$y_2 = y(x_2) = y_1 + h f(x_1, y_1) = y_1 + h\left[1 - 2x_1 y_1\right]$

$= 0.2 + 0.2\left[1 - 2(0.2)(0.2)\right] = 0.3840$

At $x = x_3 = 0.6$

$y_3 = y(x_3) = y_2 + h f(x_2, y_2) = y_2 + h\left[1 - 2x_2 y_2\right]$

$= 0.3840 + 0.2\left[1 - 2(0.4)(0.384)\right] = 0.5226$

Ex. 9 : Solve by Euler's methods, $\dfrac{dy}{dx} = x + \sqrt{y}$, $y(2) = 4$, $h = 0.2$ at $x = 3$.

Solution: $\dfrac{dy}{dx} = f(x, y) = x + \sqrt{y}$, $\quad x_0 = 2, \quad y_0 = 4$

$x_0 = 2 \quad x_1 = 2.2 \quad x_2 = 2.4 \quad\quad x_3 = 2.6 \quad\quad x_4 = 2.8 \quad\quad x_5 = 3$

At $x = x_1 = 2.2$

$$y_1 = y(x_1) = y_0 + h f(x_0, y_0) = y_0 + h\left[x_0 + \sqrt{y_0}\right]$$
$$= 4 + 0.2\left[2 + \sqrt{4}\right] = 4.8$$

At $x = x_2 = 2.4$

$$y_2 = y(x_2) = y_1 + h f(x_1, y_1) = y_1 + h\left[x_1 + \sqrt{y_1}\right]$$
$$= 4.8 + 0.2\left[(2.2) + \sqrt{4.8}\right] = 5.6782$$

At $x = x_3 = 2.6$

$$y_3 = y(x_3) = y_2 + h f(x_2, y_2) = y_2 + h\left[x_2 + \sqrt{y_2}\right]$$
$$= 5.6782 + 0.2\left[2.4 + \sqrt{5.6782}\right] = 6.6348$$

At $x = x_4 = 2.8$

$$y_4 = y(x_4) = y_3 + h f(x_3, y_3) = y_3 + h\left[x_3 + \sqrt{y_3}\right]$$
$$= 6.6348 + 0.2\left[2.6 + \sqrt{6.6348}\right] = 7.6700$$

At $x = x_5 = 3$

$$y_5 = y(x_5) = y_4 + h f(x_4, y_4) = y_4 + h\left[x_4 + \sqrt{y_4}\right]$$
$$= 7.6700 + 0.2\left[2.8 + \sqrt{7.6700}\right] = 8.7839.$$

Ex. 10: Solve $\dfrac{dy}{dx} = xy$, at $y(0) = 1$, $h = 0.1$ when $x = 0.5$

Solution: $\dfrac{dy}{dx} = f(x, y) = xy$, $x_0 = 0$, $y_0 = 1$

$x_0 = 0$ $x_1 = 0.1$ $x_2 = 0.2$ $x_3 = 0.3$ $x_4 = 0.4$ $x_5 = 0.5$

At $x = x_1 = 0.1$

$$y_1 = y(x_1) = y_0 + h f(x_0, y_0) = y_0 + h[x_0 y_0]$$
$$= 1 + 0.1\left[(0).(1)\right] = 1$$

At $x = x_2 = 0.2$

$$y_2 = y(x_2) = y_1 + h f(x_1, y_1) = y_1 + h[x_1 y_1]$$
$$= 1 + 0.1\left[(0.1)(1)\right] = 1.01$$

At $x = x_3 = 0.3$
$$y_3 = y(x_3) = y_2 + h f(x_2, y_2) = y_2 + h[x_2 y_2]$$
$$= 1.01 + 0.1[(0.2)(1.01)] = 1.0302$$

At $x = x_4 = 0.4$
$$y_4 = y(x_4) = y_3 + h f(x_3, y_3) = y_3 + h[x_3 y_3]$$
$$= 1.0302 + 0.1[(0.3)(1.0302)] = 1.0611$$

At $x = x_5 = 0.5$
$$y_5 = y(x_5) = y_4 + h f(x_4, y_4) = y_4 + h[x_4 y_4]$$
$$= 1.0611 + 0.1[(0.4)(1.0611)] = 1.1035.$$

Ex. 11: Solve $\dfrac{dy}{dx} = -y$, at $y(0) = 1$, $h = 0.01$ when $x = 0.04$.

Solution: $\dfrac{dy}{dx} = f(x, y) = -y$, $x_0 = 0$, $y_0 = 1$

$x_0 = 0$ $x_1 = 0.01$ $x_2 = 0.02$ $x_3 = 0.03$ $x_4 = 0.04$

At $x = x_1 = 0.01$
$$y_1 = y(x_1) = y_0 + h f(x_0, y_0) = y_0 + h[-y_0]$$
$$= 1 + 0.01[-1] = 0.99$$

At $x = x_2 = 0.02$
$$y_2 = y(x_2) = y_1 + h f(x_1, y_1) = y_1 + h[-y_1]$$
$$= 0.99 + 0.01[(-0.99)] = 0.9801$$

At $x = x_3 = 0.03$
$$y_3 = y(x_3) = y_2 + h f(x_2, y_2) = y_2 + h[-y_2]$$
$$= 0.9801 + 0.01[-0.9801] = 0.9703$$

At $x = x_4 = 0.04$
$$y_4 = y(x_4) = y_3 + h f(x_3, y_3) = y_3 + h[-y_3]$$
$$= 0.9703 + 0.01[-0.9703] = 0.9606$$

TEST YOUR KNOWLEDGE

1. Using Euler's method find the approximate value of y where
$\frac{dy}{dx} = 1 + y^2$, at $y(0) = 0$, $h = 0.2$ when $x = 1$. **Ans:** 1.2941

2. Using Euler's method find the approximate value of y at $x = 1$ in five steps taking $h = 0.2$ given $\frac{dy}{dx} = x + y$, $y(0) = 1$. **Ans:** 2.9766

3. Using Euler's method find the approximate value of y at $x = 0.1$ in five steps given that
$\frac{dy}{dx} = \frac{y-x}{y+x}$, $y(0) = 1$. **Ans:** 1.0927

4. Using Euler's method find the approximate value of y at $x = 1$ in five steps given that
$\frac{dy}{dx} = x + y$, $y(0) = 1$. **Ans:** 2.9766

5. Using Euler's method find the approximate value of y at $x = 1.5$ in five steps given that
$\frac{dy}{dx} = \frac{y-x}{\sqrt{xy}}$, $y(1) = 2$. **Ans:** 2.2941

6. Using Euler's method find the approximate value of y at $x = 2$ taking h=0.2, given that
$\frac{dy}{dx} = x + 2y$, $y(1) = 1$. **Ans:** 8.1619

EULER'S MODIFIED METHOD

Consider the differential equation $\frac{dy}{dx} = f(x, y)$ with initial conditions $y(x_0) = y_0$

To find the value of y at $x = x_n$ i.e y_n, divide interval $[x_0, x_n]$ into sub-intervals of equal width as per the given condition.

To find the values of $y_1, y_2, y_3, \dots y_n$ corresponding to values of $x_1, x_2, x_3, \dots x_n$, find iterations of $y_1, y_2, y_3, \dots y_n$ which are denoted by $y_1^{(1)}, y_1^{(2)}, y_1^{(3)}, \dots, y_1^{(n)}; y_2^{(1)}, y_2^{(2)}, y_2^{(3)}, \dots, y_2^{(n)}; \dots$ step by step

Step-I : Put $x = x_0$, $y = y_0$ in Euler's formula to get y_1 i.e. $y_1 = y_0 + h f(x_0, y_0)$
where y_1 is first iteration of y and denoted by $y_1^{(1)}$
$\therefore y_1^{(1)} = y_0 + h f(x_0, y_0)$

Then find the successive iterations of y_1, till we get two consecutive iterations equal

$y_1^{(2)} = y_0 + \frac{h}{2}\left[f(x_0, y_0) + f(x_1, y_1^{(1)}) \right]$

$y_1^{(3)} = y_0 + \frac{h}{2}\left[f(x_0, y_0) + f(x_1, y_1^{(2)}) \right]$

in general $y_1^{(n)} = y_0 + \frac{h}{2}\left[f(x_0, y_0) + f(x_1, y_1^{(n-1)}) \right]$ i.e. $y_1^{(n)} = y_1$ at $x = x_1$

Step-II Put $x = x_1$, $y = y_1$ in Euler's formula to get y_2 i.e. $y_2 = y_1 + h f(x_1, y_1)$
which is the first iteration of y_2 and denoted by $y_2^{(1)}$

$$y_2^{(1)} = y_1 + h f(x_1, y_1)$$

Then find the successive iterations of y_2 till we get two consecutive iterations equal

$$y_2^{(2)} = y_1 + \frac{h}{2}\left[f(x_1, y_1) + f(x_2, y_2^{(1)})\right]$$

$$y_2^{(3)} = y_1 + \frac{h}{2}\left[f(x_1, y_1) + f(x_2, y_2^{(2)})\right]$$

in general $y_2^{(n)} = y_1 + \frac{h}{2}\left[f(x_1, y_1) + f(x_2, y_2^{(n-1)})\right]$ and so on ...

Remarks : 1. Take values of n as large as possible to get best approximation of y.

2. Width of the interval is $h = \dfrac{x_n - x_0}{n}$

3. Intermediate points are obtained by the formula $x_r = x_0 + r h$

4. In Euler's Modified method, the value of x_n must be known.

5. If the value of h is not given then find the required value of y in **one step** only (i.e. **n = 1**)

Ex. 1 : Solve $\dfrac{dy}{dx} = y - x$ with $y(0) = 2$ by Euler's Modified method. At $x = 0.2$ taking $h = 0.2$.

Solution: Step-I Given $\dfrac{dy}{dx} = f(x, y) = y - x$, $x_0 = 0$, $y_0 = 2$, $x_n = 0.2$, $h = 0.2$

At $x_1 = x_0 + h = 0 + 0.2 = 0.2$

$$y_1^{(1)} = y_0 + h f(x_0, y_0)$$
$$= y_0 + h[y_0 - x_0] = 2 + 0.2[(2) - (0)] = 2.4$$

$$y_1^{(2)} = y_0 + \frac{h}{2}\left[f(x_0, y_0) + f(x_1, y_1^{(1)})\right]$$

$$= y_0 + \frac{h}{2}\left\{[y_0 - x_0] + \left[(y_1^{(1)}) - (x_1)\right]\right\}$$

$$= 2 + \frac{0.2}{2}\left\{[(2) - (0)] + [(2.4) - (0.2)]\right\} = 2.4200$$

$$y_1^{(3)} = y_0 + \frac{h}{2}\left[f(x_0, y_0) + f(x_1, y_1^{(2)})\right]$$

$$= y_0 + \frac{h}{2}\left\{[y_0 - x_0] + \left[(y_1^{(2)}) - (x_1)\right]\right\}$$

$$= 2 + \frac{0.2}{2}\left\{[(2) - (0)] + [(2.42) - (0.2)]\right\} = 2.4220$$

$$y_1^{(4)} = y_0 + \frac{h}{2}\left[f(x_0, y_0) + f(x_1, y_1^{(3)})\right]$$

$$= y_0 + \frac{h}{2}\left\{[y_0 - x_0] + \left[(y_1^{(3)}) - (x_1)\right]\right\}$$

$$= 2 + \frac{0.2}{2}\left\{[(2)-(0)] + [(2.422)-(0.2)]\right\} = 2.4222$$

$$y_1^{(5)} = y_0 + \frac{h}{2}\left[f(x_0, y_0) + f(x_1, y_1^{(4)})\right]$$

$$= y_0 + \frac{h}{2}\left\{[y_0 - x_0] + \left[(y_1^{(4)}) - (x_1)\right]\right\}$$

$$= 2 + \frac{0.2}{2}\left\{[(2)-(0)] + [(2.4222)-(0.2)]\right\} = 2.4222$$

As the values of $y_1^{(4)}$ and $y_1^{(5)}$ are equal $\therefore$ at $x = 0.2$, $\quad y_1 = 2.4222$.

Ex. 2 : Solve $\frac{dy}{dx} = 2 + \sqrt{xy}$ with $y(1) = 1$ by Euler's Modified method, at $x = 1.4$ taking $h = 0.2$.

SUK: Dec-11

Solution: Step-I Given $\frac{dy}{dx} = f(x, y) = 2 + \sqrt{xy}$, $x_0 = 1$, $y_0 = 1$ $x_n = 1.4$, $h = 0.2$

At $x_1 = x_0 + h = 1 + 0.2 = 1.2$

$$y_1^{(1)} = y_0 + h f(x_0, y_0)$$

$$= y_0 + h\left[2 + \sqrt{x_0 y_0}\right] = 1 + 0.2\left[2 + \sqrt{(1)(1)}\right] = 1.6$$

$$y_1^{(2)} = y_0 + \frac{h}{2}\left[f(x_0, y_0) + f(x_1, y_1^{(1)})\right]$$

$$= y_0 + \frac{h}{2}\left\{\left[2 + \sqrt{x_0 y_0}\right] + \left[2 + \sqrt{x_1 y_1^{(1)}}\right]\right\}$$

$$= 1 + \frac{0.2}{2}\left\{\left[2 + \sqrt{(1)(1)}\right] + \left[2 + \sqrt{(1.2)(1.6)}\right]\right\} = 1.6386$$

$$y_1^{(3)} = y_0 + \frac{h}{2}\left[f(x_0, y_0) + f(x_1, y_1^{(2)})\right]$$

$$= y_0 + \frac{h}{2}\left\{\left[2 + \sqrt{x_0 y_0}\right] + \left[2 + \sqrt{x_1 y_1^{(2)}}\right]\right\}$$

$$= 1 + \frac{0.2}{2}\left\{\left[2 + \sqrt{(1)(1)}\right] + \left[2 + \sqrt{(1.2)(1.6386)}\right]\right\} = 1.6402$$

$$y_1^{(4)} = y_0 + \frac{h}{2}\left[f(x_0, y_0) + f(x_1, y_1^{(3)})\right]$$

$$= y_0 + \frac{h}{2}\left\{\left[2 + \sqrt{x_0 y_0}\right] + \left[2 + \sqrt{x_1 y_1^{(3)}}\right]\right\}$$

$$= 1 + \frac{0.2}{2}\left\{\left[2 + \sqrt{(1)(1)}\right] + \left[2 + \sqrt{(1.2)(1.6402)}\right]\right\} = 1.6403$$

$$y_1^{(5)} = y_0 + \frac{h}{2}\left[f(x_0, y_0) + f(x_1, y_1^{(4)})\right]$$

$$= y_0 + \frac{h}{2}\left\{\left[2+\sqrt{x_0 y_0}\right] + \left[2+\sqrt{x_1 y_1^{(4)}}\right]\right\}$$

$$= 1 + \frac{0.2}{2}\left\{\left[2+\sqrt{(1)(1)}\right] + \left[2+\sqrt{(1.2)(1.6403)}\right]\right\} = 1.6403$$

As the values of $y_1^{(4)}$ and $y_1^{(5)}$ are equal   Hence for $x = 1.2$, $y_1 = 1.6403$

Step-II Again $\frac{dy}{dx} = f(x, y) = 2 + \sqrt{xy}$, $x_1 = 1.2$, $y_1 = 1.6403$ $x_2 = 1.4$, $h = 0.2$

At $x_2 = x_0 + rh = 1 + (2)(0.2) = 1.4$, or $x_2 = x_1 + h = 1.2 + 0.2 = 1.4$

$$y_2^{(1)} = y_1 + h f(x_1, y_1) = y_1 + h\left[2+\sqrt{x_1 y_1}\right]$$

$$= 1.6403 + 0.2\left[2+\sqrt{(1.2)(1.6403)}\right] = 2.3209$$

$$y_2^{(2)} = y_1 + \frac{h}{2}\left[f(x_1, y_1) + f(x_2, y_2^{(1)})\right] = y_0 + \frac{h}{2}\left\{\left[2+\sqrt{x_1 y_1}\right] + \left[2+\sqrt{x_2 y_2^{(1)}}\right]\right\}$$

$$= 1.6403 + \frac{0.2}{2}\left\{\left[2+\sqrt{(1.2)(1.6403)}\right] + \left[2+\sqrt{(1.4)(2.3209)}\right]\right\} = 2.3609$$

$$y_2^{(3)} = y_1 + \frac{h}{2}\left[f(x_1, y_1) + f(x_2, y_2^{(2)})\right] = y_0 + \frac{h}{2}\left\{\left[2+\sqrt{x_1 y_1}\right] + \left[2+\sqrt{x_2 y_2^{(2)}}\right]\right\}$$

$$= 1.6403 + \frac{0.2}{2}\left\{\left[2+\sqrt{(1.2)(1.6403)}\right] + \left[2+\sqrt{(1.4)(2.3609)}\right]\right\} = 2.3624$$

$$y_2^{(4)} = y_1 + \frac{h}{2}\left[f(x_1, y_1) + f(x_2, y_2^{(3)})\right] = y_0 + \frac{h}{2}\left\{\left[2+\sqrt{x_1 y_1}\right] + \left[2+\sqrt{x_2 y_2^{(3)}}\right]\right\}$$

$$= 1.6403 + \frac{0.2}{2}\left\{\left[2+\sqrt{(1.2)(1.6403)}\right] + \left[2+\sqrt{(1.4)(2.3624)}\right]\right\} = 2.3625$$

$$y_2^{(5)} = y_1 + \frac{h}{2}\left[f(x_1, y_1) + f(x_2, y_2^{(4)})\right] = y_0 + \frac{h}{2}\left\{\left[2+\sqrt{x_1 y_1}\right] + \left[2+\sqrt{x_2 y_2^{(4)}}\right]\right\}$$

$$= 1.6403 + \frac{0.2}{2}\left\{\left[2+\sqrt{(1.2)(1.6403)}\right] + \left[2+\sqrt{(1.4)(2.3625)}\right]\right\} = 2.3625$$

As the values of $y_2^{(4)}$ and $y_2^{(5)}$ are equal   Therefore at $x = 1.4$, $y_1 = 2.3625$.

Ex. 3: Solve $\frac{dy}{dx} = -xy^2$ with $y(0) = 2$ by Euler's Modified method. At $x = 0.2$ taking $h = 0.1$.

SUK: May-08

Solution: Step-I Given $\frac{dy}{dx} = f(x, y) = -xy^2$, $x_0 = 0$, $y_0 = 2$ $x_n = 0.2$, $h = 0.1$

At $x_1 = x_0 + h = 0 + 0.1 = 0.1$

(3.24)

$$y_1^{(1)} = y_0 + h f(x_0, y_0)$$

$$= y_0 + h\left[-x_0 y_0^2\right] = 2 + 0.1\left[-(0)(2)^2\right] = 2$$

$$y_1^{(2)} = y_0 + \frac{h}{2}\left[f(x_0, y_0) + f(x_1, y_1^{(1)})\right]$$

$$= y_0 + \frac{h}{2}\left\{\left[-x_0 y_0^2\right] + \left[-x_1 \left(y_1^{(1)}\right)^2\right]\right\}$$

$$= 2 + \frac{0.1}{2}\left\{\left[-(0)(2)^2\right] + \left[-(0.1)(2)^2\right]\right\} = 1.9800$$

$$y_1^{(3)} = y_0 + \frac{h}{2}\left[f(x_0, y_0) + f(x_1, y_1^{(2)})\right]$$

$$= y_0 + \frac{h}{2}\left\{\left[-x_0 y_0^2\right] + \left[-x_1 \left(y_1^{(2)}\right)^2\right]\right\}$$

$$= 2 + \frac{0.1}{2}\left\{\left[-(0)(2)^2\right] + \left[-(0.1)(1.98)^2\right]\right\} = 1.9804$$

$$y_1^{(4)} = y_0 + \frac{h}{2}\left[f(x_0, y_0) + f(x_1, y_1^{(3)})\right]$$

$$= y_0 + \frac{h}{2}\left\{\left[-x_0 y_0^2\right] + \left[-x_1 \left(y_1^{(3)}\right)^2\right]\right\}$$

$$= 2 + \frac{0.1}{2}\left\{\left[-(0)(2)^2\right] + \left[-(0.1)(1.9804)^2\right]\right\} = 1.9804$$

As the values of $y_1^{(3)}$ and $y_1^{(4)}$ are equal $\therefore$ at $x = 0.1$, $y_1 = 1.9804$

Step-II Again $\frac{dy}{dx} = f(x, y) = -xy^2$, $x_1 = 0.1$, $y_1 = 1.9803$ $x_2 = 0.2$, $h = 0.1$

At $x_2 = x_0 + rh = 0.1 + (2)(0.1) = 0.2$ or $x_2 = x_1 + h = 0.1 + 0.1 = 0.2$

$$y_2^{(1)} = y_1 + h f(x_1, y_1)$$

$$= y_1 + h\left[-x_1 y_1^2\right] = 1.9804 + 0.1\left[-(0.1)(1.9804)^2\right] = 1.9412$$

$$y_2^{(2)} = y_1 + \frac{h}{2}\left[f(x_1, y_1) + f(x_2, y_2^{(1)})\right]$$

$$= y_1 + \frac{h}{2}\left\{\left[-x_1 y_1^2\right] + \left[-x_2 y_2^{(1)^2}\right]\right\}$$

$$= 1.9804 + \frac{0.1}{2}\left\{\left[-(0.1)(1.9804)^2\right] + \left[-(0.2)(1.9412)^2\right]\right\} = 1.9231$$

$$y_2^{(3)} = y_1 + \frac{h}{2}\left[f(x_1, y_1) + f(x_2, y_2^{(2)})\right]$$

$$= y_1 + \frac{h}{2}\left\{\left[-x_1 y_1^2\right] + \left[-x_2 y_2^{(2)^2}\right]\right\}$$

$$= 1.9804 + \frac{0.1}{2}\left\{\left[-(0.1)(1.9804)^2\right] + \left[-(0.2)(1.9231)^2\right]\right\} = 1.9238$$

$$y_2^{(4)} = y_1 + \frac{h}{2}\left[f(x_1,y_1) + f(x_2,y_2^{(3)})\right]$$

$$= y_1 + \frac{h}{2}\left\{\left[-x_1 y_1^2\right] + \left[-x_2 y_2^{(3)^2}\right]\right\}$$

$$= 1.9804 + \frac{0.1}{2}\left\{\left[-(0.1)(1.9804)^2\right] + \left[-(0.2)(1.9238)^2\right]\right\} = 1.9238$$

As the values of $y_2^{(3)}$ and $y_2^{(4)}$ are equal $\therefore$ at $x = 0.2$, $y_1 = 1.9238$

Ex. 4 : Solve $\frac{dy}{dx} = x^2 + y$ with $y(0) = 1$ by Euler's Modified method, at $x = 0.02, 0.04, 0.06$.

SUK: Nov-12, May-10

Solution: Step-I Given $\frac{dy}{dx} = f(x, y) = x^2 + y$, $x_0 = 0$, $y_0 = 1$ $x_n = 0.06$, $h = 0.02$

At $x_1 = x_0 + h = 0 + 0.02 = 0.02$

$$y_1^{(1)} = y_0 + h f(x_0, y_0)$$

$$= y_0 + h\left[x_0^2 + y_0\right] = 1 + 0.02\left[(0)^2 + (1)\right] = 1.02$$

$$y_1^{(2)} = y_0 + \frac{h}{2}\left[f(x_0, y_0) + f(x_1, y_1^{(1)})\right]$$

$$= y_0 + \frac{h}{2}\left\{\left[x_0^2 + y_0\right] + \left[x_1^2 + (y_1^{(1)})\right]\right\}$$

$$= 1 + \frac{0.02}{2}\left\{\left[(0)^2 + (1)\right] + \left[(0.02)^2 + (1.02)\right]\right\} = 1.0202$$

$$y_1^{(3)} = y_0 + \frac{h}{2}\left[f(x_0, y_0) + f(x_1, y_1^{(2)})\right]$$

$$= y_0 + \frac{h}{2}\left\{\left[x_0^2 + y_0\right] + \left[x_1^2 + (y_1^{(2)})\right]\right\}$$

$$= 1 + \frac{0.02}{2}\left\{\left[(0)^2 + (1)\right] + \left[(0.02)^2 + (1.0202)\right]\right\} = 1.0202$$

As the values of $y_1^{(2)}$ and $y_1^{(3)}$ are equal $\therefore$ at $x = 0.02$, $y_1 = 1.0202$

Step-II Again $\frac{dy}{dx} = f(x, y) = x^2 + y$, $x_1 = 0.02$, $y_1 = 1.0202$ $x_n = 0.6$, $h = 0.02$

At $x_2 = x_1 + h = 0.02 + 0.02 = 0.04$

$$y_2^{(1)} = y_1 + h f(x_1, y_1)$$

$$= y_1 + h\left[x_1^2 + y_1\right] = 1.0202 + 0.02\left[(0.02)^2 + (1.0202)\right] = 1.0406$$

(3.26)

$$y_2^{(2)} = y_1 + \frac{h}{2}\left[f(x_1,y_1) + f(x_2,y_2^{(1)})\right]$$

$$= y_1 + \frac{h}{2}\left\{\left[x_1^2 + y_1\right] + \left[x_2^2 + (y_2^{(1)})\right]\right\}$$

$$= 1.0202 + \frac{0.02}{2}\left\{\left[(0.02)^2 + (1.0202)\right] + \left[(0.04)^2 + (1.0406)\right]\right\} = 1.0408$$

$$y_2^{(3)} = y_1 + \frac{h}{2}\left[f(x_1,y_1) + f(x_2,y_2^{(2)})\right]$$

$$= y_1 + \frac{h}{2}\left\{\left[x_1^2 + y_1\right] + \left[x_2^2 + (y_2^{(2)})\right]\right\}$$

$$= 1.0202 + \frac{0.02}{2}\left\{\left[(0.02)^2 + (1.0202)\right] + \left[(0.04)^2 + (1.0408)\right]\right\} = 1.0408$$

As the values of $y_2^{(2)}$ and $y_2^{(3)}$ are equal $\therefore$ at $x = 0.04$, $y_1 = 1.0408$

Step-III Once again $\frac{dy}{dx} = f(x,y) = x^2 + y$, $x_2 = 0.04$, $y_1 = 1.0408$ $x_n = 0.06$, $h = 0.02$

At $x_3 = x_2 + h = 0.04 + 0.02 = 0.06$

$$y_3^{(1)} = y_2 + h f(x_2, y_2)$$

$$= y_2 + h\left[x_2^2 + y_2\right] = 1.0408 + 0.02\left[(0.04)^2 + (1.0408)\right] = 1.0616$$

$$y_3^{(2)} = y_2 + \frac{h}{2}\left[f(x_2,y_2) + f(x_3,y_3^{(1)})\right]$$

$$= y_2 + \frac{h}{2}\left\{\left[x_2^2 + y_2\right] + \left[x_3^2 + (y_3^{(1)})\right]\right\}$$

$$= 1.0408 + \frac{0.02}{2}\left\{\left[(0.04)^2 + (1.0408)\right] + \left[(0.06)^2 + (1.0616)\right]\right\} = 1.0619$$

$$y_3^{(3)} = y_2 + \frac{h}{2}\left[f(x_2,y_2) + f(x_3,y_3^{(2)})\right]$$

$$= y_2 + \frac{h}{2}\left\{\left[x_2^2 + y_2\right] + \left[x_3^2 + (y_3^{(2)})\right]\right\}$$

$$= 1.0408 + \frac{0.02}{2}\left\{\left[(0.04)^2 + (1.0408)\right] + \left[(0.06)^2 + (1.0619)\right]\right\} = 1.0619$$

As the values of $y_3^{(2)}$ and $y_3^{(3)}$ are equal $\therefore$ at $x = 0.06$, $y_1 = 1.0619$

Ex. 5: Solve $\frac{dy}{dx} = \log(x+y)$ with $y(1) = 2$ by Euler's Modified method. At $x = 1.2$ and 1.4 correct to four decimal places. **SUK: Dec-13**

Solution : Step-I Given $\frac{dy}{dx} = f(x,y) = \log(x+y)$, $x_0 = 1$, $y_0 = 2$ $x_n = 1.4$, $h = 0.2$

At $x_1 = x_0 + h = 1 + 0.2 = 1.2$

$$y_1^{(1)} = y_0 + h f(x_0, y_0)$$
$$= y_0 + h[\log(x_0 + y_0)] = 2 + 0.2[\log(1+2)] = 2.2197$$
$$y_1^{(2)} = y_0 + \frac{h}{2}[f(x_0, y_0) + f(x_1, y_1^{(1)})]$$
$$= y_0 + \frac{h}{2}\{[\log(x_0 + y_0)] + [\log(x_1 + y_1^{(1)})]\}$$
$$= 2 + \frac{0.2}{2}\{[\log(1+2)] + [\log(1.2 + 2.2197)]\} = 2.2328$$
$$y_1^{(3)} = y_0 + \frac{h}{2}[f(x_0, y_0) + f(x_1, y_1^{(2)})]$$
$$= y_0 + \frac{h}{2}\{[\log(x_0 + y_0)] + [\log(x_1 + y_1^{(2)})]\}$$
$$= 2 + \frac{0.2}{2}\{[\log(1+2)] + [\log(1.2 + 2.2328)]\} = 2.2332$$
$$y_1^{(4)} = y_0 + \frac{h}{2}[f(x_0, y_0) + f(x_1, y_1^{(3)})]$$
$$= y_0 + \frac{h}{2}\{[\log(x_0 + y_0)] + [\log(x_1 + y_1^{(3)})]\}$$
$$= 2 + \frac{0.2}{2}\{[\log(1+2)] + [\log(1.2 + 2.2332)]\} = 2.2332$$

As the values of $y_1^{(3)}$ and $y_1^{(4)}$ are equal $\therefore$ at $x = 1.2$, $y_1 = 2.2332$

Step-II Again $\frac{dy}{dx} = f(x, y) = \log(x+y)$, $x_1 = 1.2$, $y_0 = 2.2332$ $x_2 = 1.4$, $h = 0.2$

At $x_2 = x_1 + h = 1.2 + 0.2 = 1.4$
$$y_2^{(1)} = y_1 + h f(x_1, y_1)$$
$$= y_1 + h[\log(x_1 + y_1)] = 2.2332 + 0.2[\log(1.2 + 2.2332)] = 2.4799$$
$$y_2^{(2)} = y_1 + \frac{h}{2}[f(x_1, y_1) + f(x_2, y_2^{(1)})]$$
$$= y_1 + \frac{h}{2}\{[\log(x_1 + y_1)] + [\log(x_2 + y_2^{(1)})]\}$$
$$= 2.2332 + \frac{0.2}{2}\{[\log(1.2 + 2.2332)] + [\log(1.4 + 2.4799)]\} = 2.4921$$
$$y_2^{(3)} = y_1 + \frac{h}{2}[f(x_1, y_1) + f(x_2, y_2^{(2)})]$$
$$= y_1 + \frac{h}{2}\{[\log(x_1 + y_1)] + [\log(x_2 + y_2^{(2)})]\}$$
$$= 2.2332 + \frac{0.2}{2}\{[\log(1.2 + 2.2332)] + [\log(1.4 + 2.4921)]\} = 2.4924$$

$$y_2^{(4)} = y_1 + \frac{h}{2}\left[f(x_1,y_1) + f(x_2,y_2^{(3)})\right]$$

$$= y_1 + \frac{h}{2}\left\{\left[\log(x_1+y_1)\right] + \left[\log(x_2+y_2^{(3)})\right]\right\}$$

$$= 2.2332 + \frac{0.2}{2}\left\{\left[\log(1.2+2.2332)\right] + \left[\log(1.4+2.4924)\right]\right\} = 2.4925$$

$$y_2^{(5)} = y_1 + \frac{h}{2}\left[f(x_1,y_1) + f(x_2,y_2^{(4)})\right]$$

$$= y_1 + \frac{h}{2}\left\{\left[\log(x_1+y_1)\right] + \left[\log(x_2+y_2^{(4)})\right]\right\}$$

$$= 2.2332 + \frac{0.2}{2}\left\{\left[\log(1.2+2.2332)\right] + \left[\log(1.4+2.4925)\right]\right\} = 2.4925$$

As the values of $y_2^{(4)}$ and $y_2^{(5)}$ are equal $\therefore$ at $x=1.4$, $y_1 = 2.4925$

Ex. 6 : Solve $\frac{dy}{dx} = x - y^2$ with $y(0) = 1$ by Euler's Modified method. At $x = 0.4$ taking $h = 0.2$.

Solution: Step-I Given $\frac{dy}{dx} = f(x,y) = x - y^2$, $x_0 = 0$, $y_0 = 1$ $x_n = 0.4$, $h = 0.2$

At $x_1 = x_0 + h = 0 + 0.2 = 0.2$

$$y_1^{(1)} = y_0 + h f(x_0, y_0)$$

$$= y_0 + h\left[x_0 - y_0^2\right] = 1 + 0.2\left[(0) - (1)^2\right] = 0.8$$

$$y_1^{(2)} = y_0 + \frac{h}{2}\left[f(x_0,y_0) + f(x_1,y_1^{(1)})\right]$$

$$= y_0 + \frac{h}{2}\left\{\left[x_0 - y_0^2\right] + \left[(x_1) - (y_1^{(1)})^2\right]\right\}$$

$$= 1 + \frac{0.2}{2}\left\{\left[(0) - (1)^2\right] + \left[(0.2) - (0.8)^2\right]\right\} = 0.8560$$

$$y_1^{(3)} = y_0 + \frac{h}{2}\left[f(x_0,y_0) + f(x_1,y_1^{(2)})\right]$$

$$= y_0 + \frac{h}{2}\left\{\left[x_0 - y_0^2\right] + \left[(x_1) - (y_1^{(2)})^2\right]\right\}$$

$$= 1 + \frac{0.2}{2}\left\{\left[(0) - (1)^2\right] + \left[(0.2) - (0.8560)^2\right]\right\} = 0.8467$$

$$y_1^{(4)} = y_0 + \frac{h}{2}\left[f(x_0,y_0) + f(x_1,y_1^{(3)})\right]$$

$$= y_0 + \frac{h}{2}\left\{\left[x_0 - y_0^2\right] + \left[(x_1) - (y_1^{(3)})^2\right]\right\}$$

$$= 1 + \frac{0.2}{2}\left\{\left[(0) - (1)^2\right] + \left[(0.2) - (0.8467)^2\right]\right\} = 0.8483$$

$$y_1^{(5)} = y_0 + \frac{h}{2}\left[f(x_0,y_0) + f(x_1,y_1^{(4)})\right]$$

$$= y_0 + \frac{h}{2}\left\{\left[x_0 - y_0^2\right] + \left[(x_1) - (y_1^{(4)})^2\right]\right\}$$

$$= 1 + \frac{0.2}{2}\left\{\left[(0) - (1)^2\right] + \left[(0.2) - (0.8483)^2\right]\right\} = 0.8480$$

$$y_1^{(6)} = y_0 + \frac{h}{2}\left[f(x_0,y_0) + f(x_1,y_1^{(5)})\right]$$

$$= y_0 + \frac{h}{2}\left\{\left[x_0 - y_0^2\right] + \left[(x_1) - (y_1^{(5)})^2\right]\right\}$$

$$= 1 + \frac{0.2}{2}\left\{\left[(0) - (1)^2\right] + \left[(0.2) - (0.8480)^2\right]\right\} = 0.8481$$

$$y_1^{(7)} = y_0 + \frac{h}{2}\left[f(x_0,y_0) + f(x_1,y_1^{(6)})\right]$$

$$= y_0 + \frac{h}{2}\left\{\left[x_0 - y_0^2\right] + \left[(x_1) - (y_1^{(6)})^2\right]\right\}$$

$$= 1 + \frac{0.2}{2}\left\{\left[(0) - (1)^2\right] + \left[(0.2) - (0.8481)^2\right]\right\} = 0.8481$$

As the values of $y_1^{(6)}$ and $y_1^{(7)}$ are equal $\therefore$ at $x = 0.2$, $y_1 = 0.8481$

Step-II Again $\frac{dy}{dx} = f(x,y) = x - y^2$, $x_1 = 0.2$, $y_1 = 0.8481$ $x_n = 0.4$, $h = 0.2$

At $x_2 = x_1 + h = 0.2 + 0.2 = 0.4$

$$y_2^{(1)} = y_1 + h f(x_1,y_1)$$

$$= y_1 + h\left[x_1 - y_1^2\right] = 1 + 0.2\left[(0.2) - (0.8481)^2\right] = 0.8961$$

$$y_2^{(2)} = y_1 + \frac{h}{2}\left[f(x_1,y_1) + f(x_2,y_2^{(1)})\right]$$

$$= y_1 + \frac{h}{2}\left\{\left[x_1 - y_1^2\right] + \left[(x_2) - (y_2^{(1)})^2\right]\right\}$$

$$= 1 + \frac{0.2}{2}\left\{\left[(0.2) - (0.8481)^2\right] + \left[(0.4) - (0.8961)^2\right]\right\} = 0.9078$$

$$y_2^{(3)} = y_1 + \frac{h}{2}\left[f(x_1,y_1) + f(x_2,y_2^{(2)})\right]$$

$$= y_1 + \frac{h}{2}\left\{\left[x_1 - y_1^2\right] + \left[(x_2) - (y_2^{(2)})^2\right]\right\}$$

$$= 1 + \frac{0.2}{2}\left\{\left[(0.2) - (0.8481)^2\right] + \left[(0.4) - (0.9078)^2\right]\right\} = 0.9057$$

$$y_2^{(4)} = y_1 + \frac{h}{2}\left[f(x_1, y_1) + f(x_2, y_2^{(3)})\right]$$

$$= y_1 + \frac{h}{2}\left\{\left[x_1 - y_1^2\right] + \left[(x_2) - (y_2^{(3)})^2\right]\right\}$$

$$= 1 + \frac{0.2}{2}\left\{\left[(0.2) - (0.8481)^2\right] + \left[(0.4) - (0.9057)^2\right]\right\} = 0.9060$$

$$y_2^{(5)} = y_1 + \frac{h}{2}\left[f(x_1, y_1) + f(x_2, y_2^{(4)})\right]$$

$$= y_1 + \frac{h}{2}\left\{\left[x_1 - y_1^2\right] + \left[(x_2) - (y_2^{(4)})^2\right]\right\}$$

$$= 1 + \frac{0.2}{2}\left\{\left[(0.2) - (0.8481)^2\right] + \left[(0.4) - (0.9060)^2\right]\right\} = 0.9060$$

As the values of $y_2^{(4)}$ and $y_2^{(5)}$ are equal $\therefore$ at $x_2 = 0.4$, $y_1 = 0.9060$

Ex. 7: Solve $\frac{dy}{dx} = 1 - y$ with $y(0) = 0$ by Euler's Modified method. At $x = 0.2$ in two step.

Solution: Step-I Given $\frac{dy}{dx} = f(x, y) = 1 - y$, $x_0 = 0$, $y_0 = 0$ $x_n = 0.2$, $h = 0.1$

At $x_1 = x_0 + h = 0 + 0.1 = 0.1$

$$y_1^{(1)} = y_0 + h f(x_0, y_0)$$

$$= y_0 + h[1 - y_0] = 0 + 0.1[1 - (0)] = 0.1$$

$$y_1^{(2)} = y_0 + \frac{h}{2}\left[f(x_0, y_0) + f(x_1, y_1^{(1)})\right]$$

$$= y_0 + \frac{h}{2}\left\{[1 - y_0] + \left[1 - (y_1^{(1)})\right]\right\}$$

$$= 0 + \frac{0.1}{2}\left\{[1 - (0)] + [1 - (0.1)]\right\} = 0.0950$$

$$y_1^{(3)} = y_0 + \frac{h}{2}\left[f(x_0, y_0) + f(x_1, y_1^{(2)})\right]$$

$$= y_0 + \frac{h}{2}\left\{[1 - y_0] + \left[1 - (y_1^{(2)})\right]\right\}$$

$$= 0 + \frac{0.1}{2}\left\{[1 - (0)] + [1 - (0.0950)]\right\} = 0.0953$$

$$y_1^{(4)} = y_0 + \frac{h}{2}\left[f(x_0, y_0) + f(x_1, y_1^{(3)})\right]$$

$$= y_0 + \frac{h}{2}\left\{[1 - y_0] + \left[1 - (y_1^{(3)})\right]\right\}$$

$$= 0 + \frac{0.1}{2}\left\{[1 - (0)] + [1 - (0.0953)]\right\} = 0.0952$$

$$y_1^{(5)} = y_0 + \frac{h}{2}\left[f(x_0, y_0) + f(x_1, y_1^{(4)})\right]$$

$$= y_0 + \frac{h}{2}\left\{[1 - y_0] + \left[1 - (y_1^{(4)})\right]\right\}$$

$$= 0 + \frac{0.1}{2}\left\{[1 - (0)] + [1 - (0.0952)]\right\} = 0.0952$$

As the values of $y_1^{(4)}$ and $y_1^{(5)}$ are equal $\therefore$ at $x_1 = 0.1$, $y_1 = 0.0952$

Step-II Again $\dfrac{dy}{dx} = f(x, y) = 1 - y$, $x_1 = 0.1$, $y_1 = 0.0952$ $x_n = 0.2$, $h = 0.1$

At $x_2 = x_1 + h = 0.1 + 0.1 = 0.2$

$y_2^{(1)} = y_1 + h f(x_1, y_1)$

$= y_1 + h[1 - y_1] = 0.0952 + 0.1[1 - (0.0952)] = 0.1857$

$y_2^{(2)} = y_1 + \dfrac{h}{2}\left[f(x_1, y_1) + f(x_2, y_2^{(1)})\right]$

$= y_1 + \dfrac{h}{2}\left\{[1 - y_1] + \left[1 - (y_2^{(1)})\right]\right\}$

$= 0.0952 + \dfrac{0.1}{2}\left\{[1 - (0.0952)] + [1 - (0.1857)]\right\} = 0.1812$

$y_2^{(3)} = y_1 + \dfrac{h}{2}\left[f(x_1, y_1) + f(x_2, y_2^{(2)})\right]$

$= y_1 + \dfrac{h}{2}\left\{[1 - y_1] + \left[1 - (y_2^{(2)})\right]\right\}$

$= 0.0952 + \dfrac{0.1}{2}\left\{[1 - (0.0952)] + [1 - (0.1812)]\right\} = 0.1814$

$y_2^{(4)} = y_1 + \dfrac{h}{2}\left[f(x_1, y_1) + f(x_2, y_2^{(3)})\right]$

$= y_1 + \dfrac{h}{2}\left\{[1 - y_1] + \left[1 - (y_2^{(3)})\right]\right\}$

$= 0.0952 + \dfrac{0.1}{2}\left\{[1 - (0.0952)] + [1 - (0.1814)]\right\} = 0.1814$

As the values of $y_2^{(3)}$ and $y_2^{(4)}$ are equal $\therefore$ at $x_2 = 0.2$, $y_2 = 0.1814$.

Ex. 8: Solve $\dfrac{dy}{dx} = 1 + xy$ with $y(0) = 1$ by Euler's Modified method, at $x = 0.1$ and $x = 0.2$.

Solution: Step-I Given $\dfrac{dy}{dx} = f(x, y) = 1 + xy$, $x_0 = 0, y_0 = 1$ $x_n = 0.2$, $h = 0.1$

At $x_1 = x_0 + h = 0 + 0.1 = 0.1$

$y_1^{(1)} = y_0 + h f(x_0, y_0)$

$= y_0 + h[1 + x_0 y_0] = 1 + 0.1[1 + (0)(1)] = 1.1000$

$$y_1^{(2)} = y_0 + \frac{h}{2}\left[f(x_0,y_0) + f(x_1,y_1^{(1)})\right]$$

$$= y_0 + \frac{h}{2}\left\{[1+x_0 y_0] + \left[1+x_1(y_1^{(1)})\right]\right\}$$

$$= 1 + \frac{0.1}{2}\left\{[1+(0)(1)] + [1+(0.1)(1.1000)]\right\} = 1.1055$$

$$y_1^{(3)} = y_0 + \frac{h}{2}\left[f(x_0,y_0) + f(x_1,y_1^{(2)})\right]$$

$$= y_0 + \frac{h}{2}\left\{[1+x_0 y_0] + \left[1+x_1(y_1^{(2)})\right]\right\}$$

$$= 1 + \frac{0.1}{2}\left\{[1+(0)(1)] + [1+(0.1)(1.1055)]\right\} = 1.1055$$

As the values of $y_1^{(2)}$ and $y_1^{(3)}$ are equal $\therefore$ at $x_1 = 0.1$, $y_1 = 1.1055$

Step-II Again $\frac{dy}{dx} = f(x,y) = 1 + xy$, $x_1 = 0.1$, $y_1 = 1.1055$ $x_n = 0.2$, $h = 0.1$

At $x_2 = x_1 + h = 0.1 + 0.1 = 0.2$

$$y_2^{(1)} = y_1 + h f(x_1, y_1)$$

$$= y_1 + h[1+x_1 y_1] = 1.1055 + 0.1[1+(0.1)(1.1055)] = 1.2166$$

$$y_2^{(2)} = y_1 + \frac{h}{2}\left[f(x_1,y_1) + f(x_2,y_2^{(1)})\right]$$

$$= y_1 + \frac{h}{2}\left\{[1+x_1 y_1] + \left[1+x_2(y_2^{(1)})\right]\right\}$$

$$= 1.1055 + \frac{0.1}{2}\left\{[1+(0.1)(1.1055)] + [1+(0.2)(1.2166)]\right\} = 1.2232$$

$$y_2^{(3)} = y_1 + \frac{h}{2}\left[f(x_1,y_1) + f(x_2,y_2^{(2)})\right]$$

$$= y_1 + \frac{h}{2}\left\{[1+x_1 y_1] + \left[1+x_2(y_2^{(2)})\right]\right\}$$

$$= 1.1055 + \frac{0.1}{2}\left\{[1+(0.1)(1.1055)] + [1+(0.2)(1.2232)]\right\} = 1.2233$$

$$y_2^{(4)} = y_1 + \frac{h}{2}\left[f(x_1,y_1) + f(x_2,y_2^{(3)})\right]$$

$$= y_1 + \frac{h}{2}\left\{[1+x_1 y_1] + \left[1+x_2(y_2^{(3)})\right]\right\}$$

$$= 1.1055 + \frac{0.1}{2}\left\{[1+(0.1)(1.1055)] + [1+(0.2)(1.2233)]\right\} = 1.2233$$

As the values of $y_2^{(3)}$ and $y_2^{(4)}$ are equal $\therefore$ at $x_2 = 0.2$, $y_1 = 1.2233$.

Ex. 9 : Solve $\dfrac{dy}{dx} = y + e^x$ with $y(0) = 0$ by Euler's Modified method. At $x = 0.3$ in one step.

Solution: Step-I Given $\dfrac{dy}{dx} = f(x, y) = y + e^x$, $x_0 = 0$, $y_0 = 0$, $x_n = 0.3$, $h = 0.3$

At $x_1 = x_0 + h = 0 + 0.3 = 0.3$

$$y_1^{(1)} = y_0 + h\, f(x_0, y_0)$$
$$= y_0 + h\left[y_0 + e^{x_0}\right] = 0 + 0.3\left[0 + e^0\right] = 0.3$$

$$y_1^{(2)} = y_0 + \dfrac{h}{2}\left[f(x_0, y_0) + f(x_1, y_1^{(1)})\right]$$
$$= y_0 + \dfrac{h}{2}\left\{\left[y_0 + e^{x_0}\right] + \left[(y_1^{(1)}) + e^{x_1}\right]\right\}$$
$$= 0 + \dfrac{0.3}{2}\left\{\left[0 + (e^0)\right] + \left[0.3 + (e^{0.3})\right]\right\} = 0.3975$$

$$y_1^{(3)} = y_0 + \dfrac{h}{2}\left[f(x_0, y_0) + f(x_1, y_1^{(2)})\right]$$
$$= y_0 + \dfrac{h}{2}\left\{\left[y_0 + e^{x_0}\right] + \left[(y_1^{(2)}) + e^{x_1}\right]\right\}$$
$$= 0 + \dfrac{0.3}{2}\left\{\left[0 + (e^0)\right] + \left[0.3975 + (e^{0.3})\right]\right\} = 0.4121$$

$$y_1^{(4)} = y_0 + \dfrac{h}{2}\left[f(x_0, y_0) + f(x_1, y_1^{(3)})\right]$$
$$= y_0 + \dfrac{h}{2}\left\{\left[y_0 + e^{x_0}\right] + \left[(y_1^{(3)}) + e^{x_1}\right]\right\}$$
$$= 0 + \dfrac{0.3}{2}\left\{\left[0 + (e^0)\right] + \left[0.4121 + (e^{0.3})\right]\right\} = 0.4143$$

$$y_1^{(5)} = y_0 + \dfrac{h}{2}\left[f(x_0, y_0) + f(x_1, y_1^{(4)})\right]$$
$$= y_0 + \dfrac{h}{2}\left\{\left[y_0 + e^{x_0}\right] + \left[(y_1^{(4)}) + e^{x_1}\right]\right\}$$
$$= 0 + \dfrac{0.3}{2}\left\{\left[0 + (e^0)\right] + \left[0.4143 + (e^{0.3})\right]\right\} = 0.4146$$

$$y_1^{(6)} = y_0 + \dfrac{h}{2}\left[f(x_0, y_0) + f(x_1, y_1^{(5)})\right]$$
$$= y_0 + \dfrac{h}{2}\left\{\left[y_0 + e^{x_0}\right] + \left[(y_1^{(5)}) + e^{x_1}\right]\right\}$$
$$= 0 + \dfrac{0.3}{2}\left\{\left[0 + (e^0)\right] + \left[0.4146 + (e^{0.3})\right]\right\} = 0.4147$$

$$y_1^{(7)} = y_0 + \frac{h}{2}\left[f(x_0, y_0) + f(x_1, y_1^{(6)})\right]$$

$$= y_0 + \frac{h}{2}\left\{\left[y_0 + e^{x_0}\right] + \left[\left(y_1^{(6)}\right) + e^{x_1}\right]\right\}$$

$$= 0 + \frac{0.3}{2}\left\{\left[0 + (e^0)\right] + \left[0.4147 + (e^{0.3})\right]\right\} = 0.4147$$

As the values of $y_1^{(6)}$ and $y_1^{(7)}$ are equal $\therefore$ at $x_1 = 0.3$, $y_1 = 0.4147$.

Ex. 10 : Solve $\dfrac{dy}{dx} = 1 + \dfrac{y}{x}$ with $y(1) = 2$ by Euler's Modified method, at $x = 1.2$, taking $h = 0.2$.

Solution : Step-I Given $\dfrac{dy}{dx} = f(x, y) = 1 + \dfrac{y}{x}$, $x_0 = 1$, $y_0 = 2$, $x_n = 1.2$, $h = 0.2$

At $x_1 = x_0 + h = 1 + 0.2 = 1.2$

$$y_1^{(1)} = y_0 + h f(x_0, y_0)$$

$$= y_0 + h\left[1 + \frac{y_0}{x_0}\right] = 2 + 0.2\left[1 + \frac{2}{1}\right] = 2.6$$

$$y_1^{(2)} = y_0 + \frac{h}{2}\left[f(x_0, y_0) + f(x_1, y_1^{(1)})\right]$$

$$= y_0 + \frac{h}{2}\left\{\left[1 + \frac{y_0}{x_0}\right] + \left[1 + \frac{\left(y_1^{(1)}\right)}{x_1}\right]\right\}$$

$$= 2 + \frac{0.2}{2}\left\{\left[1 + \frac{2}{1}\right] + \left[1 + \frac{2.6}{1.2}\right]\right\} = 2.6167$$

$$y_1^{(3)} = y_0 + \frac{h}{2}\left[f(x_0, y_0) + f(x_1, y_1^{(2)})\right]$$

$$= y_0 + \frac{h}{2}\left\{\left[1 + \frac{y_0}{x_0}\right] + \left[1 + \frac{\left(y_1^{(2)}\right)}{x_1}\right]\right\}$$

$$= 2 + \frac{0.2}{2}\left\{\left[1 + \frac{2}{1}\right] + \left[1 + \frac{2.6167}{1.2}\right]\right\} = 2.6181$$

$$y_1^{(4)} = y_0 + \frac{h}{2}\left[f(x_0, y_0) + f(x_1, y_1^{(3)})\right]$$

$$= y_0 + \frac{h}{2}\left\{\left[1 + \frac{y_0}{x_0}\right] + \left[1 + \frac{\left(y_1^{(3)}\right)}{x_1}\right]\right\}$$

$$= 2 + \frac{0.2}{2}\left\{\left[1 + \frac{2}{1}\right] + \left[1 + \frac{2.6181}{1.2}\right]\right\} = 2.6182$$

$$y_1^{(5)} = y_0 + \frac{h}{2}\left[f(x_0, y_0) + f(x_1, y_1^{(4)})\right]$$

$$= y_0 + \frac{h}{2}\left\{\left[1 + \frac{y_0}{x_0}\right] + \left[1 + \frac{(y_1^{(4)})}{x_1}\right]\right\}$$

$$= 2 + \frac{0.2}{2}\left\{\left[1 + \frac{2}{1}\right] + \left[1 + \frac{2.6182}{1.2}\right]\right\} = 2.6182$$

As the values of $y_1^{(4)}$ and $y_1^{(5)}$ are equal $\therefore$ at $x = 1.2$, $y_1 = 2.6182$

Ex. 11: Solve $\dfrac{dy}{dx} = x + \sqrt{y}$ with $y(0) = 1$ by Euler's Modified method. At $x = 0.2$

Solution: Step-I Given $\dfrac{dy}{dx} = f(x, y) = x + \sqrt{y}$, $x_0 = 0$, $y_0 = 1$, $x_n = 0.2$, $h = 0.2$

At $x_1 = x_0 + h = 0 + 0.2 = 0.2$

$$y_1^{(1)} = y_0 + h f(x_0, y_0)$$

$$= y_0 + h\left[x_0 + \sqrt{y_0}\right] = 1 + 0.2\left[0 + \sqrt{1}\right] = 1.2000$$

$$y_1^{(2)} = y_0 + \frac{h}{2}\left[f(x_0, y_0) + f(x_1, y_1^{(1)})\right]$$

$$= y_0 + \frac{h}{2}\left\{\left[x_0 + \sqrt{y_0}\right] + \left[x_1 + \sqrt{y_1^{(1)}}\right]\right\}$$

$$= 1 + \frac{0.2}{2}\left\{\left[0 + \sqrt{1}\right] + \left[0.2 + \sqrt{1.2}\right]\right\} = 1.2295$$

$$y_1^{(3)} = y_0 + \frac{h}{2}\left[f(x_0, y_0) + f(x_1, y_1^{(2)})\right]$$

$$= y_0 + \frac{h}{2}\left\{\left[x_0 + \sqrt{y_0}\right] + \left[x_1 + \sqrt{y_1^{(2)}}\right]\right\}$$

$$= 1 + \frac{0.2}{2}\left\{\left[0 + \sqrt{1}\right] + \left[0.2 + \sqrt{1.2295}\right]\right\} = 1.2309$$

$$y_1^{(4)} = y_0 + \frac{h}{2}\left[f(x_0, y_0) + f(x_1, y_1^{(3)})\right]$$

$$= y_0 + \frac{h}{2}\left\{\left[x_0 + \sqrt{y_0}\right] + \left[x_1 + \sqrt{y_1^{(3)}}\right]\right\}$$

$$= 1 + \frac{0.2}{2}\left\{\left[0 + \sqrt{1}\right] + \left[0.2 + \sqrt{1.2309}\right]\right\} = 1.2309$$

As the values of $y_1^{(3)}$ and $y_1^{(4)}$ are equal $\therefore$ at $x = 0.2$, $y_1 = 1.2309$.

Ex. 12: Solve $\dfrac{dy}{dx} = 2x - y$ with $y(0) = -1$ by Euler's Modified method. At $x = 0.2$ taking $h = 0.2$.

Solution : Step-I Given $\dfrac{dy}{dx} = f(x, y) = 2x - y$, $x_0 = 0$, $y_0 = -1$, $x_n = 0.2$, $h = 0.2$

At $x_1 = x_0 + h = 0 + 0.2 = 0.2$

$$y_1^{(1)} = y_0 + h f(x_0, y_0)$$
$$= y_0 + h[2x_0 - y_0] = -1 + 0.2[2(0) - (-1)] = -0.8$$

$$y_1^{(2)} = y_0 + \dfrac{h}{2}\left[f(x_0, y_0) + f(x_1, y_1^{(1)})\right]$$
$$= y_0 + \dfrac{h}{2}\left\{[2x_0 - y_0] + [2(x_1) - (y_1^{(1)})]\right\}$$
$$= -1 + \dfrac{0.2}{2}\left\{[2(0) - (-1)] + [2(0.2) - (-0.8)]\right\} = -7800$$

$$y_1^{(3)} = y_0 + \dfrac{h}{2}\left[f(x_0, y_0) + f(x_1, y_1^{(2)})\right]$$
$$= y_0 + \dfrac{h}{2}\left\{[2x_0 - y_0] + [2(x_1) - (y_1^{(2)})]\right\}$$
$$= -1 + \dfrac{0.2}{2}\left\{[2(0) - (-1)] + [2(0.2) - (-0.78)]\right\} = -0.7820$$

$$y_1^{(4)} = y_0 + \dfrac{h}{2}\left[f(x_0, y_0) + f(x_1, y_1^{(3)})\right]$$
$$= y_0 + \dfrac{h}{2}\left\{[2x_0 - y_0] + [2(x_1) - (y_1^{(3)})]\right\}$$
$$= -1 + \dfrac{0.2}{2}\left\{[2(0) - (-1)] + [2(0.2) - (-0.7820)]\right\} = -0.7818$$

$$y_1^{(5)} = y_0 + \dfrac{h}{2}\left[f(x_0, y_0) + f(x_1, y_1^{(4)})\right]$$
$$= y_0 + \dfrac{h}{2}\left\{[2x_0 - y_0] + [2(x_1) - (y_1^{(4)})]\right\}$$
$$= -1 + \dfrac{0.2}{2}\left\{[2(0) - (-1)] + [2(0.2) - (-0.7818)]\right\} = -0.7818$$

As the values of $y_1^{(4)}$ and $y_1^{(5)}$ are equal $\therefore$ at $x = 0.2$, $y_1 = -0.7818$.

Ex. 13: Solve $\dfrac{dy}{dx} = y^2 - \dfrac{y}{x}$ with $y(1) = 1$ by Euler's Modified method. At $x = 1.1$ taking $h = 0.05$.

Solution: Step-I Given $\dfrac{dy}{dx} = f(x,y) = y^2 - \dfrac{y}{x}$, $x_0 = 1$, $y_0 = 1$, $x_n = 1.1$, $h = 0.05$

At $x_1 = x_0 + h = 1 + 0.05 = 1.05$

$$y_1^{(1)} = y_0 + h f(x_0, y_0)$$

$$= y_0 + h\left[y_0^2 - \dfrac{y_0}{x_0}\right] = 1 + 0.05\left[(1)^2 - \dfrac{1}{1}\right] = 1.0000$$

$$y_1^{(2)} = y_0 + \dfrac{h}{2}\left[f(x_0, y_0) + f(x_1, y_1^{(1)})\right]$$

$$= y_0 + \dfrac{h}{2}\left\{\left[y_0^2 - \dfrac{y_0}{x_0}\right] + \left[y_1^{(1)} - \dfrac{(y_1^{(1)})}{x_1}\right]\right\}$$

$$= 1 + \dfrac{0.05}{2}\left\{\left[(1)^2 - \dfrac{1}{1}\right] + \left[(1)^2 - \dfrac{1}{1.05}\right]\right\} = 1.0012$$

$$y_1^{(3)} = y_0 + \dfrac{h}{2}\left[f(x_0, y_0) + f(x_1, y_1^{(2)})\right]$$

$$= y_0 + \dfrac{h}{2}\left\{\left[y_0^2 - \dfrac{y_0}{x_0}\right] + \left[y_1^{(2)} - \dfrac{(y_1^{(2)})}{x_1}\right]\right\}$$

$$= 1 + \dfrac{0.05}{2}\left\{\left[(1)^2 - \dfrac{1}{1}\right] + \left[(1.0012)^2 - \dfrac{1.0012}{1.05}\right]\right\} = 1.0012$$

As the values of $y_1^{(2)}$ and $y_1^{(3)}$ are equal $\therefore$ at $x = 1.05$, $\quad y_1 = 1.0012$

Step-II Again $\dfrac{dy}{dx} = f(x,y) = y^2 - \dfrac{y}{x}$, $x_1 = 1.05$, $y_0 = 1.0012$ $x_n = 1.1$, $h = 0.05$

At $x_2 = x_1 + h = 1.05 + 0.05 = 1.1$

$$y_2^{(1)} = y_1 + h f(x_1, y_1)$$

$$= y_1 + h\left[y_1^2 - \dfrac{y_1}{x_1}\right] = 1.0012 + 0.05\left[(1.0012)^2 - \dfrac{1.0012}{1.05}\right] = 1.0036$$

$$y_2^{(2)} = y_1 + \dfrac{h}{2}\left[f(x_1, y_1) + f(x_2, y_2^{(1)})\right]$$

$$= y_1 + \dfrac{h}{2}\left\{\left[y_1^2 - \dfrac{y_1}{x_1}\right] + \left[y_2^{(1)} - \dfrac{(y_2^{(1)})}{x_2}\right]\right\}$$

$$= 1.0012 + \dfrac{0.05}{2}\left\{\left[(1.0012)^2 - \dfrac{1.0012}{1.05}\right] + \left[(1.0036)^2 - \dfrac{1.0036}{1.1}\right]\right\} = 1.0048$$

$$y_2^{(3)} = y_1 + \frac{h}{2}\left[f(x_1, y_1) + f(x_2, y_2^{(2)})\right]$$

$$= y_1 + \frac{h}{2}\left\{\left[y_1^2 - \frac{y_1}{x_1}\right] + \left[y_2^{(2)} - \frac{(y_2^{(2)})}{x_2}\right]\right\}$$

$$= 1.0012 + \frac{0.05}{2}\left\{\left[(1.0012)^2 - \frac{1.0012}{1.05}\right] + \left[(1.0048)^2 - \frac{1.0036}{1.1}\right]\right\} = 1.0048$$

As the values of $y_1^{(2)}$ and $y_1^{(3)}$ are equal $\therefore$ at $x = 1.1$, $\quad y_1 = 1.0048$.

TEST YOUR KNOWLEDGE

1. Solve by Euler's Modified method $\frac{dy}{dx} = x + 3y$ with $x_0 = 0$, $y_0 = 1$ for x=0.1 taking h = 0.05.
   Ans: 1.3548

2. Solve $\frac{dy}{dx} = 2 + \sqrt{xy}$ $y(1.2) = 1.6403$ by Euler's Modified method. At $x = 1.6$ taking $h = 0.2$.
   Ans: 3.1695

3. Solve $\frac{dy}{dx} = x - y^2$ $y(0) = 1$ by Euler's Modified method. At $x = 0.1$ taking $h = 0.05$.
   Ans: 0.9137

4. Solve $\frac{dy}{dx} = x^2 + y$ $y(0) = 1$ by Euler's Modified method. At $x = 0.1$ taking $h = 0.05$.
   Ans: 1.1055

5. Solve $\frac{dy}{dx} = 2 + \sqrt{xy}$ $y(1) = 1$ by Euler's Modified method. At $x = 1.2$.
   Ans: 1.6440

RUNGE - KUTTA METHOD OF FOURTH ORDER:

Consider differential equation, $\frac{dy}{dx} = f(x, y)$ with the initial condition, $y(x_0) = y_0$

To solve differential equation i.e. to find value of y for given value of x. i.e for $x = x_0 + h$ then $y = y_0 + k$ where 'k' is obtain by using following formulae.

$$k_1 = h f(x_0, y_0)$$

$$k_2 = h f\left(x_0 + \frac{h}{2}, y_0 + \frac{k_1}{2}\right)$$

$$k_3 = h f\left(x_0 + \frac{h}{2}, y_0 + \frac{k_2}{2}\right)$$

$$k_4 = h f(x_0 + h, y_0 + k_3)$$

Lastly, we Calculate $k = \frac{1}{6}[k_1 + 2k_2 + 2k_3 + k_4]$

The required value of $y = y_0 + k$

EXAMPLES ON RUNGE-KUTTA METHOD

Ex. 1 : Solve by Runge-Kutta method, given $\dfrac{dy}{dx} = \dfrac{y-x}{y+x}$ with $y(0) = 1$ also find $y(0.2)$.

Solution : Given $f(x, y) = \dfrac{dy}{dx} = \dfrac{y-x}{y+x}$, $x_0 = 0$, $y_0 = 1$, $x_n = 0.2$ taking $h = 0.2$

$$k_1 = h f(x_0, y_0) = h\left(\dfrac{y_0 - x_0}{y_0 + x_0}\right) = 0.2\left(\dfrac{1-0}{1+0}\right) = 0.2$$

$$k_2 = h f\left(x_0 + \dfrac{h}{2}, y_0 + \dfrac{k_1}{2}\right)$$

$$= h\left[\dfrac{\left(y_0 + \dfrac{k_1}{2}\right) - \left(x_0 + \dfrac{h}{2}\right)}{\left(y_0 + \dfrac{k_1}{2}\right) + \left(x_0 + \dfrac{h}{2}\right)}\right] = 0.2\left[\dfrac{\left(1 + \dfrac{0.2}{2}\right) - \left(0 + \dfrac{0.2}{2}\right)}{\left(1 + \dfrac{0.2}{2}\right) + \left(0 + \dfrac{0.2}{2}\right)}\right]$$

$$= 0.2\left[\dfrac{(1.1)-(0.1)}{(1.1)+(0.1)}\right] = 0.1667$$

$$k_3 = h f\left(x_0 + \dfrac{h}{2}, y_0 + \dfrac{k_2}{2}\right)$$

$$= h\left[\dfrac{\left(y_0 + \dfrac{k_2}{2}\right) - \left(x_0 + \dfrac{h}{2}\right)}{\left(y_0 + \dfrac{k_2}{2}\right) + \left(x_0 + \dfrac{h}{2}\right)}\right] = 0.2\left[\dfrac{\left(1 + \dfrac{1.6667}{2}\right) - \left(0 + \dfrac{0.2}{2}\right)}{\left(1 + \dfrac{1.6667}{2}\right) + \left(0 + \dfrac{0.2}{2}\right)}\right]$$

$$= 0.2\left[\dfrac{(1.0833)-(0.1)}{(1.0833)+(0.1)}\right] = 0.1662$$

$$k_4 = h f(x_0 + h, y_0 + k_3)$$

$$= h\left[\dfrac{(y_0 + k_3) - (x_0 + h)}{(y_0 + k_3) + (x_0 + h)}\right] = 0.2\left[\dfrac{(1+0.1662)-(0+0.2)}{(1+0.1662)+(0+0.2)}\right] = 01414$$

and $k = \dfrac{1}{6}[k_1 + 2k_2 + 2k_3 + k_4] = \dfrac{1}{6}[0.2 + 2(0.1667) + 2(0.1662) + 0.1414] = 0.1679$

$\therefore y = y_0 + k = 1 + 0.1679 = 1.1679$

Ex. 2: Find the approximate value of y by Runge-Kutta method. Given that $\dfrac{dy}{dx} = 3x + y^2$ with $x_0 = 1$, $y_0 = 1.2$, at $x = 1.1$ **SUK: Nov-10**

Solution: Given $f(x, y) = \dfrac{dy}{dx} = 3x + y^2$, $x_0 = 1$, $y_0 = 1.2$, at $x = 1.1 \Rightarrow h = 0.1$

$$k_1 = h f(x_0, y_0) = h(3x_0 + y_0^2) = 0.1[3(1) + (1.2)^2] = 0.4440$$

$$k_2 = h f\left(x_0 + \frac{h}{2}, y_0 + \frac{k_1}{2}\right)$$

$$= h\left[3\left(x_0 + \frac{h}{2}\right) + \left(y_0 + \frac{k_1}{2}\right)^2\right] = 0.1\left[3\left(1 + \frac{0.1}{2}\right) + \left(1.2 + \frac{0.4440}{2}\right)^2\right]$$

$$= 0.5172$$

$$k_3 = h f\left(x_0 + \frac{h}{2}, y_0 + \frac{k_2}{2}\right)$$

$$= h\left[3\left(x_0 + \frac{h}{2}\right) + \left(y_0 + \frac{k_2}{2}\right)^2\right] = 0.1\left[3\left(1 + \frac{0.1}{2}\right) + \left(1.2 + \frac{0.5172}{2}\right)^2\right]$$

$$= 0.5278$$

$$k_4 = h f(x_0 + h, y_0 + k_3)$$

$$= h\left[3(x_0 + h) + (y_0 + k_3)^2\right] = 0.1\left[3(1 + 0.1) + (1.2 + 0.5277)^2\right]$$

$$= 0.6285$$

and $k = \frac{1}{6}[k_1 + 2k_2 + 2k_3 + k_4] = \frac{1}{6}[0.4440 + 2(0.5172) + 2(0.5278) + 0.6285] = 0.5271$

$\therefore y = y_0 + k = 1.2 + 0.5271 = 1.7271.$

Ex. 3 : Find the approximate value of y by Runge-Kutta method. Given that $\frac{dy}{dx} = 1 + y^2$ with $x_0 = 0$, $y_0 = 0$, at $x = 0.2$.

Solution: Given $f(x, y) = \frac{dy}{dx} = 1 + y^2$, $x_0 = 0$, $y_0 = 0$, at $x = 0.2 \Rightarrow h = 0.2$

$$k_1 = h f(x_0, y_0) = h(1 + y_0^2) = 0.2[1 + (0)^2] = 0.2000$$

$$k_2 = h f\left(x_0 + \frac{h}{2}, y_0 + \frac{k_1}{2}\right)$$

$$= h\left[1 + \left(y_0 + \frac{k_1}{2}\right)^2\right] = 0.2\left[1 + \left(0 + \frac{0.2}{2}\right)^2\right] = 0.2(1.01) = 0.2020$$

$$k_3 = h f\left(x_0 + \frac{h}{2}, y_0 + \frac{k_2}{2}\right)$$

$$= h\left[1 + \left(y_0 + \frac{k_2}{2}\right)^2\right] = 0.2\left[1 + \left(0 + \frac{0.2020}{2}\right)^2\right]$$

$$= 0.2[1 + (0.101)^2] = 0.2020$$

$$k_4 = h f(x_0 + h, y_0 + k_3)$$

$$= h\left[1 + (y_0 + k_3)^2\right] = 0.2[1 + (0 + 0.2020)^2]$$

$$= 0.2082$$

and $k = \frac{1}{6}[k_1 + 2k_2 + 2k_3 + k_4] = \frac{1}{6}[0.2 + 2(0.2020) + 2(0.2020) + 0.2082] = 0.2027$

$\therefore y = y_0 + k = 0 + 0.2027 = 0.2027$.

Ex. 4: Using Runge-Kutta method, solve $\frac{dy}{dx} = \frac{1}{x+y}$ with $y(0) = 1$ for $x = 1$. **SUK:Dec-13**

Solution: Given $f(x, y) = \frac{dy}{dx} = \frac{1}{x+y}$, $x_0 = 0$, $y_0 = 1$, $x_n = 1 \Rightarrow h = 1$

$k_1 = h f(x_0, y_0) = h\left(\frac{1}{x_0 + y_0}\right) = 1\left(\frac{1}{0+1}\right) = 1$

$k_2 = h f\left(x_0 + \frac{h}{2}, y_0 + \frac{k_1}{2}\right)$

$= h\left[\frac{1}{\left(x_0 + \frac{h}{2}\right) + \left(y_0 + \frac{k_1}{2}\right)}\right] = 1\left[\frac{1}{\left(0 + \frac{1}{2}\right) + \left(1 + \frac{1}{2}\right)}\right]$

$= 1\left[\frac{1}{(0.5) + (1.5)}\right] = 0.5$

$k_3 = h f\left(x_0 + \frac{h}{2}, y_0 + \frac{k_2}{2}\right)$

$= h\left[\frac{1}{\left(x_0 + \frac{h}{2}\right) + \left(y_0 + \frac{k_2}{2}\right)}\right] = 1\left[\frac{1}{\left(0 + \frac{1}{2}\right) + \left(1 + \frac{0.5}{2}\right)}\right]$

$= 1\left[\frac{1}{(0.5) + (1.25)}\right] = 0.5714$

$k_4 = h f(x_0 + h, y_0 + k_3)$

$= h\left[\frac{1}{(x_0 + h) + (y_0 + k_3)}\right] = 1\left[\frac{1}{(0+1) + (1+0.5714)}\right] = 0.3889$

and $k = \frac{1}{6}[k_1 + 2k_2 + 2k_3 + k_4] = \frac{1}{6}[1 + 2(0.5) + 2(0.5714) + 0.3889] = 0.5886$

$\therefore y = y_0 + k = 1 + 0.5886 = 1.5886$

Ex. 5 : Solve $\frac{dy}{dx} = xy$ with $x_0 = 1$, $y_0 = 2$, at $x = 1.4$ by Runge-Kutta method of fourth order, taking $h = 0.2$

Solution: Given $f(x, y) = \frac{dy}{dx} = xy$, $x_0 = 1$, $y_0 = 2$, $x = 1.4, h = 0.2$

Step-I At $x_1 = x_0 + h = 1 + .02 = 1.2$

For finding $y_1 = y_0 + k$

For finding k, we calculate,

$k_1 = h f(x_0, y_0) = h(xy) = 0.2[(1)(2)] = 0.4000$

$k_2 = h f\left(x_0 + \dfrac{h}{2}, y_0 + \dfrac{k_1}{2}\right)$

$= h\left[\left(x_0 + \dfrac{h}{2}\right)\left(y_0 + \dfrac{k_1}{2}\right)\right] = 0.2\left[\left(1 + \dfrac{0.2}{2}\right)\left(2 + \dfrac{0.4000}{2}\right)\right]$

$= 0.4840$

$k_3 = h f\left(x_0 + \dfrac{h}{2}, y_0 + \dfrac{k_2}{2}\right)$

$= h\left[\left(x_0 + \dfrac{h}{2}\right)\left(y_0 + \dfrac{k_2}{2}\right)\right] = 0.2\left[\left(1 + \dfrac{0.2}{2}\right)\left(2 + \dfrac{0.4840}{2}\right)\right]$

$= 0.4932$

$k_4 = h f(x_0 + h, y_0 + k_3)$

$= h[(x_0 + h)(y_0 + k_3)] = 0.2[(1 + 0.2)(2 + 0.49324)]$

$= 0.5984$

and $k = \dfrac{1}{6}[k_1 + 2k_2 + 2k_3 + k_4] = \dfrac{1}{6}[0.4000 + 2(0.4840) + 2(0.4932) + 0.5984] = 0.4921$

$\therefore y_1 = y_0 + k = 2 + 0.4921 = 2.4921.$

Step-II At $x_2 = x_1 + h = 1.2 + 0.2 = 1.4$ For finding $y_2 = y_1 + k$

Given $f(x, y) = \dfrac{dy}{dx} = xy$, $x_0 = 1.2$, $y_0 = 2.4921$, $h = 0.2$

For finding k, we calculate,

$k_1 = h f(x_0, y_0) = h(xy) = 0.2[(1.2).(2.4921)] = 0.5981$

$k_2 = h f\left(x_0 + \dfrac{h}{2}, y_0 + \dfrac{k_1}{2}\right)$

$= h\left[\left(x_0 + \dfrac{h}{2}\right)\left(y_0 + \dfrac{k_1}{2}\right)\right] = 0.2\left[\left(1.2 + \dfrac{0.2}{2}\right)\left(2.4921 + \dfrac{0.5981}{2}\right)\right]$

$= 0.7257$

$k_3 = h f\left(x_0 + \dfrac{h}{2}, y_0 + \dfrac{k_2}{2}\right)$

$= h\left[\left(x_0 + \dfrac{h}{2}\right)\left(y_0 + \dfrac{k_2}{2}\right)\right] = 0.2\left[\left(1.2 + \dfrac{0.2}{2}\right)\left(2.4921 + \dfrac{0.7257}{2}\right)\right]$

$= 0.7423$

$k_4 = h f(x_0 + h, y_0 + k_3)$

$= h[(x_0 + h)(y_0 + k_3)] = 0.2[(1.2 + 0.2)(2.4921 + 0.7423)]$

$= 0.9056$

and $k = \frac{1}{6}[k_1 + 2k_2 + 2k_3 + k_4] = \frac{1}{6}[0.5981 + 2(0.7257) + 2(0.7423) + 0.9056] = 0.7400$

$\therefore y_2 = y_1 + k = 2.4921 + 0.7400 = 3.2321.$

Ex. 6 : Solve $\frac{dy}{dx} = \sqrt{x+y}$ with $x_0 = 0$, $y_0 = 1$, at $x = 0.2$ by Runge-Kutta method of fourth order, taking $h = 0.1$.

Solution: Given $f(x, y) = \frac{dy}{dx} = \sqrt{x+y}$, $x_0 = 0$, $y_0 = 1$, $x = 0.2$, $h = 0.1$

Step-I At $x_1 = x_0 + h = 0 + 0.1 = 0.1$

For finding $y_1 = y_0 + k$

For finding k, we calculate,

$k_1 = h f(x_0, y_0) = h(\sqrt{x_0 + y_0}) = 0.1(\sqrt{0+1}) = 0.1000$

$k_2 = h f\left(x_0 + \frac{h}{2}, y_0 + \frac{k_1}{2}\right)$

$= h\left[\sqrt{\left(x_0 + \frac{h}{2}\right) + \left(y_0 + \frac{k_1}{2}\right)}\right] = 0.1\left[\sqrt{\left(0 + \frac{0.1}{2}\right) + \left(1 + \frac{0.1000}{2}\right)}\right]$

$= 0.1\sqrt{(0 + 0.05) + (1 + 0.05)} = 0.1049$

$k_3 = h f\left(x_0 + \frac{h}{2}, y_0 + \frac{k_2}{2}\right)$

$= h\left[\sqrt{\left(x_0 + \frac{h}{2}\right) + \left(y_0 + \frac{k_2}{2}\right)}\right] = 0.1\left[\sqrt{\left(0 + \frac{0.1}{2}\right) + \left(1 + \frac{0.1049}{2}\right)}\right]$

$= 0.1\sqrt{(0 + 0.05) + (1 + 0.05245)} = 0.1050$

$k_4 = h f(x_0 + h, y_0 + k_3)$

$= h\left[\sqrt{(x_0 + h) + (y_0 + k_3)}\right] = 0.1\left[\sqrt{(0 + 0.1) + (1 + 0.1050)}\right]$

$= 0.1098$

and $k = \frac{1}{6}[k_1 + 2k_2 + 2k_3 + k_4] = \frac{1}{6}[0.1000 + 2(0.1049) + 2(0.1050) + 0.1098] = 0.1049$

$\therefore y_1 = y_0 + k = 1 + 0.1049 = 1.1049.$

Step-II At $x_2 = x_1 + h = 0.1 + 0.1 = 0.2$

For finding $y_2 = y_1 + k$

Given $f(x, y) = \frac{dy}{dx} = \sqrt{x+y}$, $x_0 = 0.1$, $y_0 = 1.1049$, $h = 0.1$

For finding k, we calculate,

$k_1 = h f(x_0, y_0) = h(\sqrt{x_0 + y_0}) = 0.1(\sqrt{0.1} + 1.1049) = 0.1098$

$k_2 = h f\left(x_0 + \frac{h}{2}, y_0 + \frac{k_1}{2}\right)$

$= h\left[\sqrt{\left(x_0 + \frac{h}{2}\right) + \left(y_0 + \frac{k_1}{2}\right)}\right] = 0.1\left[\sqrt{\left(0.1 + \frac{0.1}{2}\right) + \left(1.1049 + \frac{0.1098}{2}\right)}\right]$

$= 0.1\sqrt{(0.1 + 0.05) + (1.1049 + 0.0549)} = 0.1144$

$k_3 = h f\left(x_0 + \frac{h}{2}, y_0 + \frac{k_2}{2}\right)$

$= h\left[\sqrt{\left(x_0 + \frac{h}{2}\right) + \left(y_0 + \frac{k_2}{2}\right)}\right] = 0.1\left[\sqrt{\left(0.1 + \frac{0.1}{2}\right) + \left(1.1049 + \frac{0.1144}{2}\right)}\right]$

$= 0.1\sqrt{(0.1 + 0.05) + (1.1049 + 0.0572)} = 0.1312$

$k_4 = h f(x_0 + h, y_0 + k_3)$

$= h\left[\sqrt{(x_0 + h) + (y_0 + k_3)}\right] = 0.1\left[\sqrt{(0.1 + 0.1) + (1.1049 + 0.1312)}\right]$

$= 0.1198$

and $k = \frac{1}{6}[k_1 + 2k_2 + 2k_3 + k_4] = \frac{1}{6}[0.1098 + 2(0.1144) + 2(0.1312) + 0.1198] = 0.1201$

$\therefore y_2 = y_1 + k = 1.1049 + 0.1201 = 1.2250$.

Ex. 7 : Solve $\frac{dy}{dx} = \sqrt{x + y}$ with $x_0 = 0$, $y_0 = 1$, at $x = 0.2$ by Runge-Kutta method of fourth order, taking $h = 0.2$.

Solution: Given $f(x, y) = \frac{dy}{dx} = \sqrt{x + y}$, $x_0 = 0$, $y_0 = 1$, $x = 0.2$, $h = 0.2$

At $x_1 = x_0 + h = 0 + 0.2 = 0.2$ For finding $y_1 = y_0 + k$ For finding k, we calculate,

$k_1 = h f(x_0, y_0) = h(\sqrt{x_0 + y_0}) = 0.2(\sqrt{0} + 1) = 0.2000$

$k_2 = h f\left(x_0 + \frac{h}{2}, y_0 + \frac{k_1}{2}\right)$

$= h\left[\sqrt{\left(x_0 + \frac{h}{2}\right) + \left(y_0 + \frac{k_1}{2}\right)}\right] = 0.2\left[\sqrt{\left(0 + \frac{0.2}{2}\right) + \left(1 + \frac{0.2000}{2}\right)}\right]$

$= 0.2\sqrt{(0 + 0.1) + (1 + 0.1)} = 0.2191$

$k_3 = h f\left(x_0 + \frac{h}{2}, y_0 + \frac{k_2}{2}\right)$

$= h\left[\sqrt{\left(x_0 + \frac{h}{2}\right) + \left(y_0 + \frac{k_2}{2}\right)}\right] = 0.2\left[\sqrt{\left(0 + \frac{0.2}{2}\right) + \left(1 + \frac{0.2191}{2}\right)}\right]$

$= 0.2\sqrt{(0 + 0.1) + (1 + 0.1096)} = 0.2200$

$k_4 = h f(x_0 + h, y_0 + k_3)$

$= h\left[\sqrt{(x_0 + h) + (y_0 + k_3)}\right] = 0.2\left[\sqrt{(0 + 0.2) + (1 + 0.2200)}\right]$

$= 0.2383$

and $k = \dfrac{1}{6}[k_1 + 2k_2 + 2k_3 + k_4] = \dfrac{1}{6}[0.2000 + 2(0.2191) + 2(0.2200) + 0.2383] = 0.2194$

$\therefore y_1 = y_0 + k = 1 + 0.2194 = 1.2194.$

Ex. 8 : Use Runge-Kutta method of fourth order to obtain the numerical solutions of $\dfrac{dy}{dx} = x^2 + y^2$ with $y(1) = 1.5$, at $x = 1.2$ with $h = 0.1$ **SUK: May-08, Aug-13**

Solution: Given $f(x, y) = \dfrac{dy}{dx} = x^2 + y^2$, $x_0 = 1$, $y_0 = 1.5$, at $x = 1.2 \Rightarrow h = 0.1$

Step-I $k_1 = h f(x_0, y_0) = h(x_0^2 + y_0^2) = 0.1\left[(1)^2 + (1.5)^2\right] = 0.3250$

$k_2 = h f\left(x_0 + \dfrac{h}{2}, y_0 + \dfrac{k_1}{2}\right)$

$= h\left[\left(x_0 + \dfrac{h}{2}\right)^2 + \left(y_0 + \dfrac{k_1}{2}\right)^2\right] = 0.1\left[\left(1 + \dfrac{0.1}{2}\right)^2 + \left(1.5 + \dfrac{0.3250}{2}\right)^2\right] = 0.3866$

$k_3 = h f\left(x_0 + \dfrac{h}{2}, y_0 + \dfrac{k_2}{2}\right)$

$= h\left[\left(x_0 + \dfrac{h}{2}\right)^2 + \left(y_0 + \dfrac{k_2}{2}\right)^2\right] = 0.1\left[\left(1 + \dfrac{0.1}{2}\right)^2 + \left(1.5 + \dfrac{0.3866}{2}\right)^2\right] = 0.3970$

$k_4 = h f(x_0 + h, y_0 + k_3)$

$= h\left[(x_0 + h)^2 + (y_0 + k_3)^2\right] = 0.1\left[(1 + 0.1)^2 + (1.5 + 0.3970)^2\right] = 0.4809$

and $k = \dfrac{1}{6}[k_1 + 2k_2 + 2k_3 + k_4] = \dfrac{1}{6}[0.3250 + 2(0.3870) + 2(0.3970) + 0.4809] = 0.3957$

$\therefore y = y_0 + k = 1.5 + 0.3957 = 1.8957.$

Step-II $f(x, y) = \dfrac{dy}{dx} = x^2 + y^2$, $x_0 = 1.1$, $y_0 = 1.8957$, at $x = 1.2 \Rightarrow h = 0.1$

$k_1 = h f(x_0, y_0) = h(x_0^2 + y_0^2) = 0.1\left[(1.1)^2 + (1.8957)^2\right] = 0.4803$

$k_2 = h f\left(x_0 + \dfrac{h}{2}, y_0 + \dfrac{k_1}{2}\right)$

$= h\left[\left(x_0 + \dfrac{h}{2}\right)^2 + \left(y_0 + \dfrac{k_1}{2}\right)^2\right] = 0.1\left[\left(1.1 + \dfrac{0.1}{2}\right)^2 + \left(1.8957 + \dfrac{0.4803}{2}\right)^2\right] = 0.5884$

$k_3 = h f\left(x_0 + \dfrac{h}{2}, y_0 + \dfrac{k_2}{2}\right)$

$= h\left[\left(x_0 + \dfrac{h}{2}\right)^2 + \left(y_0 + \dfrac{k_2}{2}\right)^2\right] = 0.1\left[\left(1.1 + \dfrac{0.1}{2}\right)^2 + \left(1.8957 + \dfrac{0.5884}{2}\right)^2\right] = 0.6118$

$k_4 = h f(x_0 + h, y_0 + k_3)$

$= h\left[(x_0 + h)^2 + (y_0 + k_3)^2\right] = 0.1\left[(1.1 + 0.1)^2 + (1.8957 + 0.6118)^2\right]$

$= 0.7728$

and $k = \dfrac{1}{6}[k_1 + 2k_2 + 2k_3 + k_4] = \dfrac{1}{6}[0.4803 + 2(0.5884) + 2(0.6118) + 0.7728] = 0.6089$

$\therefore y = y_0 + k = 1.8957 + 0.6089 = 2.5046.$

Ex. 9 : Compute $y(0.1)$ and $y(0.2)$ by use Runge-Kutta method of fourth order for the differential equation $\dfrac{dy}{dx} = xy + y^2$ with $y(0) = 1$.

Solution : Step-I Given

$$f(x, y) = \dfrac{dy}{dx} = xy + y^2, \qquad x_0 = 0, \ y_0 = 1, \ at \ x = 0.2 \Rightarrow h = 0.1$$

$k_1 = h f(x_0, y_0) = h(x_0 y_0 + y_0^2) = 0.1\left[(0).(1) + (1)^2\right] = 0.1$

$k_2 = h f\left(x_0 + \dfrac{h}{2}, y_0 + \dfrac{k_1}{2}\right)$

$\quad = h\left[\left(x_0 + \dfrac{h}{2}\right)\left(y_0 + \dfrac{k_1}{2}\right) + \left(y_0 + \dfrac{k_1}{2}\right)^2\right]$

$\quad = 0.1\left[\left(0 + \dfrac{0.1}{2}\right)\left(1 + \dfrac{0.1}{2}\right) + \left(1 + \dfrac{0.1}{2}\right)^2\right] = 0.1155$

$k_3 = h f\left(x_0 + \dfrac{h}{2}, y_0 + \dfrac{k_2}{2}\right)$

$\quad = h\left[\left(x_0 + \dfrac{h}{2}\right)\left(y_0 + \dfrac{k_2}{2}\right) + \left(y_0 + \dfrac{k_2}{2}\right)^2\right]$

$\quad = 0.1\left[\left(0 + \dfrac{0.1}{2}\right)\left(1 + \dfrac{0.1155}{2}\right) + \left(1 + \dfrac{0.1155}{2}\right)^2\right] = 0.1172$

$k_4 = h f(x_0 + h, y_0 + k_3)$

$\quad = h\left[(x_0 + h)(y_0 + k_3) + (y_0 + k_3)^2\right]$

$\quad = 0.1\left[(0 + 0.1)(1 + 0.1172) + (1 + 0.1172)^2\right]$

$\quad = 0.1360$

and $k = \dfrac{1}{6}[k_1 + 2k_2 + 2k_3 + k_4] = \dfrac{1}{6}[0.1 + 2(0.1155) + 2(0.1172) + 0.1360] = 0.1169$

$\therefore y = y_0 + k = 1 + 0.1169 = 1.1169.$

Step-II $f(x, y) = \dfrac{dy}{dx} = xy + y^2$,

$x_0 = 0.1, \ y_0 = 1.1169, \ at \ x = 0.2 \Rightarrow h = 0.1$

$$k_1 = hf(x_0, y_0) = h(x_0 y_0 + y_0^2)$$
$$= 0.1\left[(0.1)(1.1169) + (1.1169)^2\right] = 0.1359$$

$$k_2 = hf\left(x_0 + \frac{h}{2}, y_0 + \frac{k_1}{2}\right)$$
$$= h\left[\left(x_0 + \frac{h}{2}\right)\left(y_0 + \frac{k_1}{2}\right) + \left(y_0 + \frac{k_1}{2}\right)^2\right]$$
$$= 0.1\left[\left(0.1 + \frac{0.1}{2}\right)\left(1.1169 + \frac{0.1359}{2}\right) + \left(1.1169 + \frac{0.1359}{2}\right)^2\right] = 0.1582$$

$$k_3 = hf\left(x_0 + \frac{h}{2}, y_0 + \frac{k_2}{2}\right)$$
$$= h\left[\left(x_0 + \frac{h}{2}\right)\left(y_0 + \frac{k_2}{2}\right) + \left(y_0 + \frac{k_2}{2}\right)^2\right]$$
$$= 0.1\left[\left(0.1 + \frac{0.1}{2}\right)\left(1.1169 + \frac{0.1582}{2}\right) + \left(1.1169 + \frac{0.1582}{2}\right)^2\right] = 0.1610$$

$$k_4 = hf(x_0 + h, y_0 + k_3)$$
$$= h\left[(x_0 + h)(y_0 + k_3) + (y_0 + k_3)^2\right]$$
$$= 0.1\left[(0.1 + 0.1)(1.1169 + 0.1610) + (1.1169 + 0.1610)^2\right]$$
$$= 0.1889$$

and $k = \frac{1}{6}[k_1 + 2k_2 + 2k_3 + k_4] = \frac{1}{6}[0.1359 + 2(0.1582) + 2(0.1610) + 0.1889] = 0.1605$

$\therefore y = y_0 + k = 1.1169 + 0.1605 = 1.2774.$

Ex. 10: Find the approximate value of y by Runge-Kutta method. Given that $\frac{dy}{dx} + \frac{y}{x} = \frac{1}{x^2}$ with $y(1) = 1$, when $x = 1.1$.

Solution: Given $f(x, y) = \frac{dy}{dx} = \frac{1 - xy}{x^2}$,

$x_0 = 1$, $y_0 = 1$, at $x = 1.1 \Rightarrow h = 0.1$

$$k_1 = hf(x_0, y_0) = h\left(\frac{1-x_0 y_0}{x_0^2}\right) = 0.1\left[\frac{1-(1)(1)}{(1)^2}\right] = 0$$

$$k_2 = hf\left(x_0 + \frac{h}{2}, y_0 + \frac{k_1}{2}\right)$$

$$= h\left[\frac{1-\left(x_0+\frac{h}{2}\right)\left(y_0+\frac{k_1}{2}\right)}{\left(x_0+\frac{h}{2}\right)^2}\right]$$

$$= 0.1\left[\frac{1-\left(1+\frac{0.1}{2}\right)\left(1+\frac{0}{2}\right)}{\left(1+\frac{0.1}{2}\right)^2}\right] = -0.0045$$

$$k_3 = hf\left(x_0 + \frac{h}{2}, y_0 + \frac{k_2}{2}\right)$$

$$= h\left[\frac{1-\left(x_0+\frac{h}{2}\right)\left(y_0+\frac{k_2}{2}\right)}{\left(x_0+\frac{h}{2}\right)^2}\right] = 0.1\left[\frac{1-\left(1+\frac{0.1}{2}\right)\left(1+\frac{-0.0045}{2}\right)}{\left(1+\frac{0.1}{2}\right)^2}\right] = -0.0043$$

$$k_4 = hf(x_0+h, y_0+k_3)$$

$$= h\left[\frac{1-(x_0+h)(y_0+k_3)}{(x_0+h)^2}\right] = 0.1\left[\frac{1-(1+0.1)(1+(-0.0043))}{(1+0.1)^2}\right] = -0.0079$$

and $k = \frac{1}{6}[k_1 + 2k_2 + 2k_3 + k_4] = \frac{1}{6}[0 + 2(-0.0045) + 2(-0.0043) + (-0.0079)] = -0.0043$

$\therefore y = y_0 + k = 1 - 0.0043 = 0.9958$.

Ex. 11 : Solve by Runge-Kutta method of fourth order $\frac{dy}{dx} = x - y^2$ with $y(0) = 1$, at $x = 0.2$ with $h = 0.1$.

Solution:

Step-I $f(x,y) = \frac{dy}{dx} = x - y^2, x_0 = 0, y_0 = 1$, at $x = 0.2 \Rightarrow h = 0.1$

$k_1 = h f(x_0, y_0) = h(x_0 - y_0^2) = 0.1[(0) - (1)^2] = -0.1$

$k_2 = h f\left(x_0 + \dfrac{h}{2}, y_0 + \dfrac{k_1}{2}\right)$

$= h\left[\left(x_0 + \dfrac{h}{2}\right) - \left(y_0 + \dfrac{k_1}{2}\right)^2\right]$

$= 0.1\left[\left(0 + \dfrac{0.1}{2}\right) - \left(1 + \dfrac{-0.1}{2}\right)^2\right] = -0.0853$

$k_3 = h f\left(x_0 + \dfrac{h}{2}, y_0 + \dfrac{k_2}{2}\right)$

$= h\left[\left(x_0 + \dfrac{h}{2}\right) - \left(y_0 + \dfrac{k_2}{2}\right)^2\right]$

$= 0.1\left[\left(0 + \dfrac{0.1}{2}\right) - \left(1 + \dfrac{-0.0853}{2}\right)^2\right] = -0.0867$

$k_4 = h f(x_0 + h, y_0 + k_3)$

$= h\left[(x_0 + h) - (y_0 + k_3)^2\right]$

$= 0.1\left[(0 + 0.1) - (1 - 0.0867)^2\right] = -0.0734$

and $k = \dfrac{1}{6}[k_1 + 2k_2 + 2k_3 + k_4] = \dfrac{1}{6}[-0.1 + 2(-0.0853) + 2(-0.0867) - 0.0734] = -0.0862$

$\therefore y = y_0 + k = 1 - 0.0862 = 0.9138$.

Step-II $f(x, y) = \dfrac{dy}{dx} = x - y^2, x_0 = 0.1, y_0 = 0.9138,$ at $x = 0.2 \Rightarrow h = 0.1$,

$k_1 = h f(x_0, y_0) = h(x_0 - y_0^2)$

$= 0.1\left[(0.1) - (0.9138)^2\right] = -0.0735$

$k_2 = h f\left(x_0 + \dfrac{h}{2}, y_0 + \dfrac{k_1}{2}\right)$

$= h\left[\left(x_0 + \dfrac{h}{2}\right) - \left(y_0 + \dfrac{k_1}{2}\right)^2\right]$

$= 0.1\left[\left(0.1 + \dfrac{0.1}{2}\right) - \left(0.9138 + \dfrac{-0.0735}{2}\right)^2\right] = -0.0619$

$k_3 = h f\left(x_0 + \dfrac{h}{2}, y_0 + \dfrac{k_2}{2}\right)$

$= h\left[\left(x_0 + \dfrac{h}{2}\right) - \left(y_0 + \dfrac{k_2}{2}\right)^2\right]$

$= 0.1\left[\left(0.1 + \dfrac{0.1}{2}\right) - \left(0.9138 + \dfrac{-0.0619}{2}\right)^2\right] = -0.0629$

$k_4 = h f(x_0 + h, y_0 + k_3)$

$= h\left[(x_0 + h) - (y_0 + k_3)^2\right]$

$= 0.1\left[(0.1 + 0.1) - (0.9138 - 0.0629)^2\right] = -0.0524$

and $k = \dfrac{1}{6}[k_1 + 2k_2 + 2k_3 + k_4] = \dfrac{1}{6}[-0.0735 + 2(-0.0619) + 2(-0.0629) - 0.0524] = -0.0626$

$\therefore y = y_0 + k = 0.9138 - 0.0626 = 0.8512.$

Ex. 12: Solve $\dfrac{dy}{dx} = \dfrac{y}{x}$ with $y(1) = 1$, when $x = 1.2$ taking $h = 0.1$.

Solution: Step-I $f(x, y) = \dfrac{dy}{dx} = \dfrac{y}{x}$, $\quad x_0 = 1,\ y_0 = 1,\ at\ x = 1.2 \Rightarrow h = 0.1$

$k_1 = h f(x_0, y_0) = h\left(\dfrac{y_0}{x_0}\right) = 0.1\left[\dfrac{1}{1}\right] = 0.1$

$k_2 = h f\left(x_0 + \dfrac{h}{2},\ y_0 + \dfrac{k_1}{2}\right)$

$= h\left[\dfrac{\left(y_0 + \dfrac{k_1}{2}\right)}{\left(x_0 + \dfrac{h}{2}\right)}\right] = 0.1\left[\dfrac{\left(1 + \dfrac{0.1}{2}\right)}{\left(1 + \dfrac{0.1}{2}\right)}\right] = 0.1$

$k_3 = h f\left(x_0 + \dfrac{h}{2},\ y_0 + \dfrac{k_2}{2}\right)$

$= h\left[\dfrac{\left(y_0 + \dfrac{k_2}{2}\right)}{\left(x_0 + \dfrac{h}{2}\right)}\right] = 0.1\left[\dfrac{\left(1 + \dfrac{0.1}{2}\right)}{\left(1 + \dfrac{0.1}{2}\right)}\right] = 0.1$

$k_4 = h f(x_0 + h,\ y_0 + k_3)$

$= h\left[\dfrac{(y_0 + k_3)}{(x_0 + h)}\right] = 0.1\left[\dfrac{(1 + (0.1))}{(1 + 0.1)}\right]$

$= 0.1$

and $k = \dfrac{1}{6}[k_1 + 2k_2 + 2k_3 + k_4] = \dfrac{1}{6}[0.1 + 2(0.1) + 2(0.1) + (0.1)] = 0.1$

$\therefore y = y_0 + k = 1 + 0.1 = 1.1$

Step-II $f(x, y) = \dfrac{dy}{dx} = \dfrac{y}{x}$, $\quad x_0 = 1.1,\ y_0 = 1.1,\ at\ x = 1.2 \Rightarrow h = 0.1$

$k_1 = h f(x_0, y_0) = h\left(\dfrac{y_0}{x_0}\right) = 0.1\left[\dfrac{1.1}{1.1}\right] = 0.1$

$k_2 = h f\left(x_0 + \dfrac{h}{2},\ y_0 + \dfrac{k_1}{2}\right)$

$= h\left[\dfrac{\left(y_0 + \dfrac{k_1}{2}\right)}{\left(x_0 + \dfrac{h}{2}\right)}\right] = 0.1\left[\dfrac{\left(1.1 + \dfrac{0.1}{2}\right)}{\left(1.1 + \dfrac{0.1}{2}\right)}\right] = 0.1$

$k_3 = h f\left(x_0 + \dfrac{h}{2},\ y_0 + \dfrac{k_2}{2}\right)$

$= h\left[\dfrac{\left(y_0 + \dfrac{k_2}{2}\right)}{\left(x_0 + \dfrac{h}{2}\right)}\right] = 0.1\left[\dfrac{\left(1.1 + \dfrac{0.1}{2}\right)}{\left(1.1 + \dfrac{0.1}{2}\right)}\right] = 0.1$

$k_4 = h f(x_0 + h,\ y_0 + k_3)$

$= h\left[\dfrac{(y_0 + k_3)}{(x_0 + h)}\right] = 0.1\left[\dfrac{(1.1 + 0.1)}{(1.1 + 0.1)}\right] = 0.1$

and $k = \frac{1}{6}[k_1 + 2k_2 + 2k_3 + k_4] = \frac{1}{6}[0.1 + 2(0.1) + 2(0.1) + (0.1)] = 0.1$

$\therefore y = y_0 + k = 1.1 + 0.1 = 1.2$.

Ex. 13: Solve $\frac{dy}{dx} = 0.31 + 0.25y + 0.3x$ with $x_0 = 0$, $y_0 = 0.72$, at $x = 0.2$ by Runge-Kutta method of fourth order, taking $h = 0.2$

Solution : Given $f(x, y) = \frac{dy}{dx} = 0.31 + 0.25y + 0.3x$,

$x_0 = 0$, $y_0 = 0.72$, $x = 0.2$, $h = 0.2$

$k_1 = h f(x_0, y_0) = h[0.31 + 0.25 y_0 + 0.3 x_0]$

$= 0.2[0.31 + 0.25(0.72) + 0.3(0)] = 0.098$

$k_2 = h f\left(x_0 + \frac{h}{2}, y_0 + \frac{k_1}{2}\right)$

$= h\left[0.31 + 0.25\left(y_0 + \frac{k_1}{2}\right) + 0.3\left(x_0 + \frac{h}{2}\right)\right]$

$= 0.2\left[0.31 + 0.25\left(0.72 + \frac{0.098}{2}\right) + 0.3\left(0 + \frac{0.2}{2}\right)\right]$

$= 0.1065$

$k_3 = h f\left(x_0 + \frac{h}{2}, y_0 + \frac{k_2}{2}\right)$

$= h\left[0.31 + 0.25\left(y_0 + \frac{k_2}{2}\right) + 0.3\left(x_0 + \frac{h}{2}\right)\right]$

$= 0.2\left[0.31 + 0.25\left(0.72 + \frac{0.1065}{2}\right) + 0.3\left(0 + \frac{0.2}{2}\right)\right]$

$= 0.1067$

$k_4 = h f(x_0 + h, y_0 + k_3)$

$= h[0.31 + 0.25(y_0 + k_3) + 0.3(x_0 + h)]$

$= 0.2[0.31 + 0.25(0.72 + 0.1067) + 0.3(0 + 0.2)]$

$= 0.1153$

and $k = \frac{1}{6}[k_1 + 2k_2 + 2k_3 + k_4] = \frac{1}{6}[0.098 + 2(0.1065) + 2(0.1067) + 0.1153] = 0.1066$

$\therefore y_1 = y_0 + k = 0.72 + 0.1066 = 0.8266$.

Ex. 14: Solve $\dfrac{dy}{dx} = \dfrac{x+y}{xy}$ with $y(1) = 1.72$, when $x = 1.1$.

Solution: Given $f(x, y) = \dfrac{dy}{dx} = \dfrac{x+y}{xy}$, $x_0 = 1$, $y_0 = 1.72$, at $x = 1.1 \Rightarrow h = 0.1$

$$k_1 = h f(x_0, y_0) = h \left(\dfrac{x_0 + y_0}{x_0 y_0} \right) = 0.1 \left[\dfrac{1 + 1.72}{(1)(1.72)} \right] = 0.1581$$

$$k_2 = h f\left(x_0 + \dfrac{h}{2}, y_0 + \dfrac{k_1}{2} \right) = h \left[\dfrac{\left(x_0 + \dfrac{h}{2}\right) + \left(y_0 + \dfrac{k_1}{2}\right)}{\left(x_0 + \dfrac{h}{2}\right)\left(y_0 + \dfrac{k_1}{2}\right)} \right]$$

$$= 0.1 \left[\dfrac{\left(1 + \dfrac{0.1}{2}\right) + \left(1.72 + \dfrac{0.1581}{2}\right)}{\left(1 + \dfrac{0.1}{2}\right)\left(1.72 + \dfrac{0.1581}{2}\right)} \right] = 0.1508$$

$$k_3 = h f\left(x_0 + \dfrac{h}{2}, y_0 + \dfrac{k_2}{2} \right)$$

$$= h \left[\dfrac{\left(x_0 + \dfrac{h}{2}\right) + \left(y_0 + \dfrac{k_2}{2}\right)}{\left(x_0 + \dfrac{h}{2}\right)\left(y_0 + \dfrac{k_2}{2}\right)} \right]$$

$$= 0.1 \left[\dfrac{\left(1 + \dfrac{0.1}{2}\right) + \left(1.72 + \dfrac{0.1508}{2}\right)}{\left(1 + \dfrac{0.1}{2}\right)\left(1.72 + \dfrac{0.1508}{2}\right)} \right] = 0.1509$$

$$k_4 = h f(x_0 + h, y_0 + k_3) = h \left[\dfrac{(x_0 + h) + (y_0 + k_3)}{(x_0 + h)(y_0 + k_3)} \right]$$

$$= 0.1 \left[\dfrac{(1 + 0.1) + (1.72 + 0.1509)}{(1 + 0.1)(1.72 + 0.1509)} \right] = 0.1444$$

and $k = \dfrac{1}{6}[k_1 + 2k_2 + 2k_3 + k_4] = \dfrac{1}{6}[0.1581 + 2(0.1508) + 2(0.1509) + (0.1444)] = 0.1510$

$\therefore y = y_0 + k = 1.72 + 0.1510 = 1.8710$.

TEST YOUR KNOWLEDGE

1. Apply Runge-Kutta method to find an approximate value of y when x=0.2 given that $\frac{dy}{dx} = x + y$, $y = 1, x = 0$ at $x = 0.2$. **Ans: 1.2428**

2. Apply Runge-Kutta method to find an approximate value of y given that $\frac{dy}{dx} = x^2 + y^2$, $y = 1.5, x = 1$ in the interval $(1, 1.2)$ with $h = 0.1$. **Ans: 2.5043**

3. Apply Runge-Kutta method to find an approximate value of y at x=0.2 given that $\frac{dy}{dx} = x + y^2$, $y = 1, x = 0$ with $h = 0.1$. **Ans: 1.2736**

4. Apply Runge-Kutta method to find an approximate value of y given that $\frac{dy}{dx} = \frac{1}{x+y}$, $y = 1, x = 0$ in the interval $(0, 1)$ with $h = 0.5$. **Ans: 1.5837**

5. Apply Runge-Kutta method to find an approximate value of y at x=1 given that
   a. $(x + y)\frac{dy}{dx} = 1$, $y(0) = 1$. **Ans: 1.5837**

SIMULTANEOUS FIRST ORDER DIFFERENTIAL EQUATIONS BY RUNGE - KUTTA METHOD:

The simultaneous differential equations of the type

$$\frac{dy}{dx} = f(x, y, z)$$

and $\frac{dz}{dx} = \phi(x, y, z)$

with the initial condition $y(x_0) = y_0$ and $z(x_0) = z_0$. Then the Runge-Kutta method for the simultaneous first order differential equation is as follows

Staring at (x_0, y_0, z_0) and taking the step-sizes for x, y, z to be h, k, l respectively, we have the following formula for the Runge-Kutta method of fourth order

$k_1 = h f(x_0, y_0, z_0)$ $\qquad l_1 = h \phi(x_0, y_0, z_0)$

$k_2 = h f\left(x_0 + \frac{h}{2}, y_0 + \frac{k_1}{2}, z_0 + \frac{l_1}{2}\right)$ $\qquad l_2 = h \phi\left(x_0 + \frac{h}{2}, y_0 + \frac{k_1}{2}, z_0 + \frac{l_1}{2}\right)$

$k_3 = h f\left(x_0 + \frac{h}{2}, y_0 + \frac{k_2}{2}, z_0 + \frac{l_2}{2}\right)$ $\qquad l_3 = h \phi\left(x_0 + \frac{h}{2}, y_0 + \frac{k_2}{2}, z_0 + \frac{l_2}{2}\right)$

$k_4 = h f(x_0 + h, y_0 + k_3, z_0 + l_3)$ $\qquad l_4 = h \phi(x_0 + h, y_0 + k_3, z_0 + l_3)$

Hence $y_1 = y_0 + \frac{1}{6}[k_1 + 2k_2 + 2k_3 + k_4]$ and $z_1 = z_0 + \frac{1}{6}[l_1 + 2l_2 + 2l_3 + l_4]$

To compute y_2 and z_2, we simply replace x_0, y_0, z_0 by x_1, y_1, z_1 in the above result.

Examples on simultaneous first order differential equations by Runge-Kutta method

Ex. 1 : Solve the differential equations $\dfrac{dy}{dx} = 1 + xz$, $\dfrac{dz}{dx} = -xy$ for $x = 0.3$ using fourth order Runge-Kutta method, initial values are $x = 0, y = 0, z = 1$.

Solution: Given $\dfrac{dy}{dx} = f(x, y, z) = 1 + xz$, and $\dfrac{dz}{dx} = \phi(x, y, z) = -xy$

$x_0 = 0$, $y_0 = 0$, $z_0 = 1$. Let us take $h = 0.3$.

$$k_1 = h f(x_0, y_0, z_0)$$
$$= h(1 + x_0 z_0)$$
$$= 0.3(1 + (0)(1)) = 0.3$$

$$l_1 = h\phi(x_0, y_0, z_0)$$
$$= h(-x_0 y_0)$$
$$= 0.3[(0)(0)] = 0$$

$$k_2 = h f\left(x_0 + \dfrac{h}{2}, y_0 + \dfrac{k_1}{2}, z_0 + \dfrac{l_1}{2}\right)$$
$$= h\left[1 + \left(x_0 + \dfrac{h}{2}\right)\left(z_0 + \dfrac{l_1}{2}\right)\right]$$
$$= 0.3\left[1 + \left(0 + \dfrac{0.3}{2}\right)\left(0 + \dfrac{0}{2}\right)\right]$$
$$= 0.345$$

$$l_2 = h\phi\left(x_0 + \dfrac{h}{2}, y_0 + \dfrac{k_1}{2}, z_0 + \dfrac{l_1}{2}\right)$$
$$= h\left[-\left(x_0 + \dfrac{h}{2}\right)\left(y_0 + \dfrac{k_1}{2}\right)\right]$$
$$= 0.3\left[-\left(0 + \dfrac{0.3}{2}\right)\left(0 + \dfrac{0.3}{2}\right)\right]$$
$$= -0068$$

$$k_3 = h f\left(x_0 + \dfrac{h}{2}, y_0 + \dfrac{k_2}{2}, z_0 + \dfrac{l_2}{2}\right)$$
$$= h\left[1 + \left(x_0 + \dfrac{h}{2}\right)\left(z_0 + \dfrac{l_2}{2}\right)\right]$$
$$= 0.3\left[1 + \left(0 + \dfrac{0.3}{2}\right)\left(1 + \dfrac{-0.0068}{2}\right)\right]$$
$$= 0.3448$$

$$l_3 = h\phi\left(x_0 + \dfrac{h}{2}, y_0 + \dfrac{k_2}{2}, z_0 + \dfrac{l_2}{2}\right)$$
$$= h\left[-\left(x_0 + \dfrac{h}{2}\right)\left(y_0 + \dfrac{k_2}{2}\right)\right]$$
$$= 0.3\left[-\left(0 + \dfrac{0.3}{2}\right)\left(0 + \dfrac{0.345}{2}\right)\right]$$
$$= -0.0078$$

$$k_4 = h f(x_0 + h, y_0 + k_3, z_0 + l_3)$$
$$= h[1 + (x_0 + h)(z_0 + l_3)]$$
$$= 0.3[1 + (0 + 0.3)(1 - 0.0078)]$$
$$= 0.3893$$

$$l_4 = h\phi(x_0 + h, y_0 + k_3, z_0 + l_3)$$
$$= h[-(x_0 + h)(y_0 + k_3)]$$
$$= 0.3[-(0 + 0.3)(0 + 0.3448)]$$
$$= -0.0310$$

Hence $y_1 = y_0 + \dfrac{1}{6}[k_1 + 2k_2 + 2k_3 + k_4]$

$$= 0 + \dfrac{1}{6}[0.3 + 2(0.345) + 2(0.3448) + 0.3893] = 0.3448$$

$$z_1 = z_0 + \dfrac{1}{6}[l_1 + 2l_2 + 2l_3 + l_4]$$

$$= 1 + \dfrac{1}{6}[0 + 2(-0.0068) + 2(-0.0078) - 0.0310] = 0.9900$$

Ex. 2: Solve the differential equations $\frac{dy}{dx} = x + z$, $\frac{dz}{dx} = x - y^2$ for $x = 0.1$ using fourth order Runge-Kutta method, initial values are $y(0) = 2$, $z(0) = 1$.

Solution : Given $\frac{dy}{dx} = f(x, y, z) = x + z$, and $\frac{dz}{dx} = \phi(x, y, z) = x - y^2$

$x_0 = 0$, $y_0 = 2$, $z_0 = 1$. Let us take $h = 0.1$.

$k_1 = h f(x_0, y_0, z_0)$
$= h(x_0 + z_0)$
$= 0.1(0+1) = 0.1$

$k_2 = h f\left(x_0 + \frac{h}{2}, y_0 + \frac{k_1}{2}, z_0 + \frac{l_1}{2}\right)$
$= h\left[\left(x_0 + \frac{h}{2}\right) + \left(z_0 + \frac{l_1}{2}\right)\right]$
$= 0.1\left(0 + \frac{0.1}{2} + 1 + \frac{-0.4}{2}\right) = 0.0850$

$k_3 = h f\left(x_0 + \frac{h}{2}, y_0 + \frac{k_2}{2}, z_0 + \frac{l_2}{2}\right)$
$= h\left(x_0 + \frac{h}{2} + z_0 + \frac{l_2}{2}\right)$
$= 0.1\left(0 + \frac{0.1}{2} + 1 + \frac{-0.4153}{2}\right) = 0.0842$

$k_4 = h f(x_0 + h, y_0 + k_3, z_0 + l_3)$
$= h(x_0 + h + z_0 + l_3)$
$= 0.1(0 + 0.1 + 1 - 0.4122) = 0.0688$

$l_1 = h \phi(x_0, y_0, z_0)$
$= h(x_0 - y_0^2)$
$= 0.1(0 - 2^2) = -0.4$

$l_2 = h \phi\left(x_0 + \frac{h}{2}, y_0 + \frac{k_1}{2}, z_0 + \frac{l_1}{2}\right)$
$= h\left(x_0 + \frac{h}{2} - \left(y_0 + \frac{k_1}{2}\right)^2\right)$
$= 0.1\left(0 + \frac{0.1}{2} - \left(2 + \frac{0.1}{2}\right)^2\right) = -0.4153$

$l_3 = h \phi\left(x_0 + \frac{h}{2}, y_0 + \frac{k_2}{2}, z_0 + \frac{l_2}{2}\right)$
$= h\left(x_0 + \frac{h}{2} - \left(y_0 + \frac{k_2}{2}\right)^2\right)$
$= 0.1\left(0 + \frac{0.1}{2} - \left(2 + \frac{0.0850}{2}\right)^2\right) = -0.4122$

$l_4 = h \phi(x_0 + h, y_0 + k_3, z_0 + l_3)$
$= h(x_0 + h - (y_0 + k_3)^2)$
$= 0.1(0 + 0.1 - (2 + 0.0842)^2) = -0.4244$

Hence $y_1 = y_0 + \frac{1}{6}[k_1 + 2k_2 + 2k_3 + k_4]$

$= 2 + \frac{1}{6}[0.1 + 2(0.0850) + 2(0.0842) + 0.0688] = 2.0845$

$z_1 = z_0 + \frac{1}{6}[l_1 + 2l_2 + 2l_3 + l_4]$

$= 1 + \frac{1}{6}[-0.4 + 2(-0.4153) + 2(-0.4122) - 0.4244] = 0.5868$

Ex. 3: Solve $\dfrac{dy}{dx} = x + z$, $\dfrac{dz}{dx} = x - y$ for $x = 0.1$ and $x = 0.2$ by Runge-Kutta method, initial values are $y(0) = 0$, $z(0) = 1$.

Solution: Given $\dfrac{dy}{dx} = f(x, y, z) = x + z$, and $\dfrac{dz}{dx} = \phi(x, y, z) = x - y$

$x_0 = 0$, $y_0 = 0$, $z_0 = 1$. Let us take $h = 0.1$.

For finding $y(0.1)$ and $z(0.1)$, we have

$k_1 = h f(x_0, y_0, z_0)$
$= h(x_0 + z_0)$
$= 0.1(0 + 1) = 0.1$

$l_1 = h \phi(x_0, y_0, z_0)$
$= h(x_0 - y_0)$
$= 0.1(0 - 0) = 0$

$k_2 = h f\left(x_0 + \dfrac{h}{2}, y_0 + \dfrac{k_1}{2}, z_0 + \dfrac{l_1}{2}\right)$
$= h\left[\left(x_0 + \dfrac{h}{2}\right) + \left(z_0 + \dfrac{l_1}{2}\right)\right]$
$= 0.1\left[\left(0 + \dfrac{0.1}{2}\right) + \left(1 + \dfrac{0}{2}\right)\right] = 0.105$

$l_2 = h \phi\left(x_0 + \dfrac{h}{2}, y_0 + \dfrac{k_1}{2}, z_0 + \dfrac{l_1}{2}\right)$
$= h\left[\left(x_0 + \dfrac{h}{2}\right) - \left(y_0 + \dfrac{k_1}{2}\right)\right]$
$= 0.1\left[\left(0 + \dfrac{0.1}{2}\right) - \left(0 + \dfrac{0.1}{2}\right)\right] = 0$

$k_3 = h f\left(x_0 + \dfrac{h}{2}, y_0 + \dfrac{k_2}{2}, z_0 + \dfrac{l_2}{2}\right)$
$= h\left[\left(x_0 + \dfrac{h}{2}\right) + \left(z_0 + \dfrac{l_2}{2}\right)\right]$
$= 0.1\left[\left(0 + \dfrac{0.1}{2}\right) + \left(1 + \dfrac{0}{2}\right)\right] = 0.105$

$l_3 = h \phi\left(x_0 + \dfrac{h}{2}, y_0 + \dfrac{k_2}{2}, z_0 + \dfrac{l_2}{2}\right)$
$= h\left[\left(x_0 + \dfrac{h}{2}\right) - \left(y_0 + \dfrac{k_2}{2}\right)\right]$
$= 0.1\left[\left(0 + \dfrac{0.1}{2}\right) - \left(0 + \dfrac{0.105}{2}\right)\right] = 0.0003$

$k_4 = h f(x_0 + h, y_0 + k_3, z_0 + l_3)$
$= h\left[(x_0 + h) + (z_0 + l_3)\right]$
$= 0.1\left[(0 + 0.1) + (1 + 0.0003)\right] = 0.1100$

$l_4 = h \phi(x_0 + h, y_0 + k_3, z_0 + l_3)$
$= h\left[(x_0 + h) - (y_0 + k_3)\right]$
$= 0.1\left[(0 + 0.1) - (0 + 0.105)\right] = -0.0005$

Hence $y_1 = y_0 + \dfrac{1}{6}[k_1 + 2k_2 + 2k_3 + k_4]$

$= 0 + \dfrac{1}{6}\left[0.1 + 2(0.105) + 2(0.105) + 0.1100\right] = 0.1050$

$z_1 = z_0 + \dfrac{1}{6}[l_1 + 2l_2 + 2l_3 + l_4]$

$= 1 + \dfrac{1}{6}\left[0 + 2(0) + 2(0.0003) - 0.0005\right] = 0.9998$.

Again for finding $y(0.2)$ and $z(0.2)$, we have

$k_1 = hf(x_1, y_1, z_1)$
$= h(x_1 + z_1)$
$= 0.1(0.1 + 0.9998) = 0.1100$

$l_1 = h\phi(x_1, y_1, z_1)$
$= h(x_1 - y_1)$
$= 0.1(0.1 - 0.1050) = -0.0005$

$k_2 = hf\left(x_1 + \dfrac{h}{2}, y_1 + \dfrac{k_1}{2}, z_1 + \dfrac{l_1}{2}\right)$

$= h\left[\left(x_1 + \dfrac{h}{2}\right) + \left(z_1 + \dfrac{l_1}{2}\right)\right]$

$= 0.1\left[\left(0.1 + \dfrac{0.1}{2}\right) + \left(0.9998 + \dfrac{-0.0005}{2}\right)\right]$

$= 0.1150$

$l_2 = h\phi\left(x_1 + \dfrac{h}{2}, y_1 + \dfrac{k_1}{2}, z_1 + \dfrac{l_1}{2}\right)$

$= h\left[\left(x_1 + \dfrac{h}{2}\right) - \left(y_1 + \dfrac{k_1}{2}\right)\right]$

$= 0.1\left[\left(0.1 + \dfrac{0.1}{2}\right) - (0.1050 + 0.0550)\right]$

$= -0.0010$

$k_3 = hf\left(x_1 + \dfrac{h}{2}, y_1 + \dfrac{k_2}{2}, z_1 + \dfrac{l_2}{2}\right)$

$= h\left[\left(x_1 + \dfrac{h}{2}\right) + \left(z_1 + \dfrac{l_2}{2}\right)\right]$

$= 0.1(0.150 + 0.9998 - 0.0005)$

$= 0.1149$

$l_3 = h\phi\left(x_1 + \dfrac{h}{2}, y_1 + \dfrac{k_2}{2}, z_1 + \dfrac{l_2}{2}\right)$

$= h\left[\left(x_1 + \dfrac{h}{2}\right) - \left(y_1 + \dfrac{k_2}{2}\right)\right]$

$= 0.1[(0.150) - (0.1050 + 0.0575)]$

$= -0.0013$

$k_4 = hf(x_1 + h, y_1 + k_3, z_1 + l_3)$
$= h[(x_1 + h) + (z_1 + l_3)]$
$= 0.1(0.150 + 0.9998 - 0.0013)$
$= 0.1149$

$l_4 = h\phi(x_1 + h, y_1 + k_3, z_1 + l_3)$
$= h[(x_1 + h) - (y_1 + k_3)]$
$= 0.1[(0.150) - (0.1050 + 0.1049)]$
$= -0.0070$

Hence $y_2 = y_1 + \dfrac{1}{6}[k_1 + 2k_2 + 2k_3 + k_4]$

$= 0.1050 + \dfrac{1}{6}[0.1100 + 2(0.1150) + 2(0.1149) + 0.1149] = 0.2191$

$z_2 = z_1 + \dfrac{1}{6}[l_1 + 2l_2 + 2l_3 + l_4]$

$= 0.9998 + \dfrac{1}{6}[-0.0005 + 2(-0.0010) + 2(-0.0013) - 0.0070] = 0.9978$.

Ex. 4: Using fourth order Runge-Kutta method, Solve the differential equations $\dfrac{dy}{dx} = x + yz$, $\dfrac{dz}{dx} = x^2 - y^2$ subjected to $x_0 = 0, y_0 = 1, z_0 = \dfrac{1}{2}$
to find y and z at $x = 0.2$ taking $h = 0.2$

Solution: Given $\dfrac{dy}{dx} = f(x, y, z) = x + yz$, and $\dfrac{dz}{dx} = \phi(x, y, z) = x^2 - y^2$

$x_0 = 0, \ y_0 = 1, \ z_0 = \dfrac{1}{2}, \ h = 0.2$

$k_1 = h f(x_0, y_0, z_0)$
$= h(x_0 + y_0 z_0) = 0.2(0 + 1(0.5)) = 0.1$

$k_2 = h f\left(x_0 + \dfrac{h}{2}, y_0 + \dfrac{k_1}{2}, z_0 + \dfrac{l_1}{2}\right)$

$= h\left[\left(x_0 + \dfrac{h}{2}\right) + \left(y_0 + \dfrac{k_1}{2}\right)\left(z_0 + \dfrac{l_1}{2}\right)\right]$

$= 0.2\left[\left(0 + \dfrac{0.2}{2}\right) + \left(1 + \dfrac{0.1}{2}\right)\left(0.5 + \dfrac{-0.2}{2}\right)\right]$

$= 0.1040$

$k_3 = h f\left(x_0 + \dfrac{h}{2}, y_0 + \dfrac{k_2}{2}, z_0 + \dfrac{l_2}{2}\right)$

$= h\left[\left(x_0 + \dfrac{h}{2}\right) + \left(y_0 + \dfrac{k_2}{2}\right)\left(z_0 + \dfrac{l_2}{2}\right)\right]$

$= 0.2\left[\left(0 + \dfrac{0.2}{2}\right) + \left(1 + \dfrac{0.1040}{2}\right)\left(0.5 + \dfrac{-0.16}{2}\right)\right]$

$= 0.1084$

$k_4 = h f(x_0 + h, y_0 + k_3, z_0 + l_3)$
$= h\left[(x_0 + h) + (y_0 + k_3)(z_0 + l_3)\right]$
$= 0.2\left[(0 + 0.2) + (1 + 0.1084)(0.5 + -0.2193)\right]$
$= 0.1022$

$l_1 = h\phi(x_0, y_0, z_0)$
$= h(x_0^2 - y_0^2) = 0.2(0^2 - 1^2) = -0.2$

$l_2 = h\phi\left(x_0 + \dfrac{h}{2}, y_0 + \dfrac{k_1}{2}, z_0 + \dfrac{l_1}{2}\right)$

$= h\left[\left(x_0 + \dfrac{h}{2}\right)^2 - \left(y_0 + \dfrac{k_1}{2}\right)^2\right]$

$= 0.2\left[\left(0 + \dfrac{0.2}{2}\right)^2 - \left(1 + \dfrac{0.1}{2}\right)^2\right]$

$= -0.16$

$l_3 = h\phi\left(x_0 + \dfrac{h}{2}, y_0 + \dfrac{k_2}{2}, z_0 + \dfrac{l_2}{2}\right)$

$= h\left[\left(x_0 + \dfrac{h}{2}\right)^2 - \left(y_0 + \dfrac{k_2}{2}\right)^2\right]$

$= 0.2\left[\left(0 + \dfrac{0.2}{2}\right)^2 - \left(1 + \dfrac{0.1040}{2}\right)^2\right]$

$= -0.2193$

$l_4 = h\phi(x_0 + h, y_0 + k_3, z_0 + l_3)$
$= h\left[(x_0 + h)^2 - (y_0 + k_3)^2\right]$
$= 0.2\left[(0 + 0.2)^2 - (1 + 0.1084)^2\right]$
$= -0.2377$

Hence $y_1 = y_0 + \dfrac{1}{6}[k_1 + 2k_2 + 2k_3 + k_4]$

$= 1 + \dfrac{1}{6}[0.1 + 2(0.1040) + 2(0.1084) + 0.1022] = 1.1045$

$z_1 = z_0 + \dfrac{1}{6}[l_1 + 2l_2 + 2l_3 + l_4]$

$= 0.5 + \dfrac{1}{6}[-0.2 - 2(0.16) - 2(0.2193) - 0.2377] = 0.3006$

Ex. 5: Using Runge-Kutta method of fourth order, find the approximate values of x and y at t = 0.2 for the following system

$\frac{dx}{dt} = 2x+y$, $\frac{dy}{dt} = x-3y$ $t=0$, $x=1, y=0.5$ taking $h=0.1$.

Solution: Given $\frac{dx}{dt} = 2x+y$, and $\frac{dy}{dt} = x-3y$

$t_0 = 0, x_0 = 1, y_0 = 0.5.$ $h = 0.1$

$k_1 = h f(t_0, x_0, y_0)$ $\qquad\qquad\qquad l_1 = h\phi(t_0, x_0, y_0)$
$= h(2x_0 + y_0)$ $\qquad\qquad\qquad\quad = h(x_0 - 3y_0)$
$= 0.1[2(1)+0.5] = 0.25$ $\qquad\quad = 0.1(1-3(0.5)) = -0.05$

$k_2 = h f\left(t_0 + \frac{h}{2}, x_0 + \frac{k_1}{2}, y_0 + \frac{l_1}{2}\right)$ $\qquad l_2 = h\phi\left(t_0 + \frac{h}{2}, x_0 + \frac{k_1}{2}, y_0 + \frac{l_1}{2}\right)$
$= 0.1[2(1+0.125)+(0.5-0.025)]$ $\quad = 0.1[(1+0.125)-3(0.5-0.025)]$
$= 0.2725$ $\qquad\qquad\qquad\qquad\qquad\quad = -0.03$

$k_3 = h f\left(t_0 + \frac{h}{2}, x_0 + \frac{k_2}{2}, y_0 + \frac{l_2}{2}\right)$ $\qquad l_3 = h\phi\left(t_0 + \frac{h}{2}, x_0 + \frac{k_2}{2}, y_0 + \frac{l_2}{2}\right)$
$= 0.1[2(1+0.13625)+(0.5-0.015)]$ $= 0.1[(1+0.13625)-3(0.5-0.015)]$
$= 0.2758$ $\qquad\qquad\qquad\qquad\qquad\quad = -0.0319$

$k_4 = h f(t_0+h, x_0+k_3, y_0+l_3)$ $\qquad\quad l_4 = h\phi(t_0+h, x_0+k_3, y_0+l_3)$
$= 0.1[2(1+0.2758)+(0.5-0.0319)]$ $\ = 0.1[(1+0.2758)-3(0.5-0.0319)]$
$= 0.302$ $\qquad\qquad\qquad\qquad\qquad\qquad = -0.0129$

Hence $x_1 = x_0 + \frac{1}{6}[k_1 + 2k_2 + 2k_3 + k_4]$

$= 1 + \frac{1}{6}[0.25 + 2(0.2725) + 2(0.2758) + 0.302] = 1.2748$

$y_1 = y_0 + \frac{1}{6}[l_1 + 2l_2 + 2l_3 + l_4]$

$= 0.5 + \frac{1}{6}[-0.05 - 2(0.03) - 2(0.0319) + 0.302] - 0.0129 = 0.4689$

Replacing t_0, x_0, y_0 by t_1, x_1, y_1, we get

$k_1 = 0.3019,\ \ k_2 = 0.3314,\ \ k_3 = 0.3352,\ \ \ k_4 = 0.3692$
$l_1 = -0.0132,\ l_2 = 0.0039,\ l_3 = 0.0028,\ \ l_4 = 0.0195$
$\therefore x_2 = 1.6089$
$\therefore y_2 = 0.4722$

TEST YOUR KNOWLEDGE

1. Use Runge-Kutta method to solve $\frac{dy}{dx} = 1 + xz$, $y(0) = 0$; $\frac{dz}{dx} = -xy$, $z(0) = 1$;
   for $x = 0.3$ and $x = 0.6$

   Ans: $y(0.3) = 0.3448$, $z(0.3) = 0.99$; $y(0.6) = 0.7738$, $z(0.6) = 0.9121$

2. Find $y(0.1), z(0.1); y(0.2), z(0.2)$ from the system of equation
   $\frac{dy}{dx} = x + z,; \frac{dz}{dx} = x - y^2$, given $y(0) = 0$, $z(0) = 1$. Using Runge-Kutta method

   Ans: $y(0.1) = 2.084, z(0.1) = 0.587$

3. Solve the following simultaneous differential equation, using Runge-Kutta method for $x = 0.1$ and 0.2 $\frac{dy}{dx} = xz + 1$; $\frac{dz}{dx} = -xy$, given $y(0) = 0$, $z(0) = 1$.

   Ans: $y(0.1) = 0.105, z(0.1) = 0.999; y(0.2) = 0.22, z(0.2) = 0.997$

YEAR WISE UNIVERSITY QUESTION PAPERS -13 SEMESTERS

Dec-2013(10/12/2013)

1. Use Euler's modified method find y at $x = 1.2$ correct up to four decimal places, by taking $h = 0.2$ given that $\frac{dy}{dx} = \log(x + y)$; $y(1) = 2$.	5
2. If y satisfies the differntial equation $\frac{dy}{dx} = x^2 y - 1$ and $y = 1$ when $x = 0$ then by using Taylor's series method find y at $x = 0.03$ correct upto five decimal places	6
3. Using Runge-Kutta method solve $\frac{dy}{dx} = \frac{1}{x+y}$ with $x_0 = 0$, $y_0 = 1$ for the interval $(0,1)$ choosing $h = 0.5$.	7

August-2013(16/08/2013) Re-exam

1. Solve numerically the differential equation $\frac{dy}{dx} = y^2 - \frac{y}{x}$, $y(1) = 1$ for the interval1(0.1)1.5 by Euler's method.	6
2. Apply Runge-Kutta method to find an approximate value of y for $x = 1.1$ in one step, given $\frac{dy}{dx} = x^2 + y^2$ and $y = 1.5$ when $x = 1$.	5

May-2013(18/05/2013)

1. Use Euler's method to find y at x=1.5 in five steps, given that $f(x, y) = x^2 + y^2$; $y(1) = 1$.	5

2. Use Runge-Kutta method to solve at $x=1.1$ by taking $h=0.05$ and $x_0=1$, $y_0=1$.	6

May-2012 (29/05/2012)

1. By using Euler's method solve $\dfrac{dy}{dx} = x+y+xy$ with $y(0)=1$ at $x=0.1$. Take $h=0.025$	5
2. Find the solution of $\dfrac{dy}{dx} = y\sin x + \cos x$ at $x=0.4$ correct upto four places of decimals by Taylor's method if $y(0)=0$ and also find the series for y atleast upto the term of x^5	5

Nov-2012 (20/11/2012)

1. Determine the value of y when x=0.1 given that y(0)=1 and $\dfrac{dy}{dx} = x^2 + y$ with $y(0)=1$ By Euler's modified method.	6
2. Use Taylor's series method to solve the differential equation $\dfrac{dy}{dx} = x + y^2$ with $y(0)=0$.	5

Dec-2011 (16/12/2011)

1. Using Taylor's series method find y upto six decimal places when x=1.02 given that $(1-xy)dx + dy = 0$ and $y=2$ when $x=1$. Also write the series for y.	5
2. Solve $\dfrac{dy}{dx} = 2 + \sqrt{xy}$ $x_0 = 1.2$ and $y_0 = 1.6403$ by Euler's modified method for $x=1.4$	6
3. Use Runge-Kutta method to find y(0.1) and y(0.2) in steps of 0.1, given that $\dfrac{dy}{dx} = xy + x^2$ with $y(0)=1$.	6

May-2011 (25/05/2011)

1. Using Taylor's series method find y at x=0.1, given that $\dfrac{dy}{dx} = x - y^2$ with $y(0)=1$ take h=0.05.	6
2. Use Runge-Kutta method of fourth order to find $y(0.2)$, given that $\dfrac{dy}{dx} = xy + y^2$ with $y(0.1) = 1.1169$.	6

Nov-2010 (18/11/2010)	
1. Using Euler's method find the approximate value of y $\frac{dy}{dx} = \frac{1+y^2}{1+x^2}$ with $y(0) = 0$ taking $h = 0.2$ at $x = 1$.	5
2. Using Modified Euler's method to find the approximate value of y where $\frac{dy}{dx} = \sin(x^2 y + 1)$ with $y(0) = 1$ for $x = 0.03$.	5
3. Apply Runge-Kutta method to find an approximate value of y at x=1.1 and x=1.2 where $\frac{dy}{dx} = 3x + y^2$, $x_0 = 1$, $y_0 = 1.2$.	7

May-2010 (19/05/2010)	
1. Find the solution of $(2x - y^2)dx + (x + y^2)dy = 0$ for $x = 0.2$ if $y(0.1) = 1.0874$ by Runge-Kutta method	5
2. Determine the value of y when x=0.1 given that $\frac{dy}{dx} = x^2 + y$, $y(0) = 1$ by modified Eule's method taking $h = 0.05$.	6

May-2009 (19/05/2009)	
1. Apply Runge-Kutta method to find an approximate value of y given that $\frac{dy}{dx} = \sqrt{x^2 + y^2}$, $x_0 = 2$, $y_0 = 5$ at $x = 2.2$.	5
2. Using Euler's method, find the approximate value of y at $x = 1.5$ in five steps, given that $\frac{dy}{dx} = \frac{y-x}{\sqrt{xy}}$ and $y(1) = 2$.	6
3. Use Taylor's series method to find the solution in power of $(x-1)$ for the differential equation (up to third term) $\frac{dy}{dx} = xy - 1$ with $x_0 = 1$, $y_0 = 2$.	6

Nov-2009 (16/11/2009)	
1. Apply Runge-Kutta method to find an approximate value of y at $x = 0.2$ if $\frac{dy}{dx} = x + y^2$, given that $y = 1$ when $x = 0$ in steps of $h = 0.1$.	6
2. Using Euler's method, find the approximate value of y at $x = 1.5$ in five steps, given that $\frac{dy}{dx} = \frac{y-x}{\sqrt{xy}}$ and $y(1) = 2$.	5

3. Find the solution of $\frac{dy}{dx} = y(\sin x) + \cos x$, at $x = 0.4$ correct to four places of decimals by Taylor's series if $y(0) = 0$.	5
May-2008 (17/05/2008)	
1. Solve numerically by using Runge-Kutta fourth order formula the differential equation $\frac{dy}{dx} = x^2 + y^2$, with the given condition $x = 1, y = 1.5$ in the interval $(1, 1.2)$ with $h = 0.1$.	6
2. Use Euler's modified method to find the value of y satisfying the equation $\frac{dy}{dx} = -xy^2$, $y(0) = 2$ for $x = 0.2$.	5
Nov-2008 (10/11/2008)	
1. Use Euler's method to solve the differential equation $\frac{dy}{dx} = 2 + \sqrt{xy}$, $y(1) = 1$ for $x = 1.2$. find solution by taking 5 steps.	5
2. Apply Runge-Kutta fourth order formula to solve the differential equation $\frac{dy}{dx} = \sqrt{\sin x + \cos y}$, for $x = 1.5$.	5
3. Solve $\frac{dy}{dx} = x + y^2$ with initial condition $x0 = 0, y0 = 0.5$ by Taylor's series method for $x = 1$ in two steps.	7

UNIT - IV

SPECIAL FUNCTIONS

INTRODUCTION

Subject of integral calculus is the outcome of an effort to obtain some general method of finding an area of a plane space bounded by given curved lines. Once such method was developed, which expressed area in terms of definite integral, the idea was extended to determine the length of arc of the curve, volume of solid body, area of curved surface, etc. This also developed the concepts of Double and Triple Integrals.

Students at this stage are well versed with elementary methods of integration and evaluation of real definite integrals. Aim of this work is to take them to higher level, by introducing them to advance techniques of differentiation under the sign of integration to evaluate definite integrals. Important integrals like Beta, Gamma and Error functions which are so widely used in Engineering applications will also be discussed. Application of integration to determine length of arc of plane curves, called Rectification is also covered.

Gamma Function :

Definition: The definite integral $\int_0^\infty e^{-x} x^{n-1} dx$, $n > 0$ is denoted by the symbol $\overline{|n}$ and called as Gamma function *i.e.* $\int_0^\infty e^{-x} x^{n-1} dx = \overline{|n}$, $n > 0$.

Someone may write $\overline{|n} = \int_0^\infty e^{-x} x^{n-1} dx$, $n > 0$.

Remark : Gamma function is also known as Euler's Integral of the second kind or Improper integral.

Ex.s: $\int_0^\infty e^{-x} x^{11} dx = \overline{|10}$, $\int_0^\infty e^{-x} x^{97} dx = \overline{|96}$, $\int_0^\infty e^{-x} x^{787} dx = \overline{|786}$.

Alternative definition of Gamma function:

$$\overline{|n} = 2 \int_0^\infty e^{-x^2} x^{2n-1} dx.$$

Proof: By definition of Gamma function $\overline{|n} = \int_0^\infty e^{-x} x^{n-1} dx$

x	0	∞
t	0	∞

Put $x = t^2$, $\therefore dx = 2t\,dt$

$$\therefore \overline{|n} = \int_0^\infty e^{-t^2} t^{2n-2} 2t\,dt$$

$$\overline{|n} = 2\int_0^\infty e^{-t^2} t^{2n-1}\,dt$$

By changing the variable t to x, we get

$$\overline{|n} = 2\int_0^\infty e^{-x^2} x^{2n-1}\,dx.$$

Properties of Gamma Function:

Property 1: $\overline{|1} = 1$

Proof: By definition $\overline{|n} = \int_0^\infty e^{-x} x^{n-1}\,dx$

Put $n = 1$ $\therefore \overline{|1} = \int_0^\infty e^{-x} x^0\,dx = \int_0^\infty e^{-x}\,dx = \left[\dfrac{e^{-x}}{-1}\right]_0^\infty = 1.$

Property 2: $\overline{|n+1} = n\overline{|n}$

Proof: By definition $\overline{|n} = \int_0^\infty e^{-x} x^{n-1}\,dx$

Put $n = n+1$ $\therefore \overline{|n+1} = \int_0^\infty e^{-x} x^{n+1-1}\,dx = \int_0^\infty e^{-x} x^n\,dx,$

Integrating by parts

$$\therefore \overline{|n+1} = \left\{\left[x^n \left(\dfrac{e^{-x}}{-1}\right)\right]_0^\infty - \int_0^\infty n x^{n-1}\left(\dfrac{e^{-x}}{-1}\right)dx\right\} \qquad \because \lim_{x\to\infty} \dfrac{x^n}{e^x} = 0$$

$$= 0 + n\int_0^\infty e^{-x} x^{n-1}\,dx = n\,\overline{|n}.$$

Remark: 1. This property is also called as reduction formula for Gamma function.

2. $\overline{|n} = (n-1)\overline{|n-1}$

3. $\overline{|n+1} = n\overline{|n}$

   $= n(n-1)$ and so on, in general, if n is positive integer

   $= n(n-1)(n-2)...3.2.1\overline{|1}$

$\overline{|n+1} = n!.$

Property 3: $\Gamma\!\left(\dfrac{1}{2}\right) = \sqrt{\pi}.$

Proof: By alternative definition $\Gamma(n) = 2\int_{0}^{\infty} e^{-x^2} x^{2n-1} dx.$

Put $n = 1/2$ $\therefore \Gamma\!\left(\dfrac{1}{2}\right) = 2\int_{0}^{\infty} e^{-x^2} x^{2\cdot\frac{1}{2}-1} dx$

$$\Gamma\!\left(\dfrac{1}{2}\right) = 2\int_{0}^{\infty} e^{-x^2} x^{0} dx$$

$$= 2 \cdot \dfrac{\sqrt{\pi}}{2} = \sqrt{\pi}. \qquad \because \int_{0}^{\infty} e^{-x^2} dx = \dfrac{\sqrt{\pi}}{2}$$

Property 4: $\Gamma(0) = \infty.$

Proof: By property 2, $\Gamma(n+1) = n\,\Gamma(n)$

$\therefore \Gamma(n) = \dfrac{\Gamma(n+1)}{n}$

Put $n = 0$

$\therefore \Gamma(0) = \dfrac{\Gamma(0+1)}{0} = \dfrac{\Gamma(1)}{0} = \dfrac{1}{0} = \infty$

Property 5: $\int_{0}^{\infty} e^{-ay} y^{n-1} dy = \dfrac{\Gamma(n)}{a^n}.$

Proof: By definition, $\Gamma(n) = \int_{0}^{\infty} e^{-x} x^{n-1} dx$

Put $x = ay,$ $\therefore dx = a\,dy$

$\therefore \Gamma(n) = \int_{0}^{\infty} e^{-ay} (ay)^{n-1} a\,dy$

$$= a^n \int_{0}^{\infty} e^{-ay} y^{n-1} dy$$

$$\dfrac{\Gamma(n)}{a^n} = \int_{0}^{\infty} e^{-ay} y^{n-1} dy.$$

Some Standard Results:

1. $\Gamma(n)\,\Gamma(1-n) = \dfrac{\pi}{\sin n\pi},\quad 0 < n < 1.$

2. $\Gamma\!\left(\dfrac{1}{4}\right)\Gamma\!\left(\dfrac{3}{4}\right) = \Gamma\!\left(\dfrac{1}{4}\right)\Gamma\!\left(1-\dfrac{1}{4}\right) = \dfrac{\pi}{\sin \pi/4} = \dfrac{\pi}{1/\sqrt{2}} = \sqrt{2}\pi$

3. $\Gamma\!\left(\dfrac{1}{3}\right)\Gamma\!\left(\dfrac{2}{3}\right) = \Gamma\!\left(\dfrac{1}{3}\right)\Gamma\!\left(1-\dfrac{1}{3}\right) = \dfrac{\pi}{\sin \pi/3} = \dfrac{\pi}{\sqrt{3}/2} = \dfrac{2\pi}{\sqrt{3}}.$

Examples on Gamma function:

Type I: To evaluate the integral of the type $\overline{n} = \int_0^\infty e^{-ax^m} x^n dx$.

In such type of examples put $ax^m = t$.

Ex. 1: Prove that $\int_0^\infty x^m e^{-ax^n} dx = \dfrac{1}{n a^{\frac{m+1}{n}}} \overline{\left|\dfrac{m+1}{n}\right.}$.

Solution: Let $I = \int_0^\infty x^m e^{-ax^n} dx$

put $ax^n = t, \Rightarrow x^n = \dfrac{t}{a}$, i.e. $x = \dfrac{t^{\frac{1}{n}}}{a^{\frac{1}{n}}}$ $\therefore dx = \dfrac{1}{a^{\frac{1}{n}}} \dfrac{1}{n} t^{\frac{1}{n}-1} dt$

$\therefore I = \int_0^\infty \left(\dfrac{t^{\frac{1}{n}}}{a^{\frac{1}{n}}}\right)^m e^{-t} \dfrac{1}{a^{\frac{1}{n}}} \dfrac{1}{n} t^{\frac{1}{n}-1} dt$

$= \dfrac{1}{n a^{\frac{1}{n}}} \int_0^\infty \dfrac{t^{m/n}}{a^{m/n}} e^{-t} t^{1/n-1} dt$

$= \dfrac{1}{n a^{\frac{1}{n}+\frac{m}{n}}} \int_0^\infty e^{-t} t^{\frac{m}{n}+\frac{1}{n}-1} dt$

$= \dfrac{1}{n a^{\frac{m+1}{n}}} \overline{\left|\dfrac{m}{n} + \dfrac{1}{n}\right.}$

$= \dfrac{1}{n a^{\frac{m+1}{n}}} \overline{\left|\dfrac{m+1}{n}\right.}$.

Ex. 2: Evaluate $\int_0^\infty x^n e^{-x^m} dx$

Solution: Let $I = \int_0^\infty x^n e^{-x^m} dx$

x	0	∞
t	0	∞

put $x^m = t$ $\qquad x = t^{1/m}$ $\qquad dx = \dfrac{1}{m} t^{\frac{1}{m}-1} dt$

(4.4)

Therefore given integral becomes

$$I = \int_0^\infty t^{\frac{n}{m}} e^{-t} \frac{1}{m} t^{\frac{1}{m}-1} dt = \frac{1}{m} \int_0^\infty t^{\frac{n+1}{m}-1} e^{-t} dt = \frac{1}{m} \left\lfloor \frac{n+1}{m} \right..$$

Ex. 3: Prove that $\displaystyle\int_0^\infty e^{-ax^n} dx = \frac{1}{n a^{\frac{1}{n}}} \left\lfloor \frac{1}{n} \right..$

Solution: Let $I = \displaystyle\int_0^\infty e^{-ax^n} dx$

put $ax^n = t, \Rightarrow x^n = \dfrac{t}{a}$, i.e. $x = \dfrac{t^{\frac{1}{n}}}{a^{\frac{1}{n}}}$ $\therefore dx = \dfrac{1}{a^{\frac{1}{n}}} \dfrac{1}{n} t^{\frac{1}{n}-1} dt$

x	0	∞
t	0	∞

$\therefore I = \displaystyle\int_0^\infty e^{-t} \frac{1}{a^{\frac{1}{n}}} \frac{1}{n} t^{\frac{1}{n}-1} dt$

$= \dfrac{1}{n a^{\frac{1}{n}}} \displaystyle\int_0^\infty e^{-t} t^{1/n-1} dt = \dfrac{1}{n a^{\frac{1}{n}}} \left\lfloor \dfrac{1}{n} \right..$

Ex. 4: Evaluate $\displaystyle\int_0^\infty e^{-x^4} dx$

Solution: Put $x^4 = t, \Rightarrow x = t^{1/4}$, $\therefore dx = \dfrac{1}{4} t^{-3/4} dt$

Therefore given integral becomes

$\displaystyle\int_0^\infty e^{-x^4} dx = \int_0^\infty e^{-t} \frac{1}{4} t^{-3/4} dt$

$= \dfrac{1}{4} \displaystyle\int_0^\infty e^{-t} t^{1/4 - 1} dt$

$= \dfrac{1}{4} \left\lfloor \dfrac{1}{4} \right..$

Ex. 5: Evaluate $\displaystyle\int_0^\infty \sqrt[4]{x}\, e^{-\sqrt{x}} dx$ or $\displaystyle\int_0^\infty x^{\frac{1}{4}} e^{-\sqrt{x}} dx$ **SUK: Dec-13**

Solution: Put $\sqrt{x} = t, \Rightarrow x = t^2$, $\therefore dx = 2t\, dt$.

x	0	∞
t	0	∞

Therefore given integral becomes

$$\int_0^\infty x^{\frac{1}{4}} e^{-\sqrt{x}} dx = \int_0^\infty t^{2/4} e^{-t} 2t\, dt$$

$$= 2\int_0^\infty e^{-t} t^{\frac{3}{2}} dt$$

$$= 2\left\lfloor\frac{5}{2}\right. = 2\cdot\frac{3}{2}\left\lfloor\frac{3}{2}\right. = 2\cdot\frac{3}{2}\cdot\frac{1}{2}\left\lfloor\frac{1}{2}\right. = \frac{3\sqrt{\pi}}{2}.$$

Ex. 6: Evaluate $\displaystyle\int_0^\infty \sqrt{x}\, e^{-\sqrt[3]{x}}\, dx$

Solution: Put $x^{\frac{1}{3}} = t$, $\Rightarrow x = t^3$ $\quad \therefore dx = 3t^2\, dt$

$$\therefore \int_0^\infty x^{\frac{1}{2}} e^{-x^{\frac{1}{3}}} dx = \int_0^\infty t^{\frac{3}{2}} e^{-t} 3t^2\, dt$$

$$= 3\int_0^\infty e^{-t} t^{\frac{7}{2}} dt = 3\left\lfloor\frac{9}{2}\right. = 3\cdot\frac{7}{2}\cdot\frac{5}{2}\cdot\frac{3}{2}\cdot\frac{1}{2}\left\lfloor\frac{1}{2}\right.$$

$$= \frac{315\sqrt{\pi}}{16}.$$

Ex. 7: Evaluate $\displaystyle\int_0^\infty x^{-4} e^{-\frac{1}{x}}\, dx$ SUK: Nov-08

Solution: Put $\dfrac{1}{x} = t$, $\Rightarrow x = \dfrac{1}{t}$ $\quad \therefore dx = \dfrac{-1}{t^2} dt$

x	0	∞
t	0	∞

$$\int_\infty^0 x^{-4} e^{-\frac{1}{x}} dx = \int_0^\infty \left(\frac{1}{t}\right)^{-4} e^{-t} \left(\frac{-1}{t^2}\right) dt$$

$$= \int_0^\infty e^{-t} \left(\frac{1}{t}\right)^{-4} \left(\frac{1}{t^2}\right) dt$$

$$= \int_0^\infty e^{-t} t^{4-2}\, dt = \int_0^\infty e^{-t} t^2\, dt$$

$$= \lfloor 3 = 2!.$$

Ex. 8: Prove that $\int_0^\infty x e^{-x^8} dx \cdot \int_0^\infty x e^{-x^4} dx = \dfrac{\pi}{16\sqrt{2}}$.

Solution: Let $I_1 = \int_0^\infty x e^{-x^8} dx$ and $I_2 = \int_0^\infty x e^{-x^4} dx$

x	0	∞
t	0	∞

putting $x^8 = t \Rightarrow x = t^{\frac{1}{8}}$ $\therefore dx = \dfrac{1}{8} t^{-\frac{7}{8}} dt$

$\therefore I_1 = \int_0^\infty t^{\frac{1}{8}} e^{-t} \dfrac{1}{8} t^{-\frac{7}{8}} dt = \dfrac{1}{8} \int_0^\infty e^{-t} t^{-\frac{6}{8}} dt = \dfrac{1}{8} \overline{\left|\dfrac{1}{4}\right.}$

putting $x^4 = t \Rightarrow x = t^{\frac{1}{4}}$ $\therefore dx = \dfrac{1}{4} t^{-\frac{3}{4}} dt$

$\therefore I_2 = \int_0^\infty t^{\frac{1}{2}} e^{-t} \dfrac{1}{4} t^{-\frac{3}{4}} dt = \dfrac{1}{4} \int_0^\infty e^{-t} t^{-\frac{1}{4}} dt = \dfrac{1}{4} \overline{\left|\dfrac{3}{4}\right.}$

$\therefore I_1 \cdot I_2 = \dfrac{1}{8} \dfrac{1}{4} \overline{\left|\dfrac{1}{4}\right.} \overline{\left|\dfrac{3}{4}\right.} = \dfrac{\sqrt{2}\,\pi}{32} = \dfrac{\pi}{16\sqrt{2}}$. $\qquad \because \overline{\left|\dfrac{1}{4}\right.} \overline{\left|\dfrac{3}{4}\right.} = \sqrt{2}\,\pi$

Ex. 9: Show that $\int_0^\infty \sqrt{y}\, e^{-y^2} dy \cdot \int_0^\infty \dfrac{e^{-y^2}}{\sqrt{y}} dy = \dfrac{\pi}{2\sqrt{2}}$.

Solution: Let $I_1 = \int_0^\infty \sqrt{y}\, e^{-y^2} dy$ and $I_2 = \int_0^\infty \dfrac{e^{-y^2}}{\sqrt{y}} dy$

x	0	∞
t	0	∞

Put $y^2 = t \Rightarrow y = t^{\frac{1}{2}}$ $\therefore dy = \dfrac{1}{2} t^{-\frac{1}{2}} dt$

$I_1 = \int_0^\infty t^{\frac{1}{4}} e^{-t} \dfrac{1}{2} t^{-\frac{1}{2}} dt = \dfrac{1}{2} \int_0^\infty e^{-t} t^{-\frac{1}{4}} dt = \dfrac{1}{2} \overline{\left|\dfrac{3}{4}\right.}$

$I_2 = \int_0^\infty t^{-\frac{1}{4}} e^{-t} \dfrac{1}{2} t^{-\frac{1}{2}} dt = \dfrac{1}{2} \int_0^\infty e^{-t} t^{-\frac{3}{4}} dt = \dfrac{1}{2} \overline{\left|\dfrac{1}{4}\right.}$

$I_1 \cdot I_2 = \dfrac{1}{2} \dfrac{1}{2} \overline{\left|\dfrac{3}{4}\right.} \cdot \overline{\left|\dfrac{1}{4}\right.} = \dfrac{\sqrt{2}\,\pi}{4}$

$\therefore \int_0^\infty \sqrt{y}\, e^{-y^2} dy \cdot \int_0^\infty \dfrac{e^{-y^2}}{\sqrt{y}} dy = \dfrac{\pi}{2\sqrt{2}} = \dfrac{\pi}{2\sqrt{2}}$.

Ex. 10: Prove that $\int_0^\infty x^{n-1} e^{-h^2 x^2} dx = \dfrac{1}{2h^n} \left\lfloor \dfrac{n}{2} \right.$

Solution: Let $I = \int_0^\infty x^{n-1} e^{-h^2 x^2} dx$

x	0	∞
t	0	∞

put $h^2 x^2 = t \Rightarrow x^2 = \dfrac{t}{h^2}$ i.e. $x = \dfrac{t^{\frac{1}{2}}}{h}$ ∴ $dx = \dfrac{1}{2h} t^{-\frac{1}{2}} dt$

$I = \int_0^\infty \left(\dfrac{t^{\frac{1}{2}}}{h} \right)^{n-1} e^{-t} \dfrac{1}{2h} t^{-\frac{1}{2}} dt = \dfrac{1}{2h} \int_0^\infty \dfrac{t^{\frac{n}{2} - \frac{1}{2}}}{h^{n-1}} e^{-t} t^{-\frac{1}{2}} dt$

$= \dfrac{1}{2 h^{1+n-1}} \int_0^\infty e^{-t} t^{\frac{n}{2} - \frac{1}{2} - \frac{1}{2}} dt = \dfrac{1}{2 h^n} \int_0^\infty e^{-t} t^{\frac{n}{2} - 1} dt = \dfrac{1}{2 h^n} \left\lfloor \dfrac{n}{2} \right.$

Ex. 11: Evaluate $\int_0^\infty x^2 e^{-h^2 x^2} dx$.

Solution: Let $I = \int_0^\infty x^2 e^{-h^2 x^2} dx$

Put $h^2 x^2 = t \Rightarrow x^2 = \dfrac{t}{h^2}$ i.e. $x = \dfrac{t^{\frac{1}{2}}}{h}$ ∴ $dx = \dfrac{1}{2h} t^{\frac{-1}{2}} dt$

x	0	∞
t	0	∞

∴ $I = \int_0^\infty \dfrac{t}{h^2} e^{-t} \dfrac{1}{2h} t^{-\frac{1}{2}} dt$

$= \dfrac{1}{2 h^3} \int_0^\infty e^{-t} t^{\frac{1}{2}} dt$

$= \dfrac{1}{2 h^3} \left\lfloor \dfrac{3}{2} \right. = \dfrac{1}{2 h^3} \dfrac{1}{2} \left\lfloor \dfrac{1}{2} \right. = \dfrac{\sqrt{\pi}}{4 h^3}.$

Ex. 12: Evaluate $\int_0^\infty e^{-h^2 x^2} dx$

Solution: Put $h^2 x^2 = t \Rightarrow x^2 = \dfrac{t}{h^2}$ i.e. $x = \dfrac{t^{\frac{1}{2}}}{h}$ ∴ $dx = \dfrac{1}{2h} t^{\frac{-1}{2}} dt$

x	0	∞
t	0	∞

$$\therefore \int_0^\infty e^{-h^2 x^2} dx = \int_0^\infty e^{-t} \frac{1}{2h} t^{-\frac{1}{2}} dt = \frac{1}{2h} \left| \frac{1}{2} \right. = \frac{\sqrt{\pi}}{2h}.$$

Ex. 13: Evaluate $\int_0^\infty x^7 e^{-2x^2} dx$.   **SUK: Aug-13**

Solution: Let $I = \int_0^\infty x^7 e^{-2x^2} dx$

put $2x^2 = t$, $\Rightarrow x^2 = \frac{t}{2}$, i.e. $x = \frac{t^{\frac{1}{2}}}{2^{\frac{1}{2}}}$ $\Rightarrow x = \frac{t^{\frac{1}{2}}}{\sqrt{2}}$

$dx = \frac{1}{\sqrt{2}} \cdot \frac{1}{2} t^{-\frac{1}{2}} dt = \frac{1}{2\sqrt{2}} t^{-\frac{1}{2}} dt$

$I = \int_0^\infty \left(\frac{t^{\frac{1}{2}}}{2^{\frac{1}{2}}} \right)^7 e^{-t} \frac{1}{2\sqrt{2}} t^{-\frac{1}{2}} dt$

$= \frac{1}{2^{\frac{7}{2}+1+\frac{1}{2}}} \int_0^\infty e^{-t} t^{\frac{7}{2}-\frac{1}{2}} dt$

$= \frac{1}{2^5} \int_0^\infty e^{-t} t^3 dt = \frac{\overline{4}}{2^5} = \frac{3!}{2^5} = \frac{3}{16}$.

Ex. 14: Evaluate $\int_0^\infty (x^2 + 4) e^{-2x^2} dx$.

Solution: Let $I = \int_0^\infty (x^2 + 4) e^{-2x^2} dx$.

x	0	∞
t	0	∞

put $2x^2 = t$, $\Rightarrow x^2 = \frac{t}{2}$, i.e. $x = \frac{t^{\frac{1}{2}}}{2^{\frac{1}{2}}}$

$dx = \frac{1}{\sqrt{2}} \cdot \frac{1}{2} t^{-\frac{1}{2}} dt = \frac{1}{2\sqrt{2}} t^{-\frac{1}{2}} dt$

$$I = \int_0^\infty \left(\frac{t}{2} + 4\right) e^{-t} \frac{1}{2\sqrt{2}} t^{-\frac{1}{2}} dt$$

$$= \frac{1}{4\sqrt{2}} \int_0^\infty e^{-t} t^{\frac{1}{2}} dt + \frac{2}{\sqrt{2}} \int_0^\infty e^{-t} t^{-\frac{1}{2}} dt$$

$$= \frac{1}{4\sqrt{2}} \overline{\left|\frac{3}{2}\right.} + \frac{2}{\sqrt{2}} \overline{\left|\frac{1}{2}\right.} = \frac{1}{4\sqrt{2}} \cdot \frac{1}{2} \overline{\left|\frac{1}{2}\right.} + \frac{2}{\sqrt{2}} \overline{\left|\frac{1}{2}\right.}$$

$$= \frac{\sqrt{\pi}}{8\sqrt{2}} + \frac{2\sqrt{\pi}}{\sqrt{2}} = \frac{17\sqrt{\pi}}{8\sqrt{2}}.$$

TEST YOUR KNOWLEDGE

Evaluate the following integrals

1. $\int_0^\infty e^{-x^2} dx$ Ans: $\dfrac{\sqrt{\pi}}{2}$

2. $\int_0^\infty e^{-x^3} dx$ Ans: $\dfrac{1}{3}\overline{\left|\dfrac{1}{3}\right.}$

3. $\int_0^\infty x^5 e^{-x^2} dx$ Ans: 1

4. $\int_0^\infty x^2 e^{-x^4} dx \cdot \int_0^\infty e^{-x^4} dx$ Ans: $\dfrac{\pi}{8\sqrt{2}}$

5. $\int_0^\infty xe^{-x^8} dx \cdot \int_0^\infty x^5 e^{-x^8} dx$ Ans: $\dfrac{\pi}{32\sqrt{2}}$

6. $\int_0^\infty \sqrt{x} e^{-x^2} dx$ Ans: $\dfrac{1}{2}\overline{\left|\dfrac{3}{4}\right.}$

7. $\int_0^\infty \sqrt{x} e^{-x^3} dx$ Ans: $\dfrac{\sqrt{\pi}}{3}$ SUK : May – 08

8. $\int_0^\infty \dfrac{e^{-\sqrt{x}}}{x^{7/4}} dx$ Ans: $\dfrac{8\sqrt{\pi}}{3}$

9. $\int_0^\infty \sqrt{x} e^{-x^2} dx \cdot \int_0^\infty \dfrac{1}{\sqrt{x}} e^{-x^2} dx$ Ans: $\dfrac{\pi}{2\sqrt{2}}$

10. $\int_0^\infty \dfrac{1}{\sqrt{x}} e^{-x^3} dx \cdot \int_0^\infty x^4 e^{-x^6} dx$ Ans: $\dfrac{\pi}{9}$

11. $\int_0^\infty x^n e^{-\sqrt{ax}} dx \cdot \int_0^\infty \dfrac{1}{\sqrt{x}} e^{-x^2} dx$ Ans: $\dfrac{2}{a^{n+1}} \overline{|2n+2}$

12. $\int_0^\infty x^2 e^{-x^4} dx \cdot \int_0^\infty e^{-x^4} dx$ Ans: $\dfrac{\pi}{8\sqrt{2}}$

13. $\int_0^\infty x^{2/3} e^{-\sqrt[3]{x}} dx$ Ans: 72

14. $\int_0^\infty x^{2/3} e^{-\sqrt[3]{x}} dx$ Ans: 72

TYPE II : PROBLEM INVOLVING LOG X

Ex. 1: Prove that $\int_0^1 x^m (\log x)^n dx = \dfrac{(-1)^n \overline{|n+1}}{(m+1)^{n+1}}$.

Solution: Let $I = \int_0^1 x^m (\log x)^n dx$

x	0	∞
t	0	∞

put $\log x = -t$, $\Rightarrow x = e^{-t}$ $\therefore dx = -e^{-t} dt$

$\therefore x^m = e^{-mt}$, $(\log x)^n = (-t)^n$

$\therefore I = \int_{\infty}^{0} e^{-mt}(-t)^n(-e^{-t}) dt = -\int_{\infty}^{0}(-1)^n t^n e^{-mt-t} dt = (-1)^n \int_{0}^{\infty} e^{-(m+1)t} t^n dt$

t	0	∞
v	0	∞

put $(m+1)t = v$, $\Rightarrow t = \dfrac{v}{m+1}$, $\therefore dt = \dfrac{dv}{m+1}$

$\therefore I = (-1)^n \int_{0}^{\infty} e^{-v}\left(\dfrac{v}{m+1}\right)^n \dfrac{dv}{m+1}$

$= \dfrac{(-1)^n}{(m+1)^{n+1}} \int_{0}^{\infty} e^{-v} v^n dv = \dfrac{(-1)^n}{(m+1)^{n+1}} \overline{|n+1}$.

Remark: In particular if $m = n$, then $\int_{0}^{1}(x \log x)^n dx = \dfrac{(-1)^n \overline{|n+1}}{(n+1)^{n+1}}$.

Ex. 2: Prove that $\int_{0}^{1}(\log x)^n dx = (-1)^n\, n\overline{|n}$.

Solution: Let $I = \int_{0}^{1}(\log x)^n dx$

x	0	∞
t	0	∞

put $\log x = -t$, $\Rightarrow x = e^{-t}$ $\therefore dx = -e^{-t} dt$

$\therefore I = \int_{\infty}^{0}(-t)^n(-e^{-t}) dt = -\int_{\infty}^{0}(-1)^n t^n e^{-t} dt$

$= \int_{0}^{\infty}(-1)^n t^n e^{-t} dt = (-1)^n \int_{0}^{\infty} e^{-t} t^n dt = (-1)^n \overline{|n+1} = (-1)^n\, n\overline{|n}$.

Ex. 3: Evaluate $\int_{0}^{1}(\log x)^6 dx$. **SUK: May-09**

Solution: Let $I = \int_{0}^{1}(\log x)^6 dx$

put $\log x = -t$, $\Rightarrow x = e^{-t}$ $\therefore dx = -e^{-t} dt$

x	0	∞
t	0	∞

$$\therefore I = \int_{\infty}^{0}(-t)^{6}(-e^{-t})\,dt = -\int_{\infty}^{0}t^{6}e^{-t}\,dt$$

$$= \int_{0}^{\infty}t^{6}e^{-t}\,dt = \int_{0}^{\infty}e^{-t}t^{6}\,dt = \overline{|7} = 6!.$$

Ex. 4: Evaluate $\int_{0}^{1}(\log x)^{4}\,dx$

Solution: Put $\log x = -t$, $\Rightarrow x = e^{-t}$ $\therefore dx = -e^{-t}\,dt$

x	0	∞
t	0	∞

$$\int_{0}^{1}(\log x)^{4}\,dx = \int_{\infty}^{0}(-t)^{4}(-e^{-t})\,dt$$

$$= \int_{\infty}^{0}(-e^{-t})t^{4}\,dt = \int_{0}^{\infty}e^{-t}t^{4}\,dt = \overline{|5} = 4! = 24.$$

Ex. 5: Evaluate $\int_{0}^{1}(x\log x)^{4}\,dx$

Solution: Put $\log x = -t$, $\Rightarrow x = e^{-t}$ $\therefore dx = -e^{-t}\,dt$

x	0	∞
t	0	∞

$$\therefore \int_{0}^{1}(x\log x)^{4}\,dx = \int_{\infty}^{0}e^{-4t}(-t)^{4}(-e^{-t})\,dt$$

$$= -\int_{\infty}^{0}t^{4}e^{-5t}\,dt = \int_{0}^{\infty}t^{4}e^{-5t}\,dt$$

put $5t = v \Rightarrow t = \dfrac{v}{5}$ $\therefore dt = \dfrac{dv}{5}$

$$= \int_{0}^{\infty}\left(\dfrac{v}{5}\right)^{4}e^{-v}\dfrac{dv}{5} = \dfrac{1}{5^{4+1}}\int_{0}^{\infty}e^{-u}v^{4}\,dv = \dfrac{\overline{|5}}{5^{5}} = \dfrac{4!}{5^{5}}.$$

Ex. 6: Evaluate $\int_{0}^{1}\dfrac{1}{\sqrt{x\log x}}\,dx.$ **SUK: May-13**

Solution:

Let $I = \int_{0}^{1}\dfrac{1}{\sqrt{x\log x}}\,dx = \int_{0}^{1}(x\log x)^{\frac{-1}{2}}\,dx$ Put $\log x = -t$, $\Rightarrow x = e^{-t}$ $\therefore dx = -e^{-t}\,dt$

x	0	∞
t	0	∞

$$\therefore \int_0^1 (x\log x)^{\frac{-1}{2}} dx = \int_\infty^0 e^{-\frac{1}{2}t}(-t)^{\frac{-1}{2}}(-e^{-t})dt$$

$$= -(-1)^{\frac{-1}{2}}\int_\infty^0 (t)^{\frac{-1}{2}} e^{-\frac{1}{2}t-t} dt = (-1)^{\frac{-1}{2}} \int_0^\infty e^{-\frac{3}{2}t} (t)^{\frac{-1}{2}} dt$$

put $\dfrac{3}{2}t = v \Rightarrow t = \dfrac{2v}{3} \quad \therefore dt = \dfrac{2dv}{3}$

$$= (-1)^{\frac{-1}{2}} \int_0^\infty e^{-v} \left(\frac{2v}{3}\right)^{\frac{-1}{2}} \frac{2dv}{3}$$

$$= (-1)^{\frac{-1}{2}} \left(\frac{2}{3}\right)^{\frac{-1}{2}+1} \int_0^\infty e^{-v}(v)^{\frac{-1}{2}} dv = (-1)^{\frac{-1}{2}} \left(\frac{2}{3}\right)^{\frac{1}{2}} \overline{\left|\frac{1}{2}\right.}$$

Ex. 7: Prove that $\int_0^1 x^m \left(\log \dfrac{1}{x}\right)^n dx = \dfrac{\overline{|n+1}}{(m+1)^{n+1}}$.

Solution: $\int_0^1 x^m \left(\log \dfrac{1}{x}\right)^n dx = \int_0^1 x^m (\log 1 - \log x)^n dx$

$$= (-1)^n \int_0^1 x^m (\log x)^n dx \qquad \because \log 1 = 0$$

x	0	∞
t	0	∞

$\log x = -t, \Rightarrow x = e^{-t} \quad \therefore dx = -e^{-t} dt$

$$= (-1)^n \int_\infty^0 (e^{-t})^m (-t)^n (-e^{-t}) dt$$

$$= (-1)^n (-1)^n \int_0^\infty e^{-mt-t} t^n dt = (-1)^{2n} \int_0^\infty e^{-(m+1)t} t^n dt$$

$$= \int_0^\infty e^{-(m+1)t} t^n dt \qquad \because (-1)^{2n} = 1$$

put $(m+1)t = v, \Rightarrow t = \dfrac{v}{m+1}, \quad \therefore dt = \dfrac{dv}{m+1}$

$$\therefore I = \int_0^\infty e^{-v} \left(\frac{v}{m+1}\right)^n \frac{dv}{m+1} = \frac{1}{(m+1)^{n+1}} \int_0^\infty e^{-v} v^n dv$$

$$= \frac{1}{(m+1)^{n+1}} \overline{|n+1}.$$

Ex. 8: Evaluate $\int_0^1 x^{q-1}\left(\log\dfrac{1}{x}\right)^{p-1} dx$ **SUK: Nov-12**

Solution:

$I = \int_0^1 x^{q-1}\left(\log\dfrac{1}{x}\right)^{p-1} dx = \int_0^1 x^{q-1}(\log 1 - \log x)^{p-1} dx = (-1)^{p-1}\int_0^1 x^{q-1}(\log x)^{p-1} dx$ $\because \log 1 = 0$

$\log x = -t, \Rightarrow x = e^{-t} \quad \therefore dx = -e^{-t} dt$

x	0	∞
t	0	∞

$\therefore I = (-1)^{p-1}\int_\infty^0 (e^{-t})^{q-1}(-t)^{p-1}(-e^{-t}) dt$

$= (-1)^{p-1}(-1)^{p-1}\int_0^\infty e^{-tq+t-t}\, t^{p-1} dt = (-1)^{2(p-1)}\int_0^\infty e^{-tq}\, t^{p-1} dt = \int_0^\infty e^{-tq}\, t^{p-1} dt$

put $tq = v,\ q\,dt = dv$

x	0	∞
v	0	∞

$\therefore I = \int_0^\infty e^{-v}\left(\dfrac{v}{q}\right)^{p-1}\dfrac{dv}{q} = \dfrac{1}{q^{p-1+1}}\int_0^\infty e^{-v} v^{p-1} dv = \dfrac{1}{q^p}\overline{|p}.$

Note: Alternative substitution

Put $\log\dfrac{1}{x} = t,\ \therefore -\log x = t$ or $\log x = -t,\ \Rightarrow x = e^{-t},\ \therefore dx = -e^{-t} dt$

Ex. 9: Evaluate $\int_0^1\left(\log\dfrac{1}{y}\right)^{n-1} dy$ **SUK: Nov-12**

Solution: Let $I = \int_0^1\left(\log\dfrac{1}{y}\right)^{n-1} dy = \int_0^1 (\log 1 - \log y)^{n-1} dy$

$= \int_0^1 (-\log y)^{n-1} dy$

x	0	∞
t	0	∞

$\log y = -t,\ \Rightarrow y = e^{-t}\ \therefore dy = -e^{-t} dt$

$I = \int_\infty^0 [-(-t)]^{n-1}(-e^{-t}) dt = -\int_\infty^0 t^{n-1} e^{-t} dt = \int_0^\infty e^{-t} t^{n-1} dt = \overline{|n}$

Ex. 10: Evaluate $\int_0^1\left(\log\dfrac{1}{x}\right)^{10} dx$ **SUK: May-12**

Solution: Let $I = \int_0^1\left(\log\dfrac{1}{x}\right)^{10} dx = \int_0^1 (\log 1 - \log x)^{10} dx$

$$= \int_0^1 (-\log x)^{10} dx$$

x	0	∞
t	0	∞

$\log x = -t, \Rightarrow x = e^{-t} \therefore dx = -e^{-t} dt$

$$I = \int_\infty^0 \left[-(-t)\right]^{10} (-e^{-t}) dt = -\int_\infty^0 t^{10} e^{-t} dt = \int_0^\infty e^{-t} t^{10} dt = \overline{|11} = 10!$$

Ex. 11: Evaluate $\int_0^1 \dfrac{dx}{\sqrt{-\log x}}$

Solution: Let $I = \int_0^1 \dfrac{dx}{\sqrt{-\log x}}$

$\log x = -t, \Rightarrow x = e^{-t} \therefore dx = -e^{-t} dt$

x	0	∞
t	0	∞

$$I = \int_\infty^0 \dfrac{-e^{-t}}{\sqrt{-(-t)}} dt = -\int_\infty^0 \dfrac{e^{-t}}{t^{1/2}} dt = \int_0^\infty e^{-t} t^{-1/2} dt = \overline{\left|-\dfrac{1}{2}+1\right.} = \overline{\left|\dfrac{1}{2}\right.} = \sqrt{\pi}$$

Ex. 12: Evaluate $\int_0^1 \sqrt[3]{\log \dfrac{1}{x}} dx$

Solution: Let $I = \int_0^1 \sqrt[3]{\log \dfrac{1}{x}} dx = \int_0^1 (\log 1 - \log x)^{1/3} = \int_0^1 (-\log x)^{1/3} dx$ $\because \log 1 = 0$

x	0	∞
t	0	∞

$\log x = -t, \Rightarrow x = e^{-t} \therefore dx = -e^{-t} dt$

$$I = \int_\infty^0 \left[-(-t)\right]^{1/3} (-e^{-t}) dt = -\int_\infty^0 t^{1/3} e^{-t} dt$$

$$= \int_0^\infty e^{-t} t^{1/3} dt = \overline{\left|\dfrac{1}{3}+1\right.} = \dfrac{1}{3} \overline{\left|\dfrac{1}{3}\right.}.$$

Ex. 13: Evaluate $\int_0^1 \dfrac{dx}{\sqrt{x \log \dfrac{1}{x}}}$

Solution: Put $\log \dfrac{1}{x} = t, \therefore -\log x = t,$ or $\log x = -t, \Rightarrow x = e^{-t}, \therefore dx = -e^{-t} dt$

The integral becomes

$$\int_0^1 \frac{dx}{\sqrt{x \log \frac{1}{x}}} = \int_\infty^0 \frac{-e^{-t} dt}{\sqrt{e^{-t} \cdot t}}$$

x	0	∞
t	0	∞

$$= -\int_\infty^0 t^{-\frac{1}{2}} \left(e^{-t+1/2t}\right) dt = \int_0^\infty e^{t/2} t^{-\frac{1}{2}} dt$$

Put $\frac{t}{2} = u$, $t = 2u$, $\therefore dt = 2 du$

t	0	∞
u	0	∞

$$= \int_0^\infty e^{-u} (2u)^{-\frac{1}{2}} 2 du$$

$$= \int_0^\infty e^{-u} \sqrt{2} u^{-\frac{1}{2}} du = \sqrt{2} \, \overline{|\tfrac{1}{2}} = \sqrt{2} \, \overline{|\pi} = \sqrt{2\pi}.$$

TEST YOUR KNOWLEDGE

1. Prove that $\int_0^1 x^m (\log x)^n dx = \frac{(-1)^n \overline{|n+1}}{(m+1)^{n+1}}$.

2. Evaluate $\int_0^1 (\log x)^3 dx$ Ans: 6

3. Evaluate $\int_0^1 x^m (\log x)^m dx$ Ans: $\frac{(-1)^m \overline{|m+1}}{(m+1)^{m+1}}$

4. Evaluate $\int_0^1 (x \log x)^3 dx$ Ans: $\frac{-3}{128}$

5. Evaluate $\int_0^1 \left(\log \frac{1}{x}\right)^{p-1} dx$ Ans: $\overline{|p}$

6. Evaluate $\int_0^1 x^3 \left(\log \frac{1}{x}\right)^4 dx$ Ans: $\frac{1}{4}$ SUK : Nov09

7. Evaluate $\int_0^1 \sqrt{\log 1/x} \, dx$ Ans: $\frac{\sqrt{\pi}}{2}$.

8. Evaluate $\int_0^1 \frac{xdx}{\sqrt{\log 1/x}}$ Ans: $\sqrt{\pi/2}$.

9. Evaluate $\int_0^1 \frac{dx}{\sqrt{-\log x}}$ Ans: $\sqrt{\pi}$.

10. Evaluate $\int_0^1 \frac{dx}{\sqrt{x \log 1/x}}$ Ans: $\sqrt{2\pi}$.

11. Evaluate $\int_0^1 (\log 1/x)^{n-1} dx$ Ans: $\overline{|n}$.

12. Evaluate $\int_0^1 \sqrt{x \log 1/x} \, dx$ Ans: $\frac{1}{3}\sqrt{\frac{2}{3}} \sqrt{\pi}$.

13. $\int_0^1 x^{q-1} \left(\log \frac{1}{x}\right)^{n-1} dx$ Ans: $\frac{\overline{|n}}{a^n}$

14. $\int_0^1 x^4 \left(\log \frac{1}{x}\right)^3 dx$ Ans: $\frac{6}{625}$

15. Evaluate $\int_0^1 \sqrt[3]{x \log 1/x} \, dx$ Ans: $\left(\frac{3}{4}\right)^{4/3} \overline{|\frac{4}{3}}$.

TYPE – III PROBLEM INVOLVING (CONSTANT) (Variable)

Ex. 1: Show that $\int_0^\infty \dfrac{x^a}{a^x} dx = \dfrac{\overline{|a+1}}{(\log a)^{a+1}}$.

Solution: Put $a^x = e^t$, $\therefore x \log a = t$, $\Rightarrow x = \dfrac{t}{\log a}$, $\therefore dx = \dfrac{dt}{\log a}$

x	0	∞
t	0	∞

Given integral becomes

$$\therefore \int_0^\infty \dfrac{x^a}{a^x} dx = \int_0^\infty \left(\dfrac{t}{\log a}\right)^a \dfrac{1}{e^t} \dfrac{dt}{\log a} = \dfrac{1}{(\log a)^{a+1}} \int_0^\infty e^{-t} t^a \, dt = \dfrac{\overline{|a+1}}{(\log a)^{a+1}}.$$

Ex. 2: Evaluate $\int_0^\infty \dfrac{x^4}{4^x} dx$

Solution: Put $4^x = e^t$, $\therefore x \log 4 = t$, $\Rightarrow x = \dfrac{t}{\log 4}$, $\therefore dx = \dfrac{dt}{\log 4}$

x	0	∞
t	0	∞

$$\therefore \int_0^\infty \dfrac{x^4}{4^x} dx = \int_0^\infty \left(\dfrac{t}{\log 4}\right)^4 \dfrac{1}{e^t} \dfrac{1}{\log 4} dt$$

$$= \dfrac{1}{(\log 4)^5} \int_0^\infty e^{-t} t^4 \, dt = \dfrac{\overline{|5}}{(\log 4)^5} = \dfrac{4!}{(\log 4)^5} = \dfrac{24}{(\log 4)^5}.$$

Ex. 3: Evaluate $\int_0^\infty \dfrac{x^5}{5^x} dx$

Solution: Let $I = \int_0^\infty \dfrac{x^5}{5^x} dx$

x	0	∞
t	0	∞

Put $5^x = e^t$, $\therefore x \log 5 = t$, $\Rightarrow x = \dfrac{t}{\log 5}$, $\therefore dx = \dfrac{dt}{\log 5}$

$$I = \int_0^\infty \left(\dfrac{t}{\log 5}\right)^5 \dfrac{1}{e^t} \dfrac{dt}{\log 5} = \dfrac{1}{(\log 5)^{5+1}} \int_0^\infty t^5 e^{-t} dt = \dfrac{1}{(\log 5)^6} \int_0^\infty e^{-t} t^5 dt$$

$$\therefore I = \dfrac{\overline{|5+1}}{(\log 5)^6} = \dfrac{5!}{(\log 5)^6} = \dfrac{120}{(\log 5)^6}.$$

Ex. 4: Evaluate $\int_0^\infty \dfrac{x^2}{3^{x^2}} dx$

Solution: Put $3^{x^2} = e^t$, $\therefore x^2 \log 3 = t$, $\Rightarrow x^2 = \dfrac{t}{\log 3}$ i.e. $x = \dfrac{t^{1/2}}{\sqrt{\log 3}}$ $\therefore dx = \dfrac{\frac{1}{2}t^{-1/2}}{\sqrt{\log 3}} dt$

Given integral becomes

$$\int_0^\infty \dfrac{x^2}{3^{x^2}} dx = \int_0^\infty \dfrac{t}{\log 3} \cdot \dfrac{1}{e^t} \cdot \dfrac{\frac{1}{2}t^{-1/2}}{\sqrt{\log 3}} dt = \dfrac{1}{2(\log 3)^{3/2}} \int_0^\infty e^{-t} t^{1/2} dt$$

$$= \dfrac{1}{2(\log 3)^{3/2}} \overline{|3/2|} = \dfrac{1}{2(\log 3)^{3/2}} \cdot \dfrac{1}{2} \overline{|1/2|} = \dfrac{\sqrt{\pi}}{4(\log 3)^{3/2}}.$$

Ex. 5: Evaluate $\int_0^\infty \dfrac{dx}{3^{4x^2}}$ or $\int_0^\infty 3^{-4x^2} dx$

Solution: Let $I = \int_0^\infty \dfrac{dx}{3^{4x^2}} dx$

Put $3^{4x^2} = e^t$ $\therefore 4x^2 \log 3 = t$, $\Rightarrow x^2 = \dfrac{t}{4 \log 3}$

$\Rightarrow x = \dfrac{\sqrt{t}}{2\sqrt{\log 3}}$ $\therefore dx = \dfrac{\frac{1}{2}t^{-1/2}}{2\sqrt{\log 3}} dt$ i.e $dx = \dfrac{t^{-1/2}}{4\sqrt{\log 3}} dt$

x	0	∞
t	0	∞

$$I = \int_0^\infty \dfrac{1}{e^t} \cdot \dfrac{t^{-1/2}}{4\sqrt{\log 3}} dt = \dfrac{1}{4\sqrt{\log 3}} \int_0^\infty e^{-t} t^{-1/2} dt$$

$$= \dfrac{1}{4\sqrt{\log 3}} \overline{\left|-\dfrac{1}{2}+1\right|}$$

$$= \dfrac{1}{4\sqrt{\log 3}} \overline{\left|\dfrac{1}{2}\right|} = \dfrac{\sqrt{\pi}}{4\sqrt{\log 3}}.$$

Ex. 6: Evaluate $\int_0^\infty 7^{-4x^2} dx$

Solution: Put $7^{-4x^2} = e^{-t}$ $\therefore 7^{-4x^2} \cdot \log 7 \cdot (-8x) dx = -e^{-t} dt$

$\therefore -e^{-t} \log 7 \cdot 8 \cdot x \cdot dx = -e^{-t} dt$

$\therefore 8 . \log 7 \ . x . dx = dt$ $\because 7^{-4x^2} = e^{-t}$

Also
$$-4x^2 \log 7 = -t$$
$$\therefore x = \frac{\sqrt{t}}{2\sqrt{\log 7}}$$
$$\therefore dx = \frac{dt}{8\log 7 \cdot x} = \frac{2\sqrt{\log 7}\, dt}{8\log 7 \sqrt{t}} = \frac{t^{-1/2} dt}{4\sqrt{\log 7}}$$

$$\int_0^\infty 7^{-4x^2} dx = \int_0^\infty e^{-t} \frac{t^{-1/2}}{4\sqrt{\log 7}} dt = \frac{1}{4\sqrt{\log 7}} \int_0^\infty e^{-t} t^{-1/2} dt$$

$$= \frac{1}{4\sqrt{\log 7}} \overline{\left|\frac{1}{2}\right.} = \frac{\sqrt{\pi}}{4\sqrt{\log 7}}.$$

TEST YOUR KNOWLEDGE

1. Evaluate $\int_0^\infty a^{-4x^2} dx$ Ans: $\dfrac{\sqrt{\pi}}{4\sqrt{\log a}}$.   2. Evaluate $\int_0^\infty 5^{-4x^2} dx$ Ans: $\dfrac{\sqrt{\pi}}{4\sqrt{\log 5}}$.

3. Evaluate $\int_0^\infty \dfrac{x^{m-1}}{(m-1)^x} dx$ Ans: $\dfrac{\overline{|m}}{\left[\log(m-1)\right]^m}$.   4. Evaluate $\int_0^\infty \dfrac{x^2}{2^x} dx$ Ans: $\dfrac{2!}{(\log 2)^3}$.

5. Evaluate $\int_0^\infty \dfrac{x^7}{7^x} dx$ Ans: $\dfrac{7!}{(\log 7)^8}$.

TYPE IV : PROBLEM INVOLVING sin ax OR cos ax

Ex. 1: Show that $\int_0^\infty x^{m-1} \cos ax\, dx = \dfrac{\overline{|m}}{a^m} \cos\left(\dfrac{m\pi}{2}\right)$.

Solution: We Know that $e^{-iax} = \cos ax - i\sin ax$ $\therefore \text{Re}(e^{-iax}) = \cos ax$

We consider the real part of $I = \int_0^\infty x^{m-1} e^{-iax} dx$

Put $iax = t \Rightarrow x = \dfrac{t}{ia}$ $\therefore dx = \dfrac{dt}{ia}$

$$I = \int_0^\infty \frac{t^{m-1}}{(ia)^{m-1}} e^{-t} \frac{dt}{ia} = \frac{1}{i^m a^m} \int_0^\infty e^{-t} t^{m+1} dt$$

$$= \frac{\overline{|m}}{a^m} \cdot \frac{1}{i^m} \quad \text{As } i = \cos\frac{\pi}{2} + i\sin\frac{\pi}{2}$$

$$= \frac{\overline{|m}}{a^m} \cdot \frac{1}{\left(\cos\frac{\pi}{2} + i\sin\frac{\pi}{2}\right)^m} = \frac{\overline{|m}}{a^m} \cdot \left(\cos m\frac{\pi}{2} - i\sin m\frac{\pi}{2}\right) \quad \text{by De Moivers Theorem}$$

$$\int_0^\infty x^{m-1} \cos ax\, dx = \text{Real part of } I = \frac{\overline{|m}}{a^m} \cos m\frac{\pi}{2}.$$

Note: In above example if we equate imaginary part then we get

$$\int_0^\infty x^{m-1} \sin ax \, dx = \frac{\overline{|m}}{a^m} \sin m\frac{\pi}{2}$$

Ex. 2: Show that $\int_0^\infty \cos(ax^{1/n}) \, dx = \frac{\overline{|n+1}}{a^n} \cos\frac{n\pi}{2}$

Solution: As we know that $e^{-i(ax^{1/n})} = \cos(ax^{1/n}) - i\sin(ax^{1/n})$ $\therefore \cos(ax^{1/n}) = Re \, e^{-i(ax^{1/n})}$

Thus the integral becomes

x	0	∞
t	0	∞

$$I = Re \int_0^\infty e^{-iax^{1/n}} \, dx$$

put $i a x^{1/n} = t$, $x^{1/n} = \frac{t}{ia} \Rightarrow x = \frac{t^n}{(ia)^n}$, $\therefore dx = \frac{n t^{n-1} dt}{(ia)^n}$

$$\therefore \int_0^\infty \cos(ax^{1/n}) \, dx = Re \int_0^\infty e^{-t} \frac{n t^{n-1} dt}{(ia)^n}$$

$$= Re \frac{n}{a^n} \left(\frac{1}{i}\right)^n \int_0^\infty e^{-t} t^{n-1} dt$$

$$= Re \frac{n}{a^n} (-i)^n \overline{|n}$$

$$= Re \frac{n\overline{|n}}{a^n} \left(\cos\frac{\pi}{2} - i\sin\frac{\pi}{2}\right)^n$$

$$= \frac{\overline{|n+1}}{a^n} \cos\frac{n\pi}{2}.$$

Ex. 3: Show that $\int_0^\infty x e^{-ax} \sin bx \, dx = \frac{2ab}{(a^2+b^2)^2}$.

Solution: As we know that $e^{ibx} = \cos bx + i\sin bx$ $\therefore Im \, e^{ibx} = \sin bx$

Thus the given integral becomes

x	0	∞
t	0	∞

$$\int_0^\infty x e^{-ax} \sin bx \, dx = Im \int_0^\infty x e^{-ax} e^{ibx} \, dx = Im \int_0^\infty x e^{-(a-ib)x} \, dx$$

put $(a-ib)x = t \Rightarrow x = \frac{t}{a-ib}$ $\therefore dx = \frac{dt}{a-ib}$

(4.20)

$$= \operatorname{Im} \int_0^\infty \frac{t}{a-ib} e^{-t} \frac{dt}{a-ib} = \operatorname{Im} \frac{1}{(a-ib)^2} \int_0^\infty e^{-t} t \, dt = \operatorname{Im} \frac{1}{(a-ib)^2} \overline{|2}$$

$$= \operatorname{Im} \left[\frac{(a+ib)^2}{(a-ib)^2 (a+ib)^2} \right] . 1$$

$$= \operatorname{Im} \frac{(a+ib)^2}{(a^2+b^2)^2} = \operatorname{Im} \frac{a^2 - b^2 + 2iab}{(a^2+b^2)^2}$$

$$= \operatorname{Im} \left[\frac{a^2 - b^2}{(a^2+b^2)^2} + i \frac{2ab}{(a^2+b^2)^2} \right]$$

$$= \frac{2ab}{(a^2+b^2)^2}.$$

Ex. 4: Show that $\int_0^\infty x^{n-1} e^{-ax} \sin bx \, dx = \dfrac{\overline{|n}}{(a^2+b^2)^{n/2}} \sin \left[n \tan^{-1} \left(\dfrac{b}{a} \right) \right]$

Solution: $I = \int_0^\infty x^{n-1} e^{-ax} \sin bx \, dx$

As we know by Eulers Formula $e^{-ibx} = \cos bx - i \sin bx$ ∴ $\operatorname{Im} e^{-ibx} = \sin bx$

∴ $I = \operatorname{Im} \int_0^\infty x^{n-1} e^{-ax} e^{-ibx} \, dx = \operatorname{Im} \int_0^\infty x^{n-1} e^{-(a+ib)x} \, dx = \operatorname{Im} \dfrac{\overline{|n}}{(a+ib)^n}$

In polar form, $a = r \cos \phi$, $b = r \sin \phi$

$a + ib = r \cos \phi + i r \sin \phi$

$\qquad = r(\cos \phi + i \sin \phi) = r e^{i\phi}$

∴ $I = \operatorname{Im} \dfrac{\overline{|n}}{(re^{i\phi})^n} = \operatorname{Im} \dfrac{\overline{|n}}{r^n e^{in\phi}}$

$\qquad = \operatorname{Im} \dfrac{\overline{|n}}{r^n} e^{-in\phi}$

By Eulers Formula

∴ $I = \operatorname{Im} \dfrac{\overline{|n}}{r^n} [\cos n\phi - i \sin n\phi]$

$\qquad = \operatorname{Im} \left[\dfrac{\overline{|n}}{r^n} \cos n\phi - i \dfrac{\overline{|n}}{r^n} \sin n\phi \right]$

$\qquad = \dfrac{\overline{|n}}{r^n} \sin n\phi$

$\because a = r\cos\phi, b = r\sin\phi$

$a^2 + b^2 = r^2(\cos^2\phi + \sin^2\phi)$

$r^2 = a^2 + b^2 \quad \therefore r = (a^2+b^2)^{1/2}$

$\dfrac{b}{a} = \dfrac{r\sin\Phi}{r\cos\Phi} \quad \therefore \tan\phi = \dfrac{b}{a} \quad \therefore \phi = \tan^{-1}\dfrac{b}{a}$

$I = \dfrac{\overline{|n}}{[(a^2+b^2)^{1/2}]^n}\sin\left[n\tan^{-1}\left(\dfrac{b}{a}\right)\right]$

$= \dfrac{\overline{|n}}{(a^2+b^2)^{n/2}}\sin\left[n\tan^{-1}\left(\dfrac{b}{a}\right)\right]$

Ex. 5: Show that $\displaystyle\int_0^\infty x^{m-1}\sin ax\, dx = \dfrac{\overline{|m}}{a^m}\sin\left(\dfrac{\pi m}{2}\right)$

Solution: Let $I = \displaystyle\int_0^\infty x^{m-1}\sin ax\, dx$

As we know by Eulers Formula $e^{-iax} = \cos ax - i\sin ax \quad \therefore \operatorname{Im} e^{-iax} = \sin ax$

$\therefore I = \operatorname{Im}\displaystyle\int_0^\infty x^{m-1}e^{-iax}\, dx = \operatorname{Im}\int_0^\infty e^{-iax}x^{m-1}\, dx = \operatorname{Im}\dfrac{\overline{|m}}{i^m a^m}$

By Euler's formula, $e^{iq} = \cos\theta + i\sin\theta$ Put $\theta = \dfrac{\pi}{2}$

$e^{i\pi/2} = \cos\pi/2 + i\sin\pi/2 = 0 + i = i$

$\therefore I = \operatorname{Im}\dfrac{\overline{|m}}{\left(e^{i\pi/2}\right)^m a^m} = \operatorname{Im}\dfrac{\overline{|m}}{e^{im\pi/2}a^m} = \operatorname{Im}\dfrac{\overline{|m}}{a^m}e^{-im\pi/2}$

$= \operatorname{Im}\dfrac{\overline{|m}}{a^m}\left[\cos\left(\dfrac{\pi m}{2}\right) - i\sin\left(\dfrac{\pi m}{2}\right)\right]$

$= \operatorname{Im}\left[\dfrac{\overline{|m}}{a^m}\cos\left(\dfrac{\pi m}{2}\right) - i\dfrac{\overline{|m}}{a^m}\sin\left(\dfrac{\pi m}{2}\right)\right]$

$= \dfrac{\overline{|m}}{a^m}\sin\left(\dfrac{\pi m}{2}\right).$

TEST YOUR KNOWLEDGE

1. Prove that $\displaystyle\int_0^\infty x^{m-1}\cos ax\, dx = \dfrac{\overline{|m}}{a^m}\cos\left(\dfrac{\pi m}{2}\right)$

2. Prove that $\displaystyle\int_0^\infty x^{n-1}e^{-ax}\cos bx\, dx = \dfrac{\overline{|n}}{\left(a^2+b^2\right)^{n/2}}\cos\left(n\tan^{-1}\dfrac{b}{a}\right)$

Type V: Examples on the property $\overline{n+1} = n\overline{n}$

Ex. 1: Show that $\dfrac{2^n \overline{n+\dfrac{1}{2}}}{\sqrt{\pi}} = 1.3.5\ldots(2n-1)$

Solution: Apply $\overline{n+1} = n\overline{n}$ on $\overline{n+\dfrac{1}{2}}$

$$\overline{n+\dfrac{1}{2}} = \overline{n+\dfrac{1}{2}-1+1} = \overline{n-\dfrac{1}{2}+1} = \left(n-\dfrac{1}{2}\right)\overline{n-\dfrac{1}{2}}$$

$$= \left(n-\dfrac{1}{2}\right)\left(n-\dfrac{3}{2}\right)\overline{n-\dfrac{3}{2}} = \left(n-\dfrac{1}{2}\right)\left(n-\dfrac{3}{2}\right)\left(n-\dfrac{5}{2}\right)\overline{n-\dfrac{5}{2}}$$

...

$$= \left(n-\dfrac{1}{2}\right)\left(n-\dfrac{3}{2}\right)\left(n-\dfrac{5}{2}\right)\ldots\dfrac{3}{2}\dfrac{1}{2}\overline{\dfrac{1}{2}}$$

$$= \left(n-\dfrac{1}{2}\right)\left(n-\dfrac{3}{2}\right)\left(n-\dfrac{5}{2}\right)\ldots\dfrac{3}{2}\dfrac{1}{2}\sqrt{\pi}$$

$$= \left(\dfrac{2n-1}{2}\right)\left(\dfrac{2n-3}{2}\right)\left(\dfrac{2n-5}{2}\right)\ldots\dfrac{3}{2}\dfrac{1}{2}\sqrt{\pi}$$

$$\overline{n+\dfrac{1}{2}} = \dfrac{(2n-1)(2n-3)(2n-5)\ldots 5.3.1}{2^n}\sqrt{\pi}$$

$$\dfrac{2^n \overline{n+\dfrac{1}{2}}}{\sqrt{\pi}} = 1.3.5\ldots(2n-5)(2n-3)(2n-1).$$

Ex. 2: If $I_n = \dfrac{\dfrac{\sqrt{\pi}}{2}\overline{\dfrac{n+1}{2}}}{\overline{\dfrac{n}{2}+1}}$, show that $I_{n+2} = \dfrac{n+1}{n+2}I_n$. Hence find the value of I_5.

Solution: Given $I_n = \dfrac{\dfrac{\sqrt{\pi}}{2}\overline{\dfrac{n+1}{2}}}{\overline{\dfrac{n}{2}+1}}$ replacing n by $n+2$

$$\therefore \text{LHS} = I_{n+2} = \dfrac{\dfrac{\sqrt{\pi}}{2}\overline{\dfrac{n+2+1}{2}}}{\overline{\dfrac{n+2}{2}+1}} = \dfrac{\dfrac{\sqrt{\pi}}{2}\overline{\dfrac{n+3}{2}}}{\overline{\dfrac{n+2}{2}+1}} \quad \text{Apply } \overline{n+1} = n\overline{n}$$

$$I_{n+2} = \dfrac{\dfrac{\sqrt{\pi}}{2}\overline{\dfrac{n+3}{2}}}{\dfrac{n+2}{2}\overline{\dfrac{n+2}{2}}} = \dfrac{\dfrac{\sqrt{\pi}}{2}\overline{\dfrac{n+3}{2}-1+1}}{\dfrac{n+2}{2}\overline{\dfrac{n}{2}+1}} = \dfrac{\dfrac{\sqrt{\pi}}{2}\overline{\dfrac{n+1}{2}+1}}{\dfrac{n+2}{2}\overline{\dfrac{n}{2}+1}} = \dfrac{\dfrac{\sqrt{\pi}}{2}\dfrac{n+1}{2}\overline{\dfrac{n+1}{2}}}{\dfrac{n+2}{2}\overline{\dfrac{n}{2}+1}}$$

$$= \dfrac{n+1}{n+2}\dfrac{\dfrac{\sqrt{\pi}}{2}\overline{\dfrac{n+1}{2}}}{\overline{\dfrac{n}{2}+1}} = \dfrac{n+1}{n+2}I_n = \text{RHS}.$$

To find I_5 put $n=3$, $I_5 = \dfrac{4}{3} I_3$

Also put $n=1$, $I_3 = \dfrac{2}{3} I_1$

Given $I_n = \dfrac{\dfrac{\sqrt{\pi}}{2} \left\lceil \dfrac{n+1}{2} \right.}{\left\lceil \dfrac{n}{2}+1 \right.}$

To find I_1 put $n = 1$

$$I_1 = \dfrac{\dfrac{\sqrt{\pi}}{2}\lceil 1}{\lceil \dfrac{1}{2}+1} = \dfrac{\dfrac{\sqrt{\pi}}{2}\lceil 1}{\dfrac{1}{2}\lceil\dfrac{1}{2}} = \dfrac{\dfrac{\sqrt{\pi}}{2}\lceil 1}{\dfrac{1}{2}\sqrt{\pi}} = 1$$

Thus $I_5 = \dfrac{4}{5} \cdot \dfrac{2}{3} \cdot 1 = \dfrac{8}{15}$

BETA FUNCTION

Definition: The function of m and n (m, n > 0) defined by the integral

$\int_0^1 x^{m-1}(1-x)^{n-1}\, dx$ is called as Beta function and it is denoted by $\beta(m,n)$.

Hence $\beta(m,n) = \int_0^1 x^{m-1}(1-x)^{n-1}\, dx$.

Remark: 1. Beta function is also known as Euler's Integral of the first kind.
2. Beta function of negative numbers is not defined.

Properties of Beta function

Property 1: $\beta(m,n) = \beta(n,m)$.

Proof: By definition $\beta(m,n) = \int_0^1 x^{m-1}(1-x)^{n-1}\, dx$

x	0	∞
t	0	∞

Replace $1-x = t$, $-dx = dt$

$$\beta(m,n) = \int_1^0 (1-t)^{m-1} t^{n-1}(-dt)$$

$$= \int_0^1 t^{n-1}(1-t)^{m-1}\, dt = \beta(n,m).$$

Property 2: Relation between Beta and Gamma function $\beta(m,n) = \dfrac{\overline{|m}\,\overline{|n}}{\overline{|m+n}}$.

Proof: Please accept this property with out proof.

Property 3: $\beta(m,n) = 2\displaystyle\int_0^{\pi/2} \sin^{2m-1}\theta \, \cos^{2n-1}\theta \, d\theta$.

x	0	1
θ	0	π/2

Proof: By definition $\beta(m,n) = \displaystyle\int_0^1 x^{m-1}(1-x)^{n-1}dx$

Replace $x = \sin^2\theta$, $\quad dx = 2\sin\theta\cos\theta \, d\theta$

$\beta(m,n) = \displaystyle\int_0^{\pi/2} (\sin^2\theta)^{m-1}(1-\sin^2\theta)^{n-1} 2\sin\theta\cos\theta \, d\theta$

$= 2\displaystyle\int_0^{\pi/2} \sin^{2m-2+1}\theta \, \cos^{2n-2+1}\theta \, d\theta = 2\int_0^{\pi/2} \sin^{2m-1}\theta \, \cos^{2n-1}\theta \, d\theta$

Remark: This property is called as second form of Beta function.

Property 4: $\displaystyle\int_0^{\pi/2} \sin^p\theta \, \cos^q\theta \, d\theta = \dfrac{1}{2}\beta\left(\dfrac{p+1}{2}, \dfrac{q+1}{2}\right)$.

Proof: By Property 3 we know that $\beta(m,n) = 2\displaystyle\int_0^{\pi/2} \sin^{2m-1}\theta \, \cos^{2n-1}\theta \, d\theta$.

Replace $m = \dfrac{p+1}{2}$ and $n = \dfrac{p+1}{2}$, we get

$\dfrac{1}{2}\beta\left(\dfrac{p+1}{2}, \dfrac{q+1}{2}\right) = \displaystyle\int_0^{\pi/2} \sin^p\theta \, \cos^q\theta \, d\theta$.

Remark: If we use relation between Beta and Gamma function in property 4 then

$\displaystyle\int_0^{\pi/2} \sin^p\theta \cos^q\theta \, d\theta = \dfrac{1}{2}\dfrac{\overline{\left|\dfrac{p+1}{2}\right.}\,\overline{\left|\dfrac{q+1}{2}\right.}}{\overline{\left|\dfrac{p+q+2}{2}\right.}}$.

Property 5: $\beta(m,n) = \displaystyle\int_0^\infty \dfrac{x^{m-1}}{(1+x)^{m+n}}dx$ $\qquad$ **SUK: Nov-09**

x	0	1
t	0	∞

(4.25)

Proof: By definition $\beta(m,n) = \int_0^1 x^{m-1}(1-x)^{n-1}\,dx$

Replace $x = \dfrac{t}{1+t}$, $dx = \dfrac{(1+t).1-t}{(1+t)^2}\,dt$ i.e. $dx = \dfrac{1}{(1+t)^2}\,dt$

$$\beta(m,n) = \int_0^\infty \left(\dfrac{t}{1+t}\right)^{m-1} \left(1-\dfrac{t}{1+t}\right)^{n-1} \dfrac{1}{(1+t)^2}\,dt = \int_0^\infty \dfrac{t^{m-1}}{(1+t)^{m+n}}\,dt$$

In definite integral variables are immaterial.

Hence $\beta(m,n) = \int_0^\infty \dfrac{x^{m-1}}{(1+x)^{m+n}}\,dx$

Remark: Above property can be used as definition of Beta function

Property 6: $\left|\dfrac{1}{2}\right| = \sqrt{\pi}$.

Proof: We know that $\int_0^{\pi/2} \sin^p\theta \cos^q\theta\,d\theta = \dfrac{1}{2} \dfrac{\left|\dfrac{p+1}{2}\right|\left|\dfrac{q+1}{2}\right|}{\left|\dfrac{p+q+2}{2}\right|}$.

Replace $p=0, q=0$, $\therefore \int_0^{\pi/2} \sin^0\theta \cos^0\theta\,d\theta = \dfrac{1}{2}\dfrac{\left|\dfrac{0+1}{2}\right|\left|\dfrac{0+1}{2}\right|}{\left|\dfrac{0+0+2}{2}\right|}$

$\int_0^{\pi/2} d\theta = \dfrac{1}{2}\dfrac{\left|\dfrac{1}{2}\right|\left|\dfrac{1}{2}\right|}{\left|\dfrac{2}{2}\right|}$, $\quad [\theta]_0^{\pi/2} = \dfrac{1}{2}\dfrac{\left[\left|\dfrac{1}{2}\right|\right]^2}{\left|1\right|}$

$[\pi/2 - 0] = \dfrac{1}{2}\left[\left|\dfrac{1}{2}\right|\right]^2 \qquad \therefore \sqrt{\pi} = \left|\dfrac{1}{2}\right|$

Property 7: Legendre's Duplication formula **SUK: May-10**

$\left|m\right|\left|m+\dfrac{1}{2}\right| = \dfrac{\left|2m\right|\sqrt{\pi}}{2^{2m-1}}$. or $2^{2m-1}\left|m\right|\left|m+\dfrac{1}{2}\right| = \left|2m\right|\sqrt{\pi}$.

Proof: We know that $\int_0^{\pi/2} \sin^p\theta \cos^q\theta\,d\theta = \dfrac{1}{2}\beta\left(\dfrac{p+1}{2}, \dfrac{q+1}{2}\right)$.

θ	0	π/2
v	0	π

Replace $q = p$ $\therefore \int_0^{\pi/2} (\sin\theta \cos\theta)^p \, d\theta = \frac{1}{2}\beta\left(\frac{p+1}{2}, \frac{p+1}{2}\right)$

$\int_0^{\pi/2} \left(\frac{\sin 2\theta}{2}\right)^p d\theta = \frac{1}{2}\beta\left(\frac{p+1}{2}, \frac{p+1}{2}\right)$

Again replace $2\theta = v$ $\therefore 2d\theta = dv$

$\frac{1}{2^p} \int_0^{\pi} \sin^p v \, \frac{dv}{2} = \frac{1}{2}\beta\left(\frac{p+1}{2}, \frac{p+1}{2}\right)$

$\frac{1}{2 \cdot 2^p} \int_0^{\pi} \sin^p v \, dv = \frac{1}{2}\beta\left(\frac{p+1}{2}, \frac{p+1}{2}\right)$

$\frac{1}{2 \cdot 2^p} \int_0^{\pi/2} \left[\sin^p v + \sin^p(\pi - v)\right] dv = \frac{1}{2}\beta\left(\frac{p+1}{2}, \frac{p+1}{2}\right)$

$\because \int_0^{2a} f(x)\,dx = \int_0^a f(x) + f(2a - x)\,dx$

$\frac{2}{2 \cdot 2^p} \int_0^{\pi/2} \left[\sin^p v \cos^0 v\right] dv = \frac{1}{2}\beta\left(\frac{p+1}{2}, \frac{p+1}{2}\right)$ $\quad \sin(\pi - v) = \sin v$

$\frac{1}{2 \cdot 2^p} \beta\left(\frac{p+1}{2}, \frac{0+1}{2}\right) = \frac{1}{2}\beta\left(\frac{p+1}{2}, \frac{p+1}{2}\right)$ By property 4

$\frac{1}{2 \cdot 2^{2m-1}} \beta\left(m, \frac{0+1}{2}\right) = \frac{1}{2}\beta(m, m)$ $\quad \because \frac{p+1}{2} = m \Rightarrow p = 2m - 1$

$\frac{1}{2^{2m-1}} \beta\left(m, \frac{1}{2}\right) = \beta(m, m)$

$\frac{1}{2^{2m-1}} \cdot \frac{\overline{|m|}\overline{\left|\frac{1}{2}\right|}}{\overline{\left|m + \frac{1}{2}\right|}} = \frac{\overline{|m|}\overline{|m|}}{\overline{|2m|}} \quad \Rightarrow \frac{\overline{|2m|}\sqrt{\pi}}{2^{2m-1}} = \overline{|m|}\overline{\left|m + \frac{1}{2}\right|}.$

Remark: In above result if we put $m = \frac{1}{4}$, we get $\overline{\left|\frac{1}{4}\right|}\overline{\left|\frac{1}{4} + \frac{1}{2}\right|} = \frac{\sqrt{\pi}\,\overline{\left|2\frac{1}{4}\right|}}{2^{2\frac{1}{4} - 1}}$

$\overline{\left|\frac{1}{4}\right|}\overline{\left|\frac{3}{4}\right|} = \frac{\sqrt{\pi}\,\overline{\left|\frac{1}{2}\right|}}{2^{-\frac{1}{2}}}, \quad \Rightarrow 2^{-\frac{1}{2}}\overline{\left|\frac{1}{4}\right|}\overline{\left|\frac{3}{4}\right|}$

$= \sqrt{\pi}\sqrt{\pi}, \quad \Rightarrow \frac{1}{\sqrt{2}}\overline{\left|\frac{1}{4}\right|}\overline{\left|\frac{3}{4}\right|}$

$= \pi \quad \therefore \overline{\left|\frac{1}{4}\right|}\overline{\left|\frac{3}{4}\right|} = \sqrt{2}\pi.$

Examples on Beta function

Type-I Examples using definition of Beta function $\beta(m,n) = \int_0^1 x^{m-1}(1-x)^{n-1} dx$.

Ex. 1: Prove that $\int_0^a x^m (a-x)^n dx = a^{m+n+1} B(m+1, n+1)$

Solution: Let $I = \int_0^a x^m (a-x)^n dx$

x	0	a
t	0	1

Put $x = at$ $\therefore dx = a\,dt$ also $a - x = a - at = a(1-t)$

$\therefore I = \int_0^1 a^m t^m a^n (1-t)^n \, a\,dt$

$= a^{m+n+1} \int_0^1 t^m (1-t)^n \, dt$

$= a^{m+n+1} B(m+1, n+1)$

Ex. 2: Evaluate $\int_0^{2a} x^2 \sqrt{2ax - x^2} \, dx$.   **SUK:Nov-12**

Solution: Let $I = \int_0^{2a} x^2 \sqrt{2ax - x^2} \, dx$

x	0	2a
t	0	1

Put $x = 2at$ $\therefore dx = 2a\,dt$

$\therefore I = \int_0^1 (2at)^2 \sqrt{4a^2 t - 4a^2 t^2} \, 2a\,dt$

$= (2a)^{2+1} \int_0^1 t^2 \sqrt{4a^2 t(1-t)} \, dt = (2a)^{2+1} \int_0^1 t^2 \, 2at^{1/2} \sqrt{(1-t)} \, dt$

$= (2a)^4 \int_0^1 t^{5/2} (1-t)^{1/2} dt = 16a^4 \int_0^1 t^{7/2-1} (1-t)^{3/2-1} dt$

$= 16a^4 \beta\left(\frac{7}{2}, \frac{3}{2}\right) = 16a^4 \dfrac{\overline{\left|\tfrac{7}{2}\right.}\,\overline{\left|\tfrac{3}{2}\right.}}{\overline{|5}} = \dfrac{16}{24} a^4 \dfrac{5}{2}\dfrac{3}{2}\dfrac{1}{2}\overline{\left|\tfrac{1}{2}\right.}\overline{\left|\tfrac{1}{2}\right.} = \dfrac{15\pi a^4}{24}.$

Ex. 3: Evaluate $\int_0^{1/2} x^3\sqrt{1-4x^2}\,dx$. **SUK: May-08**

Solution: Let

x	0	½
t	0	1

$$I = \int_0^{1/2} x^3\sqrt{1-4x^2}\,dx.$$

Put $4x^2 = t$, $x^2 = \dfrac{t}{4} \Rightarrow x = \dfrac{t^{\frac{1}{2}}}{2}$ ∴ $dx = \dfrac{t^{\frac{-1}{2}}}{4}dt$

$$\therefore I = \int_0^1 \frac{t^{\frac{3}{2}}}{2^3}(1-t)^{\frac{1}{2}}\frac{t^{\frac{-1}{2}}}{4}dt$$

$$= \frac{1}{2^3} \cdot \frac{1}{4}\int_0^1 t^{\frac{3}{2}-\frac{1}{2}}(1-t)^{\frac{1}{2}}\,dt$$

$$= \frac{1}{2^5}\int_0^1 t^1(1-t)^{\frac{1}{2}}\,dt = \frac{1}{2^5}\beta\left(2,\frac{3}{2}\right)$$

Ex. 4: Evaluate $\int_0^4 \sqrt{x}(4-x)^{3/2}\,dx$.

Solution: Let $I = \int_0^4 \sqrt{x}(4-x)^{3/2}\,dx$.

x	0	4
t	0	1

Put $x = 4t$ ∴ $dx = 4\,dt$

$$\therefore I = \int_0^1 (4t)^{\frac{1}{2}}(4-4t)^{\frac{3}{2}}4\,dt = \int_0^1 2t^{\frac{1}{2}}4^{\frac{3}{2}}(1-t)^{\frac{3}{2}}4\,dt$$

$$= \int_0^1 2t^{\frac{1}{2}}2^3(1-t)^{\frac{3}{2}}2^2\,dt = 2^{1+3+2}\int_0^1 t^{\frac{1}{2}}(1-t)^{\frac{3}{2}}dt$$

$$= 2^6\int_0^1 t^{\frac{3}{2}-1}(1-t)^{\frac{5}{2}-1}dt = 64\beta\left(\frac{3}{2},\frac{5}{2}\right).$$

Ex. 5: Evaluate $\int_0^1 \dfrac{x^{2n}}{\sqrt{1-x^2}}\,dx$.

Solution: Let $I = \int_0^1 \dfrac{x^{2n}}{\sqrt{1-x^2}}\,dx$.

x	0	1
t	0	1

Put $x^2 = t \Rightarrow x = \sqrt{t}$ $\therefore dx = \dfrac{1}{2\sqrt{t}} dt$, i.e. $dx = \dfrac{1}{2} t^{-\frac{1}{2}} dt$

$$\therefore I = \int_0^1 \dfrac{x^{2n}}{\sqrt{1-x^2}} dx = \int_0^1 x^{2n} (1-x^2)^{-\frac{1}{2}} dx = \int_0^1 \left(t^{\frac{1}{2}}\right)^{2n} (1-t)^{-\frac{1}{2}} \dfrac{1}{2} t^{-\frac{1}{2}} dt$$

$$= \dfrac{1}{2} \int_0^1 t^{n-\frac{1}{2}} (1-t)^{-\frac{1}{2}} dt = \dfrac{1}{2} \beta\left(n + \dfrac{1}{2}, \dfrac{1}{2}\right).$$

Ex. 6: Prove that $\int_0^1 \left(1 - x^{\frac{1}{n}}\right)^m dx = \dfrac{m! n!}{(m+n)!}$. OR $\int_0^1 \left(1 - \sqrt[n]{x}\right)^m dx = \dfrac{m! n!}{(m+n)!}$.

Solution: Let $I = \int_0^1 \left(1 - x^{\frac{1}{n}}\right)^m dx$

x	0	1
t	0	1

Put $x^{\frac{1}{n}} = t \Rightarrow x = t^n$ $\therefore dx = n t^{n-1} dt$

$$\therefore I = \int_0^1 (1-t)^m n t^{n-1} dt = n \int_0^1 t^{n-1} (1-t)^m dt$$

$$= n \beta(n, m+1) = n \dfrac{\overline{|n|} \overline{|m+1|}}{\overline{|m+n+1|}} = \dfrac{\overline{|n+1|} \overline{|m+1|}}{\overline{|m+n+1|}} = \dfrac{n! m!}{(m+n)!}.$$

Ex. 7: Prove that $\int_0^1 x^m (1-x^n)^p dx = \dfrac{1}{n} \dfrac{\overline{\left|\dfrac{m+1}{n}\right|} \overline{|p+1|}}{\overline{\left|\dfrac{m+1}{n} + p + 1\right|}}$.

Solution: Let $I = \int_0^1 x^m (1-x^n)^p dx$

x	0	1
t	0	1

Put $x^n = t \Rightarrow x = t^{\frac{1}{n}}$ $\therefore dx = \dfrac{1}{n} t^{\frac{1}{n} - 1} dt$

$$\therefore I = \int_0^1 t^{m/n} (1-t)^p \dfrac{1}{n} t^{\frac{1}{n}-1} dt = \dfrac{1}{n} \int_0^1 t^{\frac{m}{n} + \frac{1}{n} - 1} (1-t)^p dt = \dfrac{1}{n} \beta\left(\dfrac{m+1}{n}, p+1\right) = \dfrac{1}{n} \dfrac{\overline{\left|\dfrac{m+1}{n}\right|} \overline{|p+1|}}{\overline{\left|\dfrac{m+1}{n} + p + 1\right|}}$$

Ex. 8: Evaluate $\int_0^1 x^6 (1-x^2)^{1/2} dx$

Solution: Let $I = \int_0^1 x^6 (1-x^2)^{1/2} dx$

x	0	1
t	0	1

Put $x^2 = t \Rightarrow x = t^{\frac{1}{2}}$ ∴ $dx = \frac{1}{2} t^{-\frac{1}{2}} dt$

∴ $I = \int_0^1 t^3 (1-t)^{1/2} \frac{1}{2} t^{-\frac{1}{2}} dt = \frac{1}{2} \int_0^1 t^{5/2} (1-t)^{1/2} dt = \frac{1}{2} \beta\left(\frac{7}{2}, \frac{3}{2}\right)$.

Ex. 9: Evaluate $\int_0^2 x^7 (16-x^4)^{10} dx$

Solution: Let $I = \int_0^2 x^7 (16-x^4)^{10} dx$

x	0	1
t	0	1

Put $x^4 = 16t \Rightarrow x = 2t^{\frac{1}{4}}$ ∴ $dx = 2 \cdot \frac{1}{4} t^{-\frac{3}{4}} dt$

∴ $I = \int_0^1 \left(2t^{\frac{1}{4}}\right)^7 (16)^{10} (1-t)^{10} \frac{1}{2} t^{-\frac{3}{4}} dt = \frac{1}{2} 2^7 (2^4)^{10} \int_0^1 t^{\frac{7}{4} - \frac{3}{4}} (1-t)^{10} dt$

$= 2^{46} \int_0^1 t^1 (1-t)^{10} dt = 2^{46} \beta(2, 11)$.

Ex. 10: Evaluate $\int_0^1 x^5 (1-x^3)^{10} dx$ **SUK: May-12**

Solution: Let $I = \int_0^1 x^5 (1-x^3)^{10} dx$

x	0	1
t	0	1

Put $x^3 = t \Rightarrow x = t^{\frac{1}{3}}$ ∴ $dx = \frac{1}{3} t^{-\frac{2}{3}} dt$

∴ $I = \int_0^1 t^{\frac{5}{3}} (1-t)^{10} \frac{1}{3} t^{-\frac{2}{3}} dt = \frac{1}{3} \int_0^1 t^{\frac{5}{3} - \frac{2}{3}} (1-t)^{10} dt$

$= \frac{1}{3} \int_0^1 t^1 (1-t)^{10} dt = \frac{1}{3} \beta(2, 11)$.

Ex. 11: Evaluate $\int_0^2 y^4 (8-y^3)^{-1/3} dy$

Solution: Let $I = \int_0^2 y^4 (8-y^3)^{-1/3} dy$

x	0	1
t	0	1

Put $y^3 = 8t \Rightarrow y = 2t^{\frac{1}{3}}$ $\therefore dy = \frac{2}{3} t^{-\frac{2}{3}} dt$

$\therefore I = \int_0^1 (8t)^{4/3} (8)^{-1/3} (1-t)^{-1/3} \frac{2}{3} t^{-\frac{2}{3}} dt = 8^{4/3-1/3} \frac{2}{3} \int_0^1 t^{\frac{4}{3}-\frac{2}{3}} (1-t)^{\frac{-1}{3}} dt$

$= \frac{16}{3} \int_0^1 t^{\frac{2}{3}} (1-t)^{\frac{-1}{3}} dt = \frac{16}{3} \beta\left(\frac{5}{3}, \frac{2}{3}\right).$

Ex. 12: Evaluate $\int_0^1 (1 - \sqrt[3]{x})^{11/2} dx$

Solution: Let $I = \int_0^1 (1 - \sqrt[3]{x})^{11/2} dx$

x	0	1
t	0	1

Put $\sqrt[3]{x} = t \Rightarrow x = t^3$ $\therefore dx = 3t^2 dt$

$\therefore I = \int_0^1 3t^2 (1-t)^{11/2} dt = 3\beta(3, 13/2)$

Ex. 13: Evaluate $\int_0^1 \frac{dx}{\sqrt{1-x^m}}$

Solution: Let $I = \int_0^1 \frac{dx}{\sqrt{1-x^m}}$

x	0	1
t	0	1

Put $x^m = t \Rightarrow x = t^{1/m}$ $\therefore dx = \frac{1}{m} t^{\frac{1}{m}-1} dt$

$\therefore I = \int_0^1 (1-t)^{-1/2} \frac{1}{m} t^{\frac{1}{m}-1} dt = \frac{1}{m} \beta\left(\frac{1}{m}, \frac{1}{2}\right).$

Ex. 14: Evaluate $\int_0^1 \dfrac{dx}{\sqrt{1-x^5}}$

Solution: Let $I = \int_0^1 \dfrac{dx}{\sqrt{1-x^5}}$

x	0	1
t	0	1

Put $x^5 = t \Rightarrow x = t^{1/5}$ $\therefore dx = \dfrac{1}{5} t^{-\frac{4}{5}} dt$

$\therefore I = \int_0^1 (1-t)^{-1/2} \dfrac{1}{5} t^{-\frac{4}{5}} dt = \dfrac{1}{5} \beta\left(\dfrac{1}{5}, \dfrac{1}{2}\right)$.

Ex. 15: Evaluate $\int_0^1 \sqrt{1-x^5}\, dx$

Solution: Let $I = \int_0^1 \sqrt{1-x^5}\, dx$

x	0	1
t	0	1

Put $x^5 = t \Rightarrow x = t^{1/5}$ $\therefore dx = \dfrac{1}{5} t^{-\frac{4}{5}} dt$

$\therefore I = \int_0^1 (1-t)^{1/2} \dfrac{1}{5} t^{-\frac{4}{5}} dt = \dfrac{1}{5} \beta\left(\dfrac{1}{5}, \dfrac{3}{2}\right)$.

Ex. 16: Prove that $\int_0^a \dfrac{dx}{\left[a^n - x^n\right]^{\frac{1}{n}}} = \dfrac{\pi}{n} \operatorname{cosec}\left[\dfrac{\pi}{n}\right]$

Solution: Let $I = \int_0^a \dfrac{dx}{\left[a^n - x^n\right]^{\frac{1}{n}}} = \int_0^a \left[a^n - x^n\right]^{-\frac{1}{n}} dx$

x	0	a
t	0	1

Put $x^n = a^n t \Rightarrow x = a t^{1/n}$ $\therefore dx = \dfrac{a}{n} t^{\frac{1}{n}-1} dt$

$\therefore I = \int_0^1 (a^n - a^n t)^{-1/n} \dfrac{a}{n} t^{\frac{1}{n}-1} dt = \dfrac{1}{n} \int_0^1 a^{-n/n} (1-t)^{-1/n} a\, t^{\frac{1}{n}-1} dt$

$= \dfrac{1}{n} \int_0^1 t^{\frac{1}{n}-1} (1-t)^{-1/n} dt = \dfrac{1}{n} \beta\left(\dfrac{1}{n}, \dfrac{n-1}{n}\right) = \dfrac{1}{n} \beta\left(\dfrac{1}{n}, 1-\dfrac{1}{n}\right)$

$= \dfrac{1}{n} \dfrac{\left|\dfrac{1}{n}\right| \left|1-\dfrac{1}{n}\right|}{\left|\dfrac{1}{n}+1-\dfrac{1}{n}\right|} = \dfrac{1}{n} \dfrac{\left|\dfrac{1}{n}\right| \left|1-\dfrac{1}{n}\right|}{|1|} = \dfrac{1}{n} \dfrac{\pi}{\sin\dfrac{\pi}{n}} = \dfrac{\pi}{n} \operatorname{cosec} \dfrac{\pi}{n}$ $\quad \because \overline{|1-n|n} = \dfrac{\pi}{\sin n\pi}$

TEST YOUR KNOWLEDGE
I. Prove that the following

1. $\int_0^n x^n (n-x)^m \, dx = n^{n+m+1} \beta(n+1, m+1)$. Hint put $x = nt$

2. $\int_0^1 x^{m-1} (1-x^2)^{n-1} \, dx = \frac{1}{2} \beta\left(\frac{m}{2}, n\right)$. Hint put $x^2 = t$

3. $\int_0^2 x^3 \sqrt{8-x^3} \, dx = \frac{16\pi}{9\sqrt{3}}$. Hint put $x^3 = t$

4. $\int_0^1 x^3 (1-\sqrt{x})^5 \, dx = \frac{1}{5148}$. Hint put $\sqrt{x} = t$ 5. $\int_0^1 \frac{dx}{\sqrt[3]{1-x^3}} = \frac{2\pi}{3\sqrt{3}}$. Hint put $x^3 = t$

II. Evaluate the following

1. $\int_0^9 x^{3/2} (9-x)^{1/2} \, dx$ Ans: 729

2. $\int_0^2 x^2 (2-x)^{7/2} \, dx$ Ans: $2^{13/2} \beta(3, 9/2)$

3. $\int_0^2 x^3 \sqrt{2-x} \, dx$ Ans: $\frac{512}{315}\sqrt{2}$

4. $\int_0^3 x^3 (3-x)^{5/2} \, dx$ Ans: $3^{13/2} \beta(4, 7/2)$

5. $\int_0^1 (1-\sqrt{x})^{9/2} \, dx$ Ans: $2\beta(11/2, 2)$

6. $\int_0^1 (1-\sqrt[3]{x})^{3/2} \, dx$ Ans: $5\beta(5, 5/2)$

7. $\int_0^1 x^3 \sqrt{8-x^3} \, dx$ Ans: $\frac{8}{3}\beta(2/3, 4/3)$

8. $\int_0^{2a} x^m \sqrt{2ax - x^2} \, dx$ Ans: $(2a)^{m+2} \beta(m+3/2, 3/2)$

9. $\int_0^{2a} x\sqrt{2ax - x^2} \, dx$ Ans: $\frac{\pi}{2} a^3$

10. $\int_0^2 x^3 \sqrt{2-x} \, dx$ Ans: $\frac{512\sqrt{2}}{315}$.

11. $\int_0^1 \frac{dx}{\sqrt[n]{1-x^n}}$ Ans: $\frac{1}{n}\left|\frac{1}{n}\right|\left|1 - \frac{1}{n}\right|$

12. $\int_0^1 x^2 (1-x^2)^4 \, dx$ Ans: $\frac{1}{2}\beta(3/2, 5)$

13. $\int_0^1 x^5 (1-x^3)^{10} \, dx$ Ans: $\frac{1}{3}\beta(2, 11)$

14. $\int_0^1 \frac{x^n \, dx}{\sqrt{1-x^2}}$ Ans: $\frac{1}{2}\beta(n+1/2, 1/2)$

15. $\int_0^1 \frac{x^2 \, dx}{\sqrt{1-x^4}} \int_0^1 \frac{dx}{\sqrt{1-x^4}}$ Ans: $\frac{\pi}{4}$

16. $\int_0^4 x^2 \sqrt{4x - x^2} \, dx$ Ans: 10π SUK: May–13

17. $\int_0^{2a} \frac{x^{9/2}}{\sqrt{2a-x}} \, dx$ Ans: $(2a)^5 \beta(11/2, 1/2)$

18. $\int_0^1 \sqrt{1-x^{10}} \, dx$ Ans: $\frac{1}{10}\beta(1/10, 3/2)$

19. $\int_0^1 \frac{dx}{\sqrt{1-x^{10}}}$ Ans: $\frac{1}{10}\beta(1/10, 1/2)$

20. $\int_0^1 \sqrt{1-x^n} \, dx$ Ans: $\frac{1}{n}\beta(1/n, 3/2)$

TYPE-II EXAMPLES USING TRIGONOMETRIC FORM OF BETA FUNCTION

OR Examples using property $\int_0^{\pi/2} \sin^p \theta \cos^q \theta \, d\theta = \frac{1}{2} \beta\left(\frac{p+1}{2}, \frac{q+1}{2}\right).$

Ex. 1: Evaluate $\int_0^{\pi/6} \sin^2 6\theta \cos^6 3\theta \, d\theta.$

θ	0	π/6
φ	0	π/2

Solution: Let $I = \int_0^{\pi/6} \sin^2 6\theta \cos^6 3\theta \, d\theta$

$3\theta = \phi, \therefore 3d\theta = d\phi$

$\therefore I = \int_0^{\pi/2} \sin^2 2\phi \cos^6 \phi \frac{1}{3} d\phi$

$= \int_0^{\pi/2} \frac{4}{3} \sin^2 \phi \cos^2 \phi \cos^6 \phi \, d\phi \qquad \because \sin 2\theta = 2 \sin \theta \cos \theta$

$= \frac{4}{3} \int_0^{\pi/2} \sin^2 \phi \cos^8 \phi \, d\phi \qquad$ Here $p = 2, q = 8$

$= \frac{4}{3} \cdot \frac{1}{2} \beta\left(\frac{2+1}{2}, \frac{8+1}{2}\right) = \frac{2}{3} \beta\left(\frac{3}{2}, \frac{9}{2}\right).$

Ex. 2: Evaluate $\int_0^{\pi/2} \sqrt{\tan \theta} \, d\theta.$

Solution: Let $I = \int_0^{\pi/2} \sqrt{\tan \theta} \, d\theta$

$\therefore I = \int_0^{\pi/2} \sqrt{\tan \theta} \, d\theta = \int_0^{\pi/2} \frac{\sin^{1/2} \theta}{\cos^{1/2} \theta} d\theta$

$= \int_0^{\pi/2} \sin^{1/2} \theta \cos^{-1/2} \theta \, d\theta \qquad$ here $p = \frac{1}{2}, \; q = -\frac{1}{2}$

$= \frac{1}{2} \beta\left(\frac{\frac{1}{2}+1}{2}, \frac{-\frac{1}{2}+1}{2}\right) = \frac{1}{2} \beta\left(\frac{3}{4}, \frac{1}{4}\right) = \frac{1}{2} \frac{\overline{\left|\frac{3}{4}\right.} \overline{\left|\frac{1}{4}\right.}}{\overline{\left|\frac{3}{4} + \frac{1}{4}\right.}}$

$= \frac{1}{2} \frac{\overline{\left|\frac{3}{4}\right.} \overline{\left|\frac{1}{4}\right.}}{\overline{|1}} = \frac{1}{2} \sqrt{2}\pi = \frac{\pi}{\sqrt{2}}.$

Ex. 3: Prove that $\int_0^{\pi/2} \sqrt{\tan\theta}\, d\theta \int_0^{\pi/2} \sqrt{\cot\theta}\, d\theta = \dfrac{\pi^2}{2}$.   **SUK: Aug-13**

Solution: Let $I = \int_0^{\pi/2} \sqrt{\tan\theta}\, d\theta \int_0^{\pi/2} \sqrt{\cot\theta}\, d\theta$.

$\therefore I = \int_0^{\pi/2} \sqrt{\tan\theta}\, d\theta \int_0^{\pi/2} \sqrt{\cot\theta}\, d\theta = \int_0^{\pi/2} \dfrac{\sin^{1/2}\theta}{\cos^{1/2}\theta}\, d\theta \int_0^{\pi/2} \dfrac{\cos^{1/2}\theta}{\sin^{1/2}\theta}\, d\theta$

$= \int_0^{\pi/2} \sin^{1/2}\theta \cos^{-1/2}\theta\, d\theta \int_0^{\pi/2} \sin^{-1/2}\theta \cos^{1/2}\theta\, d\theta$

$= \dfrac{1}{2}\beta\left(\dfrac{\frac{1}{2}+1}{2}, \dfrac{-\frac{1}{2}+1}{2}\right) \dfrac{1}{2}\beta\left(\dfrac{-\frac{1}{2}+1}{2}, \dfrac{\frac{1}{2}+1}{2}\right) = \dfrac{1}{2}\beta\left(\dfrac{3}{4}, \dfrac{1}{4}\right) \dfrac{1}{2}\beta\left(\dfrac{1}{4}, \dfrac{3}{4}\right)$

$= \dfrac{1}{2} \dfrac{\left\lfloor\dfrac{3}{4}\right.\left\lfloor\dfrac{1}{4}\right.}{\left\lfloor\dfrac{3}{4}+\dfrac{1}{4}\right.} \dfrac{1}{2} \dfrac{\left\lfloor\dfrac{1}{4}\right.\left\lfloor\dfrac{3}{4}\right.}{\left\lfloor\dfrac{3}{4}+\dfrac{1}{4}\right.} = \dfrac{1}{4}\dfrac{\left\lfloor\dfrac{3}{4}\right.\left\lfloor\dfrac{1}{4}\right.}{\left\lfloor 1\right.} \cdot \dfrac{\left\lfloor\dfrac{1}{4}\right.\left\lfloor\dfrac{3}{4}\right.}{\left\lfloor 1\right.} = \dfrac{1}{4}\sqrt{2\pi}\sqrt{2\pi} = \dfrac{2\pi^2}{4} = \dfrac{\pi^2}{2}$.

Ex. 4: Evaluate $\int_0^{\pi/2} \dfrac{d\theta}{\sqrt{\sin\theta}} \int_0^{\pi/2} \sqrt{\sin\theta}\, d\theta$.

Solution: Let $I = \int_0^{\pi/2} \dfrac{d\theta}{\sqrt{\sin\theta}} \int_0^{\pi/2} \sqrt{\sin\theta}\, d\theta$.

$\therefore I = \int_0^{\pi/2} \dfrac{d\theta}{\sqrt{\sin\theta}} \int_0^{\pi/2} \sqrt{\sin\theta}\, d\theta = \int_0^{\pi/2} \sin^{-1/2}\theta \cos^0\theta\, d\theta \int_0^{\pi/2} \sin^{1/2}\theta \cos^0\theta\, d\theta$

$= \dfrac{1}{2}\beta\left(\dfrac{-\frac{1}{2}+1}{2}, \dfrac{0+1}{2}\right) \dfrac{1}{2}\beta\left(\dfrac{\frac{1}{2}+1}{2}, \dfrac{0+1}{2}\right)$

$= \dfrac{1}{2}\beta\left(\dfrac{1}{4}, \dfrac{1}{2}\right) \dfrac{1}{2}\beta\left(\dfrac{3}{4}, \dfrac{1}{2}\right)$

$= \dfrac{1}{4} \dfrac{\left\lfloor\dfrac{1}{4}\right.\left\lfloor\dfrac{1}{2}\right.}{\left\lfloor\dfrac{1}{4}+\dfrac{1}{2}\right.} \dfrac{\left\lfloor\dfrac{3}{4}\right.\left\lfloor\dfrac{1}{2}\right.}{\left\lfloor\dfrac{3}{4}+\dfrac{1}{2}\right.} = \dfrac{1}{4} \dfrac{\sqrt{\pi}\sqrt{\pi} \left\lfloor\dfrac{1}{4}\right.\left\lfloor\dfrac{3}{4}\right.}{\left\lfloor\dfrac{3}{4}\right.\left\lfloor\dfrac{5}{4}\right.}$

$= \dfrac{\pi}{4} \dfrac{\left\lfloor\dfrac{1}{4}\right.}{\left\lfloor\dfrac{5}{4}\right.} = \dfrac{\pi}{4} \dfrac{\left\lfloor\dfrac{1}{4}\right.}{\dfrac{1}{4}\left\lfloor\dfrac{1}{4}\right.} = \pi$.

Ex. 5: Prove that $\int_0^{\pi/2} \tan^n \theta \, d\theta = \dfrac{\pi}{2} \sec \dfrac{n\pi}{2}$.

Solution: Let $I = \int_0^{\pi/2} \tan^n \theta \, d\theta$

$\therefore I = \int_0^{\pi/2} \dfrac{\sin^n \theta}{\cos^n \theta} d\theta = \int_0^{\pi/2} \sin^n \theta \cos^{-n} \theta \, d\theta$ here $p = n, \; q = -n$

$= \dfrac{1}{2} \beta\left(\dfrac{n+1}{2}, \dfrac{-n+1}{2}\right) = \dfrac{1}{2} \beta\left(\dfrac{n+1}{2}, \dfrac{1-n}{2}\right)$

$= \dfrac{1}{2} \dfrac{\left\lceil \dfrac{n+1}{2} \right\rceil \left\lceil \dfrac{1-n}{2} \right\rceil}{\left\lceil \dfrac{n+1}{2} + \dfrac{1-n}{2} \right\rceil}$

$= \dfrac{1}{2} \dfrac{\left\lceil \dfrac{n+1}{2} \right\rceil \left\lceil 1 - \dfrac{1+n}{2} \right\rceil}{\lceil 1 \rceil} = \dfrac{1}{2} \dfrac{\pi}{\sin\left(\dfrac{1+n}{2}\right)\pi}$ $\qquad \because \lceil n \rceil \lceil 1-n \rceil = \dfrac{\pi}{\sin n\pi}$

$= \dfrac{\pi}{2 \sin\left(\dfrac{\pi}{2} + \dfrac{\pi n}{2}\right)} = \dfrac{\pi}{2 \cos \dfrac{\pi n}{2}}$

$= \dfrac{\pi}{2} \sec \dfrac{\pi n}{2}.$

Ex. 6 : Prove that

$\int_{-\pi/4}^{\pi/4} [\sin \theta + \cos \theta]^{\frac{1}{3}} d\theta = \dfrac{1}{2^{\frac{5}{6}}} \beta\left(\dfrac{2}{3}, \dfrac{1}{2}\right). \text{ or } \int_{-\pi/4}^{\pi/4} [\cos\theta + \sin\theta]^{\frac{1}{3}} d\theta = \dfrac{1}{2^{\frac{5}{6}}} \beta\left(\dfrac{2}{3}, \dfrac{1}{2}\right).$

Solution: Let $I = \int_{-\pi/4}^{\pi/4} [\sin \theta + \cos \theta]^{\frac{1}{3}} d\theta$

θ	$-\pi/4$	$\pi/4$
t	0	$\pi/2$

$\sin\theta + \cos\theta = \sqrt{2}\left[\sin\theta \dfrac{1}{\sqrt{2}} + \cos\theta \dfrac{1}{\sqrt{2}}\right]$

$= \sqrt{2}\left[\sin\theta \cos\dfrac{\pi}{4} + \cos\theta \sin\dfrac{\pi}{4}\right] = \sqrt{2} \sin\left(\theta + \dfrac{\pi}{4}\right)$

$\therefore I = \int_{-\pi/4}^{\pi/4} \left[\sqrt{2} \sin\left(\theta + \dfrac{\pi}{4}\right)\right]^{\frac{1}{3}} d\theta = 2^{\frac{1}{6}} \int_{-\pi/4}^{\pi/4} \sin^{\frac{1}{3}}\left(\theta + \dfrac{\pi}{4}\right) d\theta$

Put $\theta + \dfrac{\pi}{4} = t \Rightarrow \theta = t - \dfrac{\pi}{4}, \; d\theta = dt$

$\therefore I = 2^{\frac{1}{6}} \int_0^{\pi/2} \sin^{\frac{1}{3}} t \, dt = 2^{\frac{1}{6}} \int_0^{\pi/2} \sin^{\frac{1}{3}} t \cos^0 t \, dt \qquad \text{Here } p = \dfrac{1}{3}, q = 0$

$= 2^{\frac{1}{6}} \dfrac{1}{2} \beta\left(\dfrac{\frac{4}{3}}{2}, \dfrac{1}{2}\right) = 2^{-\frac{5}{6}} \beta\left(\dfrac{2}{3}, \dfrac{1}{2}\right).$

Ex. 7: Evaluate $\int_0^{2\pi} \sin^2\theta(1+\cos\theta)^4\, d\theta$.

Solution: Let $I = \int_0^{2\pi} \sin^2\theta(1+\cos\theta)^4\, d\theta$

θ	0	2π
t	0	π

$$\therefore I = \int_0^{2\pi} \left(2\sin\frac{\theta}{2}\cos\frac{\theta}{2}\right)^2 \left(2\cos^2\frac{\theta}{2}\right)^4 d\theta \quad \because 2\sin\frac{\theta}{2}\cos\frac{\theta}{2} = \sin^2\frac{\theta}{2},\ 2\cos^2\frac{\theta}{2} = 1+\cos\theta$$

$$= 2^6 \int_0^{2\pi} \sin^2\frac{\theta}{2} \cos^{10}\frac{\theta}{2}\, d\theta \qquad \text{Put } \frac{\theta}{2} = t,\ d\theta = 2dt$$

$$= 2^6 \int_0^{\pi} \sin^2 t \cos^{10} t\, 2dt = 2^7 \int_0^{\pi} \sin^2 t \cos^{10} t\, dt$$

$$= 2^7 \cdot 2 \int_0^{\pi/2} \sin^2 t \cos^{10} t\, dt \quad \because \int_0^{2a} f(x)dx = 2\int_0^a f(x)dx \text{ if } f(2a-x) = f(x)$$

$$= 2^8 \cdot \frac{1}{2}\beta\left(\frac{2+1}{2}, \frac{10+1}{2}\right) = 2^7 \beta\left(\frac{3}{2}, \frac{11}{2}\right) = 2^7 \cdot \frac{\left\lfloor\frac{3}{2}\right.\left\lfloor\frac{11}{2}\right.}{\left\lfloor\frac{3}{2}+\frac{11}{2}\right.} = \frac{21\pi}{8}.$$

Ex. 8: Evaluate $\int_0^{\pi/4} \cos^3 2\theta \sin^4 4\theta\, d\theta$.

Solution: Let $I = \int_0^{\pi/4} \cos^3 2\theta \sin^4 4\theta\, d\theta$

θ	−π/4	π/4
t	0	π/2

$$\therefore I = \int_0^{\pi/4} \cos^3 2\theta [2\sin 2\theta \cos 2\theta]^4\, d\theta \qquad \because 2\sin\theta\cos\theta = \sin 2\theta$$

$$= 2^4 \int_0^{\pi/4} \cos^7 2\theta \sin^4 2\theta\, d\theta \qquad \text{Put } 2\theta = t,\ d\theta = \frac{1}{2}dt$$

$$= 16 \int_0^{\pi/2} \sin^4 t \cos^7 t \cdot \frac{1}{2}\, dt = 8 \int_0^{\pi/2} \sin^4 t \cos^7 t\, dt$$

$$= 8 \cdot \frac{1}{2}\beta\left(\frac{5}{2}, 4\right) = 4 \cdot \frac{\left\lfloor\frac{5}{2}\right.\left\lfloor 4\right.}{\left\lfloor\frac{5}{2}+4\right.} = 4 \cdot \frac{\left\lfloor\frac{5}{2}\right.\left\lfloor 4\right.}{\left\lfloor\frac{13}{2}\right.} = \frac{128}{1155}.$$

Ex. 9: Evaluate $\int_0^\pi (1-\cos\theta)^3 \, d\theta$.

Solution: Let $I = \int_0^\pi (1-\cos\theta)^3 \, d\theta$

θ	0	π
t	0	π/2

$\therefore I = \int_0^\pi 2^3 \sin^6 \frac{\theta}{2} d\theta$

Put $\frac{\theta}{2} = t \quad \therefore d\theta = 2dt$

$= 8 \int_0^{\pi/2} \sin^6 t \cdot 2dt$

$= 16 \int_0^{\pi/2} \sin^6 t \cos^0 t \, dt \quad \text{here } p=6, q=0$

$= 16 \cdot \frac{1}{2} \beta\left(\frac{7}{2}, \frac{1}{2}\right) = 8 \cdot \dfrac{\left\lfloor\frac{7}{2}\right.\left\lfloor\frac{1}{2}\right.}{\left\lfloor\frac{7}{2}+\frac{1}{2}\right.}$

$= 8 \dfrac{\frac{5}{2}\frac{3}{2}\frac{1}{2}\left\lfloor\frac{1}{2}\right.\left\lfloor\frac{1}{2}\right.}{\left\lfloor 4\right.} = 8 \dfrac{\frac{5}{2}\frac{3}{2}\frac{1}{2}\sqrt{\pi}\sqrt{\pi}}{3!} = \frac{5\pi}{2}$.

Ex. 10: Prove that $\int_0^\pi x \sin^7 x \cos^4 x \, dx = \dfrac{16\pi}{1155}$.

Solution: Let $I = \int_0^\pi x \sin^7 x \cos^4 x \, dx$

$I = \int_0^\pi (\pi - x) \sin^7(\pi - x) \cos^4(\pi - x) \, dx \qquad \because \int_0^a f(x) dx = \int_0^a f(a-x) dx$

$= \pi \int_0^\pi \sin^7 x \cos^4 x \, dx - \int_0^\pi x \sin^7 x \cos^4 x \, dx = \pi \int_0^\pi \sin^7 x \cos^4 x \, dx - I$

$2I = \pi \int_0^\pi \sin^7 x \cos^4 x \, dx$

$= \pi \left[\int_0^{\pi/2} \sin^7 x \cos^4 x \, dx + \int_0^{\pi/2} \sin^7(\pi - x) \cos^4(\pi - x) \, dx \right] \quad \because \int_0^{2a} f(x) dx = \int_0^a f(x) dx + \int_0^a f(2a-x) dx$

$$= 2\pi \int_0^{\pi/2} \sin^7 x \cos^4 x \, dx$$

$$= 2\pi \cdot \frac{1}{2} \beta\left(4, \frac{5}{2}\right) = \pi \frac{\lfloor 4 \lfloor \frac{5}{2}}{\lfloor \frac{5}{2}+4}$$

$$= \frac{3!\pi \lfloor \frac{5}{2}}{\lfloor \frac{13}{2}} = \frac{3!\pi \lfloor \frac{5}{2}}{\frac{11\,9\,7\,5}{2\,2\,2\,2} \lfloor \frac{5}{2}} = \frac{3!\pi}{\frac{11\,9\,7\,5}{2\,2\,2\,2}} = \frac{16\pi}{1155}.$$

Ex. 11: Prove that $\int_0^{\pi} x \sin^5 x \cos^4 x \, dx = \frac{8\pi}{315}.$

Solution: Let $I = \int_0^{\pi} x \sin^5 x \cos^4 x \, dx$

$$I = \int_0^{\pi} (\pi-x) \sin^5(\pi-x) \cos^4(\pi-x) \, dx \qquad \because \int_0^a f(x)dx = \int_0^a f(a-x)dx$$

$$= \pi \int_0^{\pi} \sin^5 x \cos^4 x \, dx - \int_0^{\pi} x \sin^5 x \cos^4 x \, dx = \pi \int_0^{\pi} \sin^5 x \cos^4 x \, dx - I$$

$$2I = \pi \int_0^{\pi} \sin^5 x \cos^4 x \, dx$$

$$= \pi \left[\int_0^{\pi/2} \sin^5 x \cos^4 x \, dx + \int_0^{\pi/2} \sin^5(\pi-x)\cos^4(\pi-x) \, dx \right] \qquad \because \int_0^{2a} f(x)dx = \int_0^a f(x)dx + \int_0^a f(2a-x)dx$$

$$= 2\pi \int_0^{\pi/2} \sin^5 x \cos^4 x \, dx$$

$$= 2\pi \cdot \frac{1}{2} \beta\left(3, \frac{5}{2}\right) = \pi \frac{\lfloor 3 \lfloor \frac{5}{2}}{\lfloor \frac{5}{2}+3}$$

$$= \frac{\pi \lfloor \frac{5}{2}}{\lfloor \frac{11}{2}} = \frac{\pi \lfloor \frac{5}{2}}{\frac{9\,7\,5}{2\,2\,2} \lfloor \frac{5}{2}} = \frac{\pi}{\frac{9\,7\,5}{2\,2\,2}} = \frac{8\pi}{315}.$$

Ex. 12: Evaluate $\int_0^{\infty} \frac{dx}{1+x^4}.$

Solution: Let $I = \int_0^{\infty} \frac{dx}{1+x^4}$

x	0	∞
t	0	π/2

(4.40)

Put $x^2 = \tan\theta$, $2xdx = \sec^2\theta d\theta \Rightarrow dx = \dfrac{1}{2x}\sec^2\theta d\theta = \dfrac{1}{2\sqrt{\tan\theta}}\sec^2\theta d\theta$

$$I = \int_0^{\pi/2} \dfrac{1}{1+\tan^2\theta}\dfrac{1}{2\sqrt{\tan\theta}}\sec^2\theta d\theta$$

$$= \dfrac{1}{2}\int_0^{\pi/2}\dfrac{1}{\sqrt{\tan\theta}}d\theta = \dfrac{1}{2}\int_0^{\pi/2}\sqrt{\dfrac{\cos\theta}{\sin\theta}}d\theta$$

$$= \dfrac{1}{2}\int_0^{\pi/2}\sin^{-1/2}\theta\cos^{1/2}\theta d\theta = \dfrac{1}{2}\cdot\dfrac{1}{2}\beta\left(\dfrac{1}{4},\dfrac{3}{4}\right)$$

$$= \dfrac{1}{4}\dfrac{\left|\dfrac{1}{4}\right|\dfrac{3}{4}}{\left|\dfrac{1}{4}+\dfrac{3}{4}\right|} = \dfrac{1}{4}\dfrac{\left|\dfrac{1}{4}\right|\dfrac{3}{4}}{|1|} = \dfrac{\sqrt{2}\pi}{4} = \dfrac{\pi}{2\sqrt{2}}.$$

Ex. 13: Evaluate $\int_0^\infty \dfrac{dx}{(1+x^2)^{9/2}}$.

Solution: Let $I = \int_0^\infty \dfrac{dx}{(1+x^2)^{9/2}}$

x	0	∞
t	0	π/2

Put $x = \tan\theta$, $dx = \sec^2\theta d\theta$

$$I = \int_0^{\pi/2}\dfrac{1}{(1+\tan^2\theta)^{9/2}}\sec^2\theta d\theta = \int_0^{\pi/2}\dfrac{\sec^2\theta}{(\sec^2\theta)^{9/2}}d\theta$$

$$= \int_0^{\pi/2}\dfrac{\sec^2\theta}{\sec^9\theta}d\theta = \int_0^{\pi/2}\dfrac{1}{\sec^7\theta}d\theta = \int_0^{\pi/2}\cos^7\theta d\theta$$

$$= \int_0^{\pi/2}\sin^0\theta\cos^7\theta d\theta = \dfrac{1}{2}\beta\left(\dfrac{0+1}{2},\dfrac{7+1}{2}\right) = \dfrac{1}{2}\beta\left(\dfrac{1}{2},4\right)$$

$$= \dfrac{1}{2}\dfrac{\left|\dfrac{1}{2}\right|\overline{4}}{\left|\dfrac{1}{2}+4\right|} = \dfrac{1}{2}\dfrac{3!\left|\dfrac{1}{2}\right|}{\left|\dfrac{9}{2}\right|} = \dfrac{3\left|\dfrac{1}{2}\right|}{\dfrac{7}{2}\dfrac{5}{2}\dfrac{3}{2}\dfrac{1}{2}\left|\dfrac{1}{2}\right|} = \dfrac{3}{\dfrac{7}{2}\dfrac{5}{2}\dfrac{3}{2}\dfrac{1}{2}} = \dfrac{16}{35}.$$

Ex. 14: Evaluate $\int_0^{\pi/2}\dfrac{d\phi}{\sqrt{1-\dfrac{1}{2}\sin^2\phi}}$.

Solution: Let $I = \int_0^{\pi/2}\dfrac{d\phi}{\sqrt{1-\dfrac{1}{2}\sin^2\phi}}$

Put $\cos^2\phi = \cos x$ ∴ $\sin^2\phi = 1-\cos x$

$2\cos\phi\sin\phi\,d\phi = \sin x\,dx$

$$I = \int_0^{\pi/2} \frac{1}{\sqrt{1-\frac{1}{2}(1-\cos x)}} \cdot \frac{1}{2}\frac{1}{\sqrt{\cos x}}\frac{1}{\sqrt{1-\cos x}}\sin x\,dx$$

$$= \frac{1}{\sqrt{2}}\int_0^{\pi/2} \frac{1}{\sqrt{1+\cos x}}\frac{1}{\sqrt{\cos x}}\frac{1}{\sqrt{1-\cos x}}\sin x\,dx$$

$$= \frac{1}{\sqrt{2}}\int_0^{\pi/2} \frac{1}{\sqrt{1-\cos^2 x}}\frac{1}{\sqrt{\cos x}}\sin x\,dx$$

$$= \frac{1}{\sqrt{2}}\int_0^{\pi/2} \frac{1}{\sqrt{\cos x}}\,dx = \frac{1}{\sqrt{2}}\int_0^{\pi/2}\cos^{-1/2}x\,dx$$

$$= \frac{1}{\sqrt{2}}\cdot\frac{1}{2}\beta\left(\frac{1}{2},\frac{1}{4}\right).$$

Ex. 15: If $\int_0^\infty \frac{x^{n-1}}{1+x}dx = \frac{\pi}{\sin n\pi}$, then prove that $\overline{|n|}\overline{1-n} = \frac{\pi}{\sin n\pi}$. **SUK: May-11**

Solution: Let $I = \int_0^\infty \frac{x^{n-1}}{1+x}dx$

x	0	∞
t	0	π/2

Put $x = \tan^2\theta$, ∴ $dx = 2\tan\theta\sec^2\theta\,d\theta$

$$\therefore I = \int_0^{\pi/2} \frac{\tan^{2n-2}\theta \cdot 2\tan\theta\cdot\sec^2\theta\,d\theta}{1+\tan^2\theta}$$

$$= 2\int_0^{\pi/2}\tan^{2n-1}\theta\,d\theta = 2\int_0^{\pi/2}\sin^{2n-1}\theta\cos^{1-2n}\theta\,d\theta$$

$$= 2\cdot\frac{1}{2}\beta(n,1-n) = \beta(n,1-n) = \beta(n,1-n)$$

$$= \frac{\overline{|n|}\overline{1-n}}{\overline{|n+1-n}} = \overline{|n|}\overline{1-n} = \frac{\pi}{\sin n\pi}.$$

TEST YOUR KNOWLEDGE

I. Prove that the following

1. $\int_0^{\pi/2}\sin^n\theta\,d\theta \cdot \int_0^{\pi/2}\sin^{n+1}\theta\,d\theta = \frac{\pi}{2(n+1)}$ 2. $\int_0^{\pi/2}\sin^4\theta\sec^{1/2}\theta\,d\theta = \frac{\sqrt{2}}{7\sqrt{\pi}}\left(\overline{\left|\frac{1}{4}\right.}\right)^2$

3. $\int_0^{\pi/8}\sin^4 8\theta\cos^6 4\theta\,d\theta = 2\beta\left(\frac{5}{2},\frac{11}{2}\right)$ 4. $\int_0^{\pi/4}\cos^3 2x\sin^4 4x\,dx = 4\beta\left(4,\frac{5}{2}\right)$

II. Evaluate the following

1. $\int_0^{\pi/2}\sqrt{\cot\theta}\,d\theta$ Ans: $\frac{\pi}{\sqrt{2}}$.   2. $\int_0^{\pi/2}\sqrt{\tan 2\theta}\,d\theta$ Ans: $\frac{\pi}{2\sqrt{2}}$.

3. $\int_0^{\pi/6}\cos^6 3\theta\sin^2 6\theta\,d\theta$ Ans: $\frac{7\pi}{384}$.   4. $\int_{-\pi/2}^{\pi/2}\cos^3\theta(1+\sin\theta)^2\,d\theta$ Ans: $\frac{8}{5}$.

5. $\int_0^{2\pi}\sin^2\theta(1+\cos\theta)^4\,d\theta$ Ans: $\frac{21\pi}{8}$.   6. $\int_0^\pi x\sin^5 x\cos^6 x\,dx$ Ans: $\frac{8\pi}{693}$.

7. $\int_0^\pi x\sin^6 x\cos^4 x\,dx$ Ans: $\frac{3\pi^2}{512}$.   8. $\int_0^\infty \left(\frac{x}{1+x^2}\right)^6 dx$ Ans: $\frac{3\pi}{512}$.

9. $\int_0^\infty \left(\frac{t}{1+t^2}\right)^3 dt$ Ans: $\frac{1}{4}$.

F.E. (Sem. II) M II (SU) Special Functions

Type III: Examples having form $\int_a^b (x-a)^m (b-x)^n \, dx$

For this type standard substitution is $(x-a) = (b-a)t$

Ex. 1: Prove that $\int_a^b (x-a)^m (b-x)^n \, dx = (b-a)^{m+n+1} \beta(m+1, n+1)$

Hence deduce that, $5 \int_5^9 \sqrt[4]{(x-5)(9-x)} \, dx = \dfrac{2\left(\left|\dfrac{1}{4}\right|\right)^2}{3\sqrt{\pi}}$.   SUK : Dec – 13

Solution: Let $I = \int_a^b (x-a)^m (b-x)^n \, dx$

x	a	b
t	0	1

Put $(x-a) = (b-a)t$, $\Rightarrow x = a + (b-a)t$ $\therefore dx = (b-a) dt$
and $b - x = b - a - (b-a)t \Rightarrow b - x = (b-a)(1-t)$

$\therefore I = \int_0^1 (b-a)^m t^m (b-a)^n (1-t)^n (b-a) dt$

$= (b-a)^{m+n+1} \int_0^1 t^m (1-t)^n \, dt$

$= (b-a)^{m+n+1} \beta(m+1, n+1)$.

In paticular if $a = 5, b = 9, m = 1/4, n = 1/4$

$\therefore 5 \int_a^9 \sqrt[4]{(x-5)(9-x)} \, dx = (9-5)^{\frac{1}{4}+\frac{1}{4}+1} \beta\left(\dfrac{1}{4}+1, \dfrac{1}{4}+1\right) = \dfrac{2\left(\left|\dfrac{1}{4}\right|\right)^2}{3\sqrt{\pi}}$.

Ex. 2: Evaluate $\int_3^7 (x-3)^{1/4} (7-x)^{1/4} \, dx$ **SUK: Dec-11**

Solution: Let $I = \int_3^7 (x-3)^{1/4} (7-x)^{1/4} \, dx$

x	3	7
t	0	1

Put $(x-3) = (7-3)t$, $\Rightarrow x = 3 + 4t$ $\therefore dx = 4dt$
and $7 - x = 7 - 3 - 4t \Rightarrow 7 - x = 4 - 4t$, i.e. $7 - x = 4(1-t)$

$$\therefore I = \int_0^1 4^{1/4} t^{1/4} 4^{1/4} (1-t)^{1/4} 4dt$$

$$= 4^{1/4+1/4+1} \int_0^1 t^{1/4} (1-t)^{1/4} dt$$

$$= 4^{3/2} \int_0^1 t^{1/4} (1-t)^{1/4} dt$$

$$= 4^{3/2} \frac{1}{2} \beta\left(\frac{5}{4},\frac{5}{4}\right) = 8\beta\left(\frac{5}{4},\frac{5}{4}\right).$$

$$= 8 \frac{\left\lfloor\frac{5}{4}\right.\left\lfloor\frac{5}{4}\right.}{\left\lfloor\frac{5}{4}+\frac{5}{4}\right.} = 8 \frac{\left(\left\lfloor\frac{5}{4}\right.\right)^2}{\left\lfloor\frac{5}{2}\right.}$$

$$= 8 \frac{\left(\frac{1}{4}\left\lfloor\frac{1}{4}\right.\right)^2}{\frac{3}{2}\frac{1}{2}\left\lfloor\frac{1}{2}\right.} = \frac{2\left(\left\lfloor\frac{1}{4}\right.\right)^2}{3\sqrt{\pi}}.$$

Ex. 3: Prove that $\int_{-1}^{1} (1+x)^m (1-x)^n \, dx = 2^{m+n+1} \frac{m!n!}{(m+n+1)!}$, $m,n > 0$.

Solution: Let $I = \int_{-1}^{1} (1+x)^m (1-x)^n \, dx$

Put $1+x = 2t$, $\Rightarrow x = -1+2t$ $\therefore dx = 2dt$

x	-1	1
t	0	1

$$\therefore I = \int_0^1 2^m t^m (2-2t)^n \, 2dt$$

$$= 2^{m+n+1} \int_0^1 t^m (1-t)^n \, dt$$

$$= 2^{m+n+1} \beta(m+1, n+1) = 2^{m+n+1} \frac{m!n!}{(m+n+1)!}.$$

TEST YOUR KNOWLEDGE

Evaluate the following

1. $\int_3^7 \sqrt{(x-3)(7-x)}\,dx$ Ans: 2π

2. $\int_5^9 \sqrt{(9-x)(x-5)}\,dx$ Ans: $\dfrac{2\left(\left|\dfrac{1}{4}\right|\right)^2}{3\sqrt{\pi}}$

3. $\int_3^7 \sqrt[4]{(x-3)(7-x)}\,dx$ Ans: $\dfrac{2\left(\left|\dfrac{1}{4}\right|\right)^2}{3\sqrt{\pi}}$

4. $\int_5^6 (x-5)^5 (6-x)^6\,dx$ Ans: $\beta(6,7)$

5. $\int_a^b \sqrt[n]{(x-a)(b-x)}\,dx$ Ans: $(b-a)^{\frac{2}{n}-1}\,\beta\left(\dfrac{1}{n}+1,\dfrac{1}{n}+1\right)$

6. $\int_2^5 (x-2)^{1/4}(5-x)^{1/4}\,dx\,dx$ Ans: $\dfrac{1}{4}\sqrt{\dfrac{3}{\pi}}\left(\left|\dfrac{1}{4}\right|\right)^2$

Type-IV: Beta Function as Improper Integral

OR Examples using property $\beta(m,n)=\int_0^\infty \dfrac{x^{m-1}}{(1+x)^{m+n}}\,dx$

Ex. 1: Prove that $\displaystyle\int_0^\infty \dfrac{x^{m-1}}{(a+bx)^{m+n}}\,dx = \dfrac{1}{a^n b^m}\beta(m,n).$

Hence find the value of $\displaystyle\int_0^\infty \dfrac{x^5}{(2+3x)^{16}}\,dx$

Solution: Let $I=\displaystyle\int_0^\infty \dfrac{x^{m-1}}{(a+bx)^{m+n}}\,dx$

Put $bx=\dfrac{at}{1-t} \Rightarrow x=\dfrac{a}{b}\dfrac{t}{1-t}$ $\therefore dx=\dfrac{a}{b}\left[\dfrac{(1-t)\cdot 1-t(-1)}{(1-t)^2}\right]dt \Rightarrow dx=\dfrac{a}{b}\dfrac{1}{(1-t)^2}dt$

x	0	∞
t	0	1

$a+bx = a+\dfrac{at}{1-t} = \dfrac{a(1-t)+at}{1-t} = \dfrac{a}{1-t}$

$\therefore I = \displaystyle\int_0^1 \left(\dfrac{a}{b}\right)^{m-1}\left(\dfrac{t}{1-t}\right)^{m-1}\dfrac{1}{a^{m+n}}(1-t)^{m+n}\dfrac{a}{b}\dfrac{1}{(1-t)^2}dt$

$= (a)^{m-1-m-n+1}(b)^{-m+1-1}\displaystyle\int_0^1 (t)^{m-1}(1-t)^{m+n-m+1-2}\,dt$

$= (a)^{-n}(b)^{-m}\displaystyle\int_0^1 (t)^{m-1}(1-t)^{n-1}\,dt = \dfrac{1}{a^n b^m}\beta(m,n).$ (A)

(4.45)

Again *Put* $a=2$, $b=3$, $m=6$, $n=10$ in equation (A), we get

$$\int_0^\infty \frac{x^5}{(2+3x)^{16}}dx = \frac{1}{2^{10}3^6}\beta(6,10) = \frac{1}{2^{10}3^6}\frac{\overline{|6|}\overline{|10|}}{\overline{|6+10|}} = \frac{1}{2^{10}3^6}\frac{5!9!}{15!}.$$

Remark: In particular if $a=1, b=1$ then $\int_0^\infty \frac{x^{m-1}}{(1+x)^{m+n}}dx = \beta(m,n)$. **SUK: Nov-09**

Ex. 2: Prove that $\int_0^\infty \frac{x^{m-1}+x^{n-1}}{(1+x)^{m+n}}dx = \beta(m,n)$.

Solution: We know by above remark $\beta(m,n) = \int_0^\infty \frac{x^{m-1}}{(1+x)^{m+n}}dx$

$$= \int_0^1 \frac{x^{m-1}}{(1+x)^{m+n}}dx + \int_1^\infty \frac{x^{m-1}}{(1+x)^{m+n}}dx \quad (A)$$

x	1	∞
t	1	0

Consider $I = \int_1^\infty \frac{x^{m-1}}{(1+x)^{m+n}}dx$ Put $x = \frac{1}{t}$ $\therefore dx = \frac{-1}{t^2}dt$

$$\therefore I = \int_1^0 \frac{\left(\frac{1}{t}\right)^{m-1}}{\left(1+\frac{1}{t}\right)^{m+n}} \frac{-1}{t^2}dt = \int_0^1 \frac{t^{n-1}}{(t+1)^{m+n}}dt \quad (B)$$

Substituting equation (B) in equation (A), we get

$$\beta(m,n) = \int_0^1 \frac{x^{m-1}}{(1+x)^{m+n}}dx + \int_0^1 \frac{t^{n-1}}{(t+1)^{m+n}}dt$$

$$= \int_0^1 \frac{x^{m-1}}{(1+x)^{m+n}}dx + \int_0^1 \frac{x^{n-1}}{(1+x)^{m+n}}dt \quad \text{replacing t by x}$$

$$\therefore \beta(m,n) = \int_0^1 \frac{x^{m-1}+x^{n-1}}{(1+x)^{m+n}}dx$$

Ex. 3: Prove that $\int_0^\infty \frac{x^m}{(1+x)^n}dx = \beta(m+1, n-m-1)$.

Solution: Let $I = \int_0^\infty \frac{x^m}{(1+x)^n}dx$

Put $x = \frac{t}{1-t} \Rightarrow x = \frac{t}{1-t}$ $\therefore dx = \left[\frac{(1-t).1 - t(-1)}{(1-t)^2}\right]dt \Rightarrow dx = \frac{1}{(1-t)^2}dt$

(4.46)

x	0	∞
t	0	1

$$1+x = 1+\frac{t}{1-t} = \frac{(1-t)+t}{1-t} = \frac{1}{1-t}$$

$$\therefore I = \int_0^1 \left(\frac{t}{1-t}\right)^m (1-t)^n \frac{1}{(1-t)^2} dt$$

$$= \int_0^1 t^m (1-t)^{-m+n-2} dt = \beta(m+1, n-m-1).$$

Ex. 4: Evaluate $\int_0^\infty \frac{x^{10} - x^{18}}{(1+x)^{30}} dx$

Solution: Let $I = \int_0^\infty \frac{x^{10} - x^{18}}{(1+x)^{30}} dx = \int_0^\infty \frac{x^{10}}{(1+x)^{30}} dx - \int_0^\infty \frac{x^{18}}{(1+x)^{30}} dx = I_1 - I_2$ (A)

Put $x = \frac{t}{1-t} \Rightarrow x = \frac{t}{1-t}$ $\therefore dx = \left[\frac{(1-t).1 - t(-1)}{(1-t)^2}\right] dt \Rightarrow dx = \frac{1}{(1-t)^2} dt$

x	0	∞
t	0	1

$$1+x = 1+\frac{t}{1-t} = \frac{(1-t)+t}{1-t} = \frac{1}{1-t}$$

$$\therefore I_1 = \int_0^1 \left(\frac{t}{1-t}\right)^{10} (1-t)^{30} \frac{1}{(1-t)^2} dt$$

$$= \int_0^1 t^{10} (1-t)^{18} dt = \beta(11, 19) \quad\quad (B)$$

and $I_2 = \int_0^1 \left(\frac{t}{1-t}\right)^{18} (1-t)^{30} \frac{1}{(1-t)^2} dt$

$$= \int_0^1 t^{18} (1-t)^{10} dt = \beta(19, 11) \quad\quad (C)$$

Substituting equation (B) and (C) in equation (A), we get
$$I = \beta(19, 11) - \beta(11, 19)$$
$$= \beta(19, 11) - \beta(19, 11) = 0 \quad \because \beta(m, n) = \beta(n, m)$$

$$\therefore \int_0^\infty \frac{x^{10} - x^{18}}{(1+x)^{30}} dx = 0$$

Ex. 5: Evaluate $\int_0^\infty \dfrac{x^7(1-x^{12})}{(1+x)^{28}}dx$ **SUK: May-11**

Solution: Let $I = \int_0^\infty \dfrac{x^7(1-x^{12})}{(1+x)^{28}}dx = \int_0^\infty \dfrac{x^7}{(1+x)^{28}}dx - \int_0^\infty \dfrac{x^{19}}{(1+x)^{28}}dx = I_1 - I_2$ (A)

Put $x = \dfrac{t}{1-t} \Rightarrow x = \dfrac{t}{1-t}$ $\therefore dx = \left[\dfrac{(1-t).1-t(-1)}{(1-t)^2}\right]dt \Rightarrow dx = \dfrac{1}{(1-t)^2}dt$

x	0	∞
t	0	1

$1+x = 1 + \dfrac{t}{1-t} = \dfrac{(1-t)+t}{1-t} = \dfrac{1}{1-t}$

$\therefore I_1 = \int_0^1 \left(\dfrac{t}{1-t}\right)^7 (1-t)^{28} \dfrac{1}{(1-t)^2} dt$

$= \int_0^1 t^7(1-t)^{19} dt = \beta(8, 20)$ (B)

and $I_2 = \int_0^1 \left(\dfrac{t}{1-t}\right)^{19} (1-t)^{28} \dfrac{1}{(1-t)^2} dt$

$= \int_0^1 t^{19}(1-t)^7 dt = \beta(20, 8)$ (C)

Substituting equation (B) and (C) in equation (A), we get
$I = \beta(20, 8) - \beta(8, 20)$
$= \beta(20, 8) - \beta(20, 8) = 0$ $\because \beta(m, n) = \beta(n, m)$

$\therefore \int_0^\infty \dfrac{x^7(1-x^{12})}{(1+x)^{28}}dx = 0.$

Ex. 6: Evaluate $\int_0^\infty \dfrac{x^4(1+x^5)}{(1+x)^{15}}dx$ **SUK: May-10**

Solution: Let $I = \int_0^\infty \dfrac{x^4(1+x^5)}{(1+x)^{15}}dx = \int_0^\infty \dfrac{x^4}{(1+x)^{15}}dx + \int_0^\infty \dfrac{x^9}{(1+x)^{15}}dx = I_1 + I_2$ (A)

Put $x = \dfrac{t}{1-t} \Rightarrow x = \dfrac{t}{1-t}$ $\therefore dx = \left[\dfrac{(1-t).1-t(-1)}{(1-t)^2}\right]dt \Rightarrow dx = \dfrac{1}{(1-t)^2}dt$

x	0	∞
t	0	1

$$1+x = 1+\frac{t}{1-t} = \frac{(1-t)+t}{1-t} = \frac{1}{1-t}$$

$$\therefore I_1 = \int_0^1 \left(\frac{t}{1-t}\right)^4 (1-t)^{15} \frac{1}{(1-t)^2} dt$$

$$= \int_0^1 t^4 (1-t)^9 dt = \beta(5,10) \qquad (B)$$

$$\text{and } I_2 = \int_0^1 \left(\frac{t}{1-t}\right)^9 (1-t)^{15} \frac{1}{(1-t)^2} dt$$

$$= \int_0^1 t^9 (1-t)^4 dt = \beta(10,5) \qquad (C)$$

Substituting equation (B) and (C) in equation (A), we get

$$I = \beta(5,10) + \beta(10,5)$$

$$= \beta(5,10) + \beta(5,10) \qquad \because \beta(m,n) = \beta(n,m)$$

$$= 2\beta(5,10) = \frac{1}{5005}$$

$$\therefore \int_0^\infty \frac{x^4(1+x^5)}{(1+x)^{15}} dx = \frac{1}{5005}.$$

Ex. 7: Evaluate $\int_0^\infty \frac{x^5(1+x^4)}{(1+x)^{16}} dx$

Solution: Let $I = \int_0^\infty \frac{x^5(1+x^4)}{(1+x)^{16}} dx = \int_0^\infty \frac{x^5}{(1+x)^{16}} dx + \int_0^\infty \frac{x^9}{(1+x)^{16}} dx = I_1 + I_2 \qquad (A)$

Put $x = \frac{t}{1-t} \Rightarrow x = \frac{t}{1-t}$ $\therefore dx = \left[\frac{(1-t).1 - t(-1)}{(1-t)^2}\right] dt \Rightarrow dx = \frac{1}{(1-t)^2} dt$

x	0	∞
t	0	1

$$1+x = 1+\frac{t}{1-t} = \frac{(1-t)+t}{1-t} = \frac{1}{1-t}$$

$$\therefore I_1 = \int_0^1 \left(\frac{t}{1-t}\right)^5 (1-t)^{16} \frac{1}{(1-t)^2} dt$$

$$= \int_0^1 t^5 (1-t)^9 dt = \beta(6,10) \qquad (B)$$

$$\text{and } I_2 = \int_0^1 \left(\frac{t}{1-t}\right)^9 (1-t)^{16} \frac{1}{(1-t)^2} dt$$

$$= \int_0^1 t^9 (1-t)^5 dt = \beta(10,6) \qquad (C)$$

Substituting equation (B) and (C) in equation (A), we get

$$I = \beta(6,10) + \beta(10,6) = \frac{1}{1001}$$

$$\therefore \int_0^\infty \frac{x^5(1+x^4)}{(1+x)^{16}} dx = \frac{1}{1001}.$$

Ex. 8: Evaluate $\int_0^\infty \frac{\sqrt{x}}{1+2x+x^2} dx$

Solution: Let $I = \int_0^\infty \frac{\sqrt{x}}{1+2x+x^2} dx$

Put $x = \frac{t}{1-t} \Rightarrow x = \frac{t}{1-t}$ $\therefore dx = \left[\frac{(1-t).1 - t(-1)}{(1-t)^2}\right] dt \Rightarrow dx = \frac{1}{(1-t)^2} dt$

x	0	∞
t	0	1

$$1 + x = 1 + \frac{t}{1-t} = \frac{(1-t) + t}{1-t} = \frac{1}{1-t}$$

$$\therefore I = \int_0^1 \left(\frac{t}{1-t}\right)^{1/2} (1-t)^2 \frac{1}{(1-t)^2} dt$$

$$= \int_0^1 t^{1/2} (1-t)^{-1/2} dt = \beta\left(\frac{3}{2}, \frac{1}{2}\right).$$

Ex. 9: Prove that $\int_0^\infty \frac{x^2}{(1+x^4)^3} dx = \frac{5\pi\sqrt{2}}{128}.$

Solution: Let $I = \int_0^\infty \frac{x^2}{(1+x^4)^3} dx$

x	0	∞
t	0	∞

Put $x^4 = t \Rightarrow x = t^{\frac{1}{4}}$ $\therefore dx = \frac{1}{4} t^{-\frac{3}{4}} dt$

$$\therefore I = \int_0^\infty \frac{t^{1/2}}{(1+t)^3} \frac{1}{4} t^{-\frac{3}{4}} dt = \frac{1}{4} \int_0^\infty \frac{t^{-\frac{1}{4}}}{(1+t)^3} dt$$

$$= \frac{1}{4} \int_0^\infty \frac{t^{\frac{3}{4}-1}}{(1+t)^{\frac{3}{4}+\frac{9}{4}}} dt = \frac{1}{4} \beta\left(\frac{3}{4}, \frac{9}{4}\right)$$

$$= \frac{1}{4} \frac{\left|\frac{3}{4}\right|\left|\frac{9}{4}\right|}{\left|\frac{3}{4}+\frac{9}{4}\right|} = \frac{1}{4} \frac{\frac{5}{4}\frac{1}{4}\left|\frac{3}{4}\right|\left|\frac{1}{4}\right|}{\left|3\right|} = \frac{1}{4} \frac{\frac{5}{4}\frac{1}{4}\left|\frac{3}{4}\right|\left|\frac{1}{4}\right|}{2!}$$

$$= \frac{5}{128} \left|\frac{1}{4}\right|\left|\frac{1}{4}\right| = \frac{5}{128} \frac{\pi}{\sin\frac{\pi}{4}} = \frac{5\sqrt{2}\pi}{128}. \qquad \because \left|n\right|\left|1-n\right| = \frac{\pi}{\sin n\pi}.$$

F.E. (Sem. II) M II (SU) — Special Functions

TEST YOUR KNOWLEDGE

I. Prove that the following

1. $\int_0^\infty \dfrac{x^{m-1} + x^{n-1}}{(1+x)^{m+n}} dx = 2\beta(m,n)$

2. $\int_0^\infty \dfrac{x^{m-1}}{(1+x)^{m+n}} dx = \beta(m,n)$

3. $\int_0^\infty \dfrac{x^{n-1}}{(1+x)^{m+n}} dx = \beta(n,m)$

4. $\int_1^\infty \dfrac{x^{n/2-1}}{(1+x)^n} dx = \dfrac{1}{2}\beta\left(\dfrac{n}{2},\dfrac{n}{2}\right)$.

II. Evaluate the following

1. $\int_0^\infty \dfrac{x^6(1-x^{10})}{(1+x)^{24}} dx \quad$ Ans: 0

2. $\int_0^\infty \dfrac{x^8(1-x^6)}{(1+x)^{24}} dx \quad$ Ans: 0

3. $\int_0^\infty \dfrac{x^3(1+x^8)}{(1+x)^{13}} dx \quad$ Ans: $\dfrac{1}{990}$

4. $\int_0^\infty \dfrac{x^4(1+x^5)}{(1+x)^{15}} dx \quad$ Ans: $\dfrac{1}{5005}$

5. $\int_0^\infty \dfrac{x^6 - x^3}{(1+x^3)^5} x^2 dx \quad$ Ans: 0

6. $\int_0^\infty \dfrac{x^5}{(2+3x)^{16}} dx \quad$ Ans: $\dfrac{1}{2^{10} 3^6}\beta(6,10)$ SUK : May – 13

7. $\int_0^\infty \dfrac{\sqrt{x}}{(4+12x+9x^2)^{16}} dx \quad$ Ans: $\dfrac{1}{2^{10} 3^6}\beta(6,10)$

Type V: Examples on property 2

Or Relation between Beta and Gamma function $\beta(m,n) = \dfrac{\overline{|m}\,\overline{|n}}{\overline{|m+n}}$.

Ex. 1: If $\beta(n,3) = \dfrac{1}{60}$ where n is positive integer, find the value of n.

Solution: Given $\beta(n,3) = \dfrac{1}{60}$

$\dfrac{\overline{|n}\,\overline{|3}}{\overline{|n+3}} = \dfrac{1}{60}$

$\dfrac{2!\,\overline{|n}}{(n+2)(n+1)n\,\overline{|n}} = \dfrac{1}{60} \Rightarrow \dfrac{2}{(n+2)(n+1)n} = \dfrac{1}{60}$

$120 = (n+2)(n+1)n \Rightarrow 6 \cdot 5 \cdot 4 = (n+2)(n+1)n$

$\therefore n = 4,\ n+1 = 5,\ n+2 = 6 \Rightarrow n = 4$.

Ex. 2: Prove that $\beta(m+1,n) = \dfrac{m}{m+n}\beta(m,n)$

Solution: LHS $= \beta(m+1,n) = \dfrac{\overline{|m+1}\,\overline{|n}}{\overline{|m+1+n}} = \dfrac{m\,\overline{|m}\,\overline{|n}}{(m+n)\overline{|m+n}} = \dfrac{m}{m+n}\beta(m,n) = $ RHS

(4.51)

Ex. 3: Prove that $\beta(m,n) = \beta(m, n+1) + \beta(m+1, n)$

Solution: RHS $= \beta(m, n+1) + \beta(m+1, n)$

$$= \frac{\Gamma(m)\Gamma(n+1)}{\Gamma(m+n+1)} + \frac{\Gamma(m+1)\Gamma(n)}{\Gamma(m+1+n)}$$

$$= \frac{\Gamma(m)\,n\,\Gamma(n)}{(m+n)\Gamma(m+n)} + \frac{m\,\Gamma(m)\,\Gamma(n)}{(m+n)\Gamma(m+n)}$$

$$= \frac{n\,\Gamma(m)\,\Gamma(n) + m\,\Gamma(m)\,\Gamma(n)}{(m+n)\,\Gamma(m+n)} = \frac{(m+n)\,\Gamma(m)\,\Gamma(n)}{(m+n)\,\Gamma(m+n)} = \frac{\Gamma(m)\,\Gamma(n)}{\Gamma(m+n)} = \beta(m,n) = \text{LHS}$$

Ex. 4: Prove that $\beta(n,n) = \dfrac{\sqrt{\pi}\,\Gamma(n)}{2^{2n-1}\,\Gamma\!\left(n+\dfrac{1}{2}\right)}$

Solution: LHS $= \beta(n,n)$

$$= \frac{\Gamma(n)\Gamma(n)}{\Gamma(2n)} = \frac{\Gamma(n)}{\Gamma(2n)} \cdot \frac{\Gamma(n)\,\Gamma\!\left(n+\dfrac{1}{2}\right)}{\Gamma\!\left(n+\dfrac{1}{2}\right)}$$

$$= \frac{\Gamma(n)}{\Gamma(2n)} \cdot \frac{1}{\Gamma\!\left(n+\dfrac{1}{2}\right)} \cdot \frac{\sqrt{\pi}\,\Gamma(2n)}{2^{2n-1}} \quad \text{by duplication formula}$$

$$= \frac{\sqrt{\pi}\,\Gamma(n)}{2^{2n-1}\,\Gamma\!\left(n+\dfrac{1}{2}\right)} = \text{RHS}$$

Ex. 5: Prove that $\beta(n,n)\cdot\beta\!\left(n+\dfrac{1}{2}, n+\dfrac{1}{2}\right) = \dfrac{\pi}{n}\,2^{1-4n}$.

Solution: LHS $= \beta(n,n)\cdot\beta\!\left(n+\dfrac{1}{2}, n+\dfrac{1}{2}\right)$

$$= \frac{\Gamma(n)\Gamma(n)}{\Gamma(2n)} \cdot \frac{\Gamma\!\left(n+\dfrac{1}{2}\right)\Gamma\!\left(n+\dfrac{1}{2}\right)}{\Gamma(2n+1)} = \frac{\left(\Gamma(n)\,\Gamma\!\left(n+\dfrac{1}{2}\right)\right)^2}{2n\,\Gamma(2n)\,\Gamma(2n)}$$

$$= \frac{1}{2n}\left(\frac{\Gamma(n)\,\Gamma\!\left(n+\dfrac{1}{2}\right)}{\Gamma(2n)}\right)^{\!2} = \frac{1}{2n}\left(\frac{\sqrt{\pi}}{2^{2n-1}}\right)^{\!2} = \frac{\pi}{n}\,2^{1-4n} = \text{RHS}. \quad \because \text{duplication formula}$$

Ex. 6: Prove that $\overline{|n|}\left|\dfrac{1-n}{2}\right| = \dfrac{\pi\left|\dfrac{n}{2}\right|}{2^{1-p}\cos\dfrac{n\pi}{2}}$.

Solution: We know that $\overline{|n|}\overline{|1-n|} = \dfrac{\pi}{\sin n\pi}$ Replacing n by $\dfrac{n+1}{2}$,

$$\left|\dfrac{n+1}{2}\right|\left|1-\dfrac{n+1}{2}\right| = \dfrac{\pi}{\sin\left(\dfrac{n+1}{2}\right)\pi} \qquad \left|\dfrac{n+1}{2}\right|\left|\dfrac{1-n}{2}\right| = \dfrac{\pi}{\sin\left(\dfrac{\pi}{2}+\dfrac{n\pi}{2}\right)}$$

$$\left|\dfrac{n}{2}\right|\left|\dfrac{n}{2}+\dfrac{1}{2}\right|\left|\dfrac{1-n}{2}\right| = \dfrac{\pi\left|\dfrac{n}{2}\right|}{\cos\dfrac{n\pi}{2}} \qquad \dfrac{\sqrt{\pi}\overline{|n|}}{2^{n-1}}\left|\dfrac{1-n}{2}\right| = \dfrac{\pi\left|\dfrac{n}{2}\right|}{\cos\dfrac{n\pi}{2}}$$

$$\overline{|n|}\left|\dfrac{1-n}{2}\right| = \dfrac{\sqrt{\pi}\left|\dfrac{n}{2}\right|}{2^{1-n}\cos\dfrac{n\pi}{2}}.$$

TEST YOUR KNOWLEDGE

1. If $\beta(n,3) = \dfrac{1}{60}$ where n is positive integer, find the value of n. Ans: $n = 1$.

2. If $\beta(n,2) = \dfrac{1}{42}$ where n is positive integer, find the value of n. Ans: $n = 6$.

3. Prove that $\beta\left(n+\dfrac{1}{2}, n+\dfrac{1}{2}\right) = \dfrac{\left|n+\dfrac{1}{2}\right|\sqrt{\pi}}{\overline{|n+1|}} 2^{-2n}$. 4. Prove that $\left|\dfrac{3}{2}-n\right|\left|\dfrac{3}{2}+n\right| = \left(\dfrac{1}{4}-n^2\right)\pi\sec n\pi$.

Differentiation Under Integral Sign (DUIS)

It is difficult to solve some definite integral by the traditional methods which we studied so far. But such definite integral can be easily evaluated by the rule of differentiation under integral sign i.e. This is an advance technique for evaluating certain types of definite integral which are not easily integrable.

These types of definite integrals depends upon one or more parameters, in addition to the variable of integration. We consider a definite integral involving only one parameter α and denote it as $I(\alpha) = \int_a^b f(x,\alpha)dx$ where a, b may be constants or functions of α.

Theorem: Let $I(\alpha) = \int_a^b f(x,\alpha)dx$ where a and b are independent of α

then show that $\dfrac{dI(\alpha)}{d\alpha} = \dfrac{dI}{d\alpha} = \dfrac{d}{d\alpha}\int_a^b f(x,\alpha)dx = \int_a^b\left[\dfrac{\partial}{\partial\alpha}f(x,\alpha)\right]dx$

Proof: Let $I(\alpha) = \int_a^b f(x,\alpha) dx$ $\therefore I(\alpha + \delta\alpha) = \int_a^b f(x, \alpha + \delta\alpha) dx$

By definition of derivatives $I'(\alpha) = \lim_{\delta\alpha \to 0} \dfrac{I(\alpha + \delta\alpha) - I(\alpha)}{\delta\alpha}$

Substituting the values of $I(\alpha)$ and $I(\alpha + \delta\alpha)$, we get

$$\therefore I'(\alpha) = \lim_{\delta\alpha \to 0} \dfrac{1}{\delta\alpha}\left[\int_a^b f(x, \alpha + \delta\alpha) dx - \int_a^b f(x,\alpha) dx\right]$$

$$= \lim_{\delta\alpha \to 0} \int_a^b \dfrac{f(x, \alpha + \delta\alpha) dx - f(x,\alpha)}{\delta\alpha} dx$$

$$= \int_a^b \lim_{\delta\alpha \to 0} \dfrac{f(x, \alpha + \delta\alpha) dx - f(x,\alpha)}{\delta\alpha} dx \quad \because \lim_{\delta\alpha \to 0} \int_c^d = \int_c^d \lim_{\delta\alpha \to 0}$$

$$= \int_a^b \dfrac{\partial}{\partial \alpha} f(x,\alpha) dx.$$

Note: 1. α = parameter

2. a and b are the limits of integral which may be constants or functions of α

3. x = variable of integration

4. $\dfrac{\partial}{\partial \alpha} f(x,\alpha)$ means derivative of $f(x,\alpha)$ with respect to α by keeping x as constant.

5. $\dfrac{\partial}{\partial \alpha} x^\alpha = x^\alpha \log x$

Some useful basic result:

1. $\int e^{\alpha x} \cos \beta x \, dx = \dfrac{e^{\alpha x}}{\alpha^2 + \beta^2}[\alpha \cos \beta x + \beta \sin \beta x]$.

2. $\int e^{\alpha x} \sin \beta x \, dx = \dfrac{e^{\alpha x}}{\alpha^2 + \beta^2}[\alpha \sin \beta x - \beta \cos \beta x]$.

3. $\int_0^\infty e^{-x^2} dx = \dfrac{1}{2}\left|\dfrac{1}{2}\right. = \dfrac{\sqrt{\pi}}{2}$.

4. $\int_0^\infty e^{-bx^2} dx = \dfrac{1}{2}\sqrt{\dfrac{\pi}{b}}$.

Process of Solving Examples By DUIS Rule

Step-1: First denote the given integral by $I(\alpha)$ or $I(a)$ etc

Step-2: Apply the DUIS rule $\dfrac{dI(\alpha)}{d\alpha} = \int_a^b \left[\dfrac{\partial}{\partial \alpha} f(x,\alpha)\right] dx$

Step-3: Integrate $I(\alpha)$ w. r. t. α, it involves a constant C

Step-4: Constant C can be evaluated by assigning the proper value to the parameter.

Ex.1: Prove that $\int_0^1 \dfrac{x^a - 1}{\log x} dx = \log(a+1), \ (a \geq 0)$ **SUK: Nov-08**

Solution: Let $I(a) = \int_0^1 \dfrac{x^a - 1}{\log x} dx$, here a is parameter

Applying DUIS rule $I'(a) = \int_0^1 \dfrac{\partial}{\partial a} \dfrac{x^a - 1}{\log x} dx,$

$$I'(a) = \int_0^1 \dfrac{x^a \log x}{\log x} dx$$

$$\therefore I'(a) = \int_0^1 x^a \, dx$$

Integrating w. r. t. x, we get

$$I'(a) = \left[\dfrac{x^{a+1}}{a+1}\right]_0^1 = \left[\dfrac{1}{a+1} - 0\right] = \dfrac{1}{a+1}$$

Integrating w. r. t. a,

$I(a) = \log(a+1) + C$

Put $a = 0 \ \therefore I(0) = \log(0+1) + C$

$\Rightarrow I(0) = C \qquad \because \log 1 = 0$

$\int_0^1 \dfrac{x^0 - 1}{\log x} dx = C$

$\Rightarrow \int_0^1 \dfrac{1-1}{\log x} dx = C \Rightarrow 0 = C$

Substituting the value of C, we get

$I(a) = \log(a+1)$

i.e. $\int_0^1 \dfrac{x^a - 1}{\log x} dx = \log(a+1), \ (a \geq 0)$

Ex. 2: Evaluate $\int_0^\infty \dfrac{e^{-x}}{x}(1 - e^{-ax}) dx, \ (a > -1).$ **SUK: Nov-10**

Or Prove that $\int_0^\infty \left(\dfrac{1 - e^{-ax}}{x}\right) e^{-x} dx = \log(a+1), \ (a > -1).$

Solution: Let $I(a) = \int_0^\infty \dfrac{e^{-x}}{x}(1 - e^{-ax}) dx$

Applying DUIS rule, we get

$$I'(a) = \int_0^\infty \frac{\partial}{\partial a}\left[\frac{e^{-x}}{x}(1-e^{-ax})\right]dx = \int_0^\infty \frac{e^{-x}}{x}(-e^{-ax})(-x)\,dx$$

$$= \int_0^\infty e^{-x-ax}\,dx = \int_0^\infty e^{-(a+1)x}\,dx = \left[\frac{e^{-(a+1)x}}{-(1+a)}\right]_0^\infty$$

$$\therefore I'(a) = \left[(0) - \left(\frac{1}{-(a+1)}\right)\right] = \frac{1}{a+1}$$

Integrating w. r. t. a, we get

$$I(a) = \log(a+1) + C$$

Put $a = 0$ $\therefore I(0) = \log(0+1) + C$

$\Rightarrow I(0) = C$ $\because \log 1 = 0$

$$\int_0^\infty \frac{e^{-x}}{x}(1-e^{-0})\,dx = C \Rightarrow \int_0^\infty \frac{e^{-x}}{x}(1-1)\,dx = C \Rightarrow 0 = C$$

Substituting the value of C, we get

$$I(a) = \log(a+1)$$

$$\int_0^\infty \frac{e^{-x}}{x}(1-e^{-ax})\,dx = \log(a+1) \quad (a > -1).$$

Ex. 3: Evaluate $\int_0^\infty \frac{e^{-x}}{x}\left(a - \frac{1}{x} + \frac{1}{x}e^{-ax}\right)dx$ **SUK: May-10**

Solution: Let $I(a) = \int_0^\infty \frac{e^{-x}}{x}\left(a - \frac{1}{x} + \frac{1}{x}e^{-ax}\right)dx$

Applying DUIS rule, we get

$$I'(a) = \int_0^\infty \frac{\partial}{\partial a}\left[\frac{e^{-x}}{x}\left(a - \frac{1}{x} + \frac{1}{x}e^{-ax}\right)\right]dx = \int_0^\infty \frac{e^{-x}}{x}\left(1 - 0 + \frac{1}{x}e^{-ax}(-x)\right)dx$$

$$= \int_0^\infty \frac{e^{-x}}{x}(1-e^{-ax})\,dx$$

Note that this is same as that of example 2
So Again applying DUIS rule

$$\frac{d^2 I}{da^2} = I''(a) = \int_0^\infty \frac{e^{-x}}{x} x e^{-ax}\,dx = \int_0^\infty e^{-x(a+1)}\,dx = \left[\frac{e^{-x(a+1)}}{-(a+1)}\right]_0^\infty = \frac{1}{a+1}$$

Integrating w. r. t. a, we get $I'(a) = \log(a+1) + C$

Put $a = 0$ ∴ $I'(0) = \log(0+1) + C$
$\Rightarrow I(0) = C$ ∵ $\log 1 = 0$

$\int_0^\infty \frac{e^{-x}}{x}(1-e^{-0})dx = C \Rightarrow \int_0^\infty \frac{e^{-x}}{x}(1-1)dx = C \Rightarrow 0 = C$

Substituting the value of C, we get
$I'(a) = \log(a+1)$

Again Integrating w. r. t. a by parts

$I(a) = \int \log(a+1) da$ ....(II)

$= \log(a+1)a - \int a \frac{1}{a+1} da$ ∵ $\frac{a}{a+1} = \frac{a+1-1}{a+1} = 1 - \frac{1}{a+1}$

$= a\log(a+1) - \int da + \int \frac{da}{a+1}$

$I(a) = a\log(a+1) - a + \log(a+1) + C$

Again to find C, put $a = 0$ ∴ $I(0) = C$.

By equation (II) $I(0) = \int \log(0+1) da \Rightarrow I(0) = \int 0 \, da = 0$ ∴ $C = 0$

∴ $I(a) = a\log(a+1) - a + \log(a+1)$

$\int_0^\infty \frac{e^{-x}}{x}\left(a - \frac{1}{x} + \frac{1}{x}e^{-ax}\right)dx = (a+1)\log(a+1) - a$.

Ex. 4: Prove that $\int_0^\infty e^{-\left(x^2 + \frac{a^2}{x^2}\right)} dx = \frac{\sqrt{\pi}}{2} e^{-2a}$, $a > 0$

Solution: Let $I(a) = \int_0^\infty e^{-\left(x^2 + \frac{a^2}{x^2}\right)} dx$

x	0	∞
t	∞	0

Applying DUIS rule, we get

$I'(a) = \int_0^\infty \frac{\partial}{\partial a}\left[e^{-\left(x^2 + \frac{a^2}{x^2}\right)}\right] dx = \int_0^\infty e^{-\left(x^2 + \frac{a^2}{x^2}\right)} \left(\frac{-2a}{x^2}\right) dx$

Sub $\frac{a}{x} = t$ ∴ $\frac{-a}{x^2} dx = dt$

$I'(a) = \int_\infty^0 e^{-\left(\frac{a^2}{t^2} + t^2\right)} 2 dt = -2\int_0^\infty e^{-\left(t^2 + \frac{a^2}{t^2}\right)} dt = -2 I(a)$

∴ $\frac{I'(a)}{I(a)} = -2$

Integrating w. r. t. a, we get $\log I(a) = -2a + C$

$\therefore I(a) = e^{-2a+C} = e^{-2a} e^C = e^{-2a} C_1 \quad \because C_1 = e^C$

$\therefore I(a) = C_1 e^{-2a}$

Put $a = 0 \quad \therefore I(0) = C_1$

$\Rightarrow I(0) = C_1$

$\therefore I(0) = \int_0^\infty e^{-x^2} dx = C_1 \quad \therefore \frac{\sqrt{\pi}}{2} = C_1 \quad \because \int_0^\infty e^{-x^2} dx = \frac{\sqrt{\pi}}{2}$

$\therefore \int_0^\infty e^{-\left(x^2 + \frac{a^2}{x^2}\right)} dx = \frac{\sqrt{\pi}}{2} e^{-2a}.$

Ex. 5: Prove that $\int_0^1 x^m (\log x)^n dx = \frac{(-1)^n n!}{(m+1)^{n+1}}, \quad n > 0.$

Solution: Let $I(m) = \int_0^1 x^m dx = \left[\frac{x^{m+1}}{m+1}\right]_0^1 = \frac{1}{m+1}.$

Applying DUIS rule, we get

$\int_0^1 \frac{\partial}{\partial m} x^m dx = \frac{-1}{(m+1)^2}$

$\int_0^1 x^m \log x \, dx = \frac{-1}{(m+1)^2}$

Again applying DUIS rule

$\int_0^1 \frac{\partial}{\partial m} x^m \log x \, dx = \frac{(-1)(-2)}{(m+1)^3}$

$\int_0^1 x^m (\log x)^2 dx = \frac{(-1)^2 2!}{(m+1)^3}$

Countine in this way by applying DUIS rule n times

$\therefore \int_0^1 x^m (\log x)^n dx = \frac{(-1)^n n!}{(m+1)^{n+1}}.$

Ex. 6: Prove that $\int_0^\pi \log(1 - a\cos x) dx = \pi \log\left(\frac{1 + \sqrt{1-a^2}}{2}\right) \quad |a| < 1$

Solution: Let $I(a) = \int_0^\pi \log(1 - a\cos x) dx$

x	0	π
t	∞	∞

Applying DUIS rule, we get

$$I'(a) = \int_0^\pi \frac{\partial}{\partial a}\left[\log(1-a\cos x)\right]dx = \int_0^\pi \frac{-\cos x}{1-a\cos x}dx = \frac{1}{a}\int_0^\pi \frac{-a\cos x}{1-a\cos x}dx$$

$$= \frac{1}{a}\int_0^\pi \frac{1-a\cos x - 1}{1-a\cos x}dx = \frac{1}{a}\int_0^\pi \left[1 - \frac{1}{1-a\cos x}\right]dx = \frac{1}{a}[x]_0^\pi - \frac{1}{a}\int_0^\pi \frac{1}{1-a\cos x}dx$$

Put $t = \tan\frac{x}{2}$, $x = 2\tan^{-1} t$ $\therefore dx = \frac{2dt}{1+t^2}$, $\cos x = \frac{1-t^2}{1+t^2}$, $x \to 0 \Rightarrow t \to 0$ and $x \to \pi \Rightarrow t \to \infty$

$$= \frac{1}{a}\pi - \frac{1}{a}\int_0^\infty \frac{\frac{2dt}{1+t^2}}{1-a\left[\frac{1-t^2}{1+t^2}\right]} = \frac{1}{a}\pi - \frac{2}{a}\int_0^\infty \frac{1}{1+t^2 - a[1-t^2]}dt = \frac{1}{a}\pi - \frac{2}{a}\int_0^\infty \frac{1}{1+t^2 - a + at^2}dt$$

$$= \frac{1}{a}\pi - \frac{2}{a}\int_0^\infty \frac{1}{1-a+(1+a)t^2}dt = \frac{1}{a}\pi - \frac{2}{a(1+a)}\int_0^\infty \frac{1}{\frac{1-a}{1+a} + t^2}dt$$

$$= \frac{1}{a}\pi - \frac{2}{a(1+a)}\left[\frac{1}{\sqrt{\frac{1-a}{1+a}}}\tan^{-1}\left(\frac{t}{\sqrt{\frac{1-a}{1+a}}}\right)\right]_0^\infty = \frac{1}{a}\pi - \frac{2}{a\sqrt{1-a^2}}\left[\frac{\pi}{2} - 0\right] = \frac{\pi}{a} - \frac{\pi}{a\sqrt{1-a^2}}.$$

Integrating w.r.t. a $I(a) = \pi\log a - \pi\int\frac{1}{a\sqrt{1-a^2}}da + C.$

$$I(a) = \pi\log a - \pi\log\left[\frac{1-\sqrt{1-a^2}}{a}\right] + C \quad \because \int\frac{1}{x\sqrt{1-x^2}}dx = \log\left[\frac{1-\sqrt{1-x^2}}{x}\right] + A$$

$$I(a) = \pi\log\left[\frac{a^2\left(1+\sqrt{1-a^2}\right)}{\left(1-\sqrt{1-a^2}\right)\left(1+\sqrt{1-a^2}\right)}\right] + C = \pi\log\left[\frac{a^2\left(1+\sqrt{1-a^2}\right)}{1-1+a^2}\right] + C = \pi\log\left(1+\sqrt{1-a^2}\right) + C$$

Put $a = 0$, $I(0) = \pi\log 2 + C$

But $I(0) = \int_0^\pi \log 1 dx = \int_0^\pi 0 dx = 0 \Rightarrow C = -\pi\log 2$

$$I(a) = \pi\log\left[\frac{1+\sqrt{1-a^2}}{2}\right].$$

Ex. 7: Prove that $\int_0^{\pi/2}\frac{\log(1+\cos\alpha\cos x)}{\cos x}dx = \frac{\pi^2}{8} - \frac{\alpha^2}{2}$

Solution: Let $I(\alpha) = \int_0^{\pi/2}\frac{\log(1+\cos\alpha\cos x)}{\cos x}dx$

x	0	π/2
t	0	1

Applying DUIS rule, we get

$$\text{Let } I'(\alpha) = \int_0^{\pi/2} \frac{\partial}{\partial \alpha} \frac{\log(1+\cos\alpha\cos x)}{\cos x} dx$$

$$= \int_0^{\pi/2} \frac{-\sin\alpha\cos x}{1+\cos\alpha\cos x} \cdot \frac{1}{\cos x} dx$$

$$= \int_0^{\pi/2} \frac{-\sin\alpha}{1+\cos\alpha\cos x} dx$$

Put $t = \tan\dfrac{x}{2}$, $\cos x = \dfrac{1-t^2}{1+t^2}$, $dx = \dfrac{2dt}{1+t^2}$

$$I'(\alpha) = \int_0^1 \frac{-\sin\alpha \cdot \dfrac{2dt}{1+t^2}}{1+\cos\alpha\left[\dfrac{1-t^2}{1+t^2}\right]}$$

$$= \int_0^1 \frac{-2\sin\alpha \, dt}{1+t^2+\cos\alpha(1-t^2)}$$

$$= -2\sin\alpha \int_0^1 \frac{dt}{(1+\cos\alpha)+(1-\cos\alpha)t^2}$$

$$= \frac{-2\sin\alpha}{1-\cos\alpha} \int_0^1 \frac{dt}{\dfrac{1+\cos\alpha}{1-\cos\alpha}+t^2}$$

$$= \frac{-2\sin\alpha}{2\sin^2\alpha/2} \int_0^1 \frac{dt}{\dfrac{2\cos^2\alpha/2}{2\sin^2\alpha/2}+t^2}$$

$$= \frac{-2.2\sin\alpha/2.\cos\alpha/2}{2\sin^2\alpha/2} \int_0^1 \frac{dt}{\cot^2\alpha/2+t^2}$$

$$= -2\cot\alpha/2 \frac{1}{\cot\alpha/2}\left[\tan^{-1}\frac{1}{\cot^2\alpha/2}\right]_0^1 = -2\left[\tan^{-1}\tan\alpha/2 - 0\right]$$

$I'(\alpha) = -2\alpha/2 \quad \Rightarrow I'(\alpha) = -\alpha$

Integrating w. r. t. α $\quad I(\alpha) = -\dfrac{\alpha^2}{2}+C$

Put $\alpha = \dfrac{\pi}{2}$ $\quad \therefore 0 = -\dfrac{\pi^2/4}{2}+C \quad \Rightarrow C = \dfrac{\pi^2}{8}$

$I(\alpha) = -\dfrac{\alpha^2}{2}+\dfrac{\pi^2}{8} \quad \Rightarrow I(\alpha) = \dfrac{\pi^2}{8}-\dfrac{\alpha^2}{2}$

Ex. 8: Prove that $\int_0^{\pi/2} \dfrac{\log(1+\alpha \sin^2 x)}{\sin^2 x} dx = \pi\left[\sqrt{1+\alpha}-1\right]$

Solution: Let $I(\alpha) = \int_0^{\pi/2} \dfrac{\log(1+\alpha \sin^2 x)}{\sin^2 x} dx$

x	0	π/2
t	∞	0

Applying DUIS rule, we get

$$\text{Let } I'(\alpha) = \int_0^{\pi/2} \dfrac{\partial}{\partial \alpha}\left[\dfrac{\log(1+\alpha\sin^2 x)}{\sin^2 x}\right] dx$$

$$= \int_0^{\pi/2} \dfrac{\sin^2 x}{1+\alpha \sin^2 x} \cdot \dfrac{1}{\sin^2 x} dx$$

$$= \int_0^{\pi/2} \dfrac{1}{1+\alpha \sin^2 x} dx$$

$$= \int_0^{\pi/2} \dfrac{1}{1+\dfrac{\alpha}{\text{cosec}^2 x}} dx$$

$$= \int_0^{\pi/2} \dfrac{\text{cosec}^2 x}{\text{cosec}^2 x + \alpha} dx$$

$$= \int_0^{\pi/2} \dfrac{\text{cosec}^2 x}{1+\cot^2 x + \alpha} dx$$

Put $t = \cot x$, $-\text{cosec}^2 x\, dx = dt$, $x \to 0 \Rightarrow t \to \infty$, $x \to \pi/2 \Rightarrow t \to 0$

$$I'(\alpha) = \int_\infty^0 \dfrac{-dt}{(\alpha+1)+t^2} = \int_0^\infty \dfrac{dt}{(\alpha+1)+t^2}$$

$$= \dfrac{1}{\sqrt{\alpha+1}}\left[\tan^{-1}\dfrac{t}{\sqrt{\alpha+1}}\right]_0^\infty = \dfrac{1}{\sqrt{\alpha+1}}\left[\dfrac{\pi}{2}-0\right]$$

Integrating w. r. t. α

$$I(\alpha) = \dfrac{\pi}{2} \cdot 2\sqrt{\alpha+1} + C$$

Put $\alpha = 0$ $\therefore I(0) = \pi + C \Rightarrow C = -\pi$

$I(\alpha) = \pi\sqrt{\alpha+1} - \pi \Rightarrow I(\alpha) = \pi\left[\sqrt{\alpha+1}-1\right]$

Ex. 9 : Prove that $\int_0^\infty e^{-ax} \dfrac{\sin \lambda x}{x} dx = \tan^{-1}\dfrac{\lambda}{a}$ and deduce that $\int_0^\infty \dfrac{\sin x}{x} dx$

Solution: Let $I(\lambda) = \int_0^\infty e^{-ax} \dfrac{\sin \lambda x}{x} dx$

Applying DUIS rule, we get

$$Let\ I'(\lambda) = \int_0^\infty \dfrac{\partial}{\partial \lambda}\left[e^{-ax} \dfrac{\sin \lambda x}{x} \right] dx$$

$$= \int_0^\infty \left[e^{-ax} \dfrac{x \cos \lambda x}{x} \right] dx$$

$$= \int_0^\infty \left[e^{-ax} \cos \lambda x \right] dx$$

$$= \left\{ \dfrac{e^{-ax}}{a^2 + \lambda^2}\left[-a\cos \lambda x + \lambda \sin \lambda x \right] \right\}_0^\infty$$

$$= \left\{ 0 - \dfrac{1}{a^2 + \lambda^2}[-a + 0] \right\}$$

$$I'(\lambda) = \dfrac{a}{a^2 + \lambda^2}$$

Integrating w. r. t. α

$$I'(\lambda) = \tan^{-1} \dfrac{\lambda}{a} + C$$

Put $\lambda = 0,\ \ 0 = 0 + C$

Thus $\int_0^\infty e^{-ax} \dfrac{\sin \lambda x}{x} dx = \tan^{-1} \dfrac{\lambda}{a}$

Put $a = 0,\ \lambda = 1$

$$\therefore \int_0^\infty \dfrac{\sin x}{x} dx = \tan^{-1} \dfrac{1}{0} = \dfrac{\pi}{2} \quad \Rightarrow \int_0^\infty \dfrac{\sin \lambda x}{x} dx = \dfrac{\pi}{2}$$

Ex. 10: Prove that $\int_0^\infty e^{-x^2} \cos 2\lambda x\, dx = \dfrac{\sqrt{\pi}}{2} e^{-\lambda^2}$

Solution: Let $I(\lambda) = \int_0^\infty e^{-x^2} \cos 2\lambda x\, dx$ Applying DUIS rule, we get

$$Let\ I'(\lambda) = \int_0^\infty \dfrac{\partial}{\partial \lambda}\left[e^{-x^2} \cos 2\lambda x \right] dx$$

$$= \int_0^\infty \left[e^{-x^2} \sin 2\lambda x (-2x) \right] dx$$

$$= \int_0^\infty \sin 2\lambda x \left[e^{-x^2}(-2x) \right] dx \qquad \because \int e^{f(x)} f'(x) dx = e^{f(x)}$$

$$= \left[\sin 2\lambda x \cdot e^{-x^2} \right]_0^\infty - \int_0^\infty 2\lambda \cos 2\lambda x\, e^{-x^2} dx$$

$$= [0 - 0] - 2\lambda I(\lambda)$$

$$\dfrac{I'(\lambda)}{I(\lambda)} = -2\lambda$$

Integrating w. r. t. λ

$\log I(\lambda) = -\lambda^2 + C$

$I(\lambda) = e^{-\lambda^2 + C}$

$I(\lambda) = e^{-\lambda^2} e^C$

$I(\lambda) = A e^{-\lambda^2} \qquad \because A = e^C$

Put $\lambda = 0, \quad I(0) = A$

Put $\lambda = 0 \therefore \int_0^\infty e^{-x^2} dx = A = \dfrac{\sqrt{\pi}}{2} \qquad \because \int_0^\infty e^{-x^2} dx = \dfrac{\sqrt{\pi}}{2}$

$\therefore I(\lambda) = A e^{-\lambda^2} \Rightarrow I(\lambda) = \dfrac{\sqrt{\pi}}{2} e^{-\lambda^2}.$

Ex. 11: Prove that $\int_0^\infty \dfrac{\tan^{-1} ax}{x(1+x^2)} dx = \dfrac{\pi}{2} \log(a+1)$ 	SUK: May-12

Solution: Let $I(a) = \int_0^\infty \dfrac{\tan^{-1} ax}{x(1+x^2)} dx$

Applying DUIS rule, we get $\quad$ Let $I'(a) = \int_0^\infty \dfrac{\partial}{\partial a} \left[\dfrac{\tan^{-1} ax}{x(1+x^2)} \right] dx$

$= \int_0^\infty \dfrac{1}{x(1+x^2)} \cdot \dfrac{x}{1+a^2 x^2} dx$

$= \int_0^\infty \dfrac{1}{(1+x^2) a^2 \left(x^2 + \dfrac{1}{a^2}\right)} dx$

$= \dfrac{1}{a^2} \int_0^\infty \dfrac{1}{(1+x^2)\left(x^2 + \dfrac{1}{a^2}\right)} dx$

$= \dfrac{1}{a^2 \left(\dfrac{1}{a^2} - 1\right)} \int_0^\infty \dfrac{1}{(1+x^2)} - \dfrac{1}{\left(x^2 + \dfrac{1}{a^2}\right)} dx \quad$ by applying partial fraction

$= \dfrac{1}{1-a^2} \left[\tan^{-1} x - \dfrac{1}{\dfrac{1}{a^2}} \tan^{-1} \dfrac{x}{\dfrac{1}{a^2}} \right]_0^\infty$

$= \dfrac{1}{1-a^2} \left[\tan^{-1} x - a \tan^{-1} ax \right]_0^\infty$

$= \dfrac{1}{1-a^2} \left[\left(\dfrac{\pi}{2} - a\dfrac{\pi}{2}\right) - (0-0) \right]$

$= \dfrac{1}{(1-a)(1+a)} (1-a) \dfrac{\pi}{2}$

$I'(a) = \dfrac{\pi}{2(1+a)}$

Integrating w. r. t. a

$$I(a) = \frac{\pi}{2}\log(1+a) + C$$

Put $a = 0$ ∴ $I(0) = \frac{\pi}{2}\log(1+0) + C$ ⇒ $0 = \frac{\pi}{2}\log 1 + C$ ⇒ $C = 0$

∴ $I(a) = \frac{\pi}{2}\log(1+a)$

Ex. 12: Prove that $\int_0^\infty \frac{e^{-x} - e^{-\alpha x}}{x \sec x} dx = \frac{1}{2}\log\left(\frac{\alpha^2 + 1}{2}\right)$

Solution: Let $I(\alpha) = \int_0^\infty \frac{e^{-x} - e^{-\alpha x}}{x \sec x} dx$

Applying DUIS rule, we get

$$\text{Let } I'(\alpha) = \int_0^\infty \frac{\partial}{\partial \alpha}\left[\frac{e^{-x} - e^{-\alpha x}}{x \sec x}\right] dx$$

$$= \int_0^\infty \left[\frac{0 - e^{-\alpha x}(-x)}{x \sec x}\right] dx$$

$$I'(\alpha) = \int_0^\infty e^{-\alpha x} \cos x \, dx$$

Integrating w. r. t. x

$$I'(\alpha) = \int_0^\infty e^{-\alpha x} \cos x \, dx$$

$$I'(\alpha) = \left[\frac{e^{-\alpha x}}{\alpha^2 + 1^2}(-\alpha \cos x + \sin x)\right]_0^\infty$$

$$I'(\alpha) = \left[0 - \frac{1}{\alpha^2 + 1}(-\alpha + 0)\right] = \frac{\alpha}{\alpha^2 + 1}$$

Integrating w. r. t. α

$$I(\alpha) = \frac{1}{2}\log(\alpha^2 + 1) + C$$

Put $\alpha = 1$ ∴ $I(1) = \frac{1}{2}\log(2) + C$

$0 = \frac{1}{2}\log(2) + C$ ⇒ $C = -\frac{1}{2}\log 2$

$I(\alpha) = \frac{1}{2}\log(\alpha^2 + 1) - \frac{1}{2}\log 2$ i.e. $I(\alpha) = \frac{1}{2}\log\left(\frac{\alpha^2 + 1}{2}\right)$.

Ex. 13: Prove that $\int_0^\pi \dfrac{\log(1+\sin\alpha\cos x)}{\cos x}dx = \pi\alpha$

Solution: Let $I(\alpha) = \int_0^\pi \dfrac{\log(1+\sin\alpha\cos x)}{\cos x}dx$

x	0	π
t	∞	∞

Applying DUIS rule, we get

Let $I'(\alpha) = \int_0^\pi \dfrac{\partial}{\partial\alpha}\dfrac{\log(1+\sin\alpha\cos x)}{\cos x}dx$

$= \int_0^\pi \dfrac{\cos\alpha\cos x}{1+\sin\alpha\cos x}\cdot\dfrac{1}{\cos x}dx$

$= \int_0^\pi \dfrac{\cos\alpha}{1+\sin\alpha\cos x}dx$

Put $t = \tan\dfrac{x}{2}$, $dx = \dfrac{2dt}{\sec^2 x/2}$, $dx = \dfrac{2dt}{1+t^2}$ and

$\cos x = \dfrac{1-\tan^2 x/2}{1+\tan^2 x/2} = \dfrac{1-t^2}{1+t^2}$, $x\to 0 \Rightarrow t\to 0, x\to\pi\Rightarrow t\to\infty$

$I'(\alpha) = \int_0^\infty \dfrac{\cos\alpha\dfrac{2dt}{1+t^2}}{1+\sin\alpha\left[\dfrac{1-t^2}{1+t^2}\right]}$

$= 2\cos\alpha\int_0^\infty \dfrac{dt}{(1+\sin\alpha)+(1-\sin\alpha)t^2}$

$= \dfrac{2\cos\alpha}{(1-\sin\alpha)}\int_0^\infty \dfrac{dt}{\dfrac{(1+\sin\alpha)}{(1-\sin\alpha)}+t^2}$

$= \dfrac{2\cos\alpha}{(1-\sin\alpha)}\dfrac{\sqrt{(1-\sin\alpha)}}{\sqrt{(1+\sin\alpha)}}\tan^{-1}\left[\dfrac{\sqrt{(1-\sin\alpha)}}{\sqrt{(1+\sin\alpha)}}\cdot t\right]_0^\infty$

$I'(\alpha) = \dfrac{2\cos\alpha}{\sqrt{(1-\sin^2\alpha)}}\dfrac{\pi}{2} = \pi$

Integrating w. r. t. α

$I(\alpha) = \pi\alpha + C$

Put $\alpha = 0$ $\therefore I(0) = \pi.0 + C \Rightarrow C = 0$

$I(\alpha) = \pi\alpha \Rightarrow \int_0^\pi \dfrac{\log(1+\sin\alpha\cos x)}{\cos x}dx = \pi\alpha$

Ex. 14: Prove that $\int_0^\pi \dfrac{\log(1+a\cos x)}{\cos x}dx = \pi \sin^{-1}\alpha$

Solution: Let $I(\alpha) = \int_0^\pi \dfrac{\log(1+a\cos x)}{\cos x}dx$

Applying DUIS rule, we get

Let $I'(\alpha) = \int_0^\pi \dfrac{\partial}{\partial \alpha}\dfrac{\log(1+a\cos x)}{\cos x}dx$

$= \int_0^\pi \dfrac{\cos x}{1+a\cos x} \cdot \dfrac{1}{\cos x}dx$

$= \int_0^\pi \dfrac{1}{1+a\cos x}dx$

Put $t = \tan\dfrac{x}{2}$, $dx = \dfrac{2dt}{\sec^2 x/2}$, $dx = \dfrac{2dt}{1+t^2}$ and

$\cos x = \dfrac{1-\tan^2 x/2}{1+\tan^2 x/2} = \dfrac{1-t^2}{1+t^2}$, $x \to 0 \Rightarrow t \to 0, x \to \pi \Rightarrow t \to \infty$

$I'(\alpha) = \int_0^\infty \dfrac{1\dfrac{2dt}{1+t^2}}{1+a\left[\dfrac{1-t^2}{1+t^2}\right]}$

$= 2\int_0^\infty \dfrac{dt}{(1+a)+(1-a)t^2}$

$= \dfrac{2}{(1-a)}\int_0^\infty \dfrac{dt}{\dfrac{(1+a)}{(1-a)}+t^2}$

$= \dfrac{2}{(1-a)}\dfrac{\sqrt{(1-a)}}{\sqrt{(1+a)}}\tan^{-1}\left[\dfrac{\sqrt{(1-a)}}{\sqrt{(1+a)}}\cdot t\right]_0^\infty$

$I'(\alpha) = \dfrac{2}{\sqrt{(1-a^2)}}\dfrac{\pi}{2} = \dfrac{\pi}{\sqrt{(1-a^2)}}$

Integrating w. r. t. a

$I(\alpha) = \pi\sin^{-1}a + C$

Put $a = 0$ $\therefore I(0) = \pi\sin^{-1}0 + C \Rightarrow C = 0$

$I(\alpha) = \pi\sin^{-1}a \Rightarrow \int_0^\pi \dfrac{\log(1+a\cos x)}{\cos x}dx = \pi\sin^{-1}a.$

Ex. 15: Prove that $\int_0^\infty e^{-x}\dfrac{1-\cos mx}{x}dx = \dfrac{1}{2}\log(m^2+1)$ and deduce that $\int_0^\infty \dfrac{\sin x}{x}dx$

Solution: Let $I(m) = \int_0^\infty e^{-x}\dfrac{1-\cos mx}{x}dx$

Applying DUIS rule, we get

Let $I'(m) = \int_0^\infty \dfrac{\partial}{\partial m}e^{-x}\dfrac{1-\cos mx}{x}dx$

$= \int_0^\infty \left[e^{-x}\dfrac{x\sin mx}{x}\right]dx$

$= \int_0^\infty \left[e^{-x}\sin mx\right]dx$

$= \left\{\dfrac{e^{-x}}{m^2+1^2}[-\sin x - m\cos mx]\right\}_0^\infty$

$I'(m) = \dfrac{m}{m^2+1}$

Integrating w. r. t. m

$I(m) = \dfrac{1}{2}\log(m^2+1) + C$

Put $m = 0$, $\Rightarrow 0 = 0 + C$

Thus $\int_0^\infty e^{-x}\dfrac{1-\cos mx}{x}dx = \dfrac{1}{2}\log(m^2+1)$.

Ex.16: Verify the rule of DUIS for $\int_0^\infty e^{-at}\cos bt\, dt$ **SUK: Nov-12, May-11**

Solution: Let $I(a) = \int_0^\infty e^{-at}\cos bt\, dt$

Integration by part

$\because \int_0^\infty e^{ax}\cos bx\, dx = \dfrac{e^{ax}}{a^2+b^2}(a\cos bx + b\sin bx)$

$\therefore I(a) = \left[\dfrac{e^{-at}}{a^2+b^2}(-a\cos bt + b\sin bt)\right]_0^\infty = \left[0 - \dfrac{1}{a^2+b^2}(-a+0)\right] = \dfrac{a}{a^2+b^2}$

$\therefore \dfrac{dI(a)}{da} = \left[\dfrac{(a^2+b^2)\cdot 1 - a(2a)}{(a^2+b^2)^2}\right]$

$= \dfrac{b^2-a^2}{(a^2+b^2)^2}$ (A)

Again applying DUIS rule

$$I'(a) = \int_0^\infty \frac{\partial}{\partial a} e^{-at} \cos bt \, dt = \int_0^\infty e^{-at}(-t)\cos bt \, dt$$

$$= -\int_0^\infty t e^{-at} \cos bt \, dt$$

$$= -\left\{ \left[t \frac{e^{-at}}{a^2+b^2}(-a\cos bt + b\sin bt) \right]_0^\infty - \int_0^\infty 1 \cdot \frac{e^{-at}}{a^2+b^2}(-a\cos bt + b\sin bt) \right\}$$

$$= 0 + \frac{1}{a^2+b^2} \int_0^\infty \left(-ae^{-at}\cos bt + be^{-at}\sin bt\right)$$

$$= \frac{1}{a^2+b^2}\left[-a\int_0^\infty e^{-at}\cos bt \, dt + b\int_0^\infty e^{-at}\sin bt \, dt \right]$$

$$= \frac{1}{a^2+b^2}\left\{ -a\left[\frac{e^{-at}}{a^2+b^2}(-a\cos bt + b\sin bt) \right]_0^\infty + b\left[\frac{e^{-at}}{a^2+b^2}(-a\sin bt - b\cos bt) \right]_0^\infty \right\}$$

$$= \frac{1}{a^2+b^2}\left[\frac{-a^2}{a^2+b^2} + \frac{b^2}{a^2+b^2} \right] = \frac{b^2 - a^2}{(a^2+b^2)^2} \qquad (B)$$

From Equation (A) and (B), the theorem is verified.

Ex.17: Verify the DUIS rule for $\int_a^{a^2} (\log ax) \, dx$. **SUK: Nov-09**

Solution: Let $I(a) = \int_a^{a^2} (\log ax) \, dx$.

Integration by part

Let $I(a) = \left[\log(ax)(x) \right]_a^{a^2} - \int_a^{a^2} (x) \frac{1}{ax}(a) \, dx$

$$= a^2 \log a^3 - a\log a^2 - \int_a^{a^2} 1 \cdot dx$$

$$= a^2(3\log a) - a(2\log a) - [x]_a^{a^2}$$

$$= 3a^2 \log a - 2a \log a - \left[a^2 - a\right]$$

$$\therefore I'(a) = 3a^2\left(\frac{1}{a}\right) + 6a\log a - 2a\left(\frac{1}{a}\right) - 2\log a - 2a + 1$$

$$= 3a + 6a\log a - 2 - 2\log a - 2a + 1$$

$$= a - 1 + 6a\log a - 2\log a$$

$$= a - 1 + 2\log a(3a - 1) \qquad (A)$$

Applying DUIS rule

$$I'(a) = \int_a^{a^2} \frac{\partial}{\partial a}(\log ax)\,dx + \log(a.a^2)\frac{d}{da}(a^2) - \log a.a\frac{d}{da}(a)$$

$$= \int_a^{a^2} \frac{1}{ax}(x)\,dx + \log(a^3)(2a) - \log a^2(1)$$

$$= \int_a^{a^2} \frac{1}{a}\,dx + 2a\log(a^3) - \log a^2$$

$$= \frac{1}{a}[x]_a^{a^2} + 2a(3\log a) - 2\log a$$

$$= \frac{1}{a}[a^2 - a] + 6a\log a - 2\log a = a - 1 + 2\log a(3a - 1) \quad (B)$$

From equation (A) and (B), result is verified.

Ex. 18: Prove that $\int_0^\infty \frac{e^{-ax}\sin x}{x}\,dx = \cot^{-1} x$ and deduce that $\int_0^\infty \frac{\sin x}{x}\,dx = \frac{\pi}{2}$.

Evaluate $\int_0^\infty \frac{e^{-ax}\sin x}{x}\,dx$, by DUIS rue   **SUK: Aug-13, May-09**

Solution: Let $I(\lambda) = \int_0^\infty e^{-ax}\frac{\sin x}{x}\,dx$

Applying DUIS rule, we get

Let $I'(a) = \int_0^\infty \frac{\partial}{\partial a}\left[e^{-ax}\frac{\sin x}{x}\right]dx$

$$= \int_0^\infty \left[e^{-ax}(-x)\frac{\sin x}{x}\right]dx = -\int_0^\infty \left[e^{-ax}\sin x\right]dx$$

$$= -\left\{\frac{e^{-ax}}{a^2+1^2}[-a\sin x - \cos x]\right\}_0^\infty = \left\{0 - \frac{1}{a^2+1}[0-1]\right\}$$

$$I'(a) = \frac{-1}{a^2+1}$$

Integrating w. r. t. a

$$I(a) = t\int \frac{-1}{a^2+1}\,da, \quad \therefore I(a) = \cot^{-1} a + C$$

Put $a = 0$, $\therefore I(0) = \frac{\pi}{2} + C \Rightarrow C = I(0) - \frac{\pi}{2}$

But $I(0) = \int_0^\infty \frac{\sin x}{x}\,dx$ and $I(a) = \cot^{-1}(a)$

$\therefore I(0) = \cot^{-1}(0) = \frac{\pi}{2}$

$\therefore I(0) = \int_0^\infty \frac{\sin x}{x}\,dx = \frac{\pi}{2} \quad \Rightarrow C = 0$

$\therefore I(a) = \cot^{-1} a.$

Ex. 19: Prove that $\int_0^\infty \dfrac{e^{-ax} - e^{-bx}}{x} dx = \log\left(\dfrac{b}{a}\right)$, $a > 0$, $b > 0$.

Solution: Let $I(a) = \int_0^\infty \dfrac{e^{-ax} - e^{-bx}}{x} dx$

Applying DUIS rule, we get

Let $I'(a) = \int_0^\infty \dfrac{\partial}{\partial a}\left[\dfrac{e^{-ax} - e^{-bx}}{x}\right] dx$

$= \int_0^\infty \left[\dfrac{e^{-ax}(-x) - 0}{x}\right] dx$

$I'(a) = -\int_0^\infty e^{-ax} dx = -\left[\dfrac{e^{-ax}}{-a}\right]_0^\infty = -\left[0 + \dfrac{1}{a}\right]$

$I'(a) = \dfrac{-1}{a}$.

Integrating w. r. t. a

$I(a) = -\log a + C$

Put $a = b$ $\quad \therefore I(b) = -\log b + C$

$\therefore I(b) = \int_0^\infty \dfrac{e^{-bx} - e^{-bx}}{x} dx = 0$ $\quad \therefore C = \log b$

$I(a) = -\log a + \log b = \log\left(\dfrac{b}{a}\right)$.

Ex. 20: Evaluate $\int_0^1 \dfrac{x^a - x^b}{\log x} dx$.   **SUK: Dec-11, May-08**

Solution: Let $I(a) = \int_0^1 \dfrac{x^a - x^b}{\log x} dx$.

Applying DUIS rule, we get

Let $I'(a) = \int_0^1 \dfrac{\partial}{\partial a}\left[\dfrac{x^a - x^b}{\log x}\right] dx$

$= \int_0^1 \dfrac{x^a \log x}{\log x} dx = \int_0^1 x^a dx = \left[\dfrac{x^{a+1}}{a+1}\right]_0^1 = \dfrac{1}{a+1}$

Integrating w. r. t. a

$I(a) = \log(a+1) + C$

Put $a = b$ $\quad \therefore I(b) = \log(b+1) + C$

$\therefore I(b) = \int_0^\infty \dfrac{x^b - x^b}{\log x} dx = 0$ $\quad \therefore C = -\log(b+1)$

$I(a) = \log(a+1) - \log(b+1) = \log\left(\dfrac{a+1}{b+1}\right)$.

Special Functions

TEST YOUR KNOWLEDGE

I. Prove that the following

1. $\int_0^\infty e^{-x^2} \cos 2\lambda x \, dx = \dfrac{\sqrt{\pi}}{2} e^{-\lambda^2}$

2. $\int_0^\infty e^{-x^2} \cos \lambda x \, dx = \dfrac{\sqrt{\pi}}{2} e^{-\lambda^2/4}$

3. $\int_0^\infty \dfrac{1}{x^2} \log(1+ax^2) \, dx = \pi \sqrt{a}$.

4. $\int_0^x \dfrac{1}{(x^2+a^2)^2} dx = \dfrac{1}{2a^3} \tan^{-1}\left(\dfrac{x}{a}\right) + \dfrac{x}{2a^2(x^2+a^2)}$.

II. Evaluate the following

1. $\int_0^\pi \dfrac{dx}{a+b\cos x}$, $a > 0, |b| < a$ Ans: $\dfrac{\pi}{\sqrt{a^2-b^2}}$.

2. $\int_0^{\pi/2} \log(a^2 \cos^2\theta + b^2 \sin^2\theta) d\theta$ Ans: $\pi \log\left(\dfrac{a+b}{2}\right)$.

III. verify the rule of DUIS for 1. $\int_a^{a^2} \dfrac{1}{x+a} dx$ 2. $\int_0^{a^2} \tan^{-1}\left(\dfrac{x}{a}\right) dx$.

ERROR FUNCTION

Definition: Error function of x is defined as

$$\text{erf}(x) = \dfrac{2}{\sqrt{\pi}} \int_0^x e^{-t^2} dt \qquad \text{(I)}$$

Definition: Complimentary error function of x is defined as $\text{erf}_c(x) = \dfrac{2}{\sqrt{\pi}} \int_x^\infty e^{-t^2} dt$ (II)

Remarks :

1. The variable of the error function x and variable of integrand t are independent
2. The Integrand does not contain variable x.
3. Upper limit of the integral x is called as parameter.
4. Alternative definition of $\text{erf}(x)$ and $\text{erf}_c(x)$:

Put $t^2 = u$, $t = \sqrt{u}$, $dt = \dfrac{1}{2\sqrt{u}} du$

Substituing in (I) and (II), we get

$$\text{erf}(x) = \dfrac{1}{\sqrt{\pi}} \int_0^{x^2} e^{-u} \dfrac{1}{\sqrt{u}} du$$

$$\text{erf}_c(x) = \dfrac{1}{\sqrt{\pi}} \int_{x^2}^\infty e^{-u} \dfrac{1}{\sqrt{u}} du$$

t	0	x
u	0	x^2

(4.71)

Graphs of error functions and complimentary error function

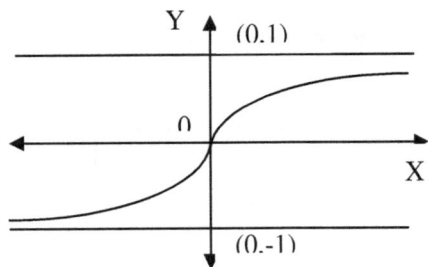

Fig: erf (x)

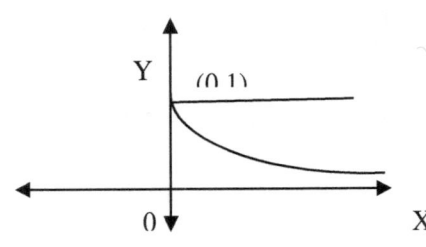

Fig: erf$_c(x)$

Properties of error function

Property 1: erf $(0) = 0$

Proof: We know the definition $\text{erf}(x) = \dfrac{2}{\sqrt{\pi}} \int_0^x e^{-t^2} dt \quad \therefore \text{erf}(0) = \dfrac{2}{\sqrt{\pi}} \int_0^0 e^{-t^2} dt = 0.$

Property 2: erf $(\infty) = 1$

Proof : We know the definition

$\text{erf}(x) = \dfrac{2}{\sqrt{\pi}} \int_0^x e^{-t^2} dt \quad \therefore \text{erf}(\infty) = \dfrac{2}{\sqrt{\pi}} \int_0^\infty e^{-t^2} dt = 0 \qquad \text{(I)}$

Put $t^2 = u,\ t = \sqrt{u},\ dt = \dfrac{1}{2\sqrt{u}} du = \dfrac{1}{2} u^{-1/2} du$

Substituing in (I), we get

$erf(\infty) = \dfrac{2}{\sqrt{\pi}} \int_0^\infty e^{-u} \dfrac{1}{2} u^{-1/2} du$

$= \dfrac{1}{\sqrt{\pi}} \int_0^\infty e^{-u} u^{-\frac{1}{2}} du$

$= \dfrac{1}{\sqrt{\pi}} \int_0^\infty e^{-u} u^{\frac{1}{2}-1} du$

$erf(\infty) = \dfrac{1}{\sqrt{\pi}} \overline{\left|\dfrac{1}{2}\right.} = \dfrac{1}{\sqrt{\pi}} \sqrt{\pi} = 1 \qquad \because \int_0^\infty e^{-x} x^{n-1} dx = \overline{|n|} \text{ and } \overline{\left|\dfrac{1}{2}\right.} = \sqrt{\pi}$

Property 3: $\text{erf}(x) + \text{erf}_c(x) = 1$

Proof: By definition of error and compliment error function,

$\text{erf}(x) + \text{erf}_c(x) = \dfrac{2}{\sqrt{\pi}} \int_0^x e^{-t^2} dt + \dfrac{2}{\sqrt{\pi}} \int_x^\infty e^{-t^2} dt$

$= \dfrac{2}{\sqrt{\pi}} \int_0^\infty e^{-t^2} dt \qquad \therefore \int_a^b + \int_b^c = \int_a^c$

$\therefore \text{erf}(x) + \text{erf}_c(x) = \text{erf}(\infty) = 1.$

Property 4: $\operatorname{erf}(-x) = -\operatorname{erf}(x)$ ($\operatorname{erf}(x)$ is odd function of x)

Proof: By definition of error function,

$$\operatorname{erf}(x) = \frac{2}{\sqrt{\pi}} \int_0^x e^{-t^2} dt \quad \therefore \operatorname{erf}(-x) = \frac{2}{\sqrt{\pi}} \int_0^{-x} e^{-t^2} dt$$

Let $t = -u$, $dt = -du$

t	0	$-x$
u	0	x

$$\therefore \operatorname{erf}(-x) = \frac{2}{\sqrt{\pi}} \int_0^x e^{-u^2} (-du)$$

$$\therefore \operatorname{erf}(-x) = \frac{-2}{\sqrt{\pi}} \int_0^x e^{-u^2} du = -\operatorname{erf}(x).$$

Property 5: Expansion of error function in power of x.

$$\operatorname{erf}(x) = \frac{2}{\sqrt{\pi}} \left[x - \frac{x^3}{3} + \frac{x^5}{5 \cdot 2!} - \frac{x^7}{7 \cdot 3!} + \ldots \right].$$

Proof: By definition of error function,

$$\operatorname{erf}(x) = \frac{2}{\sqrt{\pi}} \int_0^x e^{-t^2} dt$$

$$= \frac{2}{\sqrt{\pi}} \int_0^x \left[1 - t^2 + \frac{t^4}{2!} - \frac{t^6}{3!} + \ldots \right] dt \qquad \because e^{-x} = 1 - x + \frac{x^2}{2!} - \frac{x^3}{3!} + \ldots$$

$$= \frac{2}{\sqrt{\pi}} \left[t - \frac{t^3}{3} + \frac{t^5}{5 \cdot 2!} - \frac{t^7}{7 \cdot 3!} + \ldots \right]_0^x = \frac{2}{\sqrt{\pi}} \left[x - \frac{x^3}{3} + \frac{x^5}{5 \cdot 2!} - \frac{x^7}{7 \cdot 3!} + \ldots \right].$$

Note: 1. The value of $\operatorname{erf}(x)$ can be calculated using above series

2. $\operatorname{erf}(x)$ is a continuous function of x 3. This series is uniformly convergent

Property 6: Differentiation of error function $\dfrac{d}{dx}[\operatorname{erf}(ax)] = \dfrac{2a}{\sqrt{\pi}} e^{-a^2 x^2}$.

Proof: By definition of error function,

$$\operatorname{erf}(ax) = \frac{2}{\sqrt{\pi}} \int_0^{ax} e^{-t^2} dt$$

$$\frac{d}{dx}[\operatorname{erf}(ax)] = \frac{2}{\sqrt{\pi}} \frac{d}{dx} \left[\int_0^{ax} e^{-t^2} dt \right]$$

Applying DUIS rule w. r. t. x, we get

$$\therefore \frac{d}{dx}[\operatorname{erf}(ax)] = \frac{2}{\sqrt{\pi}} \left[\int_0^{ax} \frac{\partial}{\partial x}\left(e^{-t^2}\right) dt + e^{-a^2 x^2} \frac{d}{dx}(ax) - e^{-0} \frac{d}{dx}(0) e^{-0} \right]$$

$$\therefore \frac{d}{dx}[\operatorname{erf}(ax)] = \frac{2}{\sqrt{\pi}} \left[0 + a e^{-a^2 x^2} - 0 \right] = \frac{2a}{\sqrt{\pi}} e^{-a^2 x^2}.$$

Property 7: Differentiation of compliment error function $\dfrac{d}{dx}[\text{erf}_c(ax)] = \dfrac{-2a}{\sqrt{\pi}} e^{-a^2x^2}$.

Proof: Similar as that of property:6.

Property 8: Integration of error function $\displaystyle\int_0^t \text{erf}(ax)\,dx = t.\text{erf}(at) + \dfrac{1}{a\sqrt{\pi}}\left[e^{-a^2t^2} - 1\right]$.

Proof: By definition of error function,

$$\text{erf}(ax) = \dfrac{2}{\sqrt{\pi}} \int_0^{ax} e^{-t^2} dt$$

$\displaystyle\int_0^t \text{erf}(ax)\,dx = \int_0^t 1.\text{erf}(ax)\,dx$ Using integration by parts

$$= \left[x.\text{erf}(ax)\right]_0^t - \int_0^t x.\dfrac{2a}{\sqrt{\pi}} e^{-a^2x^2}\,dx \quad \text{By property:6}$$

$$= t.\text{erf}(at) + \dfrac{1}{a\sqrt{\pi}} \int_0^t \left(-2a^2x\right) e^{-a^2x^2}\,dx$$

$$= t.\text{erf}(at) + \dfrac{1}{a\sqrt{\pi}}\left[e^{-a^2x^2}\right]_0^t \qquad \because \int e^f f'\,dx = e^f$$

$\displaystyle\int_0^t \text{erf}(ax)\,dx = t.\text{erf}(at) + \dfrac{1}{a\sqrt{\pi}}\left[e^{-a^2t^2} - 1\right].$

Property 9: Integration of compliment error function

$\displaystyle\int_0^t \text{erf}_c(ax)\,dx = t.\text{erf}(at) - \dfrac{1}{a\sqrt{\pi}}\left[e^{-a^2t^2} - 1\right].$

Proof: Similar as that of property:8.

Examples on Error function:

Ex. 1: Show that $\text{erf}_c(-x) + \text{erf}_c(x) = 2$.

Solution: We know that $\text{erf}(x) + \text{erf}_c(x) = 1$

Replacing x by – x, we get
$\text{erf}(-x) + \text{erf}_c(-x) = 1$
$-\text{erf}(x) + \text{erf}_c(-x) = 1 \quad \because \text{erf}(-x) = -\text{erf}(x)$
$-[1 - \text{erf}_c(x)] + \text{erf}_c(-x) = 1$ by above term
$\therefore \text{erf}_c(x) + \text{erf}_c(-x) = 2$

Ex. 2: Show that $\displaystyle\int_0^\infty e^{-x^2 - 2ax}\,dx = \dfrac{\sqrt{\pi}}{2} e^{a^2}\left[1 - \text{erf}(a)\right]$.

Solution: Consider the L.H.S $= \displaystyle\int_0^\infty e^{-x^2 - 2ax}\,dx$

x	0	∞
t	a	∞

$$= \int_0^\infty e^{-x^2-2ax-a^2+a^2} dx = e^{a^2} \int_0^\infty e^{-(x+a)^2} dx$$

Put $x+a = t$ ∴ $dx = dt$

$$= e^{a^2} \int_a^\infty e^{-t^2} dt = \frac{\sqrt{\pi}}{2} e^{a^2} \frac{2}{\sqrt{\pi}} \int_a^\infty e^{-t^2} dt$$

$$= \frac{\sqrt{\pi}}{2} e^{a^2} erf_c(a) \text{ by definition}$$

$$= \frac{\sqrt{\pi}}{2} e^{a^2} [1 - erf(a)]$$

Ex. 3: Show that $\int_a^b e^{-x^2} dx = \frac{\sqrt{\pi}}{2} [erf(b) - erf(a)]$.

Solution: We know that $erf(\infty) = 1$

$$\frac{2}{\sqrt{\pi}} \int_0^\infty e^{-x^2} dx = 1$$

$$\frac{2}{\sqrt{\pi}} \left\{ \int_0^a e^{-x^2} dx + \int_a^b e^{-x^2} dx + \int_b^\infty e^{-x^2} dx \right\} = 1 \quad \because \int_a^b + \int_b^c = \int_a^c$$

$$\left\{ erf(a) + \frac{2}{\sqrt{\pi}} \int_a^b e^{-x^2} dx + erf_c(b) \right\} = 1$$

$$\left\{ erf(a) + \frac{2}{\sqrt{\pi}} \int_a^b e^{-x^2} dx \right\} = 1 - erf_c(b)$$

$$\left\{ erf(a) + \frac{2}{\sqrt{\pi}} \int_a^b e^{-x^2} dx \right\} = erf(b)$$

$$\therefore \frac{2}{\sqrt{\pi}} \int_a^b e^{-x^2} dx = erf(b) - erf(a) \Rightarrow \int_a^b e^{-x^2} dx = \frac{\sqrt{\pi}}{2} [erf(b) - erf(a)].$$

Ex. 4: Show that $erf(x) = \alpha(x\sqrt{2})$ where $\alpha(x) = \sqrt{\frac{2}{\pi}} \int_0^x e^{-t^2/2} dt$.

Solution: Given that $\alpha(x) = \sqrt{\frac{2}{\pi}} \int_0^x e^{-t^2/2} dt$

t	0	$x\sqrt{2}$
u	0	x

$$\therefore \alpha(x\sqrt{2}) = \sqrt{\frac{2}{\pi}} \int_0^{x\sqrt{2}} e^{-t^2/2} dt$$

Put $\frac{t^2}{2} = u^2$ ∴ $t^2 = 2u^2 \Rightarrow t = \sqrt{2} u$ ∴ $dt = \sqrt{2} du$

$$\therefore \alpha(x\sqrt{2}) = \sqrt{\frac{2}{\pi}} \int_0^x e^{-u^2} \sqrt{2} du$$

$$\alpha(x\sqrt{2}) = \frac{2}{\sqrt{\pi}} \int_0^x e^{-u^2} du \quad \therefore \alpha(x\sqrt{2}) = erf(x).$$

Ex. 5: Show that $\dfrac{d}{dx}\left[erf(ax^n)\right] = \dfrac{2an}{\sqrt{\pi}} x^{n-1} e^{-a^2 x^{2n}}$

Solution: By definition of error function $erf(x) = \dfrac{2}{\sqrt{\pi}} \int_0^x e^{-t^2} dt$

$$\therefore erf(ax^n) = \frac{2}{\sqrt{\pi}} \int_0^{ax^n} e^{-t^2} dt$$

Applying DUIS rule

$$\frac{d}{dx}\left[erf(ax^n)\right] = \frac{2}{\sqrt{\pi}}\left[\int_0^{ax^n} \frac{\partial}{\partial x} e^{-t^2} dt + e^{-a^2 x^{2n}} \frac{d}{dx}(ax^n) - 0\right]$$

$$\therefore \frac{d}{dx}\left[erf(ax^n)\right] = \frac{2}{\sqrt{\pi}}\left[0 + e^{-a^2 x^{2n}} \cdot nax^{n-1}\right] = \frac{2an}{\sqrt{\pi}} x^{n-1} e^{-a^2 x^{2n}}$$

Ex. 6: Show that $x\dfrac{d}{dx}[erf_c(ax)] + a\dfrac{d}{da}[erf(ax)] = 0$

Solution: By definition of error function $erf(x) = \dfrac{2}{\sqrt{\pi}} \int_0^x e^{-t^2} dt$

$$\therefore erf(ax) = \frac{2}{\sqrt{\pi}} \int_0^{ax} e^{-t^2} dt$$

$$\therefore \frac{d}{da}[erf(ax)] = \frac{2}{\sqrt{\pi}} \frac{d}{da} \int_0^{ax} e^{-t^2} dt$$

$$= \frac{2}{\sqrt{\pi}}\left[\int_0^{ax} \frac{\partial}{\partial a} e^{-t^2} dt + e^{-a^2 x^2} \cdot x - 0\right] \text{ By DUIS}$$

$$= \frac{2}{\sqrt{\pi}}\left[0 + xe^{-a^2 x^2}\right]$$

$$\therefore \frac{d}{da}[erf(ax)] = \frac{2x}{\sqrt{\pi}} e^{-a^2 x^2} \quad (I)$$

Again $erf_c(x) = \dfrac{2}{\sqrt{\pi}} \int_x^\infty e^{-t^2} dt$

$$\therefore erf_c(ax) = \frac{2}{\sqrt{\pi}} \int_{ax}^\infty e^{-t^2} dt$$

$$\therefore \frac{d}{da}[erf_c(ax)] = \frac{2}{\sqrt{\pi}} \frac{d}{da} \int_{ax}^\infty e^{-t^2} dt$$

$$= \frac{2}{\sqrt{\pi}}\left[\int_{ax}^\infty \frac{\partial}{\partial a} e^{-t^2} dt + 0 - e^{-a^2 x^2} \cdot \frac{d}{dx}(ax)\right] \text{ By DUIS}$$

$$= \frac{2}{\sqrt{\pi}}\left[0 + 0 - ae^{-a^2 x^2}\right]$$

$$\therefore \frac{d}{da}[erf_c(ax)] = \frac{-2a}{\sqrt{\pi}} e^{-a^2x^2} \qquad (II)$$

From equation (I) and (II)

$$x\frac{d}{dx}[erf_c(ax)] + a\frac{d}{da}[erf(ax)] = \frac{-2ax}{\sqrt{\pi}} e^{-a^2x^2} + \frac{2ax}{\sqrt{\pi}} e^{-a^2x^2} = 0.$$

TEST YOUR KNOWLEDGE

1. Show that $\int_0^t erf(ax) + \int_0^t erf_c(ax) = t$.

2. Show that $\int_0^\infty e^{-x^2-2bx} dx = \frac{\sqrt{\pi}}{2} e^{b^2} [1 - erf(a)]$.

3. Find $\frac{d}{dx}[erf(ax^n)]$ Ans: $\frac{2an}{\sqrt{\pi}} x^{n-1} e^{-a^2x^{2n}}$

4. Find $\frac{d}{dx}[erf(ax)]$ Ans: $\frac{2a}{\sqrt{\pi}} e^{-a^2x^2}$

5. Show that $\frac{1}{x}\frac{d}{da}[erf_c(ax)] = \frac{-1}{a}\frac{d}{dx}[erf(ax)]$

6. Find $\frac{d}{dx}[erf(ax^n) + erf_c(ax)]$ Ans: $\frac{2an}{\sqrt{\pi}} x^{n-1} e^{-a^2x^{2n}} - \frac{2a}{\sqrt{\pi}} e^{-a^2x^2}$

7. Show that $\frac{d}{dx}[erf(x)] = \frac{2}{\sqrt{\pi}} e^{-x^2}$ and $\frac{d}{dx}[erf_c(x)] = \frac{-2}{\sqrt{\pi}} e^{-x^2}$

8. Show that $\frac{d}{dt}[erf(\sqrt{t})] = \frac{1}{\sqrt{\pi t}} e^{-t}$ and $\frac{d}{dx}[erf_c(\sqrt{t})] = \frac{-1}{\sqrt{\pi t}} e^{-t}$

9. Show that $\int_0^\infty e^{-(x+a)^2} dx = \frac{\sqrt{\pi}}{2} [1 - erf(a)]$

10. Show that $\int_0^\infty e^{-st} erf(\sqrt{t}) dt = \frac{1}{s\sqrt{s+1}}$

YEAR WISE UNIVERSITY QUESTION PAPERS -13 SEMESTERS

Dec-2013(10/12/2013)

1. Evaluate $\int_0^\infty \sqrt[4]{x} e^{-\sqrt{x}} dx$.	5
2. Evaluate $\int_5^9 \sqrt{(9-x)(x-5)} dx$.	5
3. Prove that $\int_0^1 \frac{x - 2x^2 + 3x^3}{(1+x)^5} dx = \frac{1}{48}$.	6

F.E. (Sem. II) M II (SU) Special Functions

August-2013(16/08/2013) Re-exam

1. Evaluate $\int_0^\infty x^7 e^{-2x^2} dx$. — 5

2. Prove that $\int_0^{\pi/2} \sqrt{\tan\theta}\, d\theta \times \int_0^{\pi/2} \sqrt{\cot\theta}\, d\theta = \dfrac{\pi^2}{2}$. — 6

3. Evaluate $\int_0^\infty \dfrac{e^{-ax}\sin x}{x} dx$ By using rule of differentiation under integral sign. — 6

May-2013(18/05/2013)

1. Evaluate $\int_0^1 \dfrac{1}{\sqrt{x\log x}} dx$ — 5

2. Evaluate $\int_0^4 x^2\sqrt{4x-x^2}\, dx$ — 5

3. Prove that $\int_0^\infty \dfrac{x^5}{(2+3x)^{16}} dx = \dfrac{1}{2^{10} 3^6} \beta(6,10)$ — 6

May-2012 (29/05/2012)

1. Evaluate $\int_0^1 \left[\log\left(\dfrac{1}{x}\right)\right]^{10} dx$ — 5

2. Evaluate $\int_0^1 x^5 (1-x^3)^{10} dx$ — 5

3. Evaluate $\int_0^\infty \dfrac{\tan^{-1}(ax)}{x+(1+x^2)} dx$ by using method. — 6

Nov-2012(20/11/2012)

1. Define Gamma function and show that $n = \int_0^1 \left[\log\left(\dfrac{1}{y}\right)\right]^{n-1} dy$ — 5

2. Evaluate $\int_0^{2a} x\sqrt{(2ax-x^2)}\, dx$ in terms of Beta function and find its value. — 6

3. Verify the rule of DUIS for $\int_0^\infty e^{-at}\cos bt\, dt$, where a is a parameter. — 6

Dec-2011(16/12/2011)

1. Prove that $\int_0^1 x^{n-1} \log\left(\dfrac{1}{x}\right) dx = \dfrac{n}{a^n}$ $a>0$. — 5

2. Evaluate $\int_{3}^{7}(x-3)^{1/4}(7-x)^{1/4}dx$	5
3. Evaluate $\int_{0}^{1}\left(\dfrac{x^{a}-x^{b}}{\log x}\right)dx$ by using DUIS. If a is a parameter.	6
May-2011(25/05/2011)	
1. Evaluate $\int_{0}^{1}\dfrac{x^{7}(1-x^{12})}{(1+x)^{28}}dx$	5
2. If $\int_{0}^{\infty}\dfrac{x^{p-1}}{(1+x)}dx=\dfrac{\pi}{\sin p\pi}$ then prove that $p\overline{1-p}=\dfrac{\pi}{\sin p\pi}$ for $0<p<1$	6
3. Verify the rule of DUIS for the integral $\int_{0}^{\infty}e^{-at}\cos bt\,dt$ where a is a parameter.	6
Nov-2010 (18/11/2010)	
1. Evaluate $\int_{0}^{\pi/2}\sqrt[4]{\tan\theta}\,e^{-\sqrt{\tan\theta}}\sec^{2}\theta d\theta$	5
2. Evaluate $\int_{1}^{\infty}\dfrac{(x-1)^{7}}{x^{12}}dx$	6
3. Evaluate $\int_{0}^{\infty}\dfrac{e^{-x}}{x}(1-e^{-ax})dx,\ a>-1$.	5
May-2010 (19/05/2010)	
1. Evaluate $\int_{0}^{\infty}\dfrac{x^{4}(1+x^{5})}{(1+x)^{15}}dx$	5
2. Prove that $\overline{m}\,\overline{m+\dfrac{1}{2}}=\dfrac{\sqrt{\pi}}{2^{2m-1}}\overline{2m}$.	6
3. Evaluate $\int_{0}^{\infty}\dfrac{e^{-x}}{x}\left(a-\dfrac{1}{x}+\dfrac{e^{-ax}}{x}\right)dx$	6
May-2009 (19/05/2009)	
1. Evaluate $\int_{0}^{\pi}\dfrac{\sin^{4}\theta}{(1+\cos\theta)^{2}}d\theta$	4
2. Evaluate $\int_{0}^{1}x^{5}\sqrt{\dfrac{1+x^{2}}{1-x^{2}}}dx$	5

3. Evaluate $\int_0^1 (\log x)^6 \, dx$	4
4. Prove that $\int_0^\infty \dfrac{e^{-\alpha x} \sin x}{x} \, dx = \cot^{-1} \alpha.$	4
Nov-2009 (16/11/2009)	
1. Prove that $\beta(m,n) = \int_0^\infty \dfrac{x^{m-1}}{(1+x)^{m+n}} \, dx$	6
2. Evaluate $\int_0^1 x^3 \log\left(\dfrac{1}{x}\right)^4 dx$	5
3. Verify the rule of DUIS for the integral $\int_a^{a^2} \log ax \, dx$	6
May-2008 (17/05/2008)	
1. Evaluate $\int_0^1 x^5 \sin^{-1} x \, dx$	5
2. Evaluate $\int_0^{1/2} x^3 \sqrt{1-4x^2} \, dx$	4
3. Evaluate $\int_0^\infty \sqrt{x}\, e^{-x^3} \, dx$	4
4. Show that $\int_0^1 \dfrac{x^a - x^b}{\log x} \, dx = \log \dfrac{a+1}{b+1}$	4
Nov-2008 (10/11/2008)	
1. Evaluate $\int_0^\infty x^{-4} e^{-1/x} \, dx$	5
2. Evaluate $\int_0^\pi x \sin^6 x \, dx$	5
3. Prove that $\int_0^1 \dfrac{x^b - 1}{\log x} \, dx = \log(1+b), b \geq 0.$	6

UNIT - V

CURVE TRACING

INTRODUCTION

Curve tracing is the method of drawing an approximate shape of the curve (figure) by the study of some of its important characteristics such as symmetry, point of intercepts, asymptotes, tangent, nature of multiple points, region of existence etc.

For evaluating area, surface areas of revolution, volume of revolution, finding length and many other properties we need the knowledge of curve tracing.

Before studying the methods for curve tracing, let us discuss some basic definitions.

Multiple points:

Curve with implicit equation of the form $f(x,y)=0$ possess some peculiar properties because of the fact that the equation $f(x,y)=0$ may define y as a multivalued function i.e. there corresponds as many values of y to each x depending upon degree of the equation in y. These different values of y give rise to the different branches of the curve.

Hence, a point through which there pass 'n' branches of the curve is called a multiple point of order 'n' and the curve has n tangent at this point.

Through a double point, two branches of the curve pass through; a triple point three branches of the curve pass and so on. Here we shall discuss only the double point in details.

The curve has two tangents at a double point, one for each branch. The double point will be a node, cusp or isolated points according as the two tangents are different and real, coincident or imaginary.

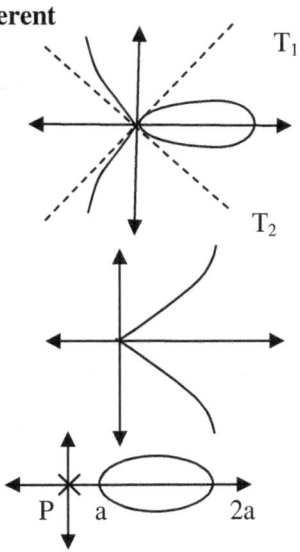

I) **Node:** If at a double point, two tangents are **real and different** then such a point on a curve is called a node.

Ex.: Consider the curve $y^2(x+a) = x^2(a-x)$

In this curve origin is a double point and two tangents are different, hence origin is a node.

II) **Cusp:** If at a double point, two tangents are **coincident**, then such a point on a curve is called a cusp.

Ex.: Consider the curve $ay^2 = x^3$

In this curve origin is a double point and two tangents are coincident, hence origin is a cusp.

III) **Isolated points (Conjugate point):** A point P is called a isolated point if the coordinates of P satisfies the equation of the curve, but no branch pass through the point P.

Tracing of Cartesian Curve:

Rules for tracing of Cartesian Curve:

Rule I: Symmetry

(A) Symmetry about X- axis: If only even powers of y occur in $f(x, y) = 0$ i.e. if the equation of the curve remains unchanged on replacing y by $-y$. $f(x,-y) = f(x, y)$ then the curve is symmetric about X axis.

Ex.: $y^2 = 4ax$.

(B) Symmetry about Y- axis: If only even powers of x occur in $f(x, y) = 0$ i.e. if the equation of the curve remains unchanged on replacing x by $-x$. $f(-x, y) = f(x, y)$ then the curve is symmetric about X axis.

Ex.: $x^2 = 4ay$.

(C) Symmetry about both X- axis and Y- axis:
If all the power of both x and y are even in $f(x, y) = 0$ then the curve is symmetric about both the axis.

Ex.: $x^2 + y^2 = a^2$.

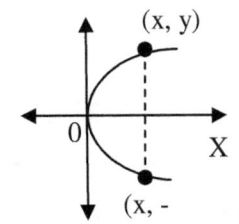

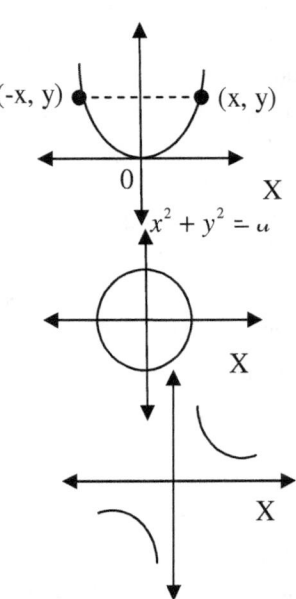

(D) Symmetry about the origin (Opposite quadrants):
If the equation of the curve remains unaltered on replacing x by $-x$ and y by $-y$ i.e. $f(-x,-y) = f(x, y)$ then the curve is symmetric about the origin.
This symmetry is also known as symmetry in opposite quadrants.

Ex.: $xy = c$.

(E) Symmetry about the line $y = x$:
If the equation of the curve remains unaltered on replacing x by y and y by x i.e. $f(y, x) = f(x, y)$

Ex.: $xy = c$.

(F) Symmetry about the line $y = -x$:
If the equation of the curve remains unaltered on replacing x by $-y$ and y by $-x$ i.e. $f(x, y) = f(-y, -x)$

Ex.: $xy = -c$.

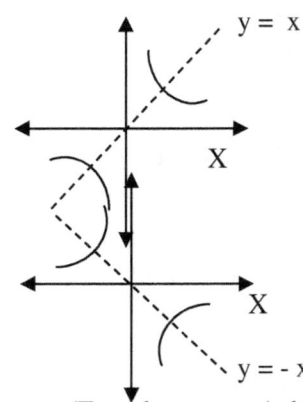

(II) Point of Intersection

(A) Origin: If the equation of curve does not contain a constant term (Zero degree term) then the curve passes through origin.

(B) Tangent at origin: If origin lies on the curve then the tangent at origin can be found out by Newton's method. (If (0, 0) is the point on the curve then only we can find the tangent at origin.)

Newton's Method: Tangent at origin can be found out by equating all lower degree term to zero in the given equation, when the equation is in rational integral algebraic form.

Ex.: Find the tangent at origin for $y^2(x+a) = x^2(3a-x)$

Solution: First we will take all the term of given equation to the left side
$y^2(x+a) - x^2(3a-x) = 0 \Rightarrow xy^2 + ay^2 - 3ax^2 + x^3 = 0$

Equating all lower degree term to zero
$ay^2 - 3ax^2 = 0 \Rightarrow ay^2 = 3ax^2 \Rightarrow y^2 = 3x^2 \therefore y = \pm\sqrt{3}x$

Thus $y = \sqrt{3}x, -\sqrt{3}x$ are the tangents at origin.

Note: In case there are two tangent at origin i.e. origin is a double point, find whether it is node, cusp or isolated point according as the tangent are equal and distinct, coincident or imaginary.

Tangent at any other point: To the nature of tangent at any point P, find $\dfrac{dy}{dx}$ at that point.

i) If $\left(\dfrac{dy}{dx}\right)_p = 0$. Then tangent at the point p is parallel to X-axis.

ii) If $\left(\dfrac{dy}{dx}\right)_p = +ve$. Then tangent at the point p makes the acute angle with X-axis.

iii) If $\left(\dfrac{dy}{dx}\right)_p = -ve$. Then tangent at the point p makes the obtuse angle with X-axis.

iv) If $\left(\dfrac{dy}{dx}\right)_p = \infty$. Then tangent at the point p is parallel to Y-axis.

(C) Intercepts: Find the point of intersection with the coordinate axis. If possible express the given equation in terms of $y = f(x) \text{ or } x = f(y)$.

i) Intersection with X-axis: Put $y = 0$ in the given equation and solve for x.

ii) Intersection with Y-axis: Put $x = 0$ in the given equation and solve for y.

iii) Points on the line of symmetry: If $y = x$ is the line of symmetry then put $y = x$ to find the point on the line of symmetry.

III) Asymptotes: Asymptotes are the tangent to the curve at infinity i.e. the curve touches the asymptote at two coincident points at infinity.

A) **Asymptotes parallel to X-axis**: Asymptotes parallel to X-axis are obtained by equating the coefficients of higher degree term in x to zero.

Ex.: Consider the equation $xy = c$

Here coefficient of x is $y \therefore y = 0$ is the asymptote parallel to X-axis.

B) **Asymptotes parallel to Y-axis**: Asymptotes parallel to Y-axis are obtained by equating the coefficients of higher degree term in y to zero.

Ex.: Consider the equation $xy = c$

Here coefficient of y is $x \therefore x = 0$ is the asymptote parallel to y-axis.

Note: If the coefficients are constant or has no real factor, the curve has no asymptotes parallel to the axes.

C) Oblique asymptotes: Asymptotes which are not parallel to x-axis or y-axis are called as oblique asymptotes.

Note: If curve is not symmetric about X-axis or Y-axis then find the oblique asymptotes.

Remark: Oblique asymptotes are obtained by following method.
Assume $y = mx + c$ as the equation of oblique asymptotes. To find the values of m and c substitute this value of y in the given equation $f(x, y) = 0$, equating to zero two successive highest power of x, we can find the values of m and c.

Ex. 1: Find the asymptotes of the equation $y = \dfrac{x-2}{2x+3}$ if any.

Solution: Given equation is $y = \dfrac{x-2}{2x+3}$, i.e. $y(2x+3) = x-2 \Rightarrow 2xy + 3y - x + 2 = 0$

i) **For Asymptotes parallel to x-axis:** Asymptotes parallel to x-axis are obtained by equating the coefficients of higher degree term in x to zero.
$2xy + 3y - x + 2 = 0 \quad \therefore (2y-1)x + 3y + 2 = 0$

$(2y-1) = 0 \Rightarrow 2y = 1, \quad \therefore y = 0.5$ is the asymptotes Parallel to x-axis.

ii) **Asymptotes parallel to y-axis:** Asymptotes parallel to y-axis are obtained by equating the coefficients of higher degree term in y to zero.
$2xy + 3y - x + 2 = 0 \quad \therefore (2x+3)y - x + 2 = 0$

$(2x+3) = 0 \Rightarrow 2x = -3, \quad \therefore x = -1.5$ is the asymptotes parallel to y-axis.

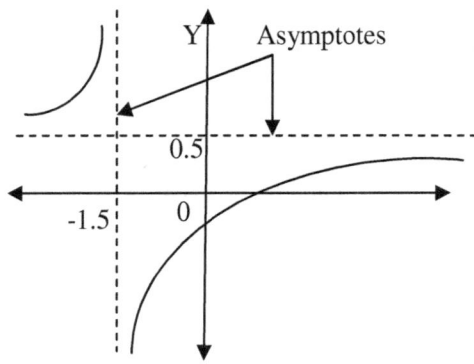

Ex. 2: Find the asymptotes of the equation $x^3 + y^3 = 3axy$ if any.

Solution: Given equation is $x^3 + y^3 = 3axy$ i.e. $x^3 + y^3 - 3axy = 0$

As the coefficients of x and y are constant (i.e.1) therefore per above note the curve has no asymptotes parallel to the axes.

We have to find the oblique asymptotes: Assume $y = mx + c$ be the asymptotes.

Therefore given equation becomes

$x^3 + (mx+c)^3 - 3ax(mx+c) = 0$

$x^3 + (m^3x^3 + 3m^2x^2c + 3mxc^2 + c^3) - 3max^2 - 3acx = 0$

$(1+m^3)x^3 + (3m^2c - 3ma)x^2 + (3mc^2 - 3ac)x + c^3 = 0$

equating to zero two successive highest power of x, we get

$1 + m^3 = 0 \Rightarrow m = -1$

$3m^2c - 3ma = 0$ As $m = -1 \Rightarrow c = -a$

∴ Obligue asymptote is $y = -x - a$ i.e. $x + y = -a$.

Ex. 3: Find the asymptotes of the equation $x^2(x^2+2) = y^3(x+5)$ if any.

Solution: Given equation is $x^4 + 2x^2 - y^3x - 5y^3 = 0$.

i) **Asymptotes parallel to x-axis:** As the coefficients of x is constant (i.e.1) therefore per above note the curve has no asymptote parallel to x-axis.

ii) **Asymptotes parallel to y-axis:**
$x^4 + 2x^2 - y^3(x+5) = 0$

∴ $x + 5 = 0 \Rightarrow x = -5$ is the asymptote parallel to y axis.

iii) **Oblique asymptotes:** We have to find the oblique asymptotes: Assume $y = mx + c$ be the asymptotes. Therefore given equation becomes

$x^4 + 2x^2 - (mx+c)^3(x+5) = 0$

$x^4 + 2x^2 - (m^3x^3 + 3m^2x^2c + 3mxc^2 + c^3)(x+5) = 0$

$x^4 + 2x^2 - m^3x^4 - 3m^2x^3c - 3mx^2c^2 - xc^3 - 5m^3x^3 - 15m^2x^2c - 15mxc^2 - 5c^3 = 0$

$(1-m^3)x^4 + (-3m^2c - 5m^3)x^3 + (2 - 3mc^2 - 15m^2c)x^2 + (-c^3 - 15mc^2) - 5c^3 = 0$

equating to zero two successive highest power of x, we get

$1 - m^3 = 0 \Rightarrow m^3 = 1$ ∴ $m = 1$

$-3m^2c - 5m^3 = 0$ As $m = 1 \Rightarrow c = -\dfrac{5}{3}$

∴ Obligue asymptote is $y = x - \dfrac{5}{3}$.

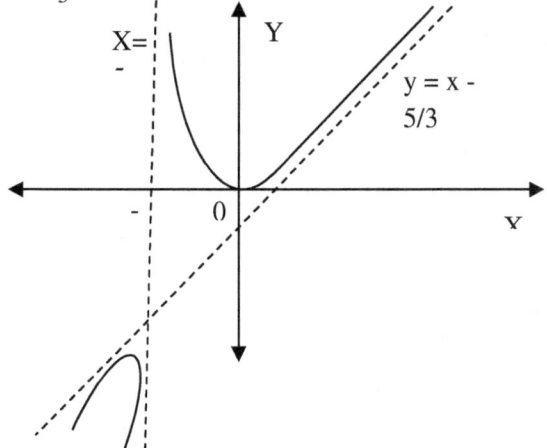

IV) Region of absence of the curve:
  i) Express the equation in the explicit form $y = f(x)$ or $x = g(y)$

  ii) If , say for $x > a$, $y^2 < 0$ (i.e. y is imaginary) then there is no branch of the curve for $x > a$.

  Also if say for $a < x < b$ (say), $y^2 < 0$ then the curve doesn't lie in the region $a < x < b$.

  iii) If say for $a < y < b$ (say), $x^2 < 0$ then the curve doesn't lie in the region $a < y < b$.

Some Important Remarks
1. Use only as many steps as necessary for tracing the curve.

2. If there are two points of the curve on any axis and if the curve does not exist on either side of the two points, then there is always a loop between the two points.

3. Similarly, If the curve is symmetric about X-axis then check for asymptotes parallel to y-axis and vise - versa.

Tracing of curve in Cartesian form: Some Standard Curve
Type I: Semi cubical parabola- Trace the curve $ay^2 = x^3$.

Solution: The given equation of the curve is $ay^2 = x^3$.

Symmetry: If only even power of y, then curve is symmetric about X-axis	The given equation of curve contain only even power of y. Therefore it is symmetrical about X-axis.
Origin: If the eqution of curve does not contain any constant term	Equation does not contain any absolute constant therefore, it passes through the origin.
Tangent at origin: Tangents at the origin are obtained by equating to zero the lowest degree terms in the equation.	As $ay^2 = x^3 \Rightarrow ay^2 - x^3 = 0$ $\therefore ay^2 = 0 \Rightarrow y^2 = 0$, $y = 0, 0$ i.e. $y = 0$ is a double point There fore X-axis is a tangent at origin.
Nature of double point: If at a double point, two tangents are coincident	Origin is a cusp.
Intercepts: Intersection with X-axis: Put $y = 0$ Intersection with Y-axis: Put $x = 0$	Put $y = 0 \therefore 0 = x^3$. $\Rightarrow x = 0$. Put $x = 0 \therefore ay^2 = 0$ i.e. $y^2 = 0 \Rightarrow y = 0$ Thus curve meets the co-ordinate axes only at $(0,0)$
Asymptotes: Asymptotes parallel to x-axis (y-axis) is obtained by equating the coefficients of higher degree term in x (y) to zero.	As the coefficients of x^3 is constant (i.e.1) therefore the curve has no asymptote parallel to X-axis. And the coefficients of y^2 is constant (i.e.a) therefore the curve has no asymptote parallel to Y-axis.
Region of absence of the curve: Find the value of x where y becomes imaginary, then curve does not exist in that region.	Given curve is $ay^2 = x^3$ At $x = -a$, $y^2 = -ve$ Therefore the curve does not exist for $x < 0$.

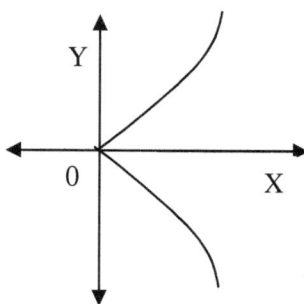

Type II: Cissiod of Diocles - Trace the curve $y^2(2a-x) = x^3$, $a > 0$.

Solution: The given equation of the curve can be written as $y^2 = \dfrac{x^3}{2a-x}$.

Symmetry: If only even power of y, then curve is symmetric about X-axis	The given equation of curve contains only even power of y. Therefore it is symmetrical about X-axis.
Origin: If the equation of curve does not contain any constant term	Equation does not contain any absolute constant therefore, it passes through the origin.
Tangent at origin: Tangents at the origin are obtained by equating to zero the lowest degree terms in the equation.	As $y^2(2a-x) = x^3 \Rightarrow 2ay^2 - xy^2 - x^3 = 0$ $\therefore 2ay^2 = 0 \Rightarrow y^2 = 0$, $y = 0,0$ i.e. $y = 0$ is a double point There fore X-axis is a tangent at origin.
Nature of double point: If at a double point, two tangents are coincident	Origin is a cusp.
Intercepts: Intersection with X-axis: Put $y = 0$ Intersection with Y-axis: Put $x = 0$	Put $y = 0 \therefore 0 = \dfrac{x^3}{2a-x}$ i.e. $0 = x^3 \Rightarrow x = 0$. Put $x = 0 \therefore y^2 = \dfrac{0}{2a-0}$ i.e. $y^2 = 0 \Rightarrow y = 0$ Thus curve meets the co-ordinate axes only at $(0,0)$
Asymptotes: Asymptotes parallel to x-axis (y-axis) is obtained by equating the coefficients of higher degree term in x (y) to zero.	As the coefficients of x^3 is constant (i.e.1) therefore the curve has no asymptote parallel to x-axis. And as $y^2(2a-x) = x^3 \therefore 2a - x = 0 \Rightarrow x = 2a$ is the asymptotes parallel to Y-axis.
Region of absence of the curve: Find the value of x where y becomes imaginary, then curve does not exist in that region.	Given curve is $y^2 = \dfrac{x^3}{2a-x}$ At $x = -a$, $y^2 = -ve$ At $x = 3a$, $y^2 = -ve$ Therefore the curve does not exist for $x < 0$ and $x > 3a$. thus the curve exist for $0 < x < 2a$.

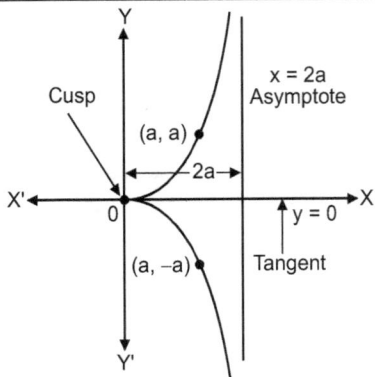

Type III: Strophoid - Trace the curve $x(x^2 + y^2) = a(x^2 - y^2)$, $a > 0$

Solution: The Given equation of the curve can be written as

$$x^3 + xy^2 = ax^2 - ay^2 \Rightarrow xy^2 + ay^2 = ax^2 - x^3$$

i.e. $y^2(a+x) = x^2(a-x)$ ∴ $y^2 = \dfrac{x^2(a-x)}{(a+x)}$.

Symmetry: If only even power of y, then curve is symmetric about X-axis	The given equation of curve contain only even power of y. Therefore it is symmetrical about X-axis.
Origin: If the equation of curve does not contain any constant	Equation does not contain any absolute constant therefore, it passes through the origin.
Tangent at origin: Tangents at the origin are obtained by equating to zero the lowest degree terms in the equation.	As $x^3 + xy^2 = ax^2 - ay^2 \Rightarrow xy^2 + ay^2 - ax^2 + x^3 = 0$ ∴ $ay^2 - ax^2 = 0 \Rightarrow y^2 = x^2$, $y = \pm x$ are the tangent at origin.
Nature of double point: If at a double point, two tangents are real and different	Origin is a node
Intercepts: Intersection with X-axis: Put $y = 0$ Intersection with Y-axis: Put $x = 0$	Put $y = 0$ ∴ $0 = \dfrac{x^2(a-x)}{(a+x)}$ i.e. $x^2(a-x) = 0 \Rightarrow x = 0$ or $x = a$. Put $x = 0$ ∴ $y^2 = \dfrac{0}{(a+0)}$ i.e. $y^2 = 0 \Rightarrow y = 0$ Thus curve meets the co-ordinate axes at $(0,0)$ and $(a,0)$
Asymptotes: Asymptotes parallel to x-axis (y-axis) is	As the coefficients of x^3 is constant (i.e.1) therefore the curve has no asymptote parallel to x-axis.

obtained by equating the coefficients of higher degree term in x (y)to zero.	And as $(a+x)y^2 - ax^2 + x^3 = 0$ $\therefore a+x=0 \Rightarrow x=-a$ is the asymptotes parallel to Y-axis.
Region of absence of the curve: Find the value of x where y becomes imaginary, then curve does not exist in that region.	Given curve is $y^2 = \dfrac{x^2(a-x)}{(a+x)}$ At $x<-a$ and $x>a$, y becomes imaginary Therefore the curve does not exist for $x<-a$ and $x>a$

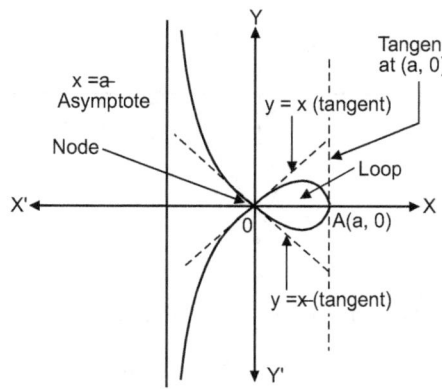

Type IV: Astroid or four cusped or Hypocycloid curve- Trace the curve $\left(\dfrac{x}{a}\right)^{\frac{2}{3}} + \left(\dfrac{y}{b}\right)^{\frac{2}{3}} = 1$.

Solution:

Symmetry: If all the power of both x and y are even, then the curve is symmetric about both the axes.	The given equation of curve contain even power of x and y. Therefore it is symmetrical about both the axes.
Origin: If the equation of curve does not contain any constant	Equation of curve contain constant therefore, it does not passes through the origin.
Intercepts: Intersection with X-axis: Put $y=0$ Intersection with Y-axis: Put $x=0$	Put $y=0$ $\therefore \left(\dfrac{x}{a}\right)^{\frac{2}{3}} + 0 = 1$. i.e. $x^2 = a^2$ $\Rightarrow x = \pm a$. Put $x=0$ $\therefore 0 + \left(\dfrac{y}{b}\right)^{\frac{2}{3}} = 1$. i.e. $y^2 = b^2$ $\Rightarrow y = \pm b$. Thus curve meets the co-ordinate axes at $(\pm a, 0)$ and $(0, \pm b)$
Asymptotes: Asymptotes parallel to x-axis (y-axis) is obtained by equating the coefficients of higher degree term in x (y)to zero.	As the coefficients of $x^{2/3}$ is constant (i.e. $1/a^{2/3}$) therefore the curve has no asymptote parallel to X-axis. And the coefficients of $y^{2/3}$ is constant (i.e. $1/b^{2/3}$) therefore the curve has no asymptote parallel to Y-axis.

| Region of absence of the curve: Find the value of x where y becomes imaginary, then curve does not exist in that region. | Given curve is $\left(\dfrac{x}{a}\right)^{\frac{2}{3}} + \left(\dfrac{y}{b}\right)^{\frac{2}{3}} = 1$. curve exist only when $-a < x < a$ and $-b < y < b$. |

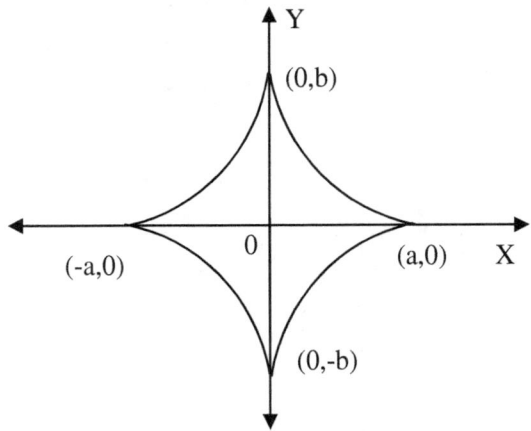

Type V: Witch of Agnesi - Trace the curve $xy^2 = a^2(a-x)$.

Solution: The Given equation of the curve can be written as $y^2 = \dfrac{a^2(a-x)}{x}$.

Symmetry: If only even power of y, then curve is symmetric about X-axis	The given equation of curve contain only even power of y. Therefore it is symmetrical about X-axis.
Origin: If the equation of curve does not contain any constant	Equation of curve contain constant therefore, it does not passes through the origin.
Intercepts: Intersection with X-axis: Put $y = 0$ Intersection with Y-axis: Put $x = 0$	Put $y = 0 \therefore 0 = \dfrac{a^2(a-x)}{x}$ .. i.e. $a^2(a-x) = 0 \Rightarrow x = a \because a \neq 0$. Put $x = 0 \Rightarrow y = 0$ Curve meets the co-ordinate axes at (a,0)
Asymptotes: Asymptotes parallel to x-axis (y-axis) is obtained by equating the coefficients of higher degree term in x (y) to zero.	As the coefficients of x is $y^2 + a^2 \Rightarrow y^2 = -a^2 \therefore y = \pm ai$ which is not real, therefore the curve has no asymptote parallel to X-axis. And as $xy^2 - a^3 + a^2x. \therefore x = 0 \Rightarrow y$ axis is the asymptotes parallel to y-axis.
Region of absence of the curve: Find the value of x where y becomes imaginary, then curve does not exist in that region.	Given curve is $y^2 = \dfrac{a^2(a-x)}{x}$ At $x = -a$ $y^2 = -ve$ At $x = 2a$ $y^2 = -ve$ $\therefore x < 0$ and $x > a$ y becomes imaginary $\therefore$ curve does not exist for $x < 0$ and $x > a$ Thus the curve exist for $0 < x < a$.

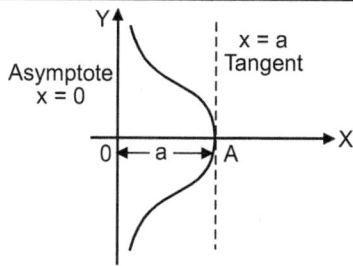

Type VI: Common catenary - Trace the curve $y = c \cosh \dfrac{x}{c}$.

Solution: The given equation of the curve is $y = c \cosh \dfrac{x}{c}$.

Symmetry: Equation remains unchanged if x is replaced by $-x$, then curve is symmetric about Y-axis.	The given equation of curve is $y = c \cosh \dfrac{x}{c}$, $\therefore y = c \cosh \dfrac{-x}{c} = c \cosh \dfrac{x}{c}$. Therefore curve is symmetric about Y-axis.
Origin: If the equation of curve does not contain any constant term	When $x = 0$ we have $y = c$ ($\because \cosh 0 = 1$). Equation of curve contain constant, therefore, it does not passes through the origin.
Intercepts: Intersection with X-axis: Put $y = 0$ Intersection with Y-axis: Put $x = 0$	Put $x = 0$ $\therefore y = c \Rightarrow (0, c)$ is the point on curve. Thus the curve meets the co-ordinate axes at $(a, 0)$. Here X-axis is called as the directrix. Curve does not cut X-axis at all. Also $\dfrac{dy}{dx} = c \sinh \dfrac{x}{c} \cdot \dfrac{1}{c} = \sinh \dfrac{x}{c}$ $\because \dfrac{d(\cosh x/c)}{dx} = \sinh \dfrac{x}{c} \cdot \dfrac{1}{c}$ $\therefore \dfrac{dy}{dx} = \sinh \dfrac{x}{c}$ $\therefore$ for $(0, c) \Rightarrow \dfrac{dy}{dx} = 0$ $\Rightarrow$ At $(0, c)$ tangent is parallel to X-axis.
Region of absence of the curve: Find the value of x where y becomes imaginary, then curve does not exist in that region.	For $y < c$ the value of x does not exist implies that curve does not exists for $y < c$. Also as x increases, y also increases from 0 to $\cdot$

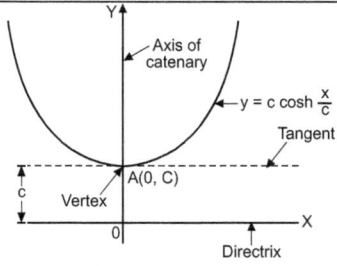

Note : This curve is known as *"The common catenary"*.

A curve in which a perfectly flexible and uniform string hangs under gravity is called *catenary*. The equation of the curve is $y = c\cosh\dfrac{x}{c}$., where c is known as *parameter* of the curve.

Type VII: Folium of Discartes - Trace the curve $x^3 + y^3 = 3axy$.

This curve is known as "Folium of Discartes"   **SUK : May-08,13; Dec-11**

Solution: The given equation of the curve is $x^3 + y^3 = 3axy$.

Symmetry: If the equation of the curve remains unaltered on replacing x by y and y by x then curve is symmetric about the line $y = x$	Given curve is symmetrical about the line $y = x$
Origin: If the equation of curve does not contain any constant term	Equation does not contain any absolute constant therefore, it passes through the origin.
Tangent at origin: Tangents at the origin are obtained by equating to zero the lowest degree terms in the equation.	As $x^3 + y^3 = 3axy$ $\therefore 3axy = 0 \Rightarrow x = 0, y = 0$ Hence $x = 0, y = 0$ are the two tangents at origin.
Intercepts: Intersection with X-axis: Put $y = 0$ Intersection with Y-axis: Put $x = 0$	Put $y = 0 \therefore x^3 + 0 = 0. \Rightarrow x^3 = 0 \therefore x = 0.$ Put $x = 0 \therefore 0 + y^3 = 0 \Rightarrow y^3 = 0 \quad y = 0.$ Also as curve is symmetric about the line $x^3 + y^3 - 3axy = 0 \Rightarrow x^3 + x^3 - 3axx = 0 \because y = x$ $y = x$ i.e. $2x^3 = 3ax^2 \therefore x = \dfrac{3a}{2}$ and $x^3 + y^3 - 3axy = 0 \Rightarrow y^3 + y^3 - 3ayy = 0 \because x = y$ i.e. $2y^3 = 3ay^2 \therefore y = \dfrac{3a}{2}$ Thus the curve meets at $(0,0)$ and $\left(\dfrac{3a}{2}, \dfrac{3a}{2}\right)$.
Asymptotes: Oblique asymptotes - Assume $y = mx + c$ as the equation of oblique asymptotes. To find the values of m and c substitute this value of y in the given equation $f(x, y) = 0$, equating to zero	As the coefficients of x and y are constant (i.e.1) moreover the curve is not symmetric about axies, therefore the curve has no asymptote parallel to x and y axis. Let us try for Oblique asymptotes.

two successive highest power of x, we can find the values of m and c.	$x^3 + y^3 = 3axy$ let $y = mx + c$ $x^3 + (mx+c)^3 = 3ax(mx+c)$ $x^3 + (m^3x^3 + 3m^2x^2c + 3mxc^2 + c^3) = 3max^2 + 3axc$ $(1+m^3)x^3 + (3m^2c - 3ma)x^2 + (3mc^2 - 3ac)x + c^3 = 0$ $1 + m^3 = 0 \Rightarrow m = -1$ and $3m^2c - 3ma = 0 \Rightarrow c = -a$ $\therefore y = -x - a$ i.e. $y + x = -a$ is the obligue asymptotes.
Region of absence of the curve: Find the value of x where y becomes imaginary, then curve does not exist in that region.	The curve exist for all values of x,y.

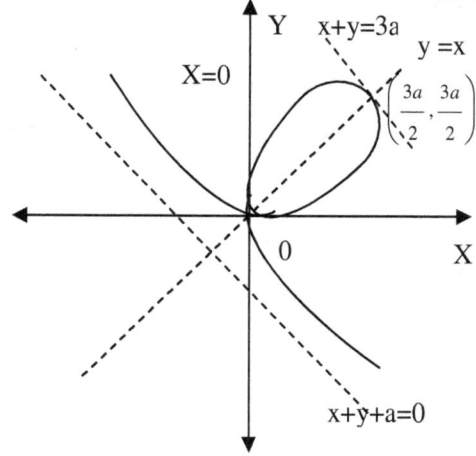

Examples on Curve tracing: Cartesion form

Ex. 1: Trace the curve with full justification $y^2(x-a) = x^2(2a-x)$.

Solution: The Given equation of the curve can be written as $y^2 = \dfrac{x^2(2a-x)}{(x-a)}$.

Symmetry: If only even power of y, then curve is symmetric about X-axis	The given equation of curve contain only even power of y. Therefore it is symmetrical about X-axis.
Intercepts: Intersection with X-axis: Put $y = 0$ Intersection with Y-axis: Put $x = 0$	Put $y = 0 \therefore 0 = x^2(2a-x)$. i.e. $x^2(2a-x) = 0$ $\Rightarrow x^2 = 0$ or $2a - x = 0 \Rightarrow x = 0,\ x = 2a$ Put $x = 0 \therefore y^2(0-a) = 0 \Rightarrow y = 0$ and $x = 2a \therefore y^2(2a-a) = 0 \Rightarrow y = 0$ Thus the curve meets the co-ordinate axes at $(0,0)$, $(2a,0)$.

Tangent at origin: can be found out by equating all lower degree term to zero	$y^2(x-a) = x^2(2a-x) \Rightarrow xy^2 - ay^2 = 2ax^2 - x^3$ $xy^2 - ay^2 - 2ax^2 + x^3 = 0$ $\therefore -ay^2 - 2ax^2 = 0 \Rightarrow 2x^2 = -y^2$. Hence no tangent at origin.
Tangent at any other point: find $\dfrac{dy}{dx}$ at the point	$\left(\dfrac{dy}{dx}\right)_{(2a,0)} = \infty \Rightarrow$ tangent at $(2a,0)$ is parallel to Y-axis
Asymptotes: Asymptotes parallel to x-axis (y-axis) is obtained by equating the coefficients of higher degree term in x (y) to zero.	As the coefficients of x is constant (i.e. 1) therefore the curve has no asymptote parallel to x-axis. And as $xy^2 - ay^2 - 2ax^2 + x^3 = 0 \Rightarrow (x-a)y^2 - 2ax^2 + x^3 = 0$ $\therefore x - a = 0 \Rightarrow x = a$ is the asymptotes parallel to Y-axis.
Region of absence of the curve: Find the value of x where y becomes imaginary, then curve does not exist in that region.	Given curve is $y^2 = \dfrac{x^2(2a-x)}{(x-a)}$. At $x = -a$ $y^2 = -ve$ At $x = a/2$ $y^2 = -ve$ At $x = 3a$ $y^2 = -ve$ At $x = 3a/2$ $y^2 = +ve$ Thus the curve exist for $0 < x < 2a$.
Nature of double point: if the coordinates of P satisfies the equation of the curve, but no branch pass through the point P.	$x = 0, y = 0$ is the point on the curve but no branch passes through from $(0,0)$ hence $(0,0)$ is a isolated point

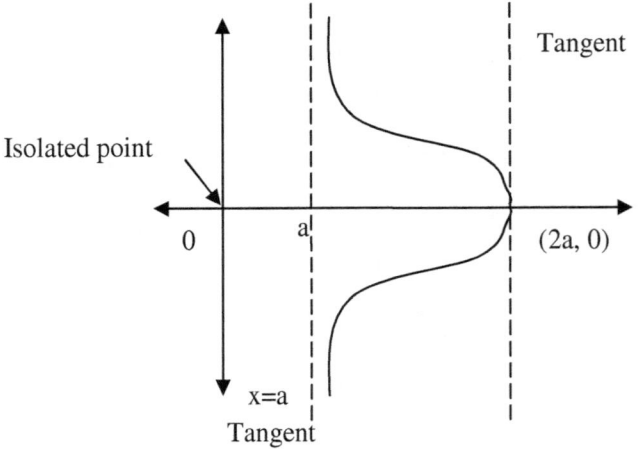

Ex. 2: Trace the curve with full justification $x=(y-1)(y-2)(y-3)$.

Solution: The given equation of the curve is $x=(y-1)(y-2)(y-3)$.

Symmetry:	No symmetry at all
Origin: If the equation of curve does not contain any constant	Equation contain constant therefore, it does not passes through the origin.
Intercepts: Intersection with X-axis: Put $y=0$. Intersection with Y-axis: Put $x=0$	Put $y=0 \therefore x=(0-1)(0-2)(0-3) \Rightarrow x=-6$ Put $x=0 \therefore 0=(y-1)(y-2)(y-3) \Rightarrow y=1,2,3$ Thus the curve meets at $(-6,0),(0,1),(0,2),(0,3)$.
Tangent at any other point: find $\dfrac{dy}{dx}$ at the point	$x=y^3-6y^2+11y-6$ $\left(\dfrac{dy}{dx}\right)_{(-6,0)}=+ve, \left(\dfrac{dy}{dx}\right)_{(0,1)}=+ve$ $\left(\dfrac{dy}{dx}\right)_{(0,2)}=-ve, \left(\dfrac{dy}{dx}\right)_{(0,3)}=+ve$ $\Rightarrow$ tangent makes acute angle with X axis at $(-6,0),(0,1),(0,3)$ and obtuse angle at $(0,2)$.
Asymptotes: Asymptotes parallel to x-axis (y-axis) is obtained by equating the coefficients of higher degree term in x (y) to zero.	As the coefficients of x and y are constant therefore the curve has no asymptote parallel to X and Y axis.
Region of absence of the curve: Find the value of x where y becomes imaginary, then curve does not exist in that region.	The odd power of x and y implies that the curve exist for all values of x and y.

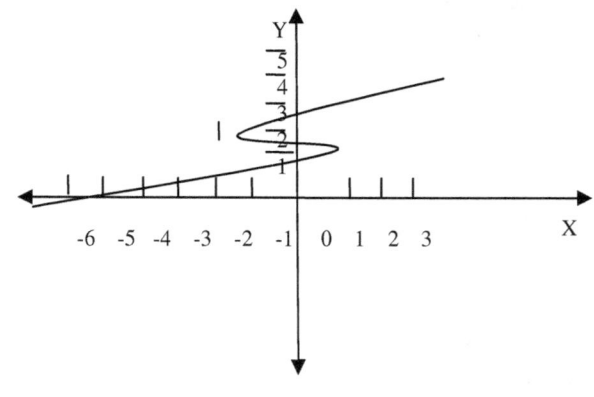

(5.15)

Ex. 3: Trace the curve with full justification $ay^2 = x^2(a-x)$ **SUK: Nov-10**

Solution: The Given equation of the curve can be written as $y^2 = \dfrac{x^2(a-x)}{a}$.

Symmetry: If only even power of y, then curve is symmetric about X-axis	The given equation of curve contain only even power of y. Therefore it is symmetrical about X-axis.
Origin: If the equation of curve does not contain any constant	Equation does not contain any absolute constant therefore, it passes through the origin.
Tangent at origin: Tangents at the origin are obtained by equating to zero the lowest degree terms in the equation.	As $ay^2 = x^2(a-x) \Rightarrow ay^2 - ax^2 + x^3 = 0$ $\therefore ay^2 - ax^2 = 0 \Rightarrow y = \pm x$ are the tangent at origin.
Nature of double point: If at a double point, two tangents are real and different	Origin is a node
Intercepts: Intersection with X-axis: Put $y=0$ Intersection with Y-axis: Put $x=0$	Put $y=0 \therefore 0 = \dfrac{x^2(a-x)}{a}$. i.e. $x^2(a-x) = 0 \Rightarrow x=0$ or $x=a$. Put $x=0 \therefore y^2 = 0$. i.e. $y^2 = 0 \Rightarrow y=0$ and $x=a \therefore y^2 = \dfrac{x^2(a-a)}{a} \Rightarrow y=0$ Thus the curve meets the co-ordinate axes at $(0,0)$ and $(a,0)$
Asymptotes: Asymptotes parallel to x-axis (y-axis) is obtained by equating the coefficients of higher degree term in x (y) to zero.	As the coefficients of x^3 and y^2 is constant therefore the curve has no asymptote parallel to X and Y axis.
Region of absence of the curve: Find the value of x where y becomes imaginary, then curve does not exist in that region.	Given curve is $ay^2 = x^2(a-x)$ At $x = -a/2$, $y^2 = +ve$ At $x = a/2$, $y^2 = +ve$ At $x = 3a$, $y^2 = -ve$ Therefore the curve exist for $x < a$

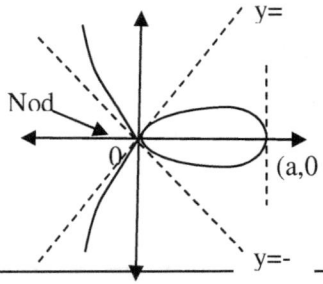

Ex. 4: Trace the curve with full justification $x^2y^2 = a^2(y^2 - x^2)$

OR Trace the curve with full justification $y^2 = \dfrac{a^2x^2}{a^2 - x^2}$.

Solution: The given equation of the curve is $x^2y^2 = a^2(y^2 - x^2)$

Symmetry: The given equation of curve contain only even power of x and y. Therefore it is symmetrical about both axis.	The curve is symmetrical about both axis.
Origin: If the equation of curve does not contain any constant	Equation does not contain any absolute constant therefore, it passes through the origin.
Tangent at origin: Tangents at the origin are obtained by equating to zero the lowest degree terms in the equation.	As $x^2y^2 = a^2(y^2 - x^2) \Rightarrow x^2y^2 - a^2y^2 + a^2x^2 = 0$ $\therefore -a^2y^2 + a^2x^2 = 0 \Rightarrow y^2 = x^2 \; y = \pm x$ are the tangent at origin.
Intercepts: Intersection with X-axis: Put $y = 0$ Intersection with Y-axis: Put $x = 0$	Put $y = 0 \therefore 0 = a^2(0 - x^2)$, i.e. $x^2 a^2 = 0 \Rightarrow x = 0$. Put $x = 0 \therefore 0 = a^2(y^2 - 0)$. i.e. $a^2 y^2 = 0 \Rightarrow y = 0$ Thus the curve meets the co-ordinate axes at $(0, 0)$
Asymptotes: Asymptotes parallel to x-axis (y-axis) is obtained by equating the coefficients of higher degree term in x (y) to zero.	As the coefficient of x^2 is $y^2 + a^2 = 0 \Rightarrow y = \pm ai$ which is not real, therefore the curve has no asymptote parallel to x-axis. And $x^2y^2 - a^2y^2 + a^2x^2 = 0 \Rightarrow (x^2 - a^2)y^2 + a^2x^2 = 0$ $\therefore x^2 - a^2 \Rightarrow x = \pm a$ are the asymptotes parallel to y-axis.
Region of absence of the curve: Find the value of x where y becomes imaginary, then curve does not exist in that region.	Given curve is $y^2 = \dfrac{a^2x^2}{a^2 - x^2}$. At $x = -2a$, $y^2 = -ve$ At $x = 3a$, $y^2 = -ve$ $\Rightarrow$ curve does not exist for $x < -a$ and $x > a$.

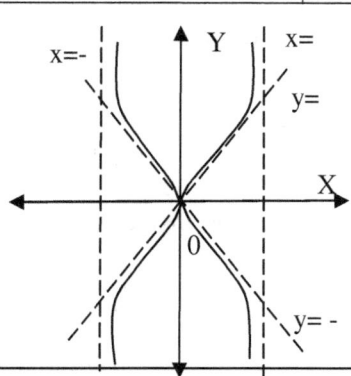

Ex. 5: Trace the curve with full justification $x^2(x^2 - 4a^2) = y^2(x^2 - a^2)$

Solution: The Given equation of the curve can be written as $y^2 = \dfrac{x^2(x^2 - 4a^2)}{(x^2 - a^2)}$.

Symmetry: The given equation of curve contain only even power of x and y. Therefore it is symmetrical about both axis.	The curve is symmetrical about both axis.
Intercepts: Intersection with X-axis: Put $y = 0$ Intersection with Y-axis: Put $x = 0$	Put $y = 0 \therefore x^2(x^2 - 4a^2) = 0$. i.e. $x^2 = 0$ or $x^2 - 4a^2 = 0 \Rightarrow x = 0, 2a, -2a$. Put $x = 0 \therefore 0 = y^2(0 - a^2)$. i.e. $a^2y^2 = 0 \Rightarrow y = 0$ Put $x = 2a \therefore 0 = y^2(4a^2 - a^2)$. i.e. $3a^2y^2 = 0 \Rightarrow y = 0$ Put $x = -2a \therefore 0 = y^2(4a^2 - a^2)$. i.e. $3a^2y^2 = 0 \Rightarrow y = 0$ Thus the curve meets the co-ordinate axes at $(0,0), (2a, 0), (-2a, 0)$
Origin: If the equation of curve does not contain any constant term	Equation does not contain any absolute constant therefore, it passes through the origin.
Tangent at origin: Tangents at the origin are obtained by equating to zero the lowest degree terms in the equation.	As $x^2(x^2 - 4a^2) = y^2(x^2 - a^2) \Rightarrow x^4 - 4a^2x^2 - x^2y^2 + y^2a^2 = 0$ $\therefore -4a^2x^2 + y^2a^2 = 0 \Rightarrow y^2a^2 = 4a^2x^2 \therefore y = \pm 2x$ are the tangent at origin.
Tangent at any other point: find $\dfrac{dy}{dx}$ at the point	$\left(\dfrac{dy}{dx}\right)_{(2a, 0)} = \infty$ and $\left(\dfrac{dy}{dx}\right)_{(-2a, 0)} = \infty$ $\Rightarrow$ tangent at $(2a, 0), (-2a, 0)$ are parallel to y-axis
Asymptotes: Asymptotes parallel to x-axis (y-axis) is obtained by equating the coefficients of higher degree term in x (y) to zero.	As the coefficients of x^4 is constant, therefore the curve has no asymptote parallel to X-axis. And $x^4 - 4a^2x^2 - x^2y^2 + y^2a^2 = 0$ $\Rightarrow x^4 - 4a^2x^2 + (a^2 - x^2)y^2 = 0$ $a^2 - x^2 = 0 \Rightarrow x = \pm a$ $\therefore x^2 - a^2 \Rightarrow x = \pm a$ are the asymptotes parallel to y-axis.

Region of absence of the curve: Find the value of x where y becomes imaginary, then curve does not exist in that region.	Given curve is $y^2 = \dfrac{x^2(x^2-4a^2)}{(x^2-a^2)}$. At $x=a/2$, $y^2 = +ve$ At $x=3a/2$, $y^2 = -ve$ At $x=3a$, $y^2 = +ve$ $\Rightarrow$ curve exist for $a < x < -a$ and $x > 2a, x > -2a$.

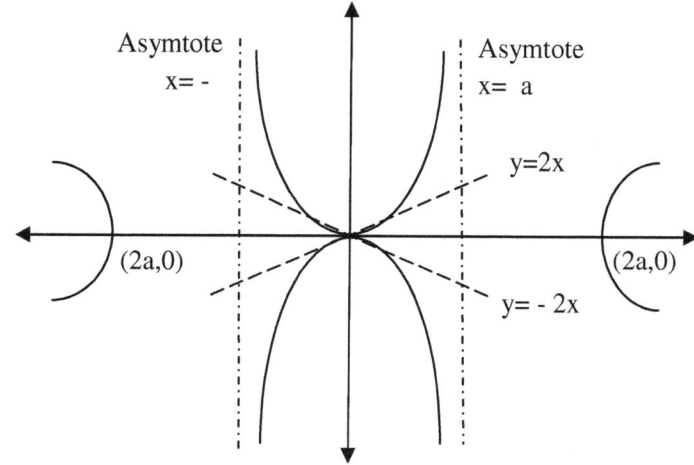

Ex. 6: Trace the curve with full justification $y^2(a^2+x^2) = a^2x^2$

Solution: The Given equation of the curve can be written as $y^2 = \dfrac{a^2x^2}{(a^2+x^2)}$.

Symmetry: The given equation of curve contain only even power of x and y. Therefore it is symmetrical about both axis.	The curve is symmetrical about both axis.
Intercepts: Intersection with X-axis: Put $y=0$ Intersection with Y-axis: Put $x=0$	Put $y=0 \therefore 0 = a^2x^2 \Rightarrow x=0$ Put $x=0 \therefore y^2(a^2+0) = 0$ i.e. $a^2y^2 = 0 \Rightarrow y=0$ Thus the curve meets the co-ordinate axes at $(0,0)$
Origin: If the equation of curve does not contain any constant term	Equation does not contain any absolute constant therefore, it passes through the origin.
Tangent at origin: Tangents at the origin are obtained by equating to zero the lowest degree terms in the equation.	As $y^2(a^2+x^2) = a^2x^2 \Rightarrow a^2y^2 + x^2y^2 - a^2x^2 = 0$ $\therefore a^2y^2 - a^2x^2 = 0 \Rightarrow y = \pm x$ are the tangent at origin.

Asymptotes: Asymptotes parallel to x-axis (y-axis) is obtained by equating the coefficients of higher degree term in x (y) to zero.	$a^2y^2 + x^2y^2 - a^2x^2 = 0 \Rightarrow a^2y^2 + (y^2 - a^2)x^2 = 0$ $\therefore y^2 - a^2 = 0 \Rightarrow y = \pm a$ are the asymptotes parallel to x axis. And $a^2y^2 + x^2y^2 - a^2x^2 = 0 \Rightarrow (a^2 + x^2)y^2 - a^2x^2 = 0$ $\therefore a^2 + x^2 = 0 \Rightarrow x^2 = -a^2 \therefore x = \pm ai$ which is not real. So there is no asymptotes parallel to y-axis.
Region of absence of the curve: Find the value of x where y becomes imaginary, then curve does not exist in that region.	Given curve is $x^2 = \dfrac{a^2y^2}{(a^2 - y^2)}$. At $y = -2a$, $x^2 = -ve$ At $y = 3a$, $x^2 = -ve$ $\Rightarrow$ curve exist for $-a < y < a$.

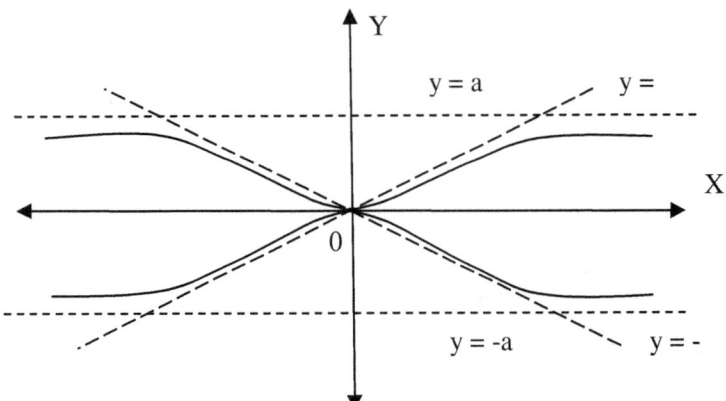

Ex. 7: Trace the curve with full justification $y = \dfrac{x}{(1+x^2)}$ or $y(1+x^2) = x$. **SUK: Dec-13**

Solution: The given equation of the curve is $y = \dfrac{x}{(1+x^2)}$.

Symmetry: Symmetry about the origin -If the equation of the curve remains unaltered on replacing x by $-x$ and y by $-y$	The curve is symmetrical about origin (opposite quadrants).
Intercepts: Intersection with X-axis: Put $y = 0$ Intersection with Y-axis: Put $x = 0$	Put $y = 0 \therefore 0 = x \Rightarrow x = 0$ Put $x = 0 \therefore y(1+0) = 0 \Rightarrow y = 0$ Thus the curve meets the co-ordinate axes at $(0, 0)$

Origin: If the equation of curve does not contain any constant term	Equation does not contain any absolute constant therefore, it passes through the origin.
Tangent at origin: Tangents at the origin are obtained by equating to zero the lowest degree terms in the equation.	As $y(1+x^2) = x \Rightarrow y + yx^2 - x = 0$ $y - x = 0 \Rightarrow y = x$ is the tangent at origin.
Asymptotes: Asymptotes parallel to x-axis (y-axis) is obtained by equating the coefficients of higher degree term in x (y) to zero.	$y(1+x^2) = x \Rightarrow y + yx^2 - x = 0$ $\therefore y = 0$ is the asymptotes parallel to x axis. And $y(1+x^2) = x \Rightarrow y(1+x^2) - x = 0$ $1 + x^2 = 0 \Rightarrow x^2 = -1$ which is imaginary. So there is no asymptotes parallel to y-axis.
Region of absence of the curve: Find the value of x where y becomes imaginary, then curve does not exist in that region.	Given curve is $y = \dfrac{x}{(1+x^2)}$. The curve exist for all x.

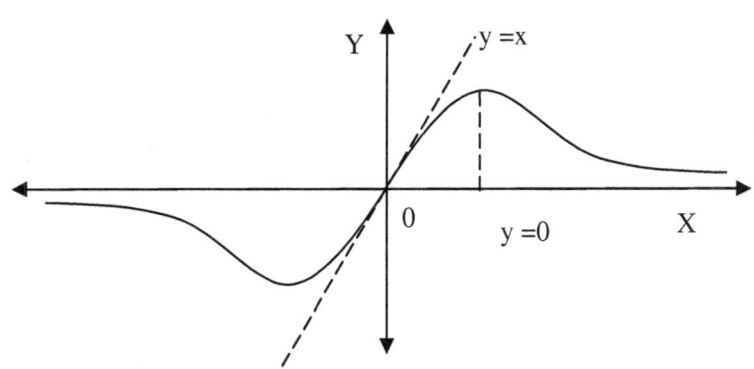

Ex. 8: Trace the curve with full justification $y(x^2 + 4a^2) = 8a^3$.

Solution:

Symmetry: Symmetry about y- axis- If only even powers of x occur	Power of x is even therefore curve is symmetry about y- axis
Intercepts: Intersection with X-axis: Put $y = 0$ Intersection with Y-axis: Put $x = 0$	Put $y = 0 \therefore 0 = 8a^3 \Rightarrow a = 0$ but $a \neq 0$ Put $x = 0 \therefore y(0 + 4a^2) = 8a^3 \Rightarrow 4a^2 y = 8a^3 \therefore y = 2a$ Thus the curve meets the co-ordinate axes at $(0, 2a)$
Origin: If the equation of curve does not contain any constant term	Equation contain constant therefore, it does not passes through the origin.

Tangent at any other point: find $\frac{dy}{dx}$ at the point	$y = \frac{8a^3}{(x^2 + 4a^2)}$ $\therefore \frac{dy}{dx} = \frac{(x^2 + 4a^2).0 - 8a^3(2x)}{(x^2 + 4a^2)^2} = \frac{-16xa^3}{(x^2 + 4a^2)^2}$ $\left(\frac{dy}{dx}\right)_{(0,2a)} = 0 \Rightarrow$ tangent at $(0, 2a)$ is parallel to X-axis
Asymptotes: Asymptotes parallel to x-axis (y-axis) is obtained by equating the coefficients of higher degree term in x (y) to zero.	$yx^2 + 4a^2 y - 8a^3 = 0$ $\therefore y = 0$ is the asymptotes parallel to X- axis. And $yx^2 + 4a^2 y - 8a^3 = 0 \Rightarrow (x^2 + 4a^2)y - 8a^3 = 0$ $x^2 + 4a^2 = 0 \Rightarrow x = \pm 2ai$ which is imaginary. So there is no asymptotes parallel to y-axis.
Region of absence of the curve: Find the value of x where y becomes imaginary, then curve does not exist in that region.	Given curve is $(x^2 + 4a^2) = \frac{8a^3}{y} \Rightarrow x^2 = \frac{8a^3}{y} - 4a^2$ At $y = -2a,\ x^2 = -ve$ At $y = 3a,\ x^2 = -ve$ The curve exist for $0 < y < 2a$. The curve also exist for all values of x.

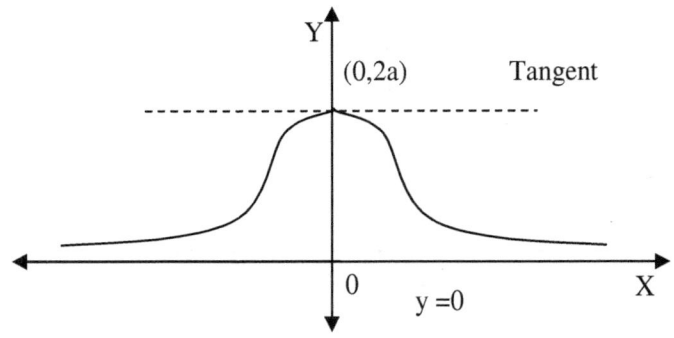

Ex. 9: Trace the curve with full justification $y^2(a^2 - x^2) = a^3 x$ SUK:May-08,11,NOV-08

Solution:

Symmetry: Symmetry about x- axis- If only even powers of y occur	Power of y is even therefore curve is symmetry about X- axis
Intercepts: Intersection with X-axis: Put $y = 0$ Intersection with Y-axis: Put $x = 0$	Put $y = 0 \therefore 0 = a^3 x \Rightarrow x = 0,\ \because a \neq 0$ Put $x = 0 \therefore y^2(a^2 - 0) = 0 \Rightarrow a^2 y^2 = 0 \therefore y = 0$ Thus the curve meets the co-ordinate axes at $(0,0)$

Origin: If the equation of curve does not contain any constant term	Equation does not contain any constant therefore, it passes through the origin.
Tangent at origin: Tangents at the origin are obtained by equating to zero the lowest degree terms in the equation.	As $y^2(a^2 - x^2) = a^3 x \Rightarrow a^2 y^2 - x^2 y^2 - a^3 x = 0$ $a^3 x = 0 \Rightarrow x = 0$ is the tangent at origin.
Asymptotes: Asymptotes parallel to x-axis (y-axis) is obtained by equating the coefficients of higher degree term in x (y) to zero.	$y^2(a^2 - x^2) = a^3 x \Rightarrow a^2 y^2 - x^2 y^2 - a^3 x = 0$ $\therefore y^2 = 0 \Rightarrow y = 0$ is the asymptotes parallel to x axis. And $y^2(a^2 - x^2) = a^3 x \Rightarrow (a^2 - x^2) y^2 - a^3 x = 0$ $a^2 - x^2 = 0 \Rightarrow x = \pm a$ are the symptotes parallel to y-axis.
Region of absence of the curve: Find the value of x where y becomes imaginary, then curve does not exist in that region.	Given curve is $y^2 = \dfrac{a^3 x}{(a^2 - x^2)}$. At $x = -2a$, $y^2 = +ve$ At $x = -a/2$, $y^2 = -ve$ At $x = a/2$, $y^2 = +ve$ At $x = 2a$, $y^2 = -ve$ The curve exist for $0 < x < a$ and $x < -a$.
Nature of double point: if the coordinates of P satisfies the equation of the curve, but no branch pass through the point P.	$x = 0$ is the point on the curve but no branch passes through from $(0, 0)$, hence $(0, 0)$ is a isolated point

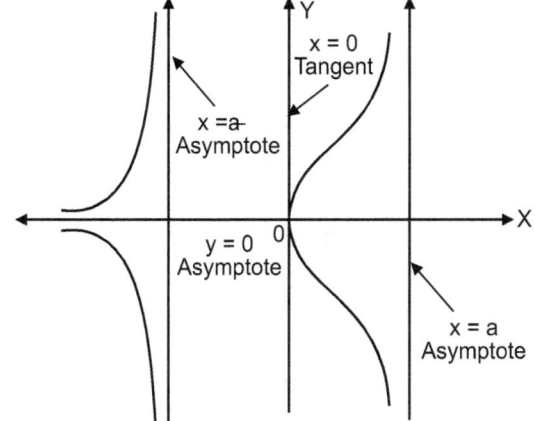

Ex. 10: Trace the curve with full justification $y^2(x^2 + a^2) = x^2(a^2 - x^2)$ **SUK: Aug-13**

Or Trace the curve with full justification $x^2(x^2 + y^2) = a^2(x^2 - y^2)$

Solution: The Given equation of the curve can be written as $y^2 = \dfrac{x^2(a^2 - x^2)}{(x^2 + a^2)}$

Symmetry: Symmetry about both x-axis and y- axis-If all the power of both x and y are even	The curve is symmetrical about both axis.
Intercepts: Intersection with X-axis: Put $y=0$ Intersection with Y-axis: Put $x=0$	Put $y=0 \therefore 0 = x^2(a^2 - x^2) \Rightarrow x^2 = 0$ or $a^2 - x^2 = 0$ $\therefore x = 0, a, -a$ Put $x = 0 \therefore y^2(0 + a^2) = 0$ i.e. $a^2 y^2 = 0 \Rightarrow y = 0$ Put $x = a \therefore y^2(a^2 + a^2) = 0$ i.e. $2a^2 y^2 = 0 \Rightarrow y = 0$ Put $x = -a \therefore y^2(a^2 + a^2) = 0$ i.e. $2a^2 y^2 = 0 \Rightarrow y = 0$ Thus curve meets the co-ordinate axes at $(0,0), (-a, 0), (a, 0)$
Origin: If the equation of curve does not contain any constant term	Equation does not contain any absolute constant therefore, it passes through the origin.
Tangent at origin: Tangents at the origin are obtained by equating to zero the lowest degree terms in the equation.	As $x^2 y^2 + a^2 y^2 - a^2 x^2 + x^4 = 0$ $\therefore a^2 y^2 - a^2 x^2 \Rightarrow y = \pm x$ are the tangent at origin.
Nature of double point: If at a double point, two tangents are real and different	Origin is a node
Asymptotes: Asymptotes parallel to x-axis (y-axis) is obtained by equating the coefficients of higher degree term in x (y) to zero.	As the coefficients of x^4 is constant therefore the curve has no asymptote parallel to X axis. and $x^2 + a^2 = 0 \Rightarrow x = \pm ai$ which is not real therefore the curve has no asymptote parallel to Y axis.
Region of absence of the curve: Find the value of x where y becomes imaginary, then curve does not exist in that region.	Given curve is $y^2 = \dfrac{x^2(a^2 - x^2)}{(x^2 + a^2)}$ At $x < -a$, $y^2 = -ve$ At $x > a$, $y^2 = -ve$ $\Rightarrow$ curve exist for $-a < x < a$.
Special point:	Since the curve passes through the origin and no branch of the curve exist to the right $x = a$ and left of $x = -a$, there fore there exist a loop between $(0, 0)$ and $(a, 0)$, $(0, 0)$ and $(-a, 0)$.

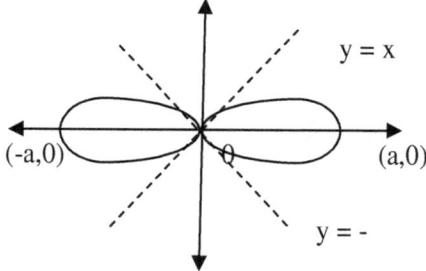

Ex. 11: Trace the curve with full justification $a^2 y^2 = x^2 (2a-x)(x-a)$

Solution:

Symmetry: Symmetry about x-axis- If only even powers of y occur	The curve is symmetrical about X-axis.
Intercepts: Intersection with X-axis: Put $y=0$ Intersection with Y-axis: Put $x=0$	Put $y=0 \therefore 0 = x^2(2a-x)(x-a)$ $\Rightarrow x^2 = 0$ or $2a-x=0$ or $x-a \therefore x = 0, 2a, a$ Put $x=0 \therefore a^2 y^2 = 0$ i.e. $a^2 y^2 = 0 \Rightarrow y = 0$ Thus curve meets co-ordinate axes at $(0,0),(a,0),(2a,0)$
Asymptotes: Asymptotes parallel to x-axis (y-axis) are obtained by equating the coefficients of higher degree term in x (y) to zero.	As the coefficients of higher power of x and y are constant therefore the curve has no asymptote parallel to x and y axis.
Region of absence of the curve: Find the value of x where y becomes imaginary, then curve does not exist in that region.	Given curve is $y^2 = \dfrac{x^2(2a-x)(x-a)}{a^2}$ At $x < 0$, $y^2 = -ve$ At $x > 2a$, $y^2 = -ve$ $\Rightarrow$ curve exist for $a < x < 2a$ and curve does not exist for $0 < x < a$.
Special point:	Since the curve passes through the origin and no branch of the curve exist to the right $x = 2a$ and left of $x = a$, there fore there exist a loop between $(a,0)$ and $(2a,0)$.
Nature of double point: If the coordinates of P satisfies the equation of the curve, but no branch pass through the point P.	$x=0, y=0$ is the point on the curve but no branch passes through from $(0,0)$, hence $(0,0)$ is a isolated point

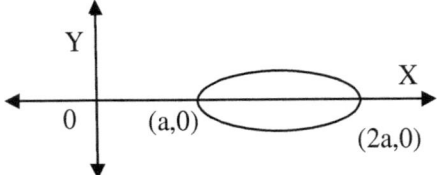

Ex. 12: Trace the curve with full justification $a^2x^2 = y^3(2a-y)$

Solution: The given equation of the curve is $a^2x^2 = y^3(2a-y)$

Symmetry: Symmetry about y-axis- If only even powers of x occur	The curve is symmetrical about Y-axis.
Intercepts: Intersection with X-axis: Put $y=0$ Intersection with Y-axis: Put $x=0$	Put $y=0 \therefore a^2x^2 = 0$ $\Rightarrow x^2 = 0$ or $a^2 = 0 \therefore x=0, a \neq 0$ Put $x=0 \therefore 0 = y^3(2a-y)$ i.e. $y^3 = 0$ or $2a-y=0 \Rightarrow y=0, 2a$ Thus the curve meets the co-ordinate axes at $(0,0), (0,2a)$
Origin: If the equation of curve does not contain any constant term	Equation does not contain any absolute constant therefore, it passes through the origin.
Tangent at origin: Tangents at the origin are obtained by equating to zero the lowest degree terms in the equation.	As $a^2x^2 - 2ay^3 + y^4 = 0$ $\therefore a^2x^2 = 0 \Rightarrow x=0,0;$ i.e. $x=0$ is the tangent at origin.
Tangent at any other point: find $\dfrac{dy}{dx}$ at the point	$a^2x^2 = y^3(2a-y)$ $2a^2x\dfrac{dx}{dy} = 6ay^2 - 4y^3$ $\Rightarrow \dfrac{dx}{dy} = \dfrac{6ay^2 - 4y^3}{2a^2x}; \dfrac{dx}{dy} = \dfrac{y^2(3a-2y)}{a^2x}$ $\left(\dfrac{dx}{dy}\right)_{(0,2a)} = -\infty$ Therefore tangent at $(0,2a)$ is parallel to X-axis.
Nature of double point: If at a double point, two tangents are real and coincident	Origin is a cusp
Asymptotes: Asymptotes parallel to x-axis (y-axis) is obtained by equating the coefficients of higher degree term in x (y) to zero.	As the coefficients of x^2 and y^4 are constant therefore the curve has no asymptote parallel to x and y axis.

Region of absence of the curve: Find the value of x where y becomes imaginary, then curve does not exist in that region.	Given curve is $x^2 = \dfrac{y^3(2a-y)}{a^2}$ When $y = a$, $x = \pm a$ for $y < 0$, $y > 2a$ x^2 becomes negative. Therefore the curve does not exist for $y > 2a$ and $y < 0$.
Special point:	Since the curve passes through the origin and no branch of the curve exist above $y = 2a$ and below $y = 0$, there fore there exist a loop between $(0,0)$ and $(0, 2a)$

(Figure: loop between origin and $(0, 2a)$ with $y = 2a$ tangent)

Ex. 13: Trace the curve $y^2(a+x) = x^2(3a-x)$ This curve is also known as "strophoid".

Solution: Given equation of the curve can be written as   SUK: Nov-12, May-10

Symmetry: Symmetry about X-axis- If only even powers of y occur	The given equation of curve contain only even power of y. Therefore it is symmetrical about X-axis.
Origin: If the equation of curve does not contain any constant	Equation does not contain any absolute constant therefore, it passes through the origin.
Tangent at origin: Tangents at the origin are obtained by equating to zero the lowest degree terms in the equation.	As $y^2(a+x) = x^2(3a-x) \Rightarrow ay^2 + xy^2 - 3ax^2 + x^3$ $\therefore ay^2 - 3ax^2 = 0 \Rightarrow y^2 = 3x^2$, $y = \pm\sqrt{3}x$ are the tangent at origin.
Nature of double point: If at a double point, two tangents are real and different	Origin is a node
Intercepts: Intersection with X-axis: Put $y = 0$ Intersection with Y-axis: Put $x = 0$	Put $y = 0 \therefore 0 = \dfrac{x^2(3a-x)}{(a+x)}$. i.e. $x^2(3a-x) = 0 \Rightarrow x = 0$ or $x = 3a$. Put $x = 0 \therefore y^2 = 0$. i.e. $y^2 = 0 \Rightarrow y = 0$ Put $x = 3a \therefore y^2 = 0$. i.e. $y^2 = 0 \Rightarrow y = 0$ Thus the curve meets the co-ordinate axes at $(0,0)$ and $(3a, 0)$

Asymptotes: Asymptotes parallel to x-axis (y-axis) is obtained by equating the coefficients of higher degree term in x (y) to zero.	As the coefficients of x^3 is constant (i.e.1) therefore the curve has no asymptote parallel to x-axis. And as $(a+x)y^2 - 3ax^2 + x^3 = 0$ $\therefore a+x=0 \Rightarrow x=-a$ is the asymptotes parallel to y-axis.
Region of absence of the curve: Find the value of x where y becomes imaginary, then curve does not exist in that region.	Given curve is $y^2 = \dfrac{x^2(3a-x)}{(a+x)}$ At $x<-a$ and $x>a$, y becomes imaginary Therefore the curve does not exist for $x<-a$ and $x>a$

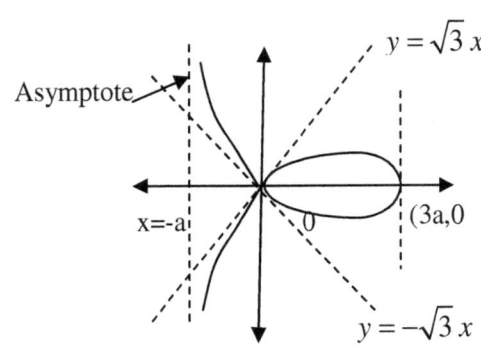

TEST YOUR KNOWLEDGE

Trace the following curves:

1. $y = x^3$
2. $y = x(x^2 - 1)$
3. $y^2(x-a) = x^2(2a-x)$
4. $27ay^2 = 4(x-2a)^3$
5. $ay^2 = x^2(a-x)$
6. $3ay^2 = x(x-a)^2$
7. $ay^2 = x(a^2 + x^2)$
8. $xy^2 = a(x^2 - a^2)$
9. $y^2(a+x) = (x-a)^3$
10. $a^2y^2 = x^2(a^2 - x^2)$
11. $a^2y^2 = x^2(x+2a)(x-a)$
12. $a^2y^2 = x^2(a-x)(x-b), b<a$
13. $y^2 = (x-1)(x-2)(x-3)$
14. $y^2(x^2 - 1) = x$
15. $y(x^2 - 1) = x^2 + 1$
16. $(x^2 - a^2)(y^2 - b^2) = a^2b^2$
17. $x^2y^2 = x^2 + 1$
18. $ay^2 = x(a^2 - x^2)$
19. $ay^2 = (x-a)(x-5a)^2$
20. $y^2 = x^5(2a-x)$
21. $y^2(x^2 + y^2) + a^2(x^2 - y^2) = 0$
22. $y^2(4-x) = x(x-2)^2$
23. $y^2(a-x) = x^3$.

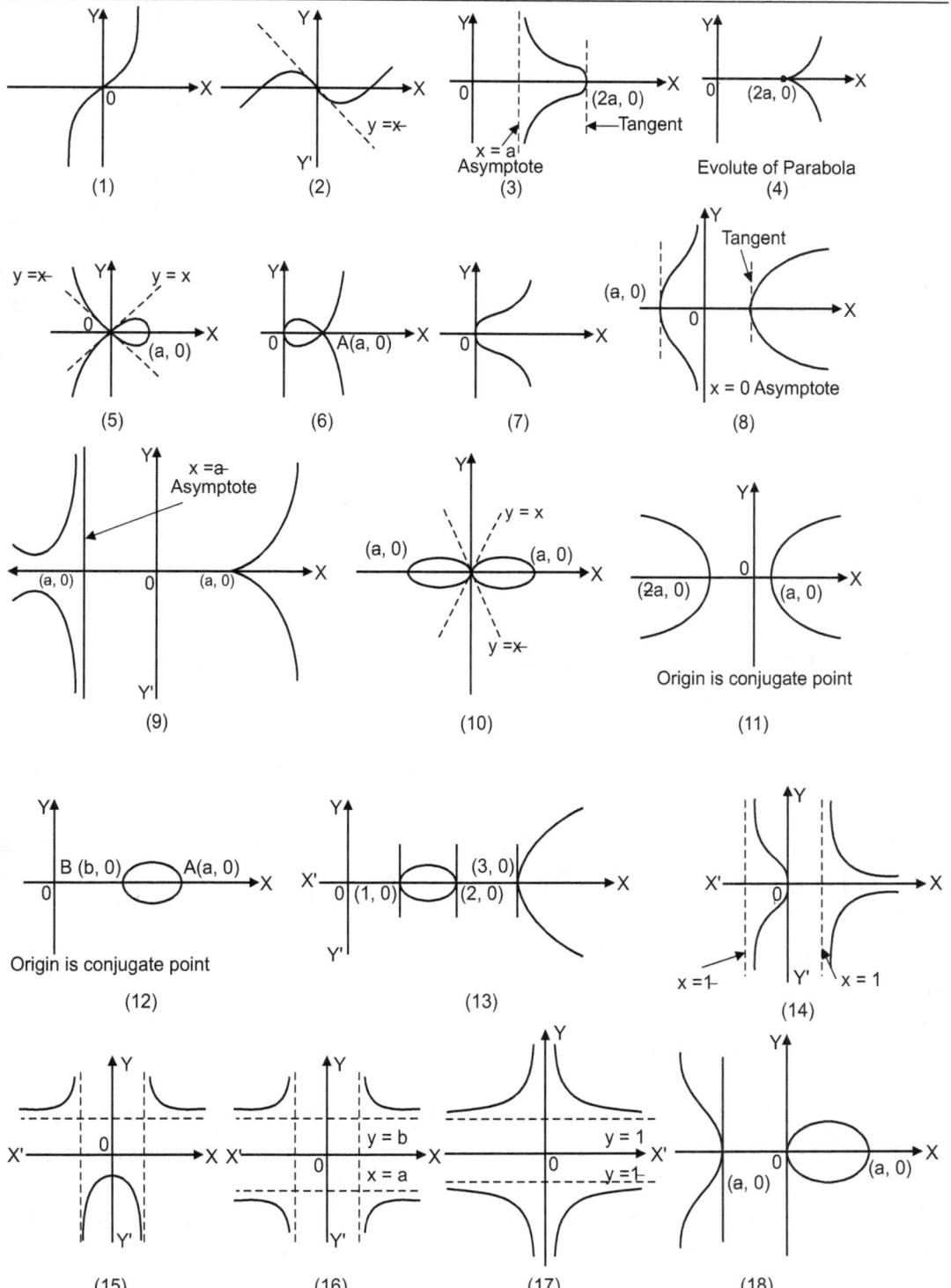

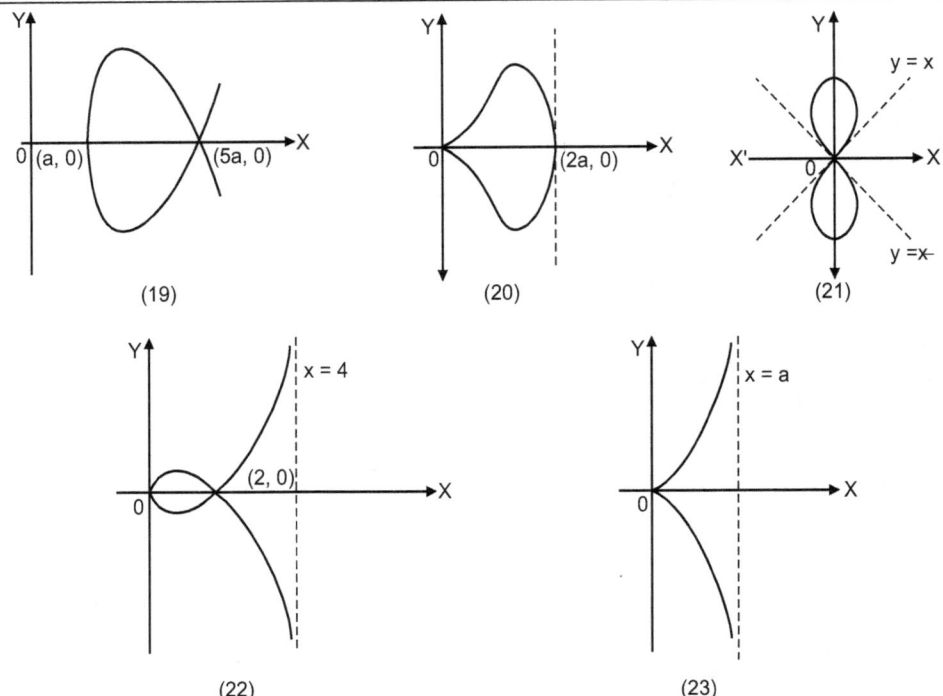

(19)　(20)　(21)

(22)　(23)

Polar Curve : We know the relation between Cartesian coordinates and Polar coordinates $x = r\cos\theta$, $y = r\sin\theta$ where $r^2 = x^2 + y^2$ and $\theta = \tan^{-1}\left(\dfrac{y}{x}\right)$.

Without loss of generality r represent the equation of circle with centre at origin, and θ (Constant) represent a family of straight lines passing through origin.

The general equation of a curve in polar coordinates (r,θ) in the explicit form is $r = f(\theta)$ or $\theta = f(r)$ and in the implicit form is $f(r,\theta) = 0$.

In polar system, the fixed point 'O' is called pole or origin. From fixed point O (pole), draw a straight line in any direction, say OX

(X-axis), then this fixed straight line OX is called as initial line.

Let P be any given point. We note that the distance OP = r is called radius vector.

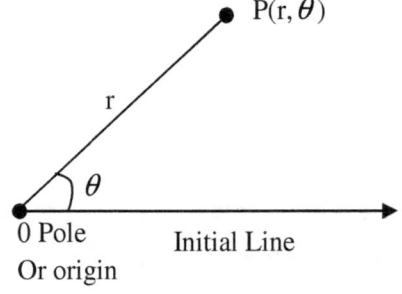

OP makes an angle θ with the initial line and is called vectorial angle measured positive in anticlockwise sense $\therefore \angle XOP = \theta$.　　OP = radius vector, any point is $P(r,\theta)$.

Co-ordinates of P in polar co-ordinates are (r,θ) and $r = f(\theta)$ is referred as polar equation of the curve. The initial line OX represents $\theta = 0$. We draw $\theta = \dfrac{\pi}{2}$ as a line perpendicular to initial line and passing through the pole.

Remark: The angle θ is the measure of rotation of a line starting from OX, the measure is positive or negative depending on whether the rotation is anticlockwise or clockwise. Guidelines for tracing a curve in polar coordinates are given below.

Rules for tracing of Polar Curve:

The equation of polar curve is often given by $r = f(\theta)$.

Rule I: Symmetry

(A) The curve is symmetric about initial line $\theta = 0$, if the equation remains unchanged when θ is replaced by $-\theta$ i.e. $f(r, -\theta) = f(r, \theta)$.

Ex.: $r = 2a\cos\theta$ i.e. $x^2 + y^2 = 2ax$ $\qquad\qquad r = a(1 + \cos\theta)$

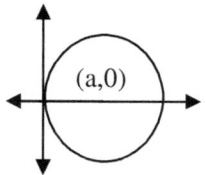
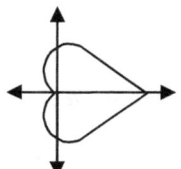

(B) The curve is symmetric about initial line $\theta = \dfrac{\pi}{2}$ (Usually positive Y-axis in cartesian coordinates) if the equation remains unchanged when θ is replaced by $(\pi - \theta)$ i.e. $f(r, \theta) = f(r, \pi - \theta)$. then curve is symmetric about Y-axis.

Ex.: $r = a(1 + \sin\theta)$

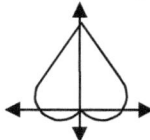

(C) If the equation remains unchanged when θ is replaced by $-\theta$ and r is replaced by $-r$ i.e. $f(-r, -\theta) = f(r, \theta)$. then curve is symmetric about y-axis.

Ex.: $r = 2a\sin\theta$ i.e. $x^2 + y^2 = 2ay$

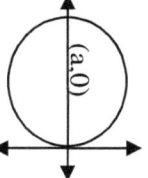

(D) The curve is symmetric about initial line $\theta = \dfrac{3\pi}{4}$ (i.e. the line $y = -x$ in Cartesian coordinates) if the equation remains unchanged when θ is replaced by $\left(\dfrac{3\pi}{4} - \theta\right)$ i.e. $f(r, \theta) = f\left(r, \dfrac{3\pi}{4} - \theta\right)$. then curve is symmetric about Y-axis.

(E) The curve is symmetric about the pole (origin), if the equation remains unchanged when r is replaced by $-r$ i.e. $f(r,\theta) = f(-r,\theta)$. i.e. even power of r. Also curve is symmetric about pole, if $f(r,\theta) = f(r,\theta+\pi)$.

Ex.: $r^2 = a^2 \cos 2\theta$ i.e. $(x^2+y^2) = a^2(x^2-y^2)$

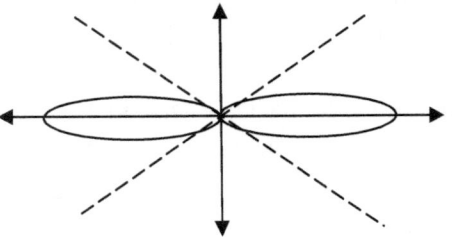

Rule II: Pole and Tangent at the pole.

If $r = f(\theta_1) = 0$ for some $\theta = \theta_1$ (i.e. if for some values of θ, r becomes zero) then the curve passes through the pole and tangent at the pole is the line $\theta = \theta_1$

Ex. 1: $r = a(1+\cos\theta)$ at $\theta = \pi$ $\therefore r = a(1+\cos\pi) = a(1-1) = 0$.

$\Rightarrow \theta = \pi$ is the tangent at origin

Ex. 2: Find the tangent at the pole $r = a\sin 3\theta$

Solution: Put $r = 0$ $\therefore a\sin 3\theta = 0$ $\Rightarrow 3\theta = 0, \pi, 2\pi, 3\pi, 4\pi...$

$\therefore \theta = 0, \dfrac{\pi}{3}, \dfrac{2\pi}{3}, \pi, \dfrac{4\pi}{3}...$ are all tangent at pole.

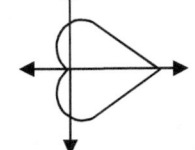

Note: To find the equation of tangent at pole, put r = 0 in the equation. The values of θ gives the equation of tangent at pole.

Rule III: Asymptotes

Find the asymptote, if any

Note: 1. If $\lim_{\theta \to \theta_1} r = \infty$, then an asymptote to the curve $r = 1/f(\theta)$ exists and is given by the relation $r\sin(\theta-\theta_1) = f'(\theta_1)$ where $\theta = \theta_1$ is a root of $f(\theta) = 0$

2. In implicit equation in cartesian form have oblique asymptote, and method of finding oblique asymptote is same as that of cartesian form.

Rule IV: Points on the curve

Put different values of θ in the equation of curve to find different points on the curve. (i.e. form the table of values of r for both positive and negative values of θ).

θ	0	$\pi/6$	$\pi/4$	...
r	...	...	...	...

Note: In polar system, distance r is measured from pole. Thus, if r = 0 then the point lies in the pole.

Rule V: Direction of tangent:

Find the angle between radius vector and the tangent $(i.e. \phi)$.

The slope of tangent at any point (r,θ) on the curve is determined from $\tan\phi = r\dfrac{d\theta}{dr} = \dfrac{r}{dr/d\theta}$ where ϕ is the angle between radius vector and the tangent. Also $\theta + \phi = \psi$.

Find the values of θ for which $\phi = 0$ or ∞.

The values of θ for which $\phi = 0$, tangent will coincide with radius vector and the values of θ for which $\phi = \pi/2$ the tangent will perpendicular to radius vector.

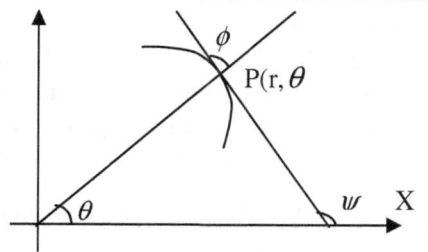

Note: 1. If necessary, transform the equation to cartesian form and use the rules of cartesian to trace the curve.

2. $\theta + \phi = \psi$ where ψ is the angle made by the tangent at point P with initial line. Hence ψ can be found by finding ϕ.

Rule VI: Region of absence of curve:

(A) If for $\alpha < \theta < \beta$, r^2 is negative then there is no branch between $\theta = \alpha$ to $\theta = \beta$.

(B) If for any value of θ maximum numerical value of r is a, then the curve lies completely in the circle r = a. If also for any value of θ, minimum numerical value of r is say, b then the curve lies outside the circle r = b.

Remark: 1. We know that $|\cos\theta| \leq 1$ and $|\sin\theta| \leq 1$

$\therefore$ For the curve $r = a\cos n\theta$ and $r = a\sin n\theta$ $r^n = a^n \cos n\theta$ and $r^n = a^n \sin n\theta$, $n > 0; |r| \leq a$

$\Rightarrow$ no curve lies outside the circle of radius a.

2. If for the curve having $\cos n\theta$ or $\sin n\theta$ each of the quadrants should be divided into n-parts.

3. If for $\alpha < \theta < \beta$, r is negative then branch of curve reflects through origin in opposite quadrant.

Examples : $r = a\cos 2\theta$ for $\dfrac{\pi}{4} < \theta < \dfrac{\pi}{2}$, $r < 0$.

This curve is present in between $\dfrac{\pi}{4}$ to $\dfrac{\pi}{2}$ but reflected through the origin in opposite quadrant.

4. The curve $r^n = a^n \cos n\theta$ for any n, then the corresponding for $r^n = a^n \sin n\theta$ can be obtained by rotating the plane through $\dfrac{\pi}{2n}$.

Ex.: $r = 2a\cos\theta$ i.e. $x^2 + y^2 = 2ax$

$r = 2a\sin\theta = 2a\cos\left(\dfrac{\pi}{2} - \theta\right)$

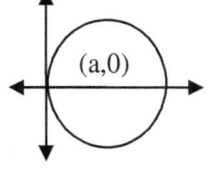

Therefore $r = 2a\sin\theta$ can be obtained by rotating the curve $r = 2a\cos\theta$ through $\dfrac{\pi}{2}$ in anticlockwise direction.

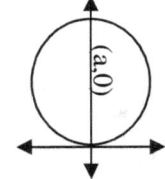

5. Loop: Curve of the type $r = 2a\sin\theta$ or $r = 2a\cos\theta$ consists of either n or 2n similar loops according as n is odd or even. Divide the region from $\theta = 0$ to $\theta = 2\pi$ into n parts and plot one loop only. Other loops can be traced using symmetry.

Tracing of curve in Polar form: Some Standard Curve

Type I: Cardioide-Trace the curve $r = a(1+\cos\theta)$. SUK: Aug-13, NOV-12

Solution: This curve is known as Cardioide. (It is a special case of Pascal's Limacon for $a = b$.

Symmetry: The curve is symmetric about initial line $\theta = 0$, if the equation remains unchanged when θ is replaced by $-\theta$.	$r = a(1+\cos(-\theta)) = a(1+\cos\theta)$. Therefore the curve is symmetric about initial line $\theta = 0$,
Pole: If $r = f(\theta_1) = 0$ for some $\theta = \theta_1$ then the curve passes through the pole and tangent at the pole is the line $\theta = \theta_1$	$r = a(1+\cos\theta)$ At $\theta = \pi \Rightarrow r = 0$ Hence curve passes through the pole. Tangent at pole is obtained by putting $r = 0$ in the equation $0 = a(1+\cos\theta) \Rightarrow 1+\cos\theta = 0 \therefore \cos\theta = -1$ $\therefore \theta = \pi$ is the tangent to the curve at pole. But since the curve is symmetric, the curve has a cusp at origin (common tangent).
Asymptotes: If $\lim_{\theta \to \theta_1} r = \infty$, then an asymptote to the curve $r = 1/f(\theta)$ exists	Since r has finite values for all θ, the curve does not have any asymptotes.
Points on the curve: Put different values of θ in the equation of curve to find different points on the curve.	See table below. Thus maximum value of r is $2a$.
Direction of tangent: Find the angle between radius vector and the tangent $\tan\phi = r\dfrac{d\theta}{dr}$	$r = a(1+\cos\theta)$ taking log $\therefore \log r = \log[a(1+\cos\theta)]$ $\log r = \log a + \log(1+\cos\theta)$ differentiating w.r.t. θ $\dfrac{1}{r}\dfrac{dr}{d\theta} = \dfrac{-\sin\theta}{1+\cos\theta} = \dfrac{-2\sin\frac{\theta}{2}\cos\frac{\theta}{2}}{2\cos^2\frac{\theta}{2}} = -\tan\frac{\theta}{2}$ $\Rightarrow r\dfrac{d\theta}{dr} = -\cot\dfrac{\theta}{2}$ $\therefore \tan\phi = r\dfrac{d\theta}{dr} = -\cot\dfrac{\theta}{2} = \tan\left(\dfrac{\pi}{2}+\dfrac{\theta}{2}\right)$ $\therefore \phi = \dfrac{\pi}{2}+\dfrac{\theta}{2} \Rightarrow \psi = \theta+\phi = \theta+\dfrac{\pi}{2}+\dfrac{\theta}{2} = \dfrac{\pi}{2}+\dfrac{3\theta}{2}$ For $\theta = 0, \phi = \dfrac{\pi}{2}$. For $\theta = \dfrac{\pi}{2}, \phi = \dfrac{3\pi}{4}$. For $\theta = \pi, \phi = \pi$.
Region of absence of curve:	Since the maximum value of r is $2a$, curve lies within a circle of radius $2a$.

θ	0	$\pi/4$	$\pi/3$	$\pi/2$	$2\pi/3$	π
r	$2a$	$a\left(1+\dfrac{1}{\sqrt{2}}\right)$	$\dfrac{3a}{2}$	a	$\dfrac{a}{2}$	0

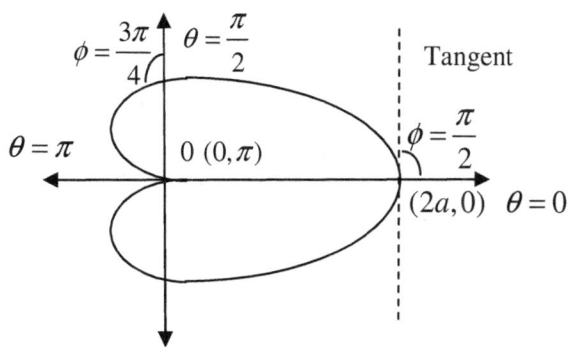

Note: 1. This curve is also known as heart-shaped curve.

Type II: Pascal's Limacon - Trace the curve with full justification $r = a + b\cos\theta$. If i) $a > b$, ii) $a < b$.

OR Trace the curve with full justification $r = a + b\cos\theta$.

Solution: Case-I: $a > b$

Symmetry: The curve is symmetric about initial line $\theta = 0$, if the equation remains unchanged when θ is replaced by $-\theta$.	$r = a + b\cos(-\theta) = a + b\cos\theta$. Therefore the curve is symmetric about initial line $\theta = 0$,
Pole: If $r = f(\theta_1) = 0$ for some $\theta = \theta_1$ then the curve passes through the pole	$r = a + b\cos\theta \Rightarrow 0 = a + b\cos\theta$, $\therefore \theta = \cos^{-1}\left(\dfrac{-a}{b}\right)$. But since $a > b \Rightarrow \dfrac{a}{b} > 1$ but there does not exist any θ for which $|\cos\theta| > 1$, since $-1 \leq \cos\theta \leq 1$ Therefore r is never zero. Thus, the curve does not pass through pole.
Asymptotes: If $\lim\limits_{\theta \to \theta_1} r = \infty$, then an asymptote to the curve $r = 1/f(\theta)$ exists	Since r has finite values for all θ, the curve does not have any asymptotes.
Points on the curve: Put different values of θ in the equation of curve to find different points on the curve.	<table><tr><td>θ</td><td>0</td><td>$\pi/4$</td><td>$\pi/2$</td><td>$3\pi/4$</td><td>π</td></tr><tr><td>r</td><td>$a+b$</td><td>$a+\dfrac{b}{\sqrt{2}}$</td><td>a</td><td>$a-\dfrac{b}{\sqrt{2}}$</td><td>$a-b$</td></tr></table> Thus, maximum value of r is $a+b$ and minimum is $a-b>0$
Direction of tangent: Find the angle between radius vector and the	$r = a + b\cos\theta$ taking log $\log r = \log(a + b\cos\theta)$ differentiating w.r.t. θ $\dfrac{1}{r}\dfrac{dr}{d\theta} = \dfrac{-b\sin\theta}{a+b\cos\theta} \Rightarrow r\dfrac{d\theta}{dr} = \dfrac{a+b\cos\theta}{-b\sin\theta}$

(5.35)

tangent $\tan\phi = r\dfrac{d\theta}{dr}$	$\therefore \tan\phi = r\dfrac{d\theta}{dr} = \dfrac{a+b\cos\theta}{-b\sin\theta}$
	For $\theta = 0$, $\tan\phi = \dfrac{a+b\cos\pi}{-b\sin 0} = \infty \Rightarrow \phi = \dfrac{\pi}{2}$.
	For $\theta = \pi$, $\tan\phi = \dfrac{a+b\cos 0}{-b\sin\pi} = \infty \Rightarrow \phi = \dfrac{\pi}{2}$.
	$\therefore \phi = 0 \Rightarrow \psi = \theta + \phi = 0 + \dfrac{\pi}{2} = \dfrac{\pi}{2}$
	$\therefore$ Angle made by tangent with initial line at A is $\dfrac{\pi}{2}$
	Hence tangent at point A is perpendicular to the initial line.
	Also $\phi = \dfrac{\pi}{2} \Rightarrow \psi = \theta + \phi = \pi + \dfrac{\pi}{2} = \dfrac{3\pi}{2}$
	$\therefore$ Angle made by tangent with initial line at B is $\dfrac{3\pi}{2}$,
	Hence tangent is perpendicular to the initial line.
Region of absence of curve:	Since the maximum value of r is $a+b$, curve lies within a circle of radius $a+b$.

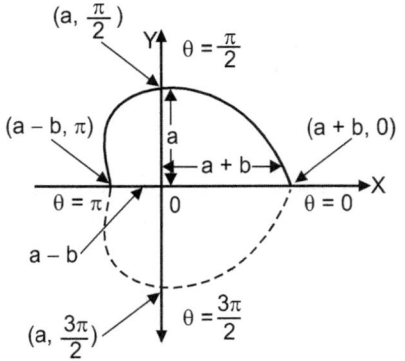

Case-II: $a < b$

Symmetry: The curve is symmetric about initial line $\theta = 0$, if the equation remains unchanged when θ is replaced by $-\theta$.	$r = a + b\cos(-\theta) = a + b\cos\theta$. Therefore the curve is symmetric about initial line $\theta = 0$,
Pole: If $r = f(\theta_1) = 0$ for some $\theta = \theta_1$ then the curve passes through the pole	$r = a + b\cos\theta \Rightarrow 0 = a + b\cos\theta$, $\therefore \theta = \cos^{-1}\left(\dfrac{-a}{b}\right)$. Since $a < b \Rightarrow \dfrac{a}{b} < 1$ ($|\cos\theta| < 1$) $\cos^{-1}\left(\dfrac{-a}{b}\right)$ has two values in the region $\theta = 0$ to $\theta = 2\pi$.

Asymptotes: If $\lim_{\theta \to \theta_1} r = \infty$, then an asymptote to the curve $r = 1/f(\theta)$ exists		One is in II quadrant and other in III quadrant. Let these values be $\theta = \theta_1$ and $\theta = \theta_2$. Thus, the curve has two tangent at pole and hence pole is a node.							
		Since r has finite values for all θ, the curve does not have any asymptotes.							
Points on the curve: Put different values of θ in the equation of curve to find different points on the curve.	θ	0	$\pi/4$	$\pi/3$	$\pi/2$	$2\pi/3$	θ_1	$\theta_1 < \theta < \pi$	π
	r	$a+b$	$a+\dfrac{b}{\sqrt{2}}$	$a+\dfrac{b}{2}$	a	$a-\dfrac{b}{2}$	0	$-ve$	$a-b<0$
	Thus maximum value of r is $a+b$ and minimum is $a-b<0$ The negative value of $r = a-b < 0$ for $\theta = \pi$ is denoted in the opposite direction.								
Direction of tangent: Find the angle between radius vector and the tangent $\tan\phi = r\dfrac{d\theta}{dr}$	$r = a + b\cos\theta$ taking log $\log r = \log(a + b\cos\theta)$ differentiating w.r.t. θ $\dfrac{1}{r}\dfrac{dr}{d\theta} = \dfrac{-b\sin\theta}{a+b\cos\theta} \Rightarrow r\dfrac{d\theta}{dr} = \dfrac{a+b\cos\theta}{-b\sin\theta}$ $\therefore \tan\phi = r\dfrac{d\theta}{dr} = \dfrac{a+b\cos\theta}{-b\sin\theta}$ For $\theta = 0$, $\tan\phi = \dfrac{a+b\cos 0}{-b\sin 0} = \infty \Rightarrow \phi = \dfrac{\pi}{2}$. For $\theta = \pi$, $\tan\phi = \dfrac{a+b\cos 0}{-b\sin\pi} = \infty \Rightarrow \phi = \dfrac{\pi}{2}$. $\therefore \phi = 0 \Rightarrow \psi = \theta + \phi = 0 + \dfrac{\pi}{2} = \dfrac{\pi}{2}$.								
Region of absence:	Since the maximum value of r is $a+b$, curve lies within a circle of radius $a+b$.								
Loop	The negative value of $r = a-b < 0$ for $\theta = \pi$, we get an inner loop between $\theta = \theta_1$ and $\theta = \theta_2$.								

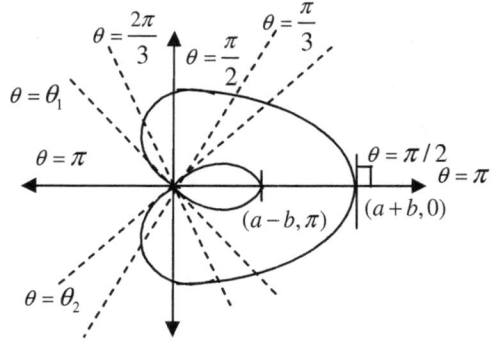

Type III: Lemniscate of Bernoulli- Trace the curve with full justification $r^2 = a^2 \cos 2\theta$.

Solution: This curve is known as Lemniscate of Bernoulli   SUK: May-08, 12

Symmetry: The curve is symmetric about initial line $\theta = 0$, if the equation remains unchanged when θ is replaced by $-\theta$.	$r^2 = a^2 \cos 2\theta = a^2 \cos 2(-\theta) = a^2 \cos 2\theta$. Therefore the curve is symmetric about initial line $\theta = 0$
The curve is symmetric about Y-axis $f(r,\theta) = f(r, \pi - \theta)$.	The curve is symmetric about y-axis. Curve is also symmetric about the pole because of even power of r.
The curve is symmetric about the pole- even power of r.	
Pole: If $r = f(\theta_1) = 0$ for some $\theta = \theta_1$ then the curve passes through the pole and tangent at the pole is the line $\theta = \theta_1$	$r^2 = a^2 \cos 2\theta \Rightarrow 0 = a^2 \cos 2\theta \therefore \cos 2\theta = 0$ $\Rightarrow 2\theta = \dfrac{\pi}{2}$ or $\dfrac{3\pi}{2}$ $\therefore \theta = \dfrac{\pi}{4}$ or $\dfrac{3\pi}{4}$. Hence curve passes through the pole. Tangent at pole is obtained by putting $r = 0$ in the equation $r^2 = a^2 \cos 2\theta \Rightarrow 0 = a^2 \cos 2\theta \therefore \cos 2\theta = 0$ $\Rightarrow 2\theta = \dfrac{\pi}{2}$ or $\dfrac{3\pi}{2}$ $\therefore \theta = \dfrac{\pi}{4}$ or $\dfrac{3\pi}{4}$. $\therefore \theta = \dfrac{\pi}{4}$ or $\dfrac{3\pi}{4}$ are the tangent to the curve at pole But since the curve is symmetric, the curve has a node at origin (tangents are different).
Asymptotes: If $\lim_{\theta \to \theta_1} r = \infty$, then an asymptote to the curve $r = 1/f(\theta)$ exists	Since r has finite values for all θ, the curve does not have any asymptotes.
Points on the curve: Put different values of θ in the equation of curve to find different points on the curve.	<table><tr><td>θ</td><td>0</td><td>$\pi/4$</td><td>$3\pi/4$</td><td>π</td><td>$5\pi/4$</td><td>$7\pi/4$</td><td>2π</td></tr><tr><td>r</td><td>a</td><td>0</td><td>0</td><td>$-a$</td><td>0</td><td>0</td><td>a</td></tr></table> Thus maximum value of r is a when $\theta = 0, r = \pm a$ Curve passes through the points $(a, 0)$ and $(-a, 0)$. Minimum value of r is 0.
Direction of tangent: Find the angle between radius vector and the tangent $\tan \phi = r \dfrac{d\theta}{dr}$	$r^2 = a^2 \cos 2\theta$. taking log $2 \log r = \log[a^2 \cos 2\theta]$ $2 \log r = 2 \log a + \log \cos 2\theta$ differentiating w.r.t. θ $\dfrac{2}{r} \dfrac{dr}{d\theta} = \dfrac{-2 \sin 2\theta}{\cos 2\theta} = -2 \tan 2\theta$

	$\Rightarrow r\dfrac{d\theta}{dr} = -\cot 2\theta$ $\therefore \tan\phi = r\dfrac{d\theta}{dr} = -\cot 2\theta = \tan\left(\dfrac{\pi}{2} + 2\theta\right)$ $\therefore \phi = \dfrac{\pi}{2} + 2\theta \Rightarrow \psi = \theta + \phi = \theta + \dfrac{\pi}{2} + 2\theta = \dfrac{\pi}{2} + 3\theta$ For $\theta = 0$, $\phi = \dfrac{\pi}{2}$ = angle made by the tangent with initial line $\therefore$ Tangent are perpendicular to the initial line at the point $(a,0)$ and $(-a,0)$.
Region of absence of curve:	Since the maximum value of r is a, curve lies within a circle of radius a.

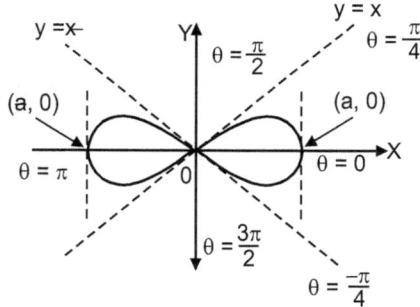

Note: To trace the curve of the type $r^2 = a^2 \sin 2\theta$, use the remark, i.e. The curve $r^n = a^n \cos n\theta$ for any n, then the corresponding for $r^n = a^n \sin n\theta$ can be obtained by rotating the plane through $\dfrac{\pi}{2n}$.

$\therefore r^2 = a^2 \sin 2\theta = a^2 \cos 2\left(\dfrac{\pi}{4} - \theta\right)$ Its value is obtaining by rotating the curve $r^2 = a^2 \cos 2\theta$ through $\dfrac{\pi}{4}$.

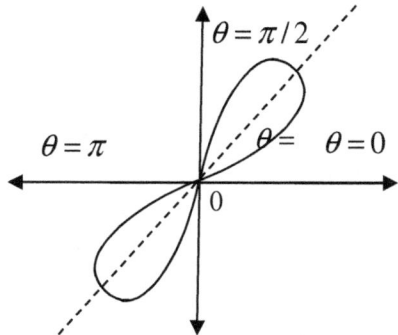

Or solve by following method

Ex. 2: Trace the curve with full justification $r^2 = a^2 \sin 2\theta$.

Solution : This curve is also known as Lemniscate of Bernoulli

Symmetry: The curve is symmetric about the pole- even power of r.	$r^2 = a^2 \sin 2\theta$. Curve is symmetric about the pole because of even power of r.
Pole: If $r = f(\theta_1) = 0$ for some $\theta = \theta_1$ then the curve passes through the pole and tangent at the pole is the line $\theta = \theta_1$	$r^2 = a^2 \sin 2\theta \Rightarrow 0 = a^2 \sin 2\theta \therefore \sin 2\theta = 0$. $\Rightarrow 2\theta = 0$ or $\pi \therefore \theta = 0$ or $\dfrac{\pi}{2}$. Hence curve passes through the pole. Tangent at pole is obtained by putting $r = 0$ in the equation $r^2 = a^2 \sin 2\theta \Rightarrow 0 = a^2 \sin 2\theta \therefore \sin 2\theta = 0$. $\Rightarrow 2\theta = 0$ or $\pi \therefore \theta = 0$ or $\dfrac{\pi}{2}$. $\therefore \theta = 0$ or $\dfrac{\pi}{2}$ are the tangent to the curve at pole. But since the curve is symmetric, the curve has a node at origin (tangents are different).
Asymptotes: If $\lim\limits_{\theta \to \theta_1} r = \infty$, then an asymptote to the curve $r = 1/f(\theta)$ exists	Since r has finite values for all θ, the curve does not have any asymptotes.
Points on the curve: Put different values of θ in the equation of curve to find different points on the curve.	<table><tr><td>θ</td><td>0</td><td>$\pi/4$</td><td>$\pi/2$</td><td>$3\pi/4$</td><td>π</td><td>$3\pi/2$</td><td>$7\pi/4$</td></tr><tr><td>r</td><td>0</td><td>$\pm a$</td><td>0</td><td>Img</td><td>0</td><td>0</td><td>Img</td></tr><tr><td>ϕ</td><td>0</td><td>$\pi/2$</td><td>π</td><td>$3\pi/2$</td><td>2π</td><td>3π</td><td>$7\pi/2$</td></tr></table>
Direction of tangent: Find the angle between radius vector and the tangent $\tan \phi = r \dfrac{d\theta}{dr}$	$r^2 = a^2 \sin 2\theta$. differentiating w.r.t. θ $2r \dfrac{dr}{d\theta} = 2a^2 \cos 2\theta$ $\therefore \tan \phi = r \dfrac{d\theta}{dr} = \dfrac{2r^2}{2a^2 \cos 2\theta} = \tan 2\theta$ $\therefore \phi = 2\theta \Rightarrow \psi = \theta + \phi = \theta + 2\theta = 3\theta$ For $\theta = 0, \phi = 0,$ For $\theta = \dfrac{\pi}{4}, \phi = \dfrac{\pi}{2}$.
Region of absence of curve:	Since the maximum value of $\sin 2\theta$ is 1, curve lies within a circle of radius a. $\sin 2\theta < 0$, for $\pi < 2\theta < 2\pi$ i.e $\pi/2 < \theta < \pi$ Similarly $\sin 2\theta < 0$, for $3\pi/2 < \theta < 2\pi$ Thus the value of r is imaginary when $\pi/2 < \theta < \pi$ and $3\pi/2 < \theta < 2\pi$ Hence the curve does not exist in II and IV quadrants.

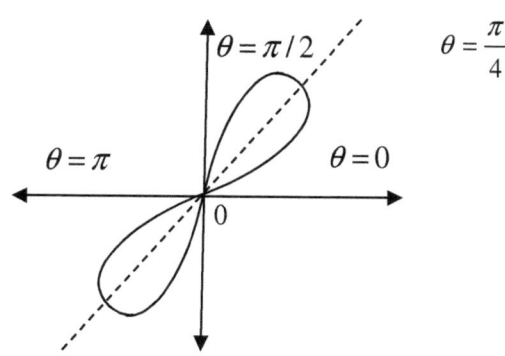

Type IV: Parabola- Trace the curve with full justification
$r(1+\cos\theta)=a$ or $r=a/1+\cos\theta$

Solution: This curve is known as Parabola

Symmetry: The curve is symmetric about initial line $\theta=0$, if the equation remains unchanged when θ is replaced by $-\theta$.	$r=a/1+\cos(-\theta)=a/1+\cos\theta$ Therefore the curve is symmetric about initial line $\theta=0$
Pole: If $r=f(\theta_1)=0$ for some $\theta=\theta_1$ then the curve passes through the pole and tangent at the pole is the line $\theta=\theta_1$	$r=a/1+\cos\theta\neq 0$, For any θ. Hence curve does not pass through the pole.
Asymptotes: If $\lim_{\theta\to\theta_1} r=\infty$, then an asymptote to the curve $r=1/f(\theta)$ exists	Since r has finite values for all θ, the curve does not have any asymptotes.

Points on the curve: Put different values of θ in the equation of curve to

θ	0	$\pi/6$	$\pi/4$	$\pi/3$	$\pi/2$	$2\pi/3$	$5\pi/6$	π
r	a/2	0.54a	0.59a	2/3a	a	2a	7a	∞

Direction of tangent: Find the angle between radius vector and the tangent $\tan\phi = r\dfrac{d\theta}{dr}$	$r=a/1+\cos\theta$ $\therefore \tan\phi = r\dfrac{d\theta}{dr} = \cot\dfrac{\theta}{2}\quad\therefore \phi = \dfrac{\pi}{2}-\dfrac{\theta}{2}$ For $\theta=0$, $\phi=\dfrac{\pi}{2}$, For $\theta=\dfrac{\pi}{2}$, $\phi=\dfrac{\pi}{4}$.
Region of absence of curve:	The curve tends to infinity as θ moves to π.

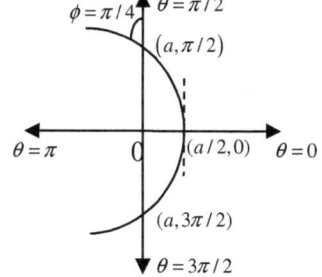

Note: To trace the curve of the type $r = a/1 + \sin\theta$, use the remark,

i.e. The curve $r^n = a^n \cos n\theta$ for any n, then the corresponding for $r^n = a^n \sin n\theta$ can be obtained by rotating the plane through $\dfrac{\pi}{2n}$. $\therefore r = a/1+\sin\theta, = a/1+\cos\left(\dfrac{\pi}{2}-\theta\right)$

Its value is obtaining by rotating the curve $r = a/1+\sin\theta$, through $\dfrac{\pi}{2}$ in anticlockwise direction.

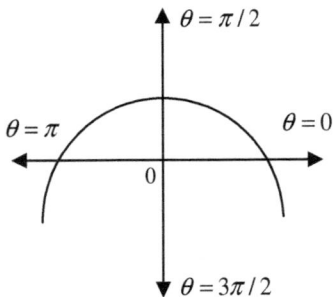

Examples on Curve tracing: Polar form

Ex. 1: Trace the curve with full justification $r = \dfrac{a}{2}(1+\cos\theta)$.

Solution:

Symmetry: The curve is symmetric about initial line $\theta = 0$, if the equation remains unchanged when θ is replaced by $-\theta$.	$r = \dfrac{a}{2}(1+\cos(-\theta)) = \dfrac{a}{2}(1+\cos\theta)$. Therefore the curve is symmetric about initial line $\theta = 0$,
Pole: If $r = f(\theta_1) = 0$ for some $\theta = \theta_1$ then the curve passes through the pole and tangent at the pole is the line $\theta = \theta_1$	$r = \dfrac{a}{2}(1+\cos\theta)$ At $\theta = \pi \Rightarrow r = 0$ Hence curve passes through the pole. Tangent at pole is obtained by putting $r = 0$ in the equation $0 = \dfrac{a}{2}(1+\cos\theta) \Rightarrow 1+\cos\theta = 0 \therefore \cos\theta = -1$ $\therefore \theta = \pi$ is the tangent to the curve at pole But since the curve is symmetric, the curve has a cusp at origin (common tangent).
Asymptotes: If $\lim\limits_{\theta \to \theta_1} r = \infty$, then an asymptote to the curve $r = 1/f(\theta)$ exists	Since r has finite values for all θ, the curve does not have any asymptotes.
Points on the curve: Put different values of θ in the equation of	θ | 0 | $\pi/2$ | π r | a | $a/2$ | 0

curve to find different points on the curve.	Thus maximum value of r is a
Direction of tangent: Find the angle between radius vector and the tangent $\tan\phi = r\dfrac{d\theta}{dr}$	$r = \dfrac{a}{2}(1+\cos\theta)$ $\therefore \tan\phi = r\dfrac{d\theta}{dr} = \dfrac{\dfrac{a}{2}(1+\cos\theta)}{\dfrac{-a}{2}\sin\theta} = -\cot\dfrac{\theta}{2} = \tan\left(\dfrac{\pi}{2}+\dfrac{\theta}{2}\right)$ $\therefore \phi = \dfrac{\pi}{2}+\dfrac{\theta}{2} \Rightarrow \psi = \theta+\phi = \theta+\dfrac{\pi}{2}+\dfrac{\theta}{2} = \dfrac{\pi}{2}+\dfrac{3\theta}{2}$ For $\theta = 0$, $\phi = \dfrac{\pi}{2}$. For $\theta = \dfrac{\pi}{2}$, $\phi = \dfrac{3\pi}{4}$. For $\theta = \pi$, $\phi = \pi$.
Region of absence of curve:	Since the maximum value of r is a, curve lies within a circle of radius a.

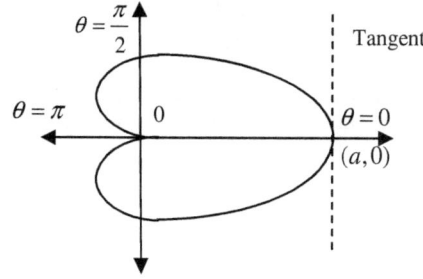

Note : 1. This curve is also known as Cardioide.

2. To trace the curve of the type $r = \dfrac{a}{2}(1+\sin\theta)$ use the remark,

i.e. The curve $r^n = a^n \cos n\theta$ for any n, then the corresponding for $r^n = a^n \sin n\theta$ can be obtained by rotating the plane through $\dfrac{\pi}{2n}$.

$\therefore r = \dfrac{a}{2}(1+\sin\theta) = \dfrac{a}{2}\left[1+\cos\left(\dfrac{\pi}{2}-\theta\right)\right]$

Its value is obtaining by rotating the curve $r = \dfrac{a}{2}(1+\sin\theta)$ through $\dfrac{\pi}{2}$ in anticlockwise direction.

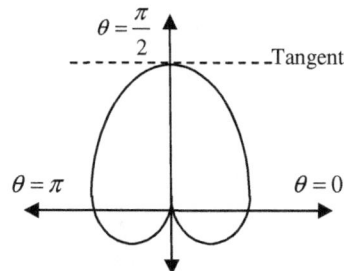

Ex. 2: Trace the curve with full justification $r = \dfrac{a}{2}(1-\cos\theta)$.

Solution:

Symmetry: The curve is symmetric about initial line $\theta = 0$, if the equation remains unchanged when θ is replaced by $-\theta$.	$r = \dfrac{a}{2}(1-\cos(-\theta)) = \dfrac{a}{2}(1-\cos\theta)$. Therefore the curve is symmetric about initial line $\theta = 0$,
Pole: If $r = f(\theta_1) = 0$ for some $\theta = \theta_1$ then the curve passes through the pole and tangent at the pole is the line $\theta = \theta_1$	$r = \dfrac{a}{2}(1-\cos\theta)$ At $\theta = 0 \Rightarrow r = 0$ Hence curve passes through the pole. Tangent at pole is obtained by putting $r = 0$ in the equation $0 = \dfrac{a}{2}(1-\cos\theta) \Rightarrow 1-\cos\theta = 0 \therefore \cos\theta = 1$ $\therefore \theta = 0$ is the tangent to the curve at pole But since the curve is symmetric, the curve has a cusp at origin (common tangent).
Asymptotes: If $\lim\limits_{\theta \to \theta_1} r = \infty$, then an asymptote to the curve $r = 1/f(\theta)$ exists	Since r has finite values for all θ, the curve does not have any asymptotes.
Points on the curve: Put different values of θ in the equation of curve to find different points on the curve.	$\begin{array}{\|c\|c\|c\|c\|} \hline \theta & 0 & \pi/2 & \pi \\ \hline r & 0 & a/2 & a \\ \hline \end{array}$ Thus maximum value of r is a
Direction of tangent: Find the angle between radius vector and the tangent $\tan\phi = r\dfrac{d\theta}{dr}$	$r = \dfrac{a}{2}(1-\cos\theta)$ taking log $\log r = \log\dfrac{a}{2} + \log(1-\cos\theta)$ differentiating w.r.t. θ $\dfrac{1}{r}\dfrac{dr}{d\theta} = \dfrac{\sin\theta}{1-\cos\theta} = \dfrac{2\sin\dfrac{\theta}{2}\cos\dfrac{\theta}{2}}{2\sin^2\dfrac{\theta}{2}} = \cot\dfrac{\theta}{2}$ $\Rightarrow r\dfrac{d\theta}{dr} = \tan\dfrac{\theta}{2}$ $\therefore \tan\phi = r\dfrac{d\theta}{dr} = \tan\dfrac{\theta}{2}$ $\therefore \phi = \dfrac{\theta}{2} \Rightarrow \psi = \theta + \phi = \theta + \dfrac{\theta}{2} = \dfrac{3\theta}{2}$ For $\theta = 0$, $\phi = 0$ $\therefore$ Tangent at pole is initial line For $\theta = \pi$, $\phi = \dfrac{\theta}{2}, \psi = \dfrac{3\pi}{2}$ $\therefore$ Tangent is perpendicular to initial line.
Region of absence of curve:	Since the maximum value of r is a, curve lies within a circle of radius a.

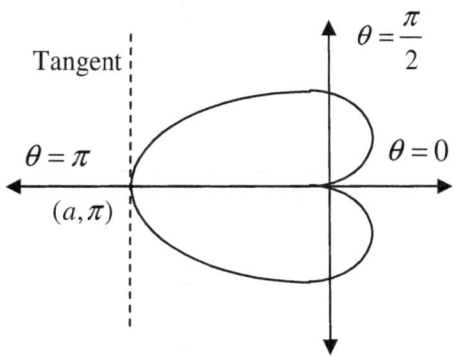

Ex. 3: Trace the curve with full justification $r(1+\cos\theta) = 2a$ or $r = 2a/1+\cos\theta$

Solution:

Symmetry: The curve is symmetric about initial line $\theta = 0$, if the equation remains unchanged when θ is replaced by $-\theta$.	$r = 2a/1+\cos(-\theta) = 2a/1+\cos\theta$ Therefore the curve is symmetric about initial line $\theta = 0$
Pole: If $r = f(\theta_1) = 0$ for some $\theta = \theta_1$ then the curve passes through the pole and tangent at the pole is the line $\theta = \theta_1$	$r = 2a/1+\cos\theta \neq 0$, For any θ. Hence curve does not pass through the pole.
Asymptotes: If $\lim_{\theta \to \theta_1} r = \infty$, then an asymptote to the curve $r = 1/f(\theta)$ exists	Since r has finite values for all θ, the curve does not have any asymptotes.
Points on the curve: Put different values of θ in the equation of curve to find different points on the curve.	<table><tr><td>θ</td><td>0</td><td>$\pi/2$</td><td>π</td></tr><tr><td>r</td><td>a</td><td>$2a$</td><td>∞</td></tr></table>
Direction of tangent: Find the angle between radius vector and the tangent $\tan\phi = r\dfrac{d\theta}{dr}$	$r = 2a/1+\cos\theta$ $\therefore \tan\phi = r\dfrac{d\theta}{dr} = \cot\dfrac{\theta}{2} = \tan\left(\dfrac{\pi}{2}-\dfrac{\theta}{2}\right)$ $\therefore \phi = \dfrac{\pi}{2}-\dfrac{\theta}{2}$ For $\theta = 0$, $\phi = \dfrac{\pi}{2}$, For $\theta = \dfrac{\pi}{2}$, $\phi = \dfrac{\pi}{4}$, For $\theta = \pi$, $\phi = 0$.
Region of absence of curve:	The curve tends to infinity as θ moves to π.

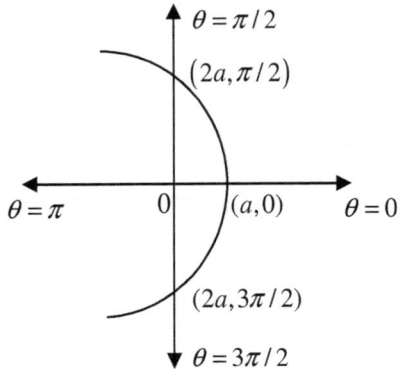

Note: 1. This curve is also known as Parabola

2. To trace the curve of the type $r = 2a/1+\sin\theta$, use the remark,

i.e. The curve $r^n = a^n \cos n\theta$ for any n, then the corresponding for $r^n = a^n \sin n\theta$ can be obtained by rotating the plane through $\dfrac{\pi}{2n}$. $\therefore r = 2a/1+\sin\theta, = 2a/1+\cos\left(\dfrac{\pi}{2}-\theta\right)$ Its value is obtaining by rotating the curve $r = 2a/1+\sin\theta$, through $\dfrac{\pi}{2}$ in anticlockwise direction.

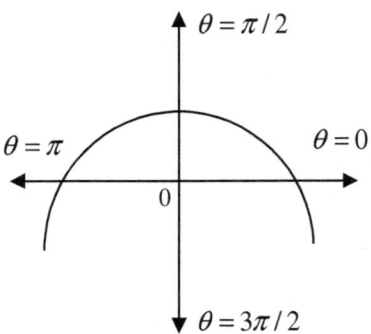

Ex. 4: Trace the curve with full justification $r = 2a\cos\theta$.

Solution: This curve is known as **circle**   SUK: May-13

Symmetry: The curve is symmetric about initial line $\theta = 0$, if the equation remains unchanged when θ is replaced by $-\theta$.	$r = 2a\cos(-\theta) = 2a\cos\theta$. Therefore the curve is symmetric about initial line $\theta = 0$
Pole: If $r = f(\theta_1) = 0$ for some $\theta = \theta_1$ then the curve passes through the pole and tangent at the	$r = 2a\cos\theta \Rightarrow 0 = 2a\cos\theta \therefore \cos\theta = 0 \Rightarrow \theta = \dfrac{\pi}{2}$. Hence curve passes through the pole. Tangent at pole is obtained by putting $r = 0$ in the equation

(5.46)

pole is the line $\theta = \theta_1$	$r = 2a\cos\theta \Rightarrow 0 = 2a\cos\theta \therefore \cos\theta = 0 \Rightarrow \theta = \dfrac{\pi}{2}$.
	$\therefore \theta = \dfrac{\pi}{2}$ is the tangent to the curve at pole
Asymptotes: If $\lim_{\theta \to \theta_1} r = \infty$, then an asymptote to curve $r = 1/f(\theta)$ exists	Since $|\cos\theta| < 1$, r has finite values for all θ the curve does not have any asymptotes.
Points on the curve: Put different values of θ in the equation of curve to find different points on the curve.	<table><tr><td>θ</td><td>0</td><td>$\pi/4$</td><td>$\pi/3$</td><td>$\pi/2$</td><td>π</td><td>$3\pi/2$</td><td>2π</td></tr><tr><td>r</td><td>$2a$</td><td>$\sqrt{2}a$</td><td>a</td><td>0</td><td>$-2a$</td><td>0</td><td>$2a$</td></tr></table> Thus maximum value of r is $2a$ when $\theta = 0, 2\pi$
Direction of tangent: Find the angle between radius vector and the tangent $\tan\phi = r\dfrac{d\theta}{dr}$	$r = 2a\cos\theta$ differentiating w.r.t. θ $\therefore \tan\phi = r\dfrac{d\theta}{dr} = \dfrac{2a\cos\theta}{-2a\sin\theta} = -\cot\theta = \tan\left(\dfrac{\pi}{2}+\theta\right)$ $\therefore \phi = \dfrac{\pi}{2}+\theta \Rightarrow \psi = \theta+\phi = \theta+\dfrac{\pi}{2}+\theta = \dfrac{\pi}{2}+2\theta$ For $\theta = 0$, $\phi = \dfrac{\pi}{2}$; For $\theta = \dfrac{\pi}{2}$, $\phi = \pi$ and so on
Region of absence of curve:	Since the maximum value of r is $2a$, curve lies within a circle of radius $2a$
Loop	The curve consist of a single loop, because n = 1.

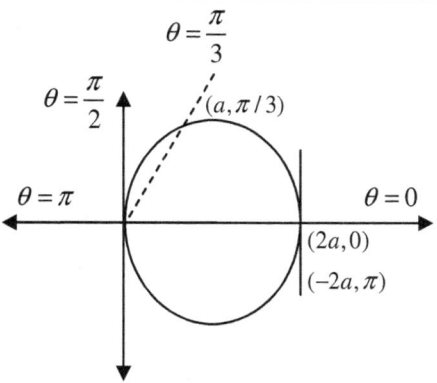

Ex. 5: Trace the curve with full justification $r = 3 + 2\cos\theta$.
(This example is a particular case of Type I: Pascal's Limacon $r = a + b\cos\theta$. If $a > b$.)
Solution: This curve is known as Dimpled Limacon.   **SUK: May-09, NOV-10**

Symmetry: The curve is symmetric about initial line $\theta = 0$, if the equation remains unchanged when θ is replaced by $-\theta$.	$r = 3 + 2\cos(-\theta) = 3 + 2\cos\theta$. Therefore the curve is symmetric about initial line $\theta = 0$,

Pole: If $r = f(\theta_1) = 0$ for some $\theta = \theta_1$, then the curve passes through the pole	$r = 3 + 2\cos\theta \Rightarrow 0 = 3 + 2\cos\theta$, $\therefore \theta = \cos^{-1}\left(\dfrac{-3}{2}\right)$. But since $3 > 2 \Rightarrow \dfrac{3}{2} > 1$ but there does not exist any θ for which $|\cos\theta| > 1$, since $-1 \leq \cos\theta \leq 1$ Therefore r is never zero. Thus, the curve does not pass through pole.
Asymptotes: If $\lim_{\theta \to \theta_1} r = \infty$, then an asymptote to the curve $r = 1/f(\theta)$ exists	Since r has finite values for all θ, the curve does not have any asymptotes.
Points on the curve: Put different values of θ in the equation of curve to find different points on the curve.	<table><tr><td>θ</td><td>0</td><td>$\pi/4$</td><td>$\pi/3$</td><td>$\pi/2$</td><td>$3\pi/4$</td><td>π</td></tr><tr><td>r</td><td>5</td><td>4.41</td><td>4</td><td>3</td><td>1.59</td><td>1</td></tr></table> Thus maximum value of r is 5 and minimum is $1 > 0$
Direction of tangent: Find the angle between radius vector and the tangent $\tan\phi = r\dfrac{d\theta}{dr}$	$r = 3 + 2\cos\theta$ taking log $\log r = \log(3 + 2\cos\theta)$ differentiating w.r.t. θ $\dfrac{1}{r}\dfrac{dr}{d\theta} = \dfrac{-2\sin\theta}{3 + 2\cos\theta} \Rightarrow r\dfrac{d\theta}{dr} = \dfrac{3 + 2\cos\theta}{-2\sin\theta}$ $\therefore \tan\phi = r\dfrac{d\theta}{dr} = \dfrac{3 + 2\cos\theta}{-2\sin\theta}$ For $\theta = 0$, $\tan\phi = \dfrac{3 + 2\cos 0}{-2\sin 0} = \infty \Rightarrow \phi = \dfrac{\pi}{2}$. For $\theta = \pi$, $\tan\phi = \dfrac{3 + 2\cos 0}{-2\sin\pi} = \infty \Rightarrow \phi = \dfrac{\pi}{2}$. $\therefore \phi = 0 \Rightarrow \psi = \theta + \phi = 0 + \dfrac{\pi}{2} = \dfrac{\pi}{2}$ $\therefore$ Angle made by tangent with initial line is $\dfrac{\pi}{2}$ Hence tangent is perpendicular to the initial line. Also $\phi = \dfrac{\pi}{2} \Rightarrow \psi = \theta + \phi = \pi + \dfrac{\pi}{2} = \dfrac{3\pi}{2}$ $\therefore$ Angle made by tangent with initial line is $\dfrac{3\pi}{2}$, Hence tangent is perpendicular to the initial line.
Region of absence of curve:	Since the maximum value of r is 5, curve lies within a circle of radius 5.

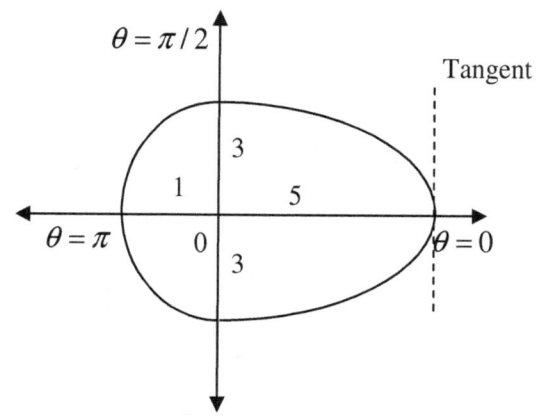

Ex. 6: Trace the curve with full justification $r = 2 + 3\cos\theta$.

Solution: (This is a particular case of Type I: Pascal's Limacon $r = a + b\cos\theta$. If $a < b$.)

Symmetry: The curve is symmetric about initial line $\theta = 0$, if the equation remains unchanged when θ is replaced by $-\theta$.	$r = 2 + 3\cos(-\theta) = 2 + 3\cos\theta$. Therefore the curve is symmetric about initial line $\theta = 0$,
Pole: If $r = f(\theta_1) = 0$ for some $\theta = \theta_1$ then the curve passes through the pole	$r = 2 + 3\cos\theta \Rightarrow 0 = 2 + 3\cos\theta$, $\therefore \theta = \cos^{-1}\left(\frac{-2}{3}\right)$. Since $2 < 3 \Rightarrow \frac{2}{3} < 1$ ($|\cos\theta| < 1$) $\cos^{-1}\left(\frac{-2}{3}\right)$ has two values in the region $\theta = 0$ to $\theta = 2\pi$. One is in II quadrant and other in III quadrant. Let these values be $\theta = \theta_1$ and $\theta = \theta_2$. Thus, the curve has two tangent at pole and hence pole is a node.
Asymptotes: If $\lim_{\theta \to \theta_1} r = \infty$, then an asymptote to the curve $r = 1/f(\theta)$ exists	Since r has finite values for all θ, the curve does not have any asymptotes.

Points on the curve: Put different values of θ in the equation of curve to find different points on the curve.	θ	0	$\pi/2$	π	$3\pi/2$	2π	$\pi/6$	$\pi/4$	$\pi/3$	$3\pi/4$
	r	5	2	-1	2	5	4.60	4.12	3.5	-0.12
	Thus maximum value of r is 5 and minimum is $-1 < 0$. The negative value of $r = -1 < 0$ for $\theta = \pi$ is denoted in the opposite direction.									

Direction of tangent: Find the angle between radius vector and the tangent $\tan\phi = r\dfrac{d\theta}{dr}$	$r = 2+3\cos\theta$ taking log $\log r = \log(2+3\cos\theta)$ differentiating w.r.t. θ $\dfrac{1}{r}\dfrac{dr}{d\theta} = \dfrac{-3\sin\theta}{2+3\cos\theta} \Rightarrow r\dfrac{d\theta}{dr} = \dfrac{2+3\cos\theta}{-3\sin\theta}$ $\therefore \tan\phi = r\dfrac{d\theta}{dr} = \dfrac{2+3\cos\theta}{-3\sin\theta}$ For $\theta = 0$, $\tan\phi = \dfrac{2+3\cos 0}{-3\sin 0} = \infty \Rightarrow \phi = \dfrac{\pi}{2}$. For $\theta = \pi$, $\tan\phi = \dfrac{2+3\cos 0}{-3\sin \pi} = \infty \Rightarrow \phi = \dfrac{\pi}{2}$. $\therefore \phi = 0 \Rightarrow \psi = \theta + \phi = 0 + \dfrac{\pi}{2} = \dfrac{\pi}{2}$.
Region of absence of curve:	Since the maximum value of r is 5, curve lies within a circle of radius 5.
Loop	The negative value of $r = -1 < 0$ for $\theta = \pi$, we get an inner loop between $\theta = \theta_1$ and $\theta = \theta_2$.

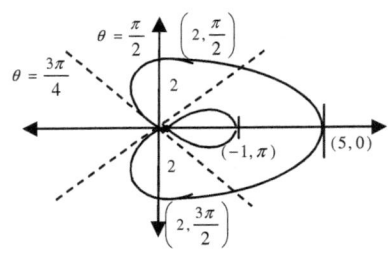

TEST YOUR KNOWLEDGE

1. $r = a(1+\sin\theta)$
2. $r = a(1-\sin\theta)$
3. $r(1+\sin\theta) = 2a$
4. $r(1-\sin\theta) = 2a$
5. $r = a\cosec\theta \pm b$
6. $r^2\theta = a^2$
7. $r = a\left[\dfrac{\sqrt{3}}{2} + \cos\dfrac{\theta}{2}\right]$
8. $r\theta = a, \ a > 0$
9. $r = a\left[\sqrt{3} + 2\cos\theta\right]$
10. $r = a(1+2\cos\theta)$
11. $r = \dfrac{a}{2}(1+\cos\theta)$.

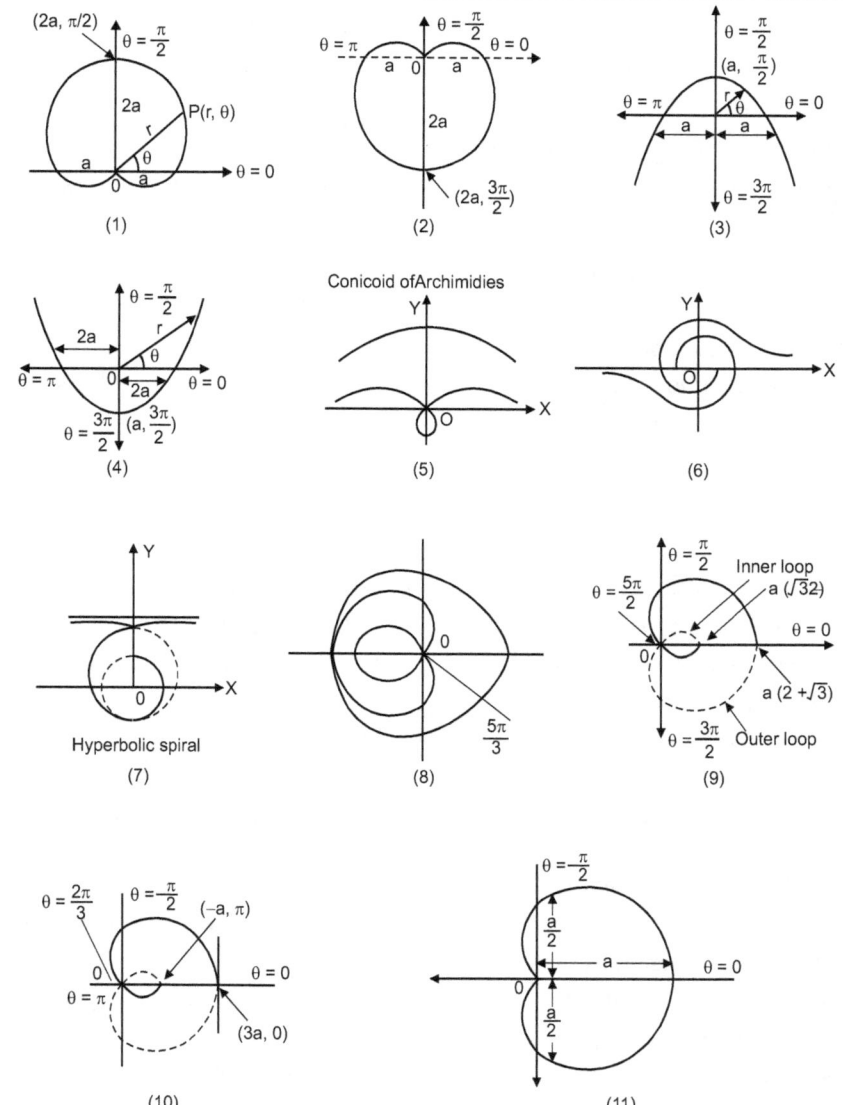

Tracing of curve in polar form: Rose curve

Rules for tracing of Polar Curve of the type $r = a\cos n\theta$ *or* $r = a\sin n\theta$:

The equation of polar curve is often given by $r = f(\theta)$.

Rule I: Symmetry

(A) The curve is symmetric about initial line $\theta = 0$, if the equation remains unchanged when θ is replaced by $-\theta$ i.e. $f(r, -\theta) = f(r, \theta)$.

Ex.: $r = a\cos 2\theta$

(B) If the equation remains unchanged when θ is replaced by $-\theta$ and r is replaced by $-r$ i.e. $f(-r,-\theta) = f(r,\theta)$. then curve is symmetric about y-axis.

Ex.: $r = a\sin 3\theta$

Rule II: Pole and Tangent at the pole.

If $r = f(\theta_1) = 0$ for some $\theta = \theta_1$ (i.e. if for some values of θ, r becomes zero) then the curve passes through the pole and tangent at the pole is the line $\theta = \theta_1$

Rule III: Points on the curve

Put different values of θ in the equation of curve to find different points on the curve. (i.e. form the table of values of r for both positive and negative values of θ).

Note: 1. Note the following values

θ	0	π/6	π/4	...
r	...	...	...	...

$\sin n\theta = 0$
For $n\theta = 0, \pi, 2\pi, 3\pi, 4\pi, 5\pi, ...$
$\Rightarrow \theta = 0, \pi/n, 2\pi/n, 3\pi/n, 4\pi/n, 5\pi/n,...$

$\cos n\theta = 0$
For $n\theta = -\pi/2, \pi/2, 3\pi/2, 5\pi/2, 7\pi/2, 9\pi/2,...$
$\Rightarrow \theta = -\pi/2n, \pi/2n, 3\pi/2n, 5\pi/2n, 7\pi/2n, 9\pi/2n,...$

2. If $r = -a$ indicates the radial distance to be taken in the opposite direction.

Rule V: Direction of tangent:

Find the angle between radius vector and the tangent $(i.e. \phi)$.

The slope of tangent at any point (r, θ) on the curve is determined from $\tan\phi = r\dfrac{d\theta}{dr} = \dfrac{r}{dr/d\theta}$ where ϕ is the angle between radius vector and the tangent. Also $\theta + \phi = \psi$.

Find the values of θ for which $\phi = 0$ or ∞.

i.e. Find the point where the tangent coincident with the radius vector or initial line.

Rule VI: Region of absence of curve:

For $r = a\cos n\theta$ or $r = a\sin n\theta$ the maximum numerical value of r is a, then the curve lies completely in the circle r = a.

Remark: 1. Since $\cos\theta$ and $\sin\theta$ are periodic functions, the values of θ from 0 to 2π should only be consider. Values of $\theta > 2\pi$ gives no new branch of the curve.

2. The curve $r = a\cos n\theta$ or $r = a\sin n\theta$ consist of

(i) n equal loops if n is odd   (ii) 2 n equal loops if n is even

3. For drawing the loops, divide each quadrant into n equal parts. For $r = a\sin n\theta$

(i) First loop is drawn along $\theta = \dfrac{\pi}{2n}$

(ii) If n is even, draw loops in two sectors consecutively from $\theta = 0$ to $\theta = 2\pi$.

(iii) If n is odd, draw loops in two sectors alternatively keeping two sectors between the loops vacant.

4. For drawing the loops, divide each quadrant into n equal parts. For $r = a\cos n\theta$

(i) First loop is drawn along $\theta = 0$

(ii) If n is even, draw loops in two sectors consecutively from $\theta = 0$ to $\theta = 2\pi$.

(iii) If n is odd, draw loops in two sectors alternatively keeping two sectors between the loops vacant.

Examples on Rose curves

Ex. 1: Trace the curve with full justification $r = a\cos 3\theta$. (Three leaved rose)

Solution:

Symmetry: The curve is symmetric about initial line $\theta = 0$, if the equation remains unchanged when θ is replaced by $-\theta$.	$r = a\cos 3(-\theta) = a\cos 3\theta$. Therefore the curve is symmetric about initial line $\theta = 0$,
Pole: If $r = f(\theta_1) = 0$ for some $\theta = \theta_1$ then the curve passes through the pole and tangent at the pole is the line $\theta = \theta_1$	$r = a\cos 3\theta = 0$ Hence curve passes through the pole. Tangent at pole is obtained by putting $r = 0$ in the equation $r = a\cos 3\theta = 0$ for $3\theta = \dfrac{\pi}{2}, \dfrac{3\pi}{2}, \dfrac{5\pi}{2}, \dfrac{7\pi}{2}, \dfrac{9\pi}{2}, \dfrac{11\pi}{2} \ldots$ $\therefore \theta = \dfrac{\pi}{6}, \dfrac{\pi}{2}, \dfrac{5\pi}{6}, \dfrac{7\pi}{6}, \dfrac{3\pi}{2}, \dfrac{11\pi}{6} \ldots$ Thus the tangent to the curve at pole are given by the lines $\theta = \dfrac{\pi}{6},\ \theta = \dfrac{\pi}{2},\ \theta = \dfrac{5\pi}{6},\ \ldots$ Since $\theta = \dfrac{\pi}{6}$ is same as the line $\theta = \pi + \dfrac{\pi}{6} = \dfrac{7\pi}{6}$ and so on...
Asymptotes: If $\lim_{\theta \to \theta_1} r = \infty$, then an asymptote to the curve $r = 1/f(\theta)$ exists	Since r has finite values for all θ, the curve does not have any asymptotes.
Points on the curve: Put different values of θ in the equation of curve to find different points on the curve.	<table><tr><td>θ</td><td>0</td><td>$\pi/6$</td><td>$\pi/\ $</td><td>$\pi/\ $</td><td>$\pi/\ $</td><td>$2\pi$</td><td>$5\pi$</td><td>$\pi$</td></tr><tr><td>r</td><td>a</td><td>0</td><td>$-a$</td><td>$-a$</td><td>0</td><td>a</td><td>0</td><td>$-a$</td></tr></table> Thus maximum value of r is a

Direction of tangent: Find the angle between radius vector and the tangent $\tan\phi = r\dfrac{d\theta}{dr}$	$r = a\cos 3\theta$ $\therefore \tan\phi = r\dfrac{d\theta}{dr} = \dfrac{\cos 3\theta}{-3\sin 3\theta}$ For $\theta = 0 \Rightarrow \tan\phi = \infty \Rightarrow \phi = \dfrac{\pi}{2}$ For $\theta = \dfrac{\pi}{2} \Rightarrow \tan\phi = 0 \Rightarrow \phi = 0$ and so on
Region of absence of curve:	Since the maximum value of r is a, curve lies within a circle of radius a.
Loop:	As θ varies from $\dfrac{\pi}{6}$ to $\dfrac{\pi}{2}$, values of r varies from $-a$ to 0. Thus, forming a loop, since $\cos\theta$ is periodic function with period 2π, $\cos 3\theta$ is periodic function with period $\dfrac{2\pi}{3}$ Hence, the curve consists of three loops.

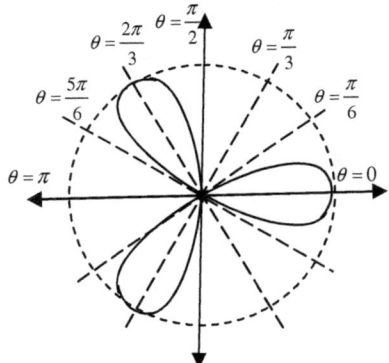

Note: The curve $r = a\sin 3\theta$ can be obtained by rotating $r = a\cos 3\theta$ through an angle $\dfrac{\pi}{6}$ in anticlockwise direction i.e. $r = a\sin 3\theta = a\cos 3\left(\dfrac{\pi}{6} - \theta\right)$. Or use the following method.

Ex. 2: Trace the curve with full justification $r = a\sin 3\theta$. (Three leaved rose) **SUK: May-10**

Solution:

Symmetry: If the equation remains unchanged when θ is replaced by $-\theta$ and r is replaced by $-r$ then curve is symmetric about Y-axis.	$r = a\sin 3\theta \Rightarrow -r = a\sin 3(-\theta) \;\therefore r = a\sin 3\theta$. Therefore the curve is symmetric about initial line $\theta = \dfrac{\pi}{2}$,
Pole: If $r = f(\theta_1) = 0$ for some $\theta = \theta_1$ then the curve passes through the pole and	$r = a\sin 3\theta \Rightarrow 0 = a\sin 3\theta \Rightarrow \sin 3\theta = 0 \;\therefore \theta = 0$ Hence curve passes through the pole. Tangent at pole is obtained by putting $r = 0$ in the equation $r = a\sin 3\theta$.

tangent at the pole is the line $\theta = \theta_1$	$\Rightarrow 0 = a\sin 3\theta \Rightarrow \sin 3\theta = 0$ $\therefore 3\theta = 0, \pi, 2\pi, 3\pi, 4\pi, \ldots \Rightarrow \theta = 0, \pi/3, 2\pi/3, \pi, 4\pi/3, \ldots$ Thus the tangent to the curve at pole are given by the lines $\theta = 0, \ \theta = \dfrac{\pi}{3}, \ \theta = \dfrac{2\pi}{3}, \ \ldots$
Asymptotes: If $\lim_{\theta \to \theta_1} r = \infty$, then an asymptote to the curve $r = 1/f(\theta)$ exists	Since r has finite values for all θ, the curve does not have any asymptotes.

Points on the curve:

θ	0	$\pi/6$	$\pi/3$	$\pi/2$	$2\pi/3$	$5\pi/6$	π	$7\pi/6$	$4\pi/3$	$3\pi/2$	$5\pi/3$	$11\pi/6$	2π
r	0	a	0	$-a$	0	a	0	$-a$	0	a	0	$-a$	0

Thus maximum value of r is a

Direction of tangent: Find the angle between radius vector and the tangent $\tan\phi = r\dfrac{d\theta}{dr}$	$r = a\sin 3\theta$ taking log $\ \therefore \log r = \log a + \log \sin 3\theta$ $\dfrac{1}{r}\dfrac{dr}{d\theta} = \dfrac{3\cos 3\theta}{\sin 3\theta} \Rightarrow r\dfrac{d\theta}{dr} = \dfrac{1}{3}\tan 3\theta$ $\therefore \tan\phi = r\dfrac{d\theta}{dr} = \dfrac{1}{3}\tan 3\theta$ For $\theta = 0, \dfrac{\pi}{3}, \dfrac{2\pi}{3}, \pi \ \Rightarrow \phi = 0$ $\psi = \theta + \phi = 0, \dfrac{\pi}{3}, \dfrac{2\pi}{3}, \pi, \ldots$ and so on Therefore the tangent are coincident with radius vectors.
Region of absence of curve:	Since the maximum value of r is a, curve lies within a circle of radius a.
Loop:	From $\theta = 0, \pi/3, 2\pi/3, \pi, 4\pi/3, \ldots$ we draw the lines and place the loops in alternate sectors. First loop between $\theta = 0$ and $\theta = \dfrac{\pi}{3}$, second between $\theta = \dfrac{2\pi}{3}$ and $\theta = \pi$, third between $\theta = \dfrac{4\pi}{3}$ and $\theta = \dfrac{5\pi}{3}$.

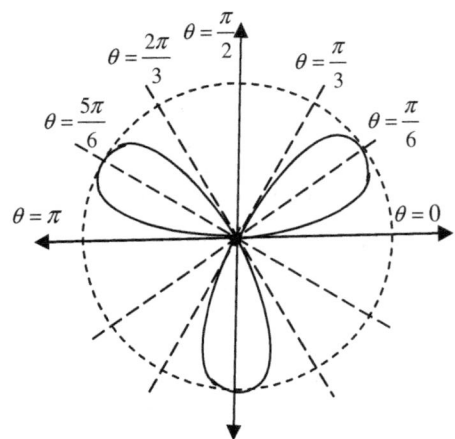

Ex. 3: Trace the curve $r = a\cos 2\theta$. (Four leaved rose)   **SUK: May-13**

Solution:

Symmetry: The curve is symmetric about initial line $\theta = 0$, if the equation remains unchanged when θ is replaced by $-\theta$.	$r = a\cos 2(-\theta) = a\cos 2\theta$. Therefore the curve is symmetric about initial line $\theta = 0$,
Pole: If $r = f(\theta_1) = 0$ for some $\theta = \theta_1$ then the curve passes through the pole and tangent at the pole is the line $\theta = \theta_1$	$r = a\cos 2\theta = 0$ Hence curve passes through the pole. Tangent at pole is obtained by putting $r = 0$ in the equation $r = a\cos 2\theta = 0$ for $2\theta = \dfrac{-\pi}{2}, \dfrac{\pi}{2}, \dfrac{3\pi}{2}, \dfrac{5\pi}{2}, \dfrac{7\pi}{2}, \dfrac{9\pi}{2}, \dfrac{11\pi}{2}\ldots$ $\therefore \theta = \dfrac{-\pi}{4}, \dfrac{\pi}{4}, \dfrac{3\pi}{4}, \dfrac{5\pi}{4}, \dfrac{7\pi}{4}, \dfrac{9\pi}{4}, \dfrac{11\pi}{4}\ldots$ Thus the tangent to the curve at pole are given by the lines $\theta = \dfrac{-\pi}{4},\ \theta = \dfrac{\pi}{4},\ \theta = \dfrac{3\pi}{4},\ \ldots$
Asymptotes: If $\lim\limits_{\theta \to \theta_1} r = \infty$, then an asymptote to the curve $r = 1/f(\theta)$ exists	Since r has finite values for all θ, the curve does not have any asymptotes.

Points on the curve: Put different values of θ in the equation of curve to find different points on the curve.

θ	0	$\pi/4$	$\pi/2$	$3\pi/4$	π	$5\pi/4$	$3\pi/2$	$7\pi/4$	2π
r	a	0	$-a$	0	a	0	$-a$	0	a

Thus maximum value of r is a

Direction of tangent: Find the angle between radius vector and the tangent $\tan \phi = r \dfrac{d\theta}{dr}$	$r = a\cos 2\theta$ $\therefore \tan \phi = r\dfrac{d\theta}{dr} = \dfrac{\cos 2\theta}{-2\sin 2\theta} = \dfrac{-1}{2}\cot 2\theta$ $= \dfrac{1}{2}\tan\left(\dfrac{\pi}{2} + 2\theta\right)$ For $\theta = \dfrac{-\pi}{4}\left(\text{or } \dfrac{7\pi}{4}\right), \dfrac{\pi}{4}, \dfrac{3\pi}{4}, \dfrac{5\pi}{4} \Rightarrow \tan\phi = 0 \Rightarrow \phi = 0$ and so on
Region of absence of curve:	Since the maximum value of r is a, curve lies within a circle of radius a.
Loop:	For $\theta = \dfrac{-\pi}{4}, \dfrac{\pi}{4}, \dfrac{3\pi}{4}, \dfrac{5\pi}{4}, \dfrac{7\pi}{4}, \dfrac{9\pi}{4}, \dfrac{11\pi}{4}\ldots$ we draw the lines and place equal loops in each division. First loop between $\theta = \dfrac{-\pi}{4}$ and $\theta = \dfrac{\pi}{4}$, second between $\theta = \dfrac{\pi}{4}$ and $\theta = \dfrac{3\pi}{4}$, third between $\theta = \dfrac{3\pi}{4}$ and $\theta = \dfrac{5\pi}{4}$, fourth between $\theta = \dfrac{5\pi}{4}$ and $\theta = \dfrac{7\pi}{4}$.

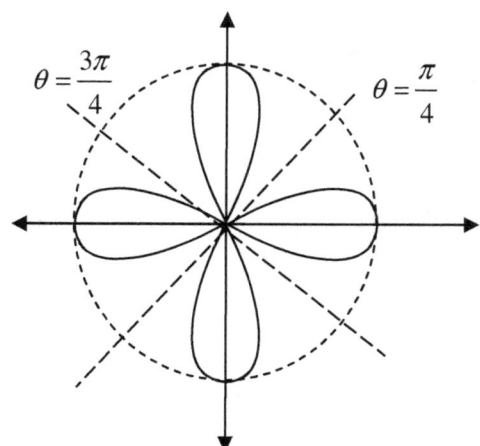

Note: The curve $r = a\sin 2\theta$. can be obtained by rotating $r = a\sin 2\theta$ through an angle $\dfrac{\pi}{4}$ in anticlockwise direction i.e. $r = a\sin 3\theta = a\cos 3\left(\dfrac{\pi}{6} - \theta\right)$.

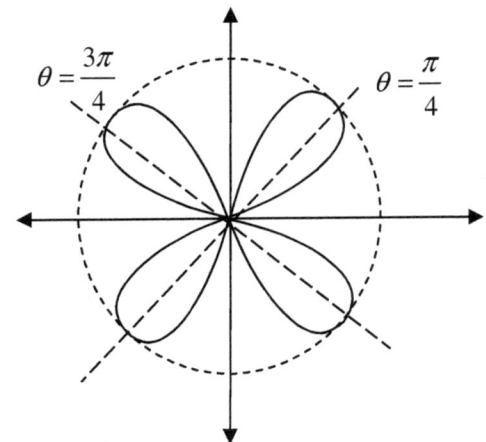

Rectification of plane curve (Cartesian and Polar form)

Definition: The process of determination of the lengths of the arcs of the plane curves between two specified points whose equations are given in Cartesian or in polar form is known as rectification.

Rectification of plane curve for Cartesian form:

Case-I: Let denote the equation of the curve by $y = f(x)$.

Consider the curve C as shown in figure below.

Consider two points $P(x, y)$, $Q(x+\delta x, y+\delta y)$, where arc $PQ = \delta s$. PM, QN are perpendiculars on

X-axis and PR is perpendicular on QN. Then

$OM = x$, $ON = x + \delta x$,

$MP = y$, $NQ = y + \delta y$,

$PR = ON - OM = \delta x$

$RQ = NQ - NR = NQ - MP = \delta y$

From right angled triangle PQR,

$PQ^2 = PR^2 + RQ^2$

or $(\delta s)^2 = (\delta x)^2 + (\delta y)^2$ (A)

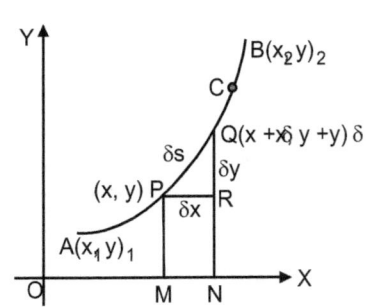

(When Q is indefinitely closer to P, arc $PQ = \delta s$ = chord PQ)

Dividing equation (A) by $(\delta x)^2$, we get

$\left(\dfrac{\delta s}{\delta x}\right)^2 = 1 + \left(\dfrac{\delta y}{\delta x}\right)^2$

Taking the limit as $Q \to P$ or $\delta x \to 0$

$$\left(\frac{ds}{dx}\right)^2 = 1 + \left(\frac{dy}{dx}\right)^2 \Rightarrow \frac{ds}{dx} = \sqrt{1 + \left(\frac{dy}{dx}\right)^2}$$

i.e. $ds = \sqrt{1 + \left(\frac{dy}{dx}\right)^2}\, dx$

On integration, we get $s = \int \sqrt{1 + \left(\frac{dy}{dx}\right)^2}\, dx$

In particular, if we want to determine arc length AB, where $A(x_1, y_1), B(x_2, y_2)$ are any two points on the curve, we substitute the limits of integration for x and we have,

$$s = \int_{x_1}^{x_2} \sqrt{1 + \left(\frac{dy}{dx}\right)^2}\, dx. \qquad (I)$$

Case-II: Let denote the equation of the curve by $x = f(y)$.

Dividing equation (A) by $(\delta y)^2$, we get

$\left(\frac{\delta s}{\delta y}\right)^2 = 1 + \left(\frac{\delta x}{\delta y}\right)^2$ Taking the limit as $Q \to P$ or $\delta y \to 0$

$\left(\frac{ds}{dy}\right)^2 = 1 + \left(\frac{dx}{dy}\right)^2 \Rightarrow \frac{ds}{dy} = \sqrt{1 + \left(\frac{dx}{dy}\right)^2}$

i.e. $ds = \sqrt{1 + \left(\frac{dx}{dy}\right)^2}\, dy$

On integration, we get $s = \int \sqrt{1 + \left(\frac{dx}{dy}\right)^2}\, dy$

In particular, if we want to determine arc length AB, where $A(x_1, y_1), B(x_2, y_2)$ are any two points on the curve, we substitute the limits of integration for y and we have,

$$s = \int_{y_1}^{y_2} \sqrt{1 + \left(\frac{dx}{dy}\right)^2}\, dy. \qquad (II)$$

Equations (I) and (II) both give the same arc length AB.
They are to be used when equation of the curve is given in cartesian form $f(x, y) = 0$.

Note: Choice between result (I) and (II) is to be made so that integration becomes simple.

Sr. No	Equation of Curve	Formula in Differential calculus (ds)	Formula in Integral calculus (s)
1.	$y = f(x)$.	$ds = \sqrt{1 + \left(\dfrac{dy}{dx}\right)^2}\, dx$	$s = \displaystyle\int_{x_1}^{x_2} \sqrt{1 + \left(\dfrac{dy}{dx}\right)^2}\, dx$
2.	$x = f(y)$.	$ds = \sqrt{1 + \left(\dfrac{dx}{dy}\right)^2}\, dy$	$s = \displaystyle\int_{y_1}^{y_2} \sqrt{1 + \left(\dfrac{dx}{dy}\right)^2}\, dy$

Method of Solving examples:

Step-I: First observe whether the given example is in cartesian or in polar.

Step-II: Observe whether limits are given directly, if not, find the limits from the given data.

Step-III: Use the appropriate result of integral calculus.

Examples on Rectification of plane curve for Cartesian form:

Example 1: Show that the arc length of the curve

$y = \log\left[\dfrac{e^x - 1}{e^x + 1}\right]$ from $x = 1$ to $x = 2$ is $\log\left[e + \dfrac{1}{e}\right]$.

Solution: Given $y = \log\left[\dfrac{e^x - 1}{e^x + 1}\right]$

$e^y = \dfrac{e^x - 1}{e^x + 1} = \dfrac{e^{x/2} - e^{-x/2}}{e^{x/2} + e^{-x/2}} = \tanh\dfrac{x}{2}. \quad \therefore y = \log\tanh\dfrac{x}{2}.$

Differentiating w. r. t. x, we get

$\dfrac{dy}{dx} = \dfrac{\dfrac{1}{2}\text{sec}^2 h\dfrac{x}{2}}{\tanh\dfrac{x}{2}} = \dfrac{1}{2\cos^2 h\dfrac{x}{2}\dfrac{\sinh x/2}{\cosh x/2}} = \dfrac{1}{2\sinh\dfrac{x}{2}\cosh\dfrac{x}{2}} = \dfrac{1}{\sinh x}$

Thus required length is $s = \displaystyle\int_{x_1}^{x_2}\sqrt{1 + \left(\dfrac{dy}{dx}\right)^2}\, dx$

$= \displaystyle\int_{1}^{2}\sqrt{1 + \left(\dfrac{1}{\sinh x}\right)^2}\, dx = \int_{1}^{2}\sqrt{1 + \text{cosech}^2 x}\, dx$

$= \displaystyle\int_{1}^{2}\sqrt{\cot h^2 x}\, dx = \int_{1}^{2} \cot h x\, dx = \Big[\log(\sinh x)\Big]_{1}^{2}$

$= \left[\log\left(\dfrac{e^x - e^{-x}}{2}\right)\right]_{1}^{2} = \left[\log\left(\dfrac{e^2 - e^{-2}}{2}\right) - \log\left(\dfrac{e^1 - e^{-1}}{2}\right)\right]$

$= \log\left\{\left(\dfrac{e^2 - e^{-2}}{2}\right)\bigg/\left(\dfrac{e^1 - e^{-1}}{2}\right)\right\} = \log\left(\dfrac{e^2 - e^{-2}}{e^1 - e^{-1}}\right)$

$= \log\left(\dfrac{(e^1 + e^{-1})(e^1 - e^{-1})}{e^1 - e^{-1}}\right) = \log(e + e^{-1}) = \log\left(e + \dfrac{1}{e}\right).$

Note: To show the length of arc of curve $y = \log\left[\tanh\dfrac{x}{2}\right]$ from $x=1$ to $x=2$ is $\log\left[e+\dfrac{1}{e}\right]$ use the same technique.

Ex. 2: Show that the length of the arc of the curve $4ax = y^2 - 2a^2 \log\left(\dfrac{y}{a}\right) - a^2$ measured from $(0, a)$ to any point is given by $\dfrac{y^2}{2a} - \dfrac{a}{2} - x$.

Solution: Given $4ax = y^2 - 2a^2 \log\left(\dfrac{y}{a}\right) - a^2$.

Required length is $s = \int\limits_{y_1}^{y_2} \sqrt{1+\left(\dfrac{dx}{dy}\right)^2}\, dy$

i.e. $s = \int\limits_{a}^{y} \sqrt{1+\left(\dfrac{dx}{dy}\right)^2}\, dy$ \hspace{1em} (I)

As $4ax = y^2 - 2a^2 \log\left(\dfrac{y}{a}\right) - a^2$

$\therefore 4a\dfrac{dx}{dy} = 2y - \dfrac{2a^2}{y/a}\cdot\dfrac{1}{a} = 2y - \dfrac{2a^2}{y}$

$\Rightarrow 4a\dfrac{dx}{dy} = \dfrac{2y^2 - 2a^2}{y}$ \hspace{1em} $\therefore \dfrac{dx}{dy} = \dfrac{2y^2 - 2a^2}{4ay} = \dfrac{y^2 - a^2}{2ay}$

$\therefore 1+\left(\dfrac{dx}{dy}\right)^2 = 1+\left(\dfrac{y^2-a^2}{2ay}\right)^2 = 1+\dfrac{y^4 - 2y^2 a^2 + a^4}{4a^2 y^2}$

$= \dfrac{4a^2 y^2 + y^4 - 2y^2 a^2 + a^4}{4a^2 y^2} = \dfrac{y^4 + 2y^2 a^2 + a^4}{4a^2 y^2} = \dfrac{(y^2+a^2)^2}{4a^2 y^2}$

Substituting in equation (I), we get

$s = \int\limits_{a}^{y}\sqrt{\dfrac{(y^2+a^2)^2}{4a^2 y^2}}\,dy = \dfrac{1}{2a}\int\limits_{a}^{y}\dfrac{(y^2+a^2)}{y}\,dy = \dfrac{1}{2a}\int\limits_{a}^{y}\left(y+\dfrac{a^2}{y}\right)dy$

$= \dfrac{1}{2a}\left[\dfrac{y^2}{2}+a^2 \log y\right]_a^y = \dfrac{1}{2a}\left[\left(\dfrac{y^2}{2}+a^2 \log y\right)-\left(\dfrac{a^2}{2}+a^2 \log a\right)\right]$

$= \dfrac{1}{2a}\left[\dfrac{y^2}{2}+a^2 \log y - a^2 \log a - \dfrac{a^2}{2}\right] = \dfrac{1}{2a}\left[\dfrac{y^2}{2}+a^2 \log\dfrac{y}{a} - \dfrac{a^2}{2}\right]$ \hspace{1em} (A)

To get the required solution, we simplify the R.H.S of the given example and show that it tallies with equation (A).

Now, $\dfrac{y^2}{2a}-\dfrac{a}{2}-x = \dfrac{y^2}{2a}-\dfrac{a}{2}-\left[\dfrac{y^2-2a^2\log\left(\dfrac{y}{a}\right)-a^2}{4a}\right]$ $\because 4ax = y^2-2a^2\log\left(\dfrac{y}{a}\right)-a^2$

$= \dfrac{y^2}{2a}-\dfrac{a}{2}-\dfrac{y^2}{4a}+\dfrac{a}{2}\log\left(\dfrac{y}{a}\right)+\dfrac{a}{4} = \left(\dfrac{y^2}{2a}-\dfrac{y^2}{4a}\right)+\dfrac{a}{2}\log\left(\dfrac{y}{a}\right)+\left(\dfrac{a}{4}-\dfrac{a}{2}\right)$

$= \dfrac{y^2}{4a}+\dfrac{a}{2}\log\left(\dfrac{y}{a}\right)-\dfrac{a}{4} = \dfrac{1}{2a}\left[\dfrac{y^2}{2}+a^2\log\left(\dfrac{y}{a}\right)-\dfrac{a^2}{2}\right]$ (B)

From equation (A) and (B) $s = \dfrac{y^2}{2a}-\dfrac{a}{2}-x.$

Ex. 3 : Show that the whole length of the loop of the curve $9y^2 = (x+7)(x+4)^2$ is $4\sqrt{3}$.
OR Find the whole length of the loop of the curve $9y^2 = (x+7)(x+4)^2$.

Solution : First we have to trace the curve.
Curve is symmetric about x-axis. And there is a loop between x = -7 to x = - 4

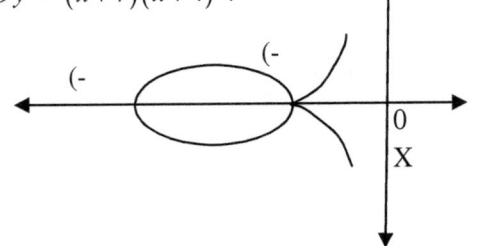

Required length is $s = \int_{x_1}^{x_2}\sqrt{1+\left(\dfrac{dy}{dx}\right)^2}\,dx$

i.e. $s = 2\int_{-7}^{-4}\sqrt{1+\left(\dfrac{dy}{dx}\right)^2}\,dx$ (I)

Given $9y^2 = (x+7)(x+4)^2$ differentiating w. r. t. x, we get

$18y\dfrac{dy}{dx} = (x+4)^2+2(x+4)(x+7) = (x+4)\left[(x+4)+(x+7).2\right]$

$\therefore \dfrac{dy}{dx} = \dfrac{(x+4)[x+4+2x+14]}{18y} = \dfrac{(x+4)(3x+18)}{18y}$

$= \dfrac{3(x+4)(x+6)}{18y} = \dfrac{(x+4)(x+6)}{6y}$

$\therefore \left(\dfrac{dy}{dx}\right)^2 = \left[\dfrac{(x+4)(x+6)}{6y}\right]^2 = \dfrac{(x+4)^2(x+6)^2}{36y^2}$

$= \dfrac{(x+4)^2(x+6)^2}{36(x+7)(x+4)^2/9}$ $\because 9y^2 = (x+7)(x+4)^2$

$\left(\dfrac{dy}{dx}\right)^2 = \dfrac{(x+6)^2}{4(x+7)}$

$\therefore 1+\left(\dfrac{dy}{dx}\right)^2 = 1+\dfrac{(x+6)^2}{4(x+7)} = \dfrac{4(x+7)+(x+6)^2}{4(x+7)}$

$= \dfrac{4x+28+x^2+12x+36}{4(x+7)}$

$= \dfrac{x^2+16x+64}{4(x+7)} = \dfrac{(x+8)^2}{4(x+7)}$

Substituting in equation (I), we get

$$s = 2\int_{-7}^{-4}\sqrt{\frac{(x+8)^2}{4(x+7)}}dx = \frac{2}{2}\int_{-7}^{-4}\frac{x+8}{\sqrt{x+7}}dx = \int_{-7}^{-4}\frac{x+7+1}{\sqrt{x+7}}dx$$

$$= \int_{-7}^{-4}\sqrt{x+7} + \frac{1}{\sqrt{x+7}}dx = \int_{-7}^{-4}(x+7)^{\frac{1}{2}} + (x+7)^{\frac{-1}{2}}dx$$

$$= \left[\frac{(x+7)^{\frac{3}{2}}}{3/2} + \frac{(x+7)^{\frac{1}{2}}}{1/2}\right]_{-7}^{-4} = \left[\left(\frac{(-4+7)^{\frac{3}{2}}}{3/2} + \frac{(-4+7)^{\frac{1}{2}}}{1/2}\right) - \left(\frac{(-7+7)^{\frac{3}{2}}}{3/2} + \frac{(-7+7)^{\frac{1}{2}}}{1/2}\right)\right]$$

$$= \frac{2}{3}(3)^{\frac{3}{2}} + 2(3)^{\frac{1}{2}} = 4\sqrt{3}.$$

Ex. 4: Show that in Catenary $y = a\cosh\frac{x}{a}$, the length of arc of the curve from vertex to any point (x, y) is (i) $s = a\sinh\left(\frac{x}{a}\right)$ (ii) $y^2 = a^2 + s^2$ (iii) $s = a\tan\psi$.

OR Find the length of arc of the Catenary $y = a\cosh\frac{x}{a}$, measured from its vertex to any point (x, y) and show that $s^2 = y^2 - a^2$. **SUK:NOV-08**

Solution: First we have to trace the curve.
Curve is symmetric about y-axis.

(i) Required length is $s = \int_{x_1}^{x_2}\sqrt{1+\left(\frac{dy}{dx}\right)^2}dx$ (I)

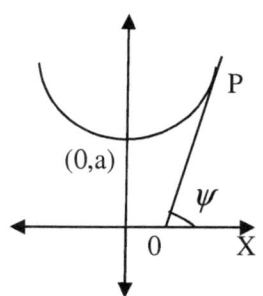

Given $y = a\cosh\frac{x}{a}$, differentiating w. r. t. x, we get

$$\frac{dy}{dx} = a\sinh\frac{x}{a}.\frac{1}{a} = \sinh\frac{x}{a} \quad \therefore \left(\frac{dy}{dx}\right)^2 = \sinh^2\frac{x}{a}$$

$$\therefore 1+\left(\frac{dy}{dx}\right)^2 = 1 + \sinh^2\frac{x}{a} = \cosh^2\frac{x}{a}.$$

Substituting in equation (I), we get

$$s = \int_0^x\sqrt{\cosh^2\frac{x}{a}}dx = \int_0^x\cosh\frac{x}{a}dx$$

$$= \left[\frac{\sinh\frac{x}{a}}{\frac{1}{a}}\right]_0^x = \left[a\sinh\frac{x}{a}\right]_0^x = \left[a\sinh\frac{x}{a} - 0\right] = a\sinh\frac{x}{a}$$

(ii) $s^2 = a^2\sinh^2\frac{x}{a} = a^2\left[\cosh^2\frac{x}{a} - 1\right]$

$$= a^2\left[\frac{y^2}{a^2} - 1\right] = y^2 - a^2. \qquad \because y = a\cosh\frac{x}{a},$$

$\therefore y^2 = s^2 + a^2.$

(iii) If the tangent at point P makes an angle ψ with the x-axis, then

$$\tan \psi = \frac{dy}{dx} = \sinh \frac{x}{a} = \frac{s}{a} \quad \therefore s = a \tan \psi.$$

Ex. 5: Find the length of the loop of the curve $3ay^2 = x(a-x)^2$.   **SUK: Dec-13**

Solution: First we have to trace the curve.
Curve is symmetric about x-axis, with $x = 0$ to $x = a$.

Hence required length is $s = 2\int_{x_1}^{x_2} \sqrt{1+\left(\frac{dy}{dx}\right)^2}\, dx$

i.e. $s = 2\int_0^a \sqrt{1+\left(\frac{dy}{dx}\right)^2}\, dx$ (I)

Given $3ay^2 = x(a-x)^2$. differentiating w. r. t. x, we get

$6ay \frac{dy}{dx} = 2x(a-x)(-1) + (a-x)^2$

$= (a-x)(a-3x)$

$\frac{dy}{dx} = \frac{(a-x)(a-3x)}{6ay} \quad \therefore \left(\frac{dy}{dx}\right)^2 = \frac{(a-x)^2(a-3x)^2}{36a^2 y^2}$

$1 + \left(\frac{dy}{dx}\right)^2 = 1 + \frac{(a-x)^2(a-3x)^2}{36a^2 y^2} = 1 + \frac{(a-x)^2(a-3x)^2}{36a^2} \cdot \frac{3a}{x(a-x)^2}$

$= 1 + \frac{(a-3x)^2}{12ax} = \frac{12ax + a^2 - 6ax + 9x^2}{12ax} = \frac{(a+3x)^2}{12ax}$

Substituting in equation (I), we get

$s = 2\int_0^a \sqrt{\frac{(a+3x)^2}{12ax}}\, dx = \frac{2}{2\sqrt{3a}} \int_0^a \frac{(a+3x)}{x^{1/2}}\, dx = \frac{1}{\sqrt{3a}} \int_0^a ax^{-1/2} + 3x^{1/2}\, dx$

$= \frac{1}{\sqrt{3a}} \left[\frac{ax^{1/2}}{1/2} + \frac{3x^{3/2}}{3/2}\right]_0^a = \frac{2}{\sqrt{3a}} \left[(a \cdot a^{1/2} + a^{3/2}) - (0)\right]$

$= \frac{2}{\sqrt{3a}} \left[a^{3/2} + a^{3/2}\right] = \frac{2}{\sqrt{3a}} \left[2a^{3/2}\right] = \frac{4}{\sqrt{3}} \left[a^{3/2} a^{-1/2}\right] = \frac{4a}{\sqrt{3}}.$

Ex. 6: Show that the length of arc of parabola $y^2 = 4ax$ cut off by the line $3y = 8x$ is $a \log 2 + \frac{15}{16}$ and that cut off by the latus rectum is $2a\left[\sqrt{2} + \log\left(1+\sqrt{2}\right)\right]$.

SUK: Aug-13, Dec-11

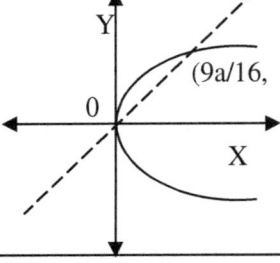

Solution: First we have to trace the curve.
Curve is symmetric about x-axis.
As $y^2 = 4ax$, $3y = 8x$

$y^2 = 4ax \Rightarrow y^2 = 4a\left(\dfrac{3y}{8}\right) = \left(\dfrac{3ay}{2}\right)$

$y^2 - \dfrac{3ay}{2} = 0 \Rightarrow \dfrac{2y^2 - 3ay}{2} = 0 \Rightarrow 2y^2 - 3ay = 0$

$(2y - 3a)y = 0 \therefore y = 0$ or $2y - 3a = 0$ i.e. $y = \dfrac{3a}{2}$

At $y = \dfrac{3a}{2} \therefore 3y = 8x \Rightarrow 3\dfrac{3a}{2} = 8x \therefore \dfrac{9a}{16} = x$

Hence required length is $s = \int_{y_1}^{y_2} \sqrt{1 + \left(\dfrac{dx}{dy}\right)^2}\, dy$

i.e. $s = \int_0^{3a/2} \sqrt{1 + \left(\dfrac{dx}{dy}\right)^2}\, dy \quad (I)$

Given $y^2 = 4ax$ differentiating w. r. t. y, we get

$2y = 4a\dfrac{dx}{dy} \Rightarrow \dfrac{dx}{dy} = \dfrac{y}{2a}$

$\therefore \left(\dfrac{dx}{dy}\right)^2 = \dfrac{y^2}{4a^2} \quad \therefore 1 + \left(\dfrac{dx}{dy}\right)^2 = 1 + \dfrac{y^2}{4a^2} = \dfrac{4a^2 + y^2}{4a^2}$

Substituting in equation (I), we get

$s = \int_0^{3a/2} \sqrt{\dfrac{4a^2 + y^2}{4a^2}}\, dy = \dfrac{1}{2a}\int_0^{3a/2} \sqrt{4a^2 + y^2}\, dy$

$= \dfrac{1}{2a}\left\{\dfrac{y\sqrt{y^2 + 4a^2}}{2} + \dfrac{4a^2}{2}\log\left(y + \sqrt{y^2 + 4a^2}\right)\right\}_0^{3a/2}$

$= \dfrac{1}{2a}\left\{\left[\dfrac{\dfrac{3a}{2}\sqrt{\left(\dfrac{3a}{2}\right)^2 + 4a^2}}{2} + \dfrac{4a^2}{2}\log\left(\dfrac{3a}{2} + \sqrt{\left(\dfrac{3a}{2}\right)^2 + 4a^2}\right)\right] - \left[0 + \dfrac{4a^2}{2}\log\left(0 + \sqrt{0 + 4a^2}\right)\right]\right\}$

$= \dfrac{1}{2a}\left\{\left[\dfrac{3a}{4}\dfrac{5a}{2} + 2a^2\log(3a/2 + 5a/2)\right] - \left[2a^2\log 2a\right]\right\}$

$= \dfrac{1}{2a}\left\{\left[\dfrac{3a}{4}\dfrac{5a}{2} + 2a^2\log\left(\dfrac{3a/2 + 5a/2}{2a}\right)\right]\right\}$

$= \dfrac{1}{2a}\left\{\dfrac{15a^2}{8} + 2a^2\log 2\right\} = \left\{\dfrac{15a}{16} + a\log 2\right\}$

$= a\left\{\dfrac{15}{16} + \log 2\right\}.$

Again, $s = 2\int_0^{2a} \sqrt{1+\left(\dfrac{dx}{dy}\right)^2}\,dy$

$s = 2\int_0^{2a} \sqrt{\dfrac{4a^2+y^2}{4a^2}}\,dy = \dfrac{2}{2a}\int_0^{2a}\sqrt{4a^2+y^2}\,dy$

$= \dfrac{1}{a}\left\{\dfrac{y\sqrt{y^2+4a^2}}{2} + 2a^2\log\left(y+\sqrt{y^2+4a^2}\right)\right\}_0^{2a}$

$= \dfrac{1}{a}\left\{\begin{bmatrix}\dfrac{2a}{2}\sqrt{4a^2+4a^2}+2a^2\log\left(2a+\sqrt{4a^2+4a^2}\right)\end{bmatrix} \\ -\begin{bmatrix}0+2a^2\log\left(0+\sqrt{0+4a^2}\right)\end{bmatrix}\right\}$

$= \dfrac{1}{a}\left\{\left[a2\sqrt{2}a + 2a^2\log\left(2a+2\sqrt{2}a\right)\right] - \left[2a^2\log 2a\right]\right\}$

$= \dfrac{1}{a}\left\{\left[2\sqrt{2}a^2 + 2a^2\log\left(\dfrac{2a+2\sqrt{2}a}{2a}\right)\right]\right\} = 2a\left\{\sqrt{2}+\log\left(1+\sqrt{2}\right)\right\}$.

Remark: Latus rectum is the chord passing through the focus perpendicular to the axis.

Example: For the parabola $y^2 = 4ax$,

$F(a,0)$ is the focus of parabola and $(a, 2a)$ and $(a,-2a)$ are the end of the latus rectum of parabola

$x = a$ is the latus rectum

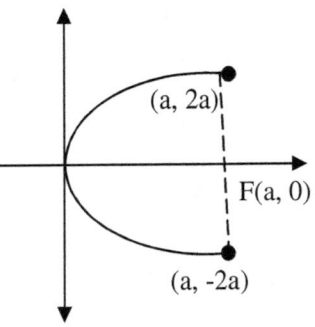

Ex. 7: Show that the length of parabola $y^2 = 4ax$ from vertex to the end of the latus rectum is $a\{\sqrt{2}+\log(1+\sqrt{2})\}$. OR Find the length of arc of parabola $y^2 = 4ax$ from vertex to one extremity of latus rectum.

Solution: First we have to trace the curve.

Given parabola is $y^2 = 4ax$, $\therefore x = a$ is the latus rectum

Therefore equation of parabola becomes

$y^2 = 4a^2$ i.e. $y = \pm 2a$ $\therefore y_1 = 0$, $y_2 = 2a$.

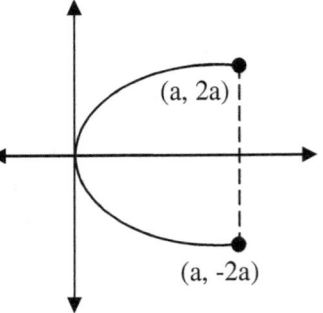

Hence required length is $s = \int_{y_1}^{y_2} \sqrt{1 + \left(\frac{dx}{dy}\right)^2} \, dy$

i.e. $s = \int_0^{2a} \sqrt{1 + \left(\frac{dx}{dy}\right)^2} \, dy$ \qquad (I)

Given $y^2 = 4ax$ differentiating w. r. t. y, we get

$2y = 4a\frac{dx}{dy} \Rightarrow \frac{dx}{dy} = \frac{y}{2a}$

$\therefore \left(\frac{dx}{dy}\right)^2 = \frac{y^2}{4a^2} \quad \therefore 1 + \left(\frac{dx}{dy}\right)^2 = 1 + \frac{y^2}{4a^2} = \frac{4a^2 + y^2}{4a^2}$

Substituting in equation (I), we get

$s = \int_0^{2a} \sqrt{\frac{4a^2 + y^2}{4a^2}} \, dy = \frac{1}{2a} \int_0^{2a} \sqrt{4a^2 + y^2} \, dy$

$= \frac{1}{2a} \left\{ \frac{y\sqrt{y^2 + 4a^2}}{2} + \frac{4a^2}{2} \log\left(y + \sqrt{y^2 + 4a^2}\right) \right\}_0^{2a}$

$= \frac{1}{2a} \left\{ \left[\frac{2a}{2}\sqrt{4a^2 + 4a^2} + 2a^2 \log\left(2a + \sqrt{4a^2 + 4a^2}\right)\right] - \left[0 + 2a^2 \log\left(0 + \sqrt{0 + 4a^2}\right)\right]\right\}$

$= \frac{1}{2a} \left\{ \left[a.2\sqrt{2} + 2a^2 \log\left(2a + 2\sqrt{2}a\right)\right] - \left[2a^2 \log 2a\right]\right\}$

$= \frac{1}{2a} \left\{ \left[2\sqrt{2}.a^2 + 2a^2 \log\left(\frac{2a + 2\sqrt{2}a}{2a}\right)\right]\right\} = a\{\sqrt{2} + \log(1 + \sqrt{2})\}.$

Ex. 8: Show that the length of the arc of the curve $ay^2 = x^3$ from origin to the point whose abscissa is b is $\frac{1}{27\sqrt{a}}(9b + 4a)^{\frac{3}{2}} - \frac{8a}{27}$.

OR Show that the length of the arc of the curve $ay^2 = x^3$ from origin to the point whose abscissa is b is $\left\{ \text{or} \left[\left(1 + \frac{9b}{4a}\right)^{\frac{3}{2}} - 1\right]\frac{8a}{27} \right\}$

Solution: First we have to trace the curve.
Given curve is symmetric about x- axis and point P is on the curve whose abscissa (x coordinate) is b.
Thus limits of integration is 0 to b.

Hence required length is $s = \int_{x_1}^{x_2} \sqrt{1 + \left(\frac{dy}{dx}\right)^2} \, dx$

i.e. $s = \int_0^b \sqrt{1 + \left(\frac{dy}{dx}\right)^2} \, dx$ \qquad (I)

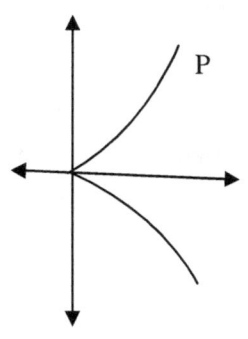

Given $ay^2 = x^3$ differentiating w. r. t. x, we get

$$2ay \frac{dy}{dx} = 3x^2 \Rightarrow \frac{dy}{dx} = \frac{3x^2}{2ay}$$

$$\therefore \left(\frac{dy}{dx}\right)^2 = \frac{9x^4}{4a^2y^2} = \frac{9x^4}{4a^2} \cdot \frac{a}{x^3} = \frac{9x}{4a} \quad \because ay^2 = x^3$$

$$1+\left(\frac{dy}{dx}\right)^2 = 1+\frac{9x}{4a} = \frac{4a+9x}{4a}$$

Substituting in equation (I), we get

$$s = \int_0^b \sqrt{\frac{4a+9x}{4a}}\,dx = \frac{1}{2\sqrt{a}}\int_0^b \sqrt{4a+9x}\,dx$$

$$= \frac{1}{2\sqrt{a}}\left[\frac{(4a+9x)^{\frac{3}{2}}}{9 \cdot \frac{3}{2}}\right]_0^b = \frac{1}{27\sqrt{a}}\left[(4a+9b)^{\frac{3}{2}} - (4a+0)^{\frac{3}{2}}\right]$$

$$= \frac{1}{27\sqrt{a}}\left[(4a+9b)^{\frac{3}{2}} - (4a)^{\frac{3}{2}}\right] = \frac{(4a+9b)^{\frac{3}{2}}}{27\sqrt{a}} - \frac{8a^{\frac{3}{2}}}{27\sqrt{a}} = \frac{(4a+9b)^{\frac{3}{2}}}{27\sqrt{a}} - \frac{8a}{27}$$

$$= \frac{8a^{\frac{3}{2}}\left(1+\frac{9b}{4a}\right)^{\frac{3}{2}}}{27\sqrt{a}} - \frac{8a}{27} = \frac{8a^{\frac{3}{2}-\frac{1}{2}}}{27}\left(1+\frac{9b}{4a}\right)^{\frac{3}{2}} - \frac{8a}{27} = \frac{8a}{27}\left(1+\frac{9b}{4a}\right)^{\frac{3}{2}} - \frac{8a}{27} = \frac{8a}{27}\left[\left(1+\frac{9b}{4a}\right)^{\frac{3}{2}} - 1\right].$$

Ex. 9 : Show that for the curve $8a^2y^2 = x^2(a^2 - x^2)$, $s = \frac{a}{2\sqrt{2}}\{2\theta + \sin\theta\cos\theta\}$ and the perimeter of one of the loops is $\frac{\pi a}{\sqrt{2}}$.

Solution: First we have to trace the curve.
Given curve is symmetric about x- axis.
We first find the arc length of the curve from origin to any point (x, y) on the curve. i.e. integrate between $x = 0$ to $x = x$

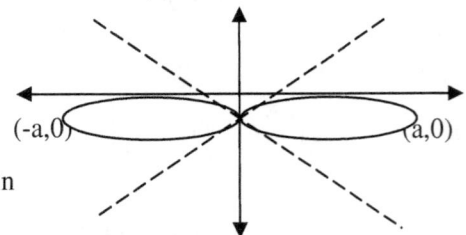

Hence required length is $s = \int_{x_1}^{x_2}\sqrt{1+\left(\frac{dy}{dx}\right)^2}\,dx$ i.e. $s = \int_0^x \sqrt{1+\left(\frac{dy}{dx}\right)^2}\,dx$ (I)

Given $8a^2y^2 = x^2(a^2 - x^2)$, differentiating w. r. t. x, we get

$8a^2y^2 = x^2(a^2 - x^2)$,

$16a^2 y \dfrac{dy}{dx} = 2x(a^2 - x^2) + x^2(-2x)$

$\qquad = 2a^2x - 2x^3 - 2x^3 = 2(a^2x - 2x^3)$

$\Rightarrow \dfrac{dy}{dx} = \dfrac{2(a^2x - 2x^3)}{16a^2y} = \dfrac{x(a^2 - 2x^2)}{8a^2 y}$

$\therefore \left(\dfrac{dy}{dx}\right)^2 = \dfrac{x^2(a^2 - 2x^2)^2}{64a^4 y^2} = \dfrac{x^2(a^2 - 2x^2)^2}{64a^4} \cdot \dfrac{8a^2}{x^2(a^2 - x^2)}$ $\qquad \therefore 8a^2y^2 = x^2(a^2 - x^2)$

$\qquad = \dfrac{(a^2 - 2x^2)^2}{8a^2(a^2 - x^2)}$

$1 + \left(\dfrac{dy}{dx}\right)^2 = 1 + \dfrac{(a^2 - 2x^2)^2}{8a^2(a^2 - x^2)} = \dfrac{8a^2(a^2 - x^2) + (a^2 - 2x^2)^2}{8a^2(a^2 - x^2)}$

$\qquad = \dfrac{8a^4 - 8a^2x^2 + a^4 - 4a^2x^2 + 4x^4}{8a^2(a^2 - x^2)} = \dfrac{9a^4 - 12a^2x^2 + 4x^4}{8a^2(a^2 - x^2)} = \dfrac{(3a^2 - 2x^2)^2}{8a^2(a^2 - x^2)}$

Substituting in equation (I), we get

$s = \int_0^x \sqrt{\dfrac{(3a^2 - 2x^2)^2}{8a^2(a^2 - x^2)}}\, dx = \int_0^x \dfrac{(3a^2 - 2x^2)}{2\sqrt{2}a\sqrt{a^2 - x^2}}\, dx = \dfrac{1}{2\sqrt{2}a} \int_0^x \dfrac{3a^2 - 2x^2}{\sqrt{a^2 - x^2}}\, dx$

Put $x = a\sin\theta \Rightarrow dx = a\cos\theta\, d\theta$

$s = \dfrac{1}{2\sqrt{2}a} \int_0^\theta \dfrac{3a^2 - 2a^2\sin^2\theta}{a\cos\theta} \cdot a\cos\theta\, d\theta$

$\quad = \dfrac{1}{2\sqrt{2}a} \int_0^\theta 3a^2 - a^2(1 - \cos 2\theta)\, d\theta$

$\quad = \dfrac{1}{2\sqrt{2}a} \int_0^\theta 2a^2 + a^2 \cos 2\theta\, d\theta$

$\quad = \dfrac{a}{2\sqrt{2}} \left[2\theta + \dfrac{\sin 2\theta}{2}\right]_0^\theta = \dfrac{a}{2\sqrt{2}}[2\theta + \sin\theta \cos\theta]$

x	0	x
θ	0	θ
upper limit of x is not known take upper limit as θ		

For the perimeter of the loop, we get

∴ $\theta = \dfrac{\pi}{2}$ when $x = a$ (Length of upper half of the loop)

$$s = \dfrac{a}{2\sqrt{2}}\left[2\dfrac{\pi}{2} + \sin\dfrac{\pi}{2}\cos\dfrac{\pi}{2}\right] = \dfrac{a\pi}{2\sqrt{2}}$$

Hence length of one loop is $= 2\dfrac{a\pi}{2\sqrt{2}} = \dfrac{a\pi}{\sqrt{2}}$.

Rectification of plane curve for Polar form:

Case-I: Let denote the equation of the curve by $r = f(\theta)$.

Let $P(r,\theta)$ and $Q(r+\delta r, \theta+\delta\theta)$ be the two adjacent points on the curve with arc $PQ = \delta s$.

Let PM perpendicular to OQ.
Then to the first order of smallness,
$$(\delta s)^2 = (\delta r)^2 + (r\delta\theta)^2 \quad (A)$$

Dividing by $(\delta\theta)^2$ and taking limits as $\delta\theta \to 0$

$$\left(\dfrac{ds}{d\theta}\right)^2 = \left(\dfrac{dr}{d\theta}\right)^2 + r^2$$

$$\therefore \dfrac{ds}{d\theta} = \sqrt{r^2 + \left(\dfrac{dr}{d\theta}\right)^2}$$

Integrating w. r. t. θ between the limits θ_1 to θ_2, we get

$$s = \int_{\theta_1}^{\theta_2}\sqrt{r^2 + \left(\dfrac{dr}{d\theta}\right)^2}\, d\theta. \quad (I)$$

Case-II: Let denote the equation of the curve by $\theta = f(r)$.

Dividing equation (A) by $(\delta r)^2$, and taking limits as $\delta r \to 0$ we get

$$\left(\dfrac{ds}{dr}\right)^2 = 1 + \left(r\dfrac{d\theta}{dr}\right)^2 \Rightarrow \dfrac{ds}{dr} = \sqrt{1 + r^2\left(\dfrac{d\theta}{dr}\right)^2}$$

Integrating w. r. t. r between the limits r_1 to r_2, we get

$$s = \int_{r_1}^{r_2}\sqrt{1 + r^2\left(\dfrac{d\theta}{dr}\right)^2}\, dr \quad (II)$$

Equations (I) and (II) both give the same arc length.
They are to be used when equation of the curve is given in polar form $f(r,\theta) = 0$.

Note: Choice between result (I) and (b) is to be made so that integration becomes simple.

Sr. No	Equation of Curve	Formula in Differential calculus (ds)	Formula in Integral calculus (s)
1.	$r = f(\theta)$.	$ds = \sqrt{r^2 + \left(\dfrac{dr}{d\theta}\right)^2}\, d\theta$	$s = \int_{\theta_1}^{\theta_2} \sqrt{r^2 + \left(\dfrac{dr}{d\theta}\right)^2}\, d\theta$
2.	$\theta = f(r)$.	$ds = \sqrt{1 + r^2 \left(\dfrac{d\theta}{dr}\right)^2}\, dr$	$s = \int_{r_1}^{r_2} \sqrt{1 + r^2 \left(\dfrac{d\theta}{dr}\right)^2}\, dr$

Examples on Rectification of plane curve for polar form:

Example1: Find the arc length of the curve $r = ae^{m\theta}$ intercepted between radii vectors r_1 and r_2.

Solution: We know that $s = \int_{r_1}^{r_2} \sqrt{1 + r^2 \left(\dfrac{d\theta}{dr}\right)^2}\, dr$ (I)

Given curve is $r = ae^{m\theta}$, differentiating w. r. t. θ we get

$\dfrac{dr}{d\theta} = ame^{m\theta} = mr \quad \therefore \left(\dfrac{dr}{d\theta}\right)^2 = m^2 r^2 \Rightarrow \left(\dfrac{d\theta}{dr}\right)^2 = \dfrac{1}{m^2 r^2}$

$\Rightarrow r^2 \left(\dfrac{dr}{d\theta}\right)^2 = r^2 \dfrac{1}{m^2 r^2} = \dfrac{1}{m^2}.$

$\therefore 1 + r^2 \left(\dfrac{dr}{d\theta}\right)^2 = 1 + \dfrac{1}{m^2} = \dfrac{m^2 + 1}{m^2}.$

Substituting in equation (I), we get

$s = \int_{r_1}^{r_2} \sqrt{\dfrac{m^2 + 1}{m^2}}\, dr = \dfrac{\sqrt{m^2 + 1}}{m} \int_{r_1}^{r_2} dr = \dfrac{\sqrt{m^2 + 1}}{m} [r]_{r_1}^{r_2}$

$s = \dfrac{\sqrt{m^2 + 1}}{m} [r_2 - r_1].$

This is the required arc length.

Ex. 2: Show that the length of spiral $r = ae^{\theta \cot \alpha}$ described as r increases from r_1 to r_2 is given by $(r_2 - r_1) \sec \alpha$.

Solution: We know that $s = \int_{r_1}^{r_2} \sqrt{1 + r^2 \left(\dfrac{d\theta}{dr}\right)^2}\, dr$ (I)

Given curve is $r = ae^{\theta \cot \alpha}$, differentiating w. r. t. θ we get

$$\frac{dr}{d\theta} = a\cot\alpha\, e^{\theta\cot\alpha} = r\cot\alpha \therefore \left(\frac{dr}{d\theta}\right)^2 = r^2\cot^2\alpha \Rightarrow \left(\frac{d\theta}{dr}\right)^2 = \frac{1}{r^2\cot^2\alpha} = \frac{\tan^2\alpha}{r^2}$$

$$\Rightarrow r^2\left(\frac{dr}{d\theta}\right)^2 = r^2\frac{\tan^2\alpha}{r^2} = \tan^2\alpha$$

$$\therefore 1 + r^2\left(\frac{dr}{d\theta}\right)^2 = 1 + \tan^2\alpha.$$

Substituting in equation (I), we get

$$s = \int_{r_1}^{r_2}\sqrt{1+\tan^2\alpha}\, dr = \int_{r_1}^{r_2}\sqrt{\sec^2\alpha}\, dr = \int_{r_1}^{r_2}\sec\alpha\, dr$$

$$= \sec\alpha\int_{r_1}^{r_2} dr = \sec\alpha\,[r]_{r_1}^{r_2} = \sec\alpha\,[r_2 - r_1].$$

Ex. 3: Find the total length of arc of the curve $r = a\sin^3\dfrac{\theta}{3}$. **SUK: NOV-12**

Solution: First we have to trace the curve
The curve is symmetric in opposite quadrants
We take the values of $\theta = 0$ to $\theta = 3\pi$.

θ	0	$\pi/2$	π	$3\pi/2$	2π	$5\pi/2$	3π
r	0	$a/8$	$3\sqrt{3}a/8$	a	$3\sqrt{3}a/8$	$a/8$	0

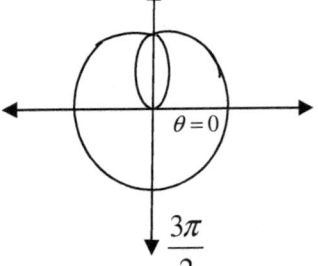

Part of the curve from $\theta = 0$ to $\theta = 3\pi/2$ is repeated from $\theta = 3\pi/2$ to $\theta = 3\pi$.

We know that $s = \int_{\theta_1}^{\theta_2}\sqrt{r^2 + \left(\dfrac{dr}{d\theta}\right)^2}\, d\theta = 2\int_0^{3\pi/2}\sqrt{r^2 + \left(\dfrac{dr}{d\theta}\right)^2}\, d\theta$ \hspace{1em} (I)

Given curve is $r = a\sin^3\dfrac{\theta}{3}$., differentiating w. r. t. θ we get

$$\frac{dr}{d\theta} = 3a\sin^2\frac{\theta}{3}\cos\frac{\theta}{3}\cdot\frac{1}{3} = a\sin^2\frac{\theta}{3}\cos\frac{\theta}{3}$$

$$\therefore \left(\frac{dr}{d\theta}\right)^2 = a^2\sin^4\frac{\theta}{3}\cos^2\frac{\theta}{3}$$

$$\Rightarrow r^2 + \left(\frac{dr}{d\theta}\right)^2 = r^2 + a^2\sin^4\frac{\theta}{3}\cos^2\frac{\theta}{3}$$

$$= a^2\sin^6\frac{\theta}{3} + a^2\sin^4\frac{\theta}{3}\cos^2\frac{\theta}{3} \quad \because r = a\sin^3\frac{\theta}{3}$$

$$= a^2\sin^4\frac{\theta}{3}\left(\sin^2\frac{\theta}{3} + \cos^2\frac{\theta}{3}\right) = a^2\sin^4\frac{\theta}{3}.$$

(5.72)

Substituting in equation (I), we get

θ	0	3π/2
t	0	π/2

$$s = 2\int_0^{3\pi/2}\sqrt{a^2\sin^4\frac{\theta}{3}}\,d\theta = 2\int_0^{3\pi/2} a\sin^2\frac{\theta}{3}\,d\theta = 2a\int_0^{3\pi/2}\sin^2\frac{\theta}{3}\,d\theta$$

Put $\dfrac{\theta}{3} = t \Rightarrow \theta = 3t \therefore d\theta = 3dt$

$$s = 2a\int_0^{\pi/2}\sin^2 t\cdot 3dt = 6a\int_0^{\pi/2}\sin^2 t\cos^0 t\,dt$$

$$= 6a\cdot\frac{1}{2}\beta\left(\frac{2+1}{2},\frac{0+1}{2}\right) \qquad \because \int_0^{\pi/2}\sin^p\theta\cos^q\theta\,d\theta = \frac{1}{2}\beta\left(\frac{p+1}{2},\frac{q+1}{2}\right)$$

$$= 3a\beta\left(\frac{3}{2},\frac{1}{2}\right) = 3a\frac{\left\lfloor\frac{3}{2}\right.\left\lfloor\frac{1}{2}\right.}{\left\lfloor\frac{3}{2}+\frac{1}{2}\right.} \qquad \because \beta(m,n) = \frac{\lfloor m\,\lfloor n}{\lfloor m+n}$$

$$= 3a\frac{\frac{1}{2}\left\lfloor\frac{1}{2}\right.\left\lfloor\frac{1}{2}\right.}{\lfloor 2} = 3a\frac{\frac{1}{2}\sqrt{\pi}\sqrt{\pi}}{\lfloor 1} = 3a\frac{\pi}{2}. \qquad \because \left\lfloor\frac{1}{2}\right. = \sqrt{\pi}$$

Ex. 4: Find the length of the upper arc of one loop of Lemniscate $r^2 = a^2\cos 2\theta$.

Solution: First we have to trace the curve
The curve is symmetric origin and initial line.

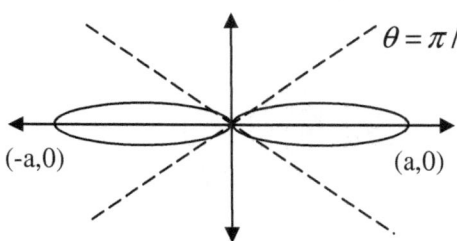

For the upper arc of one loop of the curve θ varies from $\theta = 0$ to $\theta = \pi/4$.

We know that $s = \int_{\theta_1}^{\theta_2}\sqrt{r^2 + \left(\dfrac{dr}{d\theta}\right)^2}\,d\theta = \int_0^{\pi/4}\sqrt{r^2 + \left(\dfrac{dr}{d\theta}\right)^2}\,d\theta$ (I)

Given curve is $r^2 = a^2\cos 2\theta$., differentiating w. r. t. θ we get

$$2r\frac{dr}{d\theta} = -2a^2\sin 2\theta \therefore \frac{dr}{d\theta} = \frac{-2a^2\sin 2\theta}{2r} = \frac{-2a^2\sin 2\theta}{2a\sqrt{\cos 2\theta}} = \frac{-a\sin 2\theta}{\sqrt{\cos 2\theta}} \qquad \because r^2 = a^2\cos 2\theta$$

$$\therefore \left(\frac{dr}{d\theta}\right)^2 = \frac{a^2\sin^2 2\theta}{\cos 2\theta}$$

$$\Rightarrow r^2 + \left(\frac{dr}{d\theta}\right)^2 = r^2 + \frac{a^2\sin^2 2\theta}{\cos 2\theta}$$

$$= a^2\cos 2\theta + \frac{a^2\sin^2 2\theta}{\cos 2\theta} = \frac{a^2\cos^2 2\theta + a^2\sin^2 2\theta}{\cos 2\theta} = \frac{a^2}{\cos 2\theta} \qquad \because r^2 = a^2\cos 2\theta$$

(5.73)

θ	0	π/4
t	0	π/2

Substituting in equation (I), we get

$$s = \int_0^{\pi/4} \sqrt{\frac{a^2}{\cos 2\theta}} \, d\theta = \int_0^{\pi/4} \frac{a}{\sqrt{\cos 2\theta}} \, d\theta$$

Put $2\theta = t$ ∴ $d\theta = \frac{1}{2} dt$

$$s = \int_0^{\pi/2} \frac{a}{\sqrt{\cos t}} \cdot \frac{1}{2} dt = \frac{a}{2} \int_0^{\pi/2} \sin^0 \cos^{-1/2} t \, dt$$

$$= \frac{a}{2} \cdot \frac{1}{2} \beta\left(\frac{0+1}{2}, \frac{-1/2+1}{2}\right) \quad \because \int_0^{\pi/2} \sin^p \theta \cos^q \theta \, d\theta = \frac{1}{2} \beta\left(\frac{p+1}{2}, \frac{q+1}{2}\right)$$

$$= \frac{a}{4} \beta\left(\frac{1}{2}, \frac{1}{4}\right) = \frac{a}{4} \cdot \frac{\overline{\left|\frac{1}{4}\right|} \overline{\left|\frac{1}{2}\right|}}{\overline{\left|\frac{1}{4} + \frac{1}{2}\right|}} \quad \because \beta(m,n) = \frac{\overline{|m|}\,\overline{|n|}}{\overline{|m+n|}}$$

$$= \frac{a}{4} \cdot \frac{\sqrt{\pi} \overline{\left|\frac{1}{4}\right|}}{\overline{\left|\frac{3}{4}\right|}} = \frac{a}{4} \cdot \frac{\sqrt{\pi} \left(\overline{\left|\frac{1}{4}\right|}\right)^2}{\overline{\left|\frac{1}{4}\right|}\,\overline{\left|\frac{3}{4}\right|}} \quad \because \overline{\left|\frac{1}{2}\right|} = \sqrt{\pi}$$

$$= \frac{\sqrt{\pi} a}{4} \cdot \frac{\left(\overline{\left|\frac{1}{4}\right|}\right)^2}{\sqrt{2\pi}} = \frac{a}{4\sqrt{2\sqrt{\pi}}} \left(\overline{\left|\frac{1}{4}\right|}\right)^2 \quad \because \overline{\left|\frac{1}{4}\right|}\,\overline{\left|\frac{3}{4}\right|} = \sqrt{2}\pi$$

Note: To show that the perimeter of $r^2 = a^2 \cos 2\theta$ is $\frac{a}{\sqrt{2\sqrt{\pi}}} \left(\overline{\left|\frac{1}{4}\right|}\right)^2$.

Here $s = 4 \int_{\theta_1}^{\theta_2} \sqrt{r^2 + \left(\frac{dr}{d\theta}\right)^2} \, d\theta = 4 \int_0^{\pi/4} \sqrt{r^2 + \left(\frac{dr}{d\theta}\right)^2} \, d\theta$

Solve by the same technique as that of above, we get required solution.

Ex. 5: Find the perimeter of cardiode $r = a(1 + \cos\theta)$
and show that a line $\theta = \frac{\pi}{3}$ divides upper half of the cardiode.

Solution: First we have to trace the curve
The curve is symmetric about initial line.
For the upper half arc θ varies from $\theta = 0$ to $\theta = \pi$.

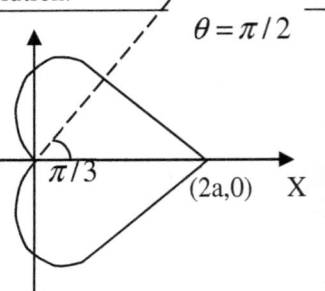

(5.74)

We know that $s = \int_{\theta_1}^{\theta_2} \sqrt{r^2 + \left(\frac{dr}{d\theta}\right)^2}\, d\theta = \int_0^{\pi} \sqrt{r^2 + \left(\frac{dr}{d\theta}\right)^2}\, d\theta$ \quad (I)

Given curve is $r = a(1+\cos\theta)$, differentiating w. r. t. θ we get

$r = a(1+\cos\theta)$

$\frac{dr}{d\theta} = -a\sin\theta \quad \therefore \left(\frac{dr}{d\theta}\right)^2 = a^2 \sin^2\theta$

$\Rightarrow r^2 + \left(\frac{dr}{d\theta}\right)^2 = r^2 + a^2\sin^2\theta = a^2(1+\cos\theta)^2 + a^2\sin^2\theta \quad \because r = a(1+\cos\theta)$

$= (a^2 + 2a^2\cos\theta + a^2\cos^2\theta + a^2\sin^2\theta)$

$= a^2(1 + 2\cos\theta + \cos^2\theta + \sin^2\theta)$

$= a^2(1 + 2\cos\theta + 1) = 2a^2(1+\cos\theta)$.

Substituting in equation (I), we get

$s = \int_0^{\pi} \sqrt{2a^2(1+\cos\theta)}\, d\theta = \int_0^{\pi} \sqrt{2}a\sqrt{1+\cos\theta}\, d\theta = \sqrt{2}a \int_0^{\pi} \sqrt{2\cos^2\frac{\theta}{2}}\, d\theta$

$= 2a\int_0^{\pi} \cos\frac{\theta}{2}\, d\theta = 4a\left[\sin\frac{\theta}{2}\right]_0^{\pi} = 4a.$

This gives length of upper half. Because of symmetry, perimeter of the cardiode is $= 2(4a) = 8a$.

Again to prove that line $\theta = \frac{\pi}{3}$ divides upper half of the cardiode.

Integrate equation (I) between the limits $\theta = 0$ to $\theta = \pi/3$.

$s = \int_0^{\pi/3} \sqrt{2a^2(1+\cos\theta)}\, d\theta = \int_0^{\pi/3} \sqrt{2}a\sqrt{1+\cos\theta}\, d\theta = \sqrt{2}a \int_0^{\pi/3} \sqrt{2\cos^2\frac{\theta}{2}}\, d\theta$

$= 2a \int_0^{\pi/3} \cos\frac{\theta}{2}\, d\theta = 4a\left[\sin\frac{\theta}{2}\right]_0^{\pi/3} = 4a\sin\frac{\pi}{6} = 4a\frac{1}{2} = 2a.$

Hence the line $\theta = \pi/3$ divides upper half.

Ex. 6: Show that the perimeter of cardioide $r = a(1+\cos\theta)$ is $8a$ and prove that an arc of the upper half of the cardioide is bisected at $\theta = \frac{\pi}{3}$.

Solution: First we have to trace the curve
The curve is symmetric about initial line.
For the upper half arc θ varies from $\theta = 0$ to $\theta = \pi$.

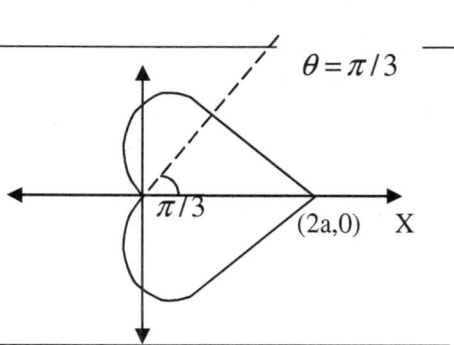

We know that $s = 2\int_{\theta_1}^{\theta_2}\sqrt{r^2+\left(\dfrac{dr}{d\theta}\right)^2}\,d\theta = 2\int_0^{\pi}\sqrt{r^2+\left(\dfrac{dr}{d\theta}\right)^2}\,d\theta$ (I)

Given curve is $r = a(1+\cos\theta)$, differentiating w. r. t. θ we get

$r = a(1+\cos\theta) \quad \therefore \dfrac{dr}{d\theta} = -a\sin\theta$

$\therefore \left(\dfrac{dr}{d\theta}\right)^2 = a^2\sin^2\theta$

$\Rightarrow r^2 + \left(\dfrac{dr}{d\theta}\right)^2 = r^2 + a^2\sin^2\theta = a^2(1+\cos\theta)^2 + a^2\sin^2\theta \quad \because r = a(1+\cos\theta)$

$= (a^2 + 2a^2\cos\theta + a^2\cos^2\theta + a^2\sin^2\theta) = a^2(1 + 2\cos\theta + \cos^2\theta + \sin^2\theta)$

$= a^2(1+2\cos\theta+1) = 2a^2(1+\cos\theta).$

Substituting in equation (I), we get

$s = 2\int_0^{\pi}\sqrt{2a^2(1+\cos\theta)}\,d\theta = 2a\int_0^{\pi}\sqrt{2(1+\cos\theta)}\,d\theta = 2a\int_0^{\pi}\sqrt{2.2\cos^2\dfrac{\theta}{2}}\,d\theta$

$= 2a\int_0^{\pi} 2\cos\dfrac{\theta}{2}\,d\theta = 8a\left[\sin\dfrac{\theta}{2}\right]_0^{\pi} = 8a.$

Again to prove that an arc of the upper half of the cardioide is bisected at $\theta = \dfrac{\pi}{3}$.

Integrate equation (I) between the limits $\theta = 0$ to $\theta = \pi/3$.

$s = \int_0^{\pi/3}\sqrt{2a^2(1+\cos\theta)}\,d\theta = \int_0^{\pi/3}\sqrt{2}a\sqrt{1+\cos\theta}\,d\theta = \sqrt{2}a\int_0^{\pi/3}\sqrt{2\cos^2\dfrac{\theta}{2}}\,d\theta$

$= 2a\int_0^{\pi/3}\cos\dfrac{\theta}{2}\,d\theta = 4a\left[\sin\dfrac{\theta}{2}\right]_0^{\pi/3} = 4a\sin\dfrac{\pi}{6} = 4a\dfrac{1}{2} = 2a.$

Hence $\theta = \pi/3$ bisected the upper half of the cardioide.

Ex. 7: Find the length of cardiode $r = a(1-\cos\theta)$ **SUK: May-10**
which lies, outside the circle $r = a\cos\theta$.

Solution: First we have to trace the curve
The equation $r = a\cos\theta$ is a circle
Passing through the pole with radius $\dfrac{a}{2}$ and centre $\left(\dfrac{a}{2},0\right)$.

At the point of intersection of two curves

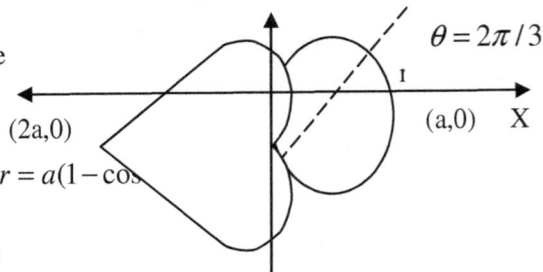

$a(1-\cos\theta) = a\cos\theta \quad \therefore \cos\theta = \dfrac{1}{2} \Rightarrow \theta = \dfrac{\pi}{3}$.

The length of the cardioide outside the circle, s is given by

$$s = 2 \times \text{Length of arc CA} = 2\int_{\theta_1}^{\theta_2}\sqrt{r^2 + \left(\dfrac{dr}{d\theta}\right)^2}\,d\theta = 2\int_{\pi/3}^{\pi}\sqrt{r^2 + \left(\dfrac{dr}{d\theta}\right)^2}\,d\theta \quad (I)$$

Since the length of the given curve is measured along cardioide, we have
$r = a(1-\cos\theta)$, differentiating w. r. t. θ we get

$\dfrac{dr}{d\theta} = a\sin\theta \qquad \therefore \left(\dfrac{dr}{d\theta}\right)^2 = a^2\sin^2\theta$

$\therefore r^2 + \left(\dfrac{dr}{d\theta}\right)^2 = r^2 + a^2\sin^2\theta = a^2(1-\cos\theta)^2 + a^2\sin^2\theta \qquad \because r = a(1-\cos\theta)$

$\qquad = a^2\left[(1-\cos\theta)^2 + \sin^2\theta\right] = a^2\left[1 - 2\cos\theta + \cos^2\theta + \sin^2\theta\right]$

$\qquad = a^2[1 - 2\cos\theta + 1] = a^2[2 - 2\cos\theta]$

$\qquad = 2a^2[1 - \cos\theta] = 2a^2\left[2\sin^2\dfrac{\theta}{2}\right] = 4a^2\sin^2\dfrac{\theta}{2}$.

Substituting in equation (I), we get

$s = 2\int_{\pi/3}^{\pi}\sqrt{4a^2\sin^2\dfrac{\theta}{2}}\,d\theta = 2\int_{\pi/3}^{\pi}2a\sin\dfrac{\theta}{2}\,d\theta$

$\quad = 4a\left[-2\cos\dfrac{\theta}{2}\right]_{\pi/3}^{\pi} = -8a\left[\cos\dfrac{\pi}{2} - \cos\dfrac{\pi}{6}\right] = -8a\left[0 - \dfrac{\sqrt{3}}{2}\right] = 4\sqrt{3}\,a$.

Ex. 8: Find the length of parabola $\dfrac{2a}{r} = 1+\cos\theta$ from the vertex to any point $P(r,\theta)$.

Solution: $s = \int_{\theta_1}^{\theta_2}\sqrt{r^2 + \left(\dfrac{dr}{d\theta}\right)^2}\,d\theta = \int_{0}^{\theta}\sqrt{r^2 + \left(\dfrac{dr}{d\theta}\right)^2}\,d\theta \qquad (I)$

Given curve is $\dfrac{2a}{r} = 1+\cos\theta \Rightarrow r = \dfrac{2a}{1+\cos\theta} = \dfrac{2a}{2\cos^2\dfrac{\theta}{2}} = a\sec^2\dfrac{\theta}{2}$

$\therefore r = a\sec^2\dfrac{\theta}{2}$. Differentiating w. r. t. θ we get

$\dfrac{dr}{d\theta} = 2a\sec^2\dfrac{\theta}{2}\tan\dfrac{\theta}{2}\cdot\dfrac{1}{2} = a\sec^2\dfrac{\theta}{2}\tan\dfrac{\theta}{2}$

$\left(\dfrac{dr}{d\theta}\right)^2 = a^2\sec^4\dfrac{\theta}{2}\tan^2\dfrac{\theta}{2}$

$r^2 + \left(\dfrac{dr}{d\theta}\right)^2 = r^2 + a^2\sec^4\dfrac{\theta}{2}\tan^2\dfrac{\theta}{2} = a^2\sec^4\dfrac{\theta}{2} + a^2\sec^4\dfrac{\theta}{2}\tan^2\dfrac{\theta}{2} \qquad \because r = a\sec^2\dfrac{\theta}{2}$

$\qquad = a^2\sec^4\dfrac{\theta}{2}\left(1 + \tan^2\dfrac{\theta}{2}\right)$.

Substituting in equation (I), we get

$$s = \int_0^\theta \sqrt{a^2 \sec^4\frac{\theta}{2}\left(1+\tan^2\frac{\theta}{2}\right)}\, d\theta = \int_0^\theta a\sec^2\frac{\theta}{2}\sqrt{1+\tan^2\frac{\theta}{2}}\, d\theta$$

Put $\tan\dfrac{\theta}{2} = t \therefore \dfrac{1}{2}\sec^2\dfrac{\theta}{2} d\theta = dt \Rightarrow \sec^2\dfrac{\theta}{2} d\theta = 2dt$

$$\therefore s = a\int_0^t \sqrt{1+t^2}\, 2dt = 2a\left[\frac{t\sqrt{1+t^2}}{2} + \frac{1}{2}\log\left(t+\sqrt{1+t^2}\right)\right]_0^t$$

$$= a\left[\tan\frac{\theta}{2}\sqrt{1+\tan^2\frac{\theta}{2}} + \log\left(\tan\frac{\theta}{2} + \sqrt{1+\tan^2\frac{\theta}{2}}\right)\right] \quad \because \tan\frac{\theta}{2} = t$$

$$= a\left[\tan\frac{\theta}{2}\sec\frac{\theta}{2} + \log\left(\tan\frac{\theta}{2} + \sec\frac{\theta}{2}\right)\right].$$

TEST YOUR KNOWLEDGE

1. Show that in the catenary $y = a\cosh\dfrac{x}{a}$, the length of arc of the curve from the vertex to any point (x, y) is given by $S = a\sinh\dfrac{x}{a}$.

2. Find the whole length of the loop of the curve $3y^2 = x(x-1)^2$. Ans. : $\dfrac{4}{\sqrt{3}}$.

3. Find the length of the arc of the curve $x = a(\cos t + t\sin t)$, $y = a(\sin t - t\cos t)$ $t = 0$ to $t = 2\pi$. Ans : $2\pi^2 a$.

4. Find the length of the arc of the parabola $3y^2 = x(x-1)^2$, $y^2 = 4x$ $y^2 = 4x$, cut off by the line $3y = 8x$. Ans: $\log 2 + \dfrac{15}{16}$.

5. Find the length of the arc of the cycloid $x = a(1-\sin\theta)$, $y = a(1-\cos\theta)$ between the two consecutive cusps. Ans: $8a$.

6. Find the length of the arc of the curve $x = e^\theta\cos\theta$, $y = e^\theta\sin\theta$ from $\theta = 0$ to $\theta = \dfrac{\pi}{2}$. Ans : $\sqrt{2}\left(e^{\pi/2} - 1\right)$.

7. Find the length of the arc of the curve $\left(\dfrac{x}{a}\right)^{2/3} + \left(\dfrac{y}{b}\right)^{2/3} = 1$, in the positive quadrant. Ans : $\dfrac{a^2 + ab + b^2}{a+b}$.

8. Show that the length of the arc of the tractrix $x = a\left(\cos t + \log\tan\dfrac{t}{2}\right)$, $y = a\sin t$ from $t = \dfrac{\pi}{2}$

To any point is $a \log \sin t$.

9. Show that the length of the arc of the curve $4ax = y^2 - 2a^2 \log \frac{y}{a} - a^2$ from $(0, a)$ to any point (x, y) is given by $S = \frac{y^2}{2a} - \frac{a}{2} - x$.

10. Evaluate $\int y^2 ds$ along the arc of the curve,
    $x = a(\cos\theta + \theta \sin\theta), \; y = a(\sin\theta - \theta \cos\theta)$. Ans: $\frac{256a^3}{15}$.

11. Find the length of the arc of the cardioide $r = a(1 - \cos\theta)$, which lies outside the circle, $r = a\cos\theta$. 	Ans: $4a\sqrt{3}$.

12. Show that the length of the arc of that part of the cardioide $r = a(1 + \cos\theta)$, which lies on the side of the line $4r = 3a \sec\theta$ remote from the pole, is equal to $4a$.

13. Show that the whole length of the arc of the limacon $r = a\cos\theta + b$ is equal to that of an ellipse whose semiaxes are equal in length to the maximum and minimum radii vectors of the limacon.

14. Find the length of any arc of the curve
    $x^{\frac{2}{3}} + y^{\frac{2}{3}} = a^{\frac{2}{3}}$. Ans: $\frac{1}{2}\left(x_2^{\frac{2}{3}} + y_2^{\frac{2}{3}}\right) - \left(x_1^{\frac{2}{3}} + y_1^{\frac{2}{3}}\right)$.

15. Find the complete arc length of the curve $x^{\frac{2}{3}} + y^{\frac{2}{3}} = a^{\frac{2}{3}}$. Ans: $6a$

YEAR WISE UNIVERSITY QUESTION PAPERS -13 SEMESTERS

Dec-2013(10/12/2013)

1. Trace the curve $y = \dfrac{x}{1+x^2}$	5
2. Trace the curve $r = a(1 - \sin\theta)$	5
3. Find the length of the loop of the curve $3ay^2 = x(x-a)^2$.	6

August-2013(16/08/2013) Re-exam

1. Trace the curve $y^2(a^2 + x^2) = x^2(a^2 - x^2)$	6
2. Trace the curve $r = a(1 + \cos\theta)$	5
3. Find the length of the arc of the parabola $y^2 = 4x$ cut off by the line $3y = 8x$	6

May-2013(18/05/2013)

1. Trace the curve $y^3 + x^3 = 3axy \; (a > 0)$	6
2. Trace the curve $r = 2\cos 2\theta$	5
3. Find the curcumberence of circle of radius a.	6

May-2012 (29/05/2012)

1. Trace the curve $y^2 = (x-1)(x-2)(x-3)$.	5
2. Trace the curve $r^2 = a^2 \cos 2\theta$	5
3. Find the perimeter of curve $r = a(1+\cos\theta)$ and show that the line $\theta = \dfrac{\pi}{3}$ divides the upper half of the curve above initial line into two equal parts.	7

Nov-2012 (20/11/2012)

1. Trace the curve $y^2(x+a) = x^2(3a-x)$.	5
2. Trace the curve $r = (a+b\cos\theta)$ for $a=b$.	5
3. Find the length of the arc of parabola $y^2 = 4ax$ cut off by the latus rectum.	6

Dec-2011 (16/12/2011)

1. Trace the curve $x^3 + y^3 = 3axy;\ a>0$	5
2. Trace the curve $r = a\sin^3\dfrac{\theta}{3}$.	5
3. Find the length of the arc of parabola $y^2 = 4ax$ cut off by the $3y = 8x$.	6

May-2011 (25/05/2011)

1. Trace the curve $y^2(x^2 - a^2) = a^3 x$	5
2. Trace the curve $r = a\cos^3\dfrac{\theta}{3}$.	5
3. Find the length of the loop of curve $y^2 = x\left(1-\dfrac{x}{3}\right)^2$	6

Nov-2010 (18/11/2010)

1. Trace the curve $3ay^2 = x^2(a-x)$	6
2. Trace the curve $r = 3 + 2\cos\theta$.	5
3. Find the total length of the curve $r = a\sin^3\dfrac{\theta}{3}$.	6

May-2010 (19/05/2010)

1. Trace the curve $y^2(x+a) = x^2(3a-x)$	5
2. Trace the curve $r = a\sin 3\theta$.	5
3. Find the length of the curve $r = a(1-\cos\theta)$ which is inside the circle $r = a\cos\theta$.	6

May-2009 (19/05/2009)

1. Trace the curve $(x+a)y^2 = a^2(a-x)$	5
2. Trace the curve $9ay^2 = x(x-3a)^2$	6
3. Trace the curve $r = 3 + 2\cos\theta$	5

4. Find the length of the loop of the curve $9y^2 = x(3-x)^2$	5
Nov-2009 (16/11/2009)	
1. Trace the curve $y^2 = (x-a)(x-b)(x-c)$ if $a<b<c$.	5
2. Trace the curve $r = a\sin^3 \dfrac{\theta}{3}$.	5
3. Find the length of arc of parabola $y^2 = 4ax$ cut off by its latus rectum.	6
May-2008 (17/05/2008)	
1. Trace the curve $y^2(a^2-x^2) = a^3 x$	5
2. Trace the curve $r^2 = a^2 \cos 2\theta$.	6
3. Trace the curve $x^3 + y^3 = 3axy$.	5
4. Find the length of arc of the curve $x = a(2\cos t - \cos 2t), y = a(2\sin t - \sin 2t)$ from $t=0$ to any point t.	
Nov-2008 (10/11/2008)	
1. Trace the curve $y^2(x^2 - a^2) = a^3 x$	6
2. Trace the curve $r = a\sin^3 \theta$	5
3. Find the length of the arc of the curve which is measured from $(0,c)$ to any point $P(x, y)$ to $y = c\cosh\dfrac{x}{c}$	6

❖ ❖ ❖

UNIT - VI

MULTIPLE INTEGRATION AND ITS APPLICATIONS

INTRODUCTION

In earlier chapters on integration, we have discussed topics like, Beta and Gamma functions, DUIS, Rectification etc. In these discussions, we came across integrals involving one variable. Applications of integration related to problems like Areas, Centre of gravity etc. require use of more than one variables. In two-dimensional problems like finding areas bounded by plane curves, moment of inertia or centre of gravity of plane laminas, we require two variables for integration, as areas in question are to be covered in two movements, one parallel to x-axis and other parallel to y-axis. Similarly in three-dimensional problems like determination of volumes, mass of solids, we shall require three variables for integration. For such types of problems, the concept of multiple integration plays an important role. Basically, it is the extension of the idea of single integration with one variable used so far. In evaluation of multiple integration problems, we have to formulate the problem first and then decide, with respect to which variable, we should carry out integration first, so that actual integration process is simplified. These and other related problems will be taken up for discussion in this chapter.

Double Integration:

Representation of Area as a Double Integral : Consider the region bounded by the curve $y = f(x)$, the ordinates $x = a, x = b$ and the X-axis. This area ABCD can be considered as the limit of the sum of an infinite number of inscribed rectangles like PMRS, where $P(x, y)$ and $Q(x + \delta x, y + \delta y)$ are two adjacent points on the curve $y = f(x)$, and the expression for the area ABCD is,

$$A = \underset{\delta x \to 0}{Lim} \sum_{x=a}^{x=b} y.\delta x$$

which is expressed in integral notation as

$$A = \int_a^b y.dx \text{ or } A = \int_a^b f(x).dx$$

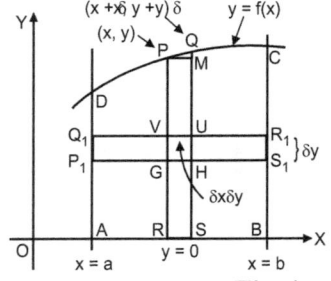

Fig. 1

Let us now consider the horizontal strip $P_1Q_1R_1S_1$ of width δy, which intersects the vertical strip PQRS in an element GHUV of area $= \delta x \delta y$. Thus we have, $\delta A = \delta x \delta y$

Now, we can first consider the summation in a vertical direction and area PQRS can be considered as the limit of a sum of an infinite number of elements like GHUV situated along the strip PQRS. Therefore, area A_1 of the strip PQRS can be expressed as,

$$A_1 = \underset{\delta y \to 0}{Lim} \left\{ \sum_{x=a}^{x=b} \delta y \right\} \delta x \quad \text{or} \quad A_1 = \left\{ \int_0^{f(x)} dy \right\} dx$$

[replacing summation sign by integral sign,

which is from $y = 0$ i.e. X-axis to $y = f(x)$ i.e. the curve]

Next we consider the summation in horizontal direction and consider the sum of all area elements like PQRS situated over the area ABCD, or in other words, we move the strip PQRS along X-axis covering the whole area ABCD and express area ABCD as,

$$A = \underset{\delta x \to 0}{Lim} \sum \left\{ \delta x \int_0^{f(x)} dy \right\}$$

or, replacing the summation sign by integral sign,

$$A = \int_{x=a}^{x=b} dx \int_{y=0}^{f(x)} dy \quad \text{or} \quad A = \int_{x=a}^{x=b} \int_{y=0}^{f(x)} dx.dy$$

Thus, the area ABCD is expressed in terms of double integral in which inner integration is carried out with respect to y treating x as constant and outer integration is then carried out with respect to x.

Question may arise as to why the area ABCD which can be computed by evaluating a single integral should be expressed in terms of double integral. Answer to this question is, double integral can handle more complicated regions than the region ABCD with simple boundaries. Then, with the help of double integral, we can compute many physical quantities like Mass, Moment of Inertia, Centre of Gravity, Centre of Pressure, etc.

Consider for example, the problem of determination of mass of area ABCD, where the density is variable and is a function of (x, y) say $f(x, y)$.

It means density varies from point to point in the region. Now, rectangular element GHUV can be considered as so small that we can treat density as constant for the region $\delta A = $ GHUV. Considering δM as the mass of element δA, we can write,

$\delta M = \rho . \delta A$ where $\rho = f(x, y)$ is density

$= f(x, y) \delta x \delta y, \qquad \delta A = \delta x \delta y$

Then, considering the summation first in a vertical direction and then in a horizontal direction, we get mass of area ABCD as,

$$M = \int_a^b \int_0^{f(x)} f(x, y) dx.dy$$ Depending upon what $f(x, y)$ represents, the double integral

$\int_a^b \int_0^{f(x)} f(x, y) dx.dy$ will represent different physical quantities in relation to area ABCD.

Irrespective of what physical quantity is represented by $\iint f(x, y) dx.dy$, we shall consider evaluation of double integral $\iint f(x, y) dx.dy$, over different regions.

We note that $\iint_R dx.dy$ represents the area of the region R and $\iint_R f(x,y)dx.dy$ represents some physical quantity related to the area of region R.

Properties of the double integrals

1. $\iint_R k f(x,y) dA = k \iint_R f(x,y) dA$ where k = constant i.e. free from x and y.

2. $\iint_R [f(x,y) \pm g(x,y)] dA = \iint_R f(x,y) dA \pm \iint_R g(x,y) dA$

3. If $R = R_1 \cup R_2$ and $R_1 \cap R_2 = \phi$ then,

$$\iint_R f(x,y) dA = \iint_{R_1} f(x,y) dA + \iint_{R_2} f(x,y) dA$$

This result holds when R is the union of two non-overlapping regions R_1 and R_2 as shown in Figure.

Evaluation of Double Integrals : Double integrals over a given region may be evaluated by three successive integrations as follows

Type-I: If limit of inner integral are functions of x

$$I = \int_a^b \int_{h(x)}^{g(x)} f(x,y) \, dx \, dy = \int_a^b \left[\int_{h(x)}^{g(x)} f(x,y) dy \right] dx.$$

We first integrate the inner integral w. r. t. y keeping x as a constant between the limits $y = h(x), y = g(x)$. Suppose we get $\phi(x)$ and then the resulting $I = \int_a^b \phi(x) dx$ be integrated w. r. t. x between the limits $x = a, \ x = b$. We get the required value of double integration.

Note: 1. Always integrate from inside outwards.

2. If limits of inner integral are functions of x, integrate it w. r. t. y

3. Limits of outmost integral are always constants

Type-II: If limit of inner integral are functions of y

$$I = \int_c^d \int_{h(y)}^{g(y)} f(x,y) \, dx \, dy = \int_c^d \left[\int_{h(y)}^{g(y)} f(x,y) dx \right] dy.$$

We first integrate the inner integral w. r. t. x keeping y as a constant between the limits $x = h(y), x = g(y)$. Suppose we get $\phi(y)$ and then the resulting $I = \int_c^d \phi(y) dy$ be integrated w. r. t. y between the limits $y = c, \ y = d$. We get the required value of double integration.

Note: 1. Always integrate from inside outwards.

2. If limits of inner integral are functions of y, integrate it w. r. t. x

3. Limits of outmost integral are always constants

Type-III: If limits of both the integrals are constants

$$I = \int_a^b \int_c^d f(x,y)dxdy = \int_a^b \left[\int_c^d f(x,y)dy\right]dx = \int_c^d \left\{\int_a^b f(x,y)dx\right\}dy.$$

If limit of both the integrals are constants then either integrate the inner integral w. r. t. x by keeping y as a constant then w. r. t. y or integrate inner integral w. r. t. y by keeping x as a constant then w. r. t. x. we get the required value of double integration.

Note: 1. Always integrate from inside outwards.

2. Integration of inner integral w. r. t. x or y is to be chosen in such a way that the evaluation of inner integral becomes possible and simple.

Examples Base on Type-I: If limit of inner integral are functions of x

$$I = \int_a^b \int_{h(x)}^{g(x)} f(x,y)\,dx\,dy = \int_a^b \left[\int_{h(x)}^{g(x)} f(x,y)dy\right]dx.$$

Ex. 1: Evaluate $\int_0^1 \int_0^{1-x} (x+y)\,dxdy.$ **SUK: Aug-13**

Solution: Here limit of inner integral is the function of x, integrating first w. r. t. y,

Let $I = \int_0^1 \int_0^{1-x} (x+y)dxdy$

$$\therefore I = \int_0^1 \left[\int_0^{1-x}(x+y)dy\right]dx$$

$$= \int_0^1 \left[x(y)+\frac{y^2}{2}\right]_0^{1-x} dx = \int_0^1 \left[\left(x(1-x)+\frac{(1-x)^2}{2}\right)-(0+0)\right]dx = \int_0^1 \left[x-x^2+\frac{1-2x+x^2}{2}\right]dx$$

$$= \int_0^1 \left[\frac{2x-2x^2+1-2x+x^2}{2}\right]dx = \frac{1}{2}\int_0^1 [1-x^2]dx = \frac{1}{2}\left[x-\frac{x^3}{3}\right]_0^1 = \frac{1}{2}\left[\left(1-\frac{1^3}{3}\right)-\left(0-\frac{0^3}{3}\right)\right] = \frac{1}{3}.$$

Ex. 2: Evaluate $\int_0^1 \int_{x^2}^x xy(x+y)\,dydx.$

Solution: Here limit of inner integral is the function of x, integrating first w. r. t. y,

Let $I = \int_0^1 \int_{x^2}^{x} xy(x+y)\,dy\,dx$.

$\therefore I = \int_0^1 \left[\int_{x^2}^{x} x^2y + xy^2\,dy \right] dx$

$= \int_0^1 \left[x^2 \frac{y^2}{2} + x\frac{y^3}{3} \right]_{x^2}^{x} dx = \int_0^1 \left[\left(x^2 \frac{x^2}{2} + x\frac{x^3}{3}\right) - \left(x^2 \frac{x^4}{2} + x\frac{x^6}{3}\right) \right] dx$

$= \int_0^1 \left[\left(\frac{x^4}{2} + \frac{x^4}{3}\right) - \left(\frac{x^6}{2} + \frac{x^7}{3}\right) \right] dx = \int_0^1 \left[\frac{5x^4}{6} - \frac{x^6}{2} - \frac{x^7}{3} \right] dx$

$= \left[\frac{5x^5}{30} - \frac{x^7}{14} - \frac{x^8}{24} \right]_0^1 = \left[\left(\frac{5 \cdot 1^5}{30} - \frac{1^7}{14} - \frac{1^8}{24}\right) - \left(\frac{5 \cdot 0^5}{30} - \frac{0^7}{14} - \frac{0^8}{24}\right) \right]$

$= \left[\frac{1}{6} - \frac{1}{14} - \frac{1}{24} \right] = \frac{3}{56}$.

Ex. 3: Evaluate $\int_0^1 \int_0^{\sqrt{a^2+x^2}} \frac{1}{a^2+x^2+y^2}\,dy\,dx$.

Solution: Here limit of inner integral is the function of x, integrating first w. r. t. y,

Let $I = \int_0^1 \int_0^{\sqrt{a^2+x^2}} \frac{1}{a^2+x^2+y^2}\,dy\,dx$

$\therefore I = \int_0^1 \left[\int_0^{\sqrt{a^2+x^2}} \frac{1}{\left(\sqrt{a^2+x^2}\right)^2 + y^2}\,dy \right] dx$

$= \int_0^1 \left[\frac{1}{\sqrt{a^2+x^2}} \tan^{-1} \frac{y}{\sqrt{a^2+x^2}} \right]_0^{\sqrt{a^2+x^2}} dx = \int_0^1 \left[\frac{1}{\sqrt{a^2+x^2}} \left(\tan^{-1} \frac{\sqrt{a^2+x^2}}{\sqrt{a^2+x^2}} - \tan^{-1} 0 \right) \right] dx$

$= \int_0^1 \left[\frac{1}{\sqrt{a^2+x^2}} \left(\tan^{-1} 1 - 0 \right) \right] dx = \int_0^1 \left[\frac{1}{\sqrt{a^2+x^2}} \cdot \frac{\pi}{4} \right] dx = \frac{\pi}{4} \int_0^1 \frac{1}{\sqrt{a^2+x^2}}\,dx$

$= \frac{\pi}{4} \left[\log\left(x + \sqrt{a^2+x^2}\right) \right]_0^1 = \frac{\pi}{4} \left[\log\left(1 + \sqrt{a^2+1}\right) - \log\left(0 + \sqrt{a^2+0}\right) \right] = \frac{\pi}{4} \left[\log\left(1 + \sqrt{a^2+1}\right) - \log a \right]$

$= \frac{\pi}{4} \log\left(\frac{1+\sqrt{a^2+1}}{a} \right)$.

Ex. 4: Evaluate $\int_0^1 \int_0^{\sqrt{1+x^2}} \frac{1}{1+x^2+y^2}\,dy\,dx$.

Solution: Here limit of inner integral is the function of x, integrating first w. r. t. y,

Let $I = \int_0^1 \int_0^{\sqrt{1+x^2}} \frac{1}{1+x^2+y^2} dy dx$

$\therefore I = \int_0^1 \left[\int_0^{\sqrt{1+x^2}} \frac{1}{\left(\sqrt{1+x^2}\right)^2 + y^2} dy \right] dx$

$= \int_0^1 \left[\frac{1}{\sqrt{1+x^2}} \tan^{-1} \frac{y}{\sqrt{1+x^2}} \right]_0^{\sqrt{1+x^2}} dx = \int_0^1 \left[\frac{1}{\sqrt{1+x^2}} \left(\tan^{-1} \frac{\sqrt{1+x^2}}{\sqrt{1+x^2}} - \tan^{-1} 0 \right) \right] dx$

$= \int_0^1 \left[\frac{1}{\sqrt{1+x^2}} \left(\tan^{-1} 1 - 0 \right) \right] dx = \int_0^1 \left[\frac{1}{\sqrt{1+x^2}} \cdot \frac{\pi}{4} \right] dx = \frac{\pi}{4} \int_0^1 \frac{1}{\sqrt{1+x^2}} dx$

$= \frac{\pi}{4} \left[\log \left(x + \sqrt{1+x^2} \right) \right]_0^1 = \frac{\pi}{4} \left[\log \left(1 + \sqrt{2} \right) - \log \left(0 + \sqrt{1+0} \right) \right] = \frac{\pi}{4} \left[\log \left(1 + \sqrt{2} \right) - \log 1 \right]$

$= \frac{\pi}{4} \log \left(1 + \sqrt{2} \right).$ $\because \log 1 = 0$

Ex. 5: Evaluate $\int_0^{a\sqrt{3}} \int_0^{\sqrt{x^2+a^2}} \frac{x}{y^2+x^2+a^2} dy dx.$ OR $\int_0^{a\sqrt{3}} \int_0^{\sqrt{x^2+a^2}} \frac{x dx dy}{x^2+y^2+a^2}$

Solution: Here limit of inner integral is the function of x, integrating first w. r. t. y,

Let $I = \int_0^{a\sqrt{3}} \int_0^{\sqrt{x^2+a^2}} \frac{x}{y^2+x^2+a^2} dy dx.$

$\therefore I = \int_0^{a\sqrt{3}} \left[\int_0^{\sqrt{x^2+a^2}} \frac{x}{y^2+\left(\sqrt{x^2+a^2}\right)^2} dy \right] dx$

$= \int_0^{a\sqrt{3}} x \left[\frac{1}{\sqrt{x^2+a^2}} \tan^{-1} \frac{y}{\sqrt{x^2+a^2}} \right]_0^{\sqrt{x^2+a^2}} dx = \int_0^{a\sqrt{3}} x \left[\frac{1}{\sqrt{x^2+a^2}} \left(\tan^{-1} \frac{\sqrt{x^2+a^2}}{\sqrt{x^2+a^2}} - \tan^{-1} 0 \right) \right] dx$

$= \int_0^{a\sqrt{3}} x \left[\frac{1}{\sqrt{x^2+a^2}} \left(\tan^{-1} 1 - 0 \right) \right] dx = \int_0^{a\sqrt{3}} x \left[\frac{1}{\sqrt{x^2+a^2}} \cdot \frac{\pi}{4} \right] dx = \frac{\pi}{4} \int_0^{a\sqrt{3}} \frac{x}{\sqrt{x^2+a^2}} dx$

$= \frac{\pi}{4} \int_0^{a\sqrt{3}} \frac{1}{2} 2x \left(x^2+a^2 \right)^{-1/2} dx$ $\because \int f'(x) f^n(x) dx = \frac{f^{n+1}(x)}{n+1}$

$= \frac{\pi}{8} \left[\frac{\left(x^2+a^2 \right)^{-1/2+1}}{-1/2+1} \right]_0^{a\sqrt{3}} = \frac{\pi}{8} \left[\frac{\left(3a^2+a^2 \right)^{1/2}}{1/2} - \frac{\left(a^2 \right)^{1/2}}{1/2} \right] = \frac{\pi}{4} \left[\left(4a^2 \right)^{1/2} - a \right] = \frac{\pi}{4} [2a - a] = \frac{a\pi}{4}.$

Ex. 6: Evaluate $\int_{-1}^1 \int_0^{1-x} x^{\frac{1}{3}} y^{\frac{-1}{2}} (1-x-y)^{\frac{1}{2}} dx dy.$

Solution: Here limit of inner integral is the function of x, integrating first w. r. t. y,

Let $I = \int_{-1}^{1}\int_{0}^{1-x} x^{\frac{1}{3}} y^{\frac{-1}{2}} (1-x-y)^{\frac{1}{2}} dxdy = \int_{-1}^{1}\left[\int_{0}^{1-x} x^{\frac{1}{3}} y^{\frac{-1}{2}} (1-x-y)^{\frac{1}{2}} dy\right] dx$ let $1-x = a$

$= \int_{-1}^{1}\left[\int_{0}^{1-x} x^{\frac{1}{3}} y^{\frac{-1}{2}} (a-y)^{\frac{1}{2}} dy\right] dx$ Put $y = at, \therefore dy = adt$

y	0	a
t	0	1

$= \int_{-1}^{1}\left[x^{\frac{1}{3}}\int_{0}^{1} (at)^{\frac{-1}{2}} (a-at)^{\frac{1}{2}} a\, dt\right] dx = \int_{-1}^{1}\left[x^{\frac{1}{3}} a\int_{0}^{1} (t)^{\frac{-1}{2}} (1-t)^{\frac{1}{2}} dt\right] dx$

$= \int_{-1}^{1}\left[x^{\frac{1}{3}} a\, \beta\left(\frac{1}{2},\frac{3}{2}\right)\right] dx = \beta\left(\frac{1}{2},\frac{3}{2}\right)\int_{-1}^{1}\left[x^{\frac{1}{3}} (1-x)\right] dx = \frac{\Gamma\frac{1}{2}\Gamma\frac{3}{2}}{\Gamma 2}\int_{-1}^{1}\left[x^{\frac{1}{3}} - x^{\frac{4}{3}}\right] dx$

$= \frac{\sqrt{\pi}\cdot\frac{1}{2}\sqrt{\pi}}{1}\left[\frac{3}{4}x^{\frac{4}{3}} - \frac{3}{7}x^{\frac{7}{3}}\right]_{-1}^{1} = \frac{\pi}{2}\left[\left(\frac{3}{4}1^{\frac{4}{3}} - \frac{3}{7}1^{\frac{7}{3}}\right) - \left(\frac{3}{4}(-1)^{\frac{4}{3}} - \frac{3}{7}(-1)^{\frac{7}{3}}\right)\right]$

$= \frac{\pi}{2}\left[\left(\frac{3}{4}-\frac{3}{7}\right) - \left(\frac{3}{4}+\frac{3}{7}\right)\right] = \frac{-3\pi}{7}$.

Ex. 7: Evaluate $\int_{0}^{1}\int_{0}^{x} e^{y/x} dxdy$.

Solution: Here limit of inner integral is the function of x, integrating first w. r. t. y,

Let $I = \int_{0}^{1}\int_{0}^{x} e^{y/x} dxdy = \int_{0}^{1}\left[\int_{0}^{x} e^{y/x} dy\right] dx = \int_{0}^{1}\left[\frac{e^{y/x}}{1/x}\right]_{0}^{x} dx = \int_{0}^{1}\left[xe^{y/x}\right]_{0}^{x} dx$

$= \int_{0}^{1}[xe - x] dx = \int_{0}^{1} x[e-1] dx = [e-1]\left[\frac{x^2}{2}\right]_{0}^{1} = [e-1]\left[\frac{1}{2}-0\right] = \frac{e-1}{2}$.

TEST YOUR KNOWLEDGE

I. Evaluate the following

1. $\int_{0}^{1}\int_{x^2}^{x} (x^2 + 3y + 2) dxdy$. Ans: $\frac{7}{12}$

2. $\int_{0}^{1}\int_{x}^{\sqrt{x}} (x^2 + y^2) dxdy$. Ans: $\frac{3}{35}$

3. $\int_{0}^{1}\int_{0}^{x^2} e^{y/x} dxdy$. Ans: $\frac{1}{2}$

4. $\int_{0}^{2a}\int_{0}^{\sqrt{2ax-x^2}} xydxdy$. Ans: $\frac{2}{3}a^4$

5. $\int_{0}^{1}\int_{x^2}^{2-x} ydxdy$. Ans: $\frac{16}{15}$

6. $\int_{0}^{1}\int_{0}^{\sqrt{1-x^2}} x^2 ydxdy$. Ans: $\frac{1}{15}$

7. $\int_{0}^{1}\int_{0}^{x} e^{x+y} dxdy$. Ans: $\frac{(e-1)^2}{2}$

8. $\int_{0}^{2}\int_{0}^{\sqrt{2x-x^2}} xdxdy$. Ans: $\frac{\pi}{2}$

9. $\int_{-2}^{1}\int_{x^2}^{2-x} ydxdy$. Ans: $\frac{36}{5}$

10. $\int_{0}^{5}\int_{0}^{x^2} x(x^2 + y^2) dxdy$. Ans: $18880\frac{5}{24}$

11. $\int_{0}^{1}\int_{x^2}^{2-x} xydxdy$. Ans: $\frac{3}{8}$

12. $\int_{0}^{1}\int_{0}^{\sqrt{1-x^2}} 4xye^{x^2} dxdy$. Ans: $e-2$

13. $\int_{0}^{1}\int_{0}^{1-x} xy\sqrt{1-x-y} dxdy$. Ans: $\frac{16}{945}$

14. $\int_{0}^{\pi}\int_{x^2}^{x} x\sin y dxdy$. Ans: $\frac{5\pi^2}{2}$

15. $\int_{1}^{\infty}\int_{x^2}^{\infty} \frac{dxdy}{x^4 + y^2}$. Ans: $\frac{\pi}{4}$

16. $\int_{0}^{\pi/2}\int_{\pi/2}^{x} \cos(x+y) dxdy$. Ans: -2

II. Prove that $\int_{0}^{1}\int_{2x^2}^{2\sqrt{x}} xy^2 dxdy = \int_{0}^{2}\int_{y^2/4}^{\sqrt{y/2}} xy^2 dxdy$. Ans: $\frac{3}{7}$

Examples Base on Type-II: If limit of inner integral are functions of y

$$I = \int_c^d \int_{h(y)}^{g(y)} f(x,y)\,dx\,dy = \int_c^d \left[\int_{h(y)}^{g(y)} f(x,y)\,dx\right] dy.$$

Ex. 1: Evaluate $\int_0^1 \int_0^y xy\,dx\,dy.$

Solution: Here limit of inner integral is the function of y, integrating first w. r. t. x,

Let $I = \int_0^1 \int_0^y xy\,dx\,dy$

$$\therefore I = \int_0^1 \left[\int_0^y xy\,dx\right] dy$$

$$= \int_0^1 \left[y \frac{x^2}{2}\right]_0^y dy = \int_0^1 \left[\left(y\frac{y^2}{2}\right) - \left(y\frac{0^2}{2}\right)\right] dy = \int_0^1 \left[\frac{y^3}{2}\right] dy$$

$$= \left[\frac{y^4}{8}\right]_0^1 = \left[\left(\frac{1^4}{8}\right) - \left(\frac{0^4}{8}\right)\right] = \frac{1}{8}.$$

Ex. 2: Evaluate $\int_0^a \int_0^{\sqrt{a^2-y^2}} \sqrt{a^2 - x^2 - y^2}\,dx\,dy.$ **SUK: May-12**

Solution: Here limit of inner integral is the function of y, integrating first w. r. t. x,

Let $I = \int_0^a \int_0^{\sqrt{a^2-y^2}} \sqrt{(a^2 - y^2) - x^2}\,dx\,dy = \int_0^a \int_0^{\sqrt{a^2-y^2}} \sqrt{\left(\sqrt{a^2-y^2}\right)^2 - x^2}\,dx\,dy$

$$= \int_0^a \left[\frac{x}{2}\sqrt{a^2 - y^2 - x^2} + \frac{(a^2 - y^2)}{2}\sin^{-1}\left(\frac{x}{\sqrt{a^2-y^2}}\right)\right]_0^{\sqrt{a^2-y^2}} dy$$

$$\because \int \sqrt{a^2 - x^2}\,dx = \frac{x}{2}\sqrt{a^2 - x^2} + \frac{a^2}{2}\sin^{-1}\left(\frac{x}{a}\right) \quad \text{here } a^2 = a^2 - y^2$$

$$= \int_0^a \left[\left\{\frac{\sqrt{a^2-y^2}}{2}\sqrt{a^2 - y^2 - \left(\sqrt{a^2-y^2}\right)^2} + \frac{(a^2-y^2)}{2}\sin^{-1}\left(\frac{\sqrt{a^2-y^2}}{\sqrt{a^2-y^2}}\right)\right\} - \left\{0 - \frac{(a^2-y^2)}{2}\sin^{-1} 0\right\}\right] dy$$

$$= \int_0^a \left[0 + \frac{(a^2-y^2)}{2}\sin^{-1} 1 - 0\right] dy = \int_0^a \frac{(a^2-y^2)}{2} \cdot \frac{\pi}{2}\,dy = \frac{\pi}{4}\int_0^a (a^2 - y^2)\,dy$$

$$= \frac{\pi}{4}\left[a^2 y - \frac{y^3}{3}\right]_0^a = \frac{\pi}{4}\left[\left(a^3 - \frac{a^3}{3}\right) - (0)\right] = \frac{\pi}{4}\left[\frac{2a^3}{3}\right] = \frac{\pi}{6}a^3.$$

Ex. 3: Evaluate $\int_0^1 \int_0^{\sqrt{\frac{1}{2}(1-y^2)}} \frac{1}{\sqrt{1-y^2-x^2}}\,dx\,dy.$ or $\int_0^1 \int_0^{\sqrt{\frac{1-y^2}{2}}} \frac{1}{\sqrt{1-x^2-y^2}}\,dx\,dy.$

Solution: Here limit of inner integral is the function of y, integrating first w. r. t. x,

Let $I = \int_0^1 \int_0^{\sqrt{\frac{1}{2}(1-y^2)}} \frac{1}{\sqrt{1-y^2-x^2}} dxdy = \int_0^1 \left[\int_0^{\sqrt{\frac{1}{2}(1-y^2)}} \frac{1}{\sqrt{(1-y^2)-x^2}} dx \right] dy$

$= \int_0^1 \left[\sin^{-1}\left(\frac{x}{\sqrt{1-y^2}}\right) \right]_0^{\sqrt{\frac{1}{2}(1-y^2)}} dy \quad \because \sin^{-1}\left(\frac{x}{a}\right) = \int \frac{1}{\sqrt{a^2-x^2}} dx$

$= \int_0^1 \left[\sin^{-1}\left(\frac{\sqrt{\frac{1}{2}(1-y^2)}}{\sqrt{1-y^2}}\right) - \sin^{-1}\left(\frac{0}{\sqrt{1-y^2}}\right) \right] dy = \int_0^1 \left[\sin^{-1}\sqrt{\frac{1}{2}} - \sin^{-1}0 \right] dy \quad \because \sin^{-1}0 = 0$

$= \int_0^1 \left[\sin^{-1}\sqrt{\frac{1}{2}} \right] dy = \int_0^1 \frac{\pi}{4} dy = \frac{\pi}{4}\int_0^1 dy = \frac{\pi}{4}[y]_0^1 = \frac{\pi}{4}[1-0] = \frac{\pi}{4}$.

Ex. 4: Evaluate $\int_0^1 \int_0^y xye^{-x^2} dxdy$.   **SUK: May-11**

Solution: Here limit of inner integral is the function of y, integrating first w. r. t. x,

Let $I = \int_0^1 \int_0^y xye^{-x^2} dxdy = -\frac{1}{2}\int_0^1 \left[\int_0^y y(-2x)e^{-x^2} dx \right] dy$

$= -\frac{1}{2}\int_0^1 y\left[e^{-x^2} \right]_0^y dy \quad \because \int f'(x)e^{f(x)} dx = e^{f(x)}$

$= -\frac{1}{2}\int_0^1 y\left[e^{-y^2} - e^0 \right] dy = -\frac{1}{2}\int_0^1 ye^{-y^2} - y\, dy = -\frac{1}{2}\int_0^1 -\frac{1}{2}(-2y)e^{-y^2} - y\, dy$

$= -\frac{1}{2}\left[-\frac{1}{2}e^{-y^2} - \frac{y^2}{2} \right]_0^1 = -\frac{1}{2}\left[\left(-\frac{1}{2}e^{-1} - \frac{1^2}{2}\right) - \left(-\frac{1}{2}e^0 - \frac{0^2}{2}\right) \right] = \frac{1}{4e}$.

Note: Alternatively put $x^2 = t$

Ex. 5: Evaluate $\int_1^2 \int_{-\sqrt{2-y}}^{\sqrt{2-y}} 2x^2y^2 \, dxdy$.

Solution: Here limit of inner integral is the function of y, integrating first w. r. t. x,

Let $I = \int_1^2 \int_{-\sqrt{2-y}}^{\sqrt{2-y}} 2x^2y^2 \, dxdy = 2\int_1^2 \left[\int_{-\sqrt{2-y}}^{\sqrt{2-y}} x^2y^2 \, dx \right] dy = 2\int_1^2 \left[y^2 \left[\frac{x^3}{3}\right]_{-\sqrt{2-y}}^{\sqrt{2-y}} \right] dy$

$= \frac{2}{3}\int_1^2 \left[y^2 \left[(2-y)^{3/2} + (2-y)^{3/2} \right] \right] dy = \frac{2}{3}\int_1^2 \left[2y^2(2-y)^{3/2} \right] dy$

$= \frac{4}{3}\int_1^2 \left[y^2(2-y)^{3/2} \right] dy$ Put $2-y = t$, $\Rightarrow y = 2-t$ $\therefore dy = -dt$ $y\to 1 \Rightarrow t = 1$ and $y \to 2 \Rightarrow t = 0$

$= \frac{4}{3}\int_1^0 \left[(2-t)^2 t^{3/2} \right](-dt) = \frac{-4}{3}\int_1^0 \left[(4-4t+t^2)t^{3/2} \right] dt = \frac{4}{3}\int_0^1 \left[4t^{3/2} - 4t^{5/2} + t^{7/2} \right] dt$

$= \frac{4}{3}\left[\frac{4t^{5/2}}{5/2} - \frac{4t^{7/2}}{7/2} + \frac{t^{9/2}}{9/2} \right]_0^1 = \frac{4}{3}\left[\frac{8}{5} - \frac{8}{7} + \frac{2}{9} \right] = \frac{856}{945}$.

Note: For evaluation of $\int_1^2 \left[2y^2(2-y)^{3/2} \right] dy$ someone may use Beta function concept.

Ex. 6: Evaluate $\int_0^1 \int_0^{1-y} x^{m-1} y^{n-1} dx dy$.

Solution: Here limit of inner integral is the function of y, integrating first w. r. t. x,

Let $I = \int_0^1 \int_0^{1-y} x^{m-1} y^{n-1} dx dy = \int_0^1 y^{n-1} \left[\int_0^{1-y} x^{m-1} dx \right] dy = \int_0^1 y^{n-1} \left[\frac{x^{m-1+1}}{m-1+1} \right]_0^{1-y} dy$

$= \frac{1}{m} \int_0^1 y^{n-1} (1-y)^m dy = \frac{1}{m} \beta(n, m+1) = \frac{1}{m} \frac{\overline{|n|} \overline{|m+1|}}{\overline{|m+n+1|}} = \frac{1}{m} \frac{\overline{|n|} \, m \overline{|m|}}{(m+n) \overline{|m+n|}} = \frac{\overline{|n|} \, \overline{|m|}}{(m+n) \overline{|m+n|}}$.

TEST YOUR KNOWLEDGE

1. Evaluate $\int_0^1 \int_{-\sqrt{y}}^{-y^2} xy \, dx dy$ Ans: $-\frac{1}{12}$

2. Evaluate $\int_0^1 \int_0^{1-y} (y - \sqrt{x}) dx dy$ Ans: $\frac{1}{10}$

3. Evaluate $\int_1^2 \int_{-\sqrt{2-y}}^{\sqrt{2-y}} 2x^2 y^2 dx dy$ Ans: $\frac{856}{945}$

4. Prove that $\int_0^2 \int_{y^2/4}^{\sqrt{y/2}} xy^2 dx dy = \int_0^1 \int_{2x^2}^{2\sqrt{x}} xy^2 dx dy$. Ans: $\frac{3}{7}$

Examples Base on Type-III: If limits of both the integrals are constants

$I = \int_a^b \int_c^d f(x,y) dx dy = \int_a^b \left[\int_c^d f(x,y) dy \right] dx = \int_c^d \left[\int_a^b f(x,y) dx \right] dy$.

Ex. 1: Evaluate $\int_0^1 \int_0^1 \frac{dx dy}{(1+x^2)(1+y^2)}$.

Solution: Here limits of both the integrals are constants

Let $I = \int_0^1 \int_0^1 \frac{dx dy}{(1+x^2)(1+y^2)}$

$= \int_0^1 \left[\int_0^1 \frac{dy}{(1+x^2)(1+y^2)} \right] dx$

$= \int_0^1 \frac{1}{(1+x^2)} \left[\tan^{-1} y \right]_0^1 dx$

$= \int_0^1 \frac{1}{(1+x^2)} \left[\tan^{-1} 1 - \tan^{-1} 0 \right] dx$

$= \int_0^1 \frac{1}{(1+x^2)} \left[\frac{\pi}{4} - 0 \right] dx$

$= \frac{\pi}{4} \int_0^1 \frac{1}{(1+x^2)} dx = \frac{\pi}{4} \left[\tan^{-1} x \right]_0^1$

$= \frac{\pi}{4} \left[\frac{\pi}{4} - 0 \right] = \frac{\pi^2}{16}$.

OR $= \int_0^1 \frac{dx}{(1+x^2)} \int_0^1 \frac{dy}{(1+y^2)}$

$= \left[\tan^{-1} y \right]_0^1 \left[\tan^{-1} x \right]_0^1$

$= \left[\tan^{-1} 1 - \tan^{-1} 0 \right] \left[\tan^{-1} 1 - \tan^{-1} 0 \right]$

$= \left[\frac{\pi}{4} - 0 \right] \left[\frac{\pi}{4} - 0 \right]$

$= \frac{\pi}{4} \cdot \frac{\pi}{4}$

$= \frac{\pi^2}{16}$.

Ex. 2: Evaluate $\int_0^\infty \int_0^\infty e^{-x^2(1+y^2)} x\,dx\,dy$.   **SUK: May-10**

Solution: Here limits of both the integrals are constants

Let $I = \int_0^\infty \int_0^\infty e^{-x^2(1+y^2)} x\,dx\,dy$.

x	0	∞
t	0	∞

Put $x^2 = t$, $2x\,dx = dt$

$\therefore I = \int_0^\infty \int_0^\infty e^{-t(1+y^2)} \dfrac{dt}{2}\,dy = \dfrac{1}{2}\int_0^\infty \left[\int_0^\infty e^{-t(1+y^2)}\,dt\right]dy = \dfrac{1}{2}\int_0^\infty \left[\dfrac{e^{-t(1+y^2)}}{-(1+y^2)}\right]_0^\infty dy = \dfrac{1}{2}\int_0^\infty \left[\left(\dfrac{e^{-\infty}}{-(1+y^2)}\right) - \left(\dfrac{e^0}{-(1+y^2)}\right)\right]dy$

$= \dfrac{1}{2}\int_0^\infty \left[(0) + \left(\dfrac{1}{1+y^2}\right)\right]dy \qquad \because e^{-\infty} = \dfrac{1}{e^\infty} = \dfrac{1}{\infty} = 0$

$= \dfrac{1}{2}\int_0^\infty \dfrac{1}{1+y^2}\,dy = \dfrac{1}{2}\left[\tan^{-1} y\right]_0^\infty = \dfrac{1}{2}\left[\tan^{-1}\infty - \tan^{-1} 0\right] = \dfrac{1}{2}\left[\dfrac{\pi}{2} - 0\right] = \dfrac{\pi}{4}$. $\because \tan^{-1}\infty = \dfrac{\pi}{2}$, $\tan^{-1} 0 = 0$

TEST YOUR KNOWLEDGE

Evaluate the following

1. $\int_0^1 \int_0^1 \dfrac{dx\,dy}{\sqrt{(1-x^2)(1-y^2)}}$ Ans: $\dfrac{\pi^2}{4}$.

2. $\int_0^1 \int_0^1 \dfrac{dx\,dy}{(1-x^2)(1-y^2)}$ Ans: $\dfrac{\pi^2}{4}$.

3. $\int_1^\infty e^{-y} \log y\,dy \int_0^1 y^x\,dx$ Ans: $\dfrac{1}{e}$.

4. $\int_0^\infty \int_0^\infty e^{-x^2(1+y^2)} x\,dx\,dy$ Ans: $\dfrac{\pi}{4}$.

5. $\int_0^\infty dx \int_0^1 e^{-x^a y}\,dy$, $a \neq 1$ Ans: $\dfrac{\sqrt{1/a}}{a-1}$.

Change of order of Integration: Some time it may happen that the integrand f(x, y) in the double integral $\int_a^b \int_{h(x)}^{g(x)} f(x,y)\,dx\,dy = \int_a^b \left[\int_{h(x)}^{g(x)} f(x,y)\,dy\right]dx$ is difficult or even impossible to integrate w. r. t. y first, but can be easily integrated w. r. t. x first, In such a situation, it becomes necessary to change (Or reverse) the order of integration in the given double integral

Similarly, in $\int_{c}^{d}\int_{h(y)}^{g(y)} f(x,y)\,dx\,dy = \int_{c}^{d}\left[\int_{h(y)}^{g(y)} f(x,y)\,dx\right]dy$ it is difficult to integrate first w. r. t. x.

In such a situation, it becomes necessary to change (Or reverse) the order of integration in the given double integral.

Method-I: Changing the strip parallel to X axis to the strip parallel to Y-axis

Let the given integral be $\int_{y=c}^{y=d}\int_{x=h(y)}^{x=g(y)} f(x,y)\,dx\,dy = \int_{y=c}^{y=d}\left[\int_{x=h(y)}^{x=g(y)} f(x,y)\,dx\right]dy$

Step-I: First write down the limits of inner most integral
i.e. $x = h(y)$, $x = g(y)$
Which implies that strip is parallel to X-axis.
Then write the limits of outer integral i.e. $y = c$, $y = d$

Step-II: From this inner and out integral draw
(Trace the curve) the figure. And find their points of interaction.(Generally outer limits curve are straight lines or curve passing through the point of intersection)

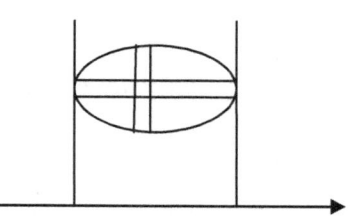

Step-III: Shade the region of integration. From this region, check whether curve is correct or wrong by taking strip parallel to X-axis (Check the limits of inner and outer integrals).

Step-IV: To change the order of integration takes the strip parallel to Y-axis in the region of integration.

Step-V: For finding the new limits

Limits of Inner integral: The lower and upper ends of the strips are the lower and upper limits respectively of the inner integral. (Find the value of y in terms of x)

Limits of outer integral: Move the strip parallel to Y-axis from left to right, then the values of x at the left and right of the strip are the lower and upper limits of outer integral. which are always constants.

Hence by changing the order of integration, we get

$\int_{x=a}^{x=b}\int_{y=h(x)}^{y=g(x)} f(x,y)\,dx\,dy = \int_{x=a}^{x=b}\left[\int_{y=h(x)}^{y=g(x)} f(x,y)\,dy\right]dx.$

Method-II: Changing the strip parallel to Y axis to the strip parallel to X-axis

Let the given integral be $I = \int_{x=a}^{x=b}\int_{y=h(x)}^{y=g(x)} f(x,y)\,dx\,dy = \int_{x=a}^{x=b}\left[\int_{y=h(x)}^{y=g(x)} f(x,y)\,dy\right]dx$

Step-I: First write down the limits of inner most integral.
i.e. $y = h(x)$, $y = g(x)$
Which implies that strip is parallel to Y-axis.
Then write the limits of outer integral i.e. $x = a$, $x = b$

Step-II: From this inner and out integral draw
(Trace the curve) the figure. And find their points of
Interaction.(Generally outer limits curve are straight lines or curve passing through the point of intersection)

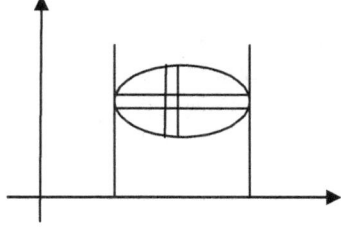

Step-III: Shade the region of integration. From this region, check whether curve is correct or wrong by taking strip parallel to Y-axis (Check the limits of inner and outer integrals).

Step-IV: To change the order of integration take the strip parallel to X-axis in the region of integration.

Step-V: For finding the new limits

Limits of Inner integral: The left and right ends of the strip are the lower and upper limits respectively of the inner integral. (Find the value of x in terms of y.)

Limits of outer integral: Move the strip parallel to X-axis from bottom to top, then the values of y at the bottom and top of the strip are the lower and upper limits of outer integral. which are always constants.

Hence by changing the order of integration, we get

$$I = \int_{y=c}^{y=d} \int_{x=h(y)}^{x=g(y)} f(x,y)\, dx\, dy = \int_{y=c}^{y=d} \left[\int_{x=h(y)}^{x=g(y)} f(x,y)\, dx \right] dy.$$

Examples on Changing the strip parallel to X axis to the strip parallel to Y-axis

Let the given integral be $\int_{y=c}^{y=d} \int_{x=h(y)}^{x=g(y)} f(x,y)\, dx\, dy = \int_{y=c}^{y=d} \left[\int_{x=h(y)}^{x=g(y)} f(x,y)\, dx \right] dy$

By changing the order of integration, we get

$$\int_{x=a}^{x=b} \int_{y=h(x)}^{y=g(x)} f(x,y)\, dx\, dy = \int_{x=a}^{x=b} \left[\int_{y=h(x)}^{y=g(x)} f(x,y)\, dy \right] dx,$$

Ex. 1: Change the order of integration and evaluate $\int_0^1 \int_{4y}^4 e^{x^2}\, dx\, dy$.

Solution: Let $I = \int_0^1 \int_{4y}^4 e^{x^2}\, dx\, dy = \int_{y=0}^{y=1} \left[\int_{x=4y}^{x=4} e^{x^2}\, dx \right] dy$ (A)

In given integral, limits of inner integral are the functions of y which implies that strip is parallel to X-axis. To change the order of integration means take the strip parallel to Y- axis. The limits of inner integral are $x = 4y$, $x = 4$ and The limits of outer integral are $y = 0$, $y = 1$.

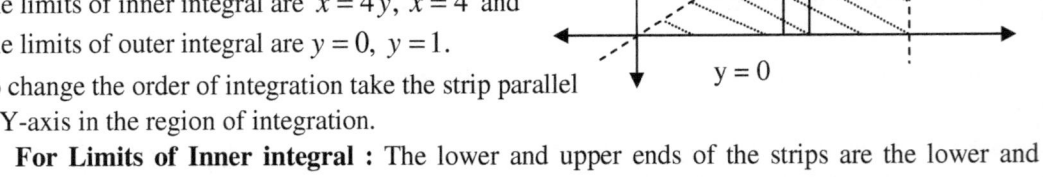

To change the order of integration take the strip parallel to Y-axis in the region of integration.

For Limits of Inner integral : The lower and upper ends of the strips are the lower and upper limits respectively of the inner integral. (Find the value of y in terms of x)

$$\therefore y = 0,\ y = \frac{x}{4}.$$

For Limits of outer integral: Move the strip parallel to Y-axis from left to right, then the values of x at the left and right of the strip are the lower and upper limits of outer integral. which are always constants. $\therefore x = 0$, $x = 4$.

Therefore from equation (A), we get

$$I = \int_{x=0}^{x=4} \left[\int_{y=0}^{y=x/4} e^{x^2} \, dy \right] dx$$

$$= \int_{x=0}^{x=4} e^{x^2} \left[[y]_0^{x/4} \right] dx = \int_{x=0}^{x=4} e^{x^2} \left[\frac{x}{4} - 0 \right] dx = \int_{x=0}^{x=4} e^{x^2} \frac{x}{4} dx$$

$$= \frac{1}{4} \int_{x=0}^{x=4} \frac{1}{2} 2x e^{x^2} \, dx = \frac{1}{8} \left[e^{x^2} \right]_0^4 = \frac{1}{8} \left[e^{4^2} - e^0 \right] = \frac{1}{8} \left[e^{16} - 1 \right].$$

Ex. 2: Evaluate $\displaystyle\int_0^1 \int_0^{\sqrt{1-y^2}} \frac{\cos^{-1} x \, dx \, dy}{\sqrt{(1-x^2-y^2)(1-x^2)}}$.

Solution: Let

$$I = \int_0^1 \int_0^{\sqrt{1-y^2}} \frac{\cos^{-1} x \, dx \, dy}{\sqrt{(1-x^2-y^2)(1-x^2)}} = \int_{y=0}^{y=1} \left[\int_{x=0}^{x=\sqrt{1-y^2}} \frac{\cos^{-1} x \, dx}{\sqrt{(1-x^2-y^2)(1-x^2)}} \right] dy \quad (A)$$

In given integral, limits of inner integral are the functions of y which implies that strip is parallel to X-axis means first integrate w. r. t. x, but it is complicated to integrate w. r. t. x.

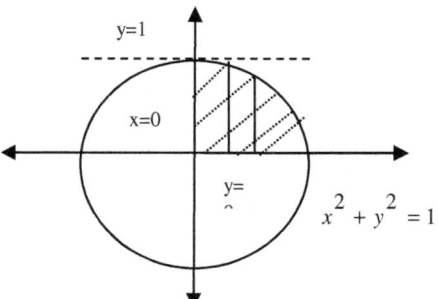

But easy to integrate w. r. t. y. Hence, it is required to change the order of integration means take the strip parallel to Y- axis.

The limits of inner integral are $x = 0$, $x = \sqrt{1-y^2}$ or $x^2 = 1 - y^2$ i.e. $x^2 + y^2 = 1$ which is a circle with centre at origin (0,0) and radius as 1. The limits of outer integral are $y = 0$, $y = 1$.

To change the order of integration take the strip parallel to Y-axis in the region of integration.

For Limits of Inner integral: The lower and upper ends of the strips are the lower and upper limits respectively of the inner integral. (Find the value of y in terms of x)

$\therefore y = 0$, $y = \sqrt{1-x^2}$.

For Limits of outer integral: Move the strip parallel to Y-axis from left to right, then the values of x at the left and right of the strip are the lower and upper limits of outer integral. which are always constants. $\therefore x = 0$, $x = 1$.

Therefore from equation (A), we get

$$I = \int_{x=0}^{x=1}\left[\int_{y=0}^{y=\sqrt{1-x^2}} \frac{\cos^{-1}x}{\sqrt{(1-x^2-y^2)(1-x^2)}}dy\right]dx = \int_{x=0}^{x=1}\frac{\cos^{-1}x}{\sqrt{(1-x^2)}}\left[\int_{y=0}^{y=\sqrt{1-x^2}}\frac{dy}{\sqrt{(1-x^2-y^2)}}\right]dx$$

$$= \int_{x=0}^{x=1}\frac{\cos^{-1}x}{\sqrt{(1-x^2)}}\left[\int_{y=0}^{y=a}\frac{dy}{\sqrt{(a^2-y^2)}}\right]dx \quad \because 1-x^2 = a^2$$

$$= \int_{x=0}^{x=1}\frac{\cos^{-1}x}{\sqrt{(1-x^2)}}\left[\sin^{-1}\frac{y}{a}\right]_0^a dx = \int_{x=0}^{x=1}\frac{\cos^{-1}x}{\sqrt{(1-x^2)}}\left[\sin^{-1}1 - \sin^{-1}0\right]dx \text{ as } \sin^{-1}1 = \frac{\pi}{2}$$

$$= \frac{\pi}{2}\int_{x=0}^{x=1}\frac{\cos^{-1}x}{\sqrt{(1-x^2)}}dx = \frac{\pi}{2}\int_{t=\pi/2}^{t=0}-t\,dt \quad \because \cos^{-1}x = t, \therefore \frac{-dx}{\sqrt{(1-x^2)}} = dt$$

$$= \frac{\pi}{2}\int_{t=0}^{t=\pi/2}t\,dt = \frac{\pi}{2}\left[\frac{t^2}{2}\right]_0^{\pi/2} = \frac{\pi}{2}\left[\frac{\pi^2}{8}\right] = \frac{\pi^3}{16}$$

x	0	1
t	$\frac{\pi}{2}$	0

Ex. 3: Evaluate $\displaystyle\int_0^a\int_0^y \frac{x\,dx\,dy}{\sqrt{(a^2-x^2)(a-y)(y-x)}}$.

Solution: Let $\displaystyle I = \int_0^a\int_0^y \frac{x\,dx\,dy}{\sqrt{(a^2-x^2)(a-y)(y-x)}} = \int_{y=0}^{y=a}\left[\int_{x=0}^{x=y}\frac{x\,dx}{\sqrt{(a^2-x^2)(a-y)(y-x)}}\right]dy$ (A)

In given integral, limits of inner integral is the functions of y which implies that strip is parallel to X-axis means first integrate w. r. t. x, but it is complicated to integrate w. r. t. x. But easy to integrate w. r. t. y. Hence, it is required to change the order of integration means take the strip parallel to Y- axis.

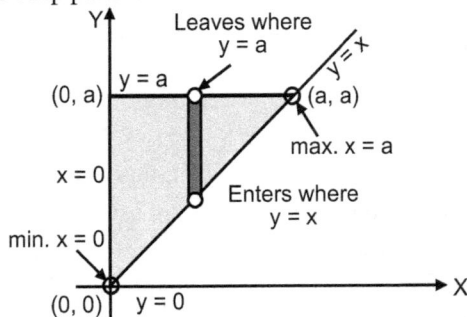

The limits of inner integral are $x = 0$, $x = y$ or $y = x$. The limits of outer integral are $y = 0$, $y = a$. To change the order of integration take the strip parallel to Y-axis in the region of integration.

For Limits of Inner integral: The lower and upper ends of the strips are the lower and upper limits respectively of the inner integral. (Find the value of y in terms of x)
∴ $y = x$, $y = a$.

For Limits of outer integral: Move the strip parallel to Y-axis from left to right, then the values of x at the left and right of the strip are the lower and upper limits of outer integral. which are always constants. ∴ $x = 0$, $x = a$.

Therefore from equation (A), we get

$$I = \int_{x=0}^{x=a} \left[\int_{y=x}^{y=a} \frac{x\,dy}{\sqrt{(a^2-x^2)(a-y)(y-x)}} \right] dx$$

$$= \int_{x=0}^{x=a} \frac{x}{\sqrt{(a^2-x^2)}} \left[\int_{y=x}^{y=a} \frac{dy}{\sqrt{(a-y)(y-x)}} \right] dx$$

Put $y - x = t^2 \Rightarrow y = x + t^2$, ∴ $dy = 2t\,dt$

y	x	a
t	0	$\sqrt{a-x}$

$$= \int_{x=0}^{x=a} \frac{x}{\sqrt{(a^2-x^2)}} \left[\int_0^{\sqrt{a-x}} \frac{2t\,dt}{\sqrt{(a-x-t^2)t^2}} \right] dx \quad \because (a-y)(y-x) = (a-x-t^2)t^2$$

$$= \int_{x=0}^{x=a} \frac{x}{\sqrt{(a^2-x^2)}} \left[2\int_0^{\sqrt{a-x}} \frac{dt}{\sqrt{(a-x)-t^2}} \right] dx = \int_{x=0}^{x=a} \frac{2x}{\sqrt{(a^2-x^2)}} \left[\sin^{-1} \frac{t}{\sqrt{a-x}} \right]_0^{\sqrt{a-x}} dx$$

$$= \int_{x=0}^{x=a} \frac{2x}{\sqrt{(a^2-x^2)}} \left[\sin^{-1} 1 - \sin^{-1} 0 \right] dx = \int_{x=0}^{x=a} \frac{2x}{\sqrt{(a^2-x^2)}} \left[\frac{\pi}{2} \right] dx$$

$$= \pi \int_{x=0}^{x=a} \frac{x}{\sqrt{(a^2-x^2)}} dx = \pi \int_{x=0}^{x=a} \frac{-1}{2} \frac{-2x}{\sqrt{(a^2-x^2)}} dx = \frac{-\pi}{2} \left[2\sqrt{(a^2-x^2)} \right]_0^a$$

$$= \frac{-\pi}{2} \left[2\sqrt{(a^2-a^2)} - 2\sqrt{(a^2-0)} \right] = \frac{-\pi}{2} [-2a] = \pi a. \quad \because \int \frac{f'(x)}{\sqrt{f(x)}} dx = 2\sqrt{f(x)}.$$

Ex. 4: Show that $\int_0^a \int_{\frac{y^2}{a}}^{y} \frac{y\,dx\,dy}{(a-x)\sqrt{ax-y^2}} = \frac{\pi a}{2}$.

Solution: Let $I = \int_0^a \int_{\frac{y^2}{a}}^{y} \frac{y\,dx\,dy}{(a-x)\sqrt{ax-y^2}} = \int_{y=0}^{y=a} \left[\int_{x=\frac{y^2}{a}}^{x=y} \frac{y\,dx}{(a-x)\sqrt{ax-y^2}} \right] dy$ (A)

Inner integral w. r. t. x is difficult to solve Hence, it is required to change the order of integration means take the strip parallel to Y- axis.

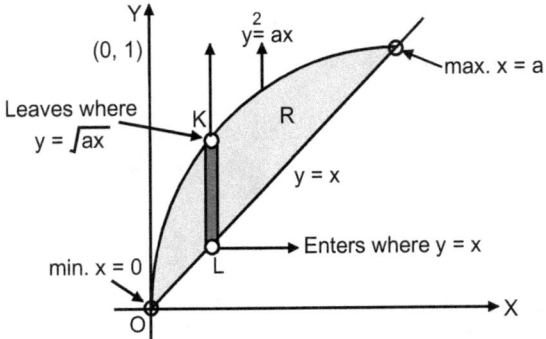

The limits of inner integral are $x = \dfrac{y^2}{a}$, i.e. $y^2 = ax$ $x = y$ or $y = x$. The limits of outer integral are $y = 0$, $y = a$.

To change the order of integration take the strip parallel to Y-axis in the region of integration.
For Limits of Inner integral: $y = x$, $y = \sqrt{ax}$.
For Limits of outer integral: $x = 0$, $x = a$.
Therefore from equation (A), we get

$$I = \int_{x=0}^{x=a}\left[\int_{y=x}^{y=\sqrt{ax}} \frac{ydy}{(a-x)\sqrt{ax-y^2}}\right]dx = \int_{x=0}^{x=a}\frac{1}{(a-x)}\left[\int_{y=x}^{y=\sqrt{ax}} \frac{ydy}{\sqrt{ax-y^2}}\right]dx$$

$$= \int_{x=0}^{x=a}\frac{1}{(a-x)}\left[\int_{y=x}^{y=\sqrt{ax}} \frac{-1}{2}\frac{-2ydy}{\sqrt{ax-y^2}}\right]dx = \frac{-1}{2}\int_{x=0}^{x=a}\frac{1}{(a-x)}\left[2\sqrt{ax-y^2}\right]_{x}^{\sqrt{ax}}dx \because \int \frac{f'(x)}{\sqrt{f(x)}}dx = 2\sqrt{f(x)}.$$

$$= -\int_{x=0}^{x=a}\frac{1}{(a-x)}\left[0 - \sqrt{ax-x^2}\right]dx = \int_{x=0}^{x=a}\frac{1}{(a-x)}\left[\sqrt{x}\sqrt{a-x}\right]dx$$

$$= \int_{x=0}^{x=a} x^{\frac{1}{2}}(a-x)^{\frac{-1}{2}}dx \text{ Put } x = at, \; dx = adt \qquad \begin{array}{|c|c|c|} \hline x & 0 & a \\ \hline t & 0 & 1 \\ \hline \end{array}$$

$$= \int_0^1 (at)^{\frac{1}{2}}(a-at)^{\frac{-1}{2}}adt = \int_0^1 (a)^{\frac{1}{2}+\frac{1}{2}}(t)^{\frac{1}{2}}(1-t)^{\frac{-1}{2}}dt = a\int_0^1 (t)^{\frac{1}{2}}(1-t)^{\frac{-1}{2}}dt$$

$$= a\beta\left(\frac{3}{2},\frac{1}{2}\right) = a\frac{\overline{\left|\frac{3}{2}\right.}\overline{\left|\frac{1}{2}\right.}}{\overline{\left|2\right.}} = a\frac{\frac{1}{2}\overline{\left|\frac{1}{2}\right.}\overline{\left|\frac{1}{2}\right.}}{\overline{\left|2\right.}} = a\frac{\frac{1}{2}\sqrt{\pi}\sqrt{\pi}}{1!} = \frac{\pi a}{2}.$$

Ex. 5: Evaluate $\displaystyle\int_0^{\pi/2}\int_0^{y} \cos 2y\sqrt{1-a^2\sin^2 x}\,dxdy$.

Solution: Let

$$I = \int_0^{\pi/2}\int_0^{y} \cos 2y\sqrt{1-a^2\sin^2 x}\,dxdy = \int_{y=0}^{y=\pi/2}\left[\int_{x=0}^{x=y} \cos 2y\sqrt{1-a^2\sin^2 x}\,dx\right]dy \quad (A)$$

Inner integral w. r. t. x is difficult to solve Hence, it is required to change the order of integration means take the strip parallel to Y- axis.

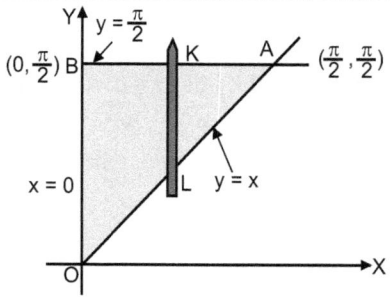

The limits of inner integral are $x = 0$, $x = y$ or $y = x$. The limits of outer integral are $y = 0$, $y = \pi/2$. To change the order of integration take the strip parallel to Y-axis in the region of integration.

For Limits of Inner integral: $y = x$, $y = \pi/2$. For Limits of outer integral: $x = 0$, $x = \pi/2$.
Therefore from equation (A), we get

$$I = \int_{x=0}^{x=\pi/2}\left[\int_{y=x}^{y=\pi/2} \cos 2y \sqrt{1-a^2 \sin^2 x}\, dy\right] dx = \int_{x=0}^{x=\pi/2} \sqrt{1-a^2 \sin^2 x}\left[\frac{\sin 2y}{2}\right]_x^{\pi/2} dx$$

$$= \int_{x=0}^{x=\pi/2} \sqrt{1-a^2 \sin^2 x}\left[\frac{\sin 2\pi/2}{2} - \frac{\sin 2x}{2}\right] dx = \int_{x=0}^{x=\pi/2} \sqrt{1-a^2 \sin^2 x}\left[0 - \frac{\sin 2x}{2}\right] dx$$

$$= \frac{-1}{2}\int_{x=0}^{x=\pi/2} \sqrt{1-a^2 \sin^2 x} \cdot \sin 2x\, dx$$

put $\sin^2 x = t$, $\therefore 2\sin x \cos x\, dx = dt$ i.e. $\sin 2x\, dx = dt$

x	0	$\pi/2$
t	0	1

$$= \frac{-1}{2}\int_0^1 \sqrt{1-a^2 t}\, dt = \frac{-1}{2}\left[\frac{(1-a^2 t)^{3/2}}{-a^2 3/2}\right]_0^1 = \frac{1}{3a^2}\left[(1-a^2)^{3/2} - 1\right].$$

Ex. 6: Show that $\displaystyle\int_0^a \int_0^{a-\sqrt{a^2-y^2}} \frac{xy \log(x+a)}{(x-a)^2} dx\,dy = \frac{a^2 (2\log a + 1)}{8}$.

Solution: Let $\displaystyle I = \int_0^a \int_0^{a-\sqrt{a^2-y^2}} \frac{xy \log(x+a)}{(x-a)^2} dx\,dy = \int_{y=0}^{y=a}\left[\int_{x=0}^{x=a-\sqrt{a^2-y^2}} \frac{xy \log(x+a)}{(x-a)^2} dx\right] dy$ (A)

Inner integral w. r. t. x is difficult to solve
Hence, it is required to change the order of integration means take the strip parallel to Y- axis. The limits of inner integral are

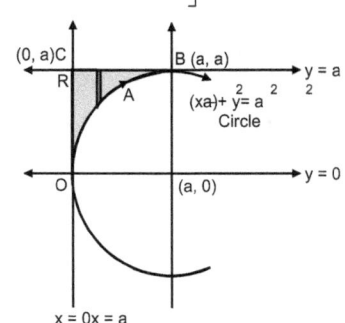

$x = 0$, $x = a - \sqrt{a^2 - y^2}$ i.e. $x - a = -\sqrt{a^2 - y^2} < 0$ or $(x-a)^2 + y^2 = a^2$ which represent a semi-circle on the negative or left side of the line $x - a = 0$ centre is at $(a, 0)$ and the radius is a The limits of outer integral are $y = 0$, $y = a$.

To change the order of integration take the strip parallel to Y-axis in the region of integration.

For Limits of Inner integral: $y = \sqrt{2ax - x^2}$, $y = a$.

For Limits of outer integral: $x = 0$, $x = a$.

Therefore from equation (A), we get

$$I = \int_{x=0}^{x=a}\left[\int_{y=\sqrt{2ax-x^2}}^{y=a} \frac{xy\log(x+a)}{(x-a)^2} dy\right] dx = \int_{x=0}^{x=a} \frac{x\log(x+a)}{(x-a)^2}\left[\int_{y=\sqrt{2ax-x^2}}^{y=a} y\,dy\right] dx$$

$$= \int_{x=0}^{x=a} \frac{x\log(x+a)}{(x-a)^2}\left[\frac{y^2}{2}\right]_{\sqrt{2ax-x^2}}^{a} dx = \int_{x=0}^{x=a} \frac{x\log(x+a)}{(x-a)^2}\left[\frac{a^2}{2} - \frac{\left(\sqrt{2ax-x^2}\right)^2}{2}\right] dx$$

$$= \int_{x=0}^{x=a} \frac{x\log(x+a)}{(x-a)^2}\left[\frac{a^2 - 2ax + x^2}{2}\right] dx = \frac{1}{2}\int_{x=0}^{x=a} \frac{x\log(x+a)}{(x-a)^2}(x-a)^2\,dx$$

$$= \frac{1}{2}\int_{x=0}^{x=a} x\log(x+a)\,dx = \frac{1}{2}\left[\log(x+a)\cdot\frac{x^2}{2}\right]_0^a - \int_0^a \frac{1}{x+a}\cdot\frac{x^2}{2}dx$$

$$= \frac{a^2}{4}[\log(2a)] - \frac{1}{4}\int_0^a \frac{x^2}{x+a}dx = \frac{a^2}{4}[\log(2a)] - \frac{1}{4}\int_0^a x - a + a^2\cdot\frac{1}{x+a}dx$$

$$\because \frac{x^2}{x+a} = \frac{x^2 - a^2 + a^2}{x+a} = \frac{(x-a)(x+a) + a^2}{x+a} = (x-a) + \frac{a^2}{x+a}.$$

$$= \frac{a^2}{4}[\log 2a] - \frac{1}{4}\left[\frac{x^2}{2} - ax + a^2\log(x+a)\right]_0^a = \frac{a^2}{8} + \frac{a^2}{4}[\log a] = \frac{a^2}{8}[1 + 2\log a].$$

Ex. 7: Change the order of integration $\int_0^a \int_{-a+\sqrt{a^2-y^2}}^{a+\sqrt{a^2-y^2}} f(x,y)dxdy$.

Solution: Let $I = \int_0^a \int_{-a+\sqrt{a^2-y^2}}^{a+\sqrt{a^2-y^2}} f(x,y)dxdy = \int_{y=0}^{y=a}\left[\int_{x=-a+\sqrt{a^2-y^2}}^{x=a+\sqrt{a^2-y^2}} f(x,y)dx\right]dy$ (A)

Inner integral w. r. t. x is difficult to solve Hence, it is required to change the order of integration means take the strip parallel to Y- axis.

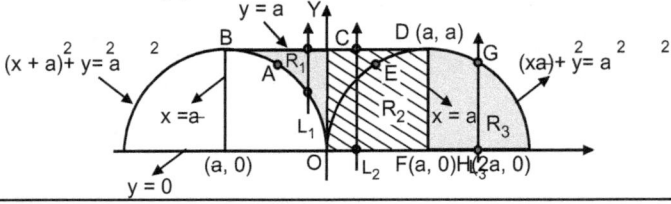

The limits of inner integral are $x = a + \sqrt{a^2 - y^2}$, i.e. $x - a = \sqrt{a^2 - y^2}$ or $(x-a)^2 + (y-0)^2 = a^2$ which represent a semi-circle with centre is at (a, 0) and the radius is a. The limits of outer integral are $x = -a + \sqrt{a^2 - y^2}$, i.e. $x + a = \sqrt{a^2 - y^2}$ or $(x+a)^2 + (y-0)^2 = a^2$ which represent a semi-circle with centre is at (-a, 0) and the radius is a. To change the order of integration take the strip parallel to Y-axis in the region of integration.

Hence the region of integration is OABCDGHFO. We divide this region into three parts by drawing the lines $x = 0$ and $x = a$

Therefore R_1 is OABC; R_2 is OCDF; R_3 is DGHF

For R_1: min $x = -a$, max $x = 0$; $y = \sqrt{a^2 - (x+a)^2}$ to $y = a$

For R_2: $x = 0$ to $x = a$; $y = 0$ to $y = a$

For R_3: min $x = a$, max $x = 2a$; $y = 0$ to $y = \sqrt{a^2 - (x-a)^2}$

$$I = \iint_{R_1} f(x,y) dx dy + \iint_{R_2} f(x,y) dx dy + \iint_{R_3} f(x,y) dx dy$$

$$\therefore I = \int_{-a}^{0} \left[\int_{\sqrt{a^2-(x+a)^2}}^{a} f(x,y) dy \right] dx + \int_{0}^{a} \left[\int_{0}^{a} f(x,y) dx \right] dy + \int_{a}^{2a} \left[\int_{0}^{\sqrt{a^2-(x-a)^2}} f(x,y) dy \right] dx.$$

Ex. 8: Change the order of integration $\int_{0}^{a} \int_{\sqrt{a^2-y^2}}^{y+a} f(x,y) dx dy$.

Solution: Let $I = \int_{0}^{a} \int_{\sqrt{a^2-y^2}}^{y+a} f(x,y) dx dy = \int_{y=0}^{y=a} \left[\int_{x=\sqrt{a^2-y^2}}^{x=y+a} f(x,y) dx \right] dy$ (A)

The limits of inner integral are

$x = \sqrt{a^2 - y^2}$, i.e. $x^2 + y^2 = a^2$ and $x = y + a$ i.e. $x - y = a$

The limits of outer integral are $y = 0$, $y = a$

Points of intersection are (0, a), (2a, a), (a, 0)
To change the order of integration take the strip parallel to Y-axis in the region of integration.
We divide the region in to two parts R_1 and R_2

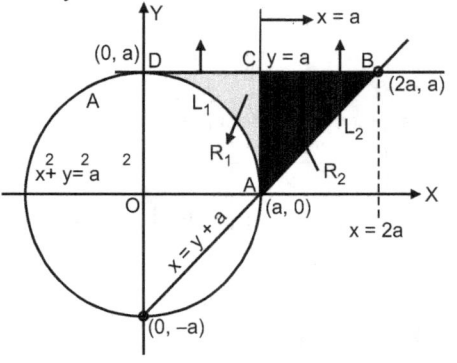

$$I = \int_{x=0}^{x=a} \left[\int_{y=\sqrt{a^2-x^2}}^{y=a} f(x,y) dy \right] dx + \int_{x=a}^{x=2a} \left[\int_{y=x-a}^{y=a} f(x,y) dy \right] dx.$$

Ex. 9 : Change the order of integration $\displaystyle\int_0^1 \int_{1-\sqrt{1-y}}^{1+\sqrt{1-y}} \frac{dxdy}{(x^2 - 2x + y - 3)^2}$.

Solution: Let $\displaystyle I = \int_0^1 \int_{1-\sqrt{1-y}}^{1+\sqrt{1-y}} \frac{dxdy}{(x^2 - 2x + y - 3)^2} = \int_{y=0}^{y=1}\left[\int_{x=1-\sqrt{1-y}}^{x=1+\sqrt{1-y}} \frac{1}{(x^2 - 2x + y - 3)^2} dx\right] dy$ ...(A)

The limits of inner integral are
$x = 1 - \sqrt{1-y}$, i.e. $(x-1)^2 = 1 - y$ and $x = 1 + \sqrt{1-y}$, i.e. $(x-1)^2 = 1 - y$
The limits of outer integral are $y = 0$, $y = 1$

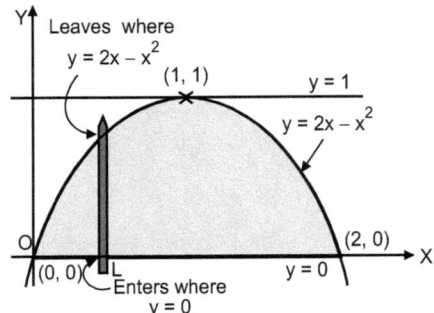

To change the order of integration take the strip parallel to Y-axis in the region of integration.

$\displaystyle I = \int_{x=0}^{x=2}\left[\int_{y=0}^{y=2x-x^2} \frac{1}{(x^2 - 2x + y - 3)^2} dy\right] dx = \int_{x=0}^{x=2}\left[\frac{-1}{(x^2 - 2x + y - 3)}\right]_0^{2x-x^2} dx$

$\displaystyle = -\int_{x=0}^{x=2}\left[\frac{1}{(x^2 - 2x + 2x - x^2 - 3)} - \frac{1}{(x^2 - 2x + 0 - 3)}\right] dx = -\int_{x=0}^{x=2}\left[\frac{1}{-3} - \frac{1}{(x^2 - 2x - 3)}\right] dx$

$\displaystyle = \int_{x=0}^{x=2}\left[\frac{1}{3} + \frac{1}{(x-3)(x+1)}\right] dx = \int_{x=0}^{x=2}\left[\frac{1}{3} + \frac{1}{4}\frac{1}{(x-3)} - \frac{1}{4}\frac{1}{(x+1)}\right] dx$

$\displaystyle = \int_{x=0}^{x=2}\left[\frac{1}{3} - \frac{1}{4}\frac{1}{(3-x)} - \frac{1}{4}\frac{1}{(x+1)}\right] dx \quad \because 0 < x < 2$

$\displaystyle = \left[\frac{1}{3}x + \frac{1}{4}\log(3-x) - \frac{1}{4}\log(x+1)\right]_0^2 = \left[\frac{2}{3} - \frac{1}{4}\log 3 - \frac{1}{4}\log 3\right] = \frac{2}{3} - \frac{1}{2}\log 3.$

Ex. 10: Show that $\displaystyle\int_0^1 \int_1^{\sqrt{2-y^2}} \frac{ydxdy}{\sqrt{(2-x^2)(1-x^2y^2)}} = 1 - \frac{\pi}{4}$.

Solution: Let $\displaystyle I = \int_0^1 \int_1^{\sqrt{2-y^2}} \frac{ydxdy}{\sqrt{(2-x^2)(1-x^2y^2)}} = \int_{y=0}^{y=1}\left[\int_{x=1}^{x=\sqrt{2-y^2}} \frac{ydx}{\sqrt{(2-x^2)(1-x^2y^2)}}\right] dy$ ...(A)

Inner integral w. r. t. x is difficult to solve Hence, it is required to change the order of integration means take the strip parallel to Y- axis.

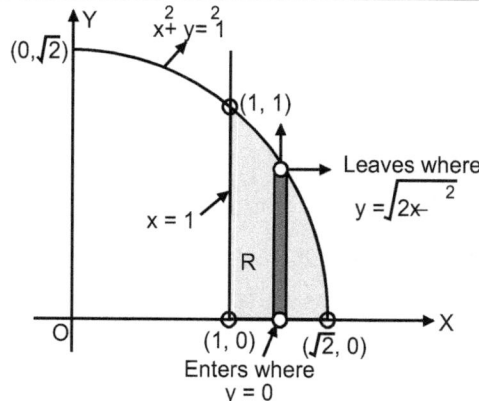

The limits of inner integral are $x=1$, $x=\sqrt{2-y^2}$ i.e. $x^2+y^2=2$ which a circle with centre is at $(0,0)$ and the radius is $\sqrt{2}$. The limits of outer integral are $y=0$, $y=1$

Points of intersections are $(\sqrt{2},0),(1,1)$.

For Limits of Inner integral: $y=0$, $y=\sqrt{2-x^2}$.

For Limits of outer integral: $x=1$, $x=\sqrt{2}$.

Therefore from equation (A), we get

$$I = \int_{x=1}^{x=\sqrt{2}} \left[\int_{y=0}^{y=\sqrt{2-x^2}} \frac{y\,dy}{\sqrt{(2-x^2)(1-x^2y^2)}} \right] dx = \int_{x=1}^{x=\sqrt{2}} \frac{dx}{\sqrt{(2-x^2)}} \left[\int_{y=0}^{y=\sqrt{2-x^2}} \frac{y\,dy}{\sqrt{(1-x^2y^2)}} \right]$$

$$= \int_{x=1}^{x=\sqrt{2}} \frac{dx}{\sqrt{(2-x^2)}} \left[\int_{y=0}^{y=\sqrt{2-x^2}} \frac{1}{-2x^2} \frac{-2x^2 y\,dy}{\sqrt{(1-x^2y^2)}} \right] = \int_{x=1}^{x=\sqrt{2}} \frac{dx}{\sqrt{(2-x^2)}} \left[\frac{1}{-2x^2} \left\{ 2\sqrt{(1-x^2y^2)} \right\}_0^{\sqrt{2-x^2}} \right]$$

$$= \int_{x=1}^{x=\sqrt{2}} \frac{dx}{\sqrt{(2-x^2)}} \left[\frac{1}{-x^2} \left\{ \sqrt{(1-x^2(2-x^2))} -1 \right\} \right] = \int_{x=1}^{x=\sqrt{2}} \frac{dx}{\sqrt{(2-x^2)}} \left[\frac{1}{x^2} \left\{ 1-\sqrt{1-2x^2+x^4} \right\} \right]$$

$$= \int_{x=1}^{x=\sqrt{2}} \frac{dx}{\sqrt{(2-x^2)}} \left[\frac{1}{x^2} \left\{ 1-\sqrt{(x^2-1)^2} \right\} \right] = \int_{x=1}^{x=\sqrt{2}} \frac{dx}{\sqrt{(2-x^2)}} \left[\frac{1}{x^2} \{1-x^2+1\} \right] = \int_{x=1}^{x=\sqrt{2}} \frac{dx}{\sqrt{(2-x^2)}} \left[\frac{2-x^2}{x^2} \right]$$

$$= \int_{x=1}^{x=\sqrt{2}} \left[\frac{\sqrt{2-x^2}}{x^2} \right] dx \quad \text{Put } x^2 = 2\sin^2\theta \Rightarrow x=\sqrt{2}\sin\theta,\ dx=\sqrt{2}\cos\theta\,d\theta$$

x	1	$\sqrt{2}$
θ	$\dfrac{\pi}{4}$	$\dfrac{\pi}{2}$

$$= \int_{\pi/4}^{\pi/2} \frac{\sqrt{2-2\sin^2\theta}}{2\sin^2\theta} \sqrt{2}\cos\theta\,d\theta = \int_{\pi/4}^{\pi/2} \frac{\cos^2\theta}{\sin^2\theta} d\theta = \int_{\pi/4}^{\pi/2} (\csc^2\theta -1)\,d\theta$$

$$= [-\cot\theta - \theta]_{\pi/4}^{\pi/2} = [(0-\pi/2)-(-1-\pi/4)] = 1-\pi/4.$$

Ex. 11: Change the orger of integration $\int_0^a \int_y^{\sqrt{ay}} \dfrac{x}{x^2+y^2} dx dy$.

Solution: Let $I = \int_0^a \int_y^{\sqrt{ay}} \dfrac{x}{x^2+y^2} dx dy = \int_{y=0}^{y=a}\left[\int_{x=y}^{x=\sqrt{ay}} \dfrac{x}{x^2+y^2} dx\right] dy$ (A)

The limits of inner integral are $x = y$, $x = \sqrt{ay}$ i.e. $x^2 = ay$. The limits of outer integral are $y = 0$, $y = a$ Points of intersections are $(0,0), (a,a)$.

For Limits of Inner integral: $y = x^2/a$, $y = x$.
For Limits of outer integral: $x = 0$, $x = a$.

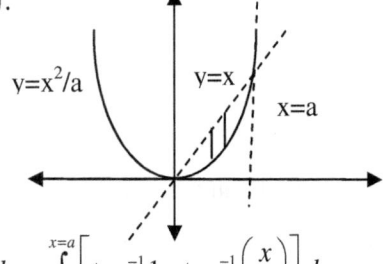

Therefore from equation (A), we get

$I = \int_{x=0}^{x=a}\left[\int_{y=x^2/a}^{y=x} \dfrac{x}{x^2+y^2} dy\right] dx = \int_{x=0}^{x=a} x\left[\dfrac{1}{x}\tan^{-1}\left(\dfrac{y}{x}\right)\right]_{x^2/a}^{x} dx = \int_{x=0}^{x=a}\left[\tan^{-1} 1 - \tan^{-1}\left(\dfrac{x}{a}\right)\right] dx$

$= \int_{x=0}^{x=a}\left[\dfrac{\pi}{4} - \tan^{-1}\left(\dfrac{x}{a}\right)\right] dx = \dfrac{\pi}{4}[x]_0^a - \left[\tan^{-1}\left(\dfrac{x}{a}\right)\int 1 dx - \int \dfrac{d}{dx}\tan^{-1}\left(\dfrac{x}{a}\right)\int 1 dx\right]_0^a$

$= \dfrac{\pi}{4}[a - 0] - \left[x\tan^{-1}\left(\dfrac{x}{a}\right) - \int \dfrac{1}{1+(x^2/a^2)} \cdot \dfrac{x}{a} dx\right]_0^a = \dfrac{\pi a}{4} - \left[x\tan^{-1}\left(\dfrac{x}{a}\right) - a\int \dfrac{x}{a^2+x^2} dx\right]_0^a$

$= \dfrac{\pi a}{4} - \left[x\tan^{-1}\left(\dfrac{x}{a}\right) - \dfrac{a}{2}\int \dfrac{2x}{a^2+x^2} dx\right]_0^a = \dfrac{\pi a}{4} - \left[x\tan^{-1}\left(\dfrac{x}{a}\right) - \dfrac{a}{2}\log(a^2+x^2)\right]_0^a$

$= \dfrac{\pi a}{4} - \left[a\left(\dfrac{\pi}{4}\right) - \dfrac{a}{2}\log(2a^2) - \left(0 - \dfrac{a}{2}\log a^2\right)\right] = \dfrac{\pi a}{4} - \left[\dfrac{a\pi}{4} - \dfrac{a}{2}\log(2a^2) + \dfrac{a}{2}\log a^2\right]$

$= \dfrac{\pi a}{4} - \dfrac{a\pi}{4} + \dfrac{a}{2}\log(2a^2) - \dfrac{a}{2}\log a^2 = \dfrac{a}{2}\left[\log(2a^2) - \log a^2\right] = \dfrac{a}{2}\log\left(\dfrac{2a^2}{a^2}\right) = \dfrac{a}{2}\log 2.$

Ex. 12: Change the order of integration and evaluate $\int_0^2 \int_{-2+\sqrt{4-y^2}}^{2+\sqrt{4-y^2}} dx dy$.

Solution: Let $I = \int_0^2 \int_{-2+\sqrt{4-y^2}}^{2+\sqrt{4-y^2}} dx dy = \int_{y=0}^{y=2}\left[\int_{x=-2+\sqrt{4-y^2}}^{x=2+\sqrt{4-y^2}} dx\right] dy$ (A)

Inner integral w. r. t. x is difficult to solve Hence, it is required to change the order of integration means take the strip parallel to Y- axis.

The limits of inner integral are

$x = 2 + \sqrt{4 - y^2}$, i.e. $x - 2 = \sqrt{4 - y^2}$ or $(x - 2)^2 = 4 - y^2 \Rightarrow (x - 2)^2 + y^2 = 4$

$x = 2 - \sqrt{4 - y^2}$, i.e. $x - 2 = -\sqrt{4 - y^2}$ or $(x - 2)^2 = 4 - y^2 \Rightarrow (x - 2)^2 + y^2 = 4$

which represent a circle with centre is at $(2, 0)$ and the radius is 2. The limits of outer integral are $y = 0$, $y = 2$

To change the order of integration take the strip parallel to Y-axis in the region of integration.

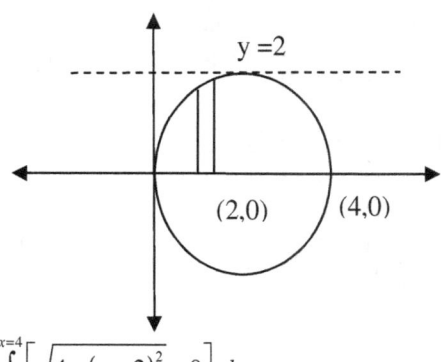

$$I = \int_{x=0}^{x=4}\left[\int_{y=0}^{y=\sqrt{4-(x-2)^2}} dy\right] dx = \int_{x=0}^{x=4}\left[[y]_0^{\sqrt{4-(x-2)^2}}\right] dx = \int_{x=0}^{x=4}\left[\sqrt{4-(x-2)^2} - 0\right] dx$$

$$= \int_{x=0}^{x=4}\left[\sqrt{(2)^2 - (x-2)^2}\right] dx = \left[\frac{(x-2)}{2}\sqrt{(2)^2 - (x-2)^2} + \frac{4}{2}\sin^{-1}\frac{(x-2)}{2}\right]_0^4$$

$$= \left[\left(0 + 2\frac{\pi}{2}\right) - \left(0 - 2\frac{\pi}{2}\right)\right] = \pi + \pi = 2\pi.$$

Ex. 13 : Combine into a single term integral $I = \int_0^a \int_0^y f(x, y)\, dy\, dx + \int_a^\infty \int_0^{a^2/y} f(x, y)\, dy\, dx$.

Solution : Region of integration for first integral on R.H.S. is bounded by the lines $x = 0$, $x = y$, $y = 0$, $y = a$ it is region A_1 shown shaded in Figure

Region for second integral on R.H.S. is bounded by $x = 0$, $x = \frac{a^2}{y}$ i.e. $xy = a^2$

$y = a$ and $y = \infty$. It is region A_2 extending upto infinity in vertical direction as shown in the figure.

In the combined region A_1, A_2 if we consider a vertical line, its lower end lies on the line $y = x$ and upper end touches hyperbola $xy = a^2$. Thus, along the vertical strip, y varies from $y = x$ to $y = \frac{a^2}{x}$.

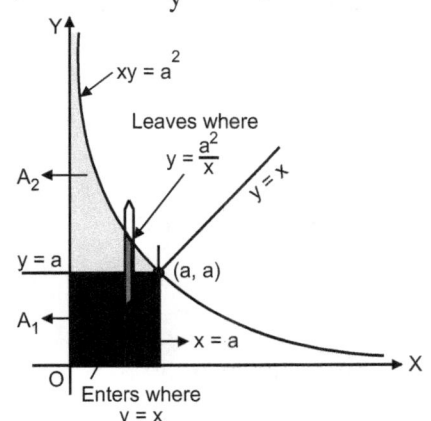

If this strip is moved horizontally to cover the whole region, x shows variation from x = 0 to x = a. Thus, by changing the order of integration, the sum of two given integrals can be combined into a single integral as,
$$I = \int_0^a \int_x^{a^2/x} f(x, y) \, dx \, dy.$$

TEST YOUR KNOWLEDGE

I. Change the order of following integral and prove that

1. $\displaystyle\int_0^1 \int_0^{\sqrt{1-y^2}} \frac{\cos^{-1} x \, dx \, dy}{\sqrt{(1-x^2-y^2)(1-x^2)}} = \frac{\pi^3}{16}$

2. $\displaystyle\int_0^1 \int_{4y}^4 e^{x^2} \, dx \, dy = \frac{e^{16}-1}{8}$

3. $\displaystyle\int_0^\infty \int_y^\infty \frac{e^{-x}}{x} \, dx \, dy = 1$

4. $\displaystyle\int_0^a \int_0^y \frac{dx \, dy}{\sqrt{(a^2+x^2)(a-y)(y-x)}} = \pi \log(1+\sqrt{2})$

II. Change the order of integration and evaluate $\displaystyle\int_0^2 \int_{2-\sqrt{4-y^2}}^{2+\sqrt{4-y^2}} dx \, dy$ **Ans. :** 2π

Hint : By changing the order, $I = \displaystyle\int_0^4 \int_0^{\sqrt{4-(x-2)^2}} dx \cdot dy$

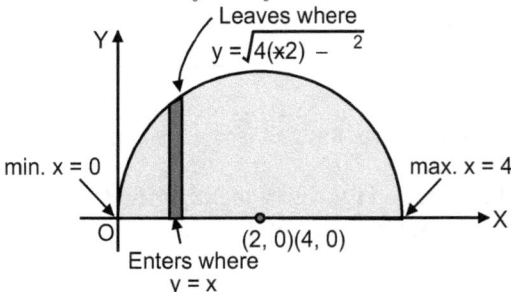

III. Change the order of integration of following double integrals :

1. $\displaystyle\int_1^2 \int_y^{y^2} f(x, y) \, dx \, dy$

2. $\displaystyle\int_{-a}^a \int_0^{\frac{y^2}{a}} f(x, y) \, dx \, dy$

3. $\displaystyle\int_0^{a\sqrt{2}} \int_y^{\sqrt{a^2-y^2}} f(x, y) \, dx \, dy$

4. $\displaystyle\int_0^3 \int_{\frac{y^2}{9}}^{\sqrt{10-y^2}} f(x, y) \, dx \, dy$

5. $\displaystyle\int_0^a \int_{\sqrt{2ay-y^2}}^{a+\sqrt{a^2-y^2}} f(x, y) \, dx \, dy$

6. $\displaystyle\int_0^1 \int_{1-\sqrt{1-y}}^{1+\sqrt{1-y}} f(x, y) \, dx \, dy$

7. $\int_{-2a}^{0}\int_{2a-\sqrt{4a^2-y^2}}^{a+\frac{y^2}{4a}} f(x,y)\,dy\,dx$

8. $\int_{0}^{b}\int_{a-\frac{a}{b}\sqrt{b^2-y^2}}^{a\frac{y^2}{b^2}} f(x,y)\,dx\,dy$

III. Express the following double integrals as single term integrals.

1. $\int_{0}^{1}\int_{-\sqrt{y}}^{\sqrt{y}} dx\,dy + \int_{1}^{2}\int_{-1}^{1} dx\,dy$ and evaluate. **Ans.:** $\dfrac{10}{3}$

2. $\int_{0}^{1}\int_{0}^{y}(x^2+y^2)\,dx\,dy + \int_{1}^{2}\int_{0}^{2-y}(x^2+y^2)\,dx\,dy$ and evaluate. **Ans.:** $\dfrac{4}{3}$

3. $\int_{-3}^{2}\int_{2-y}^{5} f(x,y)\,dx\,dy + \int_{2}^{7}\int_{y-2}^{5} f(x,y)\,dx\,dy$ **Ans.:** $\int_{0}^{5}\int_{2-x}^{2+x} f(x,y)\,dy\,dx$.

4. $\int_{1}^{2}\int_{\sqrt{x}}^{x} f(x,y)\,dy\,dx + \int_{2}^{4}\int_{\sqrt{x}}^{2} f(x,y)\,dy\,dx$. **Ans.:** $\int_{1}^{2}\int_{y}^{y^2} f(x,y)\,dx\,dy$

5. $\int_{0}^{1}\int_{0}^{y} f(x,y)\,dx\,dy + \int_{1}^{\infty}\int_{0}^{\frac{1}{y}} f(x,y)\,dx\,dy$ **Ans.:** $\int_{0}^{1}\int_{x}^{\frac{1}{x}} f(x,y)\,dy\,dx$

Method-II: Changing the strip parallel to Y axis to the strip parallel to X-axis

Let the given integral be $I = \int_{x=a}^{x=b}\int_{y=h(x)}^{y=g(x)} f(x,y)\,dx\,dy = \int_{x=a}^{x=b}\left[\int_{y=h(x)}^{y=g(x)} f(x,y)\,dy\right]dx$

Step-I: First write down the limits of inner most integral.
i.e. $y = h(x)$, $y = g(x)$

Which implies that strip is parallel to Y-axis.
Then write the limits of outer integral i.e. $x = a$, $x = b$

Step-II: From this inner and out integral draw (Trace the curve) the figure. And find their points of Interaction.(Generally outer limits curve are straight lines or curve passing through the point of intersection)

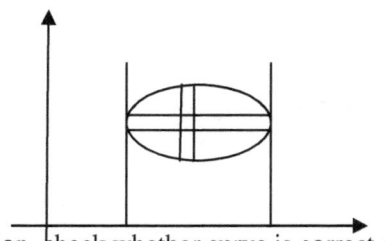

Step-III: Shade the region of integration. From this region, check whether curve is correct or wrong by taking strip parallel to Y-axis (Check the limits of inner and outer integrals).

Step-IV: To change the order of integration take the strip parallel to X-axis in the region of integration.

Step-V: For finding the new limits

Limits of Inner integral: The left and right ends of the strip are the lower and upper limits respectively of the inner integral. (Find the value of x in terms of y.)

Limits of outer integral: Move the strip parallel to X-axis from bottom to top, then the values of y at the bottom and top of the strip are the lower and upper limits of outer integral. which are always constants.

Hence by changing the order of integration, we get

$$I = \int_{y=c}^{y=d} \int_{x=h(y)}^{x=g(y)} f(x,y)\,dx\,dy = \int_{y=c}^{y=d} \left[\int_{x=h(y)}^{x=g(y)} f(x,y)\,dx \right] dy.$$

Examples on Changing the strip parallel to Y axis to the strip parallel to X-axis

Let the given integral be $I = \int_{x=a}^{x=b} \int_{y=h(x)}^{y=g(x)} f(x,y)\,dx\,dy = \int_{x=a}^{x=b} \left[\int_{y=h(x)}^{y=g(x)} f(x,y)\,dy \right] dx$

By changing the order of integration, we get

$$I = \int_{y=c}^{y=d} \int_{x=h(y)}^{x=g(y)} f(x,y)\,dx\,dy = \int_{y=c}^{y=d} \left[\int_{x=h(y)}^{x=g(y)} f(x,y)\,dx \right] dy.$$

Ex. 1: Change the order of integration $\int_{0}^{4a} \int_{x^2/4a}^{2\sqrt{ax}} f(x,y)\,dx\,dy$

Solution: Let $I = \int_{0}^{4a} \int_{x^2/4a}^{2\sqrt{ax}} f(x,y)\,dx\,dy = \int_{0}^{4a} \left[\int_{x^2/4a}^{2\sqrt{ax}} f(x,y)\,dy \right] dx$ (A)

In given integral, limits of inner integral are the functions of x which implies that strip is parallel to Y-axis. To change the order of integration means take the strip parallel to X- axis. The limits of inner integral are

$y = x^2/4a$, i.e. $x^2 = 4ay$, and $y = 2\sqrt{ax}$ i.e. $y^2 = 4ax$

and The limits of outer integral are $x = 0$, $x = 4a$.

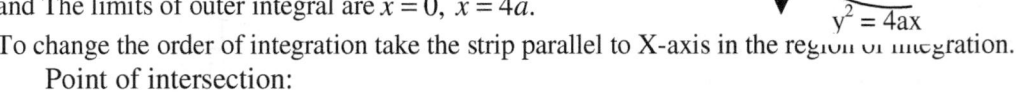

To change the order of integration take the strip parallel to X-axis in the region of integration.

Point of intersection:

As $y = x^2/4a$, and $y = 2\sqrt{ax}$

$\Rightarrow 2\sqrt{ax} = x^2/4a$

$\therefore x = 4a$ $x = 0$ $\therefore y = 4a$ $y = 0$

$\Rightarrow (4a, 4a)$ and $(0,0)$ are the points of intersections

Limits of Inner integral: The left and right ends of the strip are the lower and upper limits respectively of the inner integral. (Find the value of x in terms of y.)

$\therefore x = y^2/4a$ and $x = 2\sqrt{ay}$

Limits of outer integral: Move the strip parallel to X-axis from bottom to top, then the values of y at the bottom and top of the strip are the lower and upper limits of outer integral. which are always constants.
$\therefore y = 0$ and $y = 4a$

Therefore from equation (A), we get $\quad I = \int_0^{4a} \int_{y^2/4a}^{2\sqrt{ay}} f(x,y)\,dx\,dy.$

Ex. 2: Change the order of integration $\int_{-2}^{1} \int_{x^2}^{2-x} f(x,y)\,dx\,dy$

Solution: Let $I = \int_{-2}^{1} \int_{x^2}^{2-x} f(x,y)\,dx\,dy = \int_{-2}^{1} \left[\int_{x^2}^{2-x} f(x,y)\,dy \right] dx \quad$ (A)

In given integral, limits of inner integral are the functions of x which implies that strip is parallel to Y-axis. To change the order of integration means take the strip parallel to X- axis.
The limits of inner integral are
$y = x^2$, and $y = 2 - x$ and
The limits of outer integral are $x = -2$, $x = 1$.

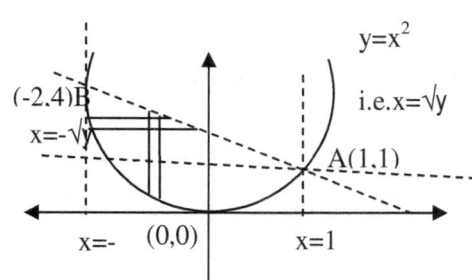

To change the order of integration take the strip parallel to X-axis in the region of integration.
Point of intersection:
As $y = x^2$ and $y = 2 - x$ i.e $x + y = 2$
$\therefore x^2 + x - 2 = 0 \Rightarrow (x+2)(x-1) = 0$
$\therefore x = -2, 1 \quad \therefore y = 4, 1$
$\Rightarrow A(1,1)$ and $C(-2, 4)$ are the points of intersections

As the strip is not moving smoothly in the given region, so divide the given region of integration into two parts ABC and ACO.

For the region ABC, left end of the strip is on $x = -\sqrt{y}$ and right end is on $x = 2 - y$ and the

Moves from $y = 1, y = 4 \qquad \therefore I_1 = \int_1^4 \int_{x=-\sqrt{y}}^{x=2-y} f(x,y)\,dx\,dy$

For the region ACO, left end of the strip is on $x = -\sqrt{y}$ and right end is on $x = \sqrt{y}$ and the

Moves from $y = 0, y = 1 \qquad \therefore I_2 = \int_0^1 \int_{x=-\sqrt{y}}^{x=\sqrt{y}} f(x,y)\,dx\,dy$

$$I = I_1 + I_2$$

Hence
$$\therefore \int_{-2}^{1}\int_{x^2}^{2-x} f(x,y)\,dx\,dy = \int_{1}^{4}\int_{x=-\sqrt{y}}^{x=2-y} f(x,y)\,dx\,dy + \int_{0}^{1}\int_{x=-\sqrt{y}}^{x=\sqrt{y}} f(x,y)\,dx\,dy$$

Ex. 3: Change the order of integration and evaluate $\int_{0}^{\infty}\int_{x}^{\infty}\dfrac{e^{-y}}{y}\,dx\,dy$

Solution: Let $I = \int_{0}^{\infty}\int_{x}^{\infty}\dfrac{e^{-y}}{y}\,dx\,dy = \int_{0}^{\infty}\left[\int_{x}^{\infty}\dfrac{e^{-y}}{y}\,dy\right]dx$ (A)

In given integral, limits of inner integral are the functions of x which implies that strip is parallel to Y-axis. To change the order of integration means take the strip parallel to X- axis.

The limits of inner integral are
$y = x$, and $y = \infty$ and

The limits of outer integral are $x = 0$, $x = \infty$.

To change the order of integration take the strip parallel to X-axis in the region of integration.

Left end of the strip is on $x = 0$ and right end is on $x = y$ and the

Moves from $y = 0, y = \infty$
$$\therefore I = \int_{0}^{\infty}\int_{0}^{y}\dfrac{e^{-y}}{y}\,dx\,dy$$

$$\therefore I = \int_{0}^{\infty}\dfrac{e^{-y}}{y}\,dy\int_{0}^{y}dx = \int_{0}^{\infty}\dfrac{e^{-y}}{y}\,y\,dy$$

$$= \int_{0}^{\infty}e^{-y}\,dy = \left[-e^{-y}\right]_{0}^{\infty} = 1$$

Ex. 4 : *Evaluate* $\int_{0}^{1}\int_{0}^{\sqrt{1-x^2}}\dfrac{dx\,dy}{(1+e^y)\sqrt{1-x^2-y^2}}$

Solution : Let, $I = \int_{0}^{1}dx\int_{0}^{\sqrt{1-x^2}}\dfrac{dy}{(1+e^y)\sqrt{1-x^2-y^2}}$.

Here integral first w.r.t. y is difficult to solve, therefore, we should change the order of integration. The given region is bounded by $x = 0$, $x = 1$, $y = 0$ and $y = +\sqrt{1^2-x^2}$, represents a positive quadrant of a circle $x^2 + y^2 = a^2$.

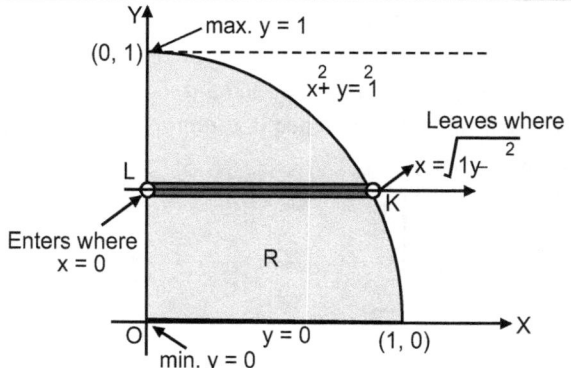

For changing the order of integration, imagine a horizontal strip LK cutting through region R as shown in Figure

Step 1 : Order is reversed.

$$I = \int \frac{dy}{1+e^y} \int \frac{dx}{\sqrt{1-y^2-x^2}}$$

Step 2 : New limits for integration,

$$I = \int_0^1 \frac{dy}{1+e^y} \int_0^{\sqrt{1-y^2}} \frac{dx}{\sqrt{1-y^2-x^2}}$$

Step 3 : Let $I_1 = \int_0^{\sqrt{1-y^2}} \frac{dx}{\sqrt{1-y^2-x^2}}$ Let $1-y^2 = b^2$

$$= \int_0^b \frac{dx}{\sqrt{b^2-x^2}} = \left[\sin^{-1}\frac{x}{b}\right]_0^b = \frac{\pi}{2} - 0 = \frac{\pi}{2}$$

Step 4 : $I = \int_0^1 \frac{dy}{1+e^y} \cdot \frac{\pi}{2} = \frac{\pi}{2} \int_0^1 \frac{1+e^y - e^y}{1+e^y} \, dy$

$$= \frac{\pi}{2} \int_0^1 \left(1 - \frac{e^y}{1+e^y}\right) dy = \frac{\pi}{2} \left[y - \log(1+e^y)\right]_0^1$$

$$= \frac{\pi}{2} \left[1 - \log(1+e) + \log 2\right] = \frac{\pi}{2} \left[\log e + \log 2 - \log(1+e)\right]$$

$$= \frac{\pi}{2} \log\left(\frac{2e}{1+e}\right)$$

Ex. 5 : Show that $\int_0^1 \int_x^{1/x} \frac{y \, dx \, dy}{(1+xy)^2 (1+y^2)} = \frac{\pi}{4} \cdot \frac{1}{4}$

Solution: Let, $I = \int_0^1 dx \int_x^{1/x} \frac{y \, dy}{(1+xy)^2 (1+y^2)}$

Here, integral first w.r.t. y is difficult to evaluate, therefore we should change the order of integration.

To evaluate first w.r.t. x and then w.r.t. y, we have to consider a horizontal strip where ends shift the curves in the vertical movement. Hence, the region is splitted up into two parts R_1, R_2 with the help of demarking line $y = 1$.

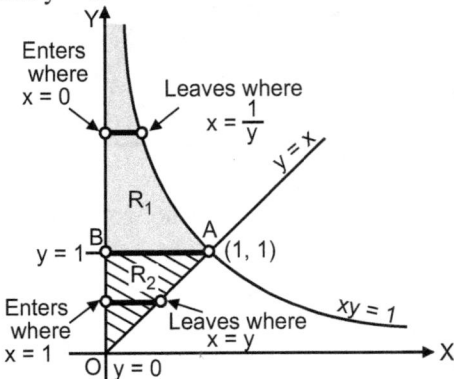

Given region is $x = 0$, $x = 1$, $y = x$, $y = \dfrac{1}{x}$ i.e. $xy = 1$.

R_1 is OAB ; R_2 is ABC. Consider two horizontal strips in R_1 and R_2 respectively.

Limits for R_1 : $y = 0$ to $y = 1$; $x = 0$ to $x = y$

Limits for R_2 : $y = 1$ to $y = \infty$; $x = 0$ to $x = \dfrac{1}{y}$.

Thus, $$I = \iint\limits_{R_1} \dfrac{y\, dy\, dx}{(1+xy)^2 (1+y^2)} + \iint\limits_{R_2} \dfrac{y\, dy\, dx}{(1+xy)^2 (1+y^2)} = I_1 + I_2.$$

$$I_1 = \int_0^1 \dfrac{y\, dy}{1+y^2} \int_0^y \dfrac{dx}{(1+xy)^2} = \int_0^1 \dfrac{y\, dy}{1+y^2} \left[\dfrac{-1}{y(1+xy)}\right]_0^y$$

$$= \int_0^1 \dfrac{dy}{1+y^2} \left[-\dfrac{1}{1+y^2} + \dfrac{1}{1}\right] = \int_0^1 -\dfrac{dy}{(1+y^2)^2} + \int_0^1 \dfrac{dy}{1+y^2}$$

In the first integral, put $y = \tan\theta$, $dy = \sec^2\theta\, d\theta$

y	0	1
θ	0	π/4

$$I_1 = -\int_0^{\pi/4} \dfrac{\sec^2\theta\, d\theta}{\sec^2\theta} + [\tan^{-1} y]_0^1 = -\int_0^{\pi/4} \dfrac{1+\cos 2\theta}{2} d\theta + \dfrac{\pi}{4}$$

$$= -\frac{1}{2}\left[\frac{\pi}{4} + \frac{\sin 2\theta}{2}\Big|_0^{\pi/4}\right] + \frac{\pi}{4} = \frac{\pi}{8} - \frac{1}{4}$$

$$I_2 = \int_1^\infty \frac{y\,dy}{1+y^2} \int_0^{1/y} \frac{dx}{(1+xy)^2} = \int_1^\infty \frac{y\,dy}{1+y^2}\left[-\frac{1}{y(1+xy)}\right]_0^{1/y}$$

$$= \int_1^\infty -\frac{dy}{1+y^2}\left[\frac{1}{2}-1\right] = \frac{1}{2}\int_1^\infty \frac{dy}{1+y^2} = \frac{1}{2}[\tan^{-1} y]_1^\infty$$

$$= \frac{1}{2}\left[\frac{\pi}{2} - \frac{\pi}{4}\right] = \frac{\pi}{8}$$

$$\therefore \quad I = \frac{\pi}{8} - \frac{1}{4} + \frac{\pi}{8} = \frac{\pi - 1}{4} \quad \ldots\ldots \text{Hence proved.}$$

Ex. 6 : Change the order of integration in the double integration $\int_0^5 \int_{2-x}^{2+x} f(x, y)\,dy\,dx$.

Solution: Let, $\quad I = \int_0^5 \left\{\int_{2-x}^{2+x} f(x, y)\,dy\right\} dx$.

Region of integration is bounded by $x = 0$, $x = 5$, $y = 2 - x$ i.e. $x + y = 2$; $y = 2 + x$. Points of intersection are $(0, 2)$, $(5, -3)$, $(5, 7)$ and the region R is shaded in Figure.

To change the order of integration, we have to integrate first w.r.t. x and then w.r.t. y i.e.

$$I = \int \left\{\int f(x, y)\,dx\right\} dy$$

∴ We have to imagine a horizontal strip and also we note that at the point $A(0, 2)$, the left end of horizontal strip changes its x-value from the straight line $x = 2 - y$ to $x = y - 2$. Therefore, we divide the region into two parts R_1, R_2 by the line AC i.e. $y = 2$.

Let R_1 is ABC and R_2 is ACD.

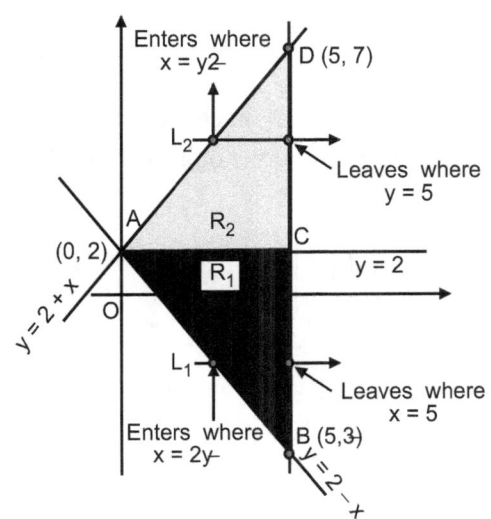

$$I = \iint_{ABCD} f(x,y)\,dx\,dy = \iint_{ABC} f(x,y)\,dx\,dy + \iint_{ACD} f(x,y)\,dx\,dy.$$

Now to find the new limits for R_1, R_2, we will imagine two horizontal strips, in regions R_1 and R_2 respectively.

By changing the order of integration, given integral becomes

$$I = \int_{-3}^{2}\left\{\int_{2-y}^{5} f(x,y)\,dx\right\}dy + \int_{2}^{7}\left\{\int_{y-2}^{5} f(x,y)\,dx\right\}dy$$

TEST YOUR KNOWLEDGE

I. Change the order of integration and prove that

1. $\displaystyle\int_0^1 \int_0^{\sqrt{1-x^2}} \frac{y\,dy\,dx}{(1+y^2)\sqrt{1-x^2-y^2}} = \frac{\pi}{4}\log 2$

2. $\displaystyle\int_0^\infty \int_0^x x\,e^{-x^2/y}\,dy\,dx = \frac{1}{2}$

3. $\displaystyle\int_0^a \int_0^x x\sqrt{(a^2-y^2)(x^2-y^2)}\,dy\,dx = \frac{8a^5}{45}$

4. $\displaystyle\int_0^\infty \int_x^\infty \frac{e^{-y}}{y}\,dx\,dy = 1$

5. $\displaystyle\int_0^a \int_0^x \frac{\tan^{-1}\frac{y}{a}\,dy\,dx}{(a^2+y^2)\sqrt{(a-x)(x-y)}} = \frac{\pi^3}{32\,a}$

6. $\displaystyle\int_0^a \int_0^x \frac{dy\,dx}{(y+a)\sqrt{(a-x)(x-y)}} = \pi\log 2$

7. $\displaystyle\int_0^a \int_0^x \frac{\sin y\,dy\,dx}{(5\cos y - 4)\sqrt{(a-x)(x-y)}} = -\frac{\pi}{5}\log(5\cos a - 4)$

II. Problems on change of order of integration.

Change the order of integration of following double integrals :

1. $\displaystyle\int_0^1 \int_x^{\frac{1}{x}} f(x,y)\,dy\,dx$

2. $\displaystyle\int_1^2 \int_0^{\frac{a^2}{x}} f(x,y)\,dy\,dx$

3. $\displaystyle\int_0^{a\cos\alpha} \int_{x\tan\alpha}^{\sqrt{a^2-x^2}} f(x,y)\,dy\,dx$

4. $\displaystyle\int_0^{4a} \int_{x^2/4a}^{2\sqrt{ax}} f(x,y)\,dy\,dx$

5. $\displaystyle\int_0^1 \int_{x^2}^{\sqrt{2-x^2}} f(x,y)\,dy\,dx$

6. $\displaystyle\int_{-1}^2 \int_{x^2}^{x+2} f(x,y)\,dy\,dx$

7. $\displaystyle\int_0^a \int_{\frac{x^2}{a}}^{2a-x} f(x,y)\, dy\, dx$
8. $\displaystyle\int_{-2}^{1} \int_{x^2}^{2-x} f(x,y)\, dy\, dx$

9. $\displaystyle\int_0^a \int_{-a+\sqrt{a^2-x^2}}^{a+\sqrt{a^2-x^2}} f(x,y)\, dy\, dx.$
10. $\displaystyle\int_0^{2a} \int_{\sqrt{2ax-x^2}}^{\sqrt{2ax}} f(x,y)\, dy\, dx$

11. $\displaystyle\int_1^2 \int_{1-\sqrt{2x-x^2}}^{1+\sqrt{2x-x^2}} f(x,y)\, dy\, dx$
12. $\displaystyle\int_{-a/2}^{0} \int_{\sqrt{-2ax-x^2}}^{\sqrt{a^2-x^2}} f(x,y)\, dy\, dx$

13. $\displaystyle\int_0^a \int_{\sqrt{a^2-x^2}}^{x+2a} f(x,y)\, dy\, dx$
14. $\displaystyle\int_0^a \int_{mx}^{nx} f(x,y)\, dy\, dx,\ n>m$

III. Express the following double integrals as single term integrals.

1. $\displaystyle\int_1^2 \int_{\sqrt{x}}^{x} f(x,y)\, dy\, dx + \int_2^4 \int_{\sqrt{x}}^{2} f(x,y)\, dy\, dx.$ **Ans. :** $\displaystyle\int_1^2 \int_y^{y^2} f(x,y)\, dx\, dy$

TRANSFORMATION OF CARTESIAN DOUBLE INTEGRAL INTO POLAR DOUBLE INTEGRAL

Consider the area OAB bounded by polar curve $r = f(\theta)$, and lines $\theta = \alpha$ and $\theta = \beta$ as shown in Fig. Let $P(r, \theta)$, $Q(r + \delta r, \theta + \delta\theta)$ be two adjacent points on curve AB. Join OP and OQ. Draw two consecutive arcs of circle of radii r and $r + \delta r$ cutting the elementary area GHUV. Arc $GV = r\, \delta\theta$, $GH = \delta r$.

$\delta A = A_{GHUV} = r\, \delta\theta\, \delta r$

Considering summation along OP (along direction of r), we get an elementary sector area OPQ known as wedge.

$$A_{OPQ} = \lim_{\delta r \to 0} \left\{ \sum_{r=0}^{f(\theta)} r\, \delta r \right\} \cdot \delta\theta = \left\{ \int_0^{f(\theta)} r\, dr \right\} \cdot \delta\theta$$

...[Replacing summation sign by integral sign]

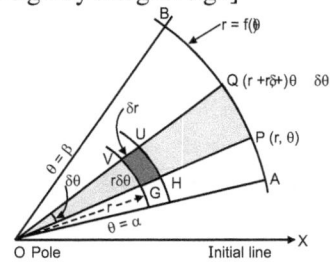

Next we can consider area OAB as consisting of infinite number of elementary areas like OPQ. Considering the summation of all such elementary areas, we get:

$$A_{OAB} = \lim_{\delta\theta \to 0} \sum_{\theta=\alpha}^{\beta} \left\{ \int_0^{f(\theta)} r\, dr \right\} \cdot \delta\theta \qquad \ldots \text{[Summation by variation of } \theta\text{]}$$

$$= \int_{\theta=\alpha}^{\beta} d\theta \int_0^{f(\theta)} r\, dr \qquad \ldots \begin{bmatrix} \text{Replacing summation sign} \\ \text{by integral sign as before} \end{bmatrix}$$

Or

$$= \int_{\alpha}^{\beta} \int_0^{f(\theta)} r\, d\theta\, dr$$

Here the inner integration is w.r.t. r, treating θ as constant and outer integration is w.r.t. θ. Order of integration can also be changed by considering summation in the direction of θ increasing first and then w.r.t. r. In most of the problems on polar double integration, *it is quite convenient to integrate w.r.t. r first and then w.r.t. θ.*

Just as $\int_{\alpha}^{\beta} \int_0^{f(\theta)} r\, d\theta\, dr$ represents the area OAB, $\int_{\alpha}^{\beta} \int_0^{f(\theta)} F(r, \theta)\, r\, d\theta\, dr$ represents some physical quantity related to the area OAB.

If $F(r, \theta)$ is density function,

$\int_{\alpha}^{\beta} \int_0^{f(\theta)} F(r, \theta)\, r\, d\theta\, dr$ represents mass of lamina OAB. Similarly, it can represent any other physical quantity depending upon nature of $F(r, \theta)$.

In many cases, it is quite advantageous to convert $\int\int f(x, y)\, dx\, dy$ into polar form by transformations $x = r\cos\theta$, $y = r\sin\theta$. Function $f(x, y)$ gets converted to $F(r, \theta)$, equations of bounding cartesian curves are expressed in polar form. The area element $dx\, dy$ is replaced by corresponding area element $r\, d\theta\, dr$.

[One may recall Jacobians from MI paper.

$$dx\, dy = |J|\, dr\, d\theta = \left| \frac{\partial(x, y)}{\partial(r, \theta)} \right| dr\, d\theta = r\, dr\, d\theta, \text{ where } x = r\cos\theta,\ y = r\sin\theta]$$

Limits in polar double integral $\int\int F(r, \theta)\, r\, d\theta\, dr$ are substituted as explained in following examples:

1. For a complete circle $x^2 + y^2 = a^2$

$$I = \int_0^{2\pi} \left\{ \int_0^a f(r, \theta) \, r \, dr \right\} d\theta$$

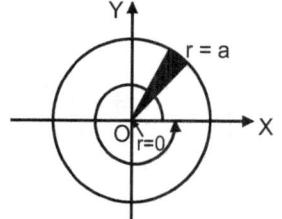

Fig.

For a semi-circle $x^2 + y^2 = a^2$, $y \geq 0$

$$I = \int_0^{\pi} \left\{ \int_0^a f(r, \theta) \, r \, dr \right\} d\theta$$

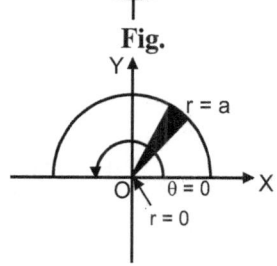

Fig.

For a positive quadrant of a circle

$$I = \int_0^{\pi/2} \left\{ \int_0^a f(r, \theta) \, r \, dr \right\} d\theta$$

Fig.

Note : In all these three cases, polar equation of circle $x^2 + y^2 = a^2$ becomes $r = a$.

2. For a circle $x^2 + y^2 = 2ax$ i.e. $x^2 - 2ax + a^2 + y^2 = a^2$
   OR $(x - a)^2 + (y - 0)^2 = a^2$ having centre $(a, 0)$, $r = a$
   We write polar equation for $x^2 + y^2 = 2ax$ as $r^2 = 2ar \cos \theta$ or $r = 2a \cos \theta$

$$I = \int_{-\pi/2}^{\pi/2} \left\{ \int_0^{2a \cos \theta} f(r, \theta) \, r \, dr \right\} d\theta$$

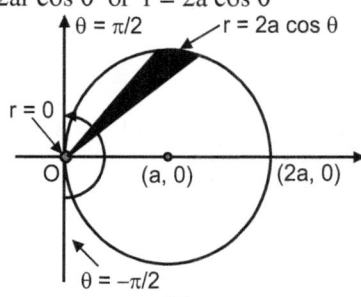

Fig.

For upper half of the circle
$x^2 + y^2 = 2ax$

$$I = \int_0^{\pi/2} \left\{ \int_0^{2a \cos \theta} f(r, \theta) \, r \, dr \right\} d\theta$$

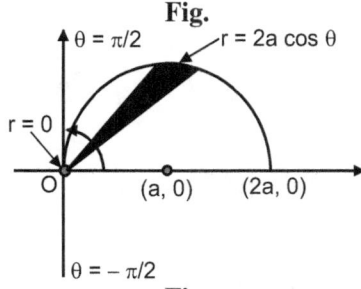

Fig.

3. For a circle $x^2 + y^2 = 2ay$ i.e. $x^2 + y^2 - 2ay + a^2 = a^2$
   i.e. $(x - 0)^2 + (y - a)^2 = a^2$ having centre $(0, a)$, $r = a$

(6.36)

Polar equation of $x^2 + y^2 = 2ay$ is $r = 2a \sin \theta$

$$I = \int_0^\pi \left\{ \int_0^{2a \sin \theta} f(r, \theta) \, r \, dr \right\} d\theta$$

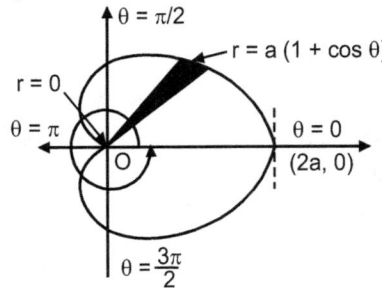

Fig.

4. For a cardioide $r = a(1 + \cos \theta)$

$$I = \int_0^{2\pi} \left\{ \int_0^{a(1+\cos \theta)} f(r, \theta) \, r \, dr \right\} d\theta$$

Fig.

For a cardioide $r = a(1 - \cos \theta)$

$$I = \int_0^{2\pi} \left\{ \int_0^{a(1-\cos \theta)} f(r, \theta) \, r \, dr \right\} d\theta$$

Fig.

5. For $r^2 = a^2 \cos 2\theta$ (Bernoullie's Lemniscate)

$$I = 2\int_{-\pi/4}^{\pi/4}\left\{\int_{0}^{a\sqrt{\cos 2\theta}} f(r,\theta)\; r\; dr\right\} d\theta \quad \text{(for whole curve i.e. two loops)}$$

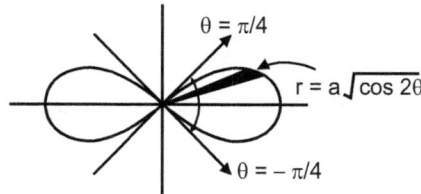

Fig.

$$I = \int_{-\pi/4}^{\pi/4}\left\{\int_{0}^{a\sqrt{\cos 2\theta}} f(r,\theta)\; r\; dr\right\} d\theta \quad \text{(for one loop)}$$

6. For a ellipse $\dfrac{x^2}{a^2} + \dfrac{y^2}{b^2} = 1$; Use $x = ar\cos\theta$, $y = br\sin\theta$, $dx\, dy = ab\, r\, dr\, d\theta$

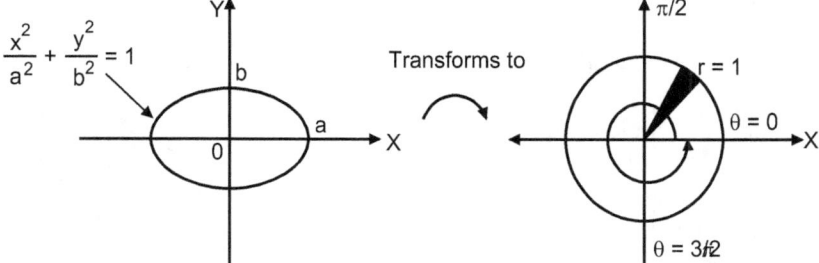

Fig.

$$I = \int_{0}^{2\pi}\left\{\int_{0}^{1} f(r,\theta)\; ab\; r\; dr\right\} d\theta \quad \text{(for complete ellipse)}$$

For a positive quadrant of an ellipse,

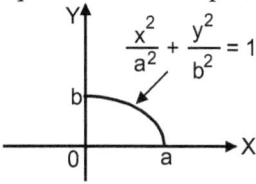
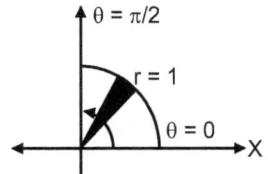

Fig.

$$I = \int_{0}^{\pi/2}\left\{\int_{0}^{1} f(r,\theta)\; ab\; r\; dr\right\} d\theta$$

7. For a triangle $y = 0$, $x = a$, $x = y$

$$I = \int_{0}^{\pi/4}\left\{\int_{0}^{a\sec\theta} f(r,\theta)\; r\; dr\right\} d\theta$$

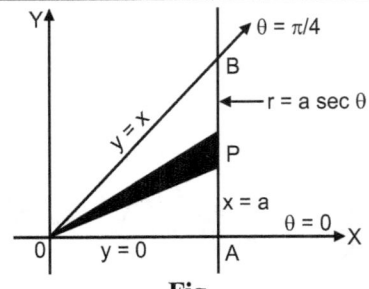

Fig.

Problems on double integration by transforming to polar form are mainly divided in the following types.

Type I : Direct evaluation.
Type II : Evaluation by finding limits of integration.
Type I : Ex. on Direct Evaluation of Double Integral by using Polar Co-ordinates

Ex. 1 : Evaluate $\displaystyle\int_0^a \int_0^{\sqrt{a^2-x^2}} \sin\left\{\frac{\pi}{a^2}(a^2-x^2-y^2)\right\} dx\, dy.$

Solution: Region of integration is bounded by $y = 0$, $y = \sqrt{a^2-x^2}$. Or $y^2 = a^2 - x^2$ i.e. $x^2 + y^2 = a^2$, $x = 0$, $x = a$ i.e. positive quadrant of circle OAB as shaded in the adjoining figure. Equation of circle in polar coordinates is $r = a$. Along radius vector OP, r varies between 0 to a and when this radius OP is rotated to cover the whole region, θ varies between $\theta = 0$ to $\theta = \dfrac{\pi}{2}$.

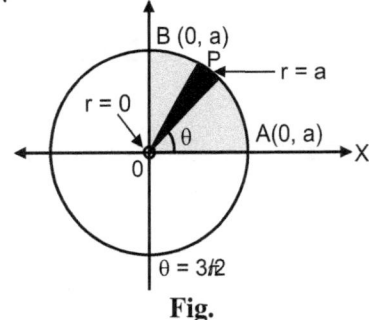

Fig.

$$I = \int_{\theta=0}^{\pi/2} \int_{r=0}^{a} \sin\left\{\frac{\pi}{a^2}(a^2-r^2)\right\} r\, d\theta\, dr$$

$$= \frac{1}{2} \int_0^{\pi/2} d\theta \int_0^a \sin\left\{\frac{\pi}{a^2}(a^2-r^2)\right\} d(r^2) \quad [2r\, dr = d(r^2)]$$

$$= \frac{1}{2} \int_0^{\pi/2} \left[\frac{-\cos\left\{\frac{\pi}{a^2}(a^2-r^2)\right\}}{-\frac{\pi}{a^2}}\right]_0^a d\theta = \frac{1}{2}\int_0^{\pi/2} \frac{a^2}{\pi}\{\cos 0 - \cos \pi\}\, d\theta$$

$$= \frac{1}{2}\frac{a^2}{\pi} \int_0^{\pi/2} \{1-(-1)\}\, d\theta = \frac{a^2}{\pi}[\theta]_0^{\pi/2} = \frac{a^2}{\pi} \cdot \frac{\pi}{2} = \frac{a^2}{2}$$

Ex. 2 : *Evaluate* $\displaystyle\int_0^a \int_{\sqrt{ax-x^2}}^{\sqrt{a^2-x^2}} \dfrac{xy}{x^2+y^2} e^{-(x^2+y^2)} \, dx\, dy$.

Solution : Region of integration is bounded by

$y = \sqrt{ax-x^2}$ i.e. $y^2 = ax - x^2$ [Polar equation $r = a\cos\theta$]

Or $x^2 + y^2 = ax$ Or $\left(x - \dfrac{a}{2}\right)^2 + y^2 = \dfrac{a^2}{4}$.

It is a circle with centre $\left(\dfrac{a}{2}, 0\right)$ and radius $= \dfrac{a}{2}$

$y = \sqrt{a^2 - x^2}$ Or $y^2 = a^2 - x^2$ i.e. $x^2 + y^2 = a^2$

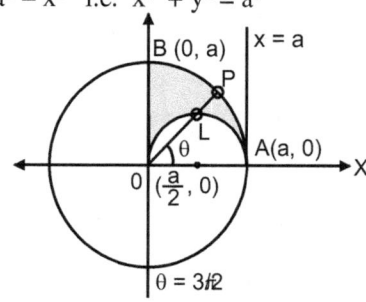

Fig. 10.33

$[r = a]$, $x = 0$, $x = a$. Region is shown shaded in Fig. 10.33.

To obtain limits, consider a radius vector OLP passing through the region, the end limits of which in the region are, $L : r = a\cos\theta$ to $P : r = a$. For the entire region, θ varies from 0 to $\pi/2$. Substituting $x = r\cos\theta$, $y = r\sin\theta$, given integral takes the form

$$I = \int_{\theta=0}^{\pi/2} \int_{r=a\cos\theta}^{a} \dfrac{r\cos\theta \, r\sin\theta}{r^2} e^{-r^2} \cdot r \, d\theta \, dr$$

$$= \int_0^{\pi/2} \int_{a\cos\theta}^{a} \sin\theta \cos\theta \, e^{-r^2} r \, dr \, d\theta = \dfrac{1}{2} \int_0^{\pi/2} \int_{a\cos\theta}^{a} \sin\theta \cos\theta \, e^{-r^2} d(r^2) \, d\theta$$

$$= \dfrac{1}{2} \int_0^{\pi/2} \sin\theta \cos\theta \left[\dfrac{e^{-r^2}}{-1}\right]_{a\cos\theta}^{a} d\theta$$

$$= -\dfrac{1}{2} \int_0^{\pi/2} \sin\theta \cos\theta \, (e^{-a^2}) \, d\theta + \dfrac{1}{2} \int_0^{\pi/2} \sin\theta \cos\theta \, e^{-a^2\cos^2\theta} \, d\theta = I_1 + I_2$$

$$I_1 = -\dfrac{1}{2} \int_0^{\pi/2} \dfrac{\sin 2\theta}{2} e^{-a^2} d\theta = -\dfrac{1}{2} e^{-a^2} \left(-\dfrac{\cos 2\theta}{4}\right)_0^{\pi/2}$$

(6.40)

$$= \frac{1}{8} e^{-a^2} [\cos \pi - \cos 0] = -\frac{1}{4} e^{-a^2}$$

$$I_2 = \frac{1}{2} \int_0^{\pi/2} e^{-a^2 \cos^2 \theta} \sin \theta \cos \theta \, d\theta \qquad \text{Put} - \cos^2 \theta = t$$
$$\therefore 2 \cos \theta \sin \theta \, d\theta = dt$$

$$= \frac{1}{4} \int_{-1}^{0} e^{a^2 t} \, dt = \frac{1}{4} \left[\frac{e^{a^2 t}}{a^2} \right]_{-1}^{0} \qquad \text{when } \theta = 0, \ t = -1 \ ; \ \theta = \frac{\pi}{2}, \ t = 0$$

$$= \frac{1}{4a^2} - \frac{1}{4a^2} e^{-a^2}$$

$$I = I_1 + I_2 = -\frac{1}{4} e^{-a^2} + \frac{1}{4a^2} - \frac{1}{4a^2} e^{-a^2} = \frac{1}{4a^2} \left[1 - (a^2 + 1) e^{-a^2} \right]$$

Ex. 3 : *Evaluate* $\displaystyle\int_0^a \int_{2\sqrt{ax}}^{\sqrt{5ax-x^2}} \frac{\sqrt{x^2 + y^2}}{y^2} \, dx \, dy.$

Solution: Region is bounded by $y = 2\sqrt{ax}$ i.e. $y^2 = 4ax$, a parabola whose polar equation is $r^2 \sin^2 \theta = 4ar \cos \theta$ i.e. $r = \dfrac{4a \cos \theta}{\sin^2 \theta}$

Circle $y = \sqrt{5ax - x^2}$ i.e. $y^2 = 5ax - x^2$
or $x^2 + y^2 = 5ax$ or $\left(x - \dfrac{5a}{2}\right)^2 + y^2 = \dfrac{25 a^2}{4}$

Polar equation of circle is $r^2 = 5ar \cos \theta$ or $r = 5a \cos \theta$. Points of intersection of parabola and circle are given by solving $y^2 = 4ax$ and $y^2 = 5ax - x^2$.
$\therefore 4ax = 5ax - x^2$ that gives $x = 0$ and $x = a$. $x = 0$ gives $y = 0$, $x = a$ gives $y = 2a$.

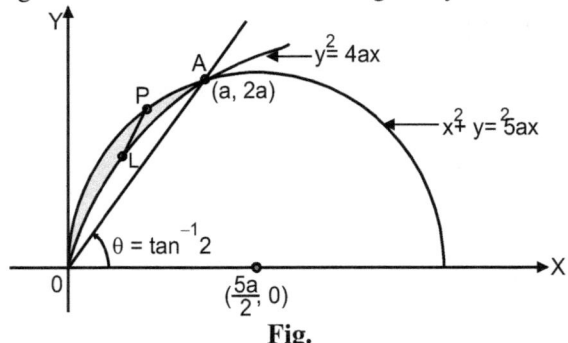

Fig.

Thus circle and parabola intersect at the points $(0, 0)$ and $(a, 2a)$.
Lines $x = 0$ and $x = a$ are the other boundaries. Region is shown shaded in Fig. 10.34
(a). Considering a radius vector in the region, r varies from $\dfrac{4 a \cos \theta}{\sin^2 \theta}$ to $r = 5a \cos \theta$ and θ varies from $\tan^{-1} 2$ (Line OA makes an angle $\tan^{-1} 2$ with x-axis) to $\dfrac{\pi}{2}$.

$$\left(\because \tan\theta = \frac{y}{x} = \frac{2a}{a} \text{ along OA}, \therefore \tan\theta = 2 \therefore \theta = \tan^{-1} 2\right)$$

$$I = \int_{\tan^{-1} 2}^{\pi/2} \int_{\frac{4a\cos\theta}{\sin^2\theta}}^{5a\cos\theta} \frac{r}{r^2 \sin^2\theta} \, r \, dr \, d\theta = \int_{\tan^{-1} 2}^{\pi/2} [r]_{4a\cos\theta/\sin^2\theta}^{5a\cos\theta} \frac{d\theta}{\sin^2\theta}$$

$$= \int_{\tan^{-1} 2}^{\pi/2} \left\{5a\cos\theta - \frac{4a\cos\theta}{\sin^2\theta}\right\} \frac{1}{\sin^2\theta} \, d\theta$$

$$= \int_{\tan^{-1} 2}^{\pi/2} [5a \csc\theta \cot\theta - 4a \csc^2\theta \csc\theta \cot\theta] \, d\theta$$

$$= \int_{\tan^{-1} 2}^{\pi/2} 5a \csc\theta \cot\theta \, d\theta + 4a \int_{\tan^{-1} 2}^{\pi/2} \csc^2\theta \, d(\csc\theta)$$

$$= [-5a \csc\theta]_{\tan^{-1} 2}^{\pi/2} + 4a \left[\frac{\csc^3\theta}{3}\right]_{\tan^{-1} 2}^{\pi/2}$$

$$= -5a + 5a\frac{\sqrt{5}}{2} + \frac{4a}{3} - \frac{4a}{3} \cdot \frac{5\sqrt{5}}{8}$$

$$\left[\text{From the triangle AOB, } \tan\theta = \frac{2}{1}, \sin\theta = \frac{2}{\sqrt{5}}, \csc\theta = \frac{\sqrt{5}}{2}\right]$$

$$= \frac{-11a}{3} + \frac{5\sqrt{5}\,a}{2}\left(1 - \frac{1}{3}\right) = \frac{-11a}{3} + \frac{5\sqrt{5}\,a}{3} = \frac{a}{3}(5\sqrt{5} - 11)$$

Ex. 4 : Sketch the area of double integration and evaluate :

$$\int_0^{a\sqrt{2}} \int_y^{\sqrt{a^2 - y^2}} \log_e(x^2 + y^2) \, dx \, dy.$$

Solution: Region of integration is bounded by $x = y$, $x = \sqrt{a^2 - y^2}$ i.e. $x^2 + y^2 = a^2$ ($r = a$) and $y = 0$, $y = \frac{a}{\sqrt{2}}$. It is shown in Fig. 10.35.

To evaluate the integral, it is simpler to transform to polars. Considering a radius vector in the region, r varies from 0 to a and θ varies from 0 to $\frac{\pi}{4}$.

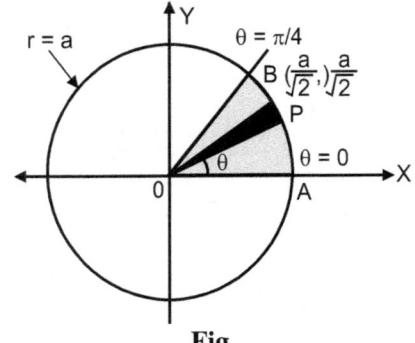

Fig.

$$I = \int_{\theta=0}^{\pi/4} \int_{r=0}^{a} \log_e (r^2) \; r \, d\theta \, dr$$

Consider inner integral

$$\int_0^a \log r^2 \cdot r \, dr = 2 \int_0^a r \log r \, dr \qquad \text{Integrating by parts,}$$

$$= 2\left[\left\{ \log r \cdot \frac{r^2}{2} \right\}_0^a - \int_0^a \frac{1}{r} \cdot \frac{r^2}{2} \, dr \right]$$

$$= a^2 \log a - \left\{ \frac{r^2}{2} \right\}_0^a \qquad \left[\lim_{r \to 0} \log r \cdot \frac{r^2}{2} = 0 \right]$$

$$= a^2 \log a - \frac{a^2}{2}$$

$$\therefore \qquad I = \int_0^{\pi/4} \left(a^2 \log a - \frac{a^2}{2} \right) d\theta = \frac{\pi}{4} a^2 \left(\log a - \frac{1}{2} \right)$$

Ex. 5 : *Show that* $\displaystyle\int_0^a \int_0^{\sqrt{a^2-x^2}} e^{-x^2-y^2} \, dx \, dy = \frac{\pi}{4}(1 - e^{-a^2})$

Solution : Transforming to polars,

$$I = \int_0^{\pi/2} \int_0^a e^{-r^2} r \, dr \, d\theta$$

$$= \int_0^{\pi/2} d\theta \left(-\frac{1}{2} \right) \int_0^a e^{-r^2} (-2r \, dr)$$

$$= -\frac{1}{2} (\pi/2) \left[e^{-r^2} \right]_0^a = \frac{\pi}{4} [1 - e^{-a^2}]$$

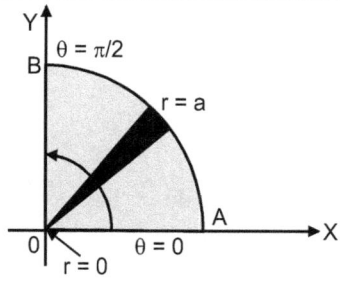

Fig.

Ex. 6 : *Evaluate* $\displaystyle\int_0^{4a}\int_{y^2/4a}^{y}\dfrac{x^2-y^2}{x^2+y^2}\,dx\,dy.$

Solution : $\displaystyle I = \int_0^{4a}\left\{\int_{y^2/4a}^{y}\dfrac{x^2-y^2}{x^2+y^2}\,dx\right\}dy$

Since the limits of inner integral are functions of y i.e. $x = \dfrac{y^2}{4a}$ i.e. $y^2 = 4ax$, $x = y$ and the limits of outer integral are $y = 0$, $y = 4a$. The points of intersection of $y = x$, $y^2 = 4ax$ is $x^2 = 4ax$ i.e. $x(x-4a) = 0$ i.e. $x = 0$, $x = 4a$. ∴ $(0, 0)$ $(4a, 4a)$ are the points of intersection.

Region of integration is as shown in Fig. 10.37.

It is difficult to evaluate the integral in cartesian co-ordinates but becomes simple in polar co-ordinates.

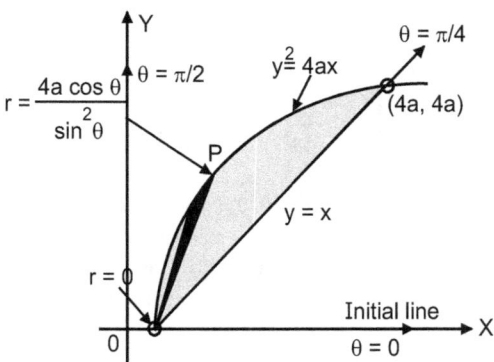

Fig.

Put $x = r\cos\theta$, $y = r\sin\theta$, $dx\,dy = r\,dr\,d\theta$, $x^2 + y^2 = r^2$,

$$I = \int\int\left(\dfrac{r^2\cos^2\theta - r^2\sin^2\theta}{r^2}\right)r\,dr\,d\theta$$

$$= \int_{\pi/4}^{\pi/2}(\cos^2\theta - \sin^2\theta)\,d\theta\int_0^{4a\cos\theta/\sin^2\theta}r\,dr$$

$$= \int_{\pi/4}^{\pi/2} (\cos^2\theta - \sin^2\theta)\, d\theta \left[\frac{r^2}{2}\right]_0^{\frac{4a\cos\theta}{\sin^2\theta}}$$

$$= 8a^2 \int_{\pi/4}^{\pi/2} (\cos^2\theta - \sin^2\theta)\frac{\cos^2\theta}{\sin^4\theta}\, d\theta = 8a^2 \int_{\pi/4}^{\pi/2} (\cot^4\theta - \cot^2\theta)\, d\theta$$

$$= 8a^2 \int_{\pi/4}^{\pi/2} \cot^2\theta\,(\cot^2\theta - 1)\, d\theta = 8a^2 \int_{\pi/4}^{\pi/2} \cot^2\theta\,[\csc^2\theta - 1 - 1]\, d\theta$$

$$= 8a^2 \int_{\pi/4}^{\pi/2} \cot^2\theta\,\csc^2\theta\, d\theta - 16a^2 \int_{\pi/4}^{\pi/2} (\csc^2\theta - 1)\, d\theta$$

$$= 8a^2 \left[-\frac{\cot^3\theta}{3}\right]_{\pi/4}^{\pi/2} - 16a^2 \left[-\cot\theta - \theta\right]_{\pi/4}^{\pi/2}$$

$$= \frac{8a^2}{3}[0+1] + 16a^2\left[0+\frac{\pi}{2}-1-\frac{\pi}{4}\right] = \frac{8a^2}{3} + 16a^2\,[\pi/4 - 1]$$

$$= 8a^2\left(\frac{\pi}{2} - \frac{5}{3}\right)$$

Ex. 7 : *Show that* $\displaystyle\int_0^a \int_y^{a+\sqrt{a^2-y^2}} \frac{dx\,dy}{(4a^2+x^2+y^2)^2} = \frac{1}{8a^2}\left(\frac{\pi}{4} - \frac{1}{\sqrt{2}}\,\tan^{-1}\frac{1}{\sqrt{2}}\right)$

Solution: Let, $I = \displaystyle\int_0^a \left\{\int_y^{a+\sqrt{a^2-y^2}} \frac{dx}{(4a^2+x^2+y^2)^2}\right\} dy$

Region of integration is bounded by $y=0$, $y=a$, $x=y$, $x=a+\sqrt{a^2-y^2}$
i.e. $x-a = \sqrt{a^2-y^2}$ OR $(x-a)^2 + (y-0)^2 = a^2$ OR $x^2+y^2 = 2ax$.

Point of intersection of circle $x^2+y^2 = 2ax$ and the line $y=x$ is (a, a). By using polar co-ordinates $x = r\cos\theta$, $y = r\sin\theta$, $x^2+y^2 = r^2$, $dx\,dy = r\,dr\,d\theta$

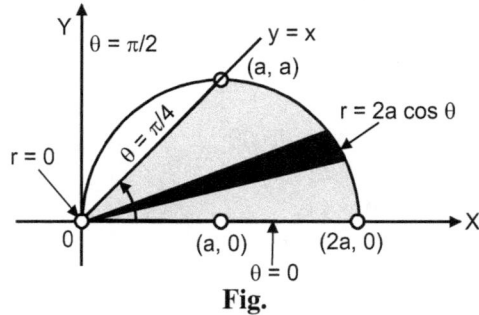

Fig.

$$I = \int_0^{\pi/4} \int_0^{2a\cos\theta} \frac{r \, dr \, d\theta}{(4a^2 + r^2)^2} = \frac{1}{2} \int_0^{\pi/4} d\theta \int_0^{2a\cos\theta} \frac{2r \, dr}{(4a^2 + r^2)^2}$$

$$= \frac{1}{2} \int_0^{\pi/4} \left[\frac{-1}{4a^2 + r^2}\right]_0^{2a\cos\theta} d\theta = \frac{1}{2} \int_0^{\pi/4} \left(\frac{-d\theta}{4a^2 + 4a^2\cos^2\theta} + \frac{d\theta}{4a^2}\right)$$

$$= \frac{1}{8a^2}\left(\frac{\pi}{4}\right) - \frac{1}{8a^2} \int_0^{\pi/4} \frac{1}{1 + \cos^2\theta} \, d\theta, \text{ divide numerator and denominator by } \cos^2\theta$$

$$= \frac{1}{8a^2}\left(\frac{\pi}{4}\right) - \frac{1}{8a^2} \int_0^{\pi/4} \frac{\sec^2\theta \, d\theta}{\sec^2\theta + 1}$$

$$= \frac{1}{8a^2}\left(\frac{\pi}{4}\right) - \frac{1}{8a^2} \int_0^{\pi/4} \frac{\sec^2\theta \, d\theta}{2 + \tan^2\theta} \quad (\text{Put } \tan\theta = t)$$

$$= \frac{1}{8a^2}\left(\frac{\pi}{4}\right) - \frac{1}{8a^2} \int_0^1 \frac{dt}{2 + t^2} = \frac{1}{8a^2}\left(\frac{\pi}{4}\right) - \frac{1}{8a^2} \left[\frac{1}{\sqrt{2}} \tan^{-1} \frac{t}{\sqrt{2}}\right]_0^1$$

$$= \frac{1}{8a^2}\left(\frac{\pi}{4}\right) - \frac{1}{8a^2}\left(\frac{1}{\sqrt{2}} \tan^{-1} \frac{1}{\sqrt{2}}\right) = \frac{1}{8a^2}\left[\frac{\pi}{4} - \frac{1}{\sqrt{2}} \tan^{-1} \frac{1}{\sqrt{2}}\right]$$

Ex. 8 : *Evaluate* $\displaystyle\int_0^2 \int_{1-\sqrt{2x-x^2}}^{1+\sqrt{2x-x^2}} \frac{dx \, dy}{(x^2 + y^2)^2}$

Solution: $I = \displaystyle\int_0^2 \left\{ \int_{1-\sqrt{2x-x^2}}^{1+\sqrt{2x-x^2}} \frac{dy}{(x^2 + y^2)^2} \right\} dx$

The region of integration R is bounded by $x = 0$, $x = 2$; $y = 1 \pm \sqrt{2x - x^2}$ i.e. $y - 1 = \pm\sqrt{2x - x^2}$ or $(y-1)^2 + x^2 - 2x + 1 = 1$ or $(x-1)^2 + (y-1)^2 = (1)^2$, a circle with centre $(1, 1)$ and $r = 1$. (Refer Fig. 10.39). By using polar co-ordinates $x = r\cos\theta$, $y = r\sin\theta$, $x^2 + y^2 = r^2$, $dx \, dy = r \, dr \, d\theta$, equation of circle becomes $(r\cos\theta - 1)^2 + (r\sin\theta - 1)^2 = 1$

$$r^2 - 2(\sin\theta + \cos\theta)r + 1 = 0$$

$$r = \frac{2(\sin\theta + \cos\theta) \pm \sqrt{4(\sin\theta + \cos\theta)^2 - 4}}{2} = \sin\theta + \cos\theta \pm \sqrt{\sin 2\theta}$$

Fig.

$$I = \iint_R \frac{dx\,dy}{(x^2+y^2)^2} = \int_0^{2\pi} \int_{\sin\theta+\cos\theta-\sqrt{\sin 2\theta}}^{\sin\theta+\cos\theta+\sqrt{\sin 2\theta}} \frac{r\,dr\,d\theta}{(r^2)^2}$$

$$= \int_0^{\pi/2} d\theta \int_{A-B}^{A+B} \frac{dr}{r^3}, \text{ where } A = \sin\theta + \cos\theta,\ B = \sqrt{\sin 2\theta}$$

$$= \int_0^{\pi/2} d\theta \left[-\frac{1}{2r^2}\right]_{A-B}^{A+B} = \frac{1}{2}\int_0^{\pi/2} \left[\frac{1}{(A-B)^2} - \frac{1}{(A+B)^2}\right] d\theta$$

$$= \frac{1}{2} \int_0^{\pi/2} \frac{4AB}{(A^2-B^2)^2} d\theta = 2\int_0^{\pi/2} (\sin\theta + \cos\theta)\sqrt{\sin 2\theta}\,d\theta$$

$$= 2\sqrt{2} \int_0^{\pi/2} \sin^{3/2}\theta \cos^{\frac{1}{2}}\theta\,d\theta + 2\sqrt{2} \int_0^{\pi/2} \sin^{\frac{1}{2}}\theta \cos^{\frac{3}{2}}\theta\,d\theta$$

$$= 2\sqrt{2}\,(2) \left[\frac{1}{2}\frac{\overline{5/4}\,\overline{3/4}}{\overline{2}}\right] = 2\sqrt{2}\,\frac{1}{4}\left|\frac{1}{4}\right|\frac{3}{4}$$

$$= \frac{1}{\sqrt{2}}\left|\frac{1}{4}\right|1-\frac{1}{4} = \frac{1}{\sqrt{2}}\frac{\pi}{\sin\frac{\pi}{4}} = \frac{1}{\sqrt{2}}(\sqrt{2}\,\pi) = \pi$$

TEST YOUR KNOWLEDGE:

I. Problems on evaluation by transforming to polar form : Prove the following :

1. $\displaystyle\int_0^1 \int_0^{\sqrt{1-x^2}} x^2 y^2\,dy\,dx = \frac{\pi}{96}$

2. $\displaystyle\int_0^1 \int_x^{\sqrt{2-x^2}} \frac{x}{\sqrt{x^2+y^2}}\,dy\,dx = 1 - \frac{1}{\sqrt{2}}$

3. $\int_0^a \int_{\sqrt{ax-x^2}}^{\sqrt{a^2-x^2}} \dfrac{dy\, dx}{\sqrt{a^2-x^2-y^2}} = a$

4. $\int_0^1 4x\, e^{-x^2}\, dx \int_0^{\sqrt{x-x^2}} \dfrac{y\, e^{-y^2}}{x^2+y^2}\, dy = \dfrac{1}{e}$

5. $\int_0^a \int_0^{\sqrt{a^2-x^2}} xy\, dx\, dy = \dfrac{a^4}{8}$

6. $\int_0^a \int_0^{\sqrt{a^2-x^2}} \sqrt{a^2-x^2-y^2}\, dy\, dx = \dfrac{\pi a^3}{6}$

7. $\int_0^1 \int_{x^2}^x \dfrac{1}{\sqrt{x^2+y^2}}\, dy\, dx = \sqrt{2} - 1$

8. $\int_0^1 \int_x^{\sqrt{2x-x^2}} (x^2+y^2)\, dy\, dx = \dfrac{3\pi}{8} - 1$

9. $\int_0^2 \int_0^{\sqrt{2x-x^2}} \dfrac{x\, dy\, dx}{\sqrt{x^2+y^2}} = \dfrac{4}{3}$

10. $\int_{-\infty}^{\infty} dx \int_{-\infty}^{\infty} \dfrac{dy}{(1+x^2+y^2)^{3/2}} = 4\pi$

11. $\int_0^a \int_y^a \dfrac{x^2\, dx\, dy}{(x^2+y^2)^{3/2}} = \dfrac{a}{\sqrt{2}}$

12. $\int_0^a \int_0^{\sqrt{ax-x^2}} (a^2-x^2-y^2)^{3/2}\, dy\, dx = \dfrac{a^5}{5}\left(\dfrac{\pi}{2} - \dfrac{8}{15}\right)$

AREA UNDER CURVES USING DOUBLE INTEGRAL

We shall discuss some important applications of double integrals which occur quite often in science and engineering. These include problems involving area, volume, mass, etc. Formulae for these in terms of multiple integrals are developed and their use in examples on these topics is illustrated.

Representation of Area as a double integral

TYPE-I: Area enclosed by plane curves expressed in Cartesian co-ordinates

Consider the area enclosed by the curves $y = f_1(x)$ and $y = f_2(x)$ and the ordinates $x = a$, $x = b$ $(a < b)$. Refer Fig.

Divide this area into vertical strips of width δx. If $P(x, y)$, $R(x + \delta x, y + \delta y)$ are two neighboring points, then the area of small rectangle PQRS = $\delta x\, \delta y$.

∴ Area of strip KL = $\underset{dy \to 0}{\text{Lim}} (\Sigma\, dx\, dy)$

Since, for all rectangles in this strip, δx is the same and y varies from $y = f_1(x)$ to $y = f_2(x)$.

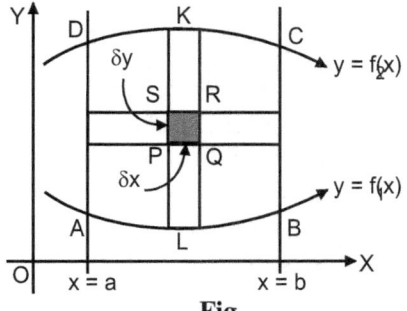

Fig.

∴ Area of the vertical strip KL = $\delta x \underset{dy \to 0}{\text{Lim}} \sum_{f_1(x)}^{f_2(x)} \delta y = \delta x \int_{f_1(x)}^{f_2(x)} dy$

(replacing summation sign by integral sign)

Now adding up all such strips from $x = a$ to $x = b$, we get the required area

$$\text{ABCD} = \lim_{dx \to 0} \left(\sum_a^b dx \right) \int_{f_1(x)}^{f_2(x)} dy$$

$$\boxed{\text{Area} = \int_a^b dx \int_{f_1(x)}^{f_2(x)} dy}$$ (replacing summation sign by integral sign)

Thus, the area ABCD is expressed in terms of double integral as,

$$\text{Area} = \int_a^b \left\{ \int_{f_1(x)}^{f_2(x)} dy \right\} dx.$$

Here inner integration is carried out w.r.t. y treating x as constant and outer integration is then carried out w.r.t. 'x'.

Similarly, dividing the area EFGH (Refer Fig. 11.2) into horizontal strips of width δy, we get the area

$$\text{EFGH} = \int_c^d \left\{ \int_{g_1(y)}^{g_2(y)} dx \right\} dy$$

$$\boxed{\text{Area} = \int_c^d dy \int_{g_1(y)}^{g_2(y)} dx}$$

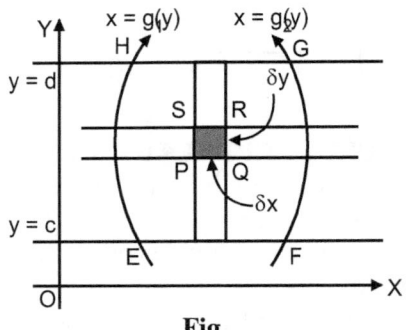

Fig.

Note :

1. The area A included by the curve $y = f(x)$, the x-axis, and the ordinates $x = a$ and $x = b$ is given by

$$\boxed{A = \int_a^b y\, dx = \int_a^b f(x)\, dx}$$

[Refer Fig. 11.3 (a)]

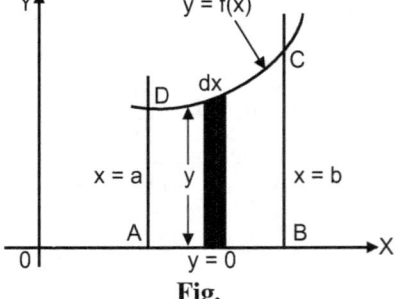

Fig.

2. The area A included by the curve $x = f(y)$, the y-axis and the abscissa $y = c$ and $y = d$ is given by

$$A = \int_c^d x\,dy = \int_c^d f(y)\,dy$$

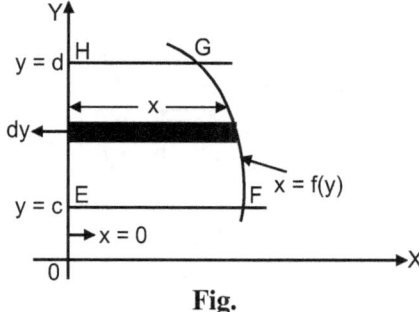

Fig.

3. Double integration is generally not suitable for parametric equations of curves. Instead we employ the following formula for area as :

Area = $\int y\,dx$ if x-axis is the boundary of the area

Area = $\int x\,dy$ if y-axis is the boundary of the area

4. Whenever we are finding the area of a plane region always consider *the symmetry*.
5. Area is always to be considered as positive.

TYPE-II: AREA ENCLOSED BY PLANE CURVES EXPRESSED IN POLAR CO-ORDINATES

Consider the area enclosed by the polar curves $r = f_1(\theta)$ and $r = f_2(\theta)$ and the line $\theta = \alpha$, $\theta = \beta$ ($\alpha < \beta$). Refer Fig. 11.4.

Let $P(r, \theta)$, $Q(r + \delta r, \theta + \delta\theta)$ be two neighboring points. Mark circular areas of radii r and $(r + \delta r)$ meeting OQ in R and OP (produced) in S.

Since arc $PR = r\,\delta\theta$ and arc $PS = \delta r$

∴ Area of the curvilinear rectangle, PQRS is approximately = (PR) (PS) = $(r\,\delta\theta)(\delta r)$. If the whole area is divided into such curvilinear rectangles, the sum $\sum\sum r\,\delta\theta\,\delta r$, taken for all these rectangles, gives in the limit the area A.

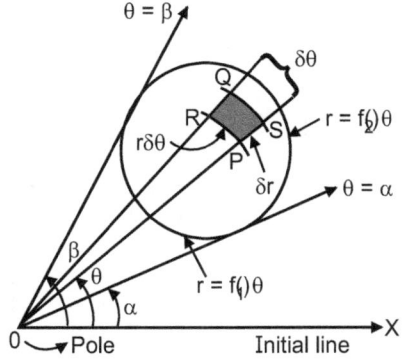

Fig.

Hence, $$A = \lim_{\substack{\delta r \to 0 \\ \delta\theta \to 0}} \sum_\alpha^\beta \sum_{f_1(\theta)}^{f_2(\theta)} r\,\delta\theta\,\delta r \qquad \text{Area} = \int_\alpha^\beta \left\{ \int_{f_1(\theta)}^{f_2(\theta)} r\,dr \right\} d\theta$$

Note :
1. The area (Refer Fig. 11.5) bounded by the curve $r = f(\theta)$ and the lines $\theta = \alpha$ and $\theta = \beta$ is

$$\text{Area} = \frac{1}{2} \int_a^b r^2 \, d\theta$$

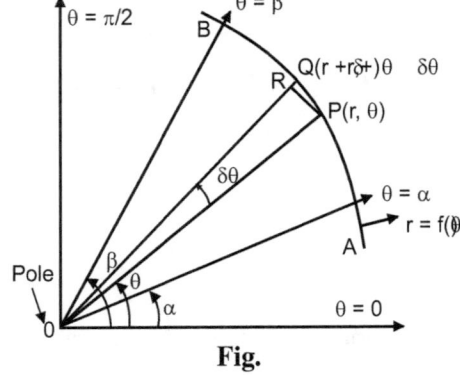

Fig.

2. For the equation of the curve in implicit form, if the loop does not lie on the x or y-axis, then it is inclined to them. In case of *inclined loop*, we change the equation to polar co-ordinates with $x = r \cos\theta$, $y = r \sin\theta$.

3. Always consider the symmetry.

Examples on Area Enclosed by Plane Curves

Ex. 1: Find the area between the curves $y^2 = 4x$ and $2x - 3y + 4 = 0$.

Solution: The points of intersection of parabola $y^2 = 4x$ and the straight line $2x - 3y + 4 = 0$ is obtained by solving the two equations i.e. $\frac{y^2}{2} = 2x$ $\therefore \frac{y^2}{2} - 3y + 4 = 0$.

OR $y^2 - 6y + 8 = 0$ OR $(y-4)(y-2) = 0$

When $y = 4$, $x = 4$ and when $y = 2$, $x = 1$. (1, 2) and (4, 4) are the points of intersection. The required area is shown shaded in Fig. 11.6. For straight line put $y = 0$, $x = -2$ and put $x = 0$, $y = \frac{4}{3}$.

Note that there is no symmetry.

$\therefore$ Required area is $A = \int \left\{ \int dy \right\} dx$.

Imagine vertical line L cutting through region R.

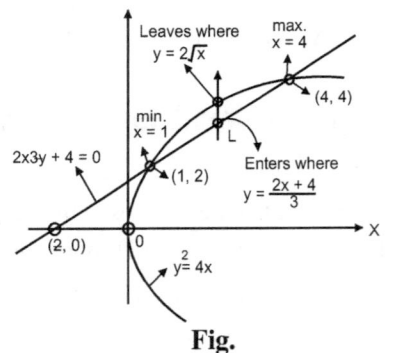

Fig.

Limits for y : $y = \frac{2x+4}{3}$ to $y = 2\sqrt{x}$; Limits for x : $x = 1$ to $x = 4$.

$$A = \int_1^4 \left\{ \int_{\frac{2x+4}{3}}^{2\sqrt{x}} dy \right\} dx = \int_1^4 [y]_{\frac{2x+4}{3}}^{2\sqrt{x}} dx$$

$$= \int_1^4 \left[2\sqrt{x} - \left(\frac{2x+4}{3}\right) \right] dx = \left[2 \frac{x^{3/2}}{3/2} - \frac{2}{3} \cdot \frac{x^2}{2} - \frac{4}{3} x \right]_1^4$$

$$= \left(\frac{32}{3} - \frac{16}{3} - \frac{16}{3}\right) - \left(\frac{4}{3} - \frac{1}{3} - \frac{4}{3}\right) = \frac{1}{3}$$

Note: We can also use $A = \int \left\{ \int dx \right\} dy$, then imagine horizontal line and

$$A = \int_2^4 \left\{ \int_{y^2/4}^{3y - 4/2} dx \right\} dy, \text{ we will get the same answer } A = \frac{1}{3}$$

Ex. 2 : Find the area between the curve $\dfrac{y+8}{x} = x - 2$ and x-axis.

Solution : $\dfrac{y+8}{x} = x - 2$ i.e. $y + 8 = x^2 - 2x$ or $y = x^2 - 2x - 8$ represents a parabolic shape. ∴ $y = (x - 4)(x + 2)$

It's intersection with x-axis is (4, 0), (−2, 0) and with y-axis is (0, −8). Hence required area lies below x-axis as shown shaded in Fig. 11.7. Since the equation of the parabola is expressed directly in terms of x (i.e. $y = x^2 - 2x - 8$), hence we will integrate first w.r.t. y and then w.r.t. x.

∴ Imagine a vertical line L cutting through region R.

Limits for y : $y = x^2 - 2x - 8$ to $y = 0$
Limits for x : $x = -2$ to $x = 4$.

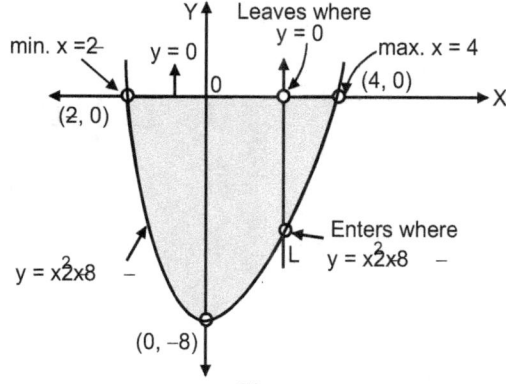

Fig.

$$\text{Area} = \int\limits_{-2}^{4} \left\{ \int dy \right\} dx = \int\limits_{-2}^{4} \left\{ \int\limits_{x^2-2x-8}^{0} dy \right\} dx$$

$$= \int\limits_{-2}^{4} [0 - (x^2 - 2x - 8)] \, dx = \int\limits_{-2}^{4} (-x^2 + 2x + 8) \, dx$$

$$= \left[\dfrac{-x^3}{3} + \dfrac{2x^2}{2} + 8x \right]_{-2}^{4} = \left(\dfrac{-64}{3} + 16 + 32 - \dfrac{8}{3} - 4 + 16 \right)$$

$$= \dfrac{108}{3} = 36$$

Ex. 3: Find by double integration the area included between the curves $y = 3x^2 - x - 3$ and $y = -2x^2 + 4x + 7$.

Solution : $y = 3x^2 - x - 3$ and $y = -2x^2 + 4x + 7$ represent parabolic shape. We will solve the two equations.

i.e. $3x^2 - x - 3 = -2x^2 + 4x + 7$ or $5x^2 - 5x - 10 = 0$ or $x^2 - x - 2 = 0$
∴ $(x - 2)(x + 1) = 0$
∴ when $x = -1$, $y = 1$; when $x = 2$, $y = 7$. Hence, (−1, 1), (2, 7) are the points of intersection (Refer Fig. 11.8).

For $y = 3x^2 - x - 3$:

x	0	1	2
y	−3	−1	7

For $y = -2x^2 + 4x + 7$:

x	0	1	2
y	7	9	7

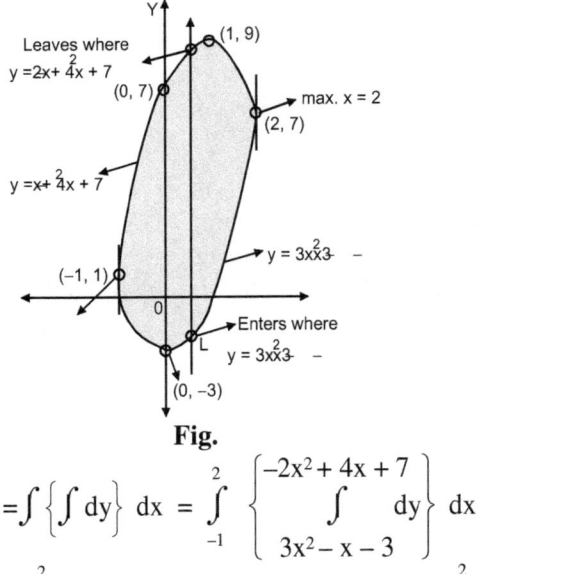

Fig.

$$\therefore \text{ Required area } = \int \left\{ \int dy \right\} dx = \int_{-1}^{2} \left\{ \int_{3x^2 - x - 3}^{-2x^2 + 4x + 7} dy \right\} dx$$

$$= \int_{-1}^{2} (-2x^2 + 4x + 7 - 3x^2 + x + 3) \, dx = \int_{-1}^{2} (-5x^2 + 5x + 10) \, dx$$

$$= \left[\frac{-5x^3}{3} + \frac{5x^2}{2} + 10x \right]_{-1}^{2} = \frac{45}{2}$$

Ex. 4 : Find the total area included between the two branches of the curve $y^2(4-x)(x-2) = x^2$ and the two asymptotes.

Solution : $\qquad y^2 = \dfrac{x^2}{(4-x)(x-2)}$

It is symmetrical about x-axis. Intersection with the co-ordinate axis is only at (0, 0). x = 2, x = 4 are the asymptotes to the given curve, when x = 3, y = ± 3. A rough sketch of the curve is as shown in Fig. 11.9. Because of the symmetry,

$$\text{Required area} = 2 \int \left\{ \int dy \right\} dx = 2 \int_{2}^{4} \int_{0}^{\frac{x}{\sqrt{(4-x)(x-2)}}} dy \, dx = 2 \int_{2}^{4} \frac{x}{\sqrt{(4-x)(x-2)}} \, dx$$

Put $x - 2 = 2 \sin^2 \theta$, $dx = 4 \sin \theta \cos \theta \, d\theta$

x	2	4
θ	0	π/2

$$\text{Area} = 2 \int_{0}^{\pi/2} \frac{(2 + 2 \sin^2 \theta) \, 4 \sin \theta \cos \theta \, d\theta}{\sqrt{(2 - 2 \sin^2 \theta) \, 2 \sin^2 \theta}}$$

$$= 8 \int_{0}^{\pi/2} (1 + \sin^2 \theta) \, d\theta = 8 \left(\frac{\pi}{2} + \frac{1}{2} \frac{\pi}{2} \right)$$

$$= 6\pi$$

Fig.

Ex. 5 : Find by double integration the area between the curve $y^2 x = 4a^2(2a - x)$ and its asymptote.

Solution : $y^2 = \dfrac{4a^2(2a-x)}{x}$

It is symmetrical about x-axis and does not pass through (0, 0). Also $x = 0$ i.e. y-axis is the asymptote to the curve and intersects x-axis at $(2a, 0)$. For $x < 0$, $x > 2a$, curve does not exist and for $x = a$, $y = \pm 2a$. This famous curve is known as "Witch of Agnesi" and it is shown shaded in Fig. 11.10. Because of the symmetry,

$$\text{Required area} = 2\int\left\{\int dy\right\}dx = 2\int_0^{2a}\int_0^{2a\sqrt{2a-x}/\sqrt{x}} dy\, dx$$

$$\text{Area} = 2\int_0^{2a} 2a\cdot\sqrt{\dfrac{2a-x}{x}}\, dx$$

$$= 4a\int_0^{2a} x^{-1/2}(2a-x)^{1/2}\, dx$$

Put $x = 2at$, $dx = 2a\, dt$

x	0	2a
t	0	1

$$\text{Area} = 4a\int_0^1 (2at)^{-1/2}(2a)^{1/2}(1-t)^{1/2}\, 2a\, dt$$

$$= 8a^2\int_0^1 t^{-1/2}(1-t)^{1/2}\, dt = 8a^2\, B(1/2, 3/2)$$

$$= 8a^2\,\dfrac{\lfloor 1/2\, \lfloor 3/2}{\lfloor 2} = 8a^2\sqrt{p}\,\dfrac{1}{2}\sqrt{p} = 4\pi a^2$$

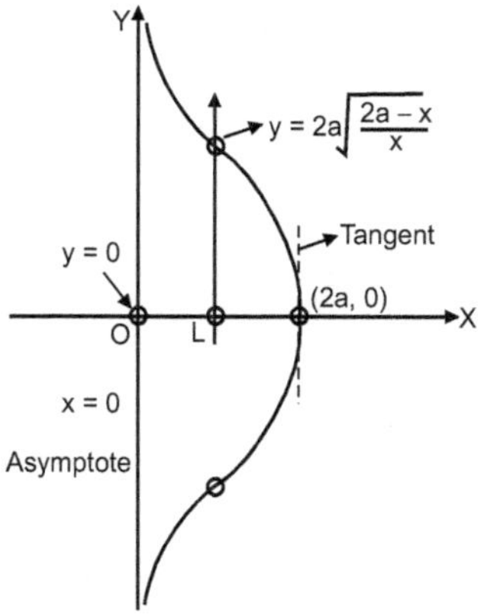

Fig.

Ex. 6 : Find the area bounded by the curve $x(x^2 + y^2) = a(y^2 - x^2)$ and its asymptote. Also find the area of the loop of the curve.

Solution : Part-I $x(x^2 + y^2) = a(y^2 - x^2)$

F.E. (Sem. II) M II (SU)   Multiple Integration and Its Applications

i.e. $ay^2 - xy^2 = x^3 + ax^2$

or $y^2(a-x) = x^2(a+x)$

i.e. $y^2 = \dfrac{x^2(a+x)}{a-x}$

It is symmetrical about x-axis and passes through (0, 0). Also $y = \pm x$ are the tangents at (0, 0). It intersects x-axis at (0, 0) (–a, 0). Here x = a is the asymptote to the given curve. The required area between the curve and its asymptote is shown shaded in Fig. 11.11. Because of symmetry,

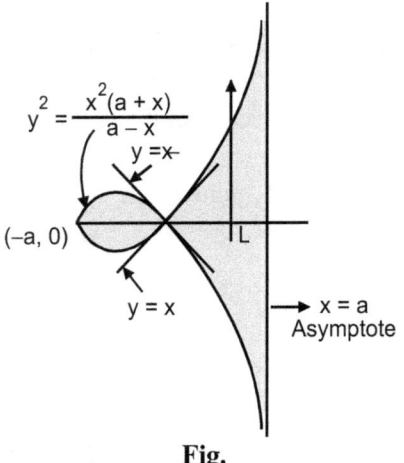

Fig.

$$\text{Area} = 2\int \left\{\int dy\right\} dx = 2\int_0^a \left\{\int_0^{x\sqrt{\frac{a+x}{a-x}}} dy\right\} dx$$

$$= 2\int_0^a \frac{x\sqrt{a+x}}{\sqrt{a-x}}\, dx = 2\int_0^a \frac{x(a+x)}{\sqrt{a^2-x^2}}\, dx$$

$$= 2\int_0^{p/2} \frac{a\sin q\,(a + a\sin q)\, a\cos q\, dq}{a\cos q} \quad \text{(by putting } x = a\sin\theta\text{)}$$

$$= 2a^2 \int_0^{p/2} (\sin\theta + \sin^2\theta)\, d\theta = 2a^2 \left[1 + \frac{1}{2}\cdot\frac{p}{2}\right] = 2a^2\left[1 + \frac{p}{4}\right]$$

Part-II To find the area of the loop, we have,

$$\text{Area} = 2\int \left\{\int dy\right\} dx = 2\int_{-a}^{0} \left\{\int_0^{x\sqrt{\frac{a+x}{a-x}}} dy\right\} dx$$

$$= 2\int_{-a}^{0} \frac{x\sqrt{a+x}}{\sqrt{a-x}}\, dx = 2\int_{-a}^{0} \frac{x(a+x)}{\sqrt{a^2-x^2}}\, dx \quad\quad \text{Put } x = -a\sin\theta$$

$$= 2\int_{p/2}^{0} \frac{(-a\sin q)(a - a\sin q)(-a\cos q\, dq)}{a\cos q}$$

$$= -2a^2 \int_0^{p/2} (\sin q - \sin^2 q)\, d\theta$$

$$= -2a^2 \left[1 - \frac{p}{4}\right] = 2a^2\left(1 - \frac{p}{4}\right) \quad \text{(numerically)}$$

Ex. 7: Show that the area of the loop of the curve $y^2(a + x) = x^2(3a - x)$ is equal to the area between the curve and its asymptote.

(6.55)

Solution : $y^2 = \dfrac{x^2(3a-x)}{a+x}$. It is symmetrical about x-axis, passes through origin and $y = \pm\sqrt{3}\, x$ are tangents at origin. It intersects x-axis at $(3a, 0)$ $(0, 0)$. Also $x = -a$ is an asymptote to the curve.

The required area is shown shaded in Fig.

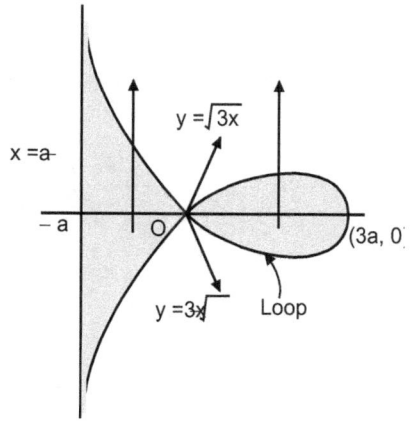

Fig.

Part-I Area of the loop $= 2 \displaystyle\int_0^{3a} \int_0^{x\sqrt{\frac{3a-x}{a+x}}} dy\, dx$

Area $= 2 \displaystyle\int_0^{3a} x\sqrt{\dfrac{3a-x}{a+x}}\, dx$

The substitution employed here is obtained by the following rule useful for integration of expressions of the type under consideration.

Rule: Half the difference between $a + x$ and $3a - x$ is $\dfrac{1}{2}[(a+x) - (3a-x)]$ i.e. $x - a$, and half their sum is $\dfrac{1}{2}[(a+x) + (3a-x)]$ i.e. $2a$.

We therefore put $x - a = 2a \sin q$ (or $x - a = 2a \cos q$) $\therefore dx = 2a \cos\theta\, d\theta$

x	0	3a
θ	−π/6	π/2

$$\text{Area of the loop} = 2 \int_{-\pi/6}^{\pi/2} \dfrac{(a + 2a\sin q)\sqrt{3a - a - 2a\sin q}}{\sqrt{a + a + 2a\sin q}} \cdot 2a \cos q\, dq$$

$$= 4a^2 \int_{-\pi/6}^{\pi/2} \dfrac{(1 + 2\sin q)\sqrt{1 - \sin q}}{\sqrt{1 + \sin q}} \cos\theta\, d\theta$$

$$= 4a^2 \int_{-\pi/6}^{\pi/2} \dfrac{(1 + 2\sin q)(1 - \sin q)}{\sqrt{1 - \sin^2 q}} \cos\theta\, d\theta$$

$$= 4a^2 \int_{-\pi/6}^{\pi/2} (1 + \sin q - 2\sin^2 q)\, d\theta$$

$$= 4a^2 \int_{-\pi/6}^{\pi/2} (1 + \sin\theta - 1 + \cos 2\theta)\, d\theta = 4a^2 \int_{-\pi/6}^{\pi/2} (\sin q + \cos 2q)\, d\theta$$

$$= 4a^2 \left[-\cos q + \dfrac{\sin 2q}{2} \right]_{-\pi/6}^{\pi/2} = 4a^2 \left[0 + \cos(-\pi/6) - \dfrac{1}{2}\sin\left(\dfrac{-p}{3}\right) \right]$$

$$= 4a^2 \left[\dfrac{\sqrt{3}}{2} - \dfrac{1}{2}\left(-\dfrac{\sqrt{3}}{2}\right) \right] = 3\sqrt{3}\, a^2 \qquad \ldots (i)$$

Part-II Area between the curve and its asymptote $= 2 \int_{-a}^{0} \int_{0}^{x\sqrt{\frac{3a-x}{a+x}}} dy\, dx$.

$$\text{Area} = 2 \int_{-a}^{0} \frac{x\sqrt{3a-x}}{\sqrt{a+x}}\, dx$$

as in the part (i) $x - a = 2a \sin \theta$

x	$-a$	0
θ	$-\pi/2$	$-\pi/6$

$$= 2 \int_{-\pi/2}^{-\pi/6} \frac{(a + 2a \sin q)\sqrt{2a(1-\sin q)}\, 2a \cos q\, dq}{\sqrt{2a(1+\sin q)}}$$

$$= 4a^2 \int_{-\pi/2}^{-\pi/6} (\sin q + \cos 2q)\, d\theta \quad \text{(As simplified in part I)}$$

$$= 4a^2 \left[-\cos q + \frac{\sin 2q}{2} \right]_{-\pi/2}^{-\pi/6} = 4a^2 \left[-\cos\left(\frac{-\pi}{6}\right) + \frac{1}{2}\sin\left(\frac{-\pi}{3}\right) - 0 \right]$$

$$= 4a^2 \left[-\cos \pi/6 - \frac{1}{2}\sin \pi/3 \right] = -4a^2 \left[\frac{\sqrt{3}}{2} + \frac{1}{2}\cdot\frac{\sqrt{3}}{2} \right]$$

$$= -4a^2 \left(\frac{3\sqrt{3}}{4} \right) = -3\sqrt{3}\, a^2$$

$$= 3\sqrt{3}\, a^2 \text{ (numerically)} \quad \ldots \text{(ii)}$$

From (i) and (ii), it is clear that
Area between the curve and its asymptote = Area of the loop of the curve.

Ex. 8 : Show that the area of the curve $a^2 x^2 = y^3 (2a - y)$ is πa^2.

Solution : $a^2 x^2 = y^3 (2a - y)$

It is symmetrical about y-axis, passes through origin and there exists a cusp at origin. It intersects y-axis at (0, 0) (0, 2a). Also $\left(\frac{dx}{dy}\right)_{(0, 2a)}$
$= \infty \Rightarrow$ tangent at (0, 2a) is parallel to x-axis. The required area is shown shaded in Fig. Since the loop is on y-axis,

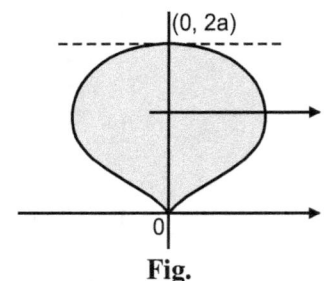

Fig.

$$\text{Area} = 2 \int x\, dy = 2 \int_{0}^{2a} \frac{y^{3/2}(2a-y)^{1/2}}{a}\, dy$$

$$= \frac{2}{a} \int_{0}^{\pi/2} (2a \sin^2 q)^{3/2} [2a(1-\sin^2 \theta)]^{1/2} \cdot 4a \sin \theta \cos \theta\, d\theta \quad \text{(putting } y = 2a \sin^2 \theta\text{)}$$

$$= 32a^2 \int_{0}^{\pi/2} \sin^4 \theta \cos^2 \theta\, d\theta = 32a^2 \left[\frac{3\cdot 1\cdot 1}{6\cdot 4\cdot 2} \right] \frac{\pi}{2} = \pi a^2$$

Ex. 9 : Find the area of the curve $x^4 - 3ax^3 + a^2(2x^2 + y^2) = 0$.

Solution : $x^4 - 3ax^3 + a^2(2x^2 + y^2) = 0$ or $a^2 y^2 = 3ax^3 - x^4 - 2a^2 x^2$

i.e. $a^2 y^2 = x^2(3ax - x^2 - 2a^2)$ or $a^2 y^2 = x^2(2a - x)(x - a)$

It is symmetrical about x-axis, passes through (0, 0). It intersects x-axis at (0, 0), (a, 0), (2a, 0). No asymptote. For $0 < x < a$, $x > 2a$, curve does not exist. The required area is shown shaded in Fig.

$$\text{Area} = 2 \int y \, dx$$

$$\text{Area} = 2 \int_a^{2a} \frac{x\sqrt{(x-a)(2a-x)}}{a} dx$$

$$= \frac{2}{a} \int_a^{2a} x\sqrt{(x-a)(2a-x)} \, dx$$

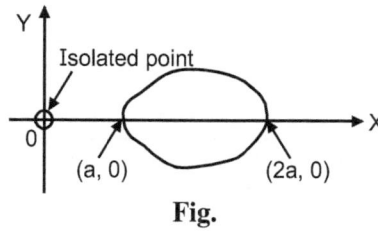

Fig.

Important Note :

$$\text{For } I = \int_a^b f(x-a, b-x) \, dx \text{ always put } x = a\cos^2 q + b\sin^2 q$$

Here, $\alpha = a$, $\beta = 2a$ ∴ We put $x = a\cos^2\theta + 2a\sin^2\theta$

∴ $x - a = a\cos^2\theta + 2a\sin^2\theta - a = 2a\sin^2\theta - a\sin^2\theta = a\sin^2\theta$

$dx = 2a\sin\theta\cos\theta \, d\theta$

x	a	2a
θ	0	π/2

$2a - x = 2a - a - a\sin^2\theta = a\cos^2\theta$

∴ $\text{Area} = \frac{2}{a} \int_0^{p/2} (a + a\sin^2 q)\sqrt{a\sin^2 q \cdot a\cos^2 q} \; (2a\sin q\cos q \, dq)$

$$= 4a^2 \left[\int_0^{p/2} \sin^2 q \cos^2 q \, dq + \int_0^{p/2} \sin^4 q \cos^2 q \, dq \right]$$

$$= 4a^2 \left[\frac{1 \cdot 1}{4 \cdot 2} \frac{p}{2} + \frac{3 \cdot 1 \cdot 1}{6 \cdot 4 \cdot 2} \frac{p}{2} \right] = \frac{3pa^2}{8}$$

Ex. 10 : Find the total area included between the two cardioides $r = a(1 + \cos\theta)$ and $r = a(1 - \cos\theta)$. **SUK : May-09, Aug-13**

Solution : Required area is as shown shaded in Fig. 11.15.

$$\text{Area} = 4 \int_0^{p/2} \left\{ \int_0^{a(1-\cos q)} r \, dr \right\} d\theta = 4 \int_0^{p/2} \frac{a^2(1 - \cos q)^2}{2} d\theta$$

$$= 2a^2 \int_0^{p/2} (1 - 2\cos\theta + \cos^2\theta) \, d\theta = 2a^2 \left[\frac{p}{2} - 2(1) + \frac{1}{2}\frac{p}{2} \right] = 2a^2 \left[\frac{3p}{4} - 2 \right]$$

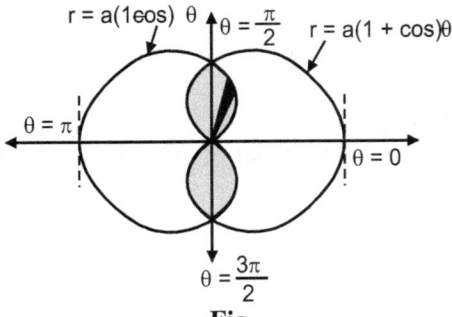
Fig.

Ex. 11 : Find the area common to the circles $x^2 + y^2 = a^2$ and $x^2 + y^2 = 2ax$.

Solution : Required area is shown shaded in Fig. 11.16. Equation of both the circles in polar co-ordinates is $r = a$, $r = 2a \cos \theta$. Solving area $a = 2a \cos \theta$, $\cos \theta = \frac{1}{2}$, $\theta = \frac{p}{3}$.

$$\text{Area} = 2 \int_0^{p/3} \left\{ \int_0^a r \, dr \right\} d\theta + 2 \int_{p/3}^{p/2} \left\{ \int_0^{2a \cos q} r \, dr \right\} d\theta$$

$$= 2 \int_0^{p/3} \frac{a^2}{2} d\theta + 2 \int_{p/3}^{p/2} \frac{4a^2 \cos^2 q}{2} d\theta = \frac{pa^2}{3} + 2a^2 \int_{p/3}^{p/2} (1 + \cos 2q) \, d\theta$$

$$= \frac{pa^2}{3} + 2a^2 \left((p/2 - p/3) + \left[\frac{\sin 2q}{2} \right]_{p/3}^{p/2} \right)$$

Fig.

$$= \frac{pa^2}{3} + 2a^2 \left(\frac{p}{6} + 0 - \frac{1}{2} \frac{\sqrt{3}}{2} \right) = \frac{pa^2}{3} + 2a^2 \left(\frac{p}{6} - \frac{\sqrt{3}}{4} \right) = \frac{2pa^2}{3} - \frac{\sqrt{3} a^2}{2}$$

Ex. 12 : Find by double integration the area inside the circle $r = a \sin \theta$ and outside the cardioide $r = a(1 - \cos \theta)$. **SUK: Nov-08**

Solution : The required area is as shown shaded in Fig. 11.17.

$$\text{Area} = \int_0^{p/2} \left\{ \int_{a(1-\cos q)}^{a \sin q} r \, dr \right\} d\theta = \frac{1}{2} \int_0^{p/2} [a^2 \sin^2 \theta - a^2 (1 - \cos \theta)^2] \, d\theta$$

$$= \frac{a^2}{2} \int_0^{p/2} [\sin^2 \theta - 1 + 2 \cos \theta - \cos^2 \theta] \, d\theta$$

$$= \frac{a^2}{2} \left[\frac{1}{2} \frac{p}{2} - \frac{p}{2} + 2(1) - \frac{1}{2} \frac{p}{2} \right] = a^2 \left(1 - \frac{p}{4} \right)$$

(6.59)

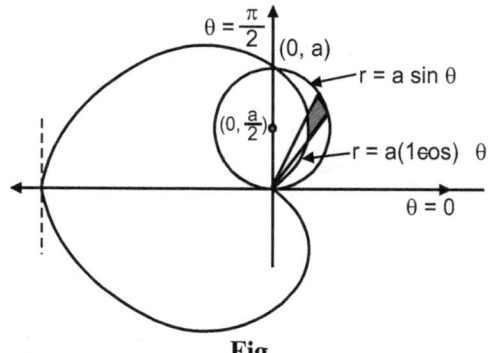

Fig.

Ex. 13 : Find the area inside the cardioide $r = 2a (1 + \cos \theta)$ and outside the parabola $r = \dfrac{2a}{1 + \cos q}$.

Solution : $r = 2a (1 + \cos \theta)$ is a cardioide and $r = \dfrac{2a}{1 + \cos q}$ is a parabola.

θ	0	π/2	π	3π/2	2π
$r = 2a (1 + \cos \theta)$	4a	2a	0	2a	4a
$r = \dfrac{2a}{1 + \cos q}$	a	2a	∞	2a	a

The required region of integration is as shown shaded in Fig. 11.18.

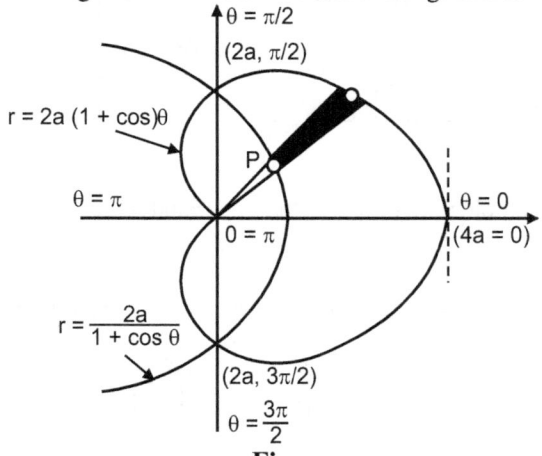

Fig.

$$\text{Area} = 2 \int_0^{\pi/2} \left\{ \int_{\frac{2a}{1+\cos q}}^{2a(1+\cos q)} r \, dr \right\} d\theta$$

$$= 2 \int_0^{\pi/2} \frac{1}{2} \left(4a^2 (1 + \cos q)^2 - \frac{4a^2}{(1 + \cos q)^2} \right) d\theta$$

(6.60)

$$= 4a^2 \int_0^{\pi/2} (1 + 2\cos\theta + \cos^2\theta)\, d\theta - 4a^2 \int_0^{\pi/2} \frac{d\theta}{4\cos^4\frac{\theta}{2}}$$

$$= 4a^2 \left[\frac{\pi}{2} + 2(1) + \frac{1}{2}\frac{\pi}{2}\right] - a^2 \int_0^{\pi/4} \sec^4 t \cdot 2\, dt \qquad \left(\because \frac{\theta}{2} = t\right)$$

$$= 4a^2 \left[\frac{3\pi}{4} + 2\right] - 2a^2 \int_0^{\pi/4} (1 + \tan^2 t)\sec^2 t\, dt \qquad (\because \tan t = u)$$

$$= 4a^2 \left[\frac{3\pi}{4} + 2\right] - 2a^2 \int_0^1 (1 + u^2)\, du = 4a^2 \left[\frac{3\pi}{4} + 2\right] - 2a^2 \left[1 + \frac{1}{3}\right]$$

$$= 4a^2 \left[\frac{3\pi}{4} + 2 - \frac{2}{3}\right] = 4a^2 \left[\frac{3\pi}{4} + \frac{4}{3}\right]$$

Ex. 14 : Find the area of the region included between the two loops of the curve $r = a(1 + 2\cos\theta)$.

Solution : Given $r = a(1 + 2\cos\theta)$. It is symmetrical about the initial line. Put $r = 0$, $\cos\theta = -\frac{1}{2}$, $\theta = \frac{2\pi}{3}$.

It passes through pole. For $2\pi/3 < \theta < \pi$, r is negative, there exists a inner loop and because of symmetry the curve is drawn as shown in Fig. 11.19.

r	3a	a	0	−a
θ	0	π/2	2π/3	π

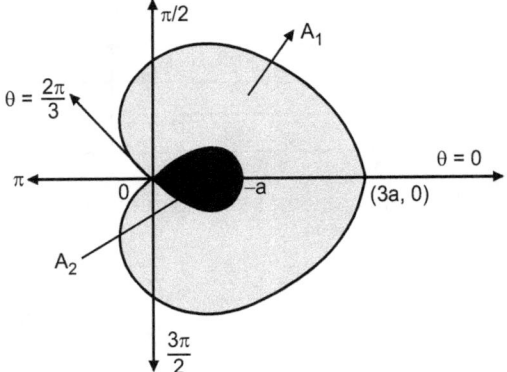

Fig.

Here we cannot use double integration as the upper and lower limits of the inner integral will be same.

$$\text{Area of outer loop} = A_1 = 2 \int_0^{2\pi/3} \frac{1}{2} r^2\, d\theta = \int_0^{2\pi/3} a^2(1 + 2\cos\theta)^2\, d\theta$$

$$A_1 = a^2 \int_0^{2\pi/3} (1 + 4\cos\theta + 4\cos^2\theta)\, d\theta = a^2 \int_0^{2\pi/3} \left[1 + 4\cos\theta + 4\frac{(1 + \cos 2\theta)}{2}\right] d\theta$$

$$= a^2 \int_0^{2\pi/3} (3 + 4\cos\theta + 2\cos 2\theta)\, d\theta = a^2 \left\{3 \cdot \frac{2\pi}{3} + [4\sin\theta + \sin 2\theta]_0^{2\pi/3}\right\}$$

$$= a^2 \left\{2\pi + \frac{4\sqrt{3}}{2} - \frac{\sqrt{3}}{2}\right\} = a^2 \left(2\pi + \frac{3\sqrt{3}}{2}\right)$$

$$\text{Area of inner loop, } A_2 = 2 \int_{2\pi/3}^{\pi} \frac{1}{2} r^2\, d\theta = \int_{2\pi/3}^{\pi} a^2(1 + 2\cos\theta)^2\, d\theta$$

$$A_2 = a^2[3\theta + 4\sin\theta + \sin 2\theta]_{2p/3}^{p}$$

$$= a^2\left[p - 4\frac{\sqrt{3}}{2} + \frac{\sqrt{3}}{2}\right] = a^2\left[p - \frac{3\sqrt{3}}{2}\right]$$

Required area $= A_1 - A_2 = a^2\left[2p + \frac{3\sqrt{3}}{2} - p + \frac{3\sqrt{3}}{2}\right]$

$$= a^2(p + 3\sqrt{3})$$

Ex. 15 : Find the area between the curve $r = a(\sec\theta + \cos\theta)$ and the asymptote $r = a\sec\theta$.

Solution : $r = a\sec\theta$ i.e. $r = \dfrac{a}{\cos q}$ or $r\cos\theta = a$ i.e. $x = a$

$$r = a(\sec\theta + \cos\theta)$$

i.e. $\sqrt{x^2 + y^2} = a\left(\dfrac{\sqrt{x^2 + y^2}}{x} + \dfrac{x}{\sqrt{x^2 + y^2}}\right)$

or $x(x^2 + y^2) = a(x^2 + y^2 + x^2)$

or $y^2 = \dfrac{x^2(2a - x)}{x - a}$

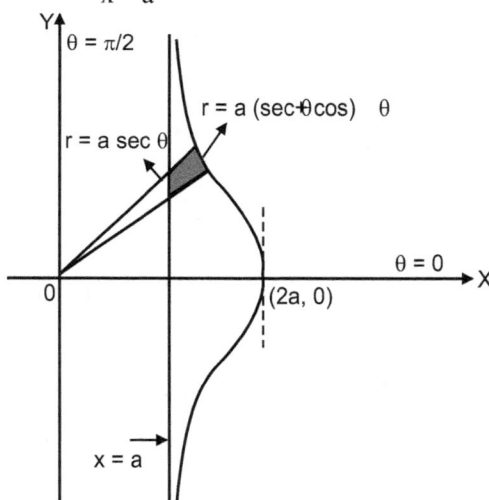

Fig.

It is symmetrical about x-axis and passes through origin (isolated point). $x = a$ is the asymptote and it intersects x-axis at $(2a, 0)$, $(0, 0)$. For $0 < x < a$, $x > 2a$ curve does not exist. The required area is as shown shaded in Fig. 11.20.

$$\text{Area} = 2\int_{0}^{p/2}\int_{a\sec q}^{a(\sec q + \cos q)} r\, dr\, d\theta$$

$$= \int_{0}^{p/2}[a^2(\sec^2\theta + 2\sec\theta\cos\theta + \cos^2\theta) - a^2\sec^2\theta]\, d\theta$$

$$= a^2\int_{0}^{p/2}(2 + \cos^2 q)\, d\theta = a^2\left[p + \frac{p}{4}\right] = \frac{5p}{4}a^2$$

(6.62)

Ex. 16 : Prove that the area of the loop of the Foulium of DesCarte's $x^3 + y^3 = 3axy$ is three times the area of one loop of $r^2 = a^2 \cos 2\theta$, Bernoullie's lemniscate.

Solution : For $x^3 + y^3 = 3axy$, it is symmetrical about $y = x$, passes through $(0, 0)$, x and y-axis are tangents at $(0, 0)$ and there exists a node at $(0, 0)$. It intersects $y = x$ at $\left(\dfrac{3a}{2}, \dfrac{3a}{2}\right)$ and $x + y + a = 0$ is the asymptote to the given curve. The curve does not exist in the third quadrant. The curve $x^2 + y^3 = 3axy$ is known as Foulium of DesCarte's and is shown shaded in Fig. 11.21 (a).

For $r^2 = a^2 \cos 2\theta$, it is symmetrical about $\theta = 0$, pole, $\theta = \dfrac{p}{2}$. Maximum value of $r = a$ and minimum value of $r = 0$. $\theta = \pi/4, 3\pi/4, 5\pi/4, 7\pi/4$ are tangents at $(0, 0)$. No asymptote. The curve $r^2 = a^2 \cos 2\theta$ is known as Bernoullie's lemniscate and is shown shaded in Fig. 11.21 (b).

Part-I Area of loop of $x^3 + y^3 = 3axy$:

In case of inclined loop, we change the equation to polar form

$$r^3 (\cos^3 \theta + \sin^3 \theta) = 3ar^2 \sin \theta \cos \theta \Rightarrow r = \frac{3a \sin \theta \cos \theta}{\cos^3 \theta + \sin^3 \theta}$$

$$\text{Area of the loop} = \frac{1}{2} \int_0^{\pi/2} r^2 d\theta = \frac{1}{2} \int_0^{\pi/2} \frac{9a^2 \sin^2 \theta \cos^2 \theta}{(\cos^3 \theta + \sin^3 \theta)^2} d\theta$$

$$= \frac{9a^2}{2} \int_0^{\pi/2} \frac{\tan^2 \theta \cdot \sec^2 \theta}{(1 + \tan^3 \theta)^2} d\theta$$

(dividing by $\cos^6 \theta$ and put $1 + \tan^3 \theta = t$)

$$= \frac{3a^2}{2} \int_1^{\infty} \frac{dt}{t^2} = \frac{3a^2}{2} \left[-\frac{1}{t}\right]_1^{\infty} = \frac{3a^2}{2} [0 + 1] = \frac{3a^2}{2} \qquad \ldots (i)$$

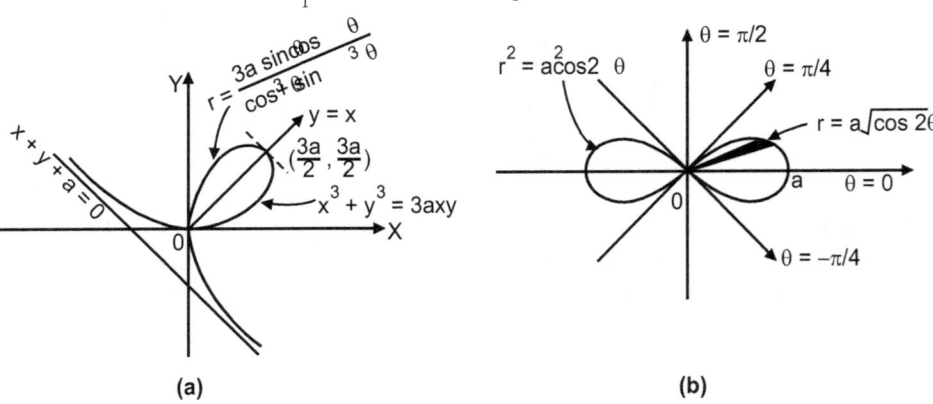

(a)   (b)

Fig.

Part-II Area of one loop of $r^2 = a^2 \cos 2\theta$:

$$\text{Area of the loop} = 2 \int_0^{\pi/4} \frac{1}{2} r^2 d\theta = \int_0^{\pi/4} a^2 \cos 2\theta \, d\theta = a^2 \left.\frac{\sin 2\theta}{2}\right|_0^{\pi/4}$$

$$= \frac{a^2}{2}(1) = \frac{a^2}{2} \qquad \ldots \text{(ii)}$$

From (i) and (ii), we note that :

Area of loop of $x^3 + y^3 = 3axy$ = 3 times area of one loop of $r^2 = a^2 \cos 2\theta$.

Ex. 17 : Find by double integration the area of the loop of curve $x^4 + y^4 = 2a^2 xy$.

Solution : It is symmetrical about $y = x$ and in opposite quadrant. It passes through (0, 0), x and y-axis are tangents at (0, 0) and there exists a node at (0, 0). It intersects the line $y = x$ at (a, a) (–a, –a). No asymptote. It does not exist in 2nd and 4th quadrants. A rough sketch of the curve is as shown in Fig. 11.22.

For the inclined loop, we convert the equation of curve to polar form

$$r^4 (\cos^4\theta + \sin^4\theta) = 2a^2 r^2 \sin\theta \cos\theta \Rightarrow r^2 = \frac{2a^2 \sin\theta \cos\theta}{\cos^4\theta + \sin^4\theta}$$

$$\text{Area} = 2 \int_0^{\pi/2} \frac{r^2}{2} d\theta$$

$$\text{Area} = \int_0^{\pi/2} \frac{2a^2 \sin\theta \cos\theta}{\cos^4\theta + \sin^4\theta} d\theta = 2a^2 \int_0^{\pi/2} \frac{\tan\theta \sec^2\theta \, d\theta}{1 + (\tan^2\theta)^2} \quad (\tan^2\theta = t)$$

$$= a^2 \int_0^\infty \frac{dt}{1+t^2} = a^2 [\tan^{-1} t]_0^\infty = a^2 [\pi/2] = \frac{\pi a^2}{2}$$

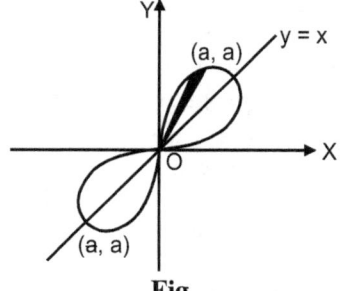

Fig.

Ex. 18: Show that the area of a loop of the curve $x^5 + y^5 = 5a\, x^2 y^2$ is $\frac{5a^2}{2}$.

Solution : It is symmetrical about $y = x$. It passes through (0, 0) and x and y-axis are tangents at origin. There exists a node at (0, 0). It intersects $y = x$ at $\left(\frac{5a}{2}, \frac{5a}{2}\right)$ and $x + y = a$ is the asymptote. The curve does not exist in 3rd quadrant. The required area of the loop is shown shaded in Fig. 11.23.

For an inclined loop, we convert the equation of curve to polar form

$$r^5 (\cos^5\theta + \sin^5\theta) = 5ar^4 \sin^2\theta \cos^2\theta \quad \text{or} \quad r = \frac{5a \sin^2 q \cos^2 q}{\cos^5 q + \sin^5 q}$$

Area of the loop = $\int_0^{\pi/2} \frac{1}{2} r^2 d\theta$

$$\text{Area} = \frac{1}{2} \int_0^{\pi/2} \frac{25a^2 \sin^4\theta \cos^4\theta \, d\theta}{(\cos^5\theta + \sin^5\theta)^2} \quad \text{(dividing by } \cos^{10}\theta\text{)}$$

$$= \frac{25a^2}{2} \int_0^{\pi/2} \frac{\tan^4\theta \sec^2\theta}{(1 + \tan^5\theta)^2} d\theta, \quad (1 + \tan^5\theta = t)$$

$$= \frac{5a^2}{2} \int_1^\infty \frac{dt}{t^2} = \frac{5a^2}{2} \left[-\frac{1}{t}\right]_1^\infty = \frac{5a^2}{2}$$

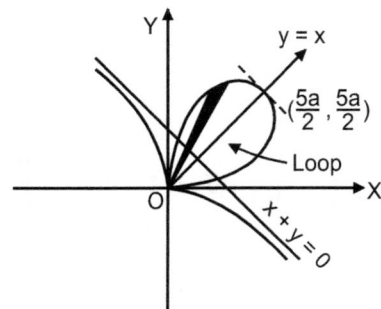

Fig.

Solution : It is symmetrical about y-axis and passes through (0, 0), maximum value of y = 2a, minimum value of y = 0 when θ = π, x = aπ, y = 2a and when θ = −π, x = −aπ, y = 2a. There exists a cusp at P(−aπ, 2a) and Q(aπ, 2a). $\frac{dy}{dx} = 0$ when θ = 0, $\frac{dy}{dx} = \infty$ when θ = ±π. The straight line PQ is called base of the cycloid, O is vertex and OY is axis of the cycloid. Curve does not exist for y < 0. The required area is as shown shaded in Fig.

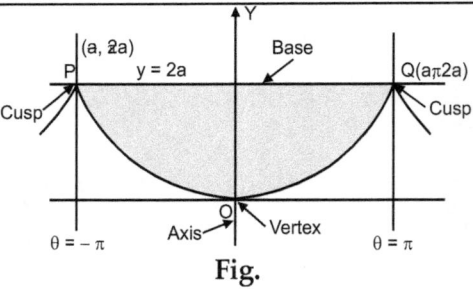

Fig.

Required area $= 2 \int x \, dy = 2 \int_0^\pi x \frac{dy}{d\theta} d\theta$

Area $= 2 \int_0^\pi a(\theta + \sin\theta) a \sin\theta \, d\theta = 2a^2 \int_0^\pi (\theta \sin\theta + \sin^2\theta) d\theta$

$= 2a^2 \left[[-\theta \cos\theta + \sin\theta]_0^\pi + 2 \cdot \frac{1}{2} \cdot \frac{\pi}{2} \right] = 2a^2 \left[\pi + \frac{\pi}{2}\right] = 3\pi a^2$

Ex. 20 : Find the total area of the Astroid $x^{2/3} + y^{2/3} = a^{2/3}$.

Solution : The parametric equations of Astroid are $x = a \cos^3 \theta$, $y = a \sin^3 \theta$. It is symmetrical about both axes and does not pass through (0, 0). Here x and y cannot exceed a. $\frac{dy}{dx} = 0$ when $\theta = 0$, $\pi \cdot \frac{dy}{dx} = \infty$ when $\theta = \frac{\pi}{2}, \frac{3\pi}{2}$.

Hence the required area is as shown shaded in Fig. 11.25.

$$\text{Area} = 4 \int x \, dy = 4 \int_0^{\pi/2} x \cdot \frac{dy}{d\theta} d\theta = 4 \int_0^{\pi/2} a \cos^3 \theta \, 3a \sin^2 \theta \cos \theta \, d\theta$$

$$= 12a^2 \int_0^{\pi/2} \sin^2 \theta \cos^4 \theta \, d\theta = 12a^2 \cdot \frac{1 \cdot 3 \cdot 1}{6 \cdot 4 \cdot 2} \cdot \frac{\pi}{2} = \frac{3\pi a^2}{8}$$

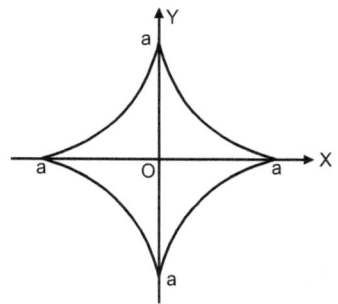

Fig.

Ex. 21 : Show that the area of a loop of the curve $r = a \cos n\theta$ is $\frac{\pi a^2}{4n}$ and state the total area in cases n is odd, n is even. Also show that the area contained between the circle $r = a$ and the curve $r = a \cos 5\theta$ is equal to three-fourth of the area of the circle.

Solution : Part-I For $r = a \cos n\theta$, put $r = 0$, $\cos n\theta = 0$

$$n\theta = -\frac{\pi}{2}, \frac{\pi}{2}, \frac{3\pi}{2}, \frac{5\pi}{2} \ldots\ldots \text{ or } \theta = -\frac{\pi}{2n}, \frac{\pi}{2n}, \frac{3\pi}{2n}, \frac{5\pi}{2n} \ldots\ldots$$

First loop lies between $-\frac{\pi}{2n}$ to $\frac{\pi}{2n}$

$$\text{Area of a loop} = \int_{-\pi/2n}^{\pi/2n} \frac{r^2}{2} d\theta = \frac{1}{2} \int_{-\pi/2n}^{\pi/2n} a^2 \cos^2 n\theta \, d\theta$$

$$= \frac{a^2}{2} \cdot 2 \int_0^{\pi/2n} \left(\frac{1 + \cos 2n\theta}{2}\right) d\theta = \frac{a^2}{2} \left[\frac{\pi}{2n} + \left(\frac{\sin 2n\theta}{2n}\right)_0^{\pi/2n}\right]$$

$$= \frac{\pi a^2}{4n}$$

∴ Total area = $n \int_{-\pi/2n}^{\pi/2n} \frac{r^2}{2} d\theta = n \cdot \frac{\pi a^2}{4n} = \frac{\pi a^2}{4}$

Case (ii) : If n is even, r = a cos nθ contains (2n) equal loops.

∴ Total area = $2n \int_{-\pi/2n}^{\pi/2n} \frac{r^2}{2} d\theta = 2n \left(\frac{\pi a^2}{4n}\right) = \frac{\pi a^2}{2}$

Hence for r = a cos nθ
$$\boxed{\begin{array}{l} \text{if n is odd, Total area} = \dfrac{\pi a^2}{4} \\ \text{if n is even, Total area} = \dfrac{\pi a^2}{2} \end{array}}$$

Part- II r = a cos 5θ contains 5 equal loops and the entire curve lies within a circle of radius r = a. Put r = 0, cos 5θ = 0.

∴ $5\theta = -\dfrac{\pi}{2}, \dfrac{\pi}{2}, \dfrac{3\pi}{2}, \dfrac{5\pi}{2}, \dfrac{7\pi}{2}, \dfrac{9\pi}{2}, \dfrac{11\pi}{2}, \dfrac{13\pi}{2}, \dfrac{15\pi}{2}, \dfrac{17\pi}{2}, \ldots$

∴ $\theta = -\dfrac{\pi}{10}, \dfrac{\pi}{10}, \dfrac{3\pi}{10}, \dfrac{\pi}{2}, \dfrac{7\pi}{10}, \dfrac{9\pi}{10}, \dfrac{11\pi}{10}, \dfrac{13\pi}{10}, \dfrac{3\pi}{2}, \dfrac{17\pi}{10}$

First loop lies between $-\dfrac{\pi}{10}$ to $\dfrac{\pi}{10}$. Place the loops between alternate division. Required area is as shown shaded in Fig. 11.26.

Area of the curve r = a cos 5θ is

$$\text{Area} = 5 \int_{-\pi/10}^{\pi/10} \frac{r^2}{2} d\theta = \frac{5}{2} \int_{-\pi/10}^{\pi/10} a^2 \cos^2 5\theta \, d\theta$$

$$= 5a^2 \int_0^{\pi/10} \cos^2 5\theta \, d\theta \quad (5\theta = t)$$

$$= 5a^2 \int_0^{\pi/2} \cos^2 t \cdot \frac{dt}{5} = a^2 \cdot \frac{1}{2} \cdot \frac{\pi}{2} = \frac{\pi a^2}{4}$$

Area of circle, r = a is πa^2.

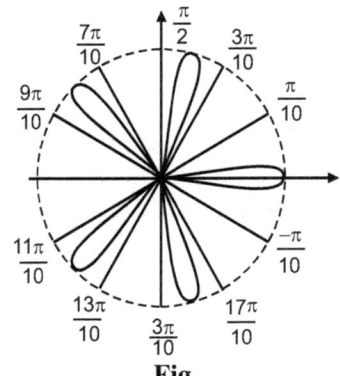

Fig.

Hence the required area $= \pi a^2 - \dfrac{\pi a^2}{4} = \dfrac{3}{4}\pi a^2$

= three-fourth of the area of the circle

TEST YOUR KNOWLEDGE:

I. Find the area bounded by :

1. $y^2 = 4x$ and $2x - y - 4 = 0$

   Ans. 9

2. $y^2 = 4ax$ and $x^2 = 4ay$.

   Ans. $\dfrac{16}{3} a^2$

3. $y^2 = x$ and $x^2 = -8y$

   Ans. $\dfrac{8}{3}$

4. $y = x(4 - x)$ and x-axis

   Ans. $\dfrac{32}{3}$

5. $y^2 = 4x$ and $y = x - 8$.

   Ans. 72

6. $y^2 = 12x$ and $y = 3(x - 5)$

   Ans. $56\dfrac{8}{9}$

7. $y = x^2 - 6x + 3$ and $y = 2x - 9$

   Ans. $\dfrac{32}{3}$

8. $x^2 = 4y$ and $x - 2y + 4 = 0$

   Ans. 9

9. $9xy = 4$ and $2x + y = 2$.

   Ans. $\dfrac{1}{3} - \dfrac{4}{9} \log 2$

10. $y^2 = 4a(x + a)$ and $y^2 = 4b(b - x)$

    Ans. $\dfrac{8}{3}(a + b)\sqrt{ab}$

11. $xy^2 = a^2(a - x)$, and $(a - x) y^2 = a^2 x$

    Ans. $(\pi - 2) a^2$

12. $\dfrac{x^2}{a^2} + \dfrac{y^2}{b^2} = 1$ and $\dfrac{x^2}{b^2} + \dfrac{y^2}{a^2} = 1$.

    Hint : Change to polars

13. $3y^2 = 25x$ and $5x^2 = 9y$.

    Ans. 5

    Ans. $4ab \tan^{-1} \dfrac{a}{b}$

14. $y = ax^2$ and $y = 1 - \dfrac{x^2}{a}$, $a > 0$, is $\dfrac{4}{3}\sqrt{\dfrac{a}{a^2 + 1}}$

15. $x^{2m} + y^{2n} = 1$ in first quadrant.

    Ans. $\dfrac{\left|\dfrac{1}{2m}\right| \left|\dfrac{1}{2n}\right|}{4mn \left|\dfrac{1}{2m} + \dfrac{1}{2n} + 1\right|}$

II. Find the area between the curve and its asymptote :

16. $y^2 (4 - x) = x(x - 2)^2$

    Ans. $2(\pi + 4)$

17. $y^2 (a + x) = (a - x)^3$

    Ans. $3\pi a^2$

18. $x(x^2 + y^2) = a(x^2 - y^2)$ **(Dec. 2011)**

19. $x^2(x^2 + y^2) = a^2(y^2 - x^2)$

Ans. $\dfrac{a^2}{2}(\pi + 4)$ Ans. $(\pi + 2)\, a^2$

20. $x^2 y^2 = a^2 (y^2 - x^2)$ 21. $(a - x)\, y^2 = x^3$

    Ans. $4a^2$ Ans. $\dfrac{3\pi a^2}{4}$

22. $x(x^2 + y^2) = a(y^2 - x^2)$ 23. $xy^2 = a^2(a - x)$

    Ans. $a^2 \left(2 + \dfrac{\pi}{2}\right)$ Ans. πa^2

24. $y(x^2 + 4a^2) = 8a^3$ 25. $x^2(1 - y)\, y = 1$

    Ans. $4\pi a^2$ Ans. 2π

III. Find the area of loop of the curve:

26. $x(x^2 + y^2) = a(x^2 - y^2)$

    Ans. $a^2 \left(2 - \dfrac{\pi}{2}\right)$

27. $y^2 (4 - x) = x(x - 2)^2$ 28. $x^4 - 2a^2 xy + a^2 y^2 = 0$ (Convert to polar)

    Ans. $2(4 - \pi)$ Ans. $\dfrac{2a^2}{3}$

29. $r(\cos\theta + \sin\theta) = 2a \sin\theta \cos\theta$ 30. $x(x^2 + y^2) = a(y^2 - x^2)$

    Ans. $\dfrac{a^2}{4}(4 - \pi)$ Ans. $a^2 \left(2 - \dfrac{\pi}{2}\right)$

31. $3ay^2 = x(x - a)^2$ 32. $a^4 y^2 = x^5 (2a - x)$

    Ans. $\dfrac{8a^2}{15\sqrt{3}}$ Ans. $\dfrac{5\pi a^2}{4}$

33. $(x + y)(x^2 + y^2) = 2axy$ 34. $y^2 = x^2(4 - x^2)$

    Ans. $a^2 \left(1 - \dfrac{\pi}{4}\right)$ Ans. $\dfrac{16}{3}$

35. $xy^2 + (x + a)^2 (x + 2a) = 0$ 36. $ay^2 = (x - a)(x - 5a)^2$

    Ans. $\dfrac{a^2}{2}(4 - \pi)$ Ans. $\dfrac{128}{15} a^2$

IV. Find the total area of the curve:

37. $x^2(x^2 + y^2) = a^2(x^2 - y^2)$ 38. $x^6 + y^6 = a^2 x^2 y^2$

    Ans. $a^2(\pi - 2)$ Ans. $\dfrac{\pi a^2}{3}$

39. $(x^2 + y^2)^2 = a^2(x^2 - y^2)$ 40. $r = a(1 + \cos\theta)$

    Ans. a^2 Ans. $\dfrac{3\pi a^2}{2}$

41. $r = a(1 - \cos\theta)$ 42. $r = a \sin 3\theta$

Ans. $\dfrac{3\pi a^2}{2}$

43. $r = a \cos 3\theta$

Ans. $\dfrac{\pi a^2}{4}$

45. $r = a \cos 2\theta$

Ans. $\dfrac{\pi a^2}{2}$

47. $\left(\dfrac{x}{a}\right)^4 + \left(\dfrac{y}{b}\right)^{10} = 1$ **Ans.** $ab\, B\left(\dfrac{11}{10}, \dfrac{1}{4}\right)$

Ans. $\dfrac{\pi a^2}{4}$

44. $r = a \sin 2\theta$

Ans. $\dfrac{\pi a^2}{2}$

46. $r = a + b \cos \theta\ (a > b)$

Ans. $\left(a^2 + \dfrac{b^2}{2}\right)\pi$

48. $a^4 y^2 = x^4(a^2 - x^2)$ **Ans.** $\dfrac{\pi a^2}{4}$

V. 49. Show that area common to the circles $x^2 + y^2 - 4y = 0$, $x^2 + y^2 - 4x - 4y + 4 = 0$ is $4\left(\dfrac{2\pi}{3} - \dfrac{\sqrt{3}}{2}\right)$.

50. Show that the area outside the circle $x^2 + y^2 = a^2$ and inside the circle $x^2 + y^2 = 2ax$ is $2\int_0^{\pi/3}\int_a^{2a\cos\theta} r\, dr\, d\theta$ and evaluate it. **Ans.** $a^2\left(\dfrac{\pi}{3} + \dfrac{\sqrt{3}}{2}\right)$

51. Show that the area outside $x^2 + y^2 = a^2$ and inside $r = a(1 + \cos\theta)$ is $\dfrac{a^2}{4}(8 + \pi)$.

52. Prove that the area of the *crescent* bounded by the circles $r = a\sqrt{2}$ and $r = 2a\cos\theta$ is a^2.

53. Prove that the area of the astroid $\left(\dfrac{x}{a}\right)^{2/3} + \left(\dfrac{y}{b}\right)^{2/3} = 1$ is $\dfrac{3}{8}\pi ab$.

54. Find the area enclosed by one arch of the cycloid $x = a(\theta - \sin\theta)$, $y = a(1 - \cos\theta)$ and its base. **Ans.** $3\pi a^2$

55. Find the area included between two loops of the curve $r = a(\sqrt{2}\cos\theta - 1)$.
Ans. $a^2(\pi + 3)$

56. Find the area included between two loops of the curve $r = a(2\cos\theta + \sqrt{3})$.
Ans. $\dfrac{a^2}{3}(10\pi + 9\sqrt{3})$.

57. Find the area enclosed by the curve $a^4 y^2 + b^2 x^4 = a^2 b^2 x^2$. **Ans.** $\dfrac{4ab}{3}$

58. Obtain the area in the first quadrant bounded by the curve $b^4 y^2 = (a^2 - x^2)^3$ and the co-ordinate axes. **Ans.** $\dfrac{3\pi a^4}{16 b^2}$

59. Find the area enclosed by the curve $y^2 = (x - a)(b - x)$, $0 < a < b$. **Ans.** $\dfrac{\pi}{4}(a - b)^2$

Mass of a Lamina

If the surface density ρ of a plane lamina is a function of the position of a point of the lamina, then the mass of an elementary area dA is ρ dA and the total mass of the lamina is $\int \rho \, dA$.

In Cartesian co-ordinates, if $\rho = f(x, y)$, the mass of the lamina, $M = \iint f(x, y) \, dx \, dy$.

In polar co-ordinates, if $\rho = F(r, \theta)$, the mass of the lamina, $M = \iint F(r, \theta) \, r \, dr \, d\theta$.

Both the integrals being taken over area of the lamina.

EXAMPLES ON APPLICATIONS OF MASS

Ex. 1 : A lamina is bounded by the curves $y = x^2 - 3x$ and $y = 2x$. If the density at any point is given by λxy, find the mass of the lamina.

Solution : The density at any point P(x, y) of the lamina is $\rho = \lambda xy$ and the mass of the elementary lamina at P is ρ dx dy i.e. $\lambda \, xy \, dx \, dy$.

$$\text{Mass of the lamina} = \iint_R \rho \cdot dA = \iint \lambda \, xy \, dx \, dy = \lambda \int_0^5 \left\{ \int_{x^2-3x}^{2x} xy \, dy \right\} dx$$

$$= \lambda \int_0^5 \left[\frac{xy^2}{2}\right]_{x^2-3x}^{2x} dx = \frac{\lambda}{2} \int_0^5 [4x^3 - x(x^2-3x)^2] \, dx$$

$$= \frac{\lambda}{2} \int_0^5 (-x^5 + 6x^4 - 5x^3) \, dx = \frac{\lambda}{2} \left[-\frac{x^6}{6} + \frac{6x^5}{5} - \frac{5x^4}{4}\right]_0^5 = \frac{4375}{24} \lambda$$

Fig.

Ex. 2 : The density at any point of a non-uniform circular lamina of radius a varies as its distance from a fixed point on the circumference of the circle. Find the mass of the lamina.

Solution : Take the fixed point in the circumference of the circle as the origin and the diameter through it as x-axis, and using the polar co-ordinates, the polar equation of the circle is r = 2a cos θ. The density at any point P(r, θ) of the lamina is ρ = λr and the mass of the elementary lamina at P is (λr) r dr dθ.

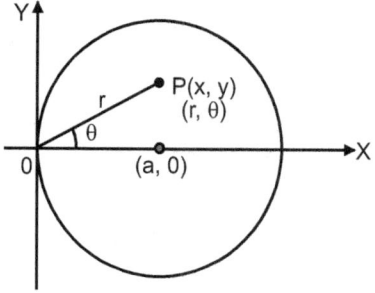

Fig.

Integrating this over the area of the circle, we have

$$\text{Mass of the lamina} = \lambda \int_{-\pi/2}^{\pi/2} d\theta \int_{0}^{2a\cos\theta} r^2 \, dr$$

$$= \frac{\lambda}{3} \int_{-\pi/2}^{\pi/2} 8a^3 \cos^3\theta \, d\theta = \frac{8\lambda a^3}{3} \cdot 2 \int_{0}^{\pi/2} \cos^3\theta \, d\theta$$

$$= \frac{16\lambda a^3}{3} \left(\frac{2}{3}\right) = \frac{32\lambda a^3}{9}$$

TEST YOUR KNOWLEDGE:

1. Find the mass distributed over the area bounded by the curve $16y^2 = x^3$ and the line $2y = x$, assuming that the density at a point of the area varies as the distance of the point from x-axis. **Ans.** $\frac{2}{3}\lambda$

2. If the density at any point on a circular lamina is k times the square of its distance from a fixed point in its circumference, find its mass. **Ans.** $\frac{3}{2}\pi\lambda a^4$

3. A lamina in the form of a parabolic segment of mass M, height h and base 2k has density at a point given by λpq^3 per unit area, where p and q are distances from the base and the axis respectively. Determine the value of λ.
   Hint : $y^2 = 4ax$ be parabola, q = y, p = h – x
   $$\rho = \lambda(h-x)y^3, \quad M = 2\int_{0}^{h}\int_{0}^{2\sqrt{ax}} \lambda(h-x)y^3 \, dx \, dy$$
   $$\therefore M = \frac{2}{3}\lambda a^2 h^4, \text{ Q (h, k) lies on } y^2 = 4ax \therefore a = \frac{k^2}{4h}$$
   Ans. $\frac{24M}{h^2 k^4}$.

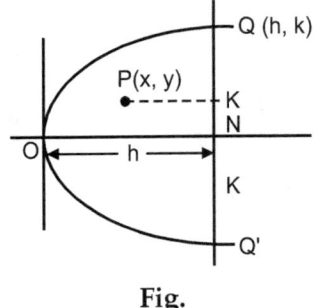

Fig.

4. The density at any point of a non-uniform circular lamina of radius unity is k times its distance from a given diameter. Find the total mass of the lamina.

Ans. $\dfrac{4k}{3}$

5. The density at any point of a cardioide $r = a(1 + \cos \theta)$ varies as the square of the distance from the axis of symmetry of the cardioide. Find the mass of the lamina.

Ans. $\dfrac{21}{32} \pi k a^4$

6. In a lamina in the form of an ellipse $\dfrac{x^2}{a^2} + \dfrac{y^2}{b^2} = 1$, the density at any point varies as the product of the distances from the axes of the ellipse. Find the mass of the lamina.

Ans. $\dfrac{k a^2 b^2}{2}$

7. If mass per unit area varies as the square of the ordinate of the point, find the mass of the lamina bounded by the cycloid $x = a(\theta + \sin \theta)$, $y = a(1 - \cos \theta)$ the ordinates from the two cusps and the tangent at the vertex.

Ans. $\dfrac{5 \lambda \pi a^4}{12}$

8. Find the mass of a lamina bounded by the curves $y^2 = ax$ and $x^2 = ay$, when the mass per unit area varies as the square of the distance of the point from the origin.

Ans. $\dfrac{6}{35} \cdot \lambda a^4$.

CENTER OF GRAVITY OF PLANE LAMINA

DEFINITIONS:

1. Centre of Mass : The centre of mass of a body is the point through which the resultant mass acts.

2. Centre of Gravity : The centre of gravity (C.G.) of a body is the point through which the resultant weight acts. Since, weight is proportional to mass, the centre of mass is the same point as the centre of gravity.

THE CENTRE OF MASS OF N POINT MASSES

A small boy on one side of a seesaw (which we regard as weightless) can balance a bigger boy on the other side. For example, the two boys in Fig. 12.1 (a) balance.

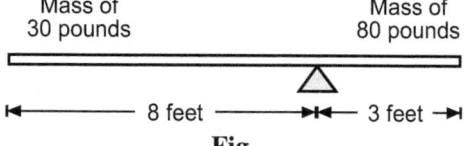
Fig.

The small mass with the long lever arm balances the large mass with the small lever arm. Each boy contributes the same tendency to turn but in opposite directions.

This tendency is called the *moment*. $\boxed{\text{Moment} = (\text{Mass}) \cdot (\text{Lever arm})}$ where the lever arm can be positive or negative.

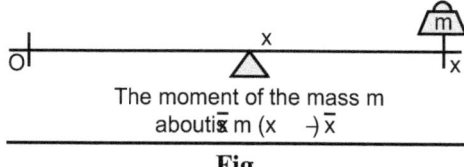
The moment of the mass m about $\bar{x}$ is $m(x - \bar{x})$
Fig.

If a mass m is located on a line at coordinate x, define its moment about the point having co-ordinate $\bar{x}$ as the product $m(x - \bar{x})$. Refer Fig. 12.1 (b).

Now, consider several point masses $m_1, m_2, m_3, \ldots m_n$. If mass m_i is located at x_i, with $i = 1, 2, \ldots, n$, then $\sum_{i=1}^{n} m_i(x_i - \bar{x})$ is the total moment of all the masses about the point $\bar{x}$.

The balancing point of masses $m_1, m_2, m_3, \ldots m_n$, located respectively at $x_1, x_2, x_3, \ldots x_n$ on x-axis, is found by solving the equation $\sum_{i=1}^{n} m_i(x_i - \bar{x}) = 0$ for the number $\bar{x}$.

$\therefore \qquad \sum_{i=1}^{n} m_i x_i = \bar{x} \sum_{i=1}^{n} m_i$

$\Rightarrow \qquad \boxed{\bar{x} = \dfrac{\sum_{i=1}^{n} m_i x_i}{\sum_{i=1}^{n} m_i}} \qquad \ldots (1)$

$\therefore$ *The number $\bar{x}$ given by equation (1) is called the centre of mass of the system of masses.*

It is the point about which all the masses balance. The centre of the mass is found by dividing the total moment about O by the total mass.

If point masses are situated in a plane, then

$$\bar{x} = \dfrac{\sum_{i=1}^{n} m_i x_i}{\sum_{i=1}^{n} m_i} \quad ; \quad \bar{y} = \dfrac{\sum_{i=1}^{n} m_i y_i}{\sum_{i=1}^{n} m_i}$$

If point masses are situated in a space, then

$$\bar{x} = \frac{\sum_{i=1}^{n} m_i x_i}{\sum_{i=1}^{n} m_i} \ ; \qquad \bar{y} = \frac{\sum_{i=1}^{n} m_i y_i}{\sum_{i=1}^{n} m_i} \ ; \qquad \bar{z} = \frac{\sum_{i=1}^{n} m_i z_i}{\sum_{i=1}^{n} m_i}$$

Instead of discrete masses, if the mass distribution is continuous (i.e. if the body is rigid body) then the summations will be replaced by the corresponding integrals and we have,

$$\bar{x} = \frac{\int x\, dm}{\int dm} \ ; \qquad \bar{y} = \frac{\int y\, dm}{\int dm} \ ; \qquad \bar{z} = \frac{\int z\, dm}{\int dm}$$

where, dm is an element of the distributed mass of the body, $(\bar{x}, \bar{y}, \bar{z})$ may be considered as C.G. of mass distribution.

Center of Gravity of a curve

Let the mass be distributed in the form of the wire "CD" in the plane XOY. Let ρ be the density per unit length. Take an elementary arc "ds" of the curve at the point P (x, y) whose equation is y = f(x). Refer Fig. 12.2.

∵ mass = density (length)

∴ The mass of this element is dm
= (ρ) (ds) and is situated at (x, y). Hence, C.G.
$(\bar{x}, \bar{y})$ of arc CD will be given by :

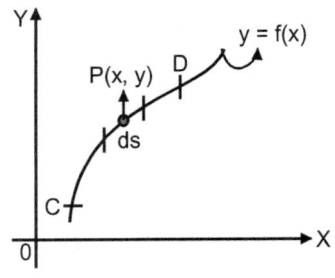

Fig.

$$\boxed{\bar{x} = \frac{\int x\, dm}{\int dm} = \frac{\int x\, \rho\, ds}{\int \rho\, ds}} \ ; \qquad \boxed{\bar{y} = \frac{\int y\, dm}{\int dm} = \frac{\int y\, \rho\, ds}{\int \rho\, ds}}$$

If ρ is constant, we have

$$\boxed{\bar{x} = \frac{\int x\, ds}{\int ds}} \ ; \qquad \boxed{\bar{y} = \frac{\int y\, ds}{\int ds}}$$

Note :

1. For y = f(x) replace ds = $\sqrt{1 + \left(\dfrac{dy}{dx}\right)^2} \cdot dx$
2. For x = f(y) replace ds = $\sqrt{1 + \left(\dfrac{dx}{dy}\right)^2} \cdot dy$

3.	For $x = f_1(t)$, $y = f_2(t)$ replace $ds = \sqrt{\left(\dfrac{dx}{dt}\right)^2 + \left(\dfrac{dy}{dt}\right)^2} \cdot dt$
4.	For $r = f(\theta)$ replace $ds = \sqrt{r^2 + \left(\dfrac{dr}{d\theta}\right)^2} \cdot d\theta$
5.	For $\theta = f(r)$ replace $ds = \sqrt{1 + r^2\left(\dfrac{d\theta}{dr}\right)^2} \cdot dr$

CENTER OF GRAVITY OF A PLANE AREA OR LAMINA

Let C be the bounding curve of a plane lamina and ρ be the mass per unit area.

∵ Mass = (Density) (Area)

∴ The mass of an elementary area dA at P(x, y) is $dm = \rho(dA)$.

Let $(\bar{x}, \bar{y})$ be the co-ordinates of C.G. of the lamina (Refer Fig. 12.3), then,

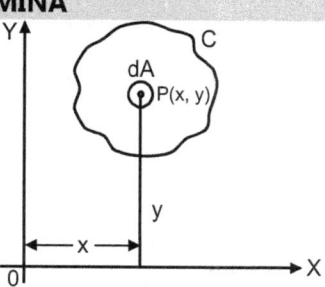

Fig.

$$\bar{x} = \frac{\int x\, dm}{\int dm} = \frac{\int x\, \rho\, dA}{\int \rho\, dA} \; ; \; \bar{y} = \frac{\int y\, dm}{\int dm} = \frac{\int y\, \rho\, dA}{\int \rho\, dA}$$

or in Double integral form, Cartesian System (dA = dx dy)

∴ $$\bar{x} = \frac{\iint x\, \rho\, dx\, dy}{\iint \rho\, dx\, dy} \; ; \; \bar{y} = \frac{\iint y\, \rho\, dx\, dy}{\iint \rho\, dx\, dy}$$

If ρ is a constant;

∴ $$\bar{x} = \frac{\iint x\, dx\, dy}{\iint dx\, dy} \; ; \; \bar{y} = \frac{\iint y\, dx\, dy}{\iint dx\, dy}$$

If the curve is given in polar co-ordinates,
$dA = r\, dr\, d\theta$; $x = r \cos \theta$; $y = r \sin \theta$; then

$$\bar{x} = \frac{\iint r \cos \theta \cdot \rho \cdot r\, dr\, d\theta}{\iint \rho r\, dr\, d\theta} \; ; \; \bar{y} = \frac{\iint r \sin \theta\, \rho r\, dr\, d\theta}{\iint \rho r\, dr\, d\theta}$$

If ρ is a constant,

∴ $$\bar{x} = \frac{\iint r \cos \theta\, r\, dr\, d\theta}{\iint r\, dr\, d\theta} \; ; \; \bar{y} = \frac{\iint r \sin \theta\, r\, dr\, d\theta}{\iint r\, dr\, d\theta}$$

Note :

The following results, for the C.G. of a plane lamina in special cases, which involve only single integrals and are also useful, are stated without proof. They can be established easily by the principles used in the above cases.

(a) For the co-ordinates of the C.G. of a plane lamina bounded by the curve y = f(x), the x-axis and the ordinates x = a and x = b, (Refer Fig. 12.4) consider strip of width dx.

If ρ is mass per unit area, dm = ρ · y · dx.

C.G. of strip is at its midpoint $\left(x, \dfrac{y}{2}\right)$.

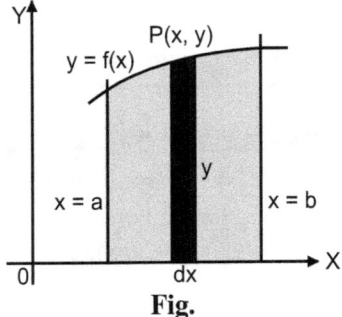

Fig.

$$\overline{x} = \dfrac{\int x\,\rho y\,dx}{\int \rho y\,dx}\,;\quad \overline{y} = \dfrac{\int \dfrac{y}{2}\rho y\,dx}{\int \rho y\,dx} = \dfrac{\dfrac{1}{2}\int \rho y^2\,dx}{\int \rho y\,dx}$$

(b) The co-ordinates of the C.G. of a sectorial element OAB, bounded by the curve r = f(θ) and the radii vectors θ = α, θ = β (Refer Fig. 12.5). Let ρ be mass per unit area. Area of ΔOPQ = $\dfrac{1}{2}r^2\,d\theta$.

$$\therefore\ dm = (\rho)\left(\dfrac{1}{2}r^2\,d\theta\right)$$

Its C.G. is on median through O at a point $\left(\dfrac{2}{3}r\cos\theta,\ \dfrac{2}{3}r\sin\theta\right)$

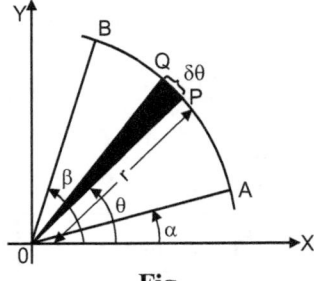

Fig.

$$\overline{x} = \dfrac{\dfrac{2}{3}\int_{\alpha}^{\beta} r^3 \cos\theta\,d\theta}{\int_{\alpha}^{\beta} r^2\,d\theta}\,;\quad \overline{y} = \dfrac{\dfrac{2}{3}\int_{\alpha}^{\beta} r^3 \sin\theta\,d\theta}{\int_{\alpha}^{\beta} r^2\,d\theta}$$

Examples on center of gravity of an area

Ex. 8 : A lamina bounded by the parabolas $y^2 = 4x$ and $2x^2 = y$ has a variable density ρ given by $\rho = 1 + xy$. Prove that $\overline{y} = 2\overline{x}$.

Solution : The points of intersection of two parabolas are (0, 0) (1, 2), density $\rho = 1 + xy$ (given).

$$\therefore \quad \bar{x} = \frac{\iint x \rho \, dx \, dy}{\iint \rho \, dx \, dy} \; ; \; \bar{y} = \frac{\iint y \rho \, dx \, dy}{\iint \rho \, dx \, dy}$$

$$\iint x \rho \, dx \, dy = \iint x (1 + xy) \, dx \, dy = \int_0^1 x \, dx \int_{2x^2}^{2\sqrt{x}} (1 + xy) \, dy$$

$$= \int_0^1 x \, dx \cdot \left[y + \frac{xy^2}{2} \right]_{2x^2}^{2\sqrt{x}} = \int_0^1 x \left[2\sqrt{x} - 2x^2 + 2x^2 - 2x^5 \right] dx$$

$$= \left(2 \cdot \frac{2x^{5/2}}{5} - 2 \frac{x^7}{7} \right) \Big|_0^1 = \frac{18}{35} \qquad \ldots \text{(i)}$$

Fig.

$$\iint y \rho \, dx \, dy = \iint y (1 + xy) \, dx \, dy$$

$$= \int_0^1 dx \int_{2x^2}^{2\sqrt{x}} (y + xy^2) \, dy = \int_0^1 dx \left[\frac{y^2}{2} + \frac{xy^3}{3} \right]_{2x^2}^{2\sqrt{x}}$$

$$= \int_0^1 \left(2x - 2x^4 + \frac{8}{3} x^{5/2} - \frac{8}{3} x^7 \right) dx = \left[x^2 - \frac{2}{5} x^5 + \frac{16}{21} x^{7/2} - \frac{x^8}{3} \right]_0^1$$

$$= \frac{36}{35} \qquad \ldots \text{(ii)}$$

$$\iint \rho \, dx \, dy = \iint (1 + xy) \, dx \, dy = \int_0^1 dx \int_{2x^2}^{2\sqrt{x}} (1 + xy) \, dy$$

$$= \int_0^1 \left[y + \frac{xy^2}{2} \right]_{2x^2}^{2\sqrt{x}} dx = \int_0^1 \left(2\sqrt{x} - 2x^2 + 2x^2 - 2x^5 \right) dx = \left[\frac{4}{3} x^{3/2} - \frac{x^6}{3} \right]_0^1 = 1 \qquad \ldots \text{(iii)}$$

From result (i), (ii) and (iii), $\bar{x} = \dfrac{18}{35}$; $\bar{y} = \dfrac{36}{35}$ $\therefore \bar{y} = 2\bar{x}$.

Ex. 9 : Find the co-ordinates of the C.G. of the area in the first quadrant, bounded by the curve $\left(\dfrac{x}{a}\right)^{2/3} + \left(\dfrac{y}{b}\right)^{2/3} = 1$, the density being given by $\rho = \lambda\, xy$, where λ is a constant.

Solution : Here, $\quad \rho = \lambda\, xy$

$\therefore \quad \bar{x} = \dfrac{\iint x\rho\, dx\, dy}{\iint \rho\, dx\, dy}$; $\bar{y} = \dfrac{\iint y\rho\, dx\, dy}{\iint \rho\, dx\, dy}$

$\iint x\rho\, dx\, dy = \iint \lambda\, x^2 y\, dx\, dy$

$= \lambda \int_0^a x^2\, dx \int_0^y y\, dy$ (Note down the limits for x and y)

$= \lambda \int_0^a x^2 \cdot \dfrac{y^2}{2} \cdot \dfrac{dx}{d\theta} \cdot d\theta$ (Putting $x = a\cos^3\theta,\ y = b\sin^3\theta$)

$= \dfrac{\lambda}{2} \int_0^{\pi/2} a^2 \cos^6\theta \cdot b^2 \sin^6\theta \cdot 3a\cos^2\theta \sin\theta \cdot d\theta$

$= \dfrac{3\lambda\, a^3 b^2}{2} \int_0^{\pi/2} \sin^7\theta \cos^8\theta\, d\theta$

$= \dfrac{3\lambda\, a^3 b^2}{2} \left[\dfrac{6 \cdot 4 \cdot 2 \cdot 7 \cdot 5 \cdot 3 \cdot 1}{15 \cdot 13 \cdot 11 \cdot 9 \cdot 7 \cdot 5 \cdot 3 \cdot 1} \right] = \dfrac{8\lambda\, a^3 b^2}{15 \cdot 13 \cdot 11}$

Fig.

$\iint y\rho\, dx\, dy = \iint \lambda\, xy^2\, dx\, dy = \lambda \int_0^a x\, dx \int_0^y y^2\, dy$

$= \dfrac{\lambda}{3} \int_0^a x \cdot y^3 \dfrac{dx}{d\theta}\, d\theta$

$= \dfrac{\lambda}{3} \int_0^{\pi/2} a\cos^3\theta \cdot b^3 \sin^9\theta \cdot (3a\cos^2\theta \sin\theta) \cdot d\theta$

$$= \lambda a^2 b^3 \int_0^{\pi/2} \sin^{10}\theta \cos^5\theta\, d\theta$$

$$= \lambda a^2 b^3 \frac{9\cdot 7\cdot 5\cdot 3\cdot 1\cdot 4\cdot 2}{15\cdot 13\cdot 11\cdot 9\cdot 7\cdot 5\cdot 3\cdot 1} = \frac{8\lambda a^2 b^3}{15\cdot 13\cdot 11}$$

$$\iint \rho\, dx\, dy = \lambda \int_0^a x\, dx \int_0^y y\, dy = \frac{\lambda}{2} \int_0^a xy^2 \frac{dx}{d\theta}\, d\theta$$

$$= \frac{\lambda}{2} \int_0^{\pi/2} a\cos^3\theta \cdot b^2 \sin^6\theta \cdot 3a\cos^2\theta \sin\theta\, d\theta$$

$$= \frac{3\lambda a^2 b^2}{2} \int_0^{\pi/2} \sin^7\theta \cdot \cos^5\theta\, d\theta$$

$$= \frac{3\lambda a^2 b^2}{2} \left(\frac{6\cdot 4\cdot 2\cdot 4\cdot 2}{12\cdot 10\cdot 8\cdot 6\cdot 4\cdot 2}\right) = \frac{\lambda a^2 b^2}{80}$$

$$\bar{x} = \frac{8\lambda a^3 b^2}{15\cdot 13\cdot 11}\frac{80}{\lambda a^2 b^2} = \frac{128\, a}{429}$$

$$\bar{y} = \frac{8\lambda a^2 b^3}{15\cdot 13\cdot 11}\frac{80}{\lambda a^2 b^2} = \frac{128\, b}{429}$$

∴ Co-ordinates of C.G. are $\left(\dfrac{128\, a}{429},\ \dfrac{128\, b}{429}\right)$.

Example 10 : Find the centroid of the loop of the curve $r^2 = a^2 \cos 2\theta$. **SUK: Aug-13**

Solution: C.G. lies on x-axis ∴ $\bar{y} = 0$ and $\bar{x} = \dfrac{\dfrac{2}{3}\displaystyle\int_{-\pi/4}^{\pi/4} r^3 \cos\theta\, d\theta}{\displaystyle\int_{-\pi/4}^{\pi/4} r^2\, d\theta} = \dfrac{N}{D}$

(Refer formula (b) given in special note after 12.4)

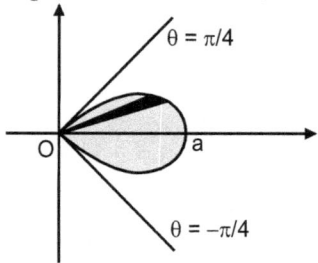

Fig.

$$N = \frac{2}{3}\int_{-\pi/4}^{\pi/4} \left(a\sqrt{\cos 2\theta}\right)^3 \cos\theta\, d\theta = \frac{4a^3}{3}\int_0^{\pi/4}(1 - 2\sin^2\theta)^{3/2} \cos\theta\, d\theta$$

∵ $2\sin^2\theta = \sin^2 t,\ \sqrt{2}\sin\theta = \sin t;\ \cos\theta\, d\theta = \dfrac{1}{\sqrt{2}}\cos t\, dt$

θ	0	π/4
t	0	π/2

$$= \frac{4a^3}{3} \int_0^{\pi/2} (1-\sin^2 t)^{3/2} \cdot \frac{1}{\sqrt{2}} \cos t\, dt = \frac{4a^3}{3\sqrt{2}} \int_0^{\pi/2} \cos^4 t\, dt$$

$$= \frac{4a^3}{3\sqrt{2}} \cdot \frac{3}{4}\frac{1}{2}\frac{\pi}{2} = \frac{\pi a^3}{4\sqrt{2}}$$

$$D = \int_{-\pi/4}^{\pi/4} a^2 \cos 2\theta\, d\theta = 2a^2 \int_0^{\pi/4} \cos 2\theta\, d\theta = 2a^2 \frac{1}{2} = a^2$$

$$\bar{x} = \frac{\pi a^3}{4\sqrt{2}\, a^2} = \frac{\pi a}{4\sqrt{2}} \qquad \therefore \text{ C.G. is } \left(\frac{\pi a}{4\sqrt{2}}, 0\right)$$

Ex. 11 : The density at a point on a circular lamina varies as the distance from a point O on the circumference. Show that the centre of gravity divides the diameter through 'O' in the ratio 3 : 2.

Solution: Take the fixed point O on the circumference as the pole, the diameter OA as the initial line and 'a' the radius of the circle.

Then the polar equation of the circle is $r = 2a\cos\theta$. By symmetry, the C.G. $(\bar{x}, \bar{y})$ of the lamina lies on the initial line, so that $\bar{y} = 0$. $\rho \propto r$. $\therefore \rho = \lambda r$.

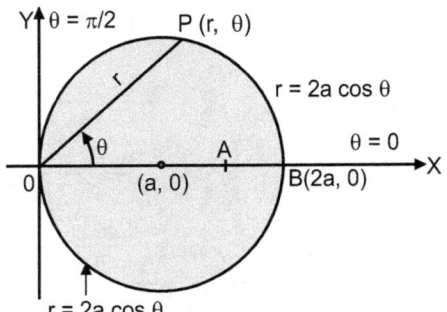

Fig.

$$\bar{x} = \frac{\iint x\rho\, dx\, dy}{\iint \rho\, dx\, dy} = \frac{\iint r\cos\theta \cdot \lambda r \cdot r\, dr\, d\theta}{\iint \lambda r \cdot r\, dr\, d\theta}$$

$$= \frac{2\lambda \int_0^{\pi/2} \cos\theta\, d\theta \int_0^{2a\cos\theta} r^3\, dr}{2\lambda \int_0^{\pi/2} d\theta \int_0^{2a\cos\theta} r^2\, dr}$$

$$= \frac{\int_0^{\pi/2} \frac{\cos\theta \cdot 16a^4 \cos^4\theta}{4}\, d\theta}{\int_0^{\pi/2} \frac{8a^3 \cos^3\theta}{3}\, d\theta} = \frac{3}{2}a \cdot \frac{\int_0^{\pi/2} \cos^5\theta\, d\theta}{\int_0^{\pi/2} \cos^3\theta\, d\theta} = \frac{3a}{2}\left(\frac{\frac{4}{5}\cdot\frac{2}{3}}{\frac{2}{3}}\right) = \frac{6a}{5}$$

$\therefore$ C.G. is $A\left(\frac{6a}{5}, 0\right)$ as shown in Fig. 12.16.

We have $OB = 2a$, $OA = \frac{6a}{5}$; $AB = OB - OA = 2a - \frac{6a}{5} = \frac{4a}{5}$

$$OA : AB = \frac{6a}{5} : \frac{4a}{5} = 3 : 2.$$

Ex. 12 : *Find the centre of mass of a homogeneous lamina having the shape of the region bounded by the parabola $y = 2 - 3x^2$ and the line $3x + 2y - 1 = 0$.*

Solution: The line intersects the parabola at $P\left(\frac{-1}{2}, \frac{5}{4}\right)$, $Q(1, -1)$.

$$\bar{x} = \frac{\iint x \, dx \, dy}{\iint dx \, dy}, \quad \bar{y} = \frac{\iint y \, dx \, dy}{\iint dx \, dy}$$

$$\iint x \, dx \, dy = \int_{-1/2}^{1} x \, dx \int_{\frac{1-3x}{2}}^{2-3x^2} dy = \int_{-1/2}^{1} x \left[2 - 3x^2 - \frac{1}{2} + \frac{3x}{2} \right] dx$$

$$= \left[\frac{3x^2}{4} - \frac{3x^4}{4} + \frac{x^3}{2} \right]_{-1/2}^{1} = \frac{27}{64}$$

Fig.

$$\iint dx \, dy = \int_{-1/2}^{1} dx \int_{\frac{1-3x}{2}}^{2-3x^2} dy = \int_{-1/2}^{1} \left(2 - 3x^2 - \frac{1}{2} + \frac{3x}{2} \right) dx$$

$$= \left[\frac{3}{2}x - x^3 + \frac{3}{4}x^2 \right]_{-1/2}^{1} = \frac{27}{16}$$

$$\iint y \, dx \, dy = \int_{-1/2}^{1} dx \int_{\frac{1-3x}{2}}^{2-3x^2} y \, dy = \frac{1}{2} \int_{-1/2}^{1} [y^2]_{\frac{1-3x}{2}}^{2-3x^2} \, dx$$

$$= \frac{1}{2} \int_{-1/2}^{1} \left[(2 - 3x^2)^2 - \left(\frac{1-3x}{2}\right)^2 \right] dx = \frac{27}{20} \text{ (after simplification)}$$

$$\bar{x} = \frac{27}{64} \times \frac{16}{27} = \frac{1}{4}$$

$$\bar{y} = \frac{27}{20} \times \frac{16}{27} = \frac{4}{5} \quad \text{Hence} \left(\frac{1}{4}, \frac{4}{5}\right) \text{ is C.G. of the area.}$$

Ex. 13 : *A plate is in the form of a quadrant of an ellipse and is of small but varying thickness, the thickness at any point being proportional to the product of the distances of the point from the axes. Find the C.G. of the plate.*

Solution: $\rho \propto x \cdot y \Rightarrow \rho = \lambda xy,$

$$\bar{x} = \frac{\iint x\rho \, dx \, dy}{\iint \rho \, dx \, dy}, \quad \bar{y} = \frac{\iint y\rho \, dx \, dy}{\iint \rho \, dx \, dy}$$

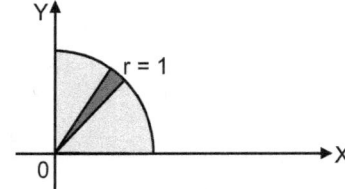

Fig.

For ellipse, $\quad \dfrac{x^2}{a^2} + \dfrac{y^2}{b^2} = 1$

We will use $\quad x = ar\cos\theta, \; y = br\sin\theta, \; dx\,dy = ab\,r\,dr\,d\theta$

Equation of ellipse reduces to $r^2 = 1$ i.e. $r = 1$

$$\iint x\rho \, dx \, dy = \iint (ar\cos\theta)^2 \, \lambda \cdot br\sin\theta \, ab\, r\, dr\, d\theta$$

$$= \lambda\, a^3 b^2 \int_0^{\pi/2} \cos^2\theta \sin\theta \, d\theta \int_0^1 r^4 dr = \lambda\, a^3 b^2 \cdot \frac{1}{3} \cdot \frac{1}{5} = \frac{\lambda\, a^3 b^2}{15}$$

Fig.

$$\iint y\rho \, dx \, dy = \iint (br\sin\theta)^2 \, \lambda \cdot ar\cos\theta \, ab\, r\, dr\, d\theta$$

$$= \lambda\, a^2 b^3 \int_0^{\pi/2} \sin^2\theta \cos\theta \, d\theta \int_0^1 r^4 dr = \frac{\lambda\, a^2 b^3}{15}$$

$$\iint \rho \, dx\, dy = \iint \lambda \cdot ar\cos\theta \cdot br\sin\theta \cdot ab\, r\, dr\, d\theta$$

$$= \lambda\, a^2 b^2 \int_0^{\pi/2} \sin\theta \cos\theta \, d\theta \int_0^1 r^3 dr = \frac{\lambda\, a^2 b^2}{8}$$

$$\bar{x} = \frac{\lambda\, a^3 b^2/15}{\lambda\, a^2 b^2/8} = \frac{8a}{15} \; ; \quad \bar{y} = \frac{\lambda\, a^2 b^3/15}{\lambda\, a^2 b^2/8} = \frac{8b}{15}$$

Co-ordinates of C.G. of the plate are $\left(\dfrac{8a}{15}, \dfrac{8b}{15}\right)$.

Ex. 14 : Find the C.G. of one loop of $r = a \sin 2\theta$.

Solution : $r = a \sin 2\theta$ contains 4 equal loops and lies within a circle of radius $r = a$. The first loop lies between $\theta = 0$ to $\theta = \dfrac{\pi}{2}$ and is symmetrical about the line $y = x$ $\left(\text{i.e. } \theta = \dfrac{\pi}{4}\right)$.

$\therefore \bar{x} = \bar{y}$. We have $\bar{x} = \dfrac{\iint x\, dx\, dy}{\iint dx\, dy}$

$$\iint x\, dx\, dy = \int_0^{\pi/2} \int_0^{a \sin 2\theta} r \cos\theta\, r\, dr\, d\theta = \int_0^{\pi/2} \cos\theta \, \dfrac{a^3 \sin^3 2\theta}{3}\, d\theta$$

$$= \dfrac{a^3}{3} \int_0^{\pi/2} \cos\theta\, (2 \sin\theta \cos\theta)^3\, d\theta$$

Fig.

$$= \dfrac{8a^3}{3} \int_0^{\pi/2} \sin^3\theta \cdot \cos^4\theta\, d\theta = \dfrac{8a^3}{3} \left(\dfrac{2 \cdot 3 \cdot 1}{7 \cdot 5 \cdot 3 \cdot 1}\right) = \dfrac{16a^3}{105}$$

$$\iint dx\, dy = \dfrac{1}{2} \int_0^{\pi/2} r^2\, d\theta = \dfrac{1}{2} \int_0^{\pi/2} a^2 \sin^2 2\theta\, d\theta$$

$$= 2a^2 \int_0^{\pi/2} \sin^2\theta \cos^2\theta\, d\theta = 2a^2 \left(\dfrac{1 \cdot 1}{4 \cdot 2} \dfrac{\pi}{2}\right) = \dfrac{\pi a^2}{8}$$

$\bar{x} = \dfrac{16a^3/105}{\pi a^2/8} = \dfrac{128\, a}{105\, \pi}$. Also $\bar{y} = \dfrac{128\, a}{105\, \pi}$

$\therefore$ C.G. is $\left(\dfrac{128\, a}{105\, \pi}, \dfrac{128\, a}{105\, \pi}\right)$

Ex. 15 : ABCD is a square plate of side a and O is the mid point of AB. If the surface density varies as the square of distance from O, show that C.G. of the plate is at a distance $\dfrac{7a}{10}$ from AB.

Solution: Take O as the origin and the side OB as the x-axis, and a line through O perpendicular to OB as y-axis. The density ρ at the point $P(x, y)$ is proportional to $(PO)^2$.

∴ $\rho \propto (x^2 + y^2) \Rightarrow \rho = \lambda(x^2 + y^2)$

As the distribution of the mass is symmetrical about OY, the C.G. of the plate is on the y-axis and $\bar{x} = 0$. ∴ $\bar{y} = \dfrac{\iint y\rho \, dx \, dy}{\iint \rho \, dx \, dy}$

By symmetry,

$$\iint y\rho \, dx \, dy = 2\iint \lambda(x^2 y + y^3) \, dx \, dy = 2\lambda \int_0^{a/2} dx \int_0^a (x^2 y + y^3) \, dy$$

$$= 2\lambda \int_0^{a/2} \left(x^2 \frac{a^2}{2} + \frac{a^4}{4}\right) dx = 2\lambda \left(\frac{a^5}{48} + \frac{a^5}{8}\right) = \frac{7\lambda a^5}{24}$$

Fig.

$$\iint \rho \, dx \, dy = \iint \lambda(x^2 + y^2) \, dx \, dy = 2\lambda \int_0^{a/2} dx \int_0^a (x^2 + y^2) \, dy$$

$$= 2\lambda \int_0^{a/2} \left(ax^2 + \frac{a^3}{3}\right) dx = 2\lambda \left(\frac{a^4}{24} + \frac{a^4}{6}\right) = \frac{5\lambda a^4}{12}$$

$$\bar{y} = \frac{7\lambda a^5 / 24}{5\lambda a^4 / 12} = \frac{7a}{10}$$

Thus, the C.G. of the plate is on the y-axis, at a distance $\dfrac{7a}{10}$ from O.

Ex. 16 : Find the C.G. of the loop of the curve $y^2(a + x) = x^2(a - x)$.

Solution: Because of symmetry, C.G. of the loop lies on x-axis, $\bar{y} = 0$.

$$\bar{x} = \frac{\int x \cdot y \cdot dx}{\int y \cdot dx}$$

$$\int xy \, dx = \int_0^a x \cdot x \sqrt{\frac{a-x}{a+x}} \, dx = \int_0^a \frac{x^2(a-x)}{\sqrt{a^2 - x^2}} \, dx \quad \text{(put } x = a \sin \theta\text{)}$$

$$= \int_0^{\pi/2} \frac{a^2 \sin^2 \theta \, (a - a \sin \theta) \cdot a \cos \theta \, d\theta}{a \cdot \cos \theta}$$

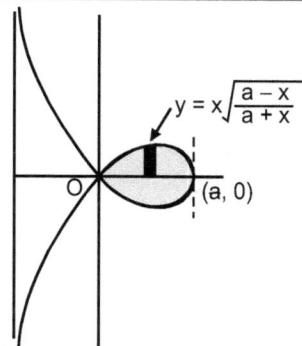

Fig.

$$= a^3 \int_0^{\pi/2} (\sin^2\theta - \sin^3\theta)\, d\theta = a^3 \left(\frac{1}{2}\frac{\pi}{2} - \frac{2}{3}\right) = a^3 \left(\frac{3\pi - 8}{12}\right)$$

$$\int y\, dx = \int_0^a x\sqrt{\frac{a-x}{a+x}}\, dx = \int_0^a \frac{x(a-x)\, dx}{\sqrt{a^2 - x^2}}$$

$$= \int_0^{\pi/2} \frac{a\sin\theta\,(a - a\sin\theta)\, a\cos\theta\, d\theta}{a\cos\theta}$$

$$= a^2 \int_0^{\pi/2} (\sin\theta - \sin^2\theta)\, d\theta = a^2\left[1 - \frac{\pi}{4}\right] = \frac{a^2}{4}(4 - \pi)$$

$$\bar{x} = \frac{a^3(3\pi - 8)/12}{a^2(4 - \pi)/4} = \frac{a(3\pi - 8)}{3(4 - \pi)} \quad \text{Required C.G. is } \left[\frac{a}{3}\left(\frac{3\pi - 8}{4 - \pi}\right), 0\right]$$

Ex. 17 : Find the position of the centroid of the area of the curve $x^{2/3} + y^{2/3} = a^{2/3}$ lying in the positive quadrant.

Solution: C.G. lies on the lines $y = x$ ∴ $\bar{x} = \bar{y}$. Also, $\bar{x} = \dfrac{\int x \cdot y \cdot dx}{\int y\, dx}$.

$$\int x \cdot y \cdot dx = \int_0^{\pi/2} a\cos^3\theta \cdot a\sin^3\theta \cdot 3a\cos^2\theta \sin\theta\, d\theta \qquad \text{Putting } \begin{cases} x = a\cos^3\theta \\ y = a\sin^3\theta \end{cases}$$

$$= 3a^3 \int_0^{\pi/2} \cos^5\theta \sin^4\theta\, d\theta = 3a^3 \cdot \frac{3 \cdot 1 \cdot 4 \cdot 2}{9 \cdot 7 \cdot 5 \cdot 3 \cdot 1} = \frac{8a^3}{105}$$

$$\int y\, dx = \int_0^{\pi/2} a\sin^3\theta\, 3a\cos^2\theta \sin\theta\, d\theta$$

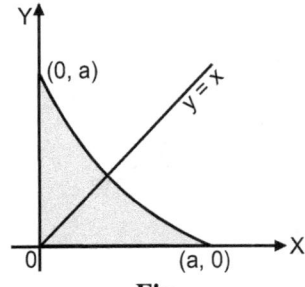
Fig.

$$= 3a^2 \int_0^{\pi/2} \sin^4\theta \cos^2\theta\, d\theta = 3a^2 \left(\frac{3\cdot 1\cdot 1}{6\cdot 4\cdot 2}\right)\frac{\pi}{2} = \frac{3\pi a^2}{32}$$

$$\bar{x} = \frac{8a^3/105}{3\pi a^2/32} = \frac{256\, a}{315\, \pi} \quad \text{and} \quad \bar{y} = \frac{256\, a}{315\, \pi}$$

Required co-ordinates of C.G. are $\left(\dfrac{256\, a}{315\, \pi},\, \dfrac{256\, a}{315\, \pi}\right)$.

Ex. 18 : Find the position of the centroid of the area bounded by the curve $y^2(2a-x) = x^3$ and its asymptote.

Solution: $y^2(2a-x) = x^3$ is known as Cissoid and is symmetrical about x-axis.

$$\therefore\ \bar{y} = 0 \qquad \bar{x} = \frac{\int x\cdot y\, dx}{\int y\, dx}$$

$$\int x\, y\, dx = \int_0^{2a} x\cdot \frac{x^{3/2}}{\sqrt{2a-x}}\, dx = \int_0^{2a} \frac{x^{5/2}}{\sqrt{2a-x}}\, dx \quad (\text{put } x = 2a\sin^2\theta)$$

$$= \int_0^{\pi/2} \frac{(2a)^{5/2}\sin^5\theta \cdot 4a\sin\theta\cos\theta\, d\theta}{(2a)^{1/2}\cos\theta} = 16a^3 \int_0^{\pi/2} \sin^6\theta\, d\theta$$

Fig.

$$= 16a^3 \left(\frac{5}{6} \cdot \frac{3}{4} \cdot \frac{1}{2} \cdot \frac{\pi}{2}\right) = \frac{5\pi a^3}{2}$$

$$\int y \, dx = \int_0^{2a} \frac{x^{3/2}}{\sqrt{2a-x}} \, dx = \int_0^{\pi/2} \frac{(2a)^{3/2} \sin^3\theta \cdot 4a \sin\theta \cos\theta \, d\theta}{(2a)^{1/2} \cos\theta}$$

$$= 8a^2 \int_0^{\pi/2} \sin^4\theta \cdot d\theta = 8a^2 \left(\frac{3}{4} \cdot \frac{1}{2} \cdot \frac{\pi}{2}\right) = \frac{3\pi a^2}{2}$$

$$\bar{x} = \frac{5\pi a^3/2}{3\pi a^2/2} = \frac{5a}{3}$$

Required co-ordinates of C.G. are $\left(\frac{5a}{3}, 0\right)$.

TEST YOUR KNOWLEDGE:

Problems on C.G. of a plane area or lamina :

5. Find the C.G. of the plate cut from the parabola $y^2 = 8x$ by its latus rectum $x = 2$, if the density is numerically equal to the distance from the latus rectum.

    Ans. $\left(\frac{6}{7}, 0\right)$

6. Find the C.G. of a plate in the form of the upper half of the cardioide $r = 2(1 + \cos\theta)$ if the density is numerically equal to the distance from the pole.

    Ans. $\left(\frac{21}{10}, \frac{96}{25\pi}\right)$

7. Find the C.G. of mass of the first quadrant part of the disk of radius 'a' with centre at the origin, if the density function is y.

    Ans. $\left(\frac{3a}{8}, \frac{3\pi a}{16}\right)$

8. Find the C.G. of the area enclosed between the curves $y^2 = ax$ and $x^2 + y^2 = 2ax$.

    Ans. $\left(a \frac{15\pi - 44}{15\pi - 40}, 0\right)$

9. Find the C.G. of the area of the cardioide $r = a(1 + \cos\theta)$ which lies above the initial line. **(Dec. 2011) Ans.** $\left(\frac{5a}{6}, \frac{16a}{9\pi}\right)$

10. Find the C.G. of the area of the cardioide $r = a(1 + \cos\theta)$. **Ans.** $\frac{5a}{6}$

11. Find the distance of the C.G. from the initial line to that half of the area of the cardioide $r = a(1 - \cos\theta)$ which lies above the initial line. **Ans.** $\bar{y} = \frac{16a}{9\pi}$

12. Find the C.G. of the area of the cardioide $r = a(1 + \cos\theta)$ if its surface density varies as its distance from the initial line. (**Hint :** $\bar{y} = 0$, $\rho = ky = kr \sin\theta$).

    Ans. $\bar{x} = \frac{4a}{5}$, $\bar{y} = 0$

13. Show that the C.G. of the area of the curve $r = 2a \sin^2 \frac{\theta}{2}$ is on the initial line at a distance $\frac{5a}{6}$ from the origin.

$\left(\textbf{Hint :} \text{ Given curve is } r = a(1 - \cos\theta) \cdot \bar{y} = 0, \bar{x} = \frac{5a}{6}\right)$

14. Find by double integration the area which is above the initial line and bounded by the straight line $\theta = \frac{\pi}{2}$, the circle $r = 2a \cos\theta$ and cardioide $r = a(1 + \cos\theta)$. Determine also the position of its C.G.

    Ans. Area $= (8 - \pi)\frac{a^2}{8}$, $\bar{y} = \left(\frac{14}{8-\pi}\right)\frac{a}{3}$, $\bar{x} = \left(\frac{16-3\pi}{8-\pi}\right)\frac{a}{2}$, $\bar{y} = \left(\frac{14a}{8-\pi}\right)\frac{a}{3}$

15. Find the C.G. of the area outside the circle $r = a$ and inside the cardioide $r = a(1 + \cos\theta)$.   **Ans.** $\left(\frac{9\pi + 44}{\pi + 8} a, 0\right)$

16. Find the C.G. of the area bounded by $r = a\sin\theta$, $r = 2a\sin\theta$.   **Ans.** $\left(0, \frac{7a}{6\pi}\right)$

17. Find the x-co-ordinate of the C.G. of the area bounded by the parabola $y^2 = 4x$ and the line $2x - y - 4 = 0$.   **Ans.** $\bar{x} = \frac{8}{5}$

18. Find the position of the C.G. of a semi-circular lamina of radius 'a' if its surface density varies as the square of the distance from the diameter.

    Hint : Take the circle above x-axis, $\rho = \lambda y^2$, $\bar{x} = 0$, $\bar{y} = \frac{32a}{15\pi}$.

19. Prove that the centroid of the smaller segment of the ellipse $\frac{x^2}{a^2} + \frac{y^2}{b^2} = 1$ cut off by the straight line $\frac{x}{a} + \frac{y}{b} = 1$ is $\left[\frac{2a}{3(\pi-2)}, \frac{2b}{3(\pi-2)}\right]$.

    Hint : Limits : $\begin{array}{l} x : 0 \text{ to } a \\ y : b\left(1 - \frac{x}{a}\right) \text{ to } \frac{b}{a}\sqrt{a^2 - x^2} \end{array}$

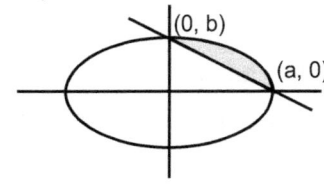

Fig.

20. Show that the C.G. of the loop of the curve $r = a\cos 3\theta$ containing the initial line lies at a distance $\frac{81\sqrt{3}}{80\pi} a$, from the pole.

21. Find the position of the C.G. of a loop of the curve $r = a\cos 2\theta$.

F.E. (Sem. II) M II (SU)   Multiple Integration and Its Applications

Ans. $\left(\dfrac{128\sqrt{2}\,a}{105\pi},\,0\right)$

22. Find the C.G. of the area enclosed by the curves $y^2 = ax$, $x^2 = ay$.

Ans. $\bar{x} = \dfrac{9a}{20} = \bar{y}$

23. Find the C.G. of the area enclosed by the curves $y^2 = 4ax$, $y = 2x$.   Ans. $\left(\dfrac{2a}{5},\,a\right)$

24. Find the C.G. of the area enclosed by the curves $y = 6x - x^2$ and $y = x$.

Ans. $\left(\dfrac{5}{2},\,5\right)$

25. Find the C.G. of the area enclosed by positive quadrant of the ellipse $\dfrac{x^2}{a^2} + \dfrac{y^2}{b^2} = 1$.

Ans. $\left(\dfrac{4a}{3\pi},\,\dfrac{4b}{3\pi}\right)$

26. Find the C.G. of the area of the cycloid $x = a(\theta + \sin\theta)$, $y = a(1 - \cos\theta)$ measured from cusp to cusp.   Ans. $\left(0,\,\dfrac{7a}{6}\right)$

27. Find the C.G. of the area bounded by y-axis, the cycloid $x = a(\theta + \sin\theta)$, $y = a$ $(1 - \cos\theta)$ and its base.

Hint : The figure is $\bar{x} = \dfrac{\int \dfrac{x}{2} x\,dy}{\int x\,dy}$, $\bar{y} = \dfrac{\int y\,x\,dx}{\int x\,dy}$ Ans. $\left(\dfrac{a(9\pi^2 - 16)}{18\pi},\,\dfrac{7a}{6}\right)$

28. Find the C.G. of the area of the cycloid $x = a(\theta - \sin\theta)$, $y = a(1 - \cos\theta)$ measured from cusp to cusp.   Ans. $\left(a\pi,\,\dfrac{5a}{6}\right)$

29. Show that $\left(\dfrac{256a}{315\pi},\,\dfrac{256b}{315\pi}\right)$ is the C.G. of the area in the first quadrant bounded by the curve $\left(\dfrac{x}{a}\right)^{2/3} + \left(\dfrac{y}{b}\right)^{2/3} = 1$.

30. Find the C.G. of the area in the first quadrant bounded by $a^4 y^2 = (a^2 - x^2)^3$.

Ans. $\left(\dfrac{16a}{15\pi},\,\dfrac{128a}{105\pi}\right)$

31. Find the distance from the origin of the C.G. of the area outside the circle $x^2 + y^2 = a^2$ and inside the circle $x^2 + y^2 = 2ax$.   Ans. $\dfrac{a}{2} \cdot \dfrac{8\pi + 3\sqrt{3}}{2\pi + 3\sqrt{3}}$

32. Find the position of the centroid of the area under the parabola $y = 4ax^2$ from $x = 0$ to $x = c$. **(May 2006) Ans.** $\left(\dfrac{3c}{4}, \dfrac{6ac^2}{5}\right)$

33. Find the C.G. of the loop of the curve $9x^2 = (2y-1)(y-2)^2$. **Ans.** $\left(0, \dfrac{8}{7}\right)$

34. Find the position of the C.G. of the area of the loop of the curve $8ay^2 = x(2a-x)^2$. **Ans.** $\bar{x} = \dfrac{6a}{7}$

MOMENT OF INERTIA

The moment of inertia of a particle of mass m about a line (or axis) is mr^2, where r is the perpendicular distance of the particle from the line (or axis).

Next, consider a body of mass M. A body is supposed to consist of an infinite number of small particles. Let the particles composing the body be taken to be of masses $m_1, m_2, m_3, \ldots\ldots$ situated at distances $r_1, r_2, r_3 \ldots\ldots$ respectively from a certain axis. Then, the moment of inertia of the body about the axis is

$$\sum mr^2 = m_1 r_1^2 + m_2 r_2^2 + m_3 r_3^2 + \ldots\ldots$$

In case the mass be in a continuously distributed form, consider an elementary particle of mass "dm" of the body. Let the distance of this element from the axis under consideration be p. Then the M.I. of this element about the axis $= p^2 dm$, so that the M.I. of the whole body $= \sum p^2 dm$. By the definition of a definite integral as the limit of a sum, we can write

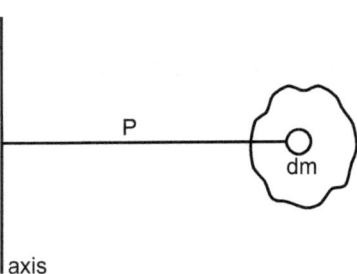

Fig.

$$\text{M.I.} = \lim_{dm \to 0} \sum p^2 dm = \int p^2 dm$$

M.I. is denoted by I :

∴ The moment of inertia I of a continuously distributed mass is $\boxed{I = \int p^2 dm}$ where the integral is to be evaluated throughout the region of the body. (Refer Fig. 12.28).

If M is the mass of a body and the M.I. of the body about an axis is denoted by MK^2 i.e. $\boxed{I = MK^2}$ then, K is said to be the *radius of gyration* of the body about the axis.

Hence, $\boxed{\text{Radius of Gyration} = K = \sqrt{\dfrac{I}{M}}}$

Note :
1. For M.I. of an area, we take $dm = dx\, dy$

∴ $I = \iint p^2 \, dx \, dy$ in cartesian form, $I = \iint p^2 r \, dr \, d\theta$ in polar form

2. For M.I. of an arc, we take $dm = ds$.

$I = \int p^2 \, ds$ and convert ds into $\dfrac{ds}{dx} dx$ or $\dfrac{ds}{dy} dy$ or $\dfrac{ds}{dt} dt$,

according to the nature of the curve.

3. If density is variable, say ρ at (x, y) or (r, θ) then the

M.I. of mass $= I = \iint p^2 \rho \, dx \, dy$ or $I = \iint p^2 \rho \, r \, dr \, d\theta$ or $I = \int p^2 \rho \, ds$

4. For M.I. of a solid, $I = \iiint p^2 \rho \, dv$.

Theorems on moment of inertia

Two important theorems on moment of inertia are given below without proof, which will be found useful in solving problems on moment of inertia.

I. Parallel Axes Theorem : If I_G is the M.I. of a body about an axis through the centroid G of the body and I_A, the M.I. of the body about any parallel axis through any point A, then

$\boxed{I_A = I_G + M d^2}$, where M is mass of the body and d is the distance between the parallel axes.

II. Perpendicular Axes Theorem : In case of a plane lamina in the XOY plane

$\boxed{I_Z = I_X + I_Y}$, where I_X and I_Y are M.I. about OX and OY and I_Z, M.I. about z-axis.

Note : This theorem is applicable to plane lamina and not to three-dimensional solids.

Some standard results

1. **For a Uniform Straight Rod :** M.I. of a uniform straight rod of length l about an axis perpendicular to the rod through (i) the mid point, (ii) an entremity.

(i) Let AB be rod of length l and O be the mid-point of AB, OY be axis through O perpendicular to AB. Consider a small element of length "dx" of the rod at a distance x from OY. If ρ is the mass per unit length of the rod, then mass of this element is $dm = \rho \cdot dx$ and the M.I. of this elementary mass about OY is $x^2 \cdot (\rho \cdot dx)$.

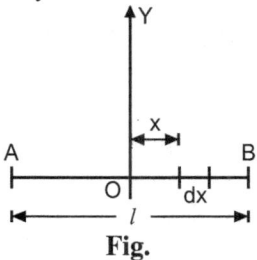
Fig.

Hence required M.I. of the rod $= \int_{-l/2}^{l/2} x^2 \cdot (\rho \, dx) = \dfrac{\rho l^3}{12}$

But $\qquad M$ = Mass of the rod $= \rho \cdot l$

M.I. of the rod about OY $= \dfrac{M \cdot l^2}{12}$

If $l = 2a$ then, M.I. of the rod of length $2a$ about OY $= M \cdot \dfrac{a^2}{3}$

The radius of gyration K is given by, $K^2 = \dfrac{a^2}{3}$

(ii) M.I. about axis through A using theorem of parallel axes,
$$I_A = I_G + M \cdot (AO)^2 = \frac{Ml^2}{12} + M \cdot \left(\frac{l}{2}\right)^2 = \frac{Ml^2}{3}$$

If $l = 2a$ then, $I_A = M\left(\frac{4a^2}{3}\right)$

2. For a Rectangle : M.I. of a rectangle of sides 'a' and 'b' about (i) a median parallel to side 'a', (ii) a median parallel to side b, (iii) an axis through centre perpendicular to the lamina.

(i) Let EF be median parallel to side 'a'. Consider a strip of width 'dx' at a distance x from EF.

$\therefore \quad dm = \rho \cdot a\, dx$

M.I. of this strip about $EF = x^2 \cdot (\rho\, a\, dx)$

M.I. of a rectangle about $EF = \int_{-b/2}^{b/2} x^2 \rho\, a\, dx = \frac{\rho\, ab^3}{12}$

But, M = Mass of rectangle = $\rho (ab)$

M.I. about median EF parallel to side 'a' $= \frac{Mb^2}{12}$

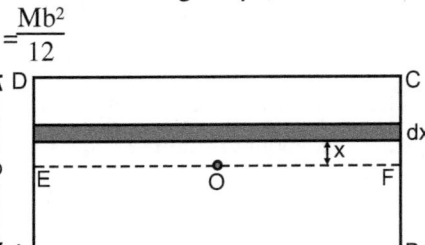

Fig.

(ii) Similarly, M.I. about median parallel to side 'b'
$$= \frac{Ma^2}{12}$$

(iii) M.I. about line through centre perpendicular to the plane of lamina
$$= \frac{Ma^2}{12} + \frac{Mb^2}{12} = \frac{M}{12}(a^2 + b^2)$$

by using perpendicular axes theorem.

3. For a Circular Ring of Radius a : M.I. of a circular ring about (i) axes through centre perpendicular to the plane of the wire, (ii) a diameter.

(i) Let 'a' be radius of circular ring and O be the centre. Let OZ be the axis perpendicular to the plane of the ring. Since, every element of the ring is at a distance a from the centre, the required M.I. is Ma^2, where M is the mass of the ring.

(ii) We have : $\quad I_z = I_x + I_y \quad$ But $\quad I_x = I_y$

$$Ma^2 = 2I_x \quad \therefore \quad I_x = \frac{Ma^2}{2}$$

M.I. of the ring about diameter $= \frac{Ma^2}{2}$.

4. For a Circular Disc : M.I. of a uniform circular disc of radius 'a' and mass M about

(i) the axis through its centre perpendicular to its plane, (ii) a diameter, (iii) tangent to the circular disc.

(i) Take the centre of the disc as the pole, so that, the polar equation of the circle is r = a and density = ρ; Mass of the disc M = $\pi a^2 \rho$. Consider element dm at a distance r from O.

$$dm = \rho (r\, dr\, d\theta)$$

M.I. of this element about OZ

$$= r^2\, dm = r^2(\rho\, r\, dr\, d\theta)$$

M.I. of disc about the line through O perpendicular to plane of disc

$$= \int_0^{2\pi} \int_0^a \rho\, r^3\, dr\, d\theta = \rho(2\pi)\frac{a^4}{4} = \frac{\rho \pi a^4}{2} = \frac{Ma^2}{2} \quad (M = \pi a^2 \rho)$$

(ii) $\quad I_z = I_x + I_y$ But $I_x = I_y$, $\dfrac{Ma^2}{2} = 2I_x$

M.I. about diameter $= \dfrac{Ma^2}{4}$

(iii) M.I. about tangent to the circular disc $= \dfrac{Ma^2}{4} + Ma^2 = \dfrac{5Ma^2}{4}$ by using parallel axes theorem.

5. M.I. of uniform solid sphere about its diameter : Divide the given sphere into an infinite number of circular discs, perpendicular to the given diameter and consider a typical disc at a distance 'x' from the centre and of thickness dx. The radius of this disc is $\sqrt{a^2 - x^2}$, where a is the radius of the sphere.

$\therefore \qquad dm = $ mass of the disc $= \rho \pi y^2\, dx \qquad \left(\because y = \sqrt{a^2 - x^2}\right)$

assuming constant density ρ.

M.I. of the disc about the line through O perpendicular to plane of the disc

$$= \frac{y^2}{2}\, dm = \frac{y^2}{2} \rho \pi y^2\, dx$$

M.I. of the sphere about diameter $= \dfrac{\pi \rho}{2} \int_{-a}^{a} y^4\, dx = \dfrac{\pi \rho}{2} \int_{-a}^{a} (a^2 - x^2)^2\, dx$

$$= \frac{\pi \rho}{2} \cdot 2 \int_0^a (a^4 - 2a^2 x^2 + x^4)\, dx = \frac{8}{15} \pi \rho a^5$$

Now, mass of the sphere, $M = \left(\dfrac{4}{3}\pi a^3\right) \cdot \rho \quad \therefore \rho = \dfrac{3M}{4\pi a^3}$

$\therefore$ M.I. of the sphere about a diameter $= \dfrac{8}{15} \pi a^5 \cdot \dfrac{3M}{4\pi a^3} = \dfrac{2}{5} Ma^2$

6. M.I. of a hollow sphere about its diameter : Here, elementary disc has a curved surface, in the form of ring of area $2\pi y\, ds$.

Let ρ be mass per unit area, then $dm = \rho(2\pi y\, ds)$

M.I. of the ring about line through the centre perpendicular to plane is ma^2.

Hence, M.I. of this ring about x-axis $= (\rho\, 2\pi y\, ds)\, y^2$

$$\text{M.I.} = 2\pi\rho \int_{-a}^{a} y^3 \, ds \qquad x = a\cos\theta, \; y = a\sin\theta$$
$$s = a\theta, \; ds = a\, d\theta$$

$$= 4\pi\rho \int_{0}^{\pi/2} a^3 \sin^3\theta \, a \, d\theta = 4\pi\rho \, a^4 \frac{2}{3} = \frac{8\pi\rho a^4}{3}$$

$$M = \text{Mass of hollow sphere} = 4\pi a^2 \rho$$

$$\therefore \quad \text{M.I.} = \frac{2Ma^2}{3}$$

7. The M.I. of a uniform triangular lamina of mass M about any axis is the same as the M.I. of the particles of mass $\frac{M}{3}$ placed at the mid points of the sides of the triangle.

Examples on Moment of inertia

Ex. 1 : Find the moment of inertia of the quadrant of the ellipse $2x^2 + y^2 = 1$ in which x and y are positive about an axis through its centre perpendicular to its plane, where mass per unit area of the ellipse varies as the abscissa of the point at which it is situated.

Solution : Let the density be $\rho \propto x$ (abscissa) $\Rightarrow \rho = Kx$. An elementary area dx dy at the point (x, y) has then the mass (Kx) (dx dy) so, dm = Kx dx dy. This mass is situated at a distance $r = \sqrt{x^2 + y^2}$ from the axis through the pole O at right angles to the plane XOY. So, the contribution to the total moment of inertia by it is :

$$r^2 \, dm = (x^2 + y^2) \, Kx \, dx \, dy = K \, x \, (x^2 + y^2) \, dx \, dy$$

The moment of inertia of the quadrant of an ellipse is $I = K \iint x \, (x^2 + y^2) \, dx \, dy$

$$2x^2 + y^2 = 1 \quad \text{or} \quad \frac{x^2}{\left(\frac{1}{\sqrt{2}}\right)^2} + \frac{y^2}{(1)^2} = 1, \quad a = \frac{1}{\sqrt{2}}, \quad b = 1$$

Put
$$x = ar\cos\theta = \frac{1}{\sqrt{2}} r \cos\theta$$
$$y = br\sin\theta = r\sin\theta$$
$$dx \, dy = ab \, r \, dr \, d\theta = \frac{1}{\sqrt{2}} r \, dr \, d\theta$$
$$2x^2 + y^2 = 1 \;\Rightarrow\; r = 1$$

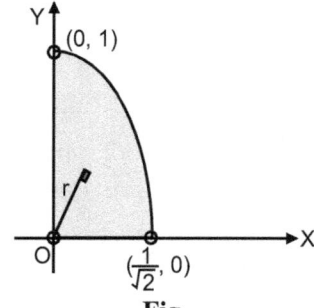

Fig.

$$I = K \int_{\theta=0}^{\pi/2} \int_{r=0}^{1} \frac{1}{\sqrt{2}} r \cos\theta \left(\frac{\cos^2\theta}{2} + \sin^2\theta\right) r^2 \cdot \frac{1}{\sqrt{2}} r \, dr \, d\theta$$

$$= \frac{K}{2} \int_{0}^{\pi/2} \left(\frac{\cos^3\theta}{2} + \sin^2\theta \cos\theta\right) d\theta \int_{0}^{1} r^4 \, dr = \frac{K}{2} \left[\frac{1}{2} \cdot \frac{2}{3} + \frac{1}{3}\right] \cdot \frac{1}{5} = \frac{K}{15}$$

Ex. 2 : Find the M.I. about the line $\theta = \frac{\pi}{2}$ of the area enclosed by $r = a(1 + \cos\theta)$.

Solution: Here, $\quad p = x = r\cos\theta \qquad I = \int p^2 \, dA$

$$\therefore \quad I = \iint r^2 \cos^2\theta \, r \, dr \, d\theta = 2 \int_{0}^{\pi} \cos^2\theta \, d\theta \int_{0}^{a(1+\cos\theta)} r^3 \, dr$$

$$= 2 \int_{0}^{\pi} \cos^2\theta \, \frac{a^4(1+\cos\theta)^4}{4} \, d\theta$$

$$= \frac{a^4}{2} \int_{0}^{\pi} \cos^2\theta \, (1 + 4\cos\theta + 6\cos^2\theta + 4\cos^3\theta + \cos^4\theta) \, d\theta$$

$$= \frac{a^4}{2} \int_{0}^{\pi} (\cos^2\theta + 4\cos^3\theta + 6\cos^4\theta + 4\cos^5\theta + \cos^6\theta) \, d\theta$$

Fig.

$$= \frac{a^4}{2} \cdot 2 \int_{0}^{\pi/2} (\cos^2\theta + 6\cos^4\theta + \cos^6\theta) \, d\theta$$

$$= a^4 \left[\frac{1}{2}\frac{\pi}{2} + 6 \cdot \frac{3}{4}\frac{1}{2}\frac{\pi}{2} + \frac{5}{6} \cdot \frac{3}{4}\frac{1}{2}\frac{\pi}{2}\right] = \frac{49\pi a^4}{32}$$

Ex. 3 : Prove that the moment of inertia of the area included between the curves $y^2 = 4ax$ and $x^2 = 4ay$ about x-axis is $\frac{144}{35} Ma^2$, where M is the mass of the area included between the curves.

Solution : M.I. about x-axis $= \int_{0}^{4a} \int_{x^2/4a}^{2\sqrt{ax}} y^2 \rho \, dx \, dy$

$$= \frac{\rho}{3} \int_0^{4a} \left(8a^{3/2} x^{3/2} - \frac{x^6}{64a^3}\right) dx = \frac{\rho}{3} \left[8a^{3/2} \frac{2x^{5/2}}{5} - \frac{x^7}{7.64a^3}\right]_0^{4a}$$

$$= \frac{\rho}{3} \left[\frac{2^9 a^4}{5} - \frac{2^8 a^4}{7}\right] = \frac{2^8 \cdot 3 \rho a^4}{35}$$

Fig.

$$\text{Mass} = M = \int_0^{4a} \int_{\frac{x^2}{4a}}^{2\sqrt{ax}} \rho \, dx \, dy$$

$$= \rho \int_0^{4a} \left(2\sqrt{ax} - \frac{x^2}{4a}\right) dx = \rho \left[2a^{1/2} \cdot \frac{2}{3} x^{3/2} - \frac{x^3}{12a}\right]_0^{4a} = \frac{16 \rho a^2}{3}$$

$$\rho = \frac{3M}{16a^2}$$

$$\therefore \quad I = \frac{2^8 \cdot 3 a^4}{35} \cdot \frac{3M}{16a^2} = \frac{144 \, Ma^2}{35}$$

Ex. 4 : Find the moment of inertia of one loop of the lemniscate $r^2 = a^2 \cos 2\theta$ about initial line.

Solution: Let ρ be constant density. Consider an element of mass $dm = \rho \, (r \, dr \, d\theta)$.

Also M.I. about initial line is $\int p^2 \, dm$, where $p = y = r \sin \theta$

$$\text{M.I.} = \iint r^2 \sin^2 \theta \cdot \rho \, r \, dr \, d\theta = 2\rho \int_0^{\pi/4} \sin^2 \theta \, d\theta \int_0^{a\sqrt{\cos 2\theta}} r^3 \, dr$$

$$= \frac{2\rho a^4}{4} \int_0^{\pi/4} \sin^2 \theta \cos^2 2\theta \, d\theta = \frac{\rho a^4}{2} \int_0^{\pi/4} \left(\frac{1 - \cos 2\theta}{2}\right) \cos^2 2\theta \, d\theta$$

Fig.

(6.97)

$$= \frac{\rho a^4}{4} \int_0^{\pi/2} (1 - \cos t) \cos^2 t \frac{dt}{2} = \frac{\rho a^4}{8} \left[\frac{1}{2}\frac{\pi}{2} - \frac{2}{3}\right] = \frac{\rho a^4}{96}(3\pi - 8)$$

$$\text{Mass} = M = \iint \rho\, r\, dr\, d\theta = 2\rho \int_0^{\pi/4} \int_0^{a\sqrt{\cos 2\theta}} r\, dr\, d\theta$$

$$M = \rho a^2 \int_0^{\pi/4} \cos 2\theta\, d\theta = \frac{\rho a^2}{2} \quad \therefore \quad \rho = \frac{2M}{a^2}$$

$$\therefore \text{ M.I. } = I = \frac{a^4(3\pi - 8)}{96}\left(\frac{2M}{a^2}\right) = \frac{(3\pi - 8)Ma^2}{48}$$

Ex. 5 : Find the moment of inertia of the portion of the parabola $y^2 = 4ax$, bounded by x-axis and latus rectum, about x-axis, if density at each point varies as the cube of the abscissa.

Solution : $\rho \propto x^3 \Rightarrow \rho = Kx^3$ also $p = y$

$$\text{M.I.} = \iint y^2 Kx^3\, dx\, dy = K \int_0^a x^3\, dx \int_0^{2\sqrt{ax}} y^2\, dy$$

$$= \frac{K}{3} \cdot 8 \cdot a^{3/2} \int_0^a x^{9/2}\, dx = \frac{16K}{33} a^7 \qquad \ldots (i)$$

Also, $M = \iint \rho\, dx\, dy = \int_0^a \int_0^{2\sqrt{ax}} Kx^3 \cdot dx\, dy$

Fig.

$$= K \int_0^a x^3 \cdot 2\sqrt{ax}\, dx = 2K\sqrt{a} \left[\frac{2}{9} x^{9/2}\right]_0^a$$

$$M = \frac{4K}{9} a^5 \quad \therefore \quad K = \frac{9M}{4a^5} \qquad \ldots (ii)$$

From (i) and (ii), $I = \frac{16a^7}{33} \cdot \frac{9m}{4a^5} = \frac{12}{11} Ma^2$

Ex. 6 : The surface density of a circular lamina varies as the square of the distance from a point on the circumference. Find the moment of inertia of the area about an axis through O perpendicular to the plane of circle.

Solution: Take the fixed point O on the circumference as the pole and the diameter through O as the initial line. Then, the polar equation of the circle is $r = 2a \cos\theta$, $\rho \propto r^2$, $\rho = Kr^2$, $p = \sqrt{x^2 + y^2} = r$.

$$\text{M.I.} = \iint p^2 \rho \, dx \, dy = \iint r^2 Kr^2 \, r \, dr \, d\theta$$

$$= K \int_0^{\pi/2} d\theta \int_0^{2a\cos\theta} r^5 \, dr = \frac{K}{6} \int_0^{\pi/2} 64 a^6 \cos^6\theta \, d\theta$$

$$= \frac{32K}{3} a^6 \cdot \frac{5}{6} \cdot \frac{3}{4} \cdot \frac{1}{2} \cdot \frac{\pi}{2} = \frac{5\pi K a^6}{3}$$

Fig.

$$\text{Mass} = M = \iint \rho \, dx \, dy = K \int_0^{\pi/2} d\theta \int_0^{2a\cos\theta} r^3 \, dr$$

$$= \frac{K}{4} \int_0^{\pi/2} 16 a^4 \cos^4\theta \, d\theta = 4 K a^4 \cdot \frac{3}{4} \cdot \frac{1}{2} \cdot \frac{\pi}{2}$$

$$M = \frac{3\pi K a^4}{4} \qquad \therefore \quad K = \frac{4M}{3\pi a^4}$$

$$\text{M.I.} = \frac{5\pi a^6}{3} \cdot \frac{4M}{3\pi a^4} = \frac{20}{9} Ma^2$$

Ex. 7 : Show that the M.I. of a rectangle of sides a and b about its diagonal is $\dfrac{M}{6}\left(\dfrac{a^2 b^2}{a^2 + b^2}\right)$ where M is the mass of rectangle. *(May 2011)*

Solution : Consider an element of area dx dy. Let P(x, y) be any point in a rectangle. Let PM ⊥ diagonal OB.

Equation of OB is $\dfrac{y}{x} = \dfrac{b}{a}$ i.e. $ay - bx = 0$.

$$\therefore \quad PM = \left|\frac{ay - bx}{\sqrt{a^2 + b^2}}\right|$$

$$\therefore \quad dm = \rho\, dx\, dy$$

And $\quad p = \dfrac{ay - bx}{\sqrt{a^2 + b^2}}$

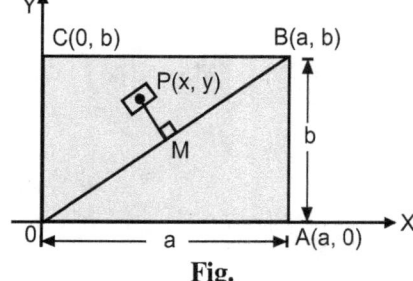

Fig.

$$M.I. = \int p^2\, dm = \int_{x=0}^{a} \int_{y=0}^{b} \frac{(ay - bx)^2}{(a^2 + b^2)} \rho\, dx\, dy$$

$$= \frac{\rho}{a^2 + b^2} \int_0^a dx \left[\frac{(ay - bx)^3}{a \cdot 3}\right]_0^b = \frac{\rho}{3a(a^2 + b^2)} \int_0^a [b^3(a - x)^3 - (-b^3 x^3)]\, dx$$

$$= \frac{\rho b^3}{3a(a^2 + b^2)} \left[\frac{(a - x)^4}{-4} + \frac{x^4}{4}\right]_0^a = \frac{\rho b^3}{12a(a^2 + b^2)}(a^4 + a^4) = \frac{\rho b^3 a^3}{6(a^2 + b^2)}$$

M = Mass of a rectangle = ρ (area) = ρ ab

$$M.I. = \frac{M}{6} \frac{a^2 b^2}{(a^2 + b^2)}$$

Ex. 8 : Find the polar M.I. of the area in XY-plane bounded by $y^2 = 2x$ and $y = x$ assuming constant density ρ.

Solution: "Polar M.I." means M.I. about the axis through the origin (pole) perpendicular to the plane of the region.

$$\therefore \quad p = \sqrt{x^2 + y^2}, \quad \rho = \text{constant}$$

Changing to polar,

$$M.I. = \iint p^2 \rho\, dx\, dy = \iint (x^2 + y^2) \rho\, dx\, dy$$

$$= \rho \iint r^2 r\, dr\, d\theta$$

$$\left[y^2 = 2x \text{ in polar} \Rightarrow r^2 \sin^2\theta = 2r \cos\theta \Rightarrow r = \frac{2 \cos\theta}{\sin^2\theta}\right]$$

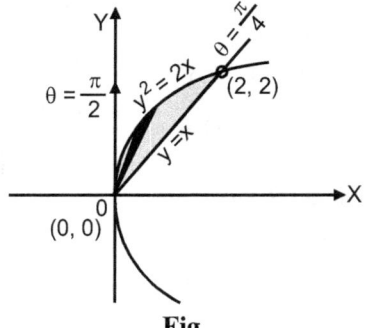

Fig.

(6.100)

$$\text{M.I.} = \rho \int_{\pi/4}^{\pi/2} d\theta \int_{0}^{\frac{2\cos\theta}{\sin^2\theta}} r^3 \, dr$$

$$= \frac{\rho}{4} \int_{\pi/4}^{\pi/2} \frac{16\cos^4\theta}{\sin^8\theta} d\theta = 4\rho \int_{\pi/4}^{\pi/2} \cot^4\theta \cdot \operatorname{cosec}^4\theta \, d\theta$$

$$= 4\rho \int_{\pi/4}^{\pi/2} \cot^4\theta \, (1 + \cot^2\theta) \operatorname{cosec}^2\theta \, d\theta$$

$$= 4\rho \left[-\frac{\cot^5\theta}{5} - \frac{\cot^7\theta}{7} \right]_{\pi/4}^{\pi/2} = 4\rho \left[0 + \frac{1}{5} + \frac{1}{7} \right] = \frac{48\,\rho}{35}$$

$$\text{Mass } M = \iint \rho \, dx \, dy = \frac{\rho}{2} \int_{\pi/4}^{\pi/2} r^2 \, d\theta$$

$$= \frac{\rho}{2} \int_{\pi/4}^{\pi/2} \frac{4\cos^2\theta}{\sin^4\theta} d\theta = 2\rho \int_{\pi/4}^{\pi/2} \cot^2\theta \operatorname{cosec}^2\theta \, d\theta$$

$$M = 2\rho \left[-\frac{\cot^3\theta}{3} \right]_{\pi/4}^{\pi/2} = 2\rho \left[0 + \frac{1}{3} \right] = \frac{2\rho}{3} \quad \therefore \quad \rho = \frac{3M}{2}$$

$$\text{M.I.} = \frac{48}{35} \left(\frac{3M}{2} \right) = \frac{72}{35} M$$

Ex. 9 : Prove that the moment of inertia of the area included between the smaller arcs of $r = 2a\cos\theta$ and $r = 2a\sin\theta$ about an axis through the pole perpendicular to the plane of the curve is $a^4 \left(\frac{3\pi}{4} - 2 \right)$.

Solution : $r = 2a\cos\theta$ is a circle with centre (a, 0) and radius a. Similarly, $r = 2a\sin\theta$ is a circle with centre (0, a) and radius a. The area included by the smaller arcs of these circles is the shaded area in the figure which is divided equally by the line $\theta = \frac{\pi}{4}$. An elementary area $r \, dr \, d\theta$ at (r, θ) is at a distance r from the axis through the pole O at right angles to the plane xoy; and thus the moment of inertia of the element about the axis is $r^2 (r \, dr \, d\theta) = r^3 \, dr \, d\theta$. Integrating this over the shaded area and using the fact that the line $\theta = \frac{\pi}{4}$ divides the region equally, we have

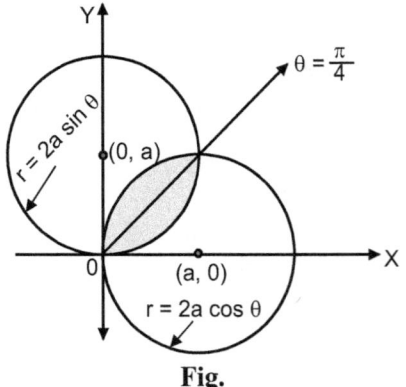

Fig.

The required moment of inertia $= 2\int_0^{\pi/4}\int_0^{2a\sin\theta} r^3\,dr\,d\theta = 8a^4\int_0^{\pi/4}\sin^4\theta\,d\theta$

$= 8a^4\int_0^{\pi/4}\frac{(1-\cos 2\theta)^2}{4}d\theta = a^4\int_0^{\pi/2}(1-\cos\phi)^2\,d\phi$, where $\phi = 2\theta$

$= a^4\int_0^{\pi/2}[1 - 2\cos\phi + \cos^2\phi]\,d\phi = a^4\left[\frac{\pi}{2} - 2 + \frac{1}{2}\frac{\pi}{2}\right] = a^4\left[\frac{3\pi}{4} - 2\right]$

Ex. 10 : Prove that the radius of gyration of semi-circular area of radius a about the line joining one end of the bounding diameter to the mid-point of the arc is $a\sqrt{\left(\frac{3}{4} - \frac{4}{3\pi}\right)}$.

Solution : Take the fixed point O on the circumference as the pole, the diameter OA as the initial line and 'a' the radius of the circle. Then the polar equation of the circle is $\quad r = 2a\cos\theta$.
Let O be one end of the diameter, C be the midpoint of the arc OCA. Join OC and equation of the line OC is $x - y = 0$.

∴ The distance of any point P(x, y) of the area from OC is $p = \left|\dfrac{x-y}{\sqrt{2}}\right|$.

Fig.

M.I. $= \iint p^2\rho\,dx\,dy = \rho\iint\dfrac{(x-y)^2}{2}dx\,dy$

$= \dfrac{\rho}{2}\iint(x^2 + y^2 - 2xy)\,dx\,dy$ (Change to polar)

$= \dfrac{\rho}{2}\int_0^{\pi/2}\int_0^{2a\cos\theta}(r^2 - 2r^2\sin\theta\cos\theta)\,r\,dr\,d\theta$

$= \dfrac{\rho}{2}\int_0^{\pi/2}(1 - 2\sin\theta\cos\theta)\,d\theta\int_0^{2a\cos\theta}r^3\,dr$

$= \dfrac{\rho}{2}\int_0^{\pi/2}(1 - 2\sin\theta\cos\theta)\dfrac{16a^4\cos^4\theta}{r}d\theta$

$= 2\rho a^4\int_0^{\pi/2}(\cos^4\theta - 2\cos^5\theta\cdot\sin\theta)\,d\theta$

$= 2\rho a^4\left[\dfrac{3}{4}\dfrac{1}{2}\dfrac{\pi}{2} - 2\cdot\dfrac{1}{6}\right] = \rho a^4\left[\dfrac{3\pi}{8} - \dfrac{2}{3}\right]$

$M = \rho$ (Area of the semi-circle) $= \rho\left(\dfrac{\pi a^2}{2}\right)$

(6.102)

$$K^2 = \frac{I}{M} = \rho a^4 \left(\frac{3\pi}{8} - \frac{2}{3}\right) \frac{2}{\rho \pi a^2} = a^2 \left(\frac{3}{4} - \frac{4}{3\pi}\right)$$

$$K = a\sqrt{\frac{3}{4} - \frac{4}{3\pi}}$$

Ex. 11 : Find the M.I. of a uniform lamina bounded by the x-axis and one arc of the cycloid $x = a(\theta - \sin\theta)$, $y = a(1 - \cos\theta)$ from $\theta = 0$ to $\theta = 2\pi$ about x-axis.

Solution: $p = y$ M.I. $= \iint p^2 \rho \, dx \, dy$

$$\text{M.I.} = \rho \int \int_0^y y^2 \, dx \, dy = \frac{\rho}{3} \int_0^{2\pi} y^3 \frac{dx}{d\theta} \cdot d\theta$$

$$= \frac{\rho}{3} \int_0^{2\pi} a^3 (1 - \cos\theta)^3 \, a (1 - \cos\theta) \, d\theta = \frac{\rho a^4}{3} \int_0^{2\pi} 16 \sin^8 \frac{\theta}{2} \, d\theta$$

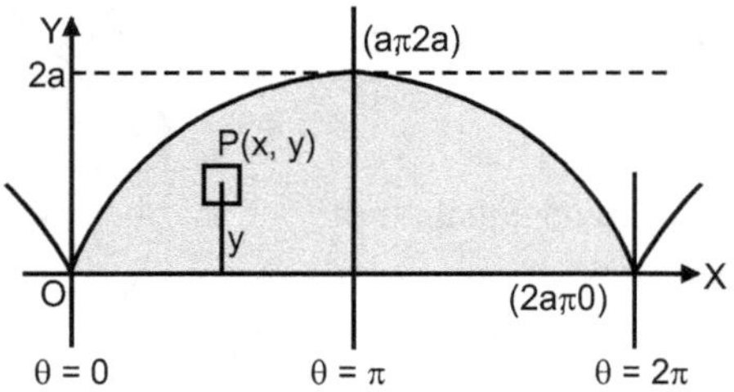

Fig. 12.41

$$= \frac{16 \rho a^4}{3} \int_0^{\pi} \sin^8 t \, 2 dt = \frac{64 \rho a^4}{3} \int_0^{\pi/2} \sin^8 t \, dt = \frac{64 \rho a^4}{3} \left(\frac{7}{8} \frac{5}{6} \frac{3}{4} \frac{1}{2} \frac{\pi}{2}\right)$$

$$= \frac{35 \pi \rho a^4}{12}$$

$$\text{Mass} = \iint \rho \, dx \, dy = \rho \int_0^{2\pi} y \frac{dx}{d\theta} \cdot d\theta$$

$$= \rho \int_0^{2\pi} a (1 - \cos\theta) \, a (1 - \cos\theta) \, d\theta = \rho a^2 \int_0^{2\pi} 4 \sin^4 \frac{\theta}{2} \, d\theta$$

$$= 4 \rho a^2 \int_0^{\pi} \sin^4 t \, 2 \, dt = 8 \rho a^2 \, 2 \int_0^{\pi/2} \sin^4 t \, dt$$

$$= 16 \rho a^2 \frac{3}{4} \frac{1}{2} \frac{\pi}{2} = 3\pi \rho a^2$$

$$\rho = \frac{M}{3\pi a^2}$$

$$\therefore \quad \text{M.I.} = \frac{35\pi a^4}{12} \frac{M}{3\pi a^2} = \frac{35}{36} Ma^2$$

Ex. 12: Find the M.I. of the area of the upper half of the circle $x^2 + y^2 = a^2$ about the line $x + y = 2a$.

Solution: The perpendicular distance of any point P(x, y) from $x + y = 2a$ is $p = \left|\dfrac{x+y-2a}{\sqrt{2}}\right|$.

$$\text{M.I.} = \iint p^2 \rho \, dx \, dy$$
$$= \rho \iint \dfrac{(x+y-2a)^2}{2} \, dx \, dy$$
$$= \dfrac{\rho}{2} \iint (x^2 + y^2 + 2xy - 4a(x+y) + 4a^2) \, dx \, dy$$
$$= \dfrac{\rho}{2} \int_0^\pi \int_0^a [r^2 + 2r^2 \sin\theta \cos\theta - 4ar(\cos\theta + \sin\theta) + 4a^2] \, r \, dr \, d\theta$$

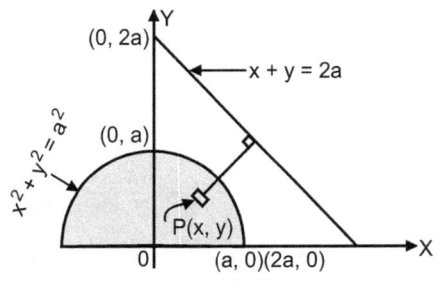

Fig. 12.42

$$= \dfrac{\rho}{2} \int_0^\pi \left(\dfrac{a^4}{4} + \dfrac{a^4}{2} \sin\theta \cos\theta - \dfrac{4a^4}{3}(\cos\theta + \sin\theta) + 2a^4 \right) d\theta$$

$$= \dfrac{\rho}{2} \left[\dfrac{9}{4} a^4 (\pi) - \dfrac{4a^4}{3}(0+2) \right] \qquad \begin{cases} \because \displaystyle\int_0^\pi \sin\theta \cos\theta \, d\theta = 0 \\ \displaystyle\int_0^\pi \cos\theta \, d\theta = 0 \end{cases}$$

$$\text{M.I.} = \rho \, a^4 \left[\dfrac{9\pi}{8} - \dfrac{4}{3} \right]$$

Problems on C.G. of an arc of a curve :

1. Find the C.G. of arc of the cycloid $x = a(\theta + \sin\theta)$, $y = a(1 - \cos\theta)$ measured from cusp to cusp.   **Ans.** $\left(0, \dfrac{2a}{3}\right)$

2. Find the position of the centroid of the arc of the cardioide $r = a(1 + \cos\theta)$ lying above the initial line.**(Dec. 2006) Ans.** $\left(\dfrac{4a}{5}, \dfrac{4a}{5}\right)$

3. Find the C.G. of an arc of the catenary $y = a \cosh \dfrac{x}{a}$ from $x = -a$ to $x = a$.

    Ans. $\left(0, \dfrac{a}{4} \cdot \dfrac{2 + \sinh 2}{\sinh 1}\right)$

4. Find the C.G. of the arc of the parabola $y^2 = 4ax$ included between the vertex and the upper extremity of the latus rectum.

Hint : C.G. of arc OA where A (a, 2a), $ds = \sqrt{\dfrac{x+a}{x}}\, dx$

Ans. $\left(\dfrac{a}{4}\dfrac{3\sqrt{2}-\log(1+\sqrt{2})}{\sqrt{2}+\log(1+\sqrt{2})},\ \dfrac{4a}{3}\dfrac{2\sqrt{2}-1}{\sqrt{2}+\log(1+\sqrt{2})}\right)$

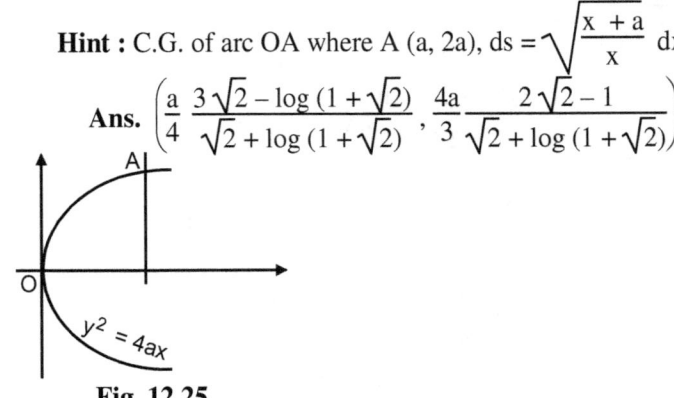

Fig. 12.25

TEST YOUR KNOWLEDGE:

1. Find the M.I. of the area enclosed by $x^{2/3} + y^{2/3} = a^{2/3}$ about x-axis. **Ans.** $\dfrac{7}{64} Ma^2$

2. Find the M.I. of an arc in the form of cardioide $r = a(1 + \cos\theta)$ about the axis through the pole perpendicular to the plane of the arc. **Ans.** $\dfrac{256 a^3 \rho}{15}$

3. Find the M.I. of a square lamina of side 'a' about one of its diagonals, density at any point (x, y) varies as the square of its distance from the diagonal. **(Dec. 09)** **Ans.** $\dfrac{Ma^2}{5}$

4. Find the M.I. of a quadrant of a circle of radius a about a line parallel to its bounding radius at a distance d (d > a) from it. **Ans.** $\rho a^2\left(\dfrac{\pi d^2}{4} - \dfrac{2ad}{3} + \dfrac{a^2\pi}{16}\right)$

5. Find the M.I. of a thin circular wire in the form of arc of a circle of a radius a which subtends an angle 2α at the centre O about :
(i) an axis through its middle point perpendicular to its plane, (ii) the radius bisecting the angle 2α. **Ans.** (i) $2a^2 M\left(1 - \dfrac{\sin\alpha}{\alpha}\right)$, (ii) $\dfrac{Ma^2}{2}\left(1 - \dfrac{\sin 2\alpha}{2\alpha}\right)$

6. Find the M.I. about x-axis of the area under the curve $y = \sin x$ from $x = 0$ to $x = \dfrac{\pi}{2}$. **Ans.** $\dfrac{2M}{9}$

7. Find the M.I. of the area enclosed by $r = a(1 - \cos\theta)$ about the line $\theta = \dfrac{\pi}{2}$. **Ans.** $\dfrac{49\pi a^4}{32}$

8. The surface density at a point of the area of the lemniscate $r^2 = a^2 \cos 2\theta$ varies as the square of its distance from the pole. Find the moment of inertia about an axis through the pole perpendicular to its plane.

   Hint: $\rho = kr^2$, $p = r$. **Ans.** $I = \dfrac{16Ma^2}{9\pi}$

9. Find the M.I. about the polar axis of the area enclosed by $r = a(1 + \cos\theta)$ in the upper half. **Ans.** $\dfrac{35\pi\rho a^4}{32}$

10. Find the M.I. of one loop of $r^2 = a^2 \sin 2\theta$ about an axis perpendicular to its plane. **Ans.** $\dfrac{\rho \pi a^4}{16}$

11. A thin plate of uniform thickness and density is in the form of lamina bounded by the parabola $x^2 = y$ and the line $y = x + 2$. Find the M.I. of the lamina about co-ordinate axis. **(Dec. 2010) Ans.** $\dfrac{47M}{14}$, $\dfrac{7M}{10}$

12. Find the M.I. of the area bounded by $x^2 + y^2 - ax = 0$, $x^2 + y^2 - 2ax = 0$ about the axis through origin perpendicular to XOY plane if density varies as distance from the origin. **Ans.** $\dfrac{496\lambda a^5}{75}$

13. Find the radius of gyration for the area of the cardioide $r = a(1 + \cos\theta)$ about the axis perpendicular to its plane through the pole when the density at any point varies as the distance of the point from the pole. **Ans.** $\dfrac{3\sqrt{21}\,a}{10}$

14. Prove that the M.I. of the disc of radius a about an axis through its centre and perpendicular to its plane is $\dfrac{3}{5}Ma^2$, where M is the mass of the disc, the density being proportional to the distance from the axis.

15. Prove that the M.I. of a lamina of mass M in the form of a right-angled triangle, having hypotenuse of length 'c' about the axis through the vertex containing the right angle perpendicular to the plane of the lamina is $\dfrac{M}{6}c^2$.

    Hint: $p = r$ and use $a^2 + b^2 = c^2$
    Limits for $x : 0$ to a, $y : 0$ to $\dfrac{b}{a}(a-x)$

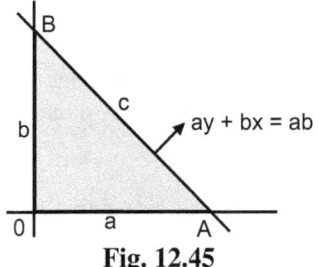

Fig. 12.45

16. Find the M.I. of a loop of the curve $r^2 = a^2 \cos 2\theta$ about a line through the pole perpendicular to its plane. **Ans.** $\dfrac{M}{8}\pi a^2$

17. A lamina in the first quadrant is bounded by $x = 0$, $y = 0$ and $x^2 + y^2 = a^2$ and $\rho = \dfrac{\lambda x^2 y}{a^3}$ where λ is constant. Find the co-ordinates of C.G. and M.I. of the lamina about z-axis. **(Dec. 2011) Ans.** $\left(\dfrac{5a}{8}, \dfrac{5\pi a}{32}\right)$, $\dfrac{5Ma^2}{7}$

18. Find the M.I. and radius of gyration of the area bounded by, $y = 20x(1-x)$ and the line $y = 0$ about (i) OX, (ii) OY. **Ans.** (i) $\dfrac{40}{7}$ M, $\sqrt{\dfrac{40}{7}}$, (ii) $\dfrac{3M}{10}$, $\sqrt{\dfrac{3}{10}}$

19. Find the M.I. of the area of the parabola $y^2 = 4ax$ bounded by a double ordinate at a distance h from the vertex about (i) an axis through the centroid perpendicular to the axis of the parabola, (ii) the tangent at the vertex, (iii) the axis.

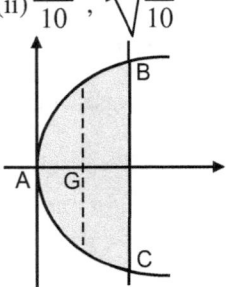

Fig. 12.46

Hint : A = vertex, BC = double ordinate, x = h

= C.G. of area BAC, $\bar{x} = \dfrac{3}{5} h$

= $\dfrac{8}{3} \rho h \sqrt{ah}$ .I. = $\rho \displaystyle\int_0^h \int_{-2\sqrt{ax}}^{2\sqrt{ax}} \left(x - \dfrac{3h}{5}\right)^2 dx\, dy$

Ans. (i) $\dfrac{12Mh^2}{175}$, (ii) tangent at vertex = y-axis, $\dfrac{3}{7}$ Mh², (iii) $\dfrac{4}{5}$ Mah.

20. Find the M.I. of a loop of Bernoulli's Lemniscate $r^2 = a^2 \cos 2\theta$ about the tangent at the pole.

Hint : tangent at pole is $\theta = \dfrac{\pi}{4}$,

$p = r \sin\left(\dfrac{\pi}{4} - \theta\right) = \dfrac{r}{\sqrt{2}} (\cos\theta - \sin\theta)$ **Ans.** $\dfrac{\pi a^4}{32}$

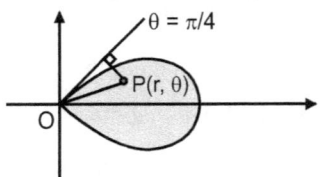

Fig. 12.47

21. An area is bounded by the curve $y = c \cosh \dfrac{x}{c}$, the axes and the ordinate $x = c$. Calculate the radius of gyration about the y-axis.

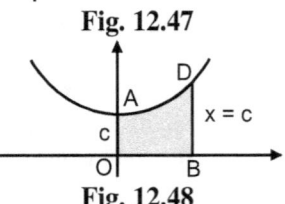

Fig. 12.48

Hint : Use $\sinh 1 = \dfrac{e - e^{-1}}{2}$, $\cosh 1 = \dfrac{e + e^{-1}}{2}$ **Ans.** $Mc^2 \left(\dfrac{e^2 - 5}{e^2 - 1}\right)$

YEAR WISE UNIVERSITY QUESTION PAPERS -13 SEMESTERS	
Dec-2013(10/12/2013)	
1. Evaluate $\displaystyle\int_0^{\pi/2} \int_0^{a\cos\theta} r\sqrt{a^2 - r^2}\, dr\, d\theta$, $a > 0$	5
2. Change the order of integration and evaluate $\displaystyle\int_0^\infty \int_x^1 e^{-xy} y\, dx\, dy$	6
3. Find the area bounded by the parabola $y^2 = 4ax$ and its latus rectum	5

4. A lamina is bounded by the curve $y = x^2 - 3x$ and $y = 2x$ if the density at any point is given by $\frac{24}{25}xy$. Then find the mass of lamina.	6
5. Find the moment of inertia about the x-axid of the area enclosed by the lines $x = 0, y = 0, \frac{x}{a} + \frac{y}{b} = 1$.	6
August-2013(16/08/2013) Re-exam	
1. Evaluate $\int_0^1 \int_0^{1-x} (x+y) dx dy$	5
2. Evaluate $\iint (x^2 + y^2) dx dy$ over the area in the positive quadrent of the ellipse $\frac{x^2}{a^2} + \frac{y^2}{b^2} = 1$.	6
3. Change into polar coordinates and hence evaluate $\int_0^a \int_y^a \frac{x^2}{(x^2+y^2)^{3/2}} dx dy$	6
4. Find the mass of an elliptical plate $\frac{x^2}{a^2} + \frac{y^2}{b^2} = 1$, if the density at any point $P(x, y)$ on it is λxy.	5
5. Calculate the volume of solid generated by the revolution of the cardioid $r = a(1 - \cos\theta)$ about its axis.	5
6. Find the area of the curve $r^2 = a^2 \cos 2\theta$ by using double integration.	6
May-2013(18/05/2013)	
1. Evaluate the following integras $\int_0^{\pi/2} \int_{a(1-\cos\theta)}^a r^2 dr d\theta$	5
2. Change the order of integration and evaluate $\int_0^{a/\sqrt{2}} \int_x^{\sqrt{a^2-x^2}} y^2 dx dy$	6
3. Show that the area enclosed by the curve $a^2 x^2 = y^3 (2a - y)$ is πa^2.	5
4. Find the moment of intertia about the x-axis of the area enclosed by the lines $x = 0, y = 0, \frac{x}{a} + \frac{y}{b} = 1$	5
5. Find the mass of the lamina bounded by the curve $y^2 = ax$ and $x^2 = ay$ if the density of the lamina at any point varies as the square of the distance from the origin.	6
May-2012 (29/05/2012)	
1. Evaluate $\int_0^a \int_0^{\sqrt{a^2-y^2}} \sqrt{a^2 - x^2 - y^2} dx dy$	5

2. Change the order of integration and evaluate $\int_0^a \int_{y^2/ax}^{y} \dfrac{ydxdy}{(a-x)\sqrt{ax-y^2}}$	6
3. Find the area common to the circles $x^2+y^2-4y=0$ and $x^2+y^2-4x-4y+4=0$ by double integrals.	5
4. Find the mass of the lamina bounded by the curve $y^2=ax$ and $x^2=ay$ if the density 'ρ' is given by x^2+y^2.	6

Nov-2012(20/11/2012)

1. By change the order of integration evaluate $\int_0^\infty \int_x^\infty \left(\dfrac{e^{-y}}{y}\right) dxdy$	6
2. Evaluate $\int_0^2 \int_0^{\sqrt{2x-x^2}} \dfrac{xdxdy}{\sqrt{x^2+y^2}}$ by changing to polar coordinates.	6
3. Find area of loop of curve $y^2=\dfrac{x^2(3a-x)}{a+x}$.	6
4. Find the mass of the lamina of the curve $a^2x^2=y^3(2a-y)$ if the density 'ρ' is proportinal to square root ot the ordinate of the point.	6

Dec-2011(16/12/2011)

1. Evaluate $\int_0^1 \int_0^x x(x^2+y^2)dxdy$	5
2. Change the order of integration and evaluate $\int_0^1 \int_0^{\sqrt{1-y^2}} \left(\dfrac{\cos^{-1}x}{\sqrt{1-x^2}\sqrt{1-x^2-y^2}}\right) dxdy$.	6
3. By change to polar coordinates evaluate $\int_0^a \int_0^x \dfrac{x^3 dxdy}{\sqrt{x^2+y^2}}$.	6
4. Find the area included between the curves $r=a(1+\cos\theta)$ and $r=a(1-\cos\theta)$.	5
5. Find the area included between the curves $9xy=4$ and $2x+y=2$ by double integration.	6
6. Find moment of inertia about the x-axis of the area enclosed by the lines $x=0;\ y=0$ and $\dfrac{x}{a}+\dfrac{y}{b}=1$	6

May-2011(20/05/2011)	
1. Evaluate $\int_0^1 \int_0^y xye^{-x^2} dxdy$	5
2. Change the order of integration and evaluate $\int_0^1 \int_0^{\sqrt{1-x^2}} \dfrac{dxdy}{(1+e^y)\sqrt{1-x^2-y^2}}$.	6
3. Find the area common to the parabola $y^2 = 4ax$ and $x^2 = 4ay$ by double integrals.	5
4. Find moment of inertia of the area included between the parabolas $y^2 = 4ax$ and $x^2 = 4ay$ about the x-axis.	5
Nov-2010 (18/11/2010)	
1. Change the order of integration and evaluate $\int_0^1 \int_{x^2}^x xy\,dxdy$.	6
2. Find the mass of the lamina in the form of an ellipse $\dfrac{x^2}{a^2}+\dfrac{y^2}{b^2}=1$ if the density at any point varies as the product of the distance from the axis of the ellipse.	6
3. Find area enclosed by the curve $x^{2/3}+y^{2/3}=a^{2/3}$.	5
4. Find the moment of inertia about the x-axis of the area enclosed by the lines $x=0,\ y=0,\ \dfrac{x}{a}+\dfrac{y}{b}=1$.	6
May-2010 (19/05/2010)	
1. Evaluate $\int_0^\infty \int_0^\infty e^{-x^2(1+y^2)}x\,dx\,dy$	5
2. Change the order of integration and evaluate $\int_0^1 \int_{x^2}^{2-x} xy\,dxdy$.	6
3. Change to polar coordinates and evaluate $\int_0^a \int_0^x \left(\dfrac{x^3 dxdy}{\sqrt{x^2+y^2}}\right)$.	6
4. Find the area between $y^2 = 4x$ and the chord AB joining the points A(1,2) and B(1,-2).	5
5. The density at any point of a non-uniform circular lamina of radius unity is k-times its distance from given diameter. Find total mass of lamina.	5
May-2009 (19/05/2009)	
1. Change the order of integration and evaluate $\int_0^a \int_{x/a}^{\sqrt{x/a}} (x^2+y^2)dxdy$	6
2. Find the whole area of the curve $r = a+b\cos\theta, a>b$.	5
3. The density of circular lamina with centre (0,0) and radius a is k times its distance from x-axis. Find its mass	5

Nov-2009 (16/11/2009)	
1. Change the order of integration and evaluate $\int_0^1 \int_0^{\sqrt{1-y^2}} \left(\dfrac{\cos^{-1} x}{\sqrt{1-x^2}\sqrt{1-x^2-y^2}} \right) dxdy.$	6
2. Find the area included between the curves $r = a(1+\cos\theta)$ and $r = a(1-\cos\theta)$.	6
3. The density at any point of a lamina in the form of an area induced by the curve $a^2 x^2 = y^3(2a - y)$ varies as the square root of the ordinate of the point. Find mass of lamina.	5
Nov-2008 (10/11/2008)	
1. Change the order of integration and evaluate $\int_0^1 \int_0^{y^2} \sqrt{8x+y^2}\, ydxdy$	7
2. Find the area inside the circle $r = a\sin\theta$ and outside the cardiode $r = a(1-\cos\theta)$.	8
3. Find the mass of the lamina of the region included between the curves $y = x,\ y = 0, x = 2,$ having uniform density.	8

✤ ✤ ✤

F.E. (Sem. II) M II (SU)   Paper Pattern

Tentative University Question Paper Pattern

First Year Engineering -All Branches Semester-II

Engineering Mathematics-II

Instructions: i) All questions are compulsory.

    ii) Figures to the right indicate full marks.

    iii) Use of non programmable calculator is allowed.

Q. No	Unit	Marks
	Section-I	
Q.1.	Unit-I: Ordinary Differential Equations of first order and first degree	Total Marks:15
a. b. c. d.	**Solve Any Three**	For each Question 05 marks
Q.2.	Unit-II: Applications Of Ordinary Differential Equations Of First Order And First Degree	Total Marks:15
a. b. c. d.	**Solve Any Three**	For each Question 05 marks
Q.3.	Unit-III: Numerical Solution Of Ordinary Differential Equations Of First Order And First Degree	Total Marks:20
a. b. c. d. e.	**Solve Any Four**	For each Question 05 marks

F.E. (Sem. II) M II (SU) — Paper Pattern

Q. No	Unit	Marks
	Section-II	
Q.4.	**Unit-IV Special Functions**	Total Marks:15
a. b. c. d.	**Solve Any Three**	For each Question 05 marks
Q.5.	**Unit-V Curve Tracing**	Total Marks:15
a. b. c. d.	**Solve Any Three**	For each Question 05 marks
Q.6.	**Unit-VI: Multiple Integration And Its Applications**	Total Marks:20
a. b. c. d. e.	**Solve Any Four**	For each Question 05 marks

(P.2)

LIST OF FORMULAE

1. $\int x^n \, dx = \dfrac{x^{n+1}}{n+1} + c \ (n \neq 1)$

2. $\int \dfrac{1}{x} \, dx = \log x + c$

3. $\int e^x \, dx = e^x + c$

4. $\int a^x \, dx = \dfrac{a^x}{\log a} + c$

5. $\int \sin x \, dx = -\cos x + c$

6. $\int \cos x \, dx = \sin x + c$

7. $\int \tan x \, dx = \log \sec x + c$

8. $\int \cot x \, dx = \log \sin x + c$

9. $\int \sec^2 x \, dx = \tan x + c$

10. $\int \operatorname{cosec}^2 x \, dx = -\cot x + c$

11. $\int \sec x \tan x \, dx = \sec x + c$

12. $\int \operatorname{cosec} x \cot x \, dx = -\operatorname{cosec} x + c$

13. $\int \sec x \, dx = \log(\sec x + \tan x) + c$

14. $\int \operatorname{cosec} x \, dx = \log(\operatorname{cosec} x - \cot x) + c$

15. $\int \dfrac{1}{\sqrt{a^2 - x^2}} \, dx = \sin^{-1}\left(\dfrac{x}{a}\right) + c$

16. $\int \dfrac{1}{\sqrt{x^2 - a^2}} \, dx = \log(x + \sqrt{x^2 - a^2}) + c$

17. $\int \dfrac{dx}{\sqrt{x^2 + a^2}} = \log(x + \sqrt{x^2 + a^2}) + c \quad \text{OR} \quad \sinh^{-1} \dfrac{x}{a} + c$

18. $\int \dfrac{dx}{a^2 - x^2} = \dfrac{1}{2a} \log\left(\dfrac{a + x}{a - x}\right) + c \quad \text{OR} \quad \dfrac{1}{a} \tanh^{-1} \dfrac{x}{a} + c$

19. $\int \dfrac{1}{x^2 - a^2} \, dx = \dfrac{1}{2a} \log \dfrac{x - a}{x + a} + c$

20. $\int \dfrac{1}{a^2 + x^2} \, dx = \dfrac{1}{a} \tan^{-1}\left(\dfrac{x}{a}\right) + c$

21. $\int \sqrt{a^2 - x^2} \, dx = \dfrac{x}{a} \sqrt{a^2 - x^2} + \dfrac{a^2}{2} \sin^{-1}\left(\dfrac{x}{a}\right) + c$

22. $\int \sqrt{x^2 - a^2} \, dx = \dfrac{x}{a} \sqrt{x^2 - a^2} - \dfrac{a^2}{2} \log[x + \sqrt{x^2 - a^2}] + c$

23. $\int \sqrt{x^2 + a^2} \, dx = \dfrac{x}{2} \sqrt{x^2 + a^2} + \dfrac{a^2}{2} \log[x + \sqrt{x^2 + a^2}] + c$

24. $\int e^x [f(x) + f'(x)] \, dx = e^x f(x)$

25. $\int e^{ax} \sin bx \, dx = \dfrac{e^{ax}}{a^2 + b^2} (a \sin bx - b \cos bx)$

26. $\int e^{ax} \cos bx \, dx = \dfrac{e^{ax}}{a^2 + b^2} (a \cos bx + b \sin bx)$

27. $\int u \cdot v \, dx = u \int v \, dx - \int \left[\frac{du}{dx} \cdot \int v \, dx \right] dx + c$ **Rule for Integration by Parts**

28. $\int [f(x)]^n f'(x) \, dx = \frac{[f(x)]^{n+1}}{n+1}, \, n \neq -1$

29. $\int \frac{f'(x)}{f(x)} \, dx = \log f(x)$

30. $\int e^{f(x)} f'(x) \, dx = e^{f(x)}$

31. $\int \sin(f(x)) f'(x) \, dx = -\cos(f(x))$

32. $\int \cos(f(x)) f'(x) \, dx = \sin(f(x))$

33. $\int \frac{f'(x)}{\sqrt{f(x)}} \, dx = 2\sqrt{f(x)}$

34. $\int \sqrt{f(x)} \cdot f'(x) \, dx = \frac{2}{3} [f(x)]^{3/2}$

35. $\int_0^a f(x) \, dx = \int_0^a f(a-x) \, dx$

36. $\int_a^b f(x) \, dx = \int_a^c f(x) \, dx + \int_c^b f(x) \, dx, \, a < c < b$

37. $\int_0^{2a} f(x) \, dx = \int_0^a f(x) \, dx + \int_0^a f(2a-x) \, dx$

38. $\int_{-a}^a f(x) \, dx = 2 \int_0^a f(x) \, dx$ if $f(x)$ is even

   $= 0$, if $f(x)$ is odd

❖ ❖ ❖